Appraisal Procedures for Counselors and Helping Professionals

FOURTH EDITION

Robert J. Drummond
University of North Florida

Merrill
an imprint of Prentice Hall
Upper Saddle River, New Jersey   *Columbus, Ohio*

Library of Congress Cataloging-in-Publication Data

Drummond, Robert J.

Appraisal procedures for counselors and helping professionals/Robert J. Drummond. —4th ed.

p. cm.

Includes bibliographical references and index.

ISBN 0-13-080590-4

1. Psychological tests. 2. Educational tests and measurements. 3. Counseling. I. title.

BF176.D78 2000

150'.28'7—dc21

99-24051

CIP

Cover art: © Super Stock
Editor: Kevin M. Davis
Editorial Assistant: Holly Jennings
Assistant Editor: Heather Doyle Fraser
Production Editor: Linda Hillis Bayma
Design Coordinator: Diane C. Lorenzo
Copyeditor: Dawn Potter
Text Designer: Mia Saunders
Cover Designer: Dan Eckel
Production Manager: Laura Messerly
Electronic Text Management: Marilyn Wilson Phelps, Karen L. Bretz, Melanie N. King
Illustrations: Christine Marrone, Janet Bidwell
Director of Marketing: Kevin Flanagan
Marketing Manager: Meghan Shepherd
Marketing Coordinator: Krista Groshong

This book was set in Garamond by Prentice Hall and was printed and bound by R.R. Donnelley & Sons Company. The cover was printed by Phoenix Color Corp.

Printed in the United States of America

10 9 8 7 6 5 4

ISBN: 0-13-080590-4

Prentice-Hall International (UK) Limited, *London*
Prentice-Hall of Australia Pty. Limited, *Sydney*
Prentice-Hall of Canada, Inc., *Toronto*
Prentice-Hall Hispanoamericana, S. A., *Mexico*
Prentice-Hall of India Private Limited, *New Delhi*
Prentice-Hall of Japan, Inc., *Tokyo*
Prentice-Hall (Singapore) Pte. Ltd., *Singapore*
Editora Prentice-Hall do Brasil, Ltda., *Rio de Janeiro*

To those who have inspired and guided me:

> *my mother*
> *my father*
> *my wife, Gloria*
> *my daughters, Robin and Heather*
> *my brother, Paul*
> *my doctoral advisor, Robert L. Thorndike*

Preface

The purpose of this text is to help current and future workers in the helping professions to become better consumers of psychological and educational tests and assessment procedures. First, users need to know the philosophical and ethical principles that relate to the field of testing. Second, they need to know when tests should be used and why. Third, they need to know how to locate and select the most valid and reliable instruments to aid in their decision making. Fourth, they need to know how to interpret and report test and assessment results. They need to be alert to the standards developed by various professional organizations and designed as guidelines for test authors and test users.

A systems approach was used to organize the knowledge base and the basic skills and competencies needed by test users. The book focuses on seven components:

1. *Models for test use and selection.* The first chapter presents a framework for conceptualizing when to use tests and why. It includes some dimensions of the historical, philosophical, and social backgrounds of the testing movement. It also introduces accountability and the competency-based movement as well as the basic skills and competencies that test administrators and examiners must master.

2. *Basic competencies needed.* Chapters 2 through 6 identify the basic measurement, statistical, and research skills needed to select, administer, and interpret tests and assessment information.

3. *Types of tests and assessment procedures.* Chapters 7 through 15 introduce the different types of tests and assessment techniques that are commonly used in the helping professions. This portion of the text covers the assessment of learning and cognitive styles and the testing of intelligence, aptitude, interest, and

personality. Assessment of the environment and development of the test taker are also discussed. The traditional pencil-and-paper tests and inventories are discussed, as are projective tests, situational tests, and the use of behavioral observation.

4. *Alternate measurement and appraisal techniques.*   Chapter 16 focuses on the use of the computer in assessment. Chapter 17 concerns the movement toward alternate and authentic assessment.

5. *Testing special populations.*   Chapters 18 through 21 focus on appraisal procedures and techniques, as well as issues, for working with different special populations, such as clients with disabilities, multicultural groups, test clients with anxiety, and school systems.

6. *Communicating test results.*   Chapter 22 presents strategies for communicating test results to clients, parents, and other professionals, and Chapter 23 looks at guidelines for writing test reports.

7. *Current issues and trends.*   Chapter 24 presents the legal and ethical standards concerned with testing that helping professionals need to know. The final chapter, Chapter 25, recapitulates some of the major trends and issues introduced in the text and predicts some future directions.

CHANGES IN THE FOURTH EDITION

Since the third edition was published, there have been a number of new tests published and others that have undergone revisions. There are many new sources of information available on testing. Many web sites are available to help professionals locate tests that are available and find critical reviews of these instruments. You can find our web site at www.prenhall.com/drummond. Many computer versions of tests and interpretative reports are now available to test users. Also, professional organizations have looked more closely at the qualifications and competencies needed by test users and even considered ethical standards for testing on the Internet. This new edition provides an update on current issues and ideas on testing.

In each chapter legal and ethical standards are emphasized, and they are reviewed and discussed in more detail in Chapter 24. The text is standards-based and considers the appraisal competencies advocated by CACREP and other national accreditation groups.

Although the overall framework of the text is the same as the third edition, new material is integrated into existing chapters. Expanded coverage is given to the theories and assessment of intelligence, the role of the computer, the movement away from traditional measurement to authentic measurement, and new directions in measurement theory. Item response theory is replacing the classical theories of measurement. Consequential validity of tests is now being debated. The computer has had dramatic impact on testing not only as an information source but through on-line testing, adaptive testing, and computerized interpretation of test results. More attention is now given to the creative use of the capabilities of the computer.

STRUCTURE OF THE TEXT

Each chapter has a similar format. A chapter overview is followed by learning objectives and a discussion of the topics related to those objectives. A brief summary is included in each chapter in addition to discussion questions, suggested activities, case studies, and additional readings. Publishers whose tests are cited in the text are listed in Appendix B, and key terms are defined in the glossary. Separate indexes are provided for authors, topics, and tests.

I have avoided evaluative critiques of most of the tests cited. I encourage readers to use the Buros home page (http://www.unl.edu/buros/) to locate the reviews that have been printed in the *Mental Measurements Yearbooks*, *Test Critiques*, or professional journals. Selection decisions should be situationally specific rather than generalized; many experts now advocate evaluating the consequential validity of the test. Myriad tests are available in almost all areas. The annotated lists included in the text are not exhaustive, nor do they represent all the exemplary tests in the field. Their purpose is to indicate the range and scope of tests in each area. The text attempts to encourage the reader's curiosity and interest and stimulate further investigation, research, reading, and experimentation to broaden knowledge, skills, and competencies in measurement and evaluation.

ACKNOWLEDGMENTS

I would like to thank the following colleagues, whose review improved this edition: Larry D. Burlew, University of Bridgeport; Claudia Flowers, University of North Carolina, Charlotte; Donna A. Henderson, Wake Forest University; Arthur E. Hernandez, University of Texas, San Antonio; and Mike Trevisan, Washington State University.

The following colleagues reviewed the previous edition: Rick Bruhn, Sam Houston State University; Judith E. Dobson, Oklahoma State University; Betty N. Dodd, Kean College of New Jersey; Bruce Growick, The Ohio State University; Patrick Hardesty, University of Louisville; Roger Herring, University of Arkansas, Little Rock; and Mark J. Miller, Louisiana Tech University.

Robert J. Drummond

Discover Companion Websites:
A Virtual Learning Environment

Technology is a constantly growing and changing aspect of our field that is creating a need for content and resources. To address this emerging need, we have developed an online learning environment for students and professors alike—Companion Websites—to support our textbooks.

In creating a Companion Website, our goal is to build on and enhance what the textbook already offers. For this reason, the content for each user-friendly website is organized by topic and provides the professor and student with a variety of meaningful resources. Common features of a Companion Website include:

For the Professor—

Every Companion Website integrates **Syllabus Manager**™, an online syllabus creation and management utility.

- **Syllabus Manager**™ provides you, the instructor, with an easy, step-by-step process to create and revise syllabi, with direct links into Companion Website and other online content without having to learn HTML.
- Students may logon to your syllabus during any study session. All they need to know is the web address for the Companion Website and the password you've assigned to your syllabus.
- After you have created a syllabus using **Syllabus Manager**™, students may enter the syllabus for their course section from any point in the Companion Website.
- Class dates are highlighted in white and assignment due dates appear in blue. Clicking on a date, the student is shown the list of activities for the assignment. The activities for each assignment are linked directly to actual content, saving time for students.

- Adding assignments consists of clicking on the desired due date, then filling in the details of the assignment—name of the assignment, instructions, and whether or not it is a one-time or repeating assignment.
- In addition, links to other activities can be created easily. If the activity is online, a URL can be entered in the space provided, and it will be linked automatically in the final syllabus.
- Your completed syllabus is hosted on our servers, allowing convenient updates from any computer on the Internet. Changes you make to your syllabus are immediately available to your students at their next logon.

For the Student—

- **Topic Overviews**—outline key concepts in topic areas
- **Electronic Blue Book**—send homework or essays directly to your instructor's email with this paperless form
- **Message Board**—serves as a virtual bulletin board to post—or respond to—questions or comments to/from a national audience
- **Web Destinations**—links to www sites that relate to each topic area
- **Professional Organizations**—links to organizations that relate to topic areas
- **Additional Resources**—access to topic specific content that enhances material found in the text

To take advantage of these resources, please visit the Companion Website for *Appraisal Procedures for Counselors and Helping Professionals,* Fourth Edition, at www.prenhall.com/drummond.

Brief Contents

CHAPTER 1   Models for Test Use and
             Selection   1
CHAPTER 2   Statistical Concepts   13
CHAPTER 3   Measurement Concepts   37
CHAPTER 4   Locating and Selecting Tests   59
CHAPTER 5   How to Administer Tests   77
CHAPTER 6   Scoring and Interpreting
             Tests   93
CHAPTER 7   Ability and Intelligence
             Testing   111
CHAPTER 8   Aptitude Testing   139
CHAPTER 9   Achievement Testing   155
CHAPTER 10   Career and Employment
             Testing   175
CHAPTER 11   Personality Testing   205
CHAPTER 12   Assessment of Adjustment   229
CHAPTER 13   Learning Styles   251
CHAPTER 14   Assessment of
             Development   267
CHAPTER 15   Environmental Assessment   283
CHAPTER 16   The Computer
             in Assessment   299

CHAPTER 17   Alternate and Authentic
             Assessment Techniques   315
CHAPTER 18   Working with Special
             Populations   337
CHAPTER 19   Multicultural Assessment   353
CHAPTER 20   Test-Taking Skills   365
CHAPTER 21   School Testing Programs   381
CHAPTER 22   Communicating Test
             Results to Clients, Parents,
             and Professionals   399
CHAPTER 23   Written Test Reports   423
CHAPTER 24   Legal and Ethical Concerns
             and Issues in Testing   441
CHAPTER 25   Current Trends and Issues   455
APPENDIX A   Tests   467
APPENDIX B   Test Publishers
             and Distributors   483
GLOSSARY   485
REFERENCES   495
NAME INDEX   509
SUBJECT INDEX   513
TEST INDEX   535

Contents

CHAPTER 1

Models for Test Use and Selection   **1**

DECISION-MAKING MODEL   2

VALUE OF TESTING   2

USES OF TESTS   3

COMPETENCIES REQUIRED OF TEST USERS   3

HISTORICAL CONTEXTS   6

CHAPTER 2

Statistical Concepts   **13**

ROLE OF STATISTICS   14

FOUR SCALES OF MEASUREMENT   14

WHAT SCORES LOOK LIKE   16

MEASURES OF CENTRAL TENDENCY   23

MEASURES OF VARIABILITY   25

MEASURES OF RELATIONSHIP   28

NORMAL CURVE   31

INFERENTIAL STATISTICS   32

CHAPTER 3

Measurement Concepts   37

    STEPS IN TEST DEVELOPMENT   38
    VALIDITY   39
    RELIABILITY   43
    PRACTICAL MEASUREMENT CONCEPTS   50

CHAPTER 4

Locating and Selecting Tests   59

    DECISION THEORY MODEL   60
    CRITERIA FOR SELECTING A TEST   70

CHAPTER 5

How to Administer Tests   77

    STANDARDS FOR ADMINISTRATION   78
    PRETESTING PROCEDURES   78
    ADMINISTERING THE TEST   84
    POSTTESTING PROCEDURES   85

CHAPTER 6

Scoring and Interpreting Tests   93

    STANDARDS FOR SCORING   94
    MODELS OF SCORING   94
    SOME EXAMPLES OF TEST SCORING   95
    INTERPRETING SCORES   96
    CRITERION-REFERENCED INTERPRETATION   96
    NORM-REFERENCED INTERPRETATION   96
    DEVELOPMENTAL INTRAINDIVIDUAL COMPARISON   101
    CONVERSION TABLES   105
    PROFILES   106

CHAPTER 7

Ability and Intelligence Testing   111

    DEFINITIONS OF INTELLIGENCE   112
    MODELS OF INTELLIGENCE   112

TYPES OF TESTS   118
TRENDS AND ISSUES   132

CHAPTER 8

Aptitude Testing   139

MULTIAPTITUDE BATTERIES   140
SPECIALIZED BATTERIES   147
ISSUES AND PROBLEM AREAS   151

CHAPTER 9

Achievement Testing   155

TYPES OF ACHIEVEMENT TESTS   156
USING ACHIEVEMENT TEST RESULTS   165
ANALYSIS OF CLASS PROFILE   169

CHAPTER 10

Career and Employment Testing   175

INTEREST INVENTORIES   176
INTEREST ASSESSMENT TECHNIQUES   180
VALUES   181
GUIDELINES FOR INTERPRETING TESTS   182
CAREER DEVELOPMENT INSTRUMENTS   182
COMBINED PROGRAMS   183
PROBLEMS OF INTEREST MEASUREMENT   184
FUTURE TRENDS IN INTEREST MEASUREMENT   185
EMPLOYMENT TESTING: ROLES AND PURPOSES   185
TEST USE IN THE PRIVATE SECTOR   185
TEST USE IN GOVERNMENT   188
TEST USE IN THE MILITARY   189
PERSONNEL SELECTION AND CLASSIFICATION TECHNIQUES   189
CURRENT TRENDS AND PERSPECTIVES   197

CHAPTER 11

Personality Testing   205

ROLE OF PERSONALITY THEORY   206
TECHNIQUES FOR MEASURING PERSONALITY   209

FORMAT OF TESTS   218

FACTOR ANALYTIC APPROACHES   219

DIMENSIONS OF PERSONALITY   220

PROBLEMS IN PERSONALITY ASSESSMENT   222

CHAPTER 12

Assessment of Adjustment   229

CLINICAL ASSESSMENT   230

TESTS IN COUNSELING   231

CURRENT TRENDS   233

BEHAVIORAL ASSESSMENT   233

ASSESSMENT APPROACHES   235

INTERVIEWS   240

WELLNESS   246

PITFALLS   247

CHAPTER 13

Learning Styles   251

PROCESSING STYLE   252

MODALITY ASSESSMENT   252

COGNITIVE STYLE   256

LEARNING PERSONALITIES   259

LEARNING STYLE INVENTORIES   260

CHAPTER 14

Assessment of Development   267

GENERAL PRINCIPLES   268

DOMAINS   268

METHODS OF ASSESSMENT   270

EARLY IDENTIFICATION   271

LANGUAGE DEVELOPMENT   272

COGNITIVE STAGES   272

PSYCHOSOCIAL DEVELOPMENT   275

MORAL DEVELOPMENT   277

CAREER DEVELOPMENT   277

CHAPTER 15

Environmental Assessment   283

    THEORETICAL BACKGROUND   284

    ASSESSMENT STRATEGIES   286

    FAMILY/HOME ENVIRONMENT   286

    SCHOOL ENVIRONMENT   289

    SCHOOL CLIMATE   292

    WORK ENVIRONMENT   293

    PERSON-ENVIRONMENT-FIT   293

CHAPTER 16

The Computer in Assessment   299

    TEST ADMINISTRATION   300

    EQUIVALENCE OF CONVENTIONAL AND COMPUTER TESTS   301

    INDIVIDUALIZATION   302

    COMPUTER-AIDED PERSONALITY TESTING   302

    EVALUATING COMPUTER-BASED ADAPTIVE TESTING   303

    PROFESSIONAL STANDARDS AND GUIDELINES   304

    SOURCES OF INFORMATION   307

    COMPUTER OPTIONS   308

    ADVANTAGES AND DISADVANTAGES OF COMPUTER APPLICATIONS   308

    COMPUTER-BASED TEST INTERPRETATION   310

    SOFTWARE FOR TEST DEVELOPMENT   310

    TRENDS AND ISSUES   310

CHAPTER 17

Alternate and Authentic Assessment Techniques   315

    OBSERVATIONAL APPROACHES   316

    METHODS OF DATA COLLECTION   322

    GUIDELINES FOR OBSERVATION   324

    INTERVIEWING   326

    PROBLEM AREAS   329

    AUTHENTIC ASSESSMENT   329

CHAPTER 18

Working with Special Populations 337

STANDARDS FOR TESTING PEOPLE WITH DISABLING CONDITIONS   338

PRESCHOOL EVALUATIONS   340

TYPES OF DISABILITIES AND DISORDERS   342

CHAPTER 19

Multicultural Assessment 353

STANDARDS FOR MULTICULTURAL ASSESSMENT   354

TEST BIAS   356

DEVELOPING GREATER MULTICULTURAL UNDERSTANDING   357

CHAPTER 20

Test-Taking Skills 365

TEST ANXIETY   366

IMPROVING TEST SCORES   369

WORKSHOP ON TEST-TAKING SKILLS   372

OTHER FACTORS   373

INFORMATION ON TEST TAKING   374

CHAPTER 21

School Testing Programs 381

GOALS AND PURPOSES OF A TESTING PROGRAM   382

STEPS IN PLANNING A TESTING PROGRAM   382

CATEGORIES OF TESTS   384

DEVELOPMENTAL MODEL   387

EVALUATION OF SCHOOL PROGRAMS   390

ISSUES AND CONCERNS   392

GOALS 2000 EDUCATION STRATEGIES   393

CHAPTER 22

Communicating Test Results to Clients, Parents, and Professionals 399

GUIDELINES FOR COMMUNICATING TEST RESULTS   400

STANDARDS FOR REPORTING TEST RESULTS   402

METHODS OF REPORTING TEST RESULTS   402

PROBLEM AREAS   404

COMMUNICATION OF TEST RESULTS TO THE PUBLIC   406

THE TESTER AS CONSULTANT: LEGAL CONSIDERATIONS   408

ETHICAL STANDARDS FOR CONSULTATION   409

CONSULTING WITH PARENTS   409

CONSULTING WITH OTHER PROFESSIONALS   417

EVALUATION OF THE CONSULTANT   417

CHAPTER 23

Written Test Reports   423

PURPOSES OF WRITTEN REPORTS   424

CONTENT OF A REPORT   424

FACTORS AFFECTING THE TEST REPORT   429

WRITING THE REPORT   430

COMPUTER-GENERATED REPORTS   435

CHAPTER 24

Legal and Ethical Concerns and Issues in Testing   441

NBCC CODE OF ETHICS   442

AMERICAN PSYCHOLOGICAL ASSOCIATION STANDARDS   443

ACA CODE OF ETHICS   444

CODES OF PROFESSIONAL RESPONSIBILITY   444

RESPONSIBLE TEST USE   446

LEGAL ASPECTS   446

EMPLOYMENT LAWS   449

COURT DECISIONS ON EDUCATIONAL TESTING   449

COURT DECISIONS ON EMPLOYMENT TESTING   450

CURRENT TRENDS AND PERSPECTIVES   452

CHAPTER 25

Current Trends and Issues   455

COMPETENCY TESTING AND THE REFORM MOVEMENT   456

LICENSURE AND CERTIFICATION EXAMINATIONS   458

TRUTH IN TESTING   459
INVASION OF PRIVACY   459
FAIRNESS TO MINORITY GROUPS   460
HOSTILE GATEKEEPER   461
HOW ASSESSMENT IS CHANGING   461

Appendix A: Tests   467
Appendix B: Test Publishers and Distributors   483
Glossary   485
References   495
Name Index   509
Subject Index   513
Test Index   535

Models for Test Use and Selection

OVERVIEW

Decision makers want to use their best judgment and appropriate information that is both relevant and accurate. Sometimes certain tests can be identified that will provide this information. Most standardized tests require objective observation and assessment of behavior under controlled conditions. Standards guide the selection, administration, and interpretation of tests.

OBJECTIVES

The chapter should enable the reader to

✔ Discuss the steps in a decision-making model

✔ Identify the purposes for giving tests

✔ List the competencies required of test users

✔ Explain the social, philosophical, and historical foundations of the testing movement as well as some of the current issues

DECISION-MAKING MODEL

In a three-step decision-making model the first step is preparation, which involves

1. Specifying the judgments and decisions to be made
2. Describing the information needed
3. Locating the information already available in files or records
4. Deciding what information is needed and when and how this information can be obtained
5. Selecting data-gathering instruments and tests to be used and reviewing the instruments for validity, reliability, usability, and interpretability

The second step of the decision-making process is data collection, which involves (1) securing the information needed through testing, observation, and other appropriate methods; and (2) recording, analyzing, and interpreting the information.

The third step of the decision-making process is evaluation, which involves (1) forming hypotheses, (2) making decisions or judgments, and (3) reporting decisions and judgments.

Tests are just one source of information; they provide a measure of an individual's behavior at a given moment. Tests only sample the domain being measured. If the limitations of the testing process are recognized, test information can be a valuable tool in decision making.

VALUE OF TESTING

Test information can be valuable to the test taker. It can improve one's self-understanding and reinforce an individual's learning. Test information can also be valuable to society. Many professions now require certification tests to screen incompetent professionals in a given field. Counselors and psychologists, for example, are required to take licensing examinations in many states. Testing programs are also designed to identify or discover talent. This was one of the purposes of the National Defense Education Act several decades ago. A fourth value of testing is that test information can help us learn more about human behavior. If the information is used properly, it can help us to make more efficient use of our social resources. For example, knowing the work values of employees aids in developing an environment that fosters job satisfaction and productivity.

Test information can be especially valuable in educational decision making because it enhances placement decisions. Public Law 94–142 requires exceptional students to be placed in the least restrictive environment, and test information helps educational personnel place these individuals in environments that will best facilitate their learning. Test data are used with different criteria in the selection of students for gifted programs, for admission to colleges and universities, and for admission to vocational and technical programs. Advanced Placement Programs and College Level Examination Programs (CLEP) are examples of widely used placement programs. Teachers are also aided by test data in their selection of instructional strategies and their evaluation of curriculum programs.

Another way of looking at the value of test data is to consider how the data are used by different groups such as administrators, teachers, counselors, psychologists, curriculum experts, students, researchers, the public, and the legislature. All these groups are consumers of test information.

USES OF TESTS

In a position statement on the use of tests, the task force of the American Association for Counseling and Development (now the American Counseling Association) (1989) identified four major uses of tests. First, test data are used in the placement and selection of individuals—in business and industry as well as in education. Second, tests can help predict success in training programs, educational programs, or actual job experiences. Third, tests can serve descriptive and diagnostic purposes. For example, a test might describe the skills a student has mastered or failed to master in reading or mathematics. Thus, the test might help diagnose why a student is having trouble in reading or math. Fourth, testing that is conducted over a long period can produce data that provide a picture of growth. For example, tests might show growth in achievement from one year to another or growth in self-concept after involvement in group therapy sessions.

The model proposed by the task force of the American Association for Counseling and Development has two other dimensions. It focuses on the type of test to be used and lists four general categories: aptitude and ability tests; achievement tests; interest, attitude, and value tests; and perceptual-motor tests. The third dimension distinguishes between individual and group tests. Often concern focuses primarily on the individual—for counseling, placement, or diagnosis. At other times decisions must involve group testing results.

COMPETENCIES REQUIRED OF TEST USERS

Certain competencies are required to use tests properly. Many negative attitudes toward testing have resulted from certain abuses or misuses of testing. The professional standards of different associations have set explicit guidelines for the selection, use, administration, and interpretation of tests. Those guidelines can be translated into competencies. Test users should be able to do the following tasks:

1. Understand basic measurement concepts such as scales of measurement, types of reliability, types of validity, and types of norms.
2. Understand the basic statistics of measurement and define, compute, and interpret measures of central tendency, variability, and relationship.
3. Compute and apply measurement formulas such as the standard error of measurement and the Spearman-Brown prophecy formula.
4. Read, evaluate, and understand test manuals and reports.
5. Follow exactly as specified the procedures for administering, scoring, and interpreting a test.

6. List and discuss major tests in their fields.

7. Identify and locate sources of test information in their fields.

8. Discuss as well as demonstrate the use of different systems of presenting test data in tabular and graphic forms.

9. Compare and contrast different types of test scores and discuss their strengths and weaknesses.

10. Explain the relative nature of norm-referenced interpretation and the use of the standard error of measurement in interpreting individual scores.

11. Help test takers and counselees to use tests as exploratory tools.

12. Aid test takers and counselees in their decision making and in their accomplishment of developmental tasks.

13. Pace an interpretative session to enhance the client's knowledge of the test results.

14. Use strategies to prepare clients for testing to maximize the accuracy of the test results.

15. Explain the test results to test takers thoughtfully and accurately but in a language they understand.

16. Use the communication skills needed in test interpretation and identify strategies for presenting the results to individuals, groups, parents, students, teachers, and professionals.

17. Shape the client's reaction to and encourage appropriate use of the test information.

18. Be alert to the verbal and nonverbal cues expressed by the client, not only in the testing situation but also during feedback situations.

19. Use appropriate strategies with clients who perceive the test results as negative.

20. Be familiar with the test interpretation forms and computerized report forms so that they can guide the client to the information and explanation.

21. Be familiar with the legal, professional, and ethical guidelines related to testing.

22. Be aware of the client's rights and the professional's responsibilities as a test administrator and counselor.

23. List and discuss the current issues and trends in testing.

24. Present results from tests both verbally and in written form and know what types of information should be presented in case studies and conferences.

25. Discuss and use strategies to assist an individual in acquiring test-taking skills and in lowering test anxiety.

26. Identify and discuss computer-assisted and computer-adaptive testing and show application to their fields.

The Test User Qualifications Working Group (AACD, 1989) identified seven factors through a factor analysis of 86 generic subelements of good testing practices. The seven factors are

1. *Comprehensive assessment:* follow-up to get facts from psychosocial history to integrate with test scores as part of interpretation

2. *Proper test use:* acceptance of responsibility for competent use of the test

3. *Psychometric knowledge:* consideration of standard error of measurement

4. *Maintaining integrity of testing:* making clear that cutoff scores imposed for placement in special programs for the gifted are questionable because they disregard measurement error
5. *Accuracy of scoring:* using checks on scoring accuracy
6. *Appropriate use of norms:* not assuming that a norm for a given job or group applies to a different job or group
7. *Interpretive feedback:* willingness and ability to give interpretation and guidance to test takers in counseling (p. 3)

In some states, individuals who wish to become school counselors must pass a certification examination. In Florida, candidates need to demonstrate competencies in eight areas:

1. Understanding basic measurement concepts such as validity, norming, reliability, standard error of measurement, and standardization
2. Identifying conditions that may affect test results
3. Demonstrating knowledge of major functions, strengths, and limitations of standardized and nonstandardized appraisal procedures
4. Demonstrating knowledge of appropriate procedures for collecting, storing, and safeguarding assessment instruments and data
5. Developing oral and written reports that provide meaningful information based upon assessment data
6. Demonstrating an understanding of statistics essential for interpretation to individual students and groups of students
7. Interpreting assessment data for professional personnel and parents in terms of growth and development of students
8. Interpreting individual student data from records and professional reports

The National Association of College Admission Counselors (NACAC) believes that counselors need certain competencies to be effective in counseling students from elementary through postsecondary school. One of the competencies that deals with testing is the ability to develop, collect, analyze, and interpret data. Every school counselor should be able to establish effective systems for conveying important data and information about students between educational levels. Specifically, counselors need to understand the proper administration and use of standardized tests and be able to interpret test scores and test-related data to students, parents, educators, institutions, agencies, and the public. The following tests are included in the NACAC list:

Advanced Placement Programs
American College Test (ACT)
College Level Examination Program (CLEP)
National Merit Scholarship Qualifying Test (NMSQT)
Preliminary American College Test (P-ACT)
Preliminary Scholastic Aptitude Test (PSAT)
Scholastic Aptitude Test (SAT)
Test of English As a Foreign Language (TOEFL)

Counselors should also understand how individual and group data and statistics are used in building class and institutional profiles, constructing student transcripts, and preparing reports.

HISTORICAL CONTEXTS

Testing is not a new idea, even though the objective test movement began only at the turn of the century (see Table 1.1). About 2200 B.C. the Chinese used essay examinations to help select civil service employees. The philosophies of Socrates and Plato emphasized the importance of assessing an individual's competencies and aptitudes in vocational selection. Throughout the centuries philosophers and educators

Table 1.1
Major events in testing during the 20th century

1900 to 1909	Jung Word Association Test Binet and Simon Intelligence Scale Standardized group tests of achievement Stone Arithmetic Test Thorndike Handwriting, Language, Spelling, and Arithmetic Tests Spearman's measurement theory Pearson's theory of correlation Thorndike's textbook on educational measurement Goddard's translation of Binet into English	1930 to 1939	Thurstone's primary mental abilities Buros's *First Mental Measurement Yearbook* Johnson's test scoring machine Graduate Record Examinations Wechsler Bellevue Intelligence Scale 1937 revision of the Stanford-Binet Intelligence Scale Murray's Thematic Apperception Test Bernreuter Personality Inventory Leiter International Performance Scale Kuder Preference Scale Record Lindquist's Iowa Every-Pupil Test Bender Gestalt Test Marino's *Sociometric Techniques* Piaget's *Origins of Intelligence* Tiegs and Clark's Progressive Achievement Test Gesell Maturity Scale
1910 to 1919	Army Alpha, Army Beta Stenquist Test of Mechanical Abilities Porteous Maze Test Seashore Measures of Musical Talents Spearman's *Factors in Intelligence* Stanford-Binet Intelligence Scale Otis Absolute Point Scale Stern's concept of mental quotient Woodworth Personal Data Sheet		
1920 to 1929	Founding of the Psychological Corporation Goodenough Draw-a-Man Test Strong Vocational Interest Blank Terman, Kelley, and Ruch's Stanford Achievement Test Clark's *Aptitude Testing* Spearman's *The Abilities of Man: Their Nature and Measurement* Morrison's School Mastery Tests Rorschach Ink Blot Test Hartshorne and May's *Character Education Inquiry* Kohs's Block Design Test	1940 to 1949	Minnesota Multiphasic Personality Inventory Wechsler Intelligence Scale for Children U.S. Employment Service's General Aptitude Test Battery Cattell Infant Intelligence Scale
		1950 to 1959	Lindquist's electronic test scoring *Standards for Educational and Psychological Testing* Guilford's *The Nature of Human Intelligence* Stevenson's *The Study of Behavior: Q-Technique and Its Methodology* Osgood's semantic differential National Defense Education Act Frederikson's in-basket assessment technique Bloom's *Taxonomy of Educational Objectives*

have devised certain scales or items to provide teachers and parents with useful information to help their children. Fitzherbert (1470–1538) identified some items to screen retarded from nonretarded individuals—for example, being able to count to 20 pence, being able to tell one's age, and being able to identify one's father and mother. Juan Huarte (1530–1589) was probably the first writer to suggest formal mental testing. His book title was translated as *The Trial of Wits: Discovering the Great Differences of Wits Among Men and What Sorts of Learning Suit Best with Each Genius.* Jean Esquirol (1772–1840), a French physician, proposed that there are several levels of mental deficiency and that language is a valid psychological criterion for differentiating among levels. Edouard Seguin (1812–1880) also worked with mentally retarded individuals and believed that they should be trained in sensory discrimination and in the development of motor control. His form board has been adapted and incorporated in some widely used performance and nonverbal IQ tests.

1960 to 1969	National Assessment of Educational Progress Flannigan's Project Talent Wechsler Preschool and Primary Scale of Intelligence 1960 revision of the Stanford-Binet Jensen's *How Much Can We Boost IQ and Scholastic Achievement?* Kuder Occupational Interest Survey Cattell's *Theory of Fluid and Crystallized Intelligence* Kirk and McCarthy's Illinois Test of Psycholinguistic Abilities Bayley Scales of Infant Development
1970 to 1979	Family Educational Rights and Privacy Act New York State Truth in Testing Act Public Law 94–142 System of Multicultural Pluralistic Assessment Wechsler Intelligence Scale for Children—Revised Revised *Standards for Educational and Psychological Testing* Rokeach Value Survey Peabody Picture Vocabulary Test *Seventh* and *Eighth Mental Measurements Yearbooks* Use of computers in testing McCarthy Scales of Children's Abilities
1980 to 1989	Thorndike, Hagen, and Stattler's revision of the Stanford-Binet Kaufman Assessment Battery for Children *Ninth* and *Tenth Mental Measurements Yearbooks* Minnesota Multiphasic Personality Inventory II Revised *Standards for Educational and Psychological Testing* Computer-adaptive and -assisted testing Wechsler Adult Intelligence Scale—Revised Nader/Nairn *The Reign of ETS* *Tests in Print III* *Mental Measurements Yearbook* reviews in Bibliographic Retrieval Service *Test Critiques*, Vols. 1 to 7
1990 to 1999	Wechsler Intelligence Scale for Children III Wechsler Individual Achievement Test Revised Scholastic Aptitude Test of CEEB *Tests III* *Test Critiques*, Vols. 8, 9, and 10 Authentic testing (direct or performance assessment) *The Eleventh, Twelfth,* and *Thirteenth Mental Measurements Yearbooks* *Standards for Educational and Psychological Measurement,* 3rd ed. Computer-adaptive version of Differential Aptitude Test *Tests in Print IV*

Alfred Binet (1857–1911) became the director of the first physiological/psychological laboratory in France, at the Sorbonne, and did his early work on the relationship of intelligence, palmistry, and phrenology. Binet and Henri were commissioned in 1896 by the Ministry of Public Education in Paris to recommend procedures whereby mentally retarded children might receive the benefits of an education. Binet claimed that his scale provided a crude means of differentiating between those children who could function in the regular classroom and those who could not.

The Victorian era marked the beginning of modern science and witnessed the influence of Darwinian biology on the studies of individuals. In 1879 in Leipzig, Wundt founded the first psychological laboratory. His work was largely concerned with sensitivity to visual, auditory, and other sensory stimuli and simple reaction time. He followed scientific procedures and rigorously controlled observations. He influenced the measurement movement by using methodology that required precision, accuracy, order, and reproducibility of data and findings. The interest in the exceptional individual broadened to include personality and behavior. Freud, Charcot, and Pinel were interested in persons with personal and social adjustment problems.

Many of the innovations and changes in the testing movement resulted from major crises. Both World War I and World War II stimulated major movements in testing. The armed services found that they needed a quick way of screening the level of mental functioning of recruits. They adapted the work of Otis, who developed an objective group test of intelligence and the Army Alpha. The original purpose of the army test was to identify those recruits whose lower intelligence would create problems for the military organization. The typical recruit had only a fifth-grade education, and many candidates were illiterate. Another problem was that America had many foreign-born candidates who had little command of the English language and thereby required a nonverbal test or pictorial form with pantomime substituted for written directions. This became the Army Beta.

The first major personality assessment was also developed for use during World War I. The armed services wanted a way to screen psychotics and other emotionally disturbed individuals. Such a test was developed from the Woodworth Personal Data Sheet, a forerunner of the modern adjustment inventories.

The successful use of tests by the armed services led to widespread adoption of tests in education and industry. Other factors also contributed to the widespread acceptance of tests. The growth in population, free public education, compulsory school attendance laws, the increase in students who were going on to institutions of higher education—all were factors that changed the philosophy and practice of testing. In addition, the egalitarian, political, and philosophical movements that championed integration, women's rights, rights of exceptional children and adults, and minority and ethnic group heritage influenced how people viewed testing. Tests were criticized for cultural bias, sexual bias, unfairness to minority groups, and unfairness to handicapped groups. These criticisms led to improved review procedures for the selection of test items and the selection of norming samples.

In recent years, however, the prevailing political philosophy in the United States has changed from a liberal to a more conservative orientation, which has caused a shift from open, humanistic education to back-to-basics and competency-based approaches. We have national assessment, state assessment, minimum- and essential-level skills tests. Many states require students to pass competency examinations prior to graduating. The 1990 Gallup Poll concludes that the public continues to oppose promotion from one grade to the next unless the student can pass examinations—presumably grade- and curriculum-appropriate examinations. Opinions on this topic have not changed significantly over a 20-year period: 68% of the group was in favor of examinations in 1990, whereas 67% favored examinations in 1978. Some states are calling for mandatory examinations for teachers to demonstrate that they can read, write, and communicate effectively; that they know methods of teaching; and that they have mastered the content of what they are to teach.

If we look back at our history, we will find that testing movements have run in recurring cycles. For example, various groups were calling for a moratorium on testing in the early 1960s. Cyclical trends have also characterized the accountability issue, the humanizing of the educational process, human rights, and other issues.

The testing movement has been stimulated by arguments within the profession. Thurstone, Spearman, and E. L. Thorndike debated the nature of intelligence as a single factor or multifactor construct. Cattell, R. L. Thorndike, and Vernon have models including both general and specific factors, or fluid and crystallized intelligence. The debate continues. Sternberg believes that there are different types of intelligence and that tests should measure different types of cognitive abilities, and Gardner has proposed a theory of multiple intelligences.

The testing movement has also been affected by technology. The computer and microcomputer have changed the scope and direction of testing administration, scoring, and interpretation. We have computer-assisted and computer-adaptive testing and a myriad of software packages to help us score and interpret everything from biographical data blanks to the Rorschach test.

It is interesting to note the tests that generated the largest number of references in the *Thirteenth Mental Measurements Yearbook*. The top test was the Beck Depression Inventory (1,026) followed by the Child Behavior Checklist (556), the Revised Hamilton Rating Scale for Depression (382), the Bayley Scales for Infant Development, Second Edition (130), the fifth edition of the California Achievement Tests (113), the Iowa Tests of Basic Skills (110), and the revised edition of the Beck Hopelessness Scale (83). Of the 396 tests reviewed, 75 (20.3%) were personality, 73 (19.8 percent) vocational.

The standards of the Council for the Accreditation of Counseling and Related Education Programs (CACREP) ask counselors to have an understanding of individual and group approaches to assessment and evaluation in eight major areas:

1. Theoretical and historical bases for assessment techniques
2. Evidence for establishing content, construct, and empirical validity
3. Methods of establishing stability, internal, and equivalent reliability
4. Appraisal methods, including environmental assessment, performance assessment, individual and group test and inventory methods, behavioral observations, and computer-managed and -assisted methods

5. Psychometric statistics, including types of assessment scores, measures of central tendency, indices of validity, standard errors, and correlations
6. Age, gender, ethnicity, language, disability, and cultural factors related to the assessment and evaluation of individuals and groups
7. Strategies for selecting, administering, interpreting, and using assessment and evaluation instruments and techniques in counseling
8. Ethical considerations in appraisal

Florida's Competency Requirements for School Counselors

Florida has seven requirements similar to CACREP's. Counselors should be able to

- Demonstrate knowledge of basic measurement concepts (validity, norming, reliability, error of measurement, and standardization)
- Identify conditions that may affect test results
- Demonstrate knowledge of the major functions, strengths, and limitations of standardized and nonstandardized appraisal procedures
- Demonstrate knowledge of appropriate procedures for collecting, storing, and safeguarding assessment instruments and data
- Demonstrate an understanding of statistics essential for interpretation to individual students and groups of students
- Interpret assessment data to professional personnel and parents in terms of the growth and development of students
- Interpret individual student data from records and professional reports

Redundant

SUMMARY

This is an information age. Many decisions need to be made, and a decision-making model is a useful guide. Test and assessment data can often help in decision making. It is important to know the types of information that can be gained from testing and the recognized and valid purposes of this procedure.

Test users need to have the skills and competencies necessary to gain reliable and valid information. They also need to be alert to the current issues and controversies in testing and to have an understanding of the historical, social, and political movements that have influenced measurement practices and procedures.

QUESTIONS FOR DISCUSSION

1. What tests have you taken during your lifetime? For what purposes were they given? How can you organize the tests into categories? In what ways was the testing valuable to you? What type of feedback did you get about the results?

2. What types of changes have you noticed in tests and testing over time?

3. Should all tests be considered within a framework of cultural diversity? Are any tests really culture-free? Can a true culture-free test be constructed?

4. Should knowledge of the historical foundations of testing be a competency required from workers in the helping professions? Why or why not?

SUGGESTED ACTIVITIES

1. Interview individuals who are working in the helping professions and find out why, when, and how they use testing. Find out what type of decision-making model they use.

2. Look through current newspapers and magazines and cut out or duplicate articles dealing with testing. Discuss those articles in class and identify the types of issues involved.

3. Write a position paper on a current issue in testing.

4. Read further about one of the critical events or one of the key figures in the history of testing and report to the class on what you have learned.

5. Compare the purposes of testing that measurement experts advocate with those that practitioners follow. Is there agreement by both groups as to the roles and functions of testing? Write a position paper on what you believe should be the role of testing and assessment in your field.

6. Report to the class about the certification requirements for your state for a psychological examiner, a school psychologist, a school counselor, or any other professional requiring expertise in testing.

ADDITIONAL READINGS

Anastasi, A. (1993). A century of psychological testing: Origins, problems, and progress. In T. K. Fagan & G. R. Vanden Bos (Eds.), *Exploring applied psychology: Origins and critical analysis* (pp. 11–36). Washington, DC: American Psychological Association.

Anastasi, one of the outstanding figures in psychological testing, provides a critical analysis of testing during the century.

Buros, O. K. (1977). Fifty years in testing: Some reminiscences, criticisms, and suggestions. *Educational Researcher, 6*(7), 9–15.

This article by one of the important figures in the testing field gives insight into where we are and where we have been.

DuBois, P. H. (1970). *The history of psychological testing*. Boston: Allyn & Bacon.

This is another good book on the history of testing.

Linden, K. W., & Linden, J. D. (1968). *Modern mental measurement: A historical perspective*. Boston: Houghton Mifflin.

This paperback provides readers with a brief history of the modern mental measurement movement.

Zeidner, M., & Most, R. (Eds.). (1992). *Psychological testing: An inside view*. Palo Alto, CA: Consulting Psychologists Press.

This book of readings provides an excellent overview of testing. The first chapter by the editors discusses the context of testing, key concepts, basic assumptions, functions and uses, classification, and major criticisms.

2

Statistical Concepts

OVERVIEW

A worker in the helping professions collects much data on individuals or groups. Statistics provide a means to organize and interpret the data in a way that can be quantified. Statistics play a major role in assessment and measurement. They provide rules and procedures to help summarize and describe data. They pro-vide a frame of reference for interpreting and evaluating test scores. Statistics also help evaluate the psychometric properties of tests or assessment instruments. For example, correlational techniques are used to compute many of the validity and reliability coefficients discussed in Chapter 3.

OBJECTIVES

The chapter should enable the reader to understand

✔ Characteristics of the four scales of measurement

✔ Ways to organize and present test data

✔ Measures of central tendency

✔ Measures of the variability of scores

✔ Shapes and types of distributions

✔ Indexes of relative position

✔ Ways of comparing individual performance on two different tests

ROLE OF STATISTICS

A professional needs to know certain statistical concepts to evaluate, use, and interpret standardized and nonstandardized instruments. Workers in the helping professions need to have a good understanding of the four scales of measurement and the different families of statistics.

Descriptive statistics are used to summarize and describe a set of data. Inferential statistics are used to draw inferences about an individual or individuals from sample data. For example, do observations of two groups of subjects differ from one another? In Chapter 3 we will look at whether there are differences in the responses of different groups—for example, in the answers of artists and engineers on an interest inventory. Multivariate statistics are used with the simultaneous investigation of two or more variable characteristics measured over a set of individuals. We might explore the relationships among the interests, values, and achievements of different occupational groups.

FOUR SCALES OF MEASUREMENT

Scores on a test, questionnaire, or assessment instrument represent the assignment of numbers to individual items or the total test in order to classify the individual or represent the standing of an individual on some variable. That is measurement—the assigning of numbers to the attributes of individuals, events, or objects according to a set of logical rules. Specific sets of rules define a scale of measurement; four of these scales—nominal, ordinal, interval, and ratio—are used to quantify variables in the behavioral sciences.

Nominal Scale

When numbers stand for names or categories that represent the way in which individuals differ, that is nominal measurement. Numbers in the nominal scales are arbitrarily assigned to code a specific variable. Here are some examples from interview schedules.

Marital status:
____ 1. Never married
____ 2. Married
____ 3. Widowed
____ 4. Divorced
____ 5. Separated

Sex:
____ 1. Male
____ 2. Female

Highest educational level completed:

___ 0. None of the following responses
___ 1. High school diploma or GED
___ 2. Vocational, business, or technical school
___ 3. Associate of arts or sciences degree
___ 4. Bachelor's degree
___ 5. Graduate degree

Ordinal Scale

When individuals or objects are ordered or ranked according to some characteristic, that is ordinal measurement. For example, a counselor who is a group facilitator might order his students along an introversion/extroversion continuum. The client who is the most introverted might be assigned the rank of 1 and the most extroverted client the highest rank. Or the percentile of individuals on an achievement test could be ranked from high to low or low to high.

Many items on schedules and questionnaires require a personal ranking on a certain characteristic. Here is just one example:

Please rate your degree of competence in the listed behaviors, using the following key: 1 = low, 3 = average, 5 = extremely high.

1.	Oral communication skills	1	2	3	4	5
2.	Written communication skills	1	2	3	4	5
3.	Listening skills	1	2	3	4	5

There are problems with the ordinal scale because the competencies may not be equally spaced. An individual might be extremely strong in certain areas, with minute differences distinguishing those competencies, and extremely weak in some others. Problems also can occur in comparing rankings across groups. The persons with number 1 rankings in each group might vary tremendously on the variable being ranked. Thus, in rank ordering, the length of the intervals can be unequal. And the numbers used for rankings do not reflect anything quantitative about the variable being ranked. Caution is needed in performing arithmetical operations on measurements derived from ordinal scales and in using and interpreting the information.

Interval Scale

When a scale differentiates among levels of an attribute and has equal distances between those levels, that is interval measurement. It uses numerical values that are equally spaced. Examples of interval scales occur in educational and psychological measurement. We often treat the scores (that is, the number of correct responses) on aptitude and ability tests as belonging to the interval scale; we assign numbers to levels of an attribute and assume that equal differences in the numbers correspond to equal differences in the attribute. That approach may be meaningful with a variable such as temperature, but we can have problems with test results. Can we say a score of 0 indicates an absence of a trait or characteristic or that someone with an IQ of 100 has twice as much intelligence as a person having an IQ of 50?

Ratio Scale

When a true or absolute zero point exists in addition to ranking and equal intervals, that is ratio measurement. Measures such as height and weight are examples of ratio scales. Response time is often an important ratio measurement in interpreting standardized tests: two minutes are twice as much as one, and there is a true zero point. Both the interval and ratio scale have interval properties and use the same statistical procedures.

WHAT SCORES LOOK LIKE

Often a visual picture of what the scores look like is needed. For example, a large number of tests might be organized by setting up the frequency distribution into some type of graphic presentation such as a histogram or frequency polygon.

Let's suppose we have just tested incarcerated youth who have been assigned to our cottage in a correctional facility. The scores of the Nowicki-Strickland Locus of Control Scale, Slosson Intelligence Test, and the Jesness Behavior Checklist are listed in Table 2.1. We have the scores on 30 youths.

Let's look first at the scores on the Nowicki-Strickland test, given in the column headed LOC. The scale purports to measure locus of control as defined by Rotter (1966). The test measures generalized expectancies for internal versus external control of reinforcement among children. Low scores indicate internality, high scores externality. As the scores are listed, it is hard to get a picture of the characteristics of this group of offenders. To visualize the data better, we could arrange the scores from high to low.

15	9,9,9	6,6	3,3,3
14	8,8,8	5,5,5,5	2,2,2
13	7,7	4,4,4,4,4	1

Arranging the scores in order helps us to see some trends in the data more quickly. We can determine at a glance the highest score and the lowest score, and we can find the approximate middle. However, when a large number of test scores have a greater range (the spread between the high and low scores), it is not as easy to organize and record the scores and see an overall picture.

Table 2.1
Scores on the Nowicki-Strickland Locus of Control Scale (LOC), Slosson Intelligence Test (SIT), and Jesness Behavior Checklist* for Cottage 1

Youth	LOC	SIT	AC	IS	CA	SO	CO	EN	RA	CM	IN	SC	CS	RE	FR	UN
1	1	110	12	27	24	17	23	18	22	20	13	12	28	37	18	26
2	3	120	18	27	28	23	27	16	20	24	15	18	29	33	19	34
3	5	99	15	30	20	21	28	23	19	21	12	16	31	34	18	27
4	3	95	12	22	23	16	22	18	19	21	19	15	26	33	19	33
5	8	93	12	28	18	17	25	18	22	19	12	15	30	36	18	26
6	3	112	15	24	24	20	20	17	22	22	20	12	24	35	19	29
7	9	108	13	26	16	15	23	15	19	17	19	16	18	34	15	31
8	8	82	9	21	19	16	22	16	14	16	18	11	22	30	11	24
9	2	115	11	30	21	17	23	18	19	24	20	18	25	41	21	26
10	14	70	19	20	19	22	21	18	21	14	14	15	30	40	17	30
11	9	99	20	28	22	25	27	13	25	21	13	16	23	37	21	35
12	5	83	8	24	23	15	18	22	18	18	10	9	24	34	15	17
13	5	88	17	29	19	22	26	20	23	18	16	18	24	29	16	31
14	15	75	12	21	15	15	20	15	17	18	17	11	19	34	18	26
15	6	102	15	25	21	21	29	16	19	16	16	14	28	32	16	32
16	7	76	13	28	16	17	19	13	14	19	17	16	22	32	16	27
17	3	85	16	28	15	21	25	17	16	19	17	17	32	41	19	30
18	2	112	14	29	21	19	24	20	18	21	20	18	25	40	20	32
19	13	79	13	17	20	14	27	17	12	18	15	12	25	18	16	25
20	2	117	16	24	22	22	23	17	15	15	15	15	25	32	16	28
21	4	113	15	27	16	20	23	18	22	17	15	15	29	33	22	27
22	9	91	9	27	17	11	18	14	21	16	15	12	26	32	14	18
23	6	107	9	20	18	15	29	16	18	13	18	15	22	28	14	29
24	5	105	18	28	25	23	24	16	20	20	17	15	25	35	19	26
25	4	109	15	27	22	22	22	19	15	20	17	15	26	39	15	23
26	4	107	18	25	25	22	30	17	17	18	18	19	29	38	18	33
27	7	83	17	27	23	22	21	16	23	21	18	15	27	33	17	28
28	4	111	16	16	16	20	25	8	16	13	11	18	21	34	20	32
29	4	109	9	20	13	13	20	18	14	14	16	12	23	28	13	19
30	8	101	17	27	19	21	26	13	21	10	16	16	28	33	20	27

*The Jesness scales are Anger Control (AC), Insight (IS), Calmness (CA), Sociability (SO), Conformity (CO), Enthusiasm (EN), Rapport (RA), Communication (CM), Independence (IN), Social Concern (SC), Consideration (CS), Responsibility (RE), Friendliness (FR), and Unobtrusiveness (UN).

Frequency Distribution

A frequency distribution is a way of summarizing and visually presenting aspects of the test data (see Table 2.2).

These steps must be followed to complete the distribution:

Table 2.2
Frequency distribution of the
Nowicki-Strickland Locus of
Control Scale

Score Value	Tally	Frequency
15	/	1
14	/	1
13	/	1
12		0
11		0
10		0
9	///	3
8	///	3
7	//	2
6	//	2
5	////	4
4	/////	5
3	////	4
2	///	3
1	//	1

1. Identify three columns to record (a) each score value, (b) a tally of the scores of each score value, and (c) a sum of each tally (frequency).
2. Arrange the scores from high to low in the first column and complete the other two columns as indicated.

A frequency distribution helps to summarize the test data on a particular scale by arranging the scores in order of magnitude and indicating how often each score was obtained.

Sometimes there is a greater range of scores because there are more items on the test and greater variability of performance among the test takers. In such a situation it is easier to group a series of score values; that grouping is called a class interval. We can visualize a frequency distribution if it has between 10 and 20 score intervals. The following formula can be used to determine the range of test score points that should be included in each interval:

$$\text{Class interval size} = \frac{\text{highest score} - \text{lowest score}}{\text{desired number of class intervals}}$$

If we establish 15 as the desired number of class intervals, then the difference between the highest and lowest scores is divided by 15, and the result is an estimate of the number of test score points to be included in each interval.

Let's turn back to Table 2.1 and look at the IQ scores, listed under SIT, for the 30 youths. The Slosson Intelligence Test, an individually administered test, yields a total intelligence score, measuring verbal reasoning, vocabulary knowledge, numerical reasoning, and abstract reasoning. To produce a group frequency distribution, we follow these steps:

1. Select the number of class intervals to be used.   10
2. Find the highest score.   120
3. Find the lowest score.   70
4. Subtract the lowest from the highest score.   50
5. Divide the range by the size of the class interval selected to   5
   determine the number of score points to be included in each interval. $10\overline{)50}$
6. Start the frequency distribution with the lowest score.

As we can see from Table 2.3, the grouped frequency distribution provides a good picture of the ability of the group. Because each interval consists of 5 test score points, we lose information about the individual scores. However, the grouping makes the data easier to interpret because there are fewer intervals, only 11 instead of the 51 there would be if individual scores with intervals of 1 were considered.

Graphic Presentations

Two types of graphic presentations of test data will be considered here—the histogram or bar graph, and the frequency polygon, a line graph. Some people prefer a visual mode of learning, and a graph quite often clarifies and simplifies the presentation of the data.

The histogram is a type of bar graph used frequently to portray the distribution of test data. Figure 2.1 presents the histogram of the locus of control scores from Table 2.1. The ordinate, or y axis (vertical line), represents the frequencies of scores appearing at each score level. The abscissa, or x axis, represents the score points. The intersection of the x and y axes represents the zero point for each.

The frequency polygon is a type of line graph, also used to portray test data. The midpoint of each score interval is used to help plot the graph. In the group frequency distribution of scores on the Slosson Intelligence Test, a score interval of 5 was used. Thus, the midpoint of the interval 70–74 is 72. If the class interval consists

Table 2.3
Group frequency distribution on the Slosson Intelligence Scale

Class Interval	Tally	Frequency
120–124	/	1
115–119	//	2
110–114	/////	5
105–109	//////	6
100–104	//	2
95–99	///	3
90–94	//	2
85–89	//	2
80–84	///	3
75–79	///	3
70–74	/	1

Figure 2.1
Histogram of Slosson Intelligence Test scores

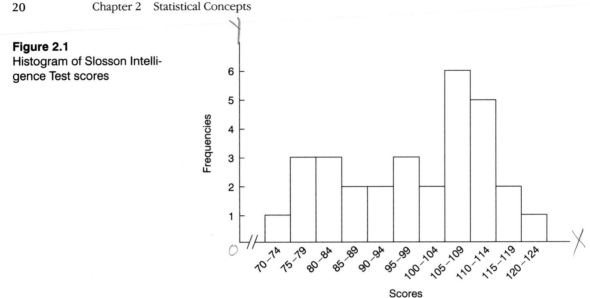

of an odd number of score points, the midpoint is a whole number; if it contains an
even number of points, the midpoint is a number +.5. Table 2.4 presents information on how the size of the class interval relates to the midpoint. A frequency polygon of the SIT scores is presented in Figure 2.2.

Smoothed Curve

If there were many more individuals and a greater number of intervals, the frequency
polygon would be a smoother curve. The shape of the curve provides useful information for the test administrator. When the curve is smoothed out, it gives a better
idea of the shape of the distribution as well as the frequency of the scores. If we

Table 2.4
Size of class interval, score range, and midpoint

Size of Class Interval	Scores	Midpoint
2	70, 71	70.5
3	70, 71, 72	71
4	70, 71, 72, 73	71.5
5	70, 71, 72, 73, 74	72
6	70, 71, 72, 73, 74, 75	72.5
7	70, 71, 72, 73, 74, 75, 76	73
8	70, 71, 72, 73, 74, 75, 76, 77	73.5
9	70, 71, 72, 73, 74, 75, 76, 77, 78	74
10	70, 71, 72, 73, 74, 75, 76, 77, 78, 79	74.5

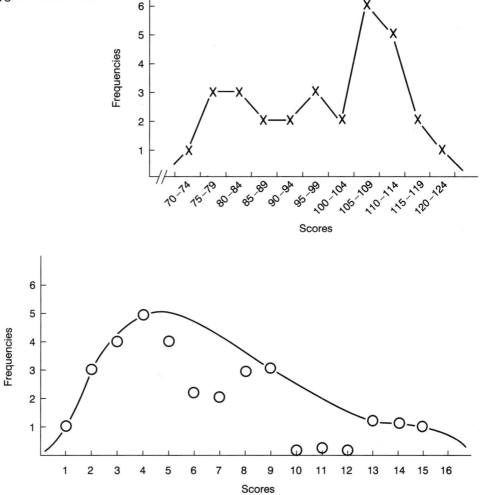

Figure 2.2
Frequency polygon of scores on
the SIT

Figure 2.3
Frequency polygon of locus-of-control curves, smoothed

made the intervals progressively smaller and increased the number of individuals
tested on the Nowicki-Strickland Locus of Control Scale, the distribution might look
like Figure 2.3.

Symmetry and Skewness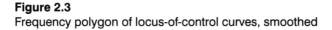

When we interpret the curve for a test, we evaluate two major characteristics—skewness and symmetry. There are two major types of curves. The curve for locus-of-con-

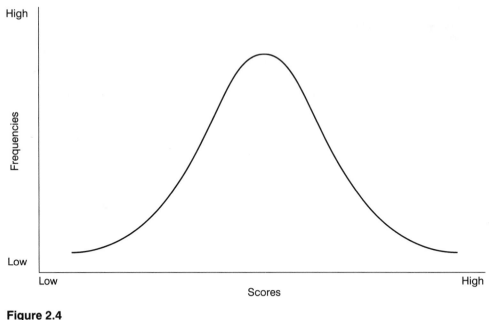

Figure 2.4
Typical curve of scores on intelligence tests

trol scores is an asymmetrical curve. The curve for the intelligence scores, when smoothed, is more of a symmetrical curve, like that in Figure 2.4. In a symmetrical distribution each side is a mirror image of the other. Later, when we look at interpretation of tests, we will focus on the normal curve, which is a special type of symmetrical curve.

The distribution of locus-of-control scores is a positively skewed distribution. Most of the youths scored near the lower end of the distribution; they were internal in their orientation. A few youths had high scores and were external in their orientation.

If we smoothed the frequency polygon for the scores on the Jesness scales, we would see that most of the scores occur at the higher score levels, with very few scores at the lower levels. This distribution would be negatively skewed. Most of the youths rated their social behavior very positively. The majority of the youths had low scores on the Nowicki-Strickland but high scores on the Jesness.

On criterion-referenced tests, in which students tend to get most of the items right, scores pile up at the upper end of the distribution. When tests are easy, most individuals make high scores, and the distribution will be negatively skewed. When test items are difficult, the test takers tend to make low scores on the test, and the scores pile up at the lower end of the distribution. A few individuals will make high scores. This distribution is positively skewed. The two types of distributions are compared in Figure 2.5.

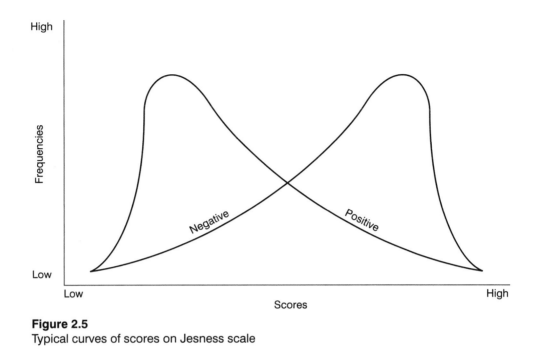

Figure 2.5
Typical curves of scores on Jesness scale

MEASURES OF CENTRAL TENDENCY

We often want to know about the typical or average performance of a group on a test. There are three measures of central tendency: mean, median, and mode. In part, the measure of central tendency depends on the scale of measurement used. With nominal data the only measure of central tendency is the mode. With ordinal data the median as well as the mode can be used. With the interval and ratio scale all three measures of central tendency can be used. The mode is the score or number that appears most frequently. The mean is the arithmetic average. The median is the middle score, or 50th percentile.

Mode

The mode is the score or numerical value that appears most frequently in a set of scores. In the ordering of the scores on the Nowicki-Strickland Scale (see Table 2.2), the mode is 4. For the Anger Control Scale on the Jesness, is the mode 9, 12, or 15?

Sometimes there is a bimodal or multimodal distribution; in other words, two or more scores may appear most frequently in the distribution. In the distribution of scores on the Friendliness Scale, the same number of people have scores of 16, 18, and 19. Certain achievement subtests produce a distribution such as the one shown in Figure 2.6. Girls tend to score higher than boys on certain scales, and vice versa, thus producing a bimodal distribution.

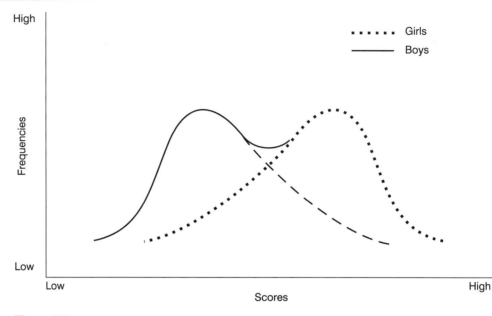

Figure 2.6
Bimodal distribution of boys' and girls' scores on reading achievement tests

The mode is often used as a quick measure of central tendency, but it is affected by various factors, such as the number of people taking the test. When the group is small, the mode does not always reflect the typical performance within the group. In a negatively or positively skewed distribution, the mode is quite often not an accurate measure of central tendency.

Mean

The mean is the arithmetic average. It is equal to the sum of the scores on a test divided by the number of individuals who took the test.

$$\overline{X} = \frac{\sum X}{N}$$

The mean ($\overline{X}$) is equal to the sum (S) of the scores (X) divided by the number of individuals (N). If we add the scores of the 30 individuals taking the Nowicki-Strickland, our total is 178. To compute the mean, we divide 178 by 30. The mean is 5.93.

The mean is the most frequently used measure of central tendency. If we subtract each score from the mean and add up the sum of the differences, the sum is 0. Each score is used to compute the mean, whereas the mode considers just the score with the highest frequency. The mean is affected by extreme scores in the distribution. A few extremely low scores will move the mean down; extremely high scores will move it up.

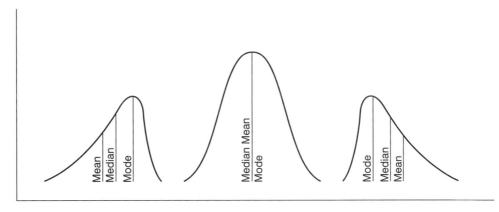

Figure 2.7
Type of distribution and measure of central tendency

Median

The median is the middle score, or the score that divides a distribution in half. There will be 50% of the scores falling below the median and 50% above. The median score on the Nowicki-Strickland is 5. When a set of scores consists of an odd number, the median is the middle score. For example, if the scores are 4, 6, 8, the median is 6. With an even number of scores—4, 6, 8, 10—the sum of the two middle scores is divided by 2; the median in this case is 7. Procedures to compute the median from grouped scores in a frequency distribution can be found in most statistical texts.

The median is a better measure of central tendency in a skewed distribution. It is not affected by extreme scores. The relationship of the mean, mode, and median is shown in Figure 2.7 for different types of distributions. The mean, median, and mode have the same score value only in a symmetrical distribution such as the normal curve.

Comparisons of Measures of Central Tendency

There is not one best measure of central tendency. The scale of measurement determines which measure of central tendency can be used, and the purpose of the measure needs to be kept in mind. The mode is the least stable statistic of central tendency. Test makers use the mean and median scores to portray typical or average performance. The mean is a statistic that has algebraic properties; it is used extensively in both descriptive and inferential statistics.

MEASURES OF VARIABILITY

Information about the variability or spread of the scores is necessary for proper interpretation of the data. Two measures of variability are used most often to interpret test scores—range and standard deviation.

Range

A quick measure of the spread of scores can be obtained by computing the range. The range is computed by subtracting the lowest score from the highest score and adding 1 to the difference. If the highest score is 3 and the lowest 1, we add 1 to the difference (2) and calculate a range of 3. The distribution would have three scores— 1, 2, and 3. In the distribution of Nowicki-Strickland scores in Table 2.1, the high score is 15 and the low score 1, making the range 15 (15 – 1 + 1 = 15).

The range is easy to compute. However, an extreme score in the distribution can make the range a misleading statistic. For example, a test might produce these scores:

1, 2, 2, 3, 3, 3, 4, 4, 5, 5, 6, 6, 40

The range here would be 40 even though the other scores are grouped closely together.

The range is a valuable statistic for test interpretation, but it is most often used in conjunction with other statistics such as standard deviation and median, mode, and mean. The range helps tell us how compact or expanded the distribution is but does not always reflect the pattern of variation in the distribution of test scores.

Variance

The variance is a statistic that provides information on how widely spread, or scattered, the scores are from the mean. The variance is computed by subtracting the mean from each score, squaring the difference, and then computing the average squared difference between the scores and the mean. In the formula, s^2 represents the variance.

$$s^2 = \frac{\sum (X - \overline{X})^2}{N}$$

Standard Deviation

The standard deviation is the square root of the variance and the most widely used statistic of variability. It is a numerical value that describes the spread of scores away from the mean and is expressed in the same units as the original scores. The wider the spread of scores, the larger the standard deviation. Because there is a small range of scores on the Nowicki-Strickland, just 15 points rather than the 51 points of the SIT, the standard deviation on the Nowicki-Strickland Locus of Control Scale will be smaller than the standard deviation on the SIT. Figure 2.8 presents a hypothetical illustration.

To compute a sample standard deviation, let's use just four scores—3, 5, 5, and 7. First, we compute the mean.

3 + 5 + 5 + 7 = 20 ÷ 4 = 5

Figure 2.8
Relationship of size of standard
deviation to type of distribution

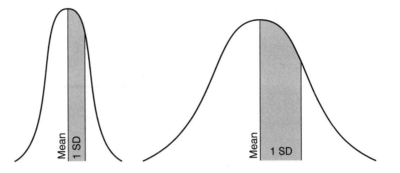

Second, we subtract the mean from each score, square the difference, and then sum the squared differences.

$$3 - 5 = -2 \qquad -2 \times -2 = +4$$
$$5 - 5 = 0 \qquad 0 \times 0 = 0$$
$$5 - 5 = 0 \qquad 0 \times 0 = 0$$
$$7 - 5 = +2 \qquad +2 \times +2 = +4$$
$$\overline{ +8}$$

To find the variance, we divide that sum by the number of scores.

$$8 \div 4 = 2$$

The standard deviation is the square root of the variance; the square root of 2 is 1.414.

It is not always convenient to use the definitional formula just illustrated because the mean may be a decimal, making arithmetic operations more complex. A computational formula for raw scores is given here and illustrated, using the scores from the previous example and letting s represent the standard deviation.

$$s = \sqrt{\frac{\Sigma X^2}{N} - \overline{X}^2}$$

X	X^2
3	9
5	25
5	25
7	49
20	108

$$s = \sqrt{\frac{108}{4} - (5)^2}$$

$$s = \sqrt{27 - 25}$$

$$s = \sqrt{2} = 1.414$$

When the scores tend to cluster around the mean, the standard deviation is smaller than when the scores are spread widely around the mean. The standard deviation is an important statistic for interpreting the relative position of an individual within a distribution of test scores. The statistic is stable and is one way of interpreting characteristics of the distribution of the test scores as well as providing a frame of reference for interpreting individual test scores.

MEASURES OF RELATIONSHIP

A statistical measure of relationship can show how two variables are related to one another. We might want to correlate the results of tests given on two different occasions or see how equivalent two forms of an intelligence or achievement test are. For tests with predictive purposes, we might want to know the relationship between intelligence and achievement or scholastic ability and grade point average. Or we might want to correlate two tests that purport to measure the same construct, such as two intelligence tests or two self-concept tests. On other occasions we might want to see whether the scales on a particular test are independent of each other.

To obtain the desired information in these cases, we would use the statistic known as the correlation coefficient. Psychologists and counselors use a number of different types of correlational procedures to measure the relationship of variables. In part, the method used will depend on the level of measurement of the variables to be compared, the type of distribution of these variables, and the number of cases to be compared.

Pearson Product Moment Correlation

The Pearson product moment correlation can be computed when we have two continuous variables and data from the interval or ratio scales. If we want to see how consistently a group performed on two different administrations of the same test, we can compute the correlation coefficient. In this case it would be the test-retest reliability coefficient. Let's assume the following scores:

Name	First (X)	Second (Y)
John	1	3
Carlo	2	2
Mary	3	4
Aziza	4	6
Heather	5	5

The formula is

$$r = \frac{N(\sum XY) - (\sum X)(\sum Y)}{\sqrt{[N(\sum X^2) - (\sum X)^2][N(\sum Y^2) - (\sum Y)^2]}}$$

Our first step would be to add each X value to find the sum (15). Our second step would be to add the Y values (20). We then need to square each of the X and Y scores and total those numbers. And we must multiply each individual X and Y score. Because we have five sets of scores, $N = 5$.

X	Y	X^2	Y^2	XY
1	3	1	9	3
2	2	4	4	4
3	4	9	16	12
4	6	16	36	24
5	5	25	25	25
15	20	55	90	68

$$r = \frac{5(68) - (15)(20)}{\sqrt{[5(55) - (15)^2][5(90) - (20)^2]}}$$

$$r = \frac{340 - 300}{\sqrt{[275 - 225][450 - 400]}} = \frac{40}{50} = .80$$

The correlation of .80 indicates a degree of association between the two testings. The correlation coefficient ranges from −1.00 to +1.00. A correlation of 0 indicates no relationship. A coefficient of +1.00 indicates a perfect positive relationship.

We could plot the scores using a scatter diagram (see Figure 2.9). The x axis represents the performance on the first test; the y axis represents the performance on the second test. With a correlation of 1.00, we would have a distribution with all the points on a straight line (see Figure 2.10). If there were an inverse relationship, with students performing in reverse order on the two tests, the correlation would be −1.00, and the scores would all fall on a straight line slanted in the opposite direction.

All kinds of combinations of the two sets of scores are possible. The correlation, however, is an index number, and we need to square it to find out the percentage of variance in one variable that is predictable from the other variable. The statistic is known as r^2 and is called the coefficient of determination. We can use Venn diagrams to illustrate the statistic (see Figure 2.11). The coefficient of determination represents the intersection of two variables and shows the proportion of variability that those variables share.

Regression

One of the major purposes of testing is prediction, and regression is one of the primary statistical tools for prediction. Regression analysis provides an equation that describes the relationship between two variables. If we know the correlation between an intelligence test and a reading test, for example, we can predict an individual's reading score from her IQ score. We can compute a regression line if we know the correlation between two variables and the means and standard deviations of each. The degree of accuracy of the prediction depends on the strength of the correlation between the two variables. The weaker the relationship, the larger the error of estimate; the stronger the relationship, the smaller the error of estimate.

Figure 2.9
Bivariate distribution

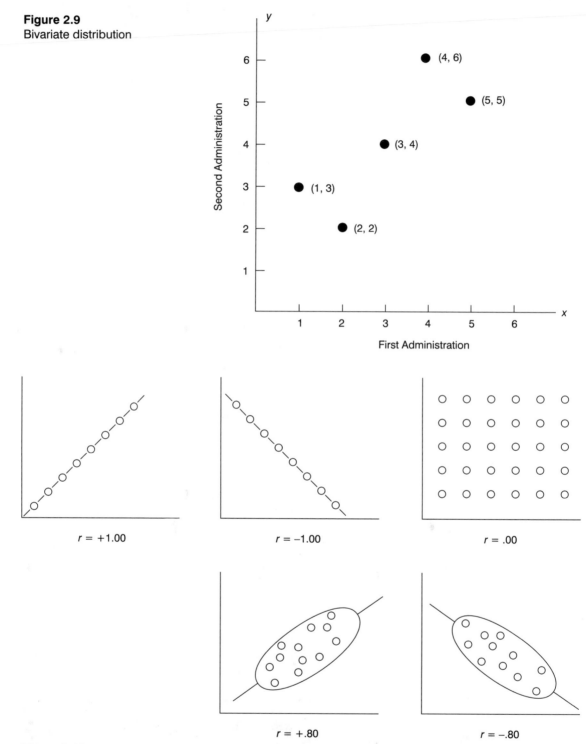

Figure 2.10
Type of distribution and magnitude of correlation coefficient

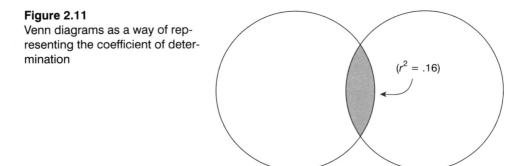

Figure 2.11
Venn diagrams as a way of representing the coefficient of determination

$(r^2 = .16)$

$r = .40$

Factor Analysis

Many tests have been derived from factor analysis, which is a statistical technique used to identify how many factors are needed to explain or account for the intercorrelation within a set of variables. Items or scales that belong to a factor have usually moderate to high correlations with the other scales in that factor. Factor analysis is a method that can systematically summarize a large matrix of correlations. If we had 50 variables, we would have a total of 1,225 correlations. Factor analysis helps remove the duplicated information from these sets of variables; it results in a smaller set of derived factors than the original number. Kachigan (1986) identifies five major uses of this technique:

1. To identify underlying factors that make up a large set of variables
2. To screen variables for inclusion in other required statistical analyses that may have to be completed in the future
3. To reduce the number of factors necessary to explain a set of variables
4. To select a small group of representative but uncorrelated variables from among a larger set in order to solve a variety of practical problems
5. To cluster people or objects into homogeneous groups based on their intercorrelations

Johnson and Holland (1986) studied the structure of the 15 Personal Problems Inventory and found that four separate and relatively distinct factors accounted for 62% of the variance: performance anxiety problems, interpersonal problems, intrapersonal problems and substance abuse problems.

NORMAL CURVE

The normal curve has many applications in the field of measurement and evaluation. It is a tool that helps us understand the nature of probability. If we obtained a distribution of most educational and psychological characteristics and graphically depicted

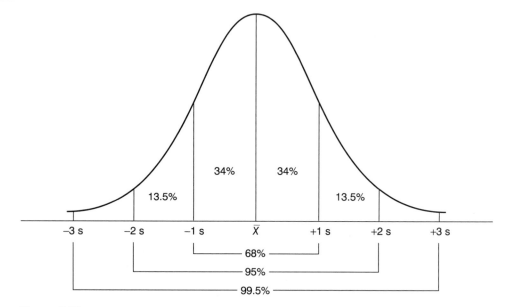

Figure 2.12
Normal curve

that distribution, the scores would fall in a bell-shaped curve called the normal curve. The theoretical normal curve serves as an important mathematical model in test interpretation.

The normal curve is a type of symmetrical distribution (see Figure 2.12). It has the following features:

The mean, mode, and median are the same score.

Most distributions accumulate near the mean.

Approximately 68% of the cases fall between −1 and +1 standard deviation.

Approximately 95% of the cases fall between −2 or +2 standard deviations.

Approximately 99.5% of the cases fall between −3 and +3 standard deviations.

We will find that errors of measurement and errors of prediction also have a normal distribution, and the table of the normal curve will help us understand the relative nature of those concepts.

INFERENTIAL STATISTICS

The table of the normal curve is used in some types of inferential statistics. We quite often must select samples of individuals because we are unable to test everyone in the population, and we are interested in seeing whether our sample statistics approximate the population statistics or whether the observed differences between two groups are probably due to something other than chance. One of the major roles of statistics is to provide an inferential measuring tool, to state our degree of confidence in the accuracy of certain measurements. We also like to generalize conclusions beyond the actual sample of observations. Inferential statistics offer the necessary techniques to make statements of certainty that there are real as opposed to chance differences between sets of observations.

An example occurred in the 1978 edition of the Wide Range Achievement Test (WRAT) (Jastak & Jastak, 1978). The males and females in each age group were compared to see whether any of the differences were statistically significant, the hypothesis being that there were no significant mean differences in reading between boys and girls. The test manual presents this information (p. 45):

Grade	N	Male Mean	SD	Female Mean	SD	Significance
5.0	200	14.83	7.43	19.31	7.35	.001
5.5	200	18.32	7.65	20.21	7.56	.05

The conclusion is that there are significant differences between reading scores of boys and girls. Girls have significantly higher means than boys. At the beginning fifth-grade level the observed difference would happen only 1 time in 1,000 by chance. At grade 5.5 the observed difference would happen only 5 times out of 100 by chance.

Test makers use inferential statistics to answer questions like these:

1. Are there statistically significant gender differences on the test? Recently one study claimed that the Scholastic Aptitude Test is an unfair instrument to use for assigning scholarship awards because men score significantly higher than women on the test.
2. Are there differences on the scales of the test between normally functioning individuals and those who have psychopathologies?
3. Are there statistically significant racial or cultural differences on the test?
4. Is the correlation coefficient between achievement and aptitude significantly different from chance for the sample selected?

SUMMARY

Statistics provide test developers and users with a way to collect, organize, and interpret test data. Frequency distributions can be used to summarize sets of test scores, and histograms and frequency polygons can help us graphically depict the scores. Measures of central tendency—the mode, mean, and median—help describe what the scores are like on the average. Measures of variability help us understand how the scores are distributed around the averages. Both range and standard deviation are statistics that are used to measure dispersion. Correlation statistics help us quantify the direction and degree of relationship between two variables. Inferential statistics are valuable tools in generalizing results from the sample of behaviors, individuals, events, and items that we have measured.

QUESTIONS FOR DISCUSSION

1. What are the four scales of measurement, and what are the advantages and disadvantages of each? Give examples of each type of scale.
2. What are the three measures of central tendency, and what are the strengths and weaknesses of each?
3. Why is variability an important construct in testing? What are the measures of dispersion that are used in testing?
4. Why are measures of relationship important to measurement consumers? What is the coefficient of determination, and how is it used?
5. What are the uses of inferential statistics in measurement contexts? Discuss the uses of multivariate statistical approaches such as factor analysis.

SUGGESTED ACTIVITIES

1. Study a test manual and identify the different types of statistics reported. Make an annotated set of cards with definitions and illustrations of the statistics identified.
2. Compute the mean, mode, and median of the Anger Control and Calmness scores that are included in Table 2.1.
3. Compute the standard deviations and range of the Anger Control and Calmness scores that are included in Table 2.1.
4. Compute a Pearson correlation between Anger Control and Calmness.
5. Construct a frequency distribution of the Sociability or Conformity Scales reported in Table 2.1. Then make a histogram and frequency polygon of the scores.

ADDITIONAL READINGS

Jaeger, R. M. (1990). *Statistics: A spectator sport* (2nd ed.). Newbury Park, CA: Sage.

The author describes basic statistical concepts using nontechnical terms and real-world examples. Chapters discuss measures of central tendency, variability, correlation, and some fundamentals of measurement.

Kachigan, S. K. (1986). *Statistical analysis: An interdisciplinary introduction to univariate and multivariate methods*. New York: Radius.

This text offers an overview of univariate and multivariate methods of statistical analysis. It provides information verbally, geometrically, graphically, and by example.

Norusis, M. J. (1993). *SPSS for Windows: Base system for user's guide.* Chicago: SPSS.

This is one of the major statistical packages available for computing statistics on a personal computer. The package can be used to compute about all of the statistical procedures used in test construction and test interpretation.

Sheskin, D. J. (1996). *Handbook of parametric and nonparametric statistical procedures.* Boca Raton, FL: CRC.

Sheskin provides a comprehensive reference for parametric and nonparametric statistics.

Measurement Concepts

OVERVIEW

Workers in the helping professions need to be able to understand and apply the fundamental concepts of measurement. Educational and psychological tests are used in a wide variety of contexts, and it is important to select and use the best possible test to obtain the desired information. Decision making should be based on accurate and valid information. However, not all tests are well constructed, and some of the criticisms leveled by practitioners and the general public are justified.

OBJECTIVES

In this chapter the measurement concepts necessary for test construction and evaluation are introduced, illustrated, and discussed. After studying this chapter, the reader should understand

✔ The essential steps in test development and the kinds of evidence with which to judge the adequacy of that development

✔ The meaning and importance of validity as well as its different types and uses

✔ The kind of evidence with which to judge the validity of a test

✔ The meaning of reliability, errors of measurement, and different types of reliability coefficients

✔ The factors that influence the reliability of a test and the evidence with which to judge the reliability of a test

✔ Practical measurement concepts that should be checked before using a test

STEPS IN TEST DEVELOPMENT

Professional standards and ethics of psychologists and counselors focus on test development. Test authors and developers are advised to provide evidence of the reliability and validity of their tests in meeting the purposes for which they were developed. Authors and developers should also provide manuals and norms to help users administer, score, and interpret the tests; they should anticipate how their tests will be used and misused and design correlative materials to foster proper use. Authors and developers have the responsibility to present information in a readily accessible form and to include summaries and interpretations to aid users in reviewing and evaluating the tests.

The test development process may vary somewhat depending upon the type of test being constructed. The following steps are involved in developing an achievement test or aptitude test.

Phase 1: Establishing the Need
1. Consider informal and formal request for such a test.
2. Conduct surveys to see if a need exists.
3. Review and critique similar tests.

Phase 2: Defining the Objectives and Test Parameters
1. Establish the purpose of the test—who is to be tested and why.
2. Define what objectives will be required of the test takers.
3. Discuss how the test information will be useful to the users as well as the test takers.
4. Consider the type of question format and the number of questions to be included.

Phase 3: Involving Advisory Committee Input
1. Select a group of experts in the field (for example, teachers, administrators, subject area specialists, consumers).
2. Review the objectives, purposes, and parameters of the test.
3. Determine the blueprint for the test.

Phase 4: Writing the Questions
1. Use subject area specialists or experts in the test domain to write the test items.
2. Have a measurement specialist review test items prior to field test; have the review panel see whether the test measures the intended domain and whether the items match the specifications in the test blueprint.

Phase 5: Conduct Field Test of the Items
1. Use test sample similar to the targeted group for which the test is being developed.
2. Compute item difficulty and discrimination indices.

Phase 6: Reviewing the Items
1. Check for sexual bias, cultural bias, and handicap bias.
2. Eliminate items that might be unfair or offensive to any group.

Phase 7: Assembling the Final Copy
1. Be sure the type and number of items meet the coverage specified in the blueprint.
2. Check validity of the scoring key with independent judges.
3. Have the test reviewed by external as well as internal committees.

Phase 8: Securing Necessary Technical Data
1. Determine sampling procedures.
2. Administer and score the test.
3. Compute reliability and validity.
4. Develop appropriate norms.

VALIDITY

Validity is defined in *Standards for Educational and Psychological Testing* (American Educational Research Association et al., 1985) as "the degree to which a certain inference from a test is appropriate or meaningful" (p. 94). The commission producing these standards stated that validity is the most important consideration in test evaluation (p. 9) and includes 25 standards dealing with the concept. Several types of inferences can be made from a score on a single test. One might, for example, be interested in the content that the test items are measuring. Or one might be interested in how the test predicts success in a given program of studies or what type of construct the test is measuring. The evidence for the validity of the test is developed through a number of different procedures. Because tests are used in a variety of ways—for description, for prediction, for measuring growth and development— there are different ways to judge the validity of the test results. Nonetheless, validity is viewed as a unitary concept, not a multidimensional one.

Three major categories are used to describe test validity. Most test manuals cite evidence of content, criterion, and construct validity. *Standards for Educational and Psychological Testing* (AERA et al., 1985) points out that "these categories are convenient, but the use of these labels does not imply that there are distinct types of validity or that a specific strategy is best for each specific inference or test use. . . . Rigorous distinctions between the categories are not possible. Evidence identified usually with the criterion-related or content-related categories is relevant also to the construct-related category" (p. 9). Currently another type of validity is receiving attention: consequential validity. It is discussed later in the chapter.

Content Validity

Content validity depends on evidence that the items on the test are representative of some defined universe or content domain and that they measure the objectives they are purported to measure. A test user is probably most concerned with the content validity of an achievement test but is also interested in the content validity of other types of tests, such as aptitude tests and interest tests. Test developers may be concerned not only with test items and objectives but also with the format or response requirements of items. Certain items may demand skills that students are not normally taught at a particular level. For example, they may require abstract reasoning of pupils who are able to use only concrete reasoning.

Content validity is often supported by expert judgment. Test companies enlist, for example, curriculum specialists, subject matter teachers, and college professors to assess the relationship of items to objectives being measured. These reviewers look at whether the items do in fact represent the defined universe or content domain. Another approach uses systematic observation of behavior. Experts or trained observers are asked to observe skills and competencies needed to perform a given task; a test or performance checklist is constructed to measure these aspects. Typical statements include the following:

> The main source of words was grade placement lists developed from studies of basal readers.

> The social studies items were selected on the basis of recommendations from 40 authorities in the field.

Face validity, a term quite often referred to by test users, relates to the extent to which the test appears to be measuring what it claims to be measuring. Usually the term relates to content validity. The test user might quickly skim over the test to see whether it covers the content generally expected in such a test. This method is a quick screening procedure, but a more thorough study of validity should be undertaken.

Criterion-Related Validity

Criterion-related validity is important in demonstrating that test scores are systematically related to one or more outcome criteria. With an aptitude test, for example, one might want evidence that the test can predict success in a training program or job field. The selection of the criterion is related to the context of particular types of clients. They may be students in a school system, clients in a counseling center, or employees in an industrial setting. The test user wants evidence that the test was applied in a context similar to that of the intended clients and that criterion studies were relevant. The goal is to have test scores accurately predicting the criterion performance of interest.

Criterion-related validity is broken down into two categories—concurrent validity and predictive validity. In computing criterion validity, test scores are correlated with criterion measures. In concurrent validity the test scores and criterion information are obtained at the same time. Concurrent validity is usually appropriate for achievement, diagnostic, and certification tests. It may reveal different test profiles for different diagnostic groups with different learning handicaps or different types of psychological adjustment problems. Examples from test manuals include the following:

The scores on the Aggressiveness Scale correlated .70 with the rating of teachers of students in their classes.

The scores on the Mechanical Aptitude Test correlated significantly with supervisory ratings of the worker's performance conducted at the same time.

If test data are used to estimate criterion scores in the future, predictive validity is determined. For example, how well does the SAT test predict a student's grade point average at the end of the freshman year of college? How well does a mechanical aptitude test predict successful performance of a job requiring mechanical aptitude? Some examples:

The SAT Verbal correlated .30 with grade point average at the end of the first semester at XYZ College.

The Spatial Relations Scale correlated .70 with success in the metal fabricating training for 136 CETA youths.

Manuals with aptitude or intelligence tests offer considerable evidence on the predictive validity of their tests. However, test users may want to check the utility of the predictor tests. Figure 3.1 presents a useful design for this purpose. A person who is predicted to pass or graduate and subsequently does pass or graduate would be tallied in the positive quadrant; someone who is predicted to pass but fails would be tallied as a false positive. The person who is predicted to fail and does so would be tallied as a negative; anyone who is predicted to fail but actually passes would be a false negative. Thus, the percentages of correct predictions can be determined and the cutoff score adjusted or a different test selected.

Figure 3.1
Design for predictive validity
check

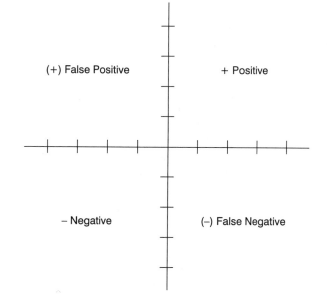

(+) False Positive   + Positive

− Negative   (−) False Negative

Theorists consider the false positive error the most important to avoid. However, these are value judgments that are partially determined by context perspective. An admissions counselor might argue that enrolling a student who subsequently fails is not all bad; at least this student is given a chance. The parent of that student, who may spend thousands of dollars for a school year with little apparent benefit, might not feel the same.

Both types of criterion-related validity require valid, reliable, and relevant measures of the criterion. The reliability and relevance of the criterion measure selected as well as the type of group tested are factors that affect the validity of the test. A heterogeneous group tends to produce greater variability in scores and therefore higher coefficients than a homogeneous group. Moreover, concurrent validity coefficients are higher than predictive validity coefficients. The criterion used is different, and predictive validity involves a time lag.

Construct Validity

The third type of validity is construct validity. A construct is a grouping of variables or behaviors (for example, locus of control, state of anxiety, cognitive ability) that is considered to vary across people. The construct is not directly observable but usually has been derived from theory, research, or observation. According to *Standards for Educational and Psychological Testing* (AERA et al., 1985), construct validity requires rational as well as statistical evidence supporting the interpretation of test scores in line with "theoretical implications associated with the construct label" (p. 90). Many authors use factor analysis. Factor analysis is a statistical multivariate procedure used to analyze the intercorrelations or covariance of the variables. The method results in the identification of a reduced number of factors needed to explain the intercorrelation of the items or variables on the test.

For example, the NEO Personality Inventory–Revised (NEO-PI-R) authors factored the 240 items. When the five varimax-rotated principal components were examined, they were found to correspond clearly with the five-factor model of personality.

On the Multidimensional Self-Esteem Inventory 1 (MSEI), a factor analysis was conducted using the total scores from each of the scales. Three factors had eigenvalues greater than 1.0 and accounted for 44.6 percent, 12.0 percent, and 9.1 percent of the variance. Factor I was labeled Overall Self-Evaluation and Effectance; Factor II, Social Self-Esteem; and Factor III, Defensiveness and Private Self-Evaluation.

Most tests attempt to measure one or more constructs. Even achievement tests measure constructs such as reading comprehension. The authors of a test should precisely define each construct and distinguish it from other constructs. Test users also want to know whether a test measures a construct under conditions that have been identified as crucially related to the construct. For example, do clients score differently on a stress scale when under stress and when not?

Authors use many different techniques to demonstrate the construct validity of their tests. A test to measure scholastic aptitude, for example, should demonstrate correlation with achievement in academic subjects and should produce results similar to those of other widely used scholastic aptitude tests. This would be an example of convergent validation, a process in which one test is correlated or compared with other tests, measures, or observations measuring the same construct. A test user would also look for evidence that the construct is unique and is not highly correlated with other scales and tests of other constructs. Anyone interpreting a scale for abstract reasoning would want the scale to have a low correlation with concrete reasoning. This would be an example of discriminant validation, a process in which a test is correlated or compared with tests, measures, or observations different from the ones in the test under consideration.

Campbell and Fisk (1959) recommend a multitrait-multimethod approach to provide evidence of the construct validity of a test. They advocate computing correlations between tests measuring the same trait by the same method, tests measuring different traits by the same method, tests measuring the same trait by different methods, and tests measuring different traits by different methods. Some examples of convergent and divergent validity include the following:

> The MSEI was correlated with the Eysenck Neuroticism and Extroversion Scales and the Guilford-Zimmerman Temperament Survey. The correlations with the Neuroticism and Extroversion scales were seen as supporting the MSEI in that the most global scales were highly correlated with other measures of global adjustment and modestly correlated with Extroversion, a scale described by Eysenck as being independent of adjustment.

> Convergent validity of the NEO is demonstrated by how the scales are correlated with alternative measures of similar constructs. The Anxiety Scale correlated high with the scores on the State-Trait Anxiety Scale.

Consequential Validity

Consequential validity refers to the incorporation of testing consequences into the validity operations. Traditional validity, on the other hand, focuses on establishing the validity of fixed interpretations of test scores. There are mixed views on whether consequential validity would complicate the development and use of tests. Cronbach (1988) emphasized that validity has to be evaluated for each testing application. That is, consequential validity demands that all phases of the process be evaluated—tasks, administration, scoring, interpretation, and use of the test scores. Taking a constructivist approach, the user asks, "What are the possible consequences of test-based interpretations to the individuals who make meaning of them in their daily lives?"

Table 3.1 summarizes the types of validity.

RELIABILITY

Reliability is defined as the degree to which test scores are consistent, dependable, and repeatable—in other words, "the degree to which test scores are free from

Table 3.1
Types of validity

Type	Purpose	Procedure	Types of Tests
Content	To compare whether the test items match the set of goals and objectives	Compare test blueprint with the school, course, program objectives Use panel of experts in content area (e.g., teachers, professors)	Survey achievement tests Criterion-referenced tests Essential skills tests Minimum-level skills tests State assessment tests Professional licensing Examinations Aptitude tests
Criterion: Concurrent	To determine whether there is a relationship between a test and an immediate criterion measure	Correlate test scores with criterion measure at or about the same time Use a rating, observation, or another test as criterion	Aptitude tests Ability tests Personality tests Employment tests
Criterion: Predictive	To determine whether there is a relationship between a test and a criterion measure to be obtained in the future	Correlate test scores with criterion measure obtained after a period of time	Scholastic aptitude tests General aptitude batteries Prognostic tests Readiness tests Personality tests Intelligence tests
Construct	To determine whether a construct exists and to understand the traits or concepts that make up the set of scores or items	Conduct multivariate statistical analysis such as factor analysis, discriminant analysis, multivariate analysis of variance	Intelligence tests Aptitude tests Personality tests

errors of measurement" (AERA et al., 1985, p. 19). A client tested on two different occasions would score differently, even on the same test. The difference is caused, in part, by errors of measurement. The test taker may guess better one time than another, know more of the content on one test form than another, or be less fatigued or less anxious at one time. These are all factors that cause errors of measurement, or changes in an individual's scores, from one occasion to another. Changes can also be due to maturation or intervention between testing periods.

Measurement errors reduce the reliability and generalizability of the scores obtained on a given test. However, the intended use of the test results influences the final judgment of the reliability of the test. A test might have sufficient reliability for appraising the achievement level of a school district but may not have sufficient reliability to screen individuals for specific placement decisions. The test developer has the major responsibility for providing evidence of a test's reliability and error measurement in each of its intended uses.

A test provides a sample of behavior at a given moment in time; it can sample only the domain being tested. Error of measurement is defined as the difference between a person's observed, or obtained, score and his true score. Thus, the obtained score represents partly a true level of ability, skill, or knowledge and partly an error component that may raise or lower the score. The true score and error score are both theoretical; we can only hypothesize what a true score might be. The standard error of measurement, which is discussed in more detail later in this chapter, is used to estimate a score range in which a true score may fall.

Reliability Coefficients

Test manuals give a number of different reliability coefficients. Reliability coefficients are computed by correlating the results of the same test given on two different occasions, alternate forms of the same test, or part scores or item scores from a single administration of a given test. A number of other coefficients are based on different theoretical assumptions. However, the three methods discussed here follow correlational procedures, which are considered in Chapter 2. The coefficient is a positive index number ranging from .00 to 1.00, with .00 indicating a lack of reliability and 1.00 indicating perfect reliability.

Test-Retest.   When the same test is given twice, the two sets of scores can be correlated and a test-retest coefficient obtained. Usually at least a day and perhaps several years will elapse between the two testings. This type of coefficient is important with aptitude, ability, and personality tests. It is also important when interest tests are used to guide clients in career decisions, which may span many years.

The test-retest method gives a coefficient of stability. Because there are two administrations of the test, a number of variables can influence an individual's performance. One variable might be the way in which the test was administered. The examiner may have made errors in timing, or an interruption may have occurred. Such errors in test administration reduce reliability. Furthermore, the test taker may vary in performance; motivation, mood, or health may fluctuate.

The interval between testings can also be a factor. Normally, this method is not used if the tests are relatively close together; test takers might remember the items and choose the same answers on the second administration, thus inflating the coefficient. The contribution of memory and practice effects must be considered in an interpretation of test-retest coefficients.

Finally, exposure to any intervention such as educational training or psychological therapy affects performance on a second testing. Consequently, the coefficient obtained after such intervention would not be a proper indicator of the stability of the constructs measured. Examples of this phenomenon include the following:

On the MSEI, the test-retest coefficient on the Global Self-Esteem Scale was .87 over a one-month interval.

The subset of 208 college students in a three-month retest on the five domains of the NEO PI resulted in coefficients of .79, .79, .80, .75, and .83 for N, E, O, A, and C, respectively.

The test-retest coefficients on the Vocational Preference Inventory (VPI) for a group of 100 females on the Realistic Scale were .79 over two weeks, .57 over two months, .86 over one year, and .58 over four years.

Alternative Forms.   Two equivalent forms of a test permit correlation of scores on the two measures to provide an estimate of reliability. This method gives a coefficient of stability because an individual's behavior is being measured at two different times. The resulting coefficient is considered to be a conservative estimate of reliability. This method also provides a coefficient of equivalence that tells how closely the two tests measure the same constructs. Sources of measurement error occur in both the two forms and the two testings.

Equivalent, or parallel, forms of a test present the same type of format and have almost equal difficulty. They are based on the same blueprint, have the same number of items, and include the same directions for administering, scoring, and interpreting the test. They do not use the same specific items, but a sample of different items forms the same domain. This method eliminates the problem of memory and practice, which affects the test-retest reliability. Most survey achievement tests, scholastic aptitude tests, and general aptitude batteries have two or more forms. Alternate forms are especially helpful when pretest and posttest comparisons are needed and high correlation is thus required. For example, on the Primary 1 Battery, Form F Reading correlated .95 with Form G Reading for 1,326 second-grade students.

Split-Half Reliability.   Split-half reliability requires only one administration of a given test. However, the test is divided into two comparable halves—for example, odd items and even items. The scores on the two subtests are then computed and correlated, and the resulting coefficient provides an estimate of the equivalence of the two forms. Because we are comparing the relationship of two halves rather than full-length tests, we adjust the coefficient, using the Spearman-Brown prophecy formula, to get an estimate of what the coefficient would be if the test halves were full length.

$$\text{total test reliability} = \left(\frac{2r}{1 + r} \right)$$

In the formula r represents the correlation between the two halves. If the correlation is .60, we can substitute the coefficient in the formula and calculate a reliability estimate for the full test.

$$\text{total} = \frac{2(.60)}{1 + (.60)} = \frac{1.20}{1.60} = .75$$

The estimated reliability of the full test is .75. In general this method tends to give a higher estimate of reliability than do the methods previously discussed. As an example, on the reading test portion of the Metropolitan Achievement Test Primary 1 Battery, the split-half coefficient corrected by the Spearman-Brown formula was .96 for a group of second graders.

Other Internal Consistency Methods.   Other methods of computing the reliability of a test consider how certain items on the test relate to other items and to the total test. The Kuder-Richardson formulas (KR 20 and KR 21) are used to estimate rational equivalence reliability. The formulas provide an estimate of reliability that is approximately equal to the average of all split-half reliabilities computed for all possible halves.

The KR 20 formula is

$$ r = \frac{n}{n-1} \left(1 - \frac{\Sigma pq}{s^2} \right) $$

In the formula r = reliability, n = number of items on the test, Σ = sum of, p = proportion of examinees getting each item correct, q = proportion of examinees getting each item incorrect, and s^2 = variance of the test. The following example illustrates the KR 20 formula.

Item	1	2	3	4	5	
p	.5	.4	.8	.6	.7	
q	.5	.6	.2	.4	.3	
pq	.25	.24	.16	.24	.21	(Σpq = 1.10)
						(s^2 = 2.00)

$$ \frac{5}{4} \left(1 - \frac{1.10}{2.00} \right) = \frac{5}{4} (.45) = .56 $$

The KR 21 formula is easier to compute. The procedure is based on the assumption that the difficulty levels are similar for all items on the test. KR 21 tends to underestimate the reliability of a test if the items vary in difficulty.

$$ r = \frac{n}{n-1} \left[1 - \frac{\overline{X}(n - \overline{X})}{n s^2} \right] $$

In this formula r = reliability, n = number of items, $\{X\}$ = mean, and s^2 = variance of the test. If n = 80, $\{X\}$ = 50, and s^2 = 100, then the KR 21 reliability is computed like this:

$$ r = \frac{80}{79} \left[1 - \frac{50(80-50)}{80(100)} \right] $$

$$ r = \frac{80}{79} \left[1 - \frac{1500}{8000} \right] $$

$$ r = 1.01 \, [1 - .19] $$

$$ r = 1.01 \, [.81] = .82 $$

Another internal consistency method of computing reliability is Cronbach's alpha (Cronbach, 1951), a method of computing the reliability of a test through using interclass correlation. It can be used when two or more scoring weights are assigned to answers and does not require the right-wrong scoring as does KR 20.

A number of problems are associated with using or interpreting estimates of internal consistency reliability. First, this method works best with a test measuring a single construct, domain, or subject area. The magnitude of the relationship is affected by the degree of homogeneity of the items on a test. If the test items measure heterogeneous dimensions, the coefficients are lower. Second, the method is not appropriate for speeded tests that consist of a series of relatively easy items or tasks, or problems that have to be completed in a strict time (such as the clerical speed and accuracy test from the Differential Aptitude Battery). The estimates of these speeded tests are inflated. The Salience Inventory, for instance, reports Cronbach's alpha coefficients on the Participation Scale of .88 for studying, .85 for working, .93 for community service, .87 for home and family, and .88 for leisure activities.

Table 3.2 summarizes the methods for assessing reliability.

Standard Error of Measurement. To apply the reliability information to the interpretation of individual scores, information is needed on the standard error of measurement and is usually contained in the test manual. The standard error of measurement is computed by using this formula.

$$SEM = s \sqrt{1 - r}$$

In the formula SEM = standard error of measurement, s = standard deviation of the test, and r = reliability coefficient of the test. If, for example, the standard deviation

Table 3.2
Methods of assessing reliability

Method	Procedure	Coefficient	Problems
Test-retest	Same test given twice with time interval between testings	Stability	Memory effect Practice effect Change over time
Alternate forms	Equivalent tests given with time between testings	Equivalence and stability	Hard to develop two equivalent tests May reflect change in behavior over time
Internal consistency	One test given at one time only (test divided into parts in split-half)	Equivalence and internal consistency	Uses shortened forms (split-half) Only good if traits are unitary or homogeneous Gives high estimate on a speeded test Hard to compute by hand

on the Erewhon IQ test is 15 and the reliability coefficient is .91, the standard error of measurement is computed thus:

$$SEM = 15 \sqrt{1 - .91}$$
$$SEM = 15 \sqrt{.09}$$
$$SEM = 15 \times .3 = 4.5$$

If the reliability of the test is .64 instead, the standard error of measurement is computed like this:

$$SEM = 15 \sqrt{1 - .64}$$
$$SEM = 15 \sqrt{.36}$$
$$SEM = 15 \times .6 = 9.0$$

The standard error of measurement tells the range within which a person's true score may fall. The range variability of an individual's score is a function of the reliability of the test. If the reliability is 1.00, the standard error is 0. The individual's obtained score would be her true score. Standard errors of measurement are distributed normally and form a normal curve. On the Metropolitan Achievement Test the standard errors are present for the raw scores, standard scores, and grade equivalent scores: Reading KR 20 = .93, Split-half= .95, SEM RS = 2.3, SEM SS = 2.7, and SEM GE = .3.

We can look at the confidence band of the range in which the true score might fall.

±1 SEM = 68 times out of 100

±2 SEM = 95 times out of 100

±3 SEM = 995 times out of 1000

In other words, 68 times out of 100 a person's true score will fall within the range formed by that person's obtained score plus or minus one standard error of measurement. If John scored 100 on the IQ test and the standard error of measurement was 4.5, we can say that 68 chances out of 100, or 68% of the time, John's true score will fall between 95.5 and 104.5. Ninety-five times out of 100, or 95% of the time, his true score will fall between 91 and 109. *Standards for Educational and Psychological Tests* (AERA et al., 1985) calls for authors and publishers to give users information on the standard error of measurement. Standard 2.9 states that the standard error of measurement should be presented for each major population for which the test is recommended (p. 22).

Factors Influencing Reliability

One of the factors influencing reliability is the length of the test. There is a trend to develop quick methods of assessing individual aptitude, as with the Career Ability Placement Survey (CAPS) (see Chapters 8 and 10). However, one of the major ways of increasing the reliability of a test is to increase its length. This works, up to a point, because more items can cover the test domain more completely and can assess a larger sample of behavior. Another version of the Spearman-Brown prophecy formula indicates the reliability of the test with increased length.

$$r = \frac{(nr)}{1 + (n - 1)r}$$

In the formula r = reliability of the test and n = number of times the test length is increased. If the reliability of a 10-minute spatial aptitude test is .50, the reliability can be increased by increasing the test length.

$$\frac{2\,(.50)}{1 + (2 - 1)(.50)} \qquad \frac{3\,(.50)}{1 + (3 - 1)(.50)} \qquad \frac{4\,(.50)}{1 + (4 - 1)(.50)}$$

Theoretically, if we increase the length of the test two, three, or four times, the reliability increases to .67, .75, or .80. There may be a point at which the test is too long, making it hard to get the test taker to attend to the tasks at hand. Fatigue and frustration may also have an effect on test performance.

A second factor that is crucial to the reliability of the test is the reliability of the scoring. Some types of tests such as multiple choice and true-false are objective, and the accuracy of the scoring can be checked readily. However, this condition is not true of some of the projective personality tests or observation or essay tests. When ratings are used as scores, rater bias can be a major source of unreliability.

A third factor that affects the reliability coefficient is the variability of the group. For instance, the reliability coefficients for individual grades or age groups will be lower than for the coefficients for an age span or grade span.

Grade 4	.82
Grade 5	.83
Grade 6	.85
Grades 4–6	.92

If the group is more homogeneous, the reliability will be lower than it is for a heterogeneous group. There is less variability of scores in a homogeneous group, more in a heterogeneous group.

A fourth factor that affects the reliability of a test is the difficulty of the items. Reliability coefficients are lower when the test is either too easy or too difficult; the distributions of scores become more homogeneous under those circumstances. On difficult tests the test takers increase the unreliability of the test by guessing.

PRACTICAL MEASUREMENT CONCEPTS

A number of practical features need to be considered in the evaluation of a test. Validity and reliability may hold more importance, but other factors merit attention also.

Time of Testing

The time it takes to give a test may be a factor. Can the test be administered during a regular class period, or does the examiner need more time? How many individually administered tests can an examiner reasonably schedule during a day? Is a short, rough approximation of a construct adequate, or is a thorough evaluation necessary? Time is a factor that is important in decision making. The purpose of the testing may determine how important that factor may be. For example, time constraints may be a critical variable when the concern is with getting information quickly to facilitate decision making. We know that the longer the test, the more reliable the results; but the question might be how much reliability is necessary for a particular purpose.

Cost of Testing

Cost is an important feature because most schools and agencies have limited budgets. Some test companies now lease tests, especially achievement batteries, rather than require the user to purchase them. Also, some test booklets are reusable, requiring the examiner to purchase only answer sheets for another testing. If computer software is available, evaluation of total cost should consider not only the purchase of test materials but also the time needed to administer, score, and interpret the tests. There are many scoring services to which most of the major tests and test batteries can be sent for scoring and interpretation—at an additional cost, of course.

Format of the Test

Just as in the evaluation of other printed material, test users should consider factors such as size of print, attractiveness of format, and clarity of illustrations. Some tests are attractively designed and use a variety of colors and print sizes. Some, however, have print that is too small or dark paper that is hard to read. Some tests may use double columns to cut down on necessary eye movements; others spread the items across the whole page. The test user should think of the test taker. An attractive format may provide more valid results.

Readability

The readability of the test is an important factor. In general, unless the intent is to test the reading level or verbal facility of the test taker, the reading level should be kept simple so that the construct is measured rather than a reading comprehension factor. Many tests report an index of readability—perhaps Dale Chall or Irving Lorge. Even a test presented on a cassette should use an appropriate reading level and vocabulary. On the Occupational Stress Inventory (Osipow & Spokane, 1987) randomly selected items from each scale and five estimates of reading levels were computed (Dale Chall 8.9, Fog 8.9, Flesch 6.9, Fry 5.0, Smog 6.0). The Millon Adolescent Personality Inventory was developed for youth who read at the sixth-grade level or above.

Ease of Administration

Chapter 5 discusses administration of tests in more detail, but readers should note here that there are different levels of tests. Some require extensive training to administer and score; others do not. Some tests are more difficult to administer because they have a number of individually timed subtests and elaborate instructions for the test taker. The test users should read through the test manual and evaluate the difficulty of test administration.

Ease of Scoring

Some tests have scoring templates and are easy to score by hand or by computer. Other tests require considerable judgment and experience on the part of the examiner. Some use differential weighing, for example. Behavioral observations may require specialized training to score. It is possible for scoring to take more time than administering a test. Even when a test is objective and has a predetermined scoring key, the test user should double-check the accuracy of the scoring.

Ease of Interpretation

Results are not useful unless they are interpretable, and both test makers and examiners are expected to provide explanations. Many tests do provide manuals of interpretation for the examiner or detailed sections in the test manual. The better tests have sample or illustrative case studies. Test users should also check to see whether there are special profile sheets or materials to guide the test takers in understanding the results.

Available Aids for Test Administrators

Quite a number of tests now exist on audiotape, some on videotape. All kinds of software packages are available for users, and many tests and questionnaires are now administered on personal computers. Available aids may make a test easier to administer. For example, a videotape of directions given in sign language might facilitate a test given to a deaf individual.

Usefulness of Test Manual

A test manual should be understandable and thorough. Here are some of the major components (AERA et al., 1985):

1. The manual should provide evidence to support any use of a single item as a basis of assessment and should caution the user about errors of that approach.
2. The manual should include evidence of the distinctiveness of the constructs being measured. The authors need to discuss how the test was developed and revised.
3. The manual should provide scientific evidence on the test.
4. The manual should provide adequate description of the domains assessed and the types of items included in the domains.

5. The manual should include a description of the course or training program for which the test was designed and the year in which the materials were prepared.
6. On interest inventories the authors should provide the extent to which average patterns of interests or abilities for an occupation are compatible with the major specialties within that occupation.
7. For adaptive tests the developers need to provide the procedures for selecting items, stopping the test, and scoring the test.
8. The manual should present the implications of the research for test design, interpretation, and use.
9. The manual should summarize evidence derived from research studies to indicate the degree to which improvement can be expected from practice or coaching.
10. The manual should explain in sufficient detail and clarity the procedures for scoring tests locally to maximize the accuracy of scoring.

	Yes	No
1. Technical manual available at time of publication of test	___	___
2. Rationale and uses of test discussed	___	___
3. User cautioned about possible misuses	___	___
4. Studies presented on general uses	___	___
5. Studies presented on specific uses	___	___
6. Special qualifications of users stated	___	___
7. Bibliography of research and studies on test presented	___	___
8. Test manual updated and revised when new edition of test was published	___	___
9. Inquiries invited from potential users	___	___
10. Relationships between test scores and criteria reported	___	___
11. Test administration conditions and modes explained	___	___
12. Interpretive aids provided for test takers	___	___
13. Promotional materials accurately supported by research base	___	___
14. Test interpretation easy to understand	___	___
15. Automated test interpretation service available	___	___
16. Rationale presented and conceptualized if cutoff scores are given	___	___
17. Validity of interpretation discussed	___	___
18. Evidence presented on whether construct being measured corresponds to nature of assessment intended	___	___
19. Rationale for specific combination of subtests and justification of interpretive relationships among scores included	___	___
20. Gender and relevant racial or ethnic group information presented	___	___
21. Method of recommended linguistic modification described in detail	___	___

Figure 3.2
Checklist for evaluating a test manual

Section 5 of *Standards for Educational and Psychological Testing* (AERA et al., 1985) is devoted to standards specifically for test publications: technical manuals and user's guides. Figure 3.2 summarizes those standards in a checklist.

SUMMARY

This chapter has focused on the measurement concepts of validity, reliability, and practicality. Validity relates to whether the test measures what it purports to measure. Content validity is established by demonstrating a similarity or relationship between what is being measured on the test and what is being taught in the targeted program. A different type of validity is established by comparing test scores with criterion measures. There are two types of criterion validity: concurrent and predictive. Concurrent validity requires that the test scores be compared to a criterion measure taken at or about the same time. In predictive validity the criterion measure is taken at some time in the future. Because most psychological variables cannot be directly measured, a third type of validity—construct validity—has to be established. Construct validity is based on statistical, experimental, and judgmental information that the construct identified is actually measured by the test. Test users need to understand the different types of validity so that they can judge a test's validity for their particular purpose. Some test makers are now advocating an additional type of validity: consequential validity. Test makers and users would have to show validity for each use of a test.

Reliability relates to the precision or accuracy of measurement. Different types of procedures are used to establish the reliability of a test: test-retest, alternate forms, split-half, and internal consistency methods. Reliability coefficients range from 0 to +1.00; the higher the coefficient, the more reliable the test. Errors of measurement interfere with the consistency and accuracy of measurement. Therefore, we use the standard error of measurement as a way of looking at the confidence we can have in interpreting a score.

Another important factor is practicality. Test users are concerned with time; cost; test format; readability; and ease of administering, scoring, and interpreting a test. It is also important to assess the helpfulness of the test manual.

QUESTIONS FOR DISCUSSION

1. What are the different types of validity, and when would each type be important to a test user?

2. What type of validity is represented by each of these questions:

    a. Do the test items match the objectives of our school?

    b. How does the new values test compare with Super's Work Values Inventory?

    c. How well does the Algebra Prognostic Test predict success or failure in Algebra I?

    d. Is there a relationship between the score on the Minnesota Rate of Manipulation Test and workers' rate of assembly of a product?

    e. Is there a relationship between the Mechanical Ability Test and performance of individuals in a six-week training program in mechanics?

    f. Is creativity a distinct factor measured by the test?

    g. Do the abstract thinking items cluster together?

3. What are the different methods of estimating the reliability of a test? What are the advantages and disadvantages of each method?

4. Criterion-reference validity is important in aptitude and ability testing. What are some of the problems in identifying appropriate criterion measures? How would you evaluate criterion measures?

5. Which factor do you believe is most important in selecting a test: validity, reliability, or practicality? Under what conditions would validity be the most important factor? Reliability? Practicality?

SUGGESTED ACTIVITIES

1. Review several standardized tests and identify the types of validity and reliability presented in the test manuals.

2. Interview psychologists and counselors and find out how they use the standard error of measurement in their testing. See whether they have completed any studies of the validity or reliability of the tests they use.

3. Construct an achievement test on the concepts introduced in this chapter and administer it to a number of students in your class. Then compute the reliability of the test using split-half and KR 20 or KR 21.

4. Write a paper or prepare a class report on one of the following topics: factors that affect test reliability, reliability, or reliability of teacher-made tests.

5. Read the critical reviews of some of the tests that you have taken and see what the reviewers say about the validity, reliability, and practicality of the test.

6. Study the following descriptions of two tests and answer the questions that follow the descriptions.

Test A: 40 items

Subscales: General self-esteem, social self-esteem, personal self-esteem, lie

Administration: Self-administering

Item format: Items in form of questions and test taker checks "yes" or "no" (example: Do you enjoy taking tests? Y N)

Scoring: Hand scoring; one template with the targeted answers and scales identified

Interpretability: Norm tables provided; illustrative case studies presented

Reliability: Test-retest for adult sample .81

Alpha coefficients: General .78, Social .57, Personal .72, Lie .54

Validity: Content—developed construct definitions for self-esteem and wrote items to cover all areas of the construct; concurrent—correlated scale with Coopersmith's Self-Esteem Inventory $r = .80$; correlation with Beck Depression Inventory and the Minnesota Multiphasic Personality Inventory also presented; construct—factor analysis completed on the scale revealed five subtests for the children's version and four for the adult version; correlations between the scales indicate General correlated .89 with Total, .67 with Social, and .79 with Personal.

Test B: 116 items

Scales: Global Self-Esteem, Competence, Lovability, Likability, Self-Control, Personal Power, Moral Self-Approval, Body Appearance, Body Functioning, Identity Integration, and Defensive Self-Enhancement

Administration: Self-administering

Item format: Client responds to each item on a five-point scale ranging from "completely true" to "completely false" and on section 2, from "almost never" to "very often" (example: People tend to like to include me in their plans.).

Scoring: The answer sheet is designed so that it can be scored immediately by ripping the answer booklet to reveal the scoring sheet and counting the numerical weights of the options chosen. There are separate profile sheets for males and females on which the T scores and percentile ranks can be identified by circling the computed raw score for each scale.

Interpretability: The manual does not have any case studies illustrating test interpretation. The manual does provide a description of what low scores and high scores mean on each scale.

Reliability: Test-retest coefficients are reported for the test and range from a high of .89 on the Body Functioning Scale to a low of .78 on the Identity Integration Scale. The alpha coefficients range from a low of .78 on Defensive Self-Enhancement to .90 on Global Self-Esteem and Body Functioning.

Validity: The test is a hierarchical model with the first level measuring global self-esteem and the second level corresponding to self-evaluations at an intermediate level of generality.

Convergent and discriminant validity: The scale was correlated with the Guilford-Zimmerman Temperament Survey, the Eysenck Personality Inventory, and the Body Cathexis Scale, among others. The average convergent correlation was .58, and discriminant coefficient was .31. Factor analysis was also conducted on the scaled scores on the test. Three factors were extracted with eigenvalues greater than 1.

a. Given this descriptive and technical information, which of the above tests would you select?

b. What additional information would you want to have to make your decision?

ADDITIONAL READINGS

Educational Measurement, 17. (1998, Summer).

   The issue contains five articles on consequential validity.

Feldt, L. S., & Brennan, R. L. (1989). Reliability. In R. L. Linn (Ed.), *Educational measurement* (3rd ed.). New York: Macmillan.

Mesick, S. (1989). Validity. In R. L. Linn (Ed.), *Educational measurement* (3rd ed.). New York: Macmillan.

   These two chapters present a thorough review and commentary on two of the important concepts in measurement.

Zeidner, M., & Most, R. (Eds.). (1992). *Psychological testing: An inside view*. Palo Alto, CA: Consulting Psychologists Press.

   The book presents an understandable and readable discussion of the major constructs in testing.

Locating and Selecting Tests

OVERVIEW

Because workers in the helping professions are often responsible for locating and selecting tests, these professionals need to be familiar with the different sources of test information that are available to them. They need to know the particular strengths and weaknesses of each source. The selection process also calls for familiarity with decision theory. The type of test selected should depend on the kinds of judgments or decisions that must be made. Helping professionals also need to be familiar with the criteria for evaluating educational and psychological tests.

OBJECTIVES

After studying this chapter, the reader should be able to

✔ Explain the decision model used to help make judgments and decisions

✔ List and discuss the sources of test information

✔ Identify and discuss the criteria that should be used to evaluate a test

DECISION THEORY MODEL

A decision theory model provides professionals with a frame of reference to guide them in deciding whether to test and how to locate and select a test. The following questions represent the various steps in a decision theory model:

1. What kinds of judgments or decisions have to be made?
2. What type of information is needed to make the best judgment or decision?
3. What type of information is already available?
4. When and how should the additional information be obtained?
5. What methods and/or instruments are available to help get the information? How should the appropriate test and instruments be located?
6. How should the tests or instruments be evaluated? What criteria should be used in selection?

Decisions and Judgments to Be Made

Workers in the helping professions are often asked to provide information to help child study teams, teachers, or other professionals decide the best type of psychological or educational program to use with a client or clients or the best type of intervention. Helping professionals are often asked to diagnose the strengths and weaknesses of a student with problems in reading or mathematics. Or they may be asked to predict the success of a student in a given educational or vocational program or a client in a treatment program. A school system may want to have a description of the basic skill competencies students have mastered. Or a client may want guidance in what career to consider.

These are only a few examples of the decisions and judgments that must be made. Sometimes the judgments focus on one individual, sometimes on a group. Sometimes their purpose is to predict behavior, sometimes to understand behavior, and sometimes to describe behavior. The key concept is that counselors need to be able to identify clearly the kind of decision or judgment that has to be made. The more specific the problem is, the easier it is to proceed to the next step in the model. The more abstract or vague the issue is, the more difficult it is to ask the right questions.

Type of Information Needed

The second step in the decision-making process is to identify the type of information needed, carefully considering the scope and range of information required. Sometimes, for a particular job a checklist can be developed of the types of information normally needed and the types of questions that should be asked. A career counselor with a client suffering from midcareer crisis might be interested in the individual's employment history as well as current and future job desires. The counselor might also want information about the client's educational background, aptitudes, values, interests, and level of achievement. Cultural and environmental factors, marital status, socioeconomic class, and age are other dimensions that might be relevant. Of course, not all of the information would be gained through testing. It is valuable to discuss a case with colleagues or other professionals to be sure all types of necessary information have been identified. Even though problems may often appear to be unique, a systematic analysis helps develop a systematic approach to identifying needed information.

Information Already Available

The next step is to identify what part of the necessary information is already available. In clinical settings there are intake questionnaires, biographical data banks, and preliminary diagnoses by clinicians and physicians. In school settings there are cumulative folders containing family information, educational history, grades, assessment and test results, anecdotal records, and attendance and health information. Unfortunately, overtesting may sometimes occur—that is, when a client is asked to repeat a recent test or take a similar one. One school district gave all of its students in grades 9 and 10 the Otis-Lennon School Ability Test, the Differential Aptitude Test, the School and College Ability Tests, and the California Test of Mental Maturity. These tests repeatedly assessed the same factors. On an individual basis it is sometimes valuable to have more than one measure of scholastic aptitude or ability. However, when clients are asked to repeat the same test in a short time frame, they may lose motivation or even become hostile. It may be helpful to develop a checklist of information normally available on clients in a particular context. Figure 4.1 presents a sample checklist for a counselor/psychologist in a school setting.

Strategies to Obtain Additional Information

After identifying the type of information needed and the information already available, the professional needs to decide how and when to obtain additional information. If the information needed is to aid in curriculum and instructional decisions for a school system, a schoolwide testing program might be desirable. If the goal is to see whether a student has some type of learning disability, an individual battery of tests would be appropriate.

The time of day, the day of the week, the physical or emotional condition of the client, and the newness of the client to the environment are some of the factors to be considered. In addition, age, grade, level of anxiety and stress, and other issues can be important. And legal aspects need attention in many contexts, especially in testing exceptional students, when parental as well as student approval is sought. Some legal requirements can be quite time-consuming. Because of the total time

	Needed?	
	Yes	No
Cumulative folder of student		
Birth date	_____	_____
Family information	_____	_____
Record of attendance	_____	_____
Record of marks awarded at each grade level	_____	_____
Previous schools attended	_____	_____
Transcripts of grades from other schools	_____	_____
Minimum level of skills test results	_____	_____
State assessment test results	_____	_____
Survey achievement test results	_____	_____
Scholastic aptitude test results	_____	_____
Health data and records	_____	_____
Hearing tests	_____	_____
Vision tests	_____	_____
Disciplinary actions	_____	_____
Anecdotal records of teachers	_____	_____
Systematic observations of teachers	_____	_____
Child study team action	_____	_____
Class records		
Current attendance	_____	_____
Grades on tests and assignments	_____	_____
Progress in reading	_____	_____
Reading level	_____	_____
Competencies mastered	_____	_____
Samples of work	_____	_____
Anecdotes on or observations of behavior	_____	_____
Notes from parent conferences	_____	_____
Skills mastered	_____	_____
Sociometric data	_____	_____
Guidance counselor's records		
Interest data	_____	_____
Behavior problems	_____	_____
Career and educational goals	_____	_____
Participation in school activities	_____	_____
Cooperative work experience data	_____	_____
Parent or guardian's records		
Nonschool activities and achievements	_____	_____
Health records	_____	_____
Previous achievement records	_____	_____
Transcripts or report cards	_____	_____
Papers or assignments	_____	_____

Figure 4.1
Sample checklist of available information

required to identify and review tests that would be appropriate in a given context and to have the booklets and answer sheets available when needed, many schools and agencies develop an approved list of tests to use for different types of decisions or judgments.

Testing also has to be coordinated with the school schedule, student schedule, or treatment schedule so that the program is not disruptive or traumatic for the client. The examiner wants cooperative and motivated test takers in order to get valid information from the testing. Students tend to perform better in the morning and quite poorly right before a holiday.

Locating Appropriate Tests

Workers in the helping professions need to know the sources of test information, which will help them get the most appropriate tests for the purposes identified. Many published as well as unpublished instruments are available, some of them copyrighted, some in the public domain. Counselors and psychologists should be able to identify and evaluate different types of test information. A list of the types of sources and their advantages and disadvantages is given in Table 4.1. The sources range from the specimen copy of the test itself to information provided by colleagues or professionals in the field. It is important to have multiple strategies to locate appropriate tests or instruments. A list of selected sources of test information is included at the end of the book. Other reference sources are included in the bibliography at the end of the chapter.

One of the major sources of information is the ERIC Clearinghouse on Assessment and Evaluation housed at the Catholic University of America (209 O'Boyle Hall, Washington, DC, 20064, 202-319-5120). The clearinghouse publishes a brief digest on hot topics in assessment and evaluation as well as the periodic *Measurement Update*. On the Internet, the ERIC/AE website includes the ETS test collection, which lists more than 10,000 commercial and noncommercial tests. Table 4.2 shows a representative selection of current ETS test collection bibliographies. ERIC/AE provides a test review locator for data bases containing the indexes to the *Mental Measurements Yearbooks*, *Tests in Print IV*, *Tests III*, and *Test Critiques*. The clearinghouse also collects essays and bibliographies on current issues in assessment and evaluation. The center provides the user with direct access to ERIC abstracts, *ERIC Digests*, *Ask ERIC Helpsheets*, Infoguides, and lesson plans and can connect the user to other websites. The ERIC/AE website may be directly accessed at http://ericae.net or through e-mail at eric_ae@cua.edu.

The Buros Institute of Mental Measurement at the University of Nebraska is another major source of test information. It can be reached on the Internet at http://www.unl.edu/buros/index.html. Links can be made to other sites, including the American Educational Research Association (AERA), the National Council of Measurement in Education (NCME), the American Psychological Association (APA), and ERIC. Available tools include the Test Review Locator. Users can also find information about various standards, codes of ethics, and Buros publications.

Table 4.1
Evaluation of sources of information

Type	Advantages	Disadvantages
Specimen sets	Can see test and test format Can read and evaluate technical information about the test Can judge validity, reliability, and interpretability of the test	Does not always include all pertinent information such as technical manual or manual for interpretation or scoring keys
Publisher's catalog	Can get current information on the cost of the test and scoring services available Can get information on new tests and services available	Sometimes presents biased picture of the test Sometimes does not have necessary technical and practical information such as time required, age or grade levels appropriate, sources from which to get complete test package, basic information to screen quickly for appropriateness, such as a description of scales or subtests
Test review volume	Contains critical reviews of the test by experts Contains bibliography of studies done using the test, such as those to assess the validity and reliability of the test	May present dated information because some volumes are published infrequently Can present a spotty or biased review because reviewers do not follow a common format Does not discuss thoroughly the purposes and possible applications of the test
Journal in the measurement field	Contains validity and reliability studies Contains reviews of certain tests Contains research on issues in testing Shows applications of a test or test procedure	Can present theoretical and technical reports Contains spotty reviews without a common format and reviews only a few tests May take two to three years to get information into print because of publication backlog
Newsletter from ERIC center, professional organization, publisher	Keeps abreast of new tests, texts, reference books in field, and issues related to test construction, administration, and interpretation Sometimes offers up-to-date bibliographies of articles and research reports using or evaluating a given test or test procedure	Can be biased Can require a subscription cost Does not index sources, so information may be hard to retrieve

Type	Advantages	Disadvantages
Abstracts (e.g., ERIC, CIJE, *Psychological Abstracts*)	Presents information that is retrievable through computerized searches Includes the major publications and information sources in the field	Identifies sources that are not always readily available May not include information on the instruments used in the study or report May use unfamiliar tests Involves a time lag between article publication and inclusion in the abstract
Test collection, specific annotated bibliography	Identifies from a variety of sources the major tests and instruments developed and used May be updated systematically and published regularly	May include dated and sometimes incomplete sources May not present information on many of the technical and practical issues, such as cost and time
Text, reference books, manual	Provides in-depth information on certain tests, instruments, or procedures Provides information on application	May present dated and biased material Can be highly technical or oversimplified Sometimes presents only one theoretical approach or styled interpretation
Manual or position paper on standards for educational and psychological tests	Provides guidelines for the construction of tests and manuals Presents criteria for interpreting and using tests	Requires background in measurement theory Requires knowledge of the history of trends and issues in testing
Colleague or person working in the field	Is abreast of the field Has firsthand experience in using certain tests Can offer guidance in administration, scoring, and interpretation of tests	May have some biases May not have had sufficient training and experience in using certain tests

Other Sources of Information on Tests

A number of professional groups publish papers on testing and testing issues. The National Center for Fair and Open Testing (342 Broadway, Cambridge, MA 02139, 616-864-4810) publishes the *Fair Test Examiner*, a quarterly source of up-to-date news and information on testing. The quarterly publication includes updates on state and federal legislation affecting testing; reports on test misuse and efforts to stop it; and profiles of promising new assessment systems at the school, university, and employment testing levels. The center also publishes monographs such as "Sex Bias in College Admissions Tests," "Beyond Standardized Tests," "SAT Coaching Coverup," and annotated bibliographies on assessment of young children, performance assessment, bilingual assessment, and the like.

Table 4.2
Representative selection of current ETS test collection bibliographies

Achievement
Achievement Batteries, Preschool–Gr. 3
Achievement Batteries, Gr. 4–6
Achievement Batteries, Gr. 7 and Above
Achievement Tests, College Level
Algebra Tests
American Government
American History
Art Achievement Tests
Art Education
Basic Skills Competency tests
Biology Achievement
Consumer Competencies
Criterion-Referenced Measures, Preschool–Gr. 3
Criterion-Referenced Measures, Gr. 4–6
Criterion-Referenced Measures, Gr. 7 and Above
Economics, Gr. 1 and Above
Environmental Education
French–Foreign Language
Geography
Geometry
//////////////

Aptitude
Artistic Aptitude
Cognitive Style and Information Processing
Concept Formation and Acquisition
Creativity and Divergent Thinking
Curiosity
General Aptitude, Adults
General Aptitude, Kindergarten–Gr. 6
Intelligence—Group Administered, Preschool–Gr. 3
Intelligence—Group, Gr. 4–6
Intelligence—Group, Gr. 7 and Above

Intelligence—Individually Administered, Preschool–Gr. 3
Intelligence—Individually Administered, Gr. 4–6
Intelligence—Individually Administered, Gr. 7 and Above
Memory
Musical Aptitude
Nonverbal Aptitude
Reasoning, Logical Thinking, Problem Solving
Scholastic Aptitude and Mental Ability
Spatial-Perceptual Relations
////////

Attitudes and Interests
Academic Interests
Children's Attitudes Toward Parents
Curriculum, Attitudes Toward
Educational Techniques, Attitudes Toward
Occupational Attitudes and Job Satisfaction
Racial Attitudes
Religious Attitudes
School and School Adjustment, Attitudes Toward
Sex Roles and Attitudes Toward Women
Social Attitudes
Values
Vocational Interests

Personality
Aggression and Hostility
Alienation
Anxiety
Ascendance-Submission
Depression
Independence-Dependence
Introversion-Extroversion

The Center for the Study of Evaluation, Standards and Student Testing (CRESST) (Center for the Study of Education Annex, 10880 Wilshire Boulevard #700, Los Angeles, CA 90024-4108) publishes a quarterly newsletter on alternative and authentic assessment.

The National Center on Post Secondary Teaching, Learning, and Assessment (NCPSTLA) (Pennsylvania State University, 403 South Allen Street, Suite 104, University Park, PA 16801-5252) releases a quarterly newsletter and occasional publications specifically on assessment.

The following are among the journals that focus on measurement:

Leadership
Locus of Control
Masculinity-Femininity
Motivation and Need-Achievement
Personality—General
Personality Adjustment
Projective Measures
Psychosexual Development
Responsibility/Perseverance
Self-Concept
Stress
Task Orientation

Sensory Motor
Auditory Skills
Motor Skills
Sensory Motor Abilities
Vision and Visual Perception, Preschool–Gr. 3

Special Populations
Adult Basic Education
American Indians
Brain and Visually Handicapped
Brain-Damaged
Bright Children and Adults
Deaf and Hearing Impaired
Disadvantaged Preschool Children
Educationally Disadvantaged Children
Educationally Disadvantaged Adults
Emotionally Disturbed, Identification
Juvenile Delinquents
Learning Disabilities
Mentally Retarded
Spanish Speakers

Vocational/Occupational
Business Skills
Clerical Aptitude and Achievement
Data Processing
Employment Interviews
Engineering Aptitude and Achievement
Mechanical Aptitude and Achievement
Nurses
Occupational Knowledge, Skilled Trades
Supervisory, Management
Teacher Assessment
Vocational Aptitude
Vocational Rating and Selection Forms
/////

Miscellaneous
Behavior Rating Scales
Biographical Inventories
Child Rearing Practices and Related Attitudes
Counseling Aids
Courtship and Marriage
Culture-Fair and Culture-Relevant Tests
Drugs—Knowledge and Abuse
Educational Record and Report Forms
Environments
Family Interaction and Related Attitudes
Group Behavior and Influences
Human Sexuality
Item Pools
Manual Dexterity
Moral Development
Piagetian Measures
Social Perception and Judgment
Social Skills
Systematic Observation Techniques

Applied Measurement in Education
Applied Psychological Measurement
Assessment and Evaluation in Higher Education Assessment
College Board Review
Educational Assessment
Educational Measurement: Issues and Practices
Educational and Psychological Measurement
Journal of Educational Measurement
Measurement and Evaluation in Counseling and Development

There are a number of other journals that publish occasional articles on tests and testing issues, such as the *American Psychologist*, the *Educational Researcher*, and the *Journal of Counseling and Development*.

Divisions of professional organizations that focus on testing publish a number of newsletters that emphasize current trends, issues, and news in the field. One is *SCORE*, a quarterly newsletter published by the division of Evaluation, Measurement, and Statistics of the American Psychological Association. The National Council on Measurement in Education also publishes a quarterly newsletter. The Association of Assessment in Counseling of the American Counseling Association publishes *Newsnotes*.

Compendia of Instruments

Many compendia of nonstandardized instruments are now available, including the following:

Chun, B. A., Cobb, C. S., & French, J. R., Jr. (1975). *Measures of psychological assessment: A guide to 3,000 original sources and their application*. Ann Arbor, MI: Institute for Social Research.

Fischer, J., & Corcoran, K. (Eds.). (1994). *Measures for clinical practice*. Vol. 1: *Couples and families* (2nd ed.). New York: Macmillan.

Goldman, B. A., & Mitchell, D. F. (1990). *Directory of unpublished experimental mental measures*. Dubuque, IA: Brown.

Rubin, R. B., Palmgreen, P., & Sypher, H. E. (Eds.). (1994). *Communication research measures: A sourcebook*. New York: Guilford.

Touliato, J., Perlmutter, B. F., & Straus, M. (Eds.). (1990). *Handbook of family measurement techniques*. Newbury Park, CA: Sage.

After locating a list of tests, the potential user might want more specific information before ordering a specimen set to review. Maintaining a file of publishers' catalogs is helpful in this regard. The type of information found in such catalogs is listed here:

Title	Content	Cost
Author	Range	Complete program
Copyright date	Norms	Manual
Brief description	Scoring/scoring services	Test booklets
Purposes	Working time required	Answer sheets
Features and benefits	Requirements for purchase	

The potential user might also choose to look at what the experts have to say about certain tests and should then consult *Mental Measurements Yearbooks*, *Test Critiques*, or some other specialized collection of reviews. The reviews in the *Mental Measurements Yearbooks* are part of a computer retrieval system. *Test Critiques* uses a standard format: introduction, practical application/uses, technical aspects, critique, and references.

If everything appears to be in order, it might be time to send for a specimen copy of the test and consider the test booklet as well as available manuals, answer sheets, and scoring services. The goal is to assess whether the test has validity for the intended purpose or purposes.

Reviewing and Evaluating Tests

Normally, a checklist should be developed for evaluating tests, and the same procedures should be systematically followed for all tests that are reviewed. Certain universal criteria should be evaluated, of course, such as the validity, reliability, interpretability, and practicability of each test. If possible, a committee should review the criteria that will be used. Perhaps the review schedule could be tried out on one or more tests to see whether it is usable and addresses the desired issues. It is better to have more than one member review each test to gain more than one perception of the test. However, if small subgroups do the initial screening, the total group should participate in the final screening.

Numerous checklists and schedules can serve as a guide. However, certain unique requirements should be considered, depending on the nature of the decision or judgment to be made. The *ERIC/AE Digest* suggests the following areas for review:

1. *Test coverage and use:* Is there a clear statement of recommended uses and a description of the population for which the test is intended?
2. *Appropriate samples for test (validation and norming):* Are there samples of adequate size used for test validation and norming of the test to support conclusions regarding the use of the instrument for the intended purpose? (See Chapter 6 for more on norms.)
3. *Test reliability:* Is the instrument sufficiently reliable to permit stable estimates of individual ability?
4. *Predictive validity:* Does the test adequately predict academic performance?
5. *Content validity:* Does the test measure the right psychological constructs?
6. *Test administration:* Does the manual contain detailed and clear instructions for administering the test?
7. *Test reporting:* Are the methods used to report test results (including scaled scores, subtest results, and combined test results) fully described along with the rationale for each method?
8. *Test and item bias:* Is the test biased regarding race, gender, native language, ethnic origin, geographic region, or other factors?

Other criteria to consider are

1. *The nature of the construct:* There are more formalized and standardized approaches to measuring scholastic aptitude but less formalized and standardized approaches to measuring learning style.
2. *The number in the testing group:* Does the examiner get the same result when using a group test as when using an individual test? Is different behavior exhibited when the test is taken in a large group rather than individually? Should a group test be administered orally to just one individual?

3. *The characteristics of the examiner:* Who is qualified to administer the test? Does the examiner have the training necessary to administer some of the individual schedules?
4. *The characteristics of the examinee:* Will any physical handicaps affect test performance? Any emotional or social handicaps?
5. *Practical constraints:* Are there any practical constraints, such as the time allotted to testing? Is cost a concern? What kinds of facilities are necessary for testing?

CRITERIA FOR SELECTING A TEST

A number of schedules and forms have been developed for evaluating a standardized test, but it is always important to have the appropriate components—test booklets, answer sheets, technical manual, administrator's manual, and any manual for interpreting the test. Not all specimen sets include these necessary components. The remainder of this chapter discusses questions that should guide helping professionals in selecting a test.

1. *Was the test designed to measure the behavior under consideration?*   Does the test manual describe the purposes of the test? Does the intended purpose correspond to one that the test was designed to accomplish? Does the test manual adequately describe the behaviors that it measures? A good test manual provides a statement of the purpose(s) of the test and a description of the behaviors it measures. Sometimes the descriptions are brief; at other times the authors provide a complex matrix of objectives as well as levels measured.
2. *Do the test items appear to be measuring the traits, objectives, or behaviors that are to be assessed?*   The next step is to review the test booklet. A survey achievement battery might have only one item measuring a specific objective in mathematics or only four or five items measuring a specific aptitude. To measure a specific competency in mathematics, a criterion-referenced test with 5 to 10 items on a given objective might be preferable. However, to gain a picture of overall achievement in a school system, the survey achievement test might be sufficient.

   In addition, it is important to look at how test items are phrased. An item could be measuring simple recall of factual information or assessing higher-level cognitive skills, such as analysis or evaluation. Items on a personality test may be direct (such as "Do you like to take tests?") or less direct (such as "In a classroom choose the situation you most prefer: taking a test, giving an oral report, doing a workbook page."). A test reviewer must sometimes make subjective judgments about items.
3. *Does the test have validity information?*   Validity is the concept that deals with whether a test measures what it was designed to measure. The test reviewer must determine whether the test is valid for the intended purpose. If the test will be used for predictive purposes, the reviewer should check the manual for

evidence of criterion-related validity. If test results will be used to describe competencies in a certain subject or in content fields, the reviewer should check the content validity of the test. Because a test includes only a limited sample of items representing the objectives or behavior to be measured, it is important that those items be as representative as possible. In addition, because tests use hypothetical constructs that have been operationally defined by the test authors, the reviewer should check the authors' evidence to support the construct validity of the test.

4. *Is the test reliable?* It is important to know how stable or consistent a test is over time, sample of items, or occasions; how precisely the test results can be interpreted; and how the score is affected by measurement errors. The reviewer should check the reliability information in the test manual, inspecting not only the types of reliability cited but also the magnitude of the coefficients reported. Coefficients will be higher for achievement tests than for personality tests and higher for high school students than for preschool students. The acceptability of the coefficient depends on the intended use of the test results. If test results will be interpreted for individuals, the reviewer should be sure the manual gives information on the standard error of measurement. A test with a large standard error of measurement might not be appropriate for individual diagnosis, placement, or prediction.

5. *Does the test provide sufficient information for the psychologist or counselor to interpret the results?* A test should provide the necessary information to make a proper interpretation. In norm-referenced tests such as survey achievement tests and scholastic ability tests, an individual's score is compared with the scores of other individuals in a selected reference or norm group. The client being tested should be represented in that norming group. Is there information on how the norming group was formulated? The examiner may want to know about the geographic areas, ages, sexual composition, school locations (such as urban, rural, suburban), cultural groups, and educational levels included in the norms. The author should explain the procedures to translate raw scores into derived scores and should provide appropriate tables for different types of scores. The author should also describe techniques for interpreting the test and should adequately explain the meaning of the various scales.

A counselor or psychologist might be interested in more than just a total score and might want specific item information. Some tests do have computerized reports that give information by objective or by item. The test reviewer should study the types of scoring services available and should have sample copies of the printout of results and interpretation.

6. *Does the test provide interpretive feedback for the examinee?* It is important to provide information to clients about their performance on a given test. With achievement tests and school testing programs the information needs to be shared not only with students but also with parents or guardians. In adaptive testing, clients taking tests on a microcomputer can get immediate feedback on the screen as well as a hard copy from the printer. Many tests have self-interpretive leaflets or booklets that examinees can use to interpret and understand their

results. However, examiners should never allow self-interpretive booklets to take the place of a counselor's communication and explanation of results. Such tools are an excellent supplement, but the counselor must be sure that all information is understood.

7. *Is the test appropriate for the examinee?* A test may measure appropriate behaviors and have excellent reliability and validity but be inappropriate for the client. One important dimension to be considered is the reading level of the items on the test. If the reading level is too difficult, the client may not be able to understand the vocabulary or sentence structure used. A second important dimension is the physical format of the test. The print size, visual layout of questions, and use of color and white space need to be considered. A third dimension is the manner of responding to questions. Are answers to be recorded on a separate answer sheet or in the test booklet, or are they to be spoken, written, marked, or performed?

Examiners must also consider whether the tasks on the test are age- or grade-appropriate; whether the test is appropriate; whether the test is appropriate for clients of different social backgrounds; whether it is appropriate for individuals with various physical, mental, or academic disabilities; and whether special equipment or facilities are needed to administer the test.

8. *Is the test free from bias?* Lately, attention has focused on cultural and sexual bias in test items. Test authors should give evidence in their manuals of the procedures used to eliminate bias. The goal is to have items that are relevant and understandable for the individuals being tested. Some older tests do contain biased language.

9. *What level of competency is needed to administer the test?* Some tests can be administered to large or small groups and have easy directions for the examiner. Other tests demand careful monitoring and can be administered only individually. In most testing programs the counselor or psychologist trains examiners and teachers to administer the less complicated group achievement and ability tests. But certain individual intelligence tests and personality tests require specialized training for the examiner. And different levels of psychological tests can be purchased and used only by qualified individuals. Sometimes tapes are available to guide test administration, and there may be separate directions for administering the test to special populations. The proper administration of a test is necessary if results are to be valid. Procedures for administering tests are discussed fully in Chapter 5.

10. *Is the test a practical one to select?* The cost of the test, answer sheets, and scoring services must be calculated. Consideration must also be given to the time factor. Quite often there is limited time to administer a test—perhaps only one 40- to 50-minute period or a few hours during one morning or afternoon. Another factor is usability. Can the test booklet be reused? Are there hand-scoring as well as machine-scoring systems available? Sending a test to be scored may take 10 days to 2 weeks. Are the results needed immediately? The ease and speed of ordering and securing materials may also be a factor. Practical considerations often are as important as some of the theoretical considerations listed earlier.

SUMMARY

A worker in the helping professions needs to know how and where to locate sources of test information. A number of data bases as well as reference sources are readily available. Other traditional sources of test information include specimen sets, publishers' catalogs, test review collections, professional journals, newsletters, ERIC, CIJE, and the *Psychological Abstract*. Peers and colleagues may also be a good source of information.

It is important to secure a specimen set of a test from the publisher and to check the face validity of the test. If the test looks promising, its validity, reliability, usability, and practicality should be checked carefully as well as various reviews by experts in the field.

QUESTIONS FOR DISCUSSION

1. What are the major steps that an examiner should follow in determining what test to use?
2. What are the different sources of test information that can be used in selecting a test? What are the advantages and disadvantages of each?
3. What practical considerations need to be included in selecting a test?
4. Would you use a test that has received a negative review by the critics? Why or why not?
5. Should a client or representative(s) from the group to be tested be involved in the selection of a test? Defend your position on this issue.

SUGGESTED ACTIVITIES

1. Make an annotated bibliography of the sources of test information.
2. Devise a checklist to use to evaluate tests.
3. Critically review a test in your field. Use the questions in this chapter to guide your evaluation.
4. Interview workers in the helping professions who use tests, and find out the procedures they use to select tests. Report your findings to the class.
5. Compare reviews of the same test found in different editions of *Mental Measurements Yearbooks* and in *Test Critiques* and professional journals. What themes did they agree on, and what were some of the sources of disagreement? What parts of the reviews were helpful to you? Write a composite evaluation of the test from these different reviews.

6. Read the following brief case study and answer the questions that follow it.

The counselor is implementing a program in (choose level) school to enhance self-concept of the students. The counselor has read in the professional journals that the self-concept of females is lower than males and that enhancing the self-concept of students leads to their increased achievement. The counselor decides to browse through professional journals and see what instruments have been used in previous research. Hearing that the two volumes on self-concept by Wylie are the definitive sources on self-concept, the counselor obtains the two volumes from the library.

a. What is the first step the counselor should have followed to find out what self-concept tests are available?
b. What are some of the problems with the approach the counselor has used?
c. Should the counselor start by reviewing the catalogs of the major publishers of psychological tests, given that these catalogs are the most recent source of test information?
d. If the counselor was using the ERIC/CIJE or Psych Info systems, what key descriptors and strategies should have been used?

ADDITIONAL READINGS

The reader should become familiar with the structure and organization of these sources of test information:

Conoley, J. C., & Kramer, J. J. (Eds.). (1994). *Supplement to the eleventh mental measurements yearbook*. Lincoln: University of Nebraska Press.

The supplement contains candid reviews of more than 100 tests.

Crosby-Milenburg, C. (1988). *Psychological and educational tests: A selected annotated guide*. Arcata, CA: Humboldt State University. (ERIC Document Reproduction Service, ED 293 896)

This book identifies books, reports, and journals about tests and includes extensive listings of references in special education, counseling, and early childhood.

ETS Test Collection Catalogs. (1986). Vol. 1: *Achievement tests and measurement devices*. (1988). Vol. 2: *Vocational tests and measurement*. (1989). Vol. 3: *Tests for special populations*. (1990). Vol. 4: *Cognitive, aptitude and intelligence tests*. (1991). Vol. 5: *Attitude tests*. Phoenix: Oryx.

ETS. (1987). *Directory of selected national testing programs*. Phoenix: Oryx.

Fabriano, E. (1989). *Index to tests used in educational dissertations*. Phoenix: Oryx.

The author lists the tests used in dissertations.

Fabriano, E., & O'Brien, N. (1987). *Testing information sources for educators*. Report TME-94. Washington, DC: American Institutes for Research, Clearinghouse on Tests, Measurement, and Evaluation.

This is a guide to more than 150 books, journals, indexes, and computer-based services and organizations that provide information about student assessment.

Impara, J. C., & Plake, B. S. (Eds.). (1998). The *thirteenth mental measurements yearbook*. Lincoln: University of Nebraska, Buros Institute.

The yearbook reviews widely used tests.

Murphy, L. L., Conoley, J., & Impara, J. C. (1994). *Tests in print IV*. Lincoln: University of Nebraska, Buros Institute.

The book contains a brief description of the instruments. It considers intended purpose; information on the test's population, administration, and scoring; and a reference list of professional literature, citing articles relevant to the instruments.

Science Directorate of the American Psychological Association. (1993). *Finding information about psychological tests: A guide for locating and using both published and unpublished tests*. Washington, DC: Author.

This is a good guide for helping individuals locate the many test sources and information.

How to Administer Tests

OVERVIEW

To produce reliable and valid test results, a test has to be administered under standardized or controlled conditions. If the examiner does not administer the test as directed, the results may be different from those obtained under standard procedures, and nonstandard results may affect the correctness of the interpretation. Other chapters will discuss the necessity for accurate scoring and reporting of the results, but administration is the important beginning. This chapter introduces, illustrates, and discusses the guidelines and procedures for test administration. In reviewing the literature on test administration, Saklofske, Kowalchuk, and Schwean (1992) identify five major competencies needed by test administrators: adequate training, knowledge of the content being measured, knowledge of test construction, awareness of measurement concepts, and knowledge of good assessment practices.

OBJECTIVES

After studying this chapter, the reader should understand

✔ What professional standards say about test administration

✔ What procedures the administrator should follow

✔ What some of the major issues are in administering tests and how to handle these issues

✔ What to do when the directions are incomplete or unclear

STANDARDS FOR ADMINISTRATION

Professional standards such as the *Standards for Educational and Psychological Testing* (AERA et al., 1985) call for proper procedures in administering tests. The test administrator is cautioned to follow carefully the standardized procedures for administration and scoring specified by the test publishers. Saklofske, Kowalchuk, and Schwean (1992) point out that test administration skills and the interpersonal style of the examiner both influence the test takers' performance. If the test administrator can build a dynamic relationship with the test taker, more valid results will be achieved.

The administrator needs to accept the responsibility for competent use and administration of the test and should be trained and qualified to use appropriate tests and to understand the content that the test measures. The National Board of Certified Counselors' *Code of Ethics* (1989) reminds counselors that there are many types of assessment techniques. Certified counselors must recognize the limits of their competence and perform only those functions for which they have adequate training.

The various standards call for the administrator to establish a comfortable testing environment with minimal distractions. Test materials need to be carefully selected to meet the developmental level of the client; that is, the test should be readable and understandable. Screens for computer-administered tests should be legible and free from glare.

In addition to being responsible for quality control, the test administrator needs to ensure the validity of the test results by eliminating opportunities for the test takers to attain scores fraudulently. The test giver needs to monitor the testing situation and must refrain from helping any favored person with answers or coaching individuals on the test items.

Any modification of standard administration procedures or scoring should be described in the test report so the reader is alert to the modifications. Users should be cautioned regarding the possible effects of such modifications on the validity of the test results. Test administrators are cautioned not to modify prescribed administration procedures to adapt to particular individuals such as reading test items to an individual, defining specific words in an item, or encouraging an individual to reconsider answers (Test Users Training Work Group, 1993).

PRETESTING PROCEDURES

The AACD (1980, 1988) statement of the responsibilities of users of standardized tests includes under test administration all the procedures to ensure that a test is presented consistently in the manner specified by the test developers and/or used in the standardization and that the individuals being tested have orientation and conditions that maximize their opportunity for optimum performance. The *Code of Ethics* of the National Board of Certified Counselors (1989) also states that counselors must provide specific orientation of information to an examinee before and after administration of an assessment instrument or technique so that the results may be put into the proper perspective with other relevant factors. The examiner must carry out a number of important duties even before the test date. A decision-making model aids in initially determining whether testing is necessary. Those steps are briefly repeated here.

1. Determine what types of decisions or judgments have to be made.
2. Translate those factors into specific information needed.
3. Check what information is already available.
4. Determine what additional information is needed.
5. Decide how and when to obtain the additional information.
6. Discover which instruments will give the information needed.
7. Determine the most valid and reliable instruments for the intended purpose(s).

According to the National Association of School Psychologists' *Principles for Professional Ethics* (1992), when conducting a psychoeducational evaluation or counseling/consultation, psychologists should consider individual differences such as age, sex, and socioeconomic and ethnic backgrounds and strive to select and use appropriate procedures, techniques, and strategies relevant to such differences.

In many situations the approval of the examinee is needed before testing can be scheduled. If the client is a minor, it is necessary to get parental approval. Most agencies and school systems have set procedures that must be followed prior to testing. Chapter 24 presents a more complete discussion of the legal and ethical procedures and guidelines that test administrators need to know. In addition to securing the appropriate permission, test administrators need to consider the privacy of the client and any ethical or legal problems that testing might raise. They also need to review the items on the test prior to administering it and to explain why the test will be given and who will get the results.

Examiner Knowledge

The first major responsibility of the examiner prior to testing is to know all about the test. The examiner needs to review the test booklet, test manuals, and answer sheet. The test administrator needs to be familiar with the content of the test, the type of test items, and the directions for administering the test. One of the best ways to become familiar with the test is to follow the procedures and actually take the test. Many tests require the examiner to read directions to the examinees; other tests also require the examiner to read the test items. The AACD (1980, 1988) statement on the responsibilities of users states that effective administration of tests requires that the administrator have knowledge of and training in the actual instruments and processes of presentation. Some individual and group tests require extensive training, and standardized tests should be administered only by qualified, experienced persons. Saklofske, Kowalchuk, and Schwean (1992) feel that the administrators also need to understand test construction, measurement concepts, and good assessment practices.

Management Details

Test companies require purchasers to furnish evidence of their qualifications to use tests. Forms request information on the training level of the purchasers, their professional credentials and educational background, the updating of their professional knowledge and skills, and any other special competencies. They are also questioned about the purposes of the testing. On the Riverside Publishing Company's form, test purchasers are asked to read five principles of effective test use and then sign the form stipulating that they will follow these guidelines:

1. Maintain the security of testing materials before and after the testing.
2. Avoid labeling students based on a single test score.
3. Adhere strictly to the copyright law and under no circumstances photocopy or otherwise reproduce answer forms, test booklets, or other materials.
4. Administer, score, interpret, and use tests exactly as specified in the manual.
5. Release results only to authorized persons in a form consistent with the accepted principles of test interpretation.

Many management tasks have to be done prior to testing. For example, it is necessary to secure the appropriate number of tests, as well as answer sheets and scoring keys. Any order should be double-checked before it is sent and when it is received. Here are some of the other tasks that need to be accomplished:

1. Scheduling the date for the test
2. Scheduling the room or facilities
3. Counting the number of booklets, answer sheets, pencils, and any other needed materials
4. Securing a stopwatch, if needed, and a do-not-disturb sign
5. Arranging materials for distribution
6. Determining the order in which tests or subtests will be administered
7. Deciding on the procedures for collecting test materials

The client must agree on the date and time of testing, and it is helpful to issue a reminder. It is usually wise to avoid testing the day before a holiday, and it is always important to schedule enough time. Time should be added for giving directions, answering questions, distributing test materials, and collecting test booklets and answer sheets. In school contexts it is important to avoid conflicts with other school activities.

Training Test Administrators

When testing a large number of clients or students, the examiner will need help from other individuals such as teachers, administrators, or counselors. The training of these assistants needs to be specific to the test being administered. They will need a general overview of the test and preferably some practice giving and taking it. Hands-on experience helps in identifying some of the types of problems that might arise—for example, what to do with clients or students who finish early. All test administrators need to know the guidelines for answering questions about the test and the importance of following standardized procedures in administering the test. Each examiner might benefit from a checklist like the one illustrated in Figure 5.1.

Awareness and Orientation

A test administrator often must be responsible for awareness and orientation. Codes of test standards remind test administrators that they have responsibility for orienta-

---

Pretesting Procedures
_____   Send out notice to remind client(s) of testing time.
_____   Send out information on testing program to public and/or parents.
_____   Get informed consent if needed.
_____   Have testing materials on hand.
_____   Check schedule to see whether there is adequate time for testing.
_____   Check date of testing to avoid conflicts.
_____   Arrange for distribution of test materials.
_____   Decide on order of administration of tests.
_____   Decide on procedures for collection of test materials.

Test Knowledge
_____   Review test manuals and test booklets.
_____   Know the makeup of the test.
_____   Read and practice the directions for administering the test.
_____   Check time limits for the test.
_____   Know the directions for recording answers.
_____   Take the test.
_____   Be familiar with scoring procedures.
_____   Prepare answers for specific questions clients might ask.

Management Details
_____   Schedule room and facilities.
_____   Make and check seating arrangements.
_____   Check lighting and ventilation.
_____   Arrange clear and adequate work space.
_____   Organize materials and arrange for distribution.
_____   Highlight directions in the manual.
_____   Develop agenda for the day.

Information for Examinees
_____   Provide sample copies, study guides, and an overview.
_____   Explain purpose of testing.
_____   Communicate the conditions under which the test is to be taken.
_____   Identify any cost of testing.
_____   Identify any special materials or tools needed.
_____   Explain what will happen with the results.
_____   Discuss test scoring procedures.

Figure 5.1
Checklist for test administrators

tion of the test takers. They recommend that the candidates for testing as well as the relevant institutions or agencies and the community be informed about testing programs. Orientation should describe the purposes of the tests, content areas measured, method of administration, and reporting and use of scores. In school contexts students and parents need to be made aware of the testing. If the test is a part of the system's overall testing program, the examiner should provide news releases not only for the school paper but also for local news media sources. Sometimes agencies

Table 5.1
Modes of test administration

Mode	Description	Advantages	Disadvantages
Self-administered	Examinees read the instructions themselves and take the test.	The examiner does not need to be present.	The motivation or attitudes of test takers are not known. They may be confused or unclear about tasks.
Group-administered	Examiner reads the directions to small or large group, answers any questions, and follows the standardized procedures outlined in the manual.	This is the most cost-effective method.	The motivation and attitude of the test takers are unknown.
Individually administered	Examiner administers test to one individual at a time, following the procedures found in the examiner's manual.	The examiner can assess the motivation and attitudes of the test taker as well as thought processes and cognitive level. The examiner can probe to gain more information.	This method is expensive, and only a few individuals can be tested each day. The examiner needs special training and experience in administering individual tests.
Computer-assisted/ Computer-adaptive	The directions for taking the test and the test itself are presented on the screen.	The test taker often can get immediate feedback. The examiner does not necessarily have to be present. This method allows for flexibility in scheduling. The computer can score, analyze, and interpret the tests of a large group of individuals. Computer-adaptive tests usually take less time to complete.	Some individuals may not perform well because of certain disabilities or because of their attitude toward computers. This method may not be practical if many individuals are to be tested.

or schools publish newsletters that include information on tests and testing programs scheduled in the near future.

Many test publishers provide information sheets and brochures about a test or testing program. These sources usually describe the type of test, the purpose(s) of the test, the types of test items used, the type of scoring, and the method of reporting the results. In some cases the cost of the testing is given, along with the time schedule for the testing and the mode of administration (see Table 5.1).

Mode	Description	Advantages	Disadvantages
Videotape-administered	Directions for taking the test and actual test items are presented on the screen.	This method allows for both audio and visual stimuli to be combined. Simulated or real situations can be presented. A wider variety of behaviors can be assessed.	The method may be inappropriate for individuals with certain disabilities.
Audiotape-administered	The test is presented on audiotape.	The examiner can circulate to see whether there are any problems. Testing time can be controlled. The quality of the recording and the type of voice can be uniformly controlled. The method is good to use with individuals with reading problems.	This method is inappropriate for individuals having hearing, listening, or attention deficits.
American Sign Language	The examiner gives directions and presents the test items using sign language.	American Sign Language is the first language of many hearing-impaired individuals.	The examiner needs to be experienced in signing and working with hearing-impaired individuals. Some hearing-impaired individuals might have learned a different system.
Pantomime	The examiner avoids oral or written directions and relies on pantomime to administer the test.	This method is appropriate for certain individuals with disabilities, such as those who are language-impaired.	The examiner must be trained in administering such tests and experienced in working with the various special populations.

The examiner must be sure that orientation makes a test relevant to the test taker(s). Seven general topics should be covered in orientation sessions:

1. Purpose of the test
2. Criteria used for selecting the test
3. Conditions under which the test is to be taken
4. Range of skills or domains to be measured
5. Administrative procedures and concerns (for example, group or individual administration, time involved, cost)
6. Types of questions on the test and an overview
7. Type of scoring, method, and schedule for reporting results to the test taker

Many standardized tests provide sample items and an overview of the test. The examiner should be sure that all who are going to take a given test have had specific practice with sample problems or have worked on test-taking skills prior to the test. This requirement is especially appropriate for aptitude, achievement, and ability testing.

ADMINISTERING THE TEST

Test administration begins with a final check to see that all is in order—lighting, ventilation, seating arrangements, clear work space for examinees, sharpened pencils, a do-not-disturb sign, and provision for the toilet needs of examinees. The test itself presents further administrative tasks. One of the most important tasks on a standardized test is to deliver verbatim instructions given in the test manual and to follow the stated sequence and timing. Any deviation may change the nature of the tasks on the test and may negate any comparison of test results with those of the norming group.

The examiner also needs to establish rapport with the examinees. For some the test may be a new and frightening experience; they may feel fear, frustration, hostility, or anxiety. In individual testing the examiner can assess these emotional and motivational factors and positively support the test taker. In group testing it is harder to establish rapport, but the examiner can be warm, friendly, and enthusiastic. The goal is for the results to give a valid picture of the attributes measured, so the examiner should encourage the examinees to do their best on each task. Saklofske, Kowalchuk, and Schwean (1992) indicate that the test administrator should demonstrate clear verbal articulation, calmness, and positive anticipation and have empathy for and social identification with the examinees. Impartial treatment of all those being tested is essential.

A list of activities for test administrators during testing is included in Figure 5.2. The examiner must be alert to what is going on in the testing situation. In addition, the examiner must be alert to the unique problems of special populations. Young children and individuals with handicaps may need shorter test periods and perhaps smaller numbers in the testing group. The examiner may have to administer tests individually or make special provisions for visual, auditory, or perceptual-motor

_____	Distribute testing materials according to plan.
_____	Caution test takers not to begin until instructed to do so.
_____	Have test takers check testing materials.
_____	Be sure that all identifying information is written on the booklet or answer sheet.
_____	Read directions from the test manual.
_____	Be polite but businesslike in providing directions and answering questions.
_____	Read clearly and loudly.
_____	Give test takers time to ask any questions they might have about taking the test.
_____	Display the starting and finishing times (on a chalkboard perhaps).
_____	Circulate to see whether test takers are marking their answers correctly, turning pages properly, stopping as directed.
_____	Replace broken pencils.
_____	Encourage test takers to check answers.
_____	Observe test behavior and note any irregularities.
_____	Guard against any cheating or other conditions that would invalidate the test results.

Figure 5.2
Checklist of activities during testing

handicaps, being sure to record any deviation from standardized administrative procedures. Many tests and assessment inventories are designed to test people with handicaps or give suggested procedures to accommodate various disabilities.

The test administrator must be a keen observer of what is going on in the testing situation. Most individual intelligence tests have observation forms on which an examiner can record test-taking behavior. Independent scales are also available, focusing attention on both normal and abnormal aspects. The examiner should record any critical incidents that may increase or reduce an individual's opportunity to perform to capacity. Chapter 17 discusses observational techniques in greater detail. If a test administrator has no direct responsibility during a test, he should circulate among the examiners and offer assistance if needed.

POSTTESTING PROCEDURES

A routine saves time. The administrator needs to collect materials according to a predetermined order, counting the test booklets and answer sheets and arranging them all face up. In addition, everything should be put back into the testing kit in the proper way so that it is ready for future use. With individual testing the examiner should take time immediately to record any incident that might invalidate scores.

Recording Test Behavior

Test behavior can be recorded on some of the standardized checklists designed to accompany various individual tests or on examiner-made scales (examples are included in Chapter 17). The examiner should determine whether any unusual behaviors might give insight into examinee performance or personality. Different rating forms usually rate examinees on physical reactions, test behavior, social behavior, and observable verbal characteristics. Sometimes it is just as important to know how the individual got an answer as to know whether the answer is right or wrong. Careful observation gives clues to typical behavior as well as to methods of problem solving and reaction to different domains.

The test administrator may want to write a short anecdotal record of an individual or an incident and file it with the test. For example, the examiner might note that John marked all the answers on his answer sheet in about two minutes and put his head down on the desk. When asked what he had done, he said, "I just put marks down on the paper to see how many items I can get right by guessing." Brief accounts can be enlightening.

Major Issues and Problems in Test Administration

Goldman (1971) points out that the problems discovered by the test administrator—such as inadequate motivation, exaggerated tensions, and response sets, with the resulting distortion in client image—are often the result of inadequate preparation for test taking. The awareness/orientation phase is an important element in helping to alleviate response set problems, anxiety, and tension. However, certain problems present themselves only during the testing situation. Some of these, with possible solutions, are detailed in Table 5.2.

Examiner and Bias

A number of factors can bias test results. Rapport (or lack thereof) is one factor. An effective interpersonal relationship must be established between the test administrator and test taker. Partly it involves encouraging test takers to do their best, to be cooperative, and to show responsiveness. Warm interpersonal relationships during testing may improve test results.

The gender, race, or ethnic heritage of the test administrator and test taker may also affect test scores. Administrators need to recognize that race, gender, socioeconomic class, and cultural and educational background can significantly influence test results. The use of reinforcement and encouragement is likewise complex because its effectiveness depends on the aforementioned factors (Saklofske, Kowalchuk, & Schwean, 1992). Other factors, such as a lack of sensitivity to the psychological, emotional, and intellectual needs of the test taker, may also bias the test results. One biasing dimension that should not be overlooked is the examiner's beliefs and attitudes. Both verbal and nonverbal cues can demonstrate bias.

Table 5.2
Problems encountered in test administration

Problem	Possible Solution
Cheating	Create an environment in which cheating is impossible because of spacing of desks, work areas, and so on.
Client asks question that is not addressed in manual	Respond with good judgment based on experience with similar tests.
Guessing	Encourage examinees to work on known items first, leaving unknown items until the latter part of the testing time. Advise clients to guess if they wish if the test does not penalize guessing.
Lack of effort	Be positive and businesslike in explaining the purpose and importance of the test and exhorting the test taker to do well.
Questions during testing	Explain in the beginning that questions will not be answered during the test session. While circulating around the test room, quietly answer only questions resulting from confusion.
Distractions	Eliminate the distraction if possible. Apologize to test takers and explain as much as possible. Allow extra time.
Refusal to answer	In individual testing repeat the questions and ask whether the test taker understands it. After testing, inquire further if the test taker should have been able to answer.
Examiner indecision in the use of praise and encouragement	Positive reinforcement may help in establishing rapport and reducing anxiety. It should not be artificial and should not be overused.
Examiner effects	Recognize personal biases and be positive but objective. Listen carefully and observe nonverbal cues.

In general, examiner bias takes six forms: race, communication skills, attitudes and expectations, gender, competence, and test ethics. Oakland and Parmelee (1985) indicate there is a popular belief that attributes the lower test scores of blacks and other minority individuals to the test administration of a white examiner. Graziano, Varca, and Levy (1982) conclude that the narrow conceptualization of this issue has resulted in oversimplified research questions and a disjointed body of literature. Although there is not strong support in the literature for their premise, Oakland and Parmelee suggest that "white examiners may contribute to anxiety, fears and suspicion, verbal constriction, strained and unnatural reactions, insecurity, latent prejudice, and other such reactions as a result of racial differences" (p. 719). On the other hand, some examiners exhibit paternalism, overidentification, and exaggerated concerns or fear of negative client reactions. In general, a test administrator might consider assigning a minority examiner to test minority clients if those clients have a strong preference to work with a minority professional.

In their metanalysis of the effects of examiner familiarity on children's test performance, Fuchs and Fuchs (1986) found that examiner familiarity raised test performance an average of .28 standard deviations. Study results indicated that differential performance favoring the familiar examiner was greater when subjects were of low socioeconomic status, were assessed on comparatively difficult tests, and had known the examiner for a relatively long duration. The authors conclude that the effects of examiner familiarity demonstrate the importance of contextual factors in testing. They see these factors as intervening between the test's sampling of skills or abilities and client performance, bringing into question the view of the test instrument as the most important, if not the exclusive, variable in test performance (p. 257).

A second factor in testing bias is the language and dialect of the examiner and test taker. Communication between the two may be impeded, and verbal and non-verbal cues may be misunderstood. Bilingual and non-English–speaking examinees quite often score higher on performance and nonlanguage tests than on verbal tests. Other factors are the attitudes and expectations of the examiner. The examiner who has warmth, empathy, or genuine concern for the examinee may behave quite differently from the examiner who rejects or is indifferent toward the examinee. Bias and prejudice may prevent an examiner from objectively understanding the characteristics of those being tested.

The fourth factor in testing bias is the sex of the examiner. Sattler (1988) concludes that female examiners tend to elicit slightly better performance than do male examiners. The competence of the examiner is another factor. Some test administrators are poorly prepared to do a clinical, behavioral, and psychoeducational assessment of certain ages or cultural groups. Others may conduct the assessment mechanically and superficially. A final factor is the ethical standards of the examiner. The APA (1992) *Ethical Principles of Psychologists* calls for the psychologist to believe in the dignity and worth of the individual and to commit to freedom of inquiry, communication, and concern for the best interests of clients, colleagues, and society in general. The psychologist is responsible for protecting the welfare of all clients.

Feedback on Test and Test Administration

In *Educational and Psychological Testing,* Nevo and Jaeger (1993) emphasize the need to get evaluative feedback from the test takers not only on their attitudes toward the test but toward the test administration, testing environment, and test orientation. Here are a few possible questions that could be included in such an evaluation:

1. How would you rate the physical environment for this testing?
2. How would you rate the performance/competencies of the test administrator?
3. Was the time allotted adequate to finish the test?
4. Was the orientation to the test helpful?
5. Do you feel that the test was fair?

SUMMARY

How a test is administered can affect the accuracy and validity of the test results. The test administrator must have important competencies. One key component is knowledge of and training with the test being administered. The attitude of the examiner toward testing and toward clients is crucial. And variables such as environmental conditions can interfere with proper results.

Many tasks—like orientation—must be completed prior to testing. Other tasks—like circulating around the room—are accomplished during testing. The administrator must be a keen observer of what is taking place during testing and should record any factors that might be important in test interpretation. The examiner should try to maintain a positive attitude, maximize achievement and motivation, and equalize advantages.

QUESTIONS FOR DISCUSSION

1. How would you compare the procedures to be followed in administering both group and individual tests?

2. What techniques should the examiner use to establish rapport with the test taker?

3. What types of behavior should an examiner avoid during test administration? Why?

4. An examiner can take certain steps in the first contact with a client prior to the testing to be sure that the test session goes smoothly; for example, the counselor can discuss the purpose of the assessment and can describe the test administrator. What other steps might be taken, and why are they important?

5. What dimensions in the testing environment might bias test results?

6. Measurement experts stress that scores are not valid when examiners deviate from standard administrative practices. Should the examiner stick rigidly to the procedures in the manual or maintain the freedom to deviate? Why? Under what circumstances, if any, should the examiner be allowed to depart from the standardized procedures?

SUGGESTED ACTIVITIES

1. Read the manual for test administration for a major controlled testing program such as the Scholastic Aptitude Test or the Graduate Record Examinations. Interview the person who is responsible for the administration of the test in your

area. What kinds of problems has the person encountered in administering the test? How adequate were the directions in the manual for handling those problem situations?

2. Observe a videotape of a test being administered, and use one of the checklists found in the chapter or one you have devised yourself to record and evaluate what the examiner is doing in the session. Rate the individual's ability to administer the test.

3. Review the literature on test bias and write an analysis of what the literature has to say about good and poor test administration practices.

4. Interview a psychologist or counselor who administers a wide variety of individual and group tests to find out that person's attitude on deviating from the standardized procedures. When have they deviated and why?

5. Design a program to train a group of counselors or teachers to administer a specific test.

6. Discuss the following four scenarios:

Scenario 1

You are scheduled to do a psychological battery on a 6-year-old child. You usually have no problems establishing rapport, but when you get into the testing room, the child says to you: "I don't like you. I am not going to take any tests for you!" The child puts her hands over her ears.

Scenario 2

You are meeting with Jose prior to setting up a testing appointment. You start to provide an orientation to the testing, explaining the purpose of the tests and the criteria used for selecting them, but are interrupted by Jose, who says: "I understand of what you are saying, but I think I would do better on the examinations if they were given in Spanish. I am originally from Mexico."

Scenario 3

You are administering a national scholastic aptitude examination, and you see evidence of a person cheating.

Scenario 4

You are administering a test to a group and have read the instructions to the individuals and gotten them started on the test. Five minutes into the test, one of the test takers raises his hand, asks a question loudly, and disrupts others who are taking the test.

7. Read this brief story about XYZ Company and answer the questions that follow:

A company administered a computer basic skills test for selection purposes. The secretary to the division supervisor administered it. There were a variety of keyboard configurations in the office where the testing took place. Since the secretary administering the test often was interrupted by telephone calls and minor crises, she paid little attention to applicants taking the test. She estimated the time.

a. What steps could be taken to ensure that the computer basic skills test is administered properly and fairly to all applicants?

b. What other procedures would you implement?

ADDITIONAL READINGS

Clemans, W. V. (1971). Test administration. In R. L. Thorndike (Ed.), *Educational measurement* (2nd ed.). Washington, DC: American Council on Education.

This chapter gives a good overview of the many details involved in administering tests.

Nevo, B., & Jaeger, R. S. (1993). *Educational and psychological testing: The test taker's outlook*. Toronto: Hofrefe & Huber.

The text deals with aspects of psychological tests in general but has specific chapters on systematic study of examinees' reactions to tests. ETS staff members show how collecting feedback from test takers can help test administrators humanize the test environment more.

Sattler, J. M. (1988). *Assessment of children's intelligence and special abilities* (3rd ed.). San Diego: Sattler.

The text has a general chapter on the examination process and specific information on administering intelligence tests.

Test Users Training Work Group of the Joint Committee on Testing Practices. (1993). *Responsible test use*. Washington, DC: APA.

CHAPTER 6

Scoring and Interpreting Tests

OVERVIEW

Scoring errors can affect how a score is interpreted. The test maker has certain responsibilities in making clear to the examiner how the test is to be scored. In addition, the examiner has specific responsibilities to ensure that the test is scored correctly. Most often the examiner calculates how many test answers fit a predetermined key or criterion. That number yields a raw score. Then, depending on the type of test score, some system is used to give meaning to the score. With criterion- or domain-referenced tests, such as a test measuring mastery of basic addition facts, the interpretation of scores relates to a functional performance level. With norm-referenced tests such as the Stanford Achievement Test, the interpretation of the scores is compared to the performance of the standardization or norming group. Counselors must proceed with caution when interpreting performances of minority group members or persons who are not represented in the norm group on which the instrument was standardized (National Board of Certified Counselors, 1989).

OBJECTIVES

The chapter should enable the reader to

✔ List and discuss the important components relative to scoring and interpreting tests that test authors should include in their test manuals

✔ Interpret different types of test scores

✔ Use several frameworks to interpret test scores

STANDARDS FOR SCORING

The standards for educational and psychological tests call for test developers to specify in sufficient detail and clarity how a test should be scored (AERA et al., 1985). Accurate scoring and reporting are essential. The standards of the American Association for Counseling and Development (1980, 1989) remind us that the measurement of human performance depends on accurate and consistent application of defined procedures for crediting the responses made by persons being tested. There are seven specific guidelines for test scoring:

1. Rescore routinely a sample of the test answer sheets to verify the accuracy of the initial scoring.
2. Employ systematic procedures to verify the accuracy and consistency of machine or computer scoring of answer sheets.
3. Obtain a separate and independent verification that appropriate scoring rules and normative conversions are used for each person tested.
4. Verify as accurate the computation to normative or descriptive scales prior to release of such information to the tested person or to users of the test results.
5. Check routinely for accuracy of computer, machine, or manual reports of test results. The person performing this task must be qualified to recognize inappropriate or impossible scores.
6. Develop and use systematic and objective procedures for observing and recording the conditions and behaviors of persons being tested and make this a part of the scores or test results that are reported.
7. Label clearly the scores that are reported and the date that a particular test was administered.

MODELS OF SCORING

There are three primary models for scoring tests: cumulative, class, and ipsative (Hammer, 1992). Cumulative models assume that the number of items endorsed or responded to that match the key represent the degree of the construct or trait the test measured. The higher the score, the greater the degree of the construct present. Many achievement, aptitude, and personality tests are based on this model. These tests often involve differential weighing of items before summing the items (for example, individual IQ tests such as the Wechsler Intelligence Scale for Children and the Wechsler Adult Intelligence Scale).

A second model is the class model that is used to categorize individuals for the purpose of description or prediction. Criterion-referenced and mastery tests are in this category. Responses may be added to compute a score but used only to determine whether the person falls into the appropriate category. Many licensure and certification examinations use this model.

The third is an ipsative model; it indicates how an individual has performed on a set of variables or scales. Certain personality, interest, and value tests use this model. The individual ranks the responses internally, and the ranks cannot be treated normatively.

SOME EXAMPLES OF TEST SCORING

Some tests demand that the test scorer judge the degree of correctness of the response or compare the responses to standards provided. For example, essay questions on many college placement examinations are scored using a holistic scoring procedure. The raters have model answers that have been given certain weights, and they compare the examinee's essays to those. Such raters are asked to assess answers on a four-point scale and make an overall rating, or holistic judgment, rather than assign a certain number of points to each possible component of the answer.

Many of the individual intelligence tests require the examiner to rate answers on a two-point scale. For example, the criterion might be the degree of abstractness or cognitive level of the answer. One child might say that orange "is a color" and receive one point; another child might say "an orange is a reddish-yellow citrus fruit containing vitamin C" and receive two points. Most test manuals have an elaborate explanation of scoring procedures and examples of typical responses of correct and incorrect answers, or one-point and two-point answers.

Examiners are expected to have supervised training before they use tests in which clinical judgment is necessary for scoring. In most situations dealing with individual intelligence testing, examiners are not making blind judgments and need to be alert to factors that may bias their judgment or influence the type of answers the clients give.

On most pencil-and-paper tests there is a predetermined key and a right or wrong answer for each item or a scoring key for a specific scale. These tests don't require individual judgment, just accuracy in calculating the number of right or appropriate answers.

Scoring Alternate and Authentic Assessment

As I have mentioned, for certain types of tests and items the scorer has to be given a scoring rubric. Let's consider writing samples that require holistic scoring procedures. Here the reader compares the writing of the student against a model. For example, the scorer might have five levels for comparison: a model of an excellent paragraph, a model of a very good paragraph, a model of a good paragraph, a model of a poor paragraph, and a model of a very poor paragraph. The examiner tries to sort the papers into these five piles.

Sometimes scorers find that there is more than one possible answer to a question. In this case examiners need the general criteria as well as a list of alternate acceptable responses. They must also check for consistency in scoring. Many times at least two readers score each paper; if there are discrepancies, the paper is checked by a third reviewer. Workshops for scoring and frequent consistency checks often improve the reliability of the scoring, and renewal sessions for readers allow them to review responses from earlier tests. Advance placement and many state assessment tests use procedures similar to these to maintain scoring consistency.

INTERPRETING SCORES

The *Code of Fair Testing Practices in Education* (Joint Committee on Testing Practice, 1988) has five guidelines to help test users interpret scores correctly. The user should first obtain information about the scale used for reporting scores, the characteristics of any norms or comparison groups, and the limitations of the scores. When interpreting scores, the test user should consider any major differences between the norms or comparison groups and the actual test takers and any differences in test administration practices or familiarity with the specific questions on the test. Counselors are cautioned not to use tests for purposes not specifically recommended by the test developer unless evidence is obtained to support an alternate use. The counselor should be able to explain how any passing scores were set, demonstrate what the results of the scores reveal, and provide evidence that the test satisfies its intended purposes.

CRITERION-REFERENCED INTERPRETATION

Criterion- or domain-referenced testing is widely used in educational contexts. Many states and school districts have set standards for students to meet—for example, mastery of essential or basic skills. Popham (1981) states that one meaning of the term *criterion-referenced* relates to referencing an individual's performance to some criterion that is a defined performance level. The individual's score is interpreted in absolute terms, such as the percentage of correct answers. The percentage of correct answers is most widely used in reporting the results of criterion- or domain-referenced tests. Table 6.1 illustrates criterion-referenced interpretation.

NORM-REFERENCED INTERPRETATION

Norm-referenced tests call for relative interpretation based on the test taker's position with respect to the normative group. Sometimes it is important for the examiner to be able to differentiate among test takers or to discriminate among individu-

Table 6.1
Criterion-referenced interpretation

Writing Tasks	Right Answers	Criterion Needed	Skill Achieved
1. Identify the plural form of nouns.	4	$3/4$	Yes
2. Use the appropriate forms of common regular verbs.	5	$4/5$	Yes
3. Make subjects and verbs agree.	4	$4/5$	Yes
4. Use the appropriate forms of common irregular verbs.	8	$7/10$	Yes
5. Include necessary information from a phone message.	3	$3/4$	Yes
6. Include necessary information in a written message.	5	$4/5$	Yes
7. Identify correct spelling of common words.	5	$7/10$	No
8. Use commas to separate words in a series	5	$4/5$	Yes
9. Use commas to separate elements in an address.	2	$3/4$	No

als on the domain being measured. The procedures used to discriminate or differentiate individual performance are based on the use of statistics of variability and central tendency. For example, T scores have a fixed mean and standard deviation and can be used to compare how high or low a score is in a distribution.

Norm-referenced test scores can be expressed in a number of different ways. In general, the interest is in the relative position of the individual within the group or in comparison to a norming group. A number of different systems can be used to express the individual's position. Two of the major ways are through the use of percentiles and standard scores.

Percentiles

Percentile ranks are one of the most widely used methods to express the relative position of the test taker on a norm-referenced test. Such rankings range from 1 to 99 and tell the percentage of persons in the norming group who score at or below that particular score. A percentile rank of 50 is the median; a test taker who has a percentile rank of 15 would surpass 15 percent of the norming group. Percentile rank, percentile score, and percentile are all used interchangeably. Table 6.2 illustrates percentile ranks.

Many standardized tests report a percentile band as well as a series of other types of scores. Some tests report a percentile band rather than a single score. The upper part of the band corresponds approximately to the percentile rank of a score one standard error of measurement above the obtained raw score. Likewise the lower part of the band corresponds to the percentile rank of the score one standard error below the obtained raw score. The Comprehensive Test of Basic Skills uses this format. Table 6.3 illustrates the use of percentile bands.

Table 6.2
Simulated percentile norms from a mathematics reasoning test for grade 8

Raw Score	Percentile Rank
45	99
44	99
43	97
42	96
41	94
40	89
39	85
38	81
//	//
31	52
30	50
29	45
//	//
15	5
14	4
13	3
12	2
0–11	1

// = omission of some scores

Table 6.3
Use of percentile bands

Test	Raw Score	Percentile Band
Reading	123	55%–75%
Mathematics	140	91%–99%
Listening	132	71%–89%
Social Studies	111	17%–49%

Standard Scores

Standard scores are a means of presenting the relative position of an individual on a test; such scores describe how many standard deviations an individual's score is from the mean. The standard deviation of the test becomes its yardstick. There are a variety of types of standard scores: z scores, T scores, deviation IQs, stanine, sten scores, and other standard score scales.

z Scores.   The z score is computed by using the formula:

$$z = \frac{x - \overline{X}}{s}$$

In the formula z = standard score, x = a given raw score on a test, $\{X\}$ = the mean on the test, and s = the standard deviation on the test. If we know that the mean on the test was 100 and the standard deviation 20, and we know that an individual scored 125 on the test, we have the data to compute the z score.

$$z = \frac{125 - 100}{20} = \frac{25}{20} = 1.25$$

Thus, the z score tells us that the person's score is 1.25 standard deviations above the mean. The mean for a distribution of z scores is 0, and the standard deviation 1.0. There are two disadvantages of using z scores. First, they will be expressed in decimals; second, about half of the z scores will have a minus sign if there is a normal distribution of test scores. A test administrator would need to check carefully to see that the scores had been properly computed and recorded, each with the appropriate sign. Table 6.4 illustrates z scores. Because the scores are linear units, they can be transformed in a number of ways without having the properties of the original raw score distribution changed. For example, z scores can be converted into the T scores described in the next section.

T Scores. T scores are standard scores using a fixed mean and standard deviation in units that eliminate the need for decimals and signs. On many tests the arbitrary or fixed mean is 50 and the arbitrary or fixed standard deviation is 10. The formula is

$$T = s(z) + \{X\}$$

If the fixed mean in one example is 50 and the fixed standard deviation is 10, and if z = −.5, then the T score is computed like this:

$$T = 10(-.50) + 50 = -5 + 50 = 45$$

The fixed mean becomes a constant that is added to each score; the fixed standard deviation becomes a constant multiplied by each z score. Negative values and decimals are eliminated through computational procedures, and whole numbers are produced. Another type of T score is known as a normalized standard score. If the distribution is skewed or deviates from a normal distribution, the percentile rank of each raw score is first computed, and then the standard score value of the rank is located in the table of the normal curve. This z unit is then used in the computation procedures.

Table 6.4
Illustration of z scores

Test	Raw Score	Mean	Standard Deviation	z Score
Reading	100	80	10	+2.00
Math	50	50	15	0.00
Science	45	55	5	−2.00
History	98	82	16	+1.00

Not all tests use the convention of 50 as the arbitrary mean and 10 as the arbitrary standard deviation. For example, the Analysis of Learning Potential uses 50 as the mean but 20 as the standard deviation. The Army General Classification Test has 100 as the mean but 20 as the standard deviation. On the Wechsler subscales 10 is the mean on the subtests and 3 the standard deviation. On the Scholastic Aptitude Test and the Graduate Record Examinations the formula used is

$$100z + 500$$

In this case the fixed mean is 500, and the fixed standard deviation 100.

Deviation IQs.   Most intelligence tests no longer compute intelligence quotients with a formula but use standard scores instead. The mean for a given age group becomes IQ 100, and the test uses a fixed standard deviation. In the past the fixed standard deviations have varied depending on the test. For example, on the 1960 revision of the Stanford-Binet the standard deviation was 16 whereas on the Wechsler scales it was 15. On the Army General Classification Test the standard deviation was 20; on the Culture-Fair Test of Intelligence scaled scores used a standard deviation of 25 as well as 15. Most of the major tests now have selected 15 as the fixed standard deviation.

It is essential for you to know the technical information about the test. What is the arbitrary standard deviation for the test? Scores of 116, 115, 120, and 125 may appear to reflect differences in magnitude but may reflect only that an individual is one standard deviation above the norming group. In looking at scores it is also important to be sure what kind of units are being expressed or reported. Percentile ranks use whole numbers containing two digits also.

Stanines.   Stanines are a widely used type of standard score using just nine score units with a mean of 5 and a standard deviation of 2. All the units except 1 and 9 are half standard deviation units. The stanine 5 extends from ¼ SD below the mean to ¼ above the mean (for example, from a z score of 2.25 to a z score of 1.25). The percentile ranks of stanines are illustrated in Table 6.5.

Sten Scores.   On the personality series—the Early School Personality Questionnaire, the Children's Personality Questionnaire, the High School Personality Questionnaire, and the Sixteen Personality Factor Questionnaire—stens are used instead of stanines. Stens are a normalized standard score scale using 10 units. Characteristics of stens are presented in Table 6.6.

Other Standard Score Scales.   The Iowa Tests of Educational Development and the American College Testing program use standard score scales with a mean of 15 and a standard deviation of 5. Other tests use 50 as the mean and 10 as the standard deviation. Test users need to make sure they know the arbitrary mean and the fixed standard deviation of tests they are using.

Normal curve equivalent (NCE) scores have been used by many schools, educators, and psychologists in working with research projects for the U.S. Office of Edu-

Table 6.5
Characteristics of stanines

Stanine	z Score Range	Percentile Rank (%)	Percent of Scores in Stanine (%)
1	to −1.75	1–4	4
2	−1.75 to −1.25	5–11	7
3	−1.25 to −.75	12–23	12
4	−.75 to −.25	24–40	17
5	−.25 to +.25	41–59	20
6	+.25 to +.75	60–76	17
7	+.75 to +1.25	77–88	12
8	+1.25 to +1.75	89–95	7
9	+1.75 to	96–99	4

Table 6.6
Characteristics of stens

Sten	Percentile Rank	Percentage of Scores in Each Category
1	1–2	2
2	3–7	5
3	8–16	9
4	17–31	15
5	32–50	19
6	51–69	19
7	70–84	15
8	85–93	9
9	94–98	5
10	99–100	2

cation, especially Title 1 or Chapter 1 reading projects. NCE scores are normalized standard scores with a mean of 50 and a standard deviation of 21.06. They are computed by calibrating the baseline of a normal curve from 1 to 99 in equal units. Percentile ranks and NCE scores are identical at 1, 50, and 99.

DEVELOPMENTAL INTRAINDIVIDUAL COMPARISON

Other frames of reference can help with interpretation of test performance. Many dimensions of the cognitive, affective, and psychomotor domains develop in a systematic, chronological manner. We are often concerned about the characteristics of individuals at different age or grade levels. Two widely used developmental scales, age norms and grade norms, implicitly compare the test taker's raw score to the average raw score of people at various developmental levels.

Age Norms

Age norms have been developed for many types of behavior and performances that change with age. One of the first authors of intelligence tests, Binet, used a system to measure the mental age of children. Age scores can be developed for many different human characteristics but have been used most widely in looking at educational and intellectual variables.

Most age scales are based on what the typical individual can do at a given age. Besides intelligence tests, some of the tests of cognitive and social maturity report age norms. The scores have meaning when the behaviors being measured vary systematically with age; however, for many behaviors the rate of growth varies from year to year (see Figure 6.1). Thus, we do not always have an even progression; there may be rapid growth during some periods and a plateau or no growth during others. The scoring units are not equal units of measurement because of this type of growth pattern.

Age scores are norm-referenced scores. We can compare an individual's performance with what most individuals typically do at that age. We might also be interested in intraindividual comparisons. We could compare an individual's mental age with her chronological age. However, we need to be cautious in our interpretation of age scores because of their psychometric properties and problems of interpretation. High age scores indicate that the individual is ahead of his peers developmentally but not necessarily able to perform the tasks characteristic of the higher age.

Figure 6.1
Age and learning curves

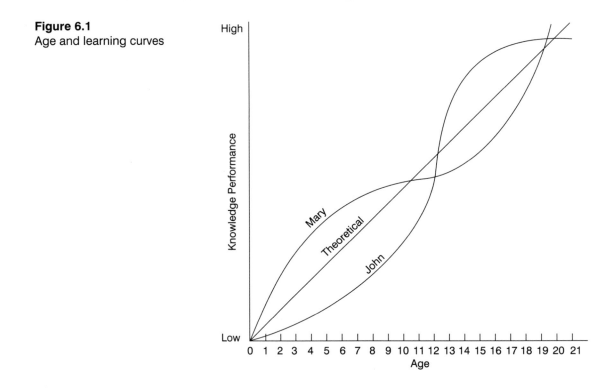

Grade Equivalent and Placement Scores

Grade equivalent scores are widely used by many of the major survey achievement batteries. These scores are based on the same assumptions that age scores are based on, but grade is the frame of reference rather than age. Grade equivalent scores are a means of comparing a student's performance with other students at a given grade level. A score of 5.0 on the Reading Comprehension subtest of the Stanford Achievement Test would mean that the student had a raw score equivalent to that made by a typical fifth-grade student on the test at the beginning of the school year. Test scores are compared to the average or sometimes the median performance at a given grade level.

Teachers, parents, and professionals must be cautious in their interpretation of grade placement scores. Such scores are computed by testing students across grade levels, computing the mean or median for each grade level, plotting the averages with as straight a line as possible, and extrapolating this line at the extremes to account for scores above and below the mean. The school year is divided into 10 segments based on a September-to-June school year. Thus, 5.0 would represent a time period at the beginning of the fifth grade, and 5.9 would represent a time period at the end of the fifth grade.

A number of problems are inherent in interpreting grade equivalent scores. A student in grade 1.9 might get all the items right on the reading comprehension test and receive a score of 4.6. Her raw score is equivalent to the mean or median raw score made by students in the middle of fourth grade. However, this does not mean the first-grade student is actually reading at the fourth-grade level. The student has perhaps gotten most of the items right on the lower primary form of the achievement test, but there were no fourth-grade-level items on the test for the first graders.

Here are some other problems and disadvantages of grade equivalent scores:

1. The scores are not equal units of measurement but are often ordinal.
2. The scores are often used as a standard, and students are expected to be at grade level.
3. Users sometimes fail to recognize that the grade placement scores are based on the average or typical performance in the norming group. Half of the students in the norming group will have higher scores, half lower.
4. Standard deviations differ for the subtests within a survey achievement test. Some distributions will have small ranges, others large. The range of grade equivalent scores will then vary for each subtest.
5. Reading comprehension tests of different publishers usually give conflicting grade placement scores.

A summary of the various types of test scores is presented in Table 6.7.

Norms

Norms are statistical or tabular data that summarize the test scores of specified groups of test takers. The *Standards for Educational and Psychological Testing* (AERA et al., 1985) calls for the presented norms to refer to clearly described groups. These

Table 6.7
Comparison of different types of test scores

Type of Score	Advantages	Disadvantages
Raw	Gives precise number of points scored on a test	Cannot be interpreted or compared
Percentile Rank	Easily understood by most test takers Requires no great sophistication in statistics Portrays relative position of scores in percentiles More appropriate for skewed data	Uses ordinal units of measurement Uses unequal units of measurement Does not permit averaging Cannot be compared unless groups are similar Greatly distorts score differences at upper and lower ends of distribution
Stanine	One-digit scores Can be averaged Used for simplicity and utility	May not provide enough scoring units to differentiate among scores Insensitive to sizable differences within a stanine Misleadingly sensitive to small differences on either side of the point separating adjacent stanines
Standard	Derived from properties of the normal curve Reflect absolute difference among scores Can be averaged and correlated Comparable from test to test if reference groups are equivalent	Inappropriate if data are markedly skewed Hard to explain to test takers
Grade and Age	Good if area measured is systematically related with age or grade level Compares an individual's performance with the average for that age or grade	Uses unequal units of measurement Leads to score interpretation that is too literal Can mislead in the case of scores, which do not signify an ability to perform or understand at the higher grade level Has little practical meaning beyond sixth grade or age 12

groups should be those with which users of the test will ordinarily wish to compare the individuals who are tested. In the test manual the test author should (1) describe who was in the norm group and (2) explain the different types of converted scores included in the tables. The test user should ask the following evaluative questions:

1. Does the norming group include the type of person with whom the test taker should be compared?
2. Do the norms include enough cases to be representative of the targeted population?

3. Do the samples include enough cases?
4. Does the manual include differentiated norms or summary information about differences among gender, ethnic, grade, or age groups?
5. Does the manual report include the year in which the normative data were collected, provide descriptive statistics, and describe the sampling design and participation rates in sufficient detail so that the norms can be evaluated?

CONVERSION TABLES

Conversion tables present every possible raw score and the derived score, such as the percentile rank or T score for a given norm group (for example, 12th-grade boys, 10th-grade girls). A conversion table for hypothetical interest scores is presented in Table 6.8. Sometimes tests present multiple group norm tables. At other times a table might present the derived T scores for several subtests (see Table 6.9).

Some tests use abbreviated or condensed norm tables in which not every raw score value is presented (see Table 6.10). Such tables require interpolation for scores that fall between two of the values presented in the table. Unfortunately, this procedure requires more of the test user's time, and necessary computation introduces greater chance for error.

Table 6.8
Sample conversion table for an interest test

Scale: Technical Group: Male	Female	T
36	36	80
35	32–35	78
34	30–31	75
33	28–29	72
//	//	//

Table 6.9
Sample norm table reporting different types of scores for several subtests

Stanine	Standard Score	Percentile Rank (%)	Grade	Raw Scores		
				ReadComp	Vocab	Total
5	50	50	11.0	30		60
5	49	48				
5	49	47			30	
5	49	46				59
5	49	45	10.9	29		

Table 6.10
Condensed norm table

Raw Score	IQ
50	140
48	135
45	130
41	125
39	120

PROFILES

Many tests provide profile sheets to aid in interpretation of the results. These forms graphically depict the scores by providing a visual interpretation. Profiles can represent the scores on a single battery or on several tests. Figure 6.2 gives an example of a profile for an individual on the COPSystem Interest Inventory.

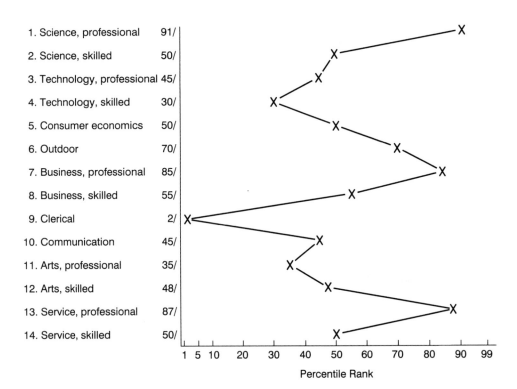

Figure 6.2
Individual profile for COPSystem Interest Inventory

Guidelines for interpreting profiles include the following:

1. Small differences should not be overinterpreted.
2. Any score represents a sample of the test taker's behavior in a given domain at a given time.
3. The standard error of measurement should be used in interpretation.
4. The normal curve can be used as a frame of reference to interpret the scores on norm-referenced tests.
5. Patterns in the shape of the profile are important (are the scores all high or low?).

SUMMARY

Studies have shown that examiners make numerous errors in scoring tests. Consequently, a number of standards and guidelines address scoring procedures. Test users need to be sure that they know how to score their tests correctly and follow systematic procedures to achieve accurate scores. Test authors need to be sure that scoring procedures are carefully described, and examiners need to read test manuals carefully.

Raw scores have to be translated into some frame of reference to give meaning to test results. Two major approaches are criterion-referenced and norm-referenced interpretation. Overall, the examiner has to ask two questions about test scores:

1. What is the nature of the score itself? What types of scoring or scaling procedures were used to arrive at the score?
2. What type of system is going to be used to interpret the score?

The examiner must know the advantages and disadvantages of each type of score and be alert to the best way of displaying and explaining the scores on a test.

In norm-referenced testing the reference group is of key importance. Examiners need to study the makeup of the norming group and see whether it is an appropriate comparison group. The validity and usefulness of test results depend on the examiner's knowledge of appropriate test interpretation strategies.

QUESTIONS FOR DISCUSSION

1. How would you handle the situation if certain test results did not appear to be accurate or did not agree with the results of previous tests you had taken? If you were the examiner and found out that you had made some errors in scoring a

client's test, what would you do? What steps and procedures should be taken to ensure the accuracy of test scores?

2. What are the differences in scoring and interpreting norm-referenced and criterion-referenced tests?

3. What are the different types of derived scores used in norm-referenced testing? Discuss when you would use each type of score, and analyze the strengths and limitations of each type of score.

4. Should you use a test if there is not an appropriate norm or representative group available for comparison purposes? Take a position and defend it.

5. If you were developing a new achievement test for college-level students, how would you select your norming group? If you were developing a new personality inventory measuring psychological types, how would you select an appropriate norming group?

SUGGESTED ACTIVITIES

1. Interview a director of testing or psychologists and counselors who test extensively. Ask what test scoring procedures they use and how they guard against errors in scoring. Discover what problems arise in scoring individual tests as well as large-group tests.

2. Locate several test manuals and read the sections on test scoring and interpretation. Compare the presentations. How clear and understandable are the procedures? Are possible problems addressed? Are models of correct answers given? Are case studies presented?

3. Write a position paper on one of the following topics: bias in test scoring, use of grade-equivalent norms, norm-referenced versus criterion-referenced interpretation, or selecting appropriate norms.

4. Give children of various ages a short, individual vocabulary test. (If vocabulary does not appeal to you, choose some other subject area.) Analyze the answers and develop a scoring system. Try writing a set of procedures for an examiner to follow to score the test.

5. Select several tests measuring the same content or constructs. Compare the types of norming groups presented in the manuals and the ways in which the groups were selected. Evaluate the tests on this dimension.

6. A third-grade teacher has brought you the following results of the spring testing on the Stanford Achievement Test. The teacher doesn't understand the types of scores and the results and wants you to guide her in interpreting the results.

Test	N	Mean Raw	Mean Scale	Percentile Rank	Stanine	Mean Grade Equivalent
Word Study Skills	19	40	613	52	5	4.0
Reading Comp	20	39	599	33	4	3.4
Vocabulary	21	19	587	9	2	2.7
Listening Comp	21	25	614	31	4	3.5
Spelling	21	29	642	94	8	5.1
Language	21	27	617	41	5	3.9
Concept of Numbers	21	19	574	15	3	3.4
Math Computation	21	28	603	43	5	4.4
Math Applications	21	22	580	30	4	3.5
Science	21	26	603	33	4	3.5
Using Information	21	24	613	39	4	3.5
Total Reading	18	78	602	36	4	3.6
Total Listening	21	44	601	15	3	3.1
Total Language	21	56	624	63	6	4.2
Total Mathematics	21	69	586	29	4	3.7

Content Clusters

	Below Average	Average	Above Average
Word Study Skills	5%	79%	16%
Structural analysis	11%	68%	21%
Phonetic analysis consonants	16%	74%	11%
Phonetic analysis vowels	11%	68%	21%
Reading Comprehension	25%	75%	0%
Textual reading	20%	70%	10%
Functional reading	30%	60%	10%
Recreational reading	20%	80%	0%
Literal comprehension	25%	65%	10%
Inferential comprehension	20%	60%	0%
Vocabulary/	48%	48%	5%
Listening Comprehension	14%	81%	5%
Retention	10%	76%	24%
Organization	19%	71%	10%
Spelling	0%	71%	29%
Sight words	0%	43%	57%
Phonetic principles	0%	76%	24%
Structured principles	0%	48%	52%
Language	0%	95%	5%
Conventions	14%	81%	5%
Language sensitivity	24%	62%	14%
Reference skills	19%	62%	19%

Concepts of Number	24%	71%	5%
Whole numbers/place value	38%	57%	5%
Fractions	0%	95%	5%
Operations and properties	29%	71%	0%
Mathematics Computation	19%	71%	10%
Addition of whole numbers	19%	67%	14%
Subtraction of whole numbers	19%	62%	19%
Multiplication of whole numbers	10%	57%	33%
Division of whole numbers	33%	62%	5%
Mathematical Applications	24%	71%	5%
Problem solving	33%	52%	14%
Geometry/measurement	19%	76%	5%
Graphs and charts	10%	67%	24%
Social Science	19%	81%	0%
Geography	19%	81%	0%
History/anthropology	19%	62%	19%
Sociology	48%	24%	29%
Political science	14%	86%	0%
Economics	29%	62%	10%
Inquiry skills	14%	67%	19%
Science	14%	81%	5%
Physical science	14%	57%	29%
Biological science	10%	86%	5%
Inquiry skills	14%	81%	5%

ADDITIONAL READINGS

Davidson, M. L. (1992). Test scores and statistics. In M. Zeidner & R. Most (Eds.), *Psychological testing: An inside view* (pp. 249–295). Palo Alto, CA: Consulting Psychologists Press.

The chapter provides a review of different types of test scores and the statistical procedures used to produce the types of derived scores.

Lyman, H. B. (1998). *Test scores and what they mean* (6th ed.). Boston: Allyn & Bacon.

The text provides guidelines for interpreting tests and examples of good and bad usage of interpretations of test results.

Ability and Intelligence Testing

OVERVIEW

One of the most controversial areas in testing is the measuring of ability and intelligence. Some of these issues are the nature-nurture controversy, the cultural bias, and the construct validity of intelligence tests. Many types of intelligence tests are widely used in education and clinical settings with all age groups and all types of individuals. Many tests have been developed during this century to measure the dimensions of intelligence—from Binet and Simon's scale to identify students who could not profit from regular classroom instruction in 1905 in France, to the revision of the Stanford-Binet developed by Thorndike, Hagen, and Sattler in 1986. Currently the most influential development in our view of intelligence has come from educational and psychological research on cognitive psychology, especially the conceptualizations by Robert Sternberg, Howard Gardner, and John Horn.

OBJECTIVES

This chapter should enable the reader to

✔ Define intelligence

✔ Discuss some of the major theories of intelligence

✔ List the major types of tests used to measure intelligence

✔ Identify what types of tests should be used and why

✔ Explain how the results of intelligence tests should be reported

✔ Identify the kinds of factors that should be considered in interpreting intelligence test results

DEFINITIONS OF INTELLIGENCE

Many different definitions of intelligence have been given by the authors of intelligence tests. Aiken (1985) indicated that the word was almost unknown in popular speech until the Victorian era. Francis Galton and Herbert Spencer used the Latin word for intelligence to refer to individual differences in mental ability. These individuals as well as other psychologists such as Cattell were influenced by Darwin to look at dimensions of individual differences. They felt that intelligence was a genetic factor, separate from special abilities. Binet and Simon (1916) conceptualized intelligence as the capacity of the individual to judge well, to reason well, and to comprehend well and postulated that intelligence was a general ability. Wechsler (1958), on the other hand, defined intelligence as the "aggregate or global ability of the individual to act purposefully, to think rationally, and to deal effectively with his environment" (p. 7). It is extremely important to check a test manual and study how the test authors define intelligence.

In general, most intelligence tests measure the individual's ability to think abstractly or use verbal, numerical, or abstract symbols. The subjects taking these tests must substitute symbols for actions and manipulate ideas that represent not only current happenings but also events remote in time and space (Stoddard, 1943). Wechsler's definition also includes the dimension of adapting to the environment and adjusting to problems and changing conditions. We must remember that the scores on an intelligence test measure how well an individual performs the set of tasks assessed by the test.

MODELS OF INTELLIGENCE

Many attempts have been made over the past century to develop models that conceptualize the facets of intelligence. One of the first theories was that of Charles Spearman, who postulated a two-factor theory of intelligence. In interpreting his statistical analysis of test performance, Spearman (1927) identified two factors—a G, or general ability, factor that each individual possesses and an S, or specific, factor that varies for each task undertaken. Thurstone (1938), on the other hand, proposed a multifactor theory. He analyzed 57 different tests taken by a high school group and concluded that there was a small group of primary factors rather than a single G factor. Thurstone (1938) termed these factors primary mental abilities and constructed a test called the Primary Mental Abilities Test. These are the seven primary abilities he identified:

1. *Number ability*—to perform basic mathematic processes accurately and rapidly
2. *Verbal ability*—to understand ideas expressed in word form
3. *Word fluency*—to speak and write fluently
4. *Memory*—to recognize and recall information such as numbers, letters, and words

5. *Reasoning*—to derive rules and solve problems inductively
6. *Spatial ability*—to visualize form relationships in three dimensions
7. *Perception*—to perceive things quickly, such as visual details and similarities and differences among pictured objects

One of the major issues during the 1920s concerned controversy over the nature of intelligence. The debate still goes on in psychological circles today. E. L. Thorndike (1927) believed that this type of debate is not productive. He disagreed with the concept of a singular and relatively independent mental process, or *G* factor, and concluded that there were many special or grouped abilities, such as mathematical and mechanical skills. He postulated that there were three major types of intelligence—abstract, practical, and social. Whether one agrees or disagrees depends partly on the individual's theoretical orientation and partly on the type of statistical analysis used with test results. Potential test users should be concerned with the purpose of an intelligence scale and the theories and approaches that will provide the most valid information.

Hierarchical Theory

Vernon (1960) proposed a hierarchical model of intelligence, which identified four levels of factors (see Figure 7.1). The trunk, or first, level includes the *G* factor, which is a general, or cognitive, factor. The two main branches of the second level are verbal-educational and practical-mechanical-spatial factors. The third level identifies component factors of these two main branches. The verbal-educational area comprises abilities such as verbal fluency and numerical ability. The practical-mechanical-spatial area includes factors such as mechanical ability, psychomotor ability, and spatial relations. The fourth level of the hierarchy consists of more special and specific factors peculiar to tests in each of the domains above it. Vernon's model presents a conceptual way of including the general intelligence dimension of Spearman's work and the multifactor approach identified by Thorndike, Thurstone, and Guilford.

Guilford's Model of Intelligence

Guilford (1967) developed a multifactor approach to intelligence. He proposed a three-dimensional model that includes five types of operations, four types of content, and six types of products. The model contains 120 cells. Operations include cognition, memory, divergent thinking, convergent thinking, and evaluation. The four types of content are figural, symbolic, semantic, and behavioral. The six products are units, classes, relations, systems, transformations, and implications. A number of tests have been developed to measure the cells of Guilford's model. His approach is an extension of the multifactor approach advocated by Thurstone.

Cattell's Fluid and Crystallized Intelligence

Cattell (1963) used factor analytic studies to identify a two-factor theory of intelligence based on fluid and crystallized intelligence. Fluid intelligence is general to

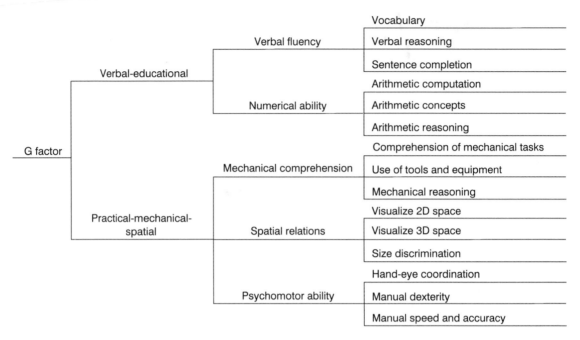

Figure 7.1
Adaptation of Vernon's hierarchical model of intelligence

many different fields and is used in tasks requiring adaptation to new situations. Heredity is an important factor in fluid intelligence. Crystallized intelligence is more specific to a given field such as education. This type of ability depends more on the environment. The Culture-Fair Intelligence Test was designed to measure fluid intelligence.

Carroll (1993) also has a factoral model that measures fluid and crystallized intelligence. In his factor analytic study of 460 data sets he identified three strata of cognitive abilities. The highest stratum is a factor often designated by *g,* for general intelligence. The second stratum consists of broad factors that include fluid intelligence, crystallized intelligence, general memory and learning, broad visual perception, broad auditory perception, broad retrieval ability, broad cognitive speediness, and processing speed. The third stratum consists of narrow abilities related to the broad areas previously listed. For example, under fluid intelligence falls general sequential reasoning, induction, and quantitative reasoning. Under crystallized intelligence falls reading comprehension, cloze ability, reading decoding, spelling ability, writing ability, foreign language proficiency, foreign language aptitude, language development, lexical knowledge, listening ability, phonetic coding, communication ability, oral production and fluency, grammatical sensitivity, and verbal language comprehension.

Horn (1989), a student of Cattell, concluded that Cattell's theory can be thought of as a theory of multiple intelligences. These intelligences are "outcroppings of distinct influences operating through development, brain functioning, genetic determination, and the adjustment, adaptations, and achievement of school and work" (p. 76).

Sternberg's Cognitive Approaches to Intelligence

Sternberg (1980, 1985) used in his theory the information-processing components of intelligence. He identifies three different types of information-processing components that are important to consider: metacomponents, performance components, and knowledge acquisition components. Metacomponents are the higher-order control processes used to oversee the planning, monitoring, and evaluating of task performance. He identifies 10 metacomponents as the most important in intelligent functioning (Sternberg, 1985, p. 62):

1. Recognition that a problem of some kind exists
2. Recognition of the nature of the problem
3. Selection of a set of lower-order, nonexecutable components
4. Selection of a strategy for task performance, combining the lower-order components
5. Selection of one or more mental representations for information
6. Decision on how to allocate additional resources
7. Monitoring one's place in the task performance—what has been done and what needs to be done
8. Monitoring one's understanding of internal and external feedback concerning the quality of the task performance
9. Knowing how to act on the feedback that is received
10. Implementing action as a result of the feedback

Sternberg identifies performance components as lower-order processes used in the execution of strategies needed to perform a task: encoding the nature of the stimulus, inferring the relations between two stimulus terms that are similar in some ways but different in others, and applying a previously inferred relation to a new situation. Knowledge acquisition components are processes involved in learning new information and storing it in memory. Sternberg considers the three most important of these components to be selective encoding, selective combination, and selective comparison. Selective encoding requires sifting out relevant from irrelevant information. Selective combination refers to the combining of information in a way that maximizes its internal coherence or connectedness. Selective comparison relates new information to information already stored in memory to maximize the connectedness of the new knowledge.

Sternberg (1985) postulated six primary sources of individual differences in information processing (pp. 64–65):

1. *Components*—One individual may use more or fewer components or even different components than those another individual uses.
2. *Combination rule for components*—Different individuals may use different rules to combine.
3. *Mode of component processing*—Different persons prefer to process particular components in different modes.
4. *Order of component processing*—Different persons may use different sequences to order components.
5. *Component time and accuracy*—One person may be able to process a particular component more quickly or accurately than another person.
6. *Mental representations on which components act*—Different individuals may use different representations of information.

Sternberg (1990) argues that memory and analytical reasoning are the operations necessary for success in school and that tacit informational knowledge rather than explicit formal knowledge is required to be successful at work. Most traditional tests are contextualized with respect to the school; the problems are relatively short, have single correct answers, and contain no "real-world" content.

Sternberg (1990) has a research form of test that includes both academic and work contexts called the Sternberg Triarchic Abilities Test. The test has overlapping grade/age levels and can be administered from kindergarten through adulthood. Included on the test are 12 types of items (pp. 216–219):

Componential: Verbal—measures test taker's ability to learn from context and pick up information from relevant context

Componential: Quantitative—measures inductive reasoning ability in the numerical domain such as extrapolation of a sequence of numbers

Coping with Novelty: Verbal—assesses the ability to think in novel ways and requires hypothetical thinking with counterfactuals or novel verbal analogies which require counterfactual reasoning

Coping with Novelty: Quantitative—assesses coping with novelty skills in the context of the quantitative domain and utilizes a numerical matrix format in which the test taker has to substitute a number in place of a given symbol

Coping with Novelty: Figural—requires test takers to complete the series in a newly mapped domain and includes items similar to the figural completion type

Automatization: Verbal—requires test takers to make rapid decisions as to whether two letters are both the same category (vowel or consonant) or are different (vowel consonant or consonant vowel)

Automatization: Quantitative—requires the test taker to make rapid judgments as to whether two numbers have the same or different properties, such as being odd or even

Automatization: Figural—measures the test taker's ability to judge whether two figures have the same or different properties such as the number of sides

Practical: Verbal—measures the test taker's ability to respond to everyday inferential reasoning problems

Practical: Quantitative—measures the test taker's ability to reason quantitatively with practical everyday problems

Practical: Figural—measures the test taker's ability to perform route planning from information given on a map or diagram

Sternberg (1986) uses three subtheories to account for intelligence. The components subtheory relates to the internal world of the individual, the experiential theory relates intelligence to the experiences of the individual with tasks and situations, and the contextual subtheory relates intelligence to the external world of the individual.

Piaget's Theory of Cognitive Development

Piaget (1970) conceptualized a theory of intellectual development by observing and interviewing children. His task was to discover the basic psychological structures that underlie the formation of concepts fundamental to philosophy and science. He was intrigued by the errors of young children on a test of reasoning and found that older children were not only quantitatively more intelligent but also qualitatively different from younger children. Piaget focused on the qualitative differences. He concluded that learning is fundamentally an internal process of construction and identified organization and adaptation as two invariant functional properties of all living organisms. Organization is the general tendency to arrange both the physical and psychological processes in a coherent system. Two important dimensions of adaptation are assimilation and accommodation. Assimilation is the process by which a child relates new objects and ideas to familiar objects and ideas. Accommodation is the process by which a child changes behavior and psychological structures in response to environmental events.

Piaget divided intellectual development into four major stages: the sensorimotor period, the preoperational period, the concrete operational period, and the formal operational period (see Figure 7.2). He further identified four factors that affect development and the transition from one stage to another: maturation, experience, transmission, and equilibration. Equilibration can be described as the relative balance that exists between the individual's psychological structures and perceived events in the environment. Developing structures continually move toward greater and greater equilibrium. Piaget's theories have been the basis of the design of curriculum materials and educational programs, and a number of scales have been published to assess an individual's stage of intellectual development.

Gardner's Theory of Multiple Intelligence

Gardner (1983) postulated a theory of intelligence that focuses on a symbol system approach and combines both factor analytical and information-processing models. He identified seven forms of intelligence: verbal/linguistic, logical/mathematical, visual/spatial, body/kinesthetic, musical/rhythmic, interpersonal, intrapersonal and environmental.

Verbal/linguistic intelligence involves word meaning and understanding, reading, grammar, and humor. Logical/mathematical intelligence involves inductive and deductive reasoning, scientific reasoning, mathematical understanding, mathemati-

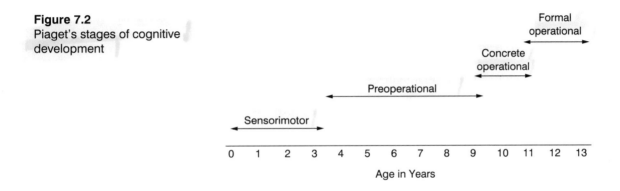

Figure 7.2
Piaget's stages of cognitive development

cal operations, and critical and abstract thinking. Visual/spatial intelligence entails understanding relationships of objects in space, mental images, graphic representation, and perception from different angles. Body/kinesthetic intelligence involves complex motor coordination, awareness control of body movements and functions, and mind and body integration. Musical/rhythmic intelligence requires sensitivity to sounds; recognition, creation, and reproduction of both melody and rhythm; and appreciation and enjoyment of the structure of music. Interpersonal intelligence requires effective verbal and nonverbal communication, sensitivity to the feelings of others, and ability to understand and work with others. Intrapersonal intelligence is dependent on metacognition, higher-order thinking, concentration, self-awareness, and other types of self-improvement skills.

Gardner (1993) states that "intelligences work together to solve problems to yield various kinds of end states—vocations, avocations, and the like" (p. 9). Interpersonal intelligence describes one's ability to detect the moods of other people and to lead those individuals. Intrapersonal intelligence depends on an understanding of one's own feelings and an ability to use self-knowledge productively.

Krechevsky (1994) has devised an observational schedule to assess students' skills based on Gardner's model of multiple intelligences. The subject areas on the rating form include visual arts, mechanical sciences, movement, music, social understanding, mathematics, science, and language. The tasks measure specific abilities that can be observed in an one-to-one situation. For example, in mathematics the scale requires observations in three areas: numerical reasoning, spatial reasoning, and logical problem solving. Can the student use estimation, find spatial patterns, and make logical inferences? Interpersonal and intrapersonal intelligences are assessed on a scale that has three components: understanding of self, understanding of others, and assumption of distinctive social roles. For example, can the student reflect on her own feelings, experiences, and accomplishments? Does the individual demonstrate knowledge of his peers and their activities? Does the student share ideas with other children?

TYPES OF TESTS

A number of methods to classify the various types of intelligence assessments and related tests are used by counselors and psychologists. Individual or group tests, verbal and nonverbal or performance tests, culture-fair tests, and developmental scales are examples. Procedures exist to measure intelligence in every age range from the infant to the senior citizen. Some tests can be classified into more than one category, and not all tests specify an IQ.

Individual Scales

Included in the list of the most cited tests in the *Thirteenth Mental Measurements Yearbook* are the Wechsler Preschool and Primary Scale of Intelligence–Revised.

The Wechsler Scales. The Wechsler Intelligence Scales are individually administered tests with appropriate forms for different age spans. There are three scales: the Wechsler Adult Intelligence Scale–Revised (WAIS-R), the Wechsler Intelligence Scale for Children–III (WISC-III), and the Wechsler Preschool and Primary Scale of Intelligence–Revised (WPPSI). The scales have 10 to 12 subtests each, about half belonging to the verbal scale, and the other half to the performance scale. The tests yield verbal, performance, and total IQ scores.

The verbal scale was designed by Wechsler to measure the examinee's ability to work with abstract symbols, the benefit the examinee received from his background, his verbal memory abilities, and his verbal fluency. The six areas included are information, digit span, arithmetic, comprehension, similarities, and vocabulary.

The information test focuses on knowledge and information acquired through educational experiences. Individuals with high scores have a wide variety of experiences, cultural opportunities, and outside interests. Low scores may show a lack of intellectual curiosity or a poor cultural environment.

The digit span test measures short-term or immediate memory. The task is to repeat digits forward as well as backward. The test demands concentration and attention; examinees with high scores have good short-term memory and can focus their attention well. This ability may relate to low anxiety or stress levels. Low scores may indicate poor attention or an inability to concentrate, resulting from anxiety or stress.

The arithmetic subtest focuses on items that require basic mathematical skills such as addition, subtraction, multiplication, and division and the ability to apply these skills. High scores are an indication of alertness, ability to concentrate, focus on tasks, and good arithmetic reasoning. Low scores may indicate a poor background in mathematical skills or reasoning and an inability to concentrate.

The comprehension subtest focuses on the individual's ability to make social judgments and requires information and knowledge of moral codes, social rules, and regulations. High scores are an indication of reality awareness, capacity for social compliance, and good judgment. Low scores may indicate poor judgment and possibly impulsiveness, antisocial tendencies, or some type of personality disturbance.

The similarities test measures reasoning and conceptual thinking ability. The test taker is presented with word pairs and must explain their similarities. The tasks demand inductive reasoning; the individuals must take specific facts and see how they fit a general rule or principle. Individuals with high scores have good verbal fluency and concept formation. Those with low scores have poor ability to think abstractly and see things flexibly.

The vocabulary test contains words from easy to difficult and from concrete to abstract. The test taker is asked to give meanings. The test measures general word knowledge and language development. This subtest is found on almost all general intelligence and scholastic aptitude tests. The performance of the individuals is influenced by cultural experiences and educational backgrounds. Those with high scores on this subtest usually have a wide range of interests, good recall, and high general intelligence. Those with low scores may have had a limited educational background or may be poorly motivated.

The performance scale includes a number of subtests: picture completion, picture arrangement, block design, object assembly, coding, and mazes.

The picture completion test requires the test taker to identify the missing part of a drawing. The subtest measures long-term visual alertness and memory as well as visual acuity. The test taker must be able to differentiate important from minor details. The tasks require perceptual alertness and concentration and an ability to organize visual material. Those with high scores on this subtest have the ability to recognize essential visual information and reveal alertness and good visual acuity. Those with low scores often have poor ability in visual organization and poor ability to concentrate. Impulsive examinees make quick responses without carefully analyzing the whole picture.

The picture arrangement test requires the examinee to put scrambled comic strip pictures in the correct order to tell a story. The test requires temporal visual sequencing, social awareness, planning ability, and nonverbal reasoning. It also requires knowledge of American subcultural values and may be inappropriate for individuals from other cultures. Those with high scores on this test have social intelligence and the ability to anticipate the consequences of initial acts. Those with low scores usually have problems in interpersonal relationships, few ideas, and poor ability to plan ahead.

The block design test requires the examinee to copy a set of designs using colored blocks. The test requires visual-spatial organization, the ability to analyze a whole into parts, and the use of nonverbal problem-solving skills. Those with high scores have good visual-motor-spatial skills and are able to concentrate. Those who score low have poor visual-motor-spatial and perceptual skills and poor visual integration. They may also have problems in concentration.

The object assembly test is a set of jigsaw puzzles that requires visual-motor speed and coordination as well as the ability to configure and organize the parts to the puzzle. Those with high scores on this test have excellent visual organizational abilities and demonstrate perceptual-motor coordination. Those with low scores have problems in visual-perceptual-motor areas and in visual concept formation.

The coding, or digit symbol, test requires quick and accurate coding of symbols that are paired with numbers of geometric shapes. The scale measures visual-motor speed and accuracy as well as short-term visual memory and the ability to follow directions. It demands an ability to learn an unfamiliar task. Those with high scores have effective visual-motor skills and are mentally efficient. They have the ability to memorize by rote new visual material. Those with low scores have poor visual-motor skills and an inadequate capacity for visual associative learning. They may have poor mental alertness.

The maze test requires children to draw an exit route out of each figure. The scale demands visual planning, visual-motor coordination, and perceptual organization. Those with high scores show an ability to plan ahead and a flexible mental orientation. Those with low scores often show impulsivity and poor visual-motor coordination and orientation to reality. A comparison of the dimensions measured in the verbal and performance scales of the Wechsler is given in Table 7.1.

Table 7.1
Comparison of verbal and performance dimensions of the Wechsler Intelligence Scales

Verbal	Performance
General	
Work with abstract symbols	Nonverbal contact with the environment
Utilization of school or educational background	Work with perceptual-motor tasks
Verbal memory abilities	Work with concrete tasks and problems
Verbal fluency	
Specific	
Computational skills	Long-term visual memory
Numerical reasoning	Visual alertness
Logical thinking	Ability to differentiate among details
Abstract thinking	Temporal visual sequencing
Ability to form verbal concepts	Social awareness
Word knowledge	Nonverbal reasoning
Language development	Planning ability
Awareness of social rules and mores	Verbal concept formation
Common sense	Whole/part analysis
Use of past experience	Visual-spatial ability
Short-term auditory memory	Sensory-motor feedback
Recall of information	Visual-motor speed, coordination, and accuracy
	Short-term visual memory
	Ability to follow directions
	Visual planning
	Ability to follow a visual pattern

The first step in interpretation of Wechsler results is to analyze the three global estimates of the client's ability—verbal, performance, and full scale. The full-scale score is used as a summary index of ability, and the examiner is advised to use ±2 standard errors of measurement to determine where a client's true score falls (La Greca & Stringer, 1985); that approach translates into a full-scale intelligence quotient (FSIQ) of ±6. Kaufman (1990) advocates using a 95 percent confidence band and interprets as a significant strength each scaled score 3 or more points above the mean and as a significant weakness each scaled score 3 or more points below the mean. The examiner can compare the individual's score with the appropriate ability classification listed in Table 7.2.

The second step is to analyze the verbal and performance scores and see whether they are significantly different; a 12-point difference is significant at the .05 level, and a 15-point difference is significant at the .01 level (Kaufman, 1976, 1994). In summarizing the research findings on significant differences between the verbal and performance scales, Groth-Marnat (1990) identified the following possible hypotheses:

Table 7.2
Classification of range of intelligence scores

IQ Range	Classification	Percentile Range
130 and above	Very Superior	98–99
120–129	Superior	91–97
110–119	High Average	75–90
90–109	Average	25–74
80–89	Low Average	9–24
70–79	Borderline	3–8
69 and below	Below Average	1–2

1. If the verbal IQ is 15 or more points above the performance IQ, it might show that the individual (a) has a high level of academic achievement, (b) comes from an urban environment, (c) has some type of neurosis (anxiety and tension state, obsessive-compulsion, or depression), (d) has learning problems of a perceptual nature, or (e) has a right-hemisphere cerebral impairment.
2. If the performance IQ is significantly higher than the verbal IQ, it might show that the individual (a) is an underachiever or has not made use of educational opportunities, (b) comes from a lower socioeconomic level or a different cultural or language background, (c) is a delinquent or a sociopath, (d) has severe reading difficulties, or (e) has left-hemisphere impairment.

The next step is to analyze and interpret the subtests. The examiner might look at the scatter of scores on the subtests and identify the highest- and lowest-scaled scores on the subtests. Kaufman (1976, 1990) reported that the average scaled score range is 7 points. The examiner might determine the number of subtests that deviate by 3 points or more from the fixed means. The subtests that are 3 points or more above the mean are identified as strengths, and those 3 points or more below the mean are identified as weaknesses. Subtest patterns are then analyzed for commonalities. Bannatyne (1971, 1974), for instance, organizes the subtests into the following categories: (1) verbal conceptual ability—comprehension, similarities, vocabulary; (2) spatial ability—block design, object assembly, picture completion; (3) sequencing ability—arithmetic, coding, digit span; and (4) acquired knowledge—arithmetic, information, vocabulary. The examiner might look at the scatter of the items within a subtest. Is there any pattern of how the individual responds to the items within the test? This is a more qualitative analysis.

The last step is to analyze the content of the responses on the various subtests. The examiner may be able to assess the client's level of thinking and identify any unusual associations as well as certain dimensions of personality and learning style. Spanish versions of the Wechsler scales are also available.

Kaufman Assessment Battery for Children. The Kaufman Assessment Battery for Children (K-ABC) (Kaufman & Kaufman, 1983) is an individually administered measure of intelligence and achievement for children ages 2 years, 6 months to 12 years, 6 months. The K-ABC is based on a theory of intelligence that distinguishes between sequential and simultaneous mental processes. Sequential processing (Kaufman, Kamphaus, & Kaufman, 1985) relates to the ability to solve problems by mentally arranging input in a sequential or serial order. Simultaneous processing refers to the ability to synthesize information from mental wholes to solve the problem. Simultaneous processing is used in such tasks as learning the shapes of letters, deriving meaning from pictorial stimuli, and determining the main idea from a paragraph of a text. Sequential processing is used in learning grammatical relationships and rules, understanding the chronology of events, and making associations between sounds and letters.

The K-ABC contains 16 subtests of mental and processing skills. Three subtests measure sequential processing, seven measure simultaneous processing, and six measure achievement. The achievement tests assess school learning in arithmetic, reading-decoding, reading-understanding, general information, early language development, and language concepts. The K-ABC also has a special nonverbal scale designed to assess the intelligence of hearing-impaired and limited English proficient children. The 10 subtests to measure mental processing skills are described in Table 7.3.

The following case study of George shows how individual testing can be used.

Table 7.3
K-ABC mental processing subtests

Subtest (ages)	Skill to Be Assessed
Magic Window (2.6 to 4.11)	Identifying and naming an object from a picture rotated behind a narrow slit that permits the picture to be only partially exposed
Face Recognition (2.6 to 4.11)	Attending closely to one or two faces in photographs that are briefly exposed and then selecting the correct face in a group photograph
Hand Movement (2.6 to 12.5)	Copying the precise sequence of taps on the table as performed by the examiner with a fist, palm, or side of the hand
Gestalt Closure (2.6 to 12.5)	Filling in the gaps in a partially completed inkblot drawing and also naming and describing the drawings
Number Recall (2.6 to 12.5)	Repeating in sequence a series of numbers orally presented by the examiner
Triangles (4.0 to 12.5)	Assembling several identical rubber triangles to match a picture of an abstract design.
Word Order (4.0 to 12.5)	Pointing with and without an interference task, to silhouettes of common objects in the same order as the objects were named by the examiner
Matrix Analogies (5.0 to 12.5)	Selecting the picture or design that best completes a 2″ × 2″ visual analogy
Spatial Memory (5.0 to 12.5)	Recalling the locations of pictures arranged randomly on a page
Photo Series (6.0 to 12.5)	Organizing in proper time sequence a randomly arranged array of photographs illustrating an event

CASE OF GEORGE

George Gray
Middletown Elementary School: Grade K
Date of birth: 3/22/91
Chronological age: 7-03
Date of examination: 7/8/98

Tests Used

Kaufman Assessment Battery for Children, Peabody Picture Vocabulary Test–Revised, Developmental Test of Visual-Motor Integration, Goodenough-Harris Draw-a-Man Test

Reasons for Referral

George Gray was referred for possible program change. He is currently participating in the language-impaired program at Middletown Elementary School.

Background Information

George was previously tested on 7/31/97. He was given the Stanford-Binet Intelligence Scale, Leiter International Performance Scale, Peabody Picture Vocabulary Test, and the Test of Visual-Motor Integration. The Stanford-Binet Intelligence Scale yielded an IQ of 48. The Leiter International Performance Scale was administered because of George's delayed language development, and an IQ score of 77 was obtained. The Peabody Picture Vocabulary Test revealed a standard score below 40, an age-equivalent score of 3 years, 6 months, and a significant deficit in the receptive vocabulary area. A communication evaluation was completed on 11/7/97 indicating that George had an articulation disorder and was severely delayed in language skills. The Vineland Adaptive Behavior Scale was completed on 6/19/98 with these results:

Scale	Age Equivalent
Receptive language	3–11
Expressive language	3–3
Written language	1–6

George's adaptive behavior composite on that evaluation equated to 60.

Another communication evaluation was conducted on 4/24/98. The speech and language pathologist reported that the two communication evaluations were consistent. George was functioning at approximately a 3-year-old level during both evaluations. Vision and hearing were found to be within acceptable limits at the school level.

Examiner Observations

George is a 7-year-old male of average stature for his chronological age. He was somewhat uncooperative by being continually out of his seat and exhibited poor listening skills. His work habits were somewhat slow, but his behavior could be described as extremely active. He was aware of his failures, and he typically gave up on a task at the very beginning if he believed he could not accomplish it. He appeared agitated after his failures. His speech was poor and his language inarticulate. At times his responses were vague, and the examiner had to encourage him to continue responding. He usually spoke only when he was spoken to. On the visual-motor tasks his reaction time was slow; he used a trial-and-error method of problem solving.

Results

Kaufman-Assessment Battery for Children gave these Global Scale standard scores:

Sequential Processing 56 ± 10
Simultaneous Processing 71 ± 9

Mental Processing Composite 63 ± 8
Achievement below 40
Nonverbal 67 ± 8

These were the Achievement standard scores:

Spaces and Places 65 ± 13
Arithmetic 62 ± 13
Riddles 59 ± 11
Reading/Decoding 67 ± 7
Reading/Understanding 0

The Mental Processing scaled scores included these scores for Sequential Processing:

Hand Movement 3
Number Recall 1
Word Order 4

These were the scores for Simultaneous Processing:

Gestalt Closure 7
Triangles 10
Matrix Analogies 6
Spatial Memory 2
Photo Series 3

These were the Nonverbal scores:

Hand Movement 3
Triangles 10
Matrix Analogies 6
Spatial Memory 2
Photo Series 3

Significant differences and overall scores were as follows:

Sequential < Simultaneous .05
Sequential > Achievement .05
Simultaneous > Achievement .01
MPC > Achievement .01
Mean Achievement Standard Score 50.6
Mean Scaled Score 4.5

These were the scores on the Peabody Picture Vocabulary Test:

Raw Score 27
Standard Score < 40
Age Equivalent 3-2

Cognitive Development and Interpretation

George was administered the K-ABC to assess his current mental processing abilities and level of achievement. The K-ABC measures one's style of problem solving. Two types of mental functioning are identified: sequential processing, which involves processing stimuli bit by bit or in serial order, and simultaneous processing, which incorporates a holistic and frequently spatial integration of stimuli.

George's Sequential Processing standard score of 56 ± 10 (95 percent confidence level) is in the educable mentally handicapped range of functioning. His Simultaneous Processing score of 71 ± 9 is in the borderline range. Thus, there is a significant difference (15 points) between his sequential processing and his simultaneous processing. This difference suggests that George has greater abilities in solving problems holistically or processing many stimuli at one time rather than stimulus by stimulus.

George's Achievement standard score of below 40 represents a significant discrepancy between his school achievement and mental processing abilities. His Simultaneous Processing standard score of 71 is significantly greater than his Achievement standard score. This difference is found in fewer than 1 percent of the individuals within George's age group and may be associated with school-related learning tasks on the test, which are usually more sequentially oriented.

George's Mental Processing Composite (MPC) of 63 ± 8 is in the educable mentally handicapped range. His true score has a 95 percent chance of being between 55 and 71. Thus, his MPC score is significantly higher than the Achievement standard score and indicates that he has greater processing potential than is being exemplified in school-related achievement.

Internal analysis of the K-ABC reveals a mean score of 4.5, which is considered in the handicapped range of functioning. A relative strength is noted on the Triangles subtest, which measures abstract concept formation. A significant weakness is noted in short-term recall via simultaneous processing (Spatial Memory). All his scores on the Mental Processing subtests, except for Triangles, are considered below the average for children within George's age group.

The Nonverbal standard score of 67 was compiled from the subtests Hand Movements, Triangles, Matrix Analogies, Spatial Memory, and Photo Series. George's Nonverbal standard score was not significantly higher than his Mental Processing score, suggesting that his abilities, as measured by the K-ABC, are not significantly different. Language impairment is the major influence, but other factors also appear to be contributing to George's low-functioning intellect.

Receptive Language

On the Peabody Picture Vocabulary Test–Revised, which requires the subject to point to one of four pictures corresponding to a word presented orally by the examiner, George received a standard score below 40. This score is greater than one standard deviation below the mean when considering chronological age and current cognitive functioning, and it represents a process deficit in the receptive language area.

Perceptual-Motor

On the Developmental Test of Visual-Motor Integration, which requires the subject to reproduce geometric designs with pencil and paper, George received a standard score of 4 and an age equivalent of 5.1. This score is within one standard deviation of the mean, when considering chronological age and current cognitive functioning, and represents adequate development in the perceptual motor area. The Goodenough-Harris Draw-a-Man Test revealed a mental age of 5.9 and an estimated IQ of 79.

Diagnostic Impressions

George is functioning in the educable mentally handicapped range. He demonstrates significantly greater abilities in simultaneous processing as compared with sequential processing. He also demonstrates a relative strength in his nonverbal concept formation and his word recognition and letter naming. A significant weakness is noted in his short-term memory recall.

George's Achievement scores are significantly lower than his potential indicates. His nonverbal abilities are not demonstrated as being significantly higher than his total Mental Processing Composite. A process deficit is noted in receptive language, consistent with his history of poor language development. Perceptual-motor abilities appear to be adequately developed. Just how much George's poor language development has affected his intellectual functioning is not known. Presently his intellectual functioning, as measured by the K-ABC, is somewhere between the educable mentally handicapped and borderline range of functioning. Current remediation strategies should address his language delay as well as his current estimated intellectual functioning.

The K-ABC does have an interpretative manual (Kaufman & Kaufman, 1983), which suggests these five steps:

1. Obtain the derived scores and describe them with bands of error, descriptive categories, national and sociocultural percentile ranks, age equivalents, and grade equivalents.
2. Compare standard scores on the Sequential Processing and Simultaneous Processing scales.
3. Compare standard scores on the Mental Processing and Achievement scales.
4. Determine strengths and weaknesses on the Mental Processing subtests.
5. Determine strengths and weaknesses on the Achievement subtests.

The K-ABC lists these primary goals: to measure intelligence from a strong theoretical and research basis, to separate acquired factual knowledge from the ability to solve unfamiliar problems, to yield scores that translate into educational interventions, to include novel tasks, to be easy to administer and objective to score, and to be sensitive to diverse needs of preschool, minority groups, and exceptional children (Kaufman & Kaufman, 1983, p. 5).

In a review of the K-ABC, Merz (1984) concludes that the authors have met the goals and that the test will fairly assess minority group members and individuals with language handicaps.

Kaufman Adolescent and Adult Intelligence Test. The Kaufman Adolescent and Adult Intelligence Test (KAIT) core battery consists of six subtests within two scales. The KAIT measures fluid intelligence, adaptability, and flexibility in problem solving through three subtests. The crystallized scale measures ability to solve problems and make decisions based on acquired knowledge, verbal conceptualization, formal and informal education, life experiences, and acculturation through subtests on auditory comprehension, double meanings, and definitions. A composite score provides a measure of overall intellectual functioning. The examiner can also add one to four additional subtests to the battery: memory for block designs, famous faces, rebus recall, and auditory recall. A rebus is a picture that stands for a word. Individuals are asked to read phrases or sentences composed of rebuses on the fluid scale, then read the phrases or sentences on the added recall test that were learned earlier during the rebus learning subtest. The KAIT can measure immediate and delayed recall. The construct validity of the KAIT is shown through studies correlating the KAIT with the WISC-R, the WAIS-R, and the K-ABC. Reliability coefficients in the .90s were reported.

Stanford-Binet Intelligence Scale. The Stanford-Binet Intelligence Scale–Fourth Edition is quite different from the edition published in 1960. The test does retain some content and a variety of tasks but no longer uses the age-scale format. All of the same type of items are grouped together, and the test now has a variety of scales. The purpose of this change is to help examiners obtain a better diagnosis of a test taker's cognitive abilities. The authors claim the test has two major strengths: (1) a continuous scale for appraising the cognitive development of the test taker from age 2 to adulthood, and (2) an adaptive-testing format that permits testing with a range of tasks best suited to the client's ability level.

The conceptual model for the fourth edition of the Stanford-Binet consists of three levels. The top level is the *G,* or generalized reasoning factor. The second level consists of three broad factors: crystallized abilities, fluid-analytical abilities, and short-term memory. The third level measures verbal, quantitative, and abstract/visual reasoning dimensions of intelligence.

The Stanford-Binet contains many of the item types from the previous edition. The criteria for selection required that the items (1) be acceptable measures of the conceptual model used, (2) be able to be scored reliably, (3) be relatively free from ethnic and gender bias, and (4) function adequately over a wide range of age groups. New items were constructed to increase the pool measuring quantitative reasoning, abstract/visual reasoning, and short-term memory.

The standardization was completed in 1985 and involved 500 examiners, 5,000 subjects, and 160 testing centers from 47 states and the District of Columbia. The standardization considered community size, ethnic group membership, age, gender, and socioeconomic status.

The Stanford-Binet consists of four factors. The verbal reasoning factor includes four subtests: vocabulary, comprehension, absurdities, and verbal relations. The abstract/visual reasoning factor also includes four subtests: pattern analysis, copying, matrices, and paper folding and cutting. The quantitative reasoning factor has three subtests: quantitative, number series, and equation building. The short-term memory factor includes four scales: bead memory, memory for sentences, memory for digits, and memory of objects. The tests report standard age scores (SAS). Each test has an SAS mean of 50 and a standard deviation of 8. The area scores and overall composite score have a fixed mean of 100 and fixed standard deviation of 15. Tables are available with 16 as the fixed standard deviation.

The items on the test are arranged in levels designated by the letters *A* through *Y.* Some tests contain 20 or more levels and cover the entire range from 2 to adulthood; others contain 10 levels and cover a narrower range of chronological age. The purpose of this format is to facilitate adaptive testing. Chronological age and performance on the vocabulary test are used to identify the level at which testing should begin. As in previous editions of the Stanford-Binet, basal and ceiling levels are established.

Other Individual Tests.   The Leiter International Performance Scale (LIPS) is a 54-item, nonverbal test used to assess the intelligence of individuals aged 2 through adulthood. It has been used to test a wide variety of individuals, including those with hearing problems, language disabilities, mental retardation, cultural disadvantages, or non-English–speaking backgrounds. The LIPS measures dimensions of perceptual and conceptual abilities. The perceptual items present tasks involving shapes, colors, block design, and visual closure. The conceptual items require clients to deduce underlying relationships, categories, and classes; demonstrate an understanding of visual-spatial relationships; and understand numerical processes. The categories are labeled symbolic transformation, quantitative discriminations, spatial imagery, genus matching, progression discriminations, and immediate recall. Matey (1984) rates the LIPS valuable for psychologists engaged in the assessment of the mental abilities of hearing-impaired children, children with severe expressive or receptive language disabilities, and adults with severe or profound mental retardation. The LIPS is also considered an appropriate instrument for those who have motor and manipulative difficulties in addition to their communication problems.

Arthur Point Scale of Performance Tests–Revised Form II is an individual scale that measures the mental abilities of individuals with reading, hearing and/or speech, emotional, or cultural problems. The Arthur Point Scale contains five tests: Knox Cube Test, Sequin Form Board, Arthur Stencil Design, Healy Picture Completion, and Porteous Maze Test.

The Peabody Picture Vocabulary Test–III measures receptive vocabulary knowledge for standard American English and provides an estimate of the verbal ability and scholastic aptitude of the test taker. The examinee is shown a plate containing four pictures and is asked to point to the picture that corresponds to the stimulus word. A new Spanish version is now available.

The Slosson Intelligence Test–Revised (SIT-R) provides a quick assessment of mental abilities of children and adults, ages 4 to 65. The SIT is a 187-item oral screening instrument with questions arranged on a scale by chronological age. The SIT-R contains 33 vocabulary items, 29 general information items, 30 similarities and difference items, 33 comprehension items, 34 quantitative items, and 28 auditory memory items. The SIT-R correlates .892 with the WISC-R verbal IQ and .863 with the WISC-III FSIQ. The KR-20 reliability coefficients are .90 or higher for all age groups. An item analysis identifies the strengths and weaknesses of an individual in eight learning areas.

The Test of Nonverbal Intelligence–2 (TONI-2) provides a language-free measure of cognitive ability. The TONI-2 is used with clients who have speech, language, or learning disabilities; who are deaf or hearing impaired; or who have suffered some other form of brain injury. It can also be used with clients who do not speak English or for whom English is not their first language. A 50-item test can be given by pantomime to the examinee, who responds by pointing to the selected answer. The test can be given to clients from ages 5 to 85, 11 months and takes 10 to 15 minutes.

The Raven's Progressive Matrices consist of a series of three nonverbal tests for different ability levels. In measuring the nonverbal component of Spearman's G factor, the items are designed to assess a client's ability to make sense of complex situations, derive meaning from events, and perceive and think clearly. It can be group-administered and has been used with mentally handicapped clients. The Coloured Progressive Matrices (CPM) (Raven, 1990) are used to spread the scores for the bottom 20 percent of the general population. Norms are available for children aged 6.5 to 16.5. The Standard Progressive Matrices (SPM) (Raven, 1993) measure the performance in the average range and consist of 5 sets of 12 problems each. The Advanced Progressive Matrices (APM) (1993) are designed to spread the scores of the top 20 percent of the population.

The Cognitive Assessment System (CAS) (Das & Naglieri, 1996) provides information about the strengths and weaknesses of four major cognitive processes and yields useful information about the intellectual strengths and weaknesses of children with mental retardation. It can be administered to children from age 2 years, 6 months to 17 years, 11 months. There are two levels. The upper preschool level is used with children between the ages of 3 years, 6 months to 6 years, 11 months and yields two scores: Verbal Ability and Nonverbal Ability. The school level also provides a composite score in Spatial Ability. Both core and diagnostic subtests are part of the assessment

Group Intelligence Tests

There are a number of widely used group intelligence tests. Such tests have been used ever since World War I, when the Army Alpha and Army Beta were used to screen recruits. The Army Alpha was the first widely used group verbal test of intelligence; the Army Beta was the first widely used group nonverbal test. Group tests measure as wide a variety of constructs as do individual tests. All types of theories and approaches are used.

It takes little training for an examiner to be competent in the administration and scoring of group tests. The directions are clearly stated in the manual, and the major task of the examiner is to read the test directions to the examinees and follow rigidly the specified time limits. Scoring keys or stencils are available, as are tables for translating the raw scores into deviation IQs or percentile ranks. Some of the widely used group tests of intelligence are described here.

The Advanced Progressive Matrices were constructed by J. C. Ravens and is a 48-item nonverbal group IQ test. The first 12 items are used to give the examinee practice for Part II. The examinee is presented with figure designs or patterns that have parts missing. Examinees are then asked to choose the correct option from among six possible parts. The test can be used with adolescents and adults. The Colored Progressive Matrices are similar to the one just described but for ages 5 to 11 and adults. It can be group-administered and has been used with mentally handicapped or impaired clients.

The Universal Nonverbal Intelligence Test (UNIT) (Bracken & McCallum, 1998) is a language-free test that requires no receptive or expressive language from the examiner or examinee. UNIT measures a number of types of intelligence and cognitive abilities. The test is made up of six subtests designed to measure the functioning of the client according to a two-tier model of intelligence, memory, and reasoning. The memory subtests are Object Memory, Spatial Memory, and Symbolic Memory. Three subtests also assess reasoning: Design, Mazes, and Analogic Reasoning. Although five of the subtests require motoric manipulation, they can be adapted for a pointing response. On the Spatial Memory test items the examinee must remember and re-create the placement of colored chips. On the Object Memory scale the examinee is shown a visual array of common objects such as a pan, a computer, and a rose for 5 seconds and then has to identify those objects from a larger array of objects in pictures. The internal consistency coefficient for 5- to 7-year-olds ranges from .83 in Analogic Reasoning to .89 in Design.

The Culture-Fair Intelligence Tests are a series developed by R. B. Cattell and A. K. S. Cattell. Scale 1 is used for ages 4 to 8; scale 2 for preadolescents, adolescents, and adults with average abilities; and scale 3 for college students and adults with above-average ability. Scales 2 and 3 are group-administered nonverbal tests measuring perceptual tasks, such as completing a series, classifying, solving incomplete designs, and evaluating conditions. The tests measure the fluid dimension of Cattell's theory (mentioned previously in this chapter).

The Cognitive Abilities Test (CogAT) was originally developed by R. L. Thorndike and E. P. Hagen and is a multilevel battery used to test children from kindergarten to grade 12. Verbal, quantitative, and nonverbal batteries are used. The verbal battery measures vocabulary, sentence completion, classification, and analogies. The quantitative battery measures relations, number series, and equation building. The nonverbal battery uses figure classification, analogies, and synthesis. The test can be group-administered to classes and hand- or computer-scored. Levels 1 and 2 are designed for kindergarten through grade 3, level A for grades 3 to 12. Testing time is about 90 minutes. A CogAT *Interpretive Guide for Teachers* and a manual, *Preparing for Testing with the CogAT*, are available to facilitate proper use and interpretation of the test. The current edition of the test is Form 5 (Thorndike & Hagen, 1993).

The Otis-Lennon School Ability Test (OLSAT) was developed by A. S. Otis and later revised by R. T. Lennon. The OLSAT is currently in its sixth edition. It has five levels: Primary I for grade 1, Primary II for grades 2 and 3, Elementary for grades 4 and 5, Intermediate for grades 6 to 8, and Advanced for grades 9 to 12. The primary batteries are read to the students by the examiner. Verbal, figural, and numerical items are rotated. The test yields one *G* score. The OLSAT is used for predicting success in cognitive, school-related areas. It also has five forms and yields a school ability index, a national PR-S, and a national NCE on total verbal and nonverbal scores. Local norms can be included in the report. The computer report provides a narrative explaining the student's performance in easy-to-understand language. That performance is analyzed by clusters, including verbal comprehension, verbal reasoning, figural reasoning, and quantitative reasoning.

The School and College Ability Tests (SCAT) are a series of group tests measuring verbal and quantitative ability from grade 3.5 to grade 14. The verbal section measures students' understanding of words and analogies, and the quantitative section measures students' understanding of fundamental number concepts. The SCAT reports scores in both verbal and quantitative areas in percentile bands.

The Test of Cognitive Skills (TCS-2) (1992) is a group test used to assess four areas of the cognitive skills of students in grades 2 to 12: analogies, sequences, memory, and verbal reasoning. The analogies test assesses students' ability to see abstract or concrete relationships and to classify objects or concepts according to common attributes. The memory test assesses students' abilities to recall information presented at the beginning of the test. The sequences test assesses students' ability to comprehend a principle or a rule implicit in a pattern or sequence of figures, letters, or numbers. The verbal reasoning test assesses students' ability to discern relationships and reason logically. The TCS-2 yields scores in each of the four areas and provides a verbal, nonverbal, and total IQ.

The Primary Test of Cognitive Skills (PTCS) (1990) was developed by Huttenlocher and Levine to measure the cognitive skills of children in kindergarten and first grade and has four subscales: verbal, spatial, memory, and concepts. These four subscales are combined to yield a cognitive skills index, using a mean of 100 and a standard deviation of 10.

These are not all of the many group tests that are used but are representative of the types of tests that are available and reflect the variety of approaches used by test authors. For example, the Culture-Fair Intelligence Tests yield only one score, whereas the CogAT and TCS-2 yield a series of scores. Scores are reported in different ways. Some tests use percentile bands; others use deviation IQ scores. Certain tests are designed to be culture-free. Some tests—such as the OLSAT, CogAT, SCAT, and TCS-2—are often given along with major survey achievement batteries because they may provide useful information to the counselor and teacher about students' cognitive abilities that are not assessed as completely on the achievement tests. Some tests use primarily verbal and numeric material, while others, such as the Culture-Free Scales, use only perceptual stimuli. Some, of course, measure all three areas.

TRENDS AND ISSUES

Intelligence testing is still a center of controversy. Many definitions of the construct of intelligence have led to the development of many different models, theories, and tests. There is no shared agreement as to what intelligence is and how it should be measured. We are not even sure of what words we should use to describe the construct—ability, aptitude, cognitive abilities, intelligence, or potential. The cognitive and information processing movements in psychology have had an impact on the theories and have influenced how we interpret and title our tests. Instead of "intelligence" in the title, many tests now refer to "cognitive abilities."

Many models have been developed to help us conceptualize intelligence, such as those by Spearman, Thurstone, E. L. Thorndike, Guilford, Gardner, Horn, Piaget, Sternberg, Wagner, Vernon, and Jensen. The controversy still centers around the issue of whether intelligence is a general attribute or has many specific attributes.

The heredity and environment issue is also still debated. Social scientists have been divided for a long time over the relative importance of heredity and environment in relation to intelligence. Most recently, in their book *The Bell Curve* (1994), Herrnstein and Murray conclude that heredity plays an important role in intelligence. Among other evidence, they note that IQ scores are highly correlated with academic success, job performance, and infant mortality. Children of low-IQ women tend to die more often in infancy than those of higher-IQ parents. Current studies are exploring how the interaction between heredity and environment affects intelligence.

Neither are we in agreement as to the purposes of intelligence testing. Sternberg and Wagner believe the tests should be used to provide useful information for understanding and improving the learning process of individuals tested.

Much concern is still focused on the biased nature of IQ tests. White middle-class test takers score better than individuals from different racial and cultural groups. Loehlin, Lindzey, and Spohler (1975) concluded that such distinctions reflect biases in the tests themselves, differences in the environments of the groups, and differences in the genetic makeup of the individuals studied. The three factors are viewed as interactive but not necessarily independent. Attempts were made, for example, on the Wechsler Intelligence Scale for Children to minimize bias. Statistics were computed to identify and eliminate items preferential to certain age, ethnic, or gender groups in the current third edition.

Another question often debated deals with the stability of intelligence over time. Research has indicated that IQ scores are very unstable in early childhood. Later, scores may decline with age on some types of items and increase on others. IQ is not viewed as a fixed entity. Some dimensions may be influenced by genetic makeup, but typically one develops greater general knowledge, problem-solving ability, and comprehension with age. On the other hand, the psychomotor performance of an individual might decrease with age.

SUMMARY

The chapter focused on the individual and group-intelligence scales that are most widely used today. The tests cited illustrate that there are many definitions and models of intelligence. They help teachers make instructional decisions about what methods and materials would be best for their students. They help workers in the helping professions to develop realistic expectations for their clients and students. The information from intelligence tests is also valuable in guiding individuals to make educational and vocational decisions. The tests provide a frame of reference for looking at cognitive abilities and making placement and classification decisions on the basis of such scores. Intelligence tests are also used for descriptive and predictive purposes.

Kamphaus, Petoskey, and Morgan (1997) point out that there have been four major approaches to intelligence test interpretation. The first was to design a system to classify individuals according to their abilities. Remember the early work of Binet and others was to classify individuals into specific groups based upon the scores they made on intelligence tests.

The second was to use profile analysis to help achieve a more complete understanding of an individual's cognitive skills. Rapaport and Wechsler led this second wave of test interpretations.

The third wave was the use of psychometric profile analysis stimulated by the availability of the computer and statistical software packages. Scales on the Wechsler tests were factor-analyzed. Cohen was the leader in this movement and helped clinicians understand the necessity of considering subtest score interpretation. Kaufman extended our understanding of the problems associated with profile analysis.

The fourth wave was applying theory to intelligence test interpretation. Integrative approaches emphasized that results can only be interpreted meaningfully in the context of other test results such as clinical findings, background information, and the like. Findings were seen as meaningful if supported by research evidence. Knowledge of theory is a key element in helping the examiner conceptualize a client's score.

QUESTIONS FOR DISCUSSION

1. Compare the different theories of intelligence. What theory do you find most acceptable and why? Why are theories important?

2. What are the advantages and disadvantages of group intelligence tests? Of individual tests? When would you use each?

3. E. L. Thorndike said there were three types of intelligence: abstract, social, and practical. Do you agree with his view? How do they compare with Sternberg's and Gardner's types?

4. Turn back to the "Case of George." He was given the Stanford-Binet, the Leiter International Performance Scale, the Peabody Picture Vocabulary Test, the Goodenough-Harris Drawing Test, and the Developmental Test of Visual-Motor Integration. Why was each test given? Why are there differences in the scores on these tests? Would you have given George any other test? Why or why not?

5. Do you feel that most tests are biased in favor of the white middle-class examinee? Do you believe that we should use only culture-fair tests? Defend your beliefs.

6. What factors influence how an individual performs on an IQ test? Do you believe that items on the intelligence tests should be radically changed so the test can be of more use? Why or why not?

SUGGESTED ACTIVITIES

1. Critique a group or an individual intelligence test discussed in this chapter.

2. Interview psychologists and counselors who use intelligence tests. Find out which tests they use and why and when they test. Report your results to the class.

3. Make an annotated bibliography of the intelligence and scholastic aptitude tests you would use in your field.

4. Write a review of the literature or a position paper on one of the following topics: bias in intelligence testing, history of intelligence testing, socioeconomic

class and intelligence, genetic studies of intelligence, computer-adaptive intelligence testing.

5. Take a group IQ test, score it, and write a report of the results.

6. Read *The Bell Curve* and be prepared to discuss the book in class.

7. Read the following case and answer the questions at the end.

Case of Roberta

Roberta is a grade 9 student who was referred to the school psychologists for psychoeducational evaluation to assess possible causes of her unacceptable behavior and poor peer/adult relationships.

School personnel are concerned about Roberta's inability to function in a school setting. She is frequently off task, asks inappropriate questions, comes unprepared, wanders about the classroom, and seeks to make herself the center of attention. Roberta is making just fair grades in average group classes. She appears to be preoccupied and also seems to fear her parents, not wanting them to know what happens in school.

Examiner observations:

Roberta is a thin, pale girl with unkempt hair. She has an excellent vocabulary and a good sense of humor. However, she does not know how to respond to teasing or correction and seemed to enjoy telling stories about how she got back at people who offended her. Her speech was affected, leaning toward the theatrical, and she appeared to enjoy the attention testing afforded.

She was observed in the class and in the halls. She was unprepared for class, not having paper. This seemed to be a common occurrence. She responded to questions in a mumble. When asked to speak louder, she became quite dramatic. In the halls she keeps to herself. She leaves class late and hurries to her next class. She stands out in the crowd. Her mannerisms and dress set her apart.

Results:

Stanford-Binet (full scale) 142

Wide Range Achievement Test

Subject	Grade Equivalent	Standard Score	Percentile
1. Reading	12.7	139	99.1
2. Spelling	11.7	127	96
3. Arithmetic	10.0	114	82
4. Arithmetic (untimed)	12.8	133	99

WISC-III

Verbal Tests	Raw Score	Scaled Score
1. Information	28	16
2. Similarities	29	19
3. Arithmetic	17	14
4. Vocabulary	61	19
5. Comprehension	25	10
6. (Digit Span)[1]	(19)	(13)
7. Verbal Score	78	

---

1. Parentheses indicate that the subtest is optional.

Performance Tests	*Raw Score*	*Scaled Score*	
1. Picture Completion	20	9	
2. Picture Arrangement	23	7	
3. Block Design	52	13	
4. Object Assembly	21	7	
5. Coding	40	5	
6. Performance Score		41	
Composite Scores	*Raw Score*	*Scaled Score*	*IQ*
1. Verbal Score		78	136
2. Performance Score		41	87
3. Full-Scale Score		119	113

a. Describe Roberta's intellectual abilities.

b. Are the results similar for different tests?

c. What additional information would you like to have about Roberta?

ADDITIONAL READINGS

Flanagan, D. P., Genshaft, J. L., & Harrison, P. L. (1997). *Contemporary intellectual assessment: Theories, tests, and issues.* New York: Guilford.

The authors cover the origins of intellectual assessment, contemporary and emerging theories, new tests and alternate techniques for assessing intelligence, and integration and synthesis of current theories and trends.

Gardner, H. (1983). *Frames of mind: The theory of multiple intelligence.* New York: Basic Books.

Gardner, H. (1993). *Multiple intelligences: The theory in practice.* New York: Basic Books.

Gardner discusses his theory of multiple intelligences, which takes into consideration the psychological, biological, and cultural dimensions of cognition.

Jensen, A. R. (1980). *Bias in mental testing.* New York: Free Press.

Jensen, A. R. (1981). *Straight talk about mental tests.* New York: Free Press.

The writings of Jensen have stimulated debate about the role of heredity and environment in the formation of intelligence.

Kamphaus, R. W. (1993). *Clinical assessment of children's intelligence: A handbook for professional practice.* Boston: Allyn & Bacon.

The author provides examples and cases to facilitate understanding and interpretation of the WISC-III, the Stanford-Binet, the Kaufman ABS, and the Woodcock-Johnson. Information is presented on the use of tests for infant and preschool assessment.

Kaufman, A. S. (1990). *Assessing adolescent and adult intelligence.* Boston: Allyn & Bacon.

The author discusses the clinical and neuropsychological assessment of the intelligence of adolescents and adults with special attention given to the Wechsler Adult Intelligence Scale–Revised.

McGrew, K. S. (1994). *Clinical interpretation of the Woodcock-Johnson Tests of Cognitive Abilities–Revised.* Boston: Allyn & Bacon.

The author presents a detailed, step-by-step analysis of the 21 WJTCA tests and includes a special strengths and weaknesses worksheet as well as diagrams and figures to help examiners understand and interpret the test.

Sternberg, R. J. (1985). *Beyond IQ: A triarchic theory of human intelligence*. Cambridge: Cambridge University Press.

Sternberg is one of the leading writers on the topic of the role and function of intelligence.

Sternberg, R. J., & Davidson, J. E. (Eds.). (1990). Intelligence and intelligence testing [Special issue]. *Educational Psychologist, 25*(3–4).

Sternberg, R. J., & Detterman, D. K. (Eds). (1986). *What is intelligence? Contemporary viewpoints on its nature and definition.* Norwood, NJ: Ablex.

Wagner, R. K., & Sternberg, R. J. (1984). Alternative conceptions of intelligence and their implications for education. *Review of Educational Research, 54*(2), 179–223.

The authors of these last three titles make a case for different conceptualizations of intelligence.

CHAPTER 8

Aptitude Testing

OVERVIEW

Aptitude testing has been used in education and psychology since the 1920s to predict what people can learn. Aptitude was considered by some early theorists to be innate but now is viewed as the result of learning experiences. The current operational definition of the construct addresses an individual's ability to learn certain skills or tasks if given the opportunity. Aptitude tests measure an individual's capacity, or potential, for performing a given skill or task and are used to predict behavior—will the individual be successful in a given educational program, vocational program, or occupational situation?

OBJECTIVES

After studying this chapter, the reader should be able to identify and discuss the

✔ Uses of major multiaptitude test batteries

✔ Uses of special abilities tests

✔ Uses of work-sample aptitude tests

✔ Problems and issues related to aptitude testing

✔ Uses of scholastic aptitude tests

The content of intelligence, achievement, and aptitude tests overlaps. For example, vocabulary items are a part of all three types, as are numerical computation and reasoning items. One of the primary differences among these tests is how the tests are used. Scholastic aptitude, general aptitude, intelligence, and special abilities tests are often used for predictive purposes, whereas achievement tests measure what has been learned and are most often used for descriptive purposes and assessment of growth and change. A variety of specialized achievement tests are used for diagnostic purposes.

MULTIAPTITUDE BATTERIES

Multiaptitude batteries are tests that measure a number of relatively broad ability areas, such as verbal reasoning, numerical reasoning, mechanical reasoning, and abstract reasoning. The most widely used and highly rated multiaptitude batteries are the Armed Services Vocational Aptitude Battery (ASVAB), the Differential Aptitude Test (DAT), and the General Aptitude Test Battery (GATB).

Such tests are used primarily for educational and vocational counseling. They permit intraindividual comparisons, showing the highs and lows of an individual's performance on the various subtests. Studies are made of the construct and criterion-reference validity of these tests. The potential test user wants a battery with subtests that are relatively independent of one another (that is, measuring different abilities and having low intercorrelations) and that have a high correlation of success in various educational and vocational programs. Unfortunately, the factors on most aptitude batteries have moderate to high intercorrelations with each other.

Armed Services Vocational Aptitude Battery

The ASVAB was first developed in 1966 and has gone through a number of revisions since: Forms 18 and 19 are the current versions. Multiple aptitude batteries are a fundamental component of a comprehensive counseling program. Results from these batteries help students assess their aptitudes, predict performance in academic and occupational areas, select career exploration activities, and make tentative career choices. The ASVAB measures aptitudes for general academic areas and career areas that encompass most civilian and military work. The test is used with clients in grade 11 and higher. The authors claim the test is valuable for military and nonmilitary purposes because it can be used for academic and career counseling. The ASVAB consists of 10 subtests, which are described in Table 8.1. The test takes 3 hours to complete—144 minutes of testing and 36 minutes of administrative time.

The ASVAB provides three academic composite scores:

Academic Ability—word knowledge, paragraph comprehension, and arithmetic reasoning

Verbal—word knowledge, paragraph comprehension, and general science

Math—mathematics knowledge and arithmetic reasoning

Table 8.1
Subtests of the Armed Services Vocational Aptitude Battery

Scale	Time (min.)	Items	Description
General Science	11	25	Measures knowledge of the physical and biological sciences
Arithmetic Reasoning	36	30	Measures ability to solve arithmetic word problems
Word Knowledge	11	35	Measures ability to select correct meaning of words in context and best synonym for a given word
Paragraph Comprehension	13	15	Measures ability to obtain information from written passages
Numerical Operations	3	50	Measures ability to perform arithmetic computations in a speeded context
Coding Speed	7	84	Measures ability to use a key in assigning code numbers to words in a speeded context
Auto and Shop	11	25	Measures knowledge of automobiles, tools, and shop terminology and practices
Mathematics Knowledge	24	25	Measures knowledge of high school mathematics principles
Mechanical Comprehension	19	25	Measures knowledge of mechanical and physical principles and ability to visualize how illustrated objects work
Electronics Information	9	20	Measures knowledge of electricity and electronics

Source: From the counselor's manual of the *Armed Services Vocational Aptitude Battery (Form 16).*
1991. North Chicago: U.S. Military Processing Command.

The test has four occupational components:

> *Mechanical and Crafts*—arithmetic reasoning, mechanical comprehension, and auto, shop, and electronics information
>
> *Business and Clerical*—word knowledge, paragraph comprehension, mathematics knowledge, and coding speed
>
> *Electronics and Electrical*—arithmetic reasoning, mathematical knowledge, electronics information, and general science
>
> *Health, Social, and Technology*—word knowledge and paragraph meaning, arithmetic reasoning, and mechanical comprehension

The number of items included on some of the subtests has been increased to help improve the reliability of the subtests. The test was normed on a national representative sample of 12,000 men and women aged 16 to 23. There are guides for both the counselor and test takers, and a computerized profile is given to the test takers. Figure 8.1 shows an example of a profile.

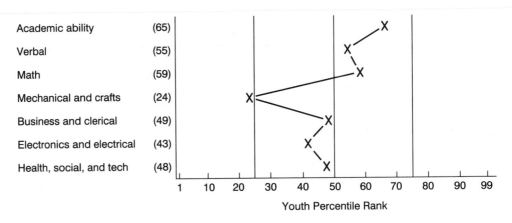

Figure 8.1
Individual profile of performance on the Armed Services Vocational Aptitude Battery

Jensen (1988) considers the ASVAB to be a test that measures general ability plus interests rather than differential aptitude. He concludes that the ASVAB is an excellent group test of general ability but states that there are shorter tests available that measure *G* with satisfactory reliability.

Differential Aptitude Test Battery

The DAT is a battery of eight subtests used for vocational and educational guidance purposes with students in grades 7 through 12 and adults. The test was originally developed in 1947 by Bennett, Seashore, and Wesman and published by the Psychological Corporation. The current revision is the fifth edition (1990). The test takes 235 minutes—181 minutes of actual testing time and 54 minutes of administration. The computer-adapted version takes about 90 minutes. The eight subtests are verbal reasoning, numerical reasoning, abstract reasoning, perceptual speed and accuracy, mechanical reasoning, space relations, spelling, and language usage. The verbal reasoning and numerical ability scores are combined to make a composite index of scholastic aptitude.

The authors claim the results help students plan their futures soundly. The test is also viewed as a tool for the early identification of students with superior intellectual promise.

Available with the DAT is a Career Interest Inventory and a computerized report form that provides a combined assessment of interests and aptitudes that may then be linked to potential occupations.

Reviewers such as Linn (1982) and Pennock-Roman (1988) consider the DAT useful in exploring a student's academic and vocational possibilities. Test limitations relate to the lack of independence of some of the scales and the separate sex norms. Support materials—a manual and the book *Counseling from Profiles* by Bennett, Seashore, and Wesman (1977), a student workbook, and *Using Test Results for Deci-*

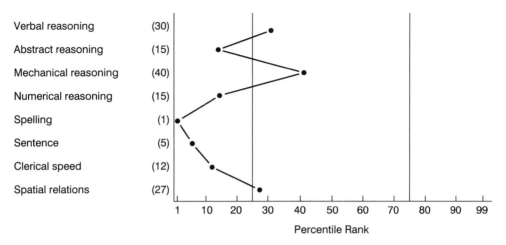

Figure 8.2
Individual profile of performance on the Differential Aptitude Test Battery

sion Making: A Guide for Parents and Students—are valuable to counselors and test takers. Both computerized scoring services and hand-scoring stencils are available for the test. A computer-adaptive edition of the DAT is available. The form is parallel to the printed test but results in reduced testing time, and immediate scoring reports are available on completion of the tests. An example of a profile from the DAT is presented in Figure 8.2.

General Aptitude Battery

The U.S. Employment Service (USES) General Aptitude Test Battery (GATB) is one of the most widely used batteries for assessment in vocational counseling. It is used primarily by the employment service but administered in some secondary schools and in employment projects. The test takes 150 minutes of total time but only 48 minutes of actual testing time. The GATB is a pencil-and-paper test that measures nine dimensions: verbal, numerical, spatial, form perception, clerical perception, motor coordination, finger dexterity, manual dexterity, and general learning ability. Support systems for the counselor include the *Guide for Occupational Exploration, Dictionary of Occupational Titles*, and the *Bridge of the World of Work*. Keesling and Healy (1988) conclude that the GATB, despite its psychometric limitations, may help clients to make reasonable estimates of their standings on the aptitudes relative to working adults.

Career Ability Placement Survey

The CAPS is a quick, 50-minute battery used to assess abilities for a majority of jobs in 14 occupational clusters. The CAPS contains eight tests:

1. Mechanical reasoning (MR) measures understanding of mechanical principles.
2. Spatial relations (SR) measures the ability to think and visualize in three dimensions.
3. Verbal reasoning (VR) measures the ability to reason with words.
4. Numerical ability (NA) measures the ability to reason with and use numbers.
5. Language usage (LU) measures recognition and use of proper grammar and punctuation.
6. Word knowledge (WK) measures understanding of the meaning and precise use of words.
7. Perceptual speed and accuracy (PSA) measures rapid and accurate perception of small details.
8. Manual speed and dexterity (MSD) measures rapid and accurate hand movement.

There are both self-scoring and machine-scoring forms of the test, and the Educational and Industrial Testing Service (EdITS) provides computerized scoring and reporting for CAPS.

The test authors L. F. Kapp and R. R. Kapp say that the test has five major uses:

1. Classroom career exploration units, matching individual students' ability with occupational requirements
2. School course or training program selection
3. Curriculum evaluation
4. Career development in conjunction with the COPSystem Interest Inventory and COPES, a values profile
5. Employee evaluation

All types of supportive materials are available for the counselor and the client: a self-interpretation profile sheet and guide, occupational cluster charts, COPSystem Career Briefs Kit, and COPSystem Career Cluster Booklet Kits, in addition to an examiner's manual, tapes for administration, and visuals for orientation.

Table 8.2 compares the subtests of the ASVAB, the DAT, the GATB, and the CAPS.

Table 8.2
Comparison of subtests on multiaptitude scales

ASVAB	DAT	GATB	CAPS
Arithmetic reasoning	Abstract reasoning	Clerical perception	Manual speed and dexterity
Auto and shop	Clerical speed	Finger dexterity	Language usage
Coding speed	Mechanical reasoning	Form perception	Mechanical reasoning
General science	Numerical reasoning	General learning	Perceptual speed and accuracy
Electronics information	Sentence	Manual dexterity	Spatial relations
Mathematics knowledge	Spatial relations	Motor coordination	Verbal reasoning
Numerical operations	Verbal reasoning	Numerical	Word knowledge
Paragraph comprehension	Spelling	Spatial	Numerical ability
Word knowledge		Verbal	

Career Ability Tests

Ability tests assess the maximum performance of the individual and her present ability to perform a task. Aptitude tests assess the future level of the individual to perform a task. There are similarities between these two types of tests, and the differentiation is somewhat unclear. In career counseling situations the counselor is concerned about eventual success of the client on the job. Anastasi (1996) has concluded that all ability tests, regardless of how they are labeled (multiaptitude, achievement, general intelligence), measure the level of development attained by the test taker in one or more abilities.

Harrington (1995) identified 14 major abilities: artistic, clerical, interpersonal, language, leadership, manual, musical/dramatic, numerical/mathematical, organizational, persuasive, reading, social, spatial, and technical/mechanical. Multiaptitude test do not measure all of the abilities identified by Harrington and also have limited value in predicting success. Goldman (1971) feels the main contribution of aptitude tests is to facilitate the self-concept of the test taker.

Admissions Tests. A number of specialized tests are used as one source of information to help admissions counselors in their decision making. Two major national testing programs are used by colleges and universities for admissions decisions: the American College Testing Program (ACT) and the Scholastic Aptitude Test (SAT).

The ACT contains a series of tests: English Usage, Mathematics, Social Studies, and Natural Sciences. The test taker receives scores in each subject area in addition to a composite score. The mathematics test assesses knowledge of algebra and geometry. The science and social studies scales assess the examinee's ability to interpret written paragraphs on science or social studies topics.

The new SAT has two major forms—I and II. SAT I is broken into two sections, Verbal and Mathematical Reasoning. The verbal emphasizes critical reading skills and the understanding of words in context. The mathematics section allows students to use calculators; 29 of the questions require answers generated by the test taker. SAT II includes an English essay and other verbal and quantitative achievement tests in various subject areas. The verbal section measures verbal reasoning and comprehension of textlike material, whereas the quantitative section measures basic principles of algebra and geometry. The PSAT, taken by students in their junior year of high school, helps students become familiar with the types of skills and competencies measured by the test. The SAT is used by high school counselors to help guide students in their educational decisions. Some colleges use the PSAT results to make scholarship decisions. The SAT has been criticized for its inherent bias against minorities and its relative lack of importance in helping make college admissions decisions.

Graduate School Admissions Tests. On this level also, competitive examinations are used by schools and universities for guidance in admissions decisions. The Graduate Record Examinations (GRE) are scholastic aptitude tests required by many graduate and professional schools and scholarship sponsors. The tests are given world-wide at testing centers approved by the Educational Testing Service. The GRE was developed by the Graduate Record Examination Board and is administered by the Educational Testing Service. The GRE General Test assesses verbal, quantitative, and analytical abilities. The seven 30-minute sections require 3½ hours of testing time. There are 17 subject tests, each of which requires 2 hours and 50 minutes of testing time. Subject tests are available in biology, chemistry, computer science, economics, education, engineering, French, geology, history, literature in English, mathematics, music, physics, political science, psychology, sociology, and Spanish.

The education test contains 200 questions covering five major areas:

1. *Education Goals*—philosophical; historical; psychological, including physical, emotional, intellectual; role of education in a pluralistic society
2. *School Administration and Supervision*—sources of authority; psychological concerns such as grouping practices; sociological considerations such as teacher and student rights
3. *Curriculum*—historical and philosophical considerations; relation to development and learning factors; relation to societal demands
4. *Teaching-Learning*—historical and philosophical concerns; nature of learning and teaching; sociological factors such as social class
5. *Evaluation and Research*—meaning of research conclusions; elementary statistical and measurement concepts; sociological concerns such as uses of pupil records

If requests are made in advance, special arrangements and test materials are available for individuals with verbal, physical, hearing, or learning disabilities. For example, the General Test is available in Braille (1972 Nemeth Code), in large type, with large-type answer sheets, and on cassettes. French and Spanish versions of the test are given once a year.

The reliability of the GRE test has been computed using the KR 20 formula. This coefficient provides an estimate of the internal consistency of the test and alternate form reliability. The test bulletin reports that the reliabilities on the general tests and subject tests range from .88 to .96. The content validity of the subject examinations is extremely critical and is evaluated by a committee of professors working with ETS test development specialists. The main type of validity for the test is its predictive validity—to predict success in graduate school.

The Miller's Analogies Test (MAT) is an objective, group-administered test of mental ability, consisting of 100 multiple-choice analogy items. The content for the analogies comes from literature, social sciences, chemistry, physics, mathematics, and general information. The test is given only at controlled testing centers and requires 50 minutes of testing time. It is used primarily for the selection of students for graduate schools and is published by the Psychological Corporation. The MAT is a short test but seems to have good predictive validity.

Other widely used admission tests in higher education include the Medical College Admissions Test (MCAT), Law School Admissions Test (LSAT), and the Graduate Management Admission Test (GMAT). The most important consideration in the use of these tests is whether the validity of the test for a particular program has been established, especially through studies at a local college or university.

SPECIALIZED BATTERIES

Two of the most widely used specialized aptitude tests historically have been the Minnesota Clerical Test (MCT) (Andrew, Peterson, & Longstaff, 1979) and the Bennett Mechanical Comprehension Test (1980). The MCT consists of two parts: number checking and name checking. There are 200 pairs of numbers and 200 pairs of names. The test taker is to check each pair in which the items are identical. The test is speeded, and the examinee has eight minutes for the number section and seven minutes for the name section.

The Bennett Mechanical Comprehension Test has both English and Spanish forms to measure an individual's understanding of mechanical relationships and the laws of physics in practical situations. The test is used to screen job applicants for positions requiring complex machine operation and repair and other types of positions requiring practical application of mechanical principles. Norms are available for industrial job applicants, industrial employees, and students. A taped version of the test is available for applicants with limited reading skill. The test requires 30 minutes of testing time.

Clerical Ability

Quite a few clerical tests other than the Minnesota Clerical Test are used by counselors:

The Clerical Aptitude Test is a three-part pencil-and-paper test that includes number checking; business practice; and date, name, and address checking.

The Curtis Verbal-Clerical Skills Test assesses clerical and verbal abilities and measures practical arithmetic, checking and perceptual speed and accuracy, and reading comprehension.

The General Clerical Test measures three types of abilities needed for clerical jobs—clerical speed and accuracy, numerical ability, and verbal ability.

The Hay Aptitude Test Battery is a general battery that measures number perception, name finding, and number series completion and predicts aptitude for a variety of positions, including accounting, keypunching, typing, filing, stockroom work, and mail sorting. Cassette tapes are available for administering and timing the tests.

The Office Skills Test assesses clerical abilities of entry-level applicants and contains 12 subtests—checking, coding, filing, forms completion, grammar, numerical skills, oral directions, punctuation, reading comprehension, spelling, typing, and vocabulary.

The Personnel Research Institute Clerical Battery consists of a number of tests—alphabetizing, arithmetic reasoning, classification, filing, name comparison, number comparison, spelling, tabulation, shorthand skills, basic checking, audio checking, numeric computation, numerical reasoning, and verbal usage.

The PSI Basic Skills Tests for Business, Industry, and Government include a number of subtests—classifying, coding, computation, decision making, filing names, filing numbers, following oral directions, forms checking, language skills, memory, problem solving, reading comprehension, reasoning, typing practice copy, typing revised copy, typing straight copy, typing tables, visual speed and accuracy, and vocabulary.

The SRA Clerical Aptitude Test measures general aptitude necessary for clerical work through three pencil-and-paper tests of office vocabulary, office arithmetic, and office checking.

The USES Clerical Skills Test assesses six types of clerical skills—typing from plain copy, taking dictation, spelling, statistical typing, and spelling medical and legal terms.

The descriptions of these tests reveal that some of the subtests are similar to certain subtests on some of the group intelligence and scholastic aptitude tests and to some of the scales on the DAT, the ASVAB, and the GATB. Verbal and numerical skills are as important as perceptual speed and accuracy skills. Ability to follow directions and short- and long-term memory are also included on some of the tests. In addition, job-related or job-specific skills such as typing and filing are measured on some of the batteries.

Mechanical Ability

There are a number of other pencil-and-paper tests of mechanical ability besides the Bennett Mechanical Comprehension Test and the mechanical subtests on the multi-aptitude batteries:

The Mechanical Aptitude Test is a 45-minute test for high school students and adults that measures comprehension of mechanical tasks, use of tools and materials, and matching tools with operations.

The SRA Mechanical Aptitude Test is a 35-minute test for high school students and adults that measures mechanical knowledge, space relations, and shop arithmetic.

The SRA Test of Mechanical Concepts is a 35- to 40-minute test for adults measuring the individual's ability to visualize and understand basic mechanical and spatial interrelationships. It contains three subtests—mechanical interrelationships, mechanical tools and devices, and spatial relations.

Some of these tests of mechanical aptitude contain subtests of spatial relations. The classic tests in the field to measure spatial relations are the Minnesota Spatial Relations Test and the Minnesota Paper Formboard. They require the test taker to visualize objects in three dimensions and manipulate them to produce a particular configuration.

Psychomotor Ability

Quite a few individual tests measure psychomotor abilities, especially fine and gross motor skills and manual dexterity:

The Crawford Small Parts Dexterity Test (CSPDT) is designed to measure fine hand-eye coordination and is used in job selection for occupational areas such as engraving, watch repairing, and telephone installing. Part 1 requires use of tweezers to assemble pin and collar assemblies; Part 2 requires putting small screws into threaded holes in a plate and screwing them down.

The Hand-Tool Dexterity Test involves wrenches and screwdrivers and requires the examinee to take apart 12 assemblies of nuts, bolts, and washers from a wooden frame and then reassemble them.

The Minnesota Manual Dexterity Test measures the capacity for rapid, simple hand-eye coordination needed for semiskilled shop and clerical operations such as wrapping, sorting, and packing. The test taker is given a long board containing four rows of holes. In the placing test, pegs are to be transferred to the empty board just as they were presented, using only one hand. In the turning test, the pegs are to be removed with one hand one at a time, turned over, transferred to the other hand, and replaced in the same position on the board.

The Minnesota Rate of Manipulation Test measures finger-hand-arm dexterity and is used to select employees for jobs that require manual dexterity and can be part of vocational and rehabilitation training programs. There are five subtests in the battery—placing, turning, displacing, one-hand turning and placing, and two-hand turning and placing. The test also uses a test board with round holes arranged in four rows and round blocks painted orange and yellow.

The O'Connor Finger Dexterity Test measures finger dexterity and is useful in determining aptitude for assembly jobs requiring rapid handwork. This test uses a smaller board containing a shallow well and many holes arranged in 10 rows. The test taker is given a set of 300 pins and is required to place three in each hole. The test has been useful in predicting success in machine and lathe work, watch and clock repair, and assembly of small parts.

The O'Connor Tweezer Dexterity Test measures fine hand-eye coordination and the ability to use small hand tools. The test uses a small board with small holes in it, just like the board for the O'Connor Finger Dexterity Test. However, the test taker is given 100 pins and is required to put one in each hole, using only a small tweezer. This type of skill is required of laboratory workers, medical personnel, watch repairers, and even stamp collectors.

The Purdue Pegboard Test measures hand-finger-arm coordination required for certain types of business or industries. The test taker works with pegs, washers, and collars—putting in the pegs, placing washers over them, and then putting on the collars.

The Stromberg Dexterity Test measures manipulative skills in sorting by color and by sequence. The test taker is given an assembly board and disks and is asked to discriminate among, sort, and move and place the biscuit-sized disks as fast as possible.

All of these tests are individually administered and require adequate facilities and space for their administration. The Valpar Component Work Sample System assesses vocational and functional skills and is designed for use with other testing instruments. Valpar System 2000 integrates aptitude, interest, and work history assessment through computer technology. The interest survey is video-based and uses actual job situations. Counselors use both clinical observation and test results from Valpar and other instruments to help clients in selection of training programs and in job placement. The information is also useful in designing educational or rehabilitation plans for a client.

Artistic Aptitude

Three classic tests measure dimensions of art aptitude:

The Graves Design Judgment Test presents 90 sets of two- or three-dimensional designs that vary in unity, balance, symmetry, or other aspects of aesthetic order. The test taker is asked to select the best in each set.

The Meier Art Test: Aesthetic Perception presents four versions of the same work, each differing in terms of proportion, unity, form, or design. The test taker is asked to rank each set in order of merit.

The Meier Art Test: Art Judgment consists of 100 pairs of pictures of famous works of art. One of the pair has been altered, and the test taker is asked to choose the better of the two pictures.

Musical Aptitude

A number of tests have been developed to measure musical aptitude. The classic test in this field is Seashore Measures of Musical Talents. The test takes about 1 hour of testing time and can be administered to students in grade 4 and above and to adults. The test presents on tape six subtests measuring dimensions of auditory discrimination: pitch, loudness, time, timbre, rhythm, and tonal memory. Unfortunately, the test lacks sufficient documentation of validity and reliability.

Other tests also purport to measure musical aptitude:

The Kwalwasser Music Talent Test is a 50-item orally administered pencil-and-paper test to assess musical aptitude of students from grade 4 to college. It presents three-tone patterns that are repeated with variations in pitch, tone, rhythm, or loudness.

The Musical Aptitude Profile is an aptitude test that uses violin and cello. Pairs of selections are played, and the test taker is asked whether the two are the same or which of the two represents a better performance. The three subtests are tonal imagery (melody and harmony), rhythm imagery (tempo and meter), and musical sensitivity (phrasing, balance, and style). The test is used for 4th to 12th graders and takes about 2 hours to administer.

Unfortunately, research has been limited on the value of these tests. Music teachers tend to rely more on their own clinical judgment and look for individual performance of music as it is written.

Computer Aptitude

Computer literacy is being taught in kindergarten. Microcomputers have become inexpensive and readily available, and a number of instruments have been developed to assess aptitude in this field:

> The Computer Operator Aptitude Battery is a pencil-and-paper test designed to help predict the performance of computer operators. It takes 45 minutes and has three subtests—sequence recognition, format checking, and logical thinking.

> The Computer Programmer Aptitude Battery (CPAB) is a 75-minute pencil-and-paper test for adults. It is used to measure potential for success in the computer programming field. The five tests are verbal meaning, reasoning, letter series, number ability, and diagramming, which includes problem analysis and logical solutions.

> The Programmer Aptitude Competence Test System (PACTS) assesses the ability to write good computer programs through a simulated experience. The client is given an instruction book to study for 30 to 50 minutes about a general computer programming language for a hypothetical computer. He then is given problems to solve that are scored for correctness, efficiency, compactness, problem difficulty, and completion time.

ISSUES AND PROBLEM AREAS

The trait and factors approach has been a venerable theme in career guidance, rooted in the psychology of individual differences, applied psychology, and differential psychology (McDaniel & Gysbers, 1992). The trait and factor approach views each person as a pattern of traits. These aptitude, achievement, personality, and interest dimensions are identified through objective psychological testing and can be profiled to represent the individual's potential. Occupations are treated in the same way. The degree of fit between the two profiles can be identified. Herr and Cramer

(1984) conclude that many variables enter into career decision making—work values, occupational stereotypes and expectations, residence, family socioeconomic status, child-rearing practices, general adjustment, personality factors including needs and propensity for risk taking, educational achievement, level of aspiration, and gender.

Regarding abilities, specific aptitudes tend to correlate more with success in training than with success in performance. Super and Crites (1962) conclude that there might be a level of intelligence necessary to learn a certain occupation, but intelligence tends "to have no special effects on the individual's success in that occupation" (p. 99). The follow-up studies of Thorndike and Hagen (1959) of 10,000 men who had taken the Air Corps Test Battery in 1943 found that there were near zero correlations between the scores on that battery and the criteria of success in the occupations. The average variability of the scores within each of the occupational groups was almost as great as the variability of the scales across occupational groups. Project Talent, a large longitudinal study of 440,000 high school students begun in 1960, studied the relation of 22 aptitude and achievement tests, an interest inventory, and a student activities inventory with later educational and career attainments. The results are similar to those found by Thorndike and Hagen.

Emphasis now seems to focus more on decision making and career and educational choice; less emphasis is being placed on aptitude testing. Most of the major batteries are combined with other tests to provide the client with more information. In the COPSystem, interests, values, and aptitude information are combined to provide a starting point to study more about occupations related to these factors.

The various subtests of the special aptitude tests present considerable overlap. The tests are designed to focus on the skills and abilities necessary to be successful in further training or employment in a given field. We must remember, though, that aptitude tests give only one source of information. Brown (1983) points out that there are new trends in this field, such as the integration of testing with cognitive psychology and the use of adaptive testing to individualize testing.

SUMMARY

Multifactor aptitude batteries are used in educational and business contexts. Many aptitude batteries are a part of career guidance systems. The most widely used batteries are the Armed Services Vocational Aptitude Battery (ASVAB), the General Aptitude Test Battery (GATB), and the Differential Aptitude Test Battery (DAT).

Specialized aptitude tests are designed to measure the ability to acquire proficiency in a specific area of activity, such as art or music. Mechanical and clerical aptitude tests have been used by vocational education, business, industry personnel to counsel, evaluate, classify, and place test takers. Both multifactor and special aptitude tests are designed to help the test takers gain a better understanding of their own special abilities.

QUESTIONS FOR DISCUSSION

1. What are the major multifactor aptitude batteries? When should they be used and why? What are the advantages and disadvantages of this type of test?

2. When would you use special aptitude batteries and why? What are the advantages and disadvantages of such tests?

3. Critics have said that multiaptitude tests provide little differential prediction and are of little value. Do you agree with their evaluation? If you have taken aptitude tests, what value did the results have for you? Did the scores provide a useful framework for looking at your aptitudes and abilities?

4. Some school districts require that all students be given an aptitude battery at some time during their four years of high school. Do you agree or disagree with this requirement? Why or why not?

5. Do you feel that there can be a pencil-and-paper aptitude test to measure aptitudes in art, music, and mechanics? Why or why not?

SUGGESTED ACTIVITIES

1. Write a critique of a widely used multiaptitude or special aptitude test.

2. Interview workers in the helping professions who use aptitude tests—employment counselors, career counselors, and school counselors—and find out what tests they use and why. Report your findings to the class.

3. Take a multifactor or specialized aptitude test and write a report detailing the results and your reaction to the test.

4. Make an annotated bibliography of aptitude tests you would use in your field.

5. Write a critical review of the literature on one of the following topics: validity of aptitude tests, new directions in aptitude testing, computer-adaptive aptitude testing, performance aptitude tests.

6. Study the case that follows and answer the questions at the end.

Case of Albert

Albert is a 23-year-old Caucasian male who dropped out of school in the 10th grade. He is enrolled in a high school equivalency program at a local community college sponsored by the Private Industry Council. He has had numerous jobs in the food service industry but has not been able to hold on to them. He has a wife and three children and realizes now he needs further training and education to support his family.

The Private Industry Council arranged for some vocational testing. He was administered the DAT with the following results:

Verbal Reasoning 40%

Numerical Reasoning 55%

Abstract Reasoning 20%

Mechanical Reasoning 55%

Spatial Relations 30%

Spelling 3%

Sentence 5%

Clerical Speed 45%

a. How would you characterize Albert's aptitudes?

b. What additional information about Albert would you like to have?

c. If you were a counselor, what educational and vocational directions would you encourage him to explore?

ADDITIONAL READINGS

Kapes, J. T., & Mastie, M. M. (1999). *A counselor's guide to vocational guidance instruments* (4th ed.). Falls Church, VA: National Vocational Guidance Association.

This text reviews multiaptitude batteries as well as other aptitude batteries used with special populations.

Lowman, R. L. (1991). *The clinical practice of career assessment: Interest, abilities, and personality.* Washington, DC: American Psychological Association.

Lowman provides guidelines for and examples of tests of the affective domain.

Achievement Testing

OVERVIEW

Achievement testing is the primary type of testing used in educational programs at all levels. Achievement tests measure acquired knowledge and skills, whereas aptitude tests measure potential, or the ability to learn new tasks. The main distinctions between achievement and aptitude testing relate to the type of learning being measured and the intended use of the test results. Achievement tests come in a variety of types:

1. *Survey achievement batteries*—Partially norm-referenced and partially criterion-referenced tests that measure knowledge and skill in reading, mathematics, language arts, social studies, and science
2. *Subject area tests*—Achievement tests in a single subject area, such as algebra, plane geometry, American history, and chemistry

3. *Criterion-referenced tests*—Tests that measure knowledge and comprehension of a specific skill or competency, such as the ability to draw inferences from pictorial or written matter or the ability to read a metric scale and give the weight of an object in metric and English units
4. *Minimum-level skills tests*—Tests that measure objectives or minimum skills that have to be achieved to pass from one level or grade to another
5. *Individual achievement tests*—Tests that are administered individually across a wide age or grade level to measure achievement
6. *Diagnostic tests*—Tests that are used to assess the strengths and weaknesses of individuals in a subject area by measuring a limited number of skills thoroughly

OBJECTIVES

After studying this chapter, the reader should be able to

✔ List and discuss the different types of achievement tests

✔ Identify situations in which each type of test would be used

✔ Explain the problems and issues in achievement testing

✔ Interpret the results of an achievement test

TYPES OF ACHIEVEMENT TESTS

Survey Achievement Tests

The most widely used achievement test, the survey battery is part of most school testing programs. It usually has a number of subtests—such as reading, mathematics, social studies, and science—and measures the objectives that are typically addressed in grades K through 12. A number of different levels or separate tests are in the achievement battery, which is most often given at the beginning or end of the school year. Some districts give the test both times and use the scores as one criterion of whether a student passes to the next grade. The test provides teachers and administrators with a picture of what the student has learned or achieved.

The survey achievement battery subtests are all coordinated with standardized administration and scoring procedures, a common format, and little content overlap. In addition, all of the subtests are normed on the same sampling group. Comparisons between the tests are thus more valid than when each subtests is normed on a different sample. Some widely used achievement batteries are described here:

The California Achievement Test (CAT) (Fifth Ed., 1992) is divided into 10 overlapping levels and is administered to students in grades K through 12.9. Level 10 is a readiness instrument for kindergarten students. The test measures achievement in traditional school areas—reading, language, mathematics, reference skills, and spelling.

The Comprehensive Test of Basic Skills (CTBS/4) (1993) is a multilevel achievement battery consisting of 10 levels and measuring three to seven areas, such as reading, language, mathematics, science, social studies, spelling, and reference skills. The CTBS was standardized along with the Short Form Test of Academic Aptitude (California Test of Mental Ability). The test has forms for students in grades K through 12.9.

The Iowa Tests of Basic Skills (ITBS) assess the skills of students in grades K through 9 in reading, language, spelling, capitalization, punctuation, usage, work-study, visual materials, reference materials, mathematics concepts, problem solving, computation, word analysis, and listening.

The Metropolitan Achievement Test–Seventh Edition (MAT-7) is an eight-level achievement test that measures reading comprehension, mathematics, and language skills of kindergartners through 12th graders. Social science and science subtests are included in the higher levels of the battery. The MAT-7 has an abridged version containing just the reading, mathematics, and language tests; each test takes about 30 minutes.

The National Educational Development Series (Educational Services) is used with students in grades 9 and 10. The test reliably predicts student performance on the PSAT and ACT and provides information useful for career and individual counseling.

The Sequential Tests of Educational Progress (STEP) assess English, reading, and mathematics skills. The preschool and primary test diagnoses the instructional needs of students and measures their interests, problem-solving and reading skills, mathematics concepts, and psychomotor skills. The upper-grade test measures achievement levels in English expression, reading, mechanics of writing, mathematics computation, mathematics basic concepts, science, and social studies.

The SRA Achievement Series (ACH 1-2) measures achievement in reading, mathematics, science, and social studies. Forms are available for grades K through 12.

The Stanford Achievement Test–Ninth Edition (SAT9) is a modular survey achievement test that allows for choice of open-ended subtests in reading, mathematics, writing, science, and social science or traditional multiple-choice formats to assess reading, mathematics, science, social science, language, spelling, study skills, and listening—or a combination of both formats. The test also aligns with National Assessment of Educational Progress (NAEP) standards. The reading passages are from works by well-known authors.

Criterion-Referenced Tests

Criterion-referenced tests, sometimes called domain-referenced tests, measure specific objectives and skills. They differ from norm-referenced tests and survey achievement tests in that they focus on mastery of a given objective or skill. Norm-referenced tests usually include only one or two items to measure a given objective, whereas criterion-referenced tests include many items on a specific objective. The criterion-referenced test is scored to an absolute standard, usually the percentage of correct answers. The teacher may be required to assign grades to the test takers, or students may be required to meet a certain score—say, 70 percent—as evidence of mastery. In systems requiring mastery of objectives, the test taker is not allowed to go on to the next unit until he has passed the one being studied.

Criterion-referenced tests can be used for other purposes also:

1. To evaluate the curriculum
2. To identify topics that should be remediated or enriched
3. To provide information for the counselor to use in educational and vocational planning with students

4. To help students select courses
5. To document student mastery of objectives
6. To provide systematic evidence of student attainment of objectives across levels and fields over time
7. To help the counselor mark the progress of the child over time

Here are a few examples of criterion-referenced tests and testing systems:

The Criterion Test of Basic Skills is a multiple-item criterion-referenced test assessing the reading and mathematics skills of students in grades 1 through 6. The reading subtests measure letter recognition, letter sounding, blending, sequencing, recognition of sight words, and recognition of special sounds. The mathematics subtests assess number and numerical recognition skills, addition, subtraction, multiplication, and division.

The Instructional Objectives Exchange (IOX) has a series of tests available for teachers to use to assess specific skills and objectives in reading, mathematics, and writing.

Multiscore is a system that provides criterion-referenced assessment of reading, language arts, mathematics, science, social studies, and life skills. It offers a pool of more than 5,500 items and catalogs of instructional objectives. The test service is available from Riverside Publishing Company.

Item Banks

Commercial and public domain test item banks are available for educational purposes. Item banks allow school districts to custom-design achievement tests for specific objectives. Aiken (1985) points out that these item banks have several disadvantages, such as the problem of deciding on an acceptable passing score or mastery level for each test, the limited reliability of the many subtests used to measure given instructional goals or objectives, and the questionable validity of the items as representative of the objective being measured.

Westinghouse Learning Corporation, Science Research Associates, and Houghton Mifflin, among other publishers, provide item banks. Publishers who market survey achievement batteries have a large pool of items from old editions not included in current editions. Many states and consortiums have also developed for school districts item banks that come from tests developed under federal or state grants; these should be screened for local applicability.

Minimum-Level Skills Tests

Many districts establish minimum-level skills tests in each subject area that require mastery for a student to pass to the next grade level. Absolute standards are often set, frequently 75 percent. These essential-skills tests are criterion-referenced and are designed to measure the reading and mathematics skills of students in elementary schools. Often locally constructed, the tests are based upon the instructional management system guiding the progress of students in reading and mathematics. In addition, commercial tests are available that focus on minimum-level skills:

> The Basic Skills Assessment Program (BSAP), used with 10th- to 12th-grade students, is a 210-item pencil-and-paper test measuring skills in reading, mathematics, and writing. The test assesses the ability of students to understand consumer information, read newspapers, and complete job applications.

> The Everyday Skills Test (EDST) measures routine skills needed in mathematics and reading, such as reading and comprehending labels and telephone directories.

State Assessment Tests

A number of states require school districts to administer assessment tests in selected grades. Sometimes these tests focus only on essential skills. Other times they survey student knowledge, skills, and understanding in a given subject area such as science, social studies, reading, mathematics, health and nutrition, career education, citizenship, music, and fine arts. The purpose is to help school districts identify problem areas and evaluate their curriculum.

Some states require a minimum level of performance for student advancement. For example, Florida college students are required to pass reading, mathematics, language, and writing tests at a set level to be able to register for upper-division courses.

Another Florida test, the Florida Comprehensive Assessment Test (FCAT), will be administered at three grade levels to all students in the public schools: the FCAT Reading Test to grades 4, 8, and 10; the FCAT Mathematics Test to grades 5, 8, and 10. The tests will be based on the Sunshine State Standards and will contain items that are challenging for students at all levels of academic achievement. For example, the mathematics test for grade 10 will contain some Sunshine State Standards that are currently taught in Geometry and Algebra II classes. All exams will contain multiple-choice questions and short- and extended-response performance tasks. A short-response task, for example, may require a student to explain the main idea of a reading passage in three or four sentences or write an equation that will solve a mathematical problem. The mathematics test will require students to write and grid numerical solutions on the answer grid.

Here is a typical goal statement based on the FCAT Reading Test:

Goal:
Students will be able to construct meaning from informational text.

Content:
Nonfiction articles, textbooks, reference materials, and primary sources

Objectives:
To recognize or explain the main idea, the author's point of view, and cause-and-effect relationships

To differentiate between fact and opinion

To compare similarities and differences within and across texts

To demonstrate knowledge of vocabulary

To retell or summarize the meaning of a passage

To select and use information from a passage to perform a task

National Assessment of Educational Progress

The National Assessment of Educational Progress (NAEP) is a national program to assess the knowledge, skills, and attitudes of 9-, 13-, 17-, and 25- to 35-year-olds. Currently, the assessment focuses on 4th-, 8th-, and 12th-grade students. In the past, 10 subject areas were selected for study: art, career and occupational development, citizenship, literature, mathematics, music, reading, science, social studies, and writing. The testing began in 1969 in response to the charge given to the commissioner of education to determine the progress of education in this country. Normally, two subject areas are tested each year using a stratified random sample. Comparisons are made across age, geographic region, type of community, sex, socioeducational status, and race. Reading is assessed each year, along with two or three other subject areas. In 1990, approximately 87,000 students participated in the national assessment and another 100,000 participated in state assessments of eighth-grade mathematics. The 1992 assessments involved approximately 419,000 students in 12,000 schools. Since 1992, tests have been available for state assessment programs.

Subject Area Tests

Subject area tests differ from subtests on a survey achievement battery. The survey subtests cover the general curriculum areas of an educational program—reading, mathematics, science, spelling, language, and social studies. These fundamental concepts and skills become competencies upon which more advanced study is based. Survey achievement batteries may provide some measure of students' basic skills but little information on achievement in a given subject. Subject area achievement tests provide more reliable and valid information.

Subject area tests have somewhat the same use as achievement batteries in that student performance can be compared against national norms. A number of subject area tests are available to high schools. Test questions are often derived from instruction across many school districts and states. Some states require students to pass subject area examinations or minimum-level skills tests in all high school subject areas in order to graduate. Subject area tests are part of major national testing programs used by colleges and universities to determine advanced placement or credit; they may also be one of the criteria for admission. Many states and professional organizations require licensing examinations, which are really specialized types of subject area achievement tests.

National achievement testing programs include the College Board Achievement Tests, the American College Testing (ACT) Proficiency Tests, the College Board Advanced Placement Programs, and the College-Level Examination Program (CLEP).

A number of publishers and organizations publish subject area achievement tests. A few examples are given here:

> The Ohio Vocational Education Achievement Testing Program covers most vocational areas—agricultural business, agricultural mechanics, farm management, horticulture, production agriculture, stenography, clerk typing, data processing, general office clerking, word processing, carpentry, construction electricity, air conditioning and refrigeration, cosmetology, auto body mechanics, and so on.

> The Riverside Curriculum Assessment System is designed for use with secondary students and tests such areas as algebra, geometry, physics, chemistry, biology, world history, American history, consumer economics, and computer literacy.

Many professional societies have developed achievement tests. The American Chemical Society, for example, offers achievement tests in general organic-biological chemistry, inorganic chemistry, instrumental determination analysis, general chemistry, and so on.

Individual Achievement Tests

Workers in the helping professions often use individual achievement tests to assess a client's achievement and cognitive processes. The tests provide useful information on the attitudes and motivation of the test takers and may be a single subject or a survey achievement type:

> The Basic Achievement Skills Individual Screener (BASIS), published by the Psychological Corporation, is designed for pupils from grades 1 through 8. It includes three subtests—reading, spelling, and mathematics—and an optional writing exercise. Both criterion-referenced and norm-referenced, the test provides beginning-of-the-grade and end-of-the-grade norms as well as age and adult norms. It takes about 1 hour to administer and is designed to help examiners formulate individual educational plans for exceptional and special populations.

> The Keymath Diagnostic Arithmetic Test–Revised (KMDAT) (Connolly, 1988), published by the American Guidance Service, is a single-subject individual test used to diagnose children's strengths and weaknesses in mathematics. It measures the test taker's knowledge of operations (addition, subtraction, multiplication, division, mental computation, and numerical reasoning); mathematical applications (word problems, missing elements, money, measurement, and time); and content areas such as numeration, fractions, geometry, and symbols. The examiner uses test plates and records the test taker's performance on an individual record form.

> The Peabody Individual Achievement Test (PIAT), published by the American Guidance Service, can be a survey battery and is given to clients aged 5 to adulthood. The PIAT takes 30 to 50 minutes to administer and provides information on achievement in reading, mathematics, spelling, and general knowledge (science, social studies, fine arts, and sports) as well as diagnostic information. The

examiner uses easel kits and test plates. The PIAT yields grade equivalents, age percentile ranks, and standard scores by age or grade.

The Wide Range Achievement Test–Revised (WRAT-3) is usually administered individually, although the spelling and arithmetic subtests are suitable for group administration. The reading subtest calls for the test taker to recognize and name letters and pronounce printed words; the examiner is encouraged to analyze error patterns. The test is given to people between the ages of 5 and 75.

The Wechsler Individual Achievement Test (WIAT) (1992) was developed for use in conjunction with Wechsler Intelligence Scale for Children–III (WISC-III) and was co-normed. Subtests include basic reading, mathematical reasoning, spelling, reading comprehension, listening comprehension, mathematics computation, oral expression, and written expression. The test can be given to students aged 5 through 19.

The Woodcock-Johnson Test of Achievement (WJTA) (1990) has two forms that measure achievement in reading, mathematics, written language, and knowledge in the way they are typically taught in schools. The WJTA can be given to individuals aged 2 to 90.

Some examiners individually administer other survey and subject area achievement tests, especially if a student has a disability. Individually administered tests do not rely as heavily on reading speed and accuracy. Individual oral administration of a test can be used as a validity check of the scores on a group-administered test.

Authentic and Alternate Assessment

The major trend in achievement testing is authentic and alternate assessment. Authentic and performance assessment are replacing traditional norm-referenced testing that relies on multiple-choice questions. One such system developed by a major test publisher is the Integrated Assessment System (Farr & Farr, 1992). The series consists of performance tasks in language arts, mathematics, and science for grades 1 through 8. The IAS Language Arts (1990) consists of a series of reading passages and guided writing activities that assess reading comprehension, writing performance, and higher-level thinking in one integrated activity. The IAS Language Arts portfolio provides a flexible framework for collecting the ongoing work of students. The system encourages collaboration between students and teachers in reviewing the products of the work in the portfolios. Mathematics problems are given requiring students to produce original responses in writing as they select strategies to solve the given problems. Holistic and analytic scoring procedures are explained in the scoring guide. Scores are based on the quality of work, presence and number of flaws, knowledge of concepts, problem-solving abilities, reasoning skills, computational proficiency, and ability to follow directions.

Criterion-referenced skills analysis is provided by most survey achievement series. For example, the Iowa Tests of Basic Skills, the Tests of Achievement and Proficiency, and the Iowa Tests of Educational Development give users the number of correct answers by objective, number attempted, number correct by each student, class average percentage correct, and national average correct.

More information is presented on authentic assessment in Chapter 21.

Curriculum-Based Measurement

Curriculum-based measurement (CBM) is an alternate approach to monitoring student progress in academic areas. It is used for a variety of purposes, such as screening, referral, and identification for special education services and for evaluating student progress over time. It is a useful tool in single-subject evaluation and research studies. Key features of CBM are repeated assessments, the linking of instruction and assessment, and the use of material from local curriculum. The focus is on long-term goals rather than short-term objectives. CBM are based upon four properties: technical adequacy, ease of administration, repeated and frequent measurement, and low cost in terms of money and time.

Here is an example of how CBM works:

1. Select a reading passage of about 300 words from material you plan to cover with the student this academic year.
2. Make two copies of the passage—one for you, one for the student.
3. Count the words in the passage and make a note of the exact number.
4. Read the following directions to the student:

   When I say, "Begin," read the passage aloud, beginning with the first line on the page. Try to read each word. If you are stuck, I'll tell you the word you don't know how to read. [Give the student 4 seconds before supplying the word.]

5. Follow along on your copy while the student reads. Circle omissions, substitutions, mispronunciations, and reversals. Count the number of words that were pronounced correctly.
6. At the end of 1 minute, say, "Stop."

This format can be used to test spelling, written expressions, and mathematics.

A major problem with CBM is the amount of time it takes for individual assessment. Group approaches and computer-assisted systems are currently being developed.

Adult Achievement Tests

I have already discussed many tests that can be used to measure the achievement of adults—for example, the Wide Range Achievement Test and the Peabody Individual Achievement Test. Most major testing programs, such as the Graduate Record and College Board tests, have achievement tests that are used with adults. In 1989 the General Educational Development Test, a high school equivalence examination, was administered to approximately 683,000 people in the United States, Canada, and U.S. territories. More than 376,000 of these test takers earned diplomas.

Certain tests are designed specifically for use with adult populations:

The Adult Language Assessment Scale (AdultLAS) (Duncan & DeAvila, 1991) is designed to assess how well non-native English speakers can function. It can be used as a screening test for the ESL population to plan individual instruction, to measure growth in English proficiency, and to help employers design appropriate training.

The General Educational Performance Index, published by Steck-Vaughn, is used by workers in the helping professions to measure an adult's readiness to take the General Educational Development Test. It measures skills in writing, social studies, mathematics, and reading.

The Test of Adult Basic Education (TABE), published by CTB/McGraw-Hill, measures adult proficiency in reading, mathematics, and language. The TABE is used as a diagnostic tool and has three forms: a second- to fourth-grade reading level version, a fourth- to sixth-grade reading level version, and a sixth- to ninth-grade reading level version. The reading test assesses vocabulary and comprehension; the language test measures mechanics, expression, and spelling; and the mathematics test evaluates computation skills, knowledge of concepts, and problem solving. A locator test is used first to determine which is the most appropriate form; then a practice exercise is available to reduce the test taker's anxiety. Depending on the form, the test requires 1½ to 2½ hours of testing time. There is also a Spanish version of the TABE. TABE-PC (1994) is a computer-assisted version of Forms 5 and 6. The locator test is also on the system and places the student at the correct test level. There is a Spanish PC version.

Diagnostic Tests

One of the major purposes of achievement testing is to diagnose strengths and weaknesses. Diagnostic tests are based on the essential skills and competencies needed for success in a given subject area or educational program, and they use numerous items to measure a skill or objective. The tests can be given individually or in groups, and the information provides a profile of strengths and weaknesses in a particular area of concern. Many of the tests already discussed are used for diagnostic purposes—for example, the Peabody Individual Achievement Test, the Wide Range Achievement Test, and the Keymath Diagnostic Arithmetic Test. In addition, some tests are used specifically for diagnostic purposes. One of the most widely used tests, the Woodcock-Johnson Psycho-Educational Battery (WJPEB), is an individually administered test consisting of 27 subtests designed to measure cognitive ability, scholastic aptitude, academic achievement, interest level, and independent behavior. The test battery is recommended for use in individual assessment, screening, and diagnosis of strengths and weaknesses in cognitive, achievement, and interest areas. It is also used for evaluation of individual growth and program effectiveness, research purposes, and teaching purposes (e.g., training in individual test administration).

Some special diagnostic tests concern only reading. The Gates-McKillop-Horowitz Reading Diagnostic Test has 15 individually administered subtests to provide a profile of a student's ability to recognize words and their component sounds. The test enables the teacher to diagnose weaknesses in areas such as coding skills, sight-word recognition, auditory blending, auditory discrimination, spelling, and written expression.

USING ACHIEVEMENT TEST RESULTS

Workers in the helping professions can use the results from standardized achievement tests in a variety of ways. One of the primary uses is instructional. Test results can help teachers evaluate individual and group progress as well as materials and methods of instruction. An achievement test is just one source of information, but it is a systematic approach using standardized methods and items that are carefully screened. Achievement test information can be useful in selection and placement decisions; it can be used to help place students and to check on the validity of such placements. Achievement data may show growth in content areas or specific subject areas over time and can serve as one of the criteria to evaluate a school's curriculum.

The following case shows how achievement tests may be used.

CASE OF JAMES

The case of James illustrates steps in interpreting achievement test data from a survey achievement test. James is in fifth grade and is having some academic difficulties in school. He is 10.3 years old, weighs 80 pounds, and is 4 feet 9 inches tall. His profile on the Stanford Achievement Test is given in Figure 9.1. The derived scores plotted in the profile are percentile ranks and represent how the student performed in relation to students in the national sample.

A profile often has peaks and valleys representing the learner's relative strengths and weaknesses. The median is the 50th percentile and represents typical or average performance. Some tests use different systems to classify superior or poor performance. Workers in the helping professions need to be familiar not only with what scores mean but also with what is measured by each subtest and which scores are combined to give total scores. In this case the test user needs to be familiar with the *Teacher's Guide for Interpretation* of the Intermediate Level I battery of the Stanford Achievement Test. Table 9.1 describes some of the subtests and types of items included.

A total listening score is based on the combination of the Vocabulary and Listening Comprehension scores, which provide data on the learner's ability to understand and remember information presented orally. A total reading score helps test users identify students who might have deficiencies in reading comprehension as well as overall scholastic achievement.

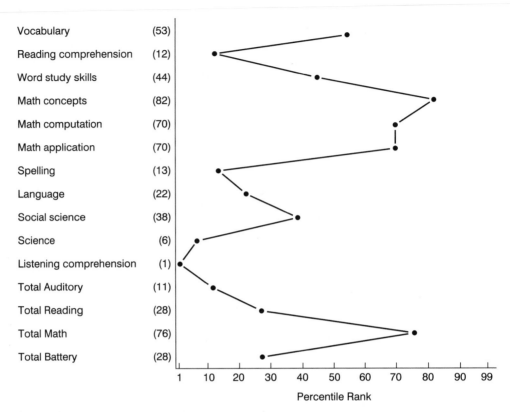

Figure 9.1
Profile of James's scores on the Stanford Achievement Test

The authors of the test believe that factors other than test scores should also be taken into consideration:

1. *Grade level*—The test measures what has been taught in this and preceding grades.
2. *Number of years at current school*—Students who move often and change schools may be at a disadvantage.
3. *Age*—Students who are in the age range typically served by a grade level tend to achieve higher scores than younger students or students who have been retained a year or more.
4. *Out-of-school experience*—Students who travel and read independently and have peers at home who are interested in learning tend to achieve at a higher level.

5. *Health and nutrition*—Healthy individuals who eat a balanced diet tend to score higher than those who do not.
6. *Self-concept*—Students with positive academic and general self-concepts tend to achieve higher scores than those with negative self-concepts.
7. *Socioeconomic level*—Students from lower socioeconomic levels may not have an equal opportunity to learn.
8. *School environment*—The quality of the classroom environment and the attitude of the teacher(s) toward the students can influence performance.
9. *Test content*—The test content may not reflect completely what is taught in a particular district. Also, certain questions may be biased and unfair to certain students,

Table 9.1
Sample of dimensions measured by the Stanford Achievement Test

Subtest	Type of Items (total number)
Vocabulary (60)	Selecting proper or correct meaning of a word: reading and literature (13), nonfiction and reference (18), mathematics and science (11), social science (14), arts and crafts (4)
Reading Comprehension (72)	Identifying meaning after reading given passage: global meaning (7), explicit meaning (27), implicit meaning (10), meaning determined by context (9), inferential meaning (19)
Word Study Skills (130)	Analyzing words: phonetic analysis (35), consonant sounds (7), long-vowel sounds (10), variant vowels (13), short-vowel sounds (5), structural analysis (30), affixes (8), syllables (7), accent (8), disconnected syllables (7)
Mathematics Concepts (32)	Understanding sets, ordinals, fractions, Roman numerals, powers, value changes, number sentences, associative properties, algorithms, size relationships, length, mean, ordered pairs: numbers (9), notation (7), operations (9), geometry and measurement (7)
Mathematics Computation (40)	Using fundamental facts and solving simple math sentences and algorithms: knowledge of primary facts (18), addition and subtraction algorithms (9), multiplication and division algorithms (13)
Mathematics Application (40)	Selecting proper operation and solving two-step problems: solution of one-step problem (12), analysis and development of solution design (8), rate and scale problems (6), measurement (6), graph reading and interpretation (8)

and not all students have the same opportunity to experience and learn certain material.

10. *Test administration*—Proper administrative procedures, time limits, and monitoring of student test-taking behavior are all important.

Additional Information Needed for the Case of James

One of the first questions to consider is how James's test performance compares to his performance in class. His teacher reports that he is an average student in mathematics but has problems in reading comprehension and following directions. He does not seem to listen at times and cannot remember what he is to do. His problems in reading comprehension also create problems in understanding his science and social studies materials.

A second question is how his current test profile compares with other test results. On a local essential skills test (a minimum-level or basic skills criterion-referenced test), James failed the following areas (i.e., he had fewer than 75% of the items correct): vocabulary, listening comprehension, synonyms, antonyms, sequencing, facts and opinions, recalling details, main idea, and sentence completion. The problem of comprehension is very real; James scored at the 12th percentile on the Stanford Achievement Test Reading Comprehension, 82 out of a possible 133 right. In mathematics he failed only word problems and association of numbers with words. James scored 111 out of 125 on this test, with a passing score being 94. His reading comprehension problem did not seem to affect his performance on the section on mathematics word problems: he scored at the 70th percentile. Test results are inconsistent in this dimension. Previous standardized achievement scores were low average in reading, average in mathematics, and average in social studies.

A third question is how James performs in relation to his ability. Many school districts no longer include scholastic aptitude testing as part of the school testing program. If the student is referred to a child study team, the counselor may give the student an individual test such as the Peabody Picture Vocabulary Test, the Slosson Intelligence Test, or even a group IQ test such as the Otis-Lennon School Ability Test. The psychologist may administer the Stanford-Binet or the Wechsler Intelligence Scale for Children. Scholastic aptitude or intelligence testing would help in developing an individually prescribed learning program for James, but no scholastic aptitude or intelligence data were available in his cumulative folder.

A fourth question is whether there are other factors that should be taken into consideration in interpreting the test results. James has progressed normally in school; he was never retained at a grade level and has been at the same school since the beginning of the third grade. He did attend two schools in other states prior to that time. James has had all the normal childhood diseases but is healthy and has not missed many days of school.

James is the oldest child of three siblings; he has an 8-year-old brother and a 3-year-old sister. He lives with his mother and stepfather, who works as a carpenter for a construction company. His mother works part time as a checkout clerk in a supermarket. His father is

in the Navy, and his parents were divorced when James was in kindergarten.

James's mother is concerned about his progress and is open to any suggestions the teacher or counselor may have to improve his academic performance. James relates fairly well with his classmates but gets easily frustrated when he cannot understand his lessons or recite correctly for the teacher. He likes to perform duties around the classroom and has become strongly attached to his teacher.

Two other questions relate to an analysis of the data. How does James perform in relation to the national norms? And how is he mastering the objectives required for the fifth grade? The scores on the Stanford Achievement Test profile show that he scored high in relation to other fifth graders in math concepts and just slightly lower in math computation and application. Clearly, his strongest area of achievement is mathematics. In the two listening tests, he scored average in vocabulary and poor in listening comprehension. His total listening performance is below average compared to his peers. He is also below average in spelling, language, science, and reading comprehension. His word study skills are average as are his scores in social science. James is in danger of being retained in the fifth grade because his reading scores are below the criterion for promotion. He has a second chance to pass the essential skills test but needs help to accomplish that task.

Although each item on the survey achievement test relates to a specific behavioral objective, often only one or two items measure a specific objective. An item analysis on such a test may provide good information for the teacher who has a total class profile, but it is of limited value in diagnosing James's educational problem. The essential skills test is based specifically on the behavioral objectives taught in James's class, whereas the Stanford Achievement Test is based on a wide sampling of objectives and textbooks from schools across the nation. Teachers and counselors should check the face validity and content validity of a norm-referenced test and determine what percentage of local objectives are assessed by the test battery. Fewer differences are apt to be found in mathematics and reading than in science and social studies.

Postscript

James was referred to the child study team and observed and tested by the school psychologist. On the basis of the information collected by the team, he was assigned to work in a specific learning disabilities resource room.

ANALYSIS OF CLASS PROFILE

A sixth-grade teacher or counselor who had given the Stanford Achievement Test early in the school year (grade level 6.2) might have the test scores reported in Table 9.2 and might want to be able to answer questions like these:

1. How are class members achieving in relation to their ability?
2. How is the class achieving in each subject area?
3. Are there any students who need help or who are having problems in one or more achievement areas?

The achievement test scores in Table 9.2 are reported in grade-equivalent form. The IQ scores are from the Otis-Lennon School Ability Test, which yields one score—a deviation IQ with the mean of 100 and a standard deviation of 15. The scores are listed to permit comparison of achievement and scholastic ability.

Assuming that the Stanford Achievement Test is a valid instrument to measure achievement in this school district, students with average ability should score around grade level, and students with below-average ability should score below grade level. Care should be taken not to overinterpret minor differences in individual scores. Student 19, for example, is technically below grade placement in seven achievement areas, but the 5.8 in Mathematics Concepts is not significantly lower than grade placement when the standard error of measurement is considered.

The teacher might graph the scores of the class or compute some measures of central tendency; the median Battery Median score is 6.15, and the median on the vocabulary is 6.1. The means could be computed: the mean for science is 7.00 and for vocabulary 6.21. Or the teacher might simply count how many students are at or above grade level and how many are below. There are 12 at or above grade placement in vocabulary and 12 below, 11 at or above grade placement in mathematical application and 13 below, and 15 at or above in science and 9 below. This type of analysis is fast, but the ability levels of the group must be kept in mind. The teacher might also be interested in looking at item information, perhaps the specific items that presented problems to the class.

In all cases the purpose of the test should be considered. The scores in this example might be low in some areas because the test was given early in the year,

Table 9.2
Achievement test results for a sixth-grade class*

Student	Sex	IQ	BM	WM	PM	SP	LG	AC	ACP	AA	SS	SC
1	G	127	8.3	8.7	8.7	10.5	8.0	6.3	6.6	9.6	6.8	9.2
2	G	116	8.3	7.8	8.7	7.0	9.0	5.6	7.3	9.1	8.3	10.0
3	G	130	8.0	7.5	8.0	7.8	10.7	6.5	8.0	9.1	9.0	7.2
4	G	132	7.8	8.0	7.8	8.8	10.5	6.3	7.6	7.4	7.9	7.8
5	G	121	7.3	7.3	9.6	7.0	8.8	6.2	6.3	7.7	8.5	6.0
6	B	122	7.0	6.7	7.0	5.4	8.5	5.8	6.8	7.7	11.4	10.0
7	G	116	6.9	6.9	7.0	8.2	10.0	5.9	6.8	6.8	7.0	5.8
8	B	118	6.8	6.8	7.0	5.6	6.7	5.8	6.3	7.7	7.4	6.9
9	G	110	6.7	7.3	7.2	6.3	6.7	5.8	5.4	7.2	7.2	8.1
10	G	114	6.6	6.6	6.9	8.0	9.3	5.4	6.6	5.7	5.6	6.0
11	B	115	6.5	6.6	6.5	6.0	7.2	5.8	5.9	5.4	8.1	9.2
12	B	104	6.2	5.6	6.2	5.7	6.0	5.8	6.3	7.7	6.3	6.4
13	B	117	6.1	5.4	6.1	4.1	6.2	6.0	7.3	5.9	6.4	9.2
14	G	115	6.0	7.3	6.7	6.6	5.7	5.9	5.9	4.9	6.0	9.0
15	B	115	5.8	5.6	6.1	4.7	7.0	7.0	5.4	6.5	6.6	5.8
16	B	109	5.8	5.5	6.6	4.7	7.1	5.8	4.8	5.6	5.9	6.7
17	B	108	5.6	5.6	5.6	4.3	5.8	5.4	6.3	5.6	5.6	6.7
18	B	103	5.6	3.9	4.9	3.0	5.6	5.2	5.9	5.9	6.8	5.8
19	G	102	5.6	4.7	5.6	3.6	5.3	5.8	6.5	5.6	6.3	4.1
20	G	93	5.5	5.5	5.9	4.7	6.6	4.6	5.4	4.4	6.3	6.6
21	G	112	5.4	4.9	6.4	5.1	5.4	5.6	4.8	5.4	5.3	5.8
22	G	112	5.3	4.7	6.1	6.9	4.6	5.8	5.4	3.8	5.3	4.2
23	B	89	5.1	5.2	4.7	3.4	4.3	5.6	6.1	5.1	5.2	4.3
24	B	96	4.9	5.4	6.1	4.3	5.5	4.4	4.5	3.8	4.9	6.4

*IQ = intelligence quotient, BM = battery median, WM = word meaning, PM = paragraph meaning, SP = spelling, LG = language, AC = mathematics concepts, ACP = mathematics computation, AA = mathematics application, SS = social studies, SC = science

before the students had been exposed to many of the concepts and objectives taught in the sixth grade. Some school districts intentionally give this test at the beginning of the year to obtain an overall estimate of the entry level of the students.

SUMMARY

Achievement tests are used at all age and grade levels to measure what individuals have learned. They are used for a wide variety of purposes, such as diagnosis, placement, growth, and description. A variety of achievement tests include individual and group; norm- and criterion-referenced; survey batteries and single-subject; and diagnostic, prognostic, and readiness tests.

Local school districts, states, and the federal government are involved in assessing achievement. Local school districts develop a series of criterion tests to measure how well students are achieving the minimum-level skills and essential-level skills being taught. The tests are valuable for educational and vocational guidance purposes, evaluation of curriculum and teaching methods, and demonstration of growth from grade to grade.

Achievement tests are used for placement, selection, and classification of students. They should not be used as a primary criterion for evaluating teacher performance. Achievement tests are not free from controversy. Critics are concerned that some tests and test items may be biased against certain groups.

QUESTIONS FOR DISCUSSION

1. Compare survey achievement and criterion-referenced tests. In what situations would each be the best measure to use?

2. Is it necessary to give both survey achievement tests and minimum-level and essential-level skills tests within one district? Defend your position.

3. How would you go about developing a minimum-level skills test in a content field in junior or senior high school?

4. For what purposes should survey achievement tests be used? For what purposes should we avoid using the tests?

5. Look at the scores found in Table 9.2 and answer these questions: (a) How are class members achieving in relation to their ability? (b) How is the class achieving in each subject area? (c) Are there any students who need help or who are having problems in one or more achievement areas?

6. State your position on one of the following issues: (a) Testing controls what is taught in schools. (b) The best predictor of future success is past achievement, not aptitude. (c) Achievement tests should be banned from use.

SUGGESTED ACTIVITIES

1. Select one of the major achievement tests and write a critique of it.

2. Assemble an annotated bibliography of achievement tests related to your field of interest.

3. Interview workers in the helping professions who use achievement tests in their work. Find out what tests they use and why and how they use the results. Report your findings to the class.

4. Administer an individual achievement test or diagnostic test and write a report of the results.

5. Review the research and write a paper on one of the following topics: bias in achievement testing, sex differences in achievement testing, the national assessment program, current trends and issues in achievement testing, criterion-referenced testing.

6. Read the case that follows and answer the questions at the end:

Case of Danzel

A teacher noticed Danzel's constant battle with fellow classmates in class. Danzel doesn't seem to have any friends. When his other teachers were asked about him, a mystery seemed to exist.

Elementary School Record

First Grade		Second Grade		Third Grade		Third Grade (This year)	
Reading	D	Reading	D	Reading	D	Reading	C
Spelling	C	Spelling	D	Spelling	D	Spelling	C
Writing	C	Writing	D	Writing	C	Writing	C
Math	D	Math	D	Math	F	Math	C
				Lang. Arts	F	Lang. Arts	D
				Soc. St.	D	Soc. St.	D
				Science	F	Science	C

Attendance Record

Absent	23	25	30	21

Current test record:
Grade 3 (current)
Minibattery of Achievement

	Subject	Score
1.	Reading	2.7
2.	Math	2.6
3.	Writing	2.0
4.	Factual	2.2

WISC-III

	Area	Score
1.	Verbal	98
2.	Performance	105
3.	Total	101

Health record:
Danzel's physical condition is good. He has had the normal childhood diseases.

Family background:
Danzel's father is a heating and air conditioning technician and a high school graduate; his mother is a housewife and has an eighth-grade education. The parents are separated, and Danzel lives with his grandparents. He has lived with his grandparents since he was 4 years of age, when he was taken out of St. John's Orphanage. Home conditions are average considering that his grandparents are old. They lack interest in how he is doing at school.

Social life:

Danzel belongs to no organizations or clubs, and he does not have any close friends. He frequently starts arguments in class and on the playground. He is very outspoken.

Interests and abilities:

Danzel has a lot of interest in making things; this is evident in his science projects and art. He has special skills in making things with his hands. He does little reading but watches lots of TV. He fails to do his homework most of the time.

Other teachers' assessment of Danzel:

They comment on his family environment and say that his grandparents' continual moving has deprived Danzel of companions. They say that he acts out to gain attention.

a. Provide a capsule summary of Danzel's achievement and aptitude.
b. What additional information about Danzel would you like to have?
c. Do his test results correlate with his grades?

ADDITIONAL READINGS

Berk, R. A. (Ed.). (1980). *Criterion-referenced measurement: The state of the art*. Baltimore: Johns Hopkins University Press.

This is a good resource book on criterion-referenced testing.

Farr, R. (1994). *Portfolio and performance assessment*. San Antonio, TX: Psychological Corporation.

Farr provides specific procedures and techniques for using portfolios and integrating them into the instructional program and school assessment practices.

Millman, J., & Greene, J. (1989). The specification and development of tests of achievement and ability. In R. Linn (Ed.), *Educational measurement* (3rd ed.). New York: Collier Macmillan.

Oakland, T., & Hambleton, R. K. (1995). *International perspectives on academic assessment*. Boston: Klower.

The book provides an overview of tests used with children and youth internationally.

Reynolds, C. R., & Kamphaus, R. W. (1990). *Handbook of psychological and educational assessment of children*. Vol. 1, *Intelligence and Achievement*.

The book discusses major assessment instruments as well as ways of assessing special populations. Attention is also given to current issues.

Wiggins, G. P. (1993). *Assessing student performance: Exploring the purpose and limits of testing*. San Francisco: Jossey-Bass.

Wiggins critically reviews testing practices and the problematic practices operating today in the field. He discusses the usefulness of timely feedback and suggests a new system of assessment that provides teachers and policymakers with more useful and credible feedback.

CHAPTER 10

Career and Employment Testing

OVERVIEW

The first part of this chapter discusses tests and assessment procedures to measure interests, values, and career maturity. Many studies have been made of nonintellectual characteristics of individuals and the relationship of those characteristics to achievement and success in different educational and vocational fields. Information about these nonacademic areas is invaluable to counselors working with students or with adults making career and educational decisions. The test results are also important for counselors and psychologists working with clients who have personal prob-

lems or teachers and counselors working with children who have educational problems.

The second part of the chapter focuses on employment testing. Tests are widely used in employment contexts in both the public and the private sectors. The usefulness of tests for employment and career development within an organization was demonstrated through the testing programs developed during World War II. Since most employees no longer stay in one career field all their lives but try five to seven careers, these test programs have extended use.

OBJECTIVES

After studying this chapter, the reader should be able to

✔ Identify widely used interest, values, and career guidance inventories

✔ Discuss when these inventories are used and explain how they are interpreted

✔ Identify and discuss some of the issues and problems in interpreting tests

✔ Identify specific sources of information concerning vocational and career guidance instruments

✔ Discuss some of the trends in career guidance testing

✔ Identify the roles, purposes, and procedures of employment testing

✔ Discuss the trends, problems, and issues in employment testing

INTEREST INVENTORIES

According to English and English (1958), the word *interest* has several elusive meanings. The first meaning is the attitude or set of attending; that is individuals respond consistently in the same way to a given stimulus. The second meaning is the tendency to give selective attention to something. The third meaning is an attitude or feeling that an object or event makes a difference or is of concern to oneself. Some psychological theorists hold to the doctrine that learning cannot take place without a feeling of interest. Sometimes interest is synonymous with motivation. Career developmental theorists have pointed out the importance of interests. Strong (1927) postulated that interest is in the domain of motivation and there are clusters of attitudes, interests, and personality factors related to choice of and satisfaction with an occupation (Shertzer & Linden, 1979, p. 270).

A wide variety of techniques are used to measure interests, such as checklists, structured and unstructured interviews and questionnaires, and informal and standardized inventories. Interest inventories have been used in the helping professions for more than half a century. E. K. Strong published his first version of the Strong Vocational Interest Blank in 1927. A revised version of the test, the Strong Interest Inventory, is widely used in the field today. It provides a profile of how an individual's interests compare with those of successful people in certain occupational fields. Another interest inventory, the Kuder Preference Record–Vocational, was first published in 1932. Test takers were asked to choose the item they liked most and the one they liked least in each cluster of three. Kuder's test initially measured interest in 10 general areas, such as outdoor, literary, musical, artistic, and scientific. Interest tests can be one source of information to help with educational and vocational decisions; they are not appropriate for selection purposes, however.

Self-Directed Search

The Self-Directed Search (SDS) is one of the most widely used interest inventories. It was first published in 1971 and has gone through a number of revisions. The SDS guides examinees through an evaluation of their abilities and interests. The 16-page test is a tool for high school and college students and for adults returning to the work force to find occupations that best fit their interests and abilities. It can be used by anyone between the ages of 15 and 70 in need of career guidance. The author and publisher claim that the SDS is easy and uncomplicated to administer and score. It can even be self-administered and scored. Special answer sheets, proctors, computer scoring, or scoring stencils are not needed. The SDS is designed to provide immediate feedback, which, according to the author, aids in examinees' self-understanding and career exploration.

Specifically, the examinees are asked to list their daydreams, activities liked or disliked, competencies, occupations of interest, and self-appraisals in mechanical, scientific, teaching, sales, and clerical fields. Examinees use the Occupational Finder (Holland, 1985), which lists 1,156 of the most common occupations in the United States. The occupations are coded by letter to indicate which of Holland's personality types they represent: realistic, investigative, artistic, social, enterprising, or conventional. The manual also gives a single-digit number to indicate the level of general educational development required along with the nine-digit number given by the *Dictionary of Occupational Titles* (DOT, 1991) used for each occupation listed. Here is an example:

Type	*Title*	*Number*
RAS	Cook Apprentice Pastry	313.381-018 ED 4
RAS	Cook Pastry	313.381-026 ED 4

Educational levels of 5 and 6 require college training or more; levels 3 and 4 high school and some college, technical, or business training. Levels 1 and 2 require no special training.

To help the examiner, the *Professional Manual* (1994) provides guidance, and the sourcebook *Making Vocational Choices: A Theory of Vocational Personalities and Work Environments* (Holland, 1997) provides a more complete review of the theory and research behind the test. Additional materials can facilitate the assessment, including *Occupational Finder, You and Your Career, Leisure Activity Finder*, and *College Majors Finder*. A number of versions are available for counselors to use with clients, such as Form CP Career Planning, Form E–Canadian Edition: French, Form E–Canadian Edition: English, Edition En Español, Vietnamese Edition, Form R–Braille Edition, and Form R–Computer Version.

Strong Interest Inventory

The Strong Interest Inventory (SII), Fourth Edition, is an expansion of previous editions and includes six general occupational themes (realistic, investigative, artistic, social, enterprising, conventional—i.e., Holland's six personality types, also called RIASEC), 23 basic interest scales, 207 occupational scales (including 34 additional vocational/technical ones), and 12 new professional scales. The inventory also includes an academic comfort scale and 10 administrative indexes. Correlative materials are available to help the counselor and client in interpreting the results, including the *User's Guide*, a career exploration worksheet, a career finder, a college major exploration sheet, an introduction for career counselors, a guide to understanding results, a Strong and Myers-Briggs Type Indicator (MBTI) career development guide, an introduction for organizational settings, a workshop leader's guide, a Strong-Hansen occupational guide, and a video about career options. The authors designed the SII to

1. Help individuals make educational choices
2. Introduce lifestyle issues for exploration as possible career enhancements
3. Stimulate discussions among counselors, students, and parents
4. Identify shared interests with people successfully employed in an occupation
5. Identify careers to explore for possible midcareer change
6. Help identify an interest in management
7. Help counselors understand an employee's job satisfaction or dissatisfaction
8. Aid in retirement planning

The SII is also proposed as a research tool for individuals, groups, and cultures.

The authors claim that the SII is an interesting exercise and provides a thorough measure of client interests. The profile uses John Holland's taxonomy for ease of interpretation. The test takes only about 30 minutes to complete and compares examinee interests with those of persons successfully employed in a wide variety of fields. The authors claim that the occupational scales predict one's eventual occupational choice regardless of sex or racial background. The test can be administered and scored on a microcomputer if the user wants immediate feedback.

In addition to the *User's Guide*, a manual is available that explains the three types of scales—General Occupational Themes, Basic Interest Scales, and Occupational Scales—and discusses what to do with clients who have either elevated or depressed profiles. The authors also provide suggestions for using the test with adults, cross-cultural groups, and special populations. A number of different types of reports are available such as a profile report, an expanded interpretive report, an original interpretive report, a college major report, and topic reports on areas such as leadership/management style or organizational specialty, leisure, and individual summary.

Career Occupational Preference System

The Career Occupational Preference System (COPSystem) has three components. The first section is designed to measure interests and presents a profile in 14 areas:

Science Professional	Business Skilled
Science Skilled	Clerical
Technology Professional	Communication
Technology Skilled	Arts Professional
Consumer Economics	Arts Skilled
Outdoor	Service Professional
Business Professional	Service Skilled

The second part of the test battery is an aptitude test (CAPS). It includes eight 5-minute subtests—mechanical reasoning, spatial relations, verbal reasoning, numerical ability, language usage, word knowledge, perceptual speed and accuracy, and manual speed and dexterity.

The third part of the battery measures work values (COPES). It, too, has eight scales—accepting/investigative, carefree/practical, conformity/independence, supportive/leadership, noncompulsive/orderliness, privacy/recognition, realistic/aesthetic, and self-concern/social.

There are several forms of the test. COPS-P measures interest at the professional level. COPS-R is written at a sixth-grade reading level and the unit is presented in a single, easy-to-follow programmed booklet. COPS-II is used to measure the interests of younger students and those at higher grade levels for whom reading or language presents difficulties or for whom motivation might be a problem.

The test summary provides a profile of the 14 career groups, showing the highs on all three tests, and clients are urged to consider groups in which their interest, abilities, and values are all high. Thereafter, they are instructed to look at the groups for which interests and aptitudes are both high.

The *COPSystem Comprehensive Career Guide* provides support for the client. The COPS interest test can be completed in a 20- to 30-minute period and is self-scoring. COPES takes approximately 40 to 50 minutes, while CAPS requires 50 minutes. Both self-scoring and machine-scoring forms are available. The CAPS also has administration available on tape. A *COPSystem Career Brief Kit* for clients to use with their test results and *Career Cluster Booklets* provide correlative information about the different occupational fields.

Other Interest Inventories

Many other interest tests are available. Critical reviews can be found in *Reports of the AMEG* (now the Association for Assessment in Counseling) *Committee to Screen Career Guidance Instruments* (Association of Measurement and Evaluation in Counseling and Development, 1986), *A Counselor's Guide to Vocational Guidance Instruments* (Kapes & Mastie, 1994), and *Mental Measurement Yearbooks*. A special annotated bibliography on personality and vocational assessment instruments is part of the ETS Test Collection volumes available from Ornx.

Some of the other widely used inventories are identified here:

The Campbell Interest and Skills Survey (CISS) focuses on careers that require a postsecondary education and is most appropriate for use with individuals who have completed college or plan to attend. The CISS adds a parallel skill scale that reports the estimate of the individual's confidence in his or her ability to perform various occupational activities.

The Career Assessment Inventory (CAI) provides scores on 6 general occupational theme scales, 22 basic interest scales, and 89 occupational scales. The CAI also has administrative indices and four nonoccupational scales.

The Harrington-O'Shea Career Decision-Making System–Revised (COM-R) is designed for use with junior high school students to adults and provides scale scores in six interest areas (e.g., crafts, arts, scientific, social). The COM-R surveys abilities, values, school subject preferences, and interests. A Spanish version is available. Another version is written at the fourth-grade level and is designed for use with individuals with low reading skills, special education students, and adults.

The Interest Determination, Exploration, and Assessment System provides scores on scales such as mechanical, electronics, nature/outdoor, science, numbers, writing, arts/crafts, social service, child care, medical service, business, sales, office practice, and food service. The test is designed for use in grades 6 through 12.

The Jackson Vocational Interest Survey (JVIS) is used with high school students and adults and has 34 basic interest scales, including creative arts, performing arts, mathematics, skilled trades, dominant leadership, business, sales, law, human relations, management, and professional advising. It also has 10 occupational themes such as assertive, enterprising, helping, and logical. The test reports similarities of examinee interests and 24 areas of major study in college.

The Judgment of Occupational Behavior–Orientation (JOB-O) is used with seventh graders to adults and provides scores for 120 job titles, with decision-making information included on the answer sheet.

The Kuder General Interest Survey (Form E) is used with 6th- to 12th-grade students. It measures broad vocational interests and is used for counseling and vocational exploration. The 10 scales are outdoor, mechanical, computational, scientific, persuasive, artistic, literary, musical, social service, and clerical.

The Kuder Occupational Interest Survey (Form DD) has 126 occupational and 48 college major scales.

The Ohio Vocational Interest Survey: Second Edition (OVIS–II) provides scales such as manual work, basic services, machine operations, quality control, clerical health services, crafts and precise operations, skilled personal services, sports and recreation, customer service, regulations enforcement, communications, numerical, visual arts, agricultural and life sciences, engineering and physical sciences, music, performing arts, marketing, legal services, management, education and social work, and medical service.

The Vocational Interest, Experience, and Skills Assessment (VIESA) is used with 8th- to 12th-grade students and combines two ACT instruments: the ACT Interest Inventory and the Career-Related Experience Inventory. The information is clustered around the themes of data, ideas, people, and things.

INTEREST ASSESSMENT TECHNIQUES

Several techniques can be used to measure interest. Super and Crites (1962) identified four methods:

1. *Expressed interests*—what clients say their interests are
2. *Manifest interests*—what clients are observed doing
3. *Testing*—what clients know about various fields
4. *Interest inventories*—what clients check about their interests and preferences

The helping professional may want to check the validity of test or inventory results by asking clients about their interests and activities, inquiring about their preferences, and finding out why areas are liked and disliked. Individuals may have had no experience or opportunity in certain areas, and some likes and dislikes may be influenced by parents, spouse, or family attitudes. Interests cannot be determined by how clients spend their time. Time may be spent doing things under pressure from parents, spouse, family, or peers. Or individuals simply may not have time to do the things they most enjoy.

Client performance should be considered on more than just interest tests. In many situations, aptitude and achievement data also help in the decision-making process. Clients may learn and like what they do best, but not necessarily. A number of other factors may be involved, such as opportunity and experience.

VALUES

Values are an important dimension of personality, and value assessment is an important component of career guidance testing. Most large computerized guidance systems include value measurement and definitions as an important part of the system. Some tests measure general values; others only work values:

The Hall Occupational Orientation Inventory (Hall & Tarrier, 1976) is based on Maslow's personality theory and Roe's theory of occupational choice. The authors argue that occupational decisions reflect inner values, needs, and beliefs; abilities; and interests perceived as important. The first 10 scales assess client values and needs—for example, creativity, independence, risk, belonging-ness, security, aspiration, esteem, location concern, and extremism.

The Minnesota Importance Questionnaire measures 20 psychological needs and six underlying values related to work satisfaction. The values assessed are achievement, altruism, autonomy, comfort, safety, and status. The needs scales provide scores in areas such as security, social status, compensation, achievement, authority, creativity, and moral values.

The Salience Inventory (Research Edition) measures the importance of five major life roles—student, worker, homemaker, leisurite, and citizen. Each role is assessed from three perspectives: participation, commitment, and value expectations. There are 170 behavioral and affective items that are rated on a four-point scale.

The Values Scale was developed to measure intrinsic and extrinsic life/career values. The test has some scales similar to the Work Values Inventory (for example, achievement, aesthetics, altruism, economic returns, prestige, and variety), but it also has scales such as ability utilization, advancement, authority, creativity, lifestyle, personal development, physical activity, risk, social interaction, social relations, working conditions, cultural identity, physical prowess, and economic security.

The Work Values Inventory (WVI) measures 15 extrinsic and intrinsic values important to the world of work. The WVI is a short 45-item test yielding scores in areas such as altruism, aesthetics, creativity, intellectual stimulation, independence, achievement, prestige, management, economic returns, security, surroundings, supervisory relations, associates, variety, and way of life.

GUIDELINES FOR INTERPRETING TESTS

Consider these general guidelines when interpreting interest and values tests:

1. Scale titles should be translated into terms clients can understand. Clients may be confused by actual scale titles such as altruism and aesthetics.
2. Clients may be encouraged to plot their own scores and make profiles, identifying their own high and low scores. This is a type of ipsative interpretation, with clients making their own intraindividual comparisons.
3. Client profiles can be compared with norming groups and available vocational and educational groups.
4. If key items are identified by research, specific responses may be considered and discussed with the client.
5. The meaning of values and interests in work and career fields should be discussed.

CAREER DEVELOPMENT INSTRUMENTS

Career development and maturity instruments were developed to help counselors assess career awareness and knowledge. Used to evaluate the effectiveness of career guidance and education programs, they were widely used when there was more federal and state support of career education programs in the schools. These instruments can provide counselors with valuable information about the career development and educational needs of individual clients and can provide survey information to help in planning career guidance programs:

The Career Awareness Inventory has two forms—an elementary form for grades 3 to 6 and an advanced form for grades 7 to 12. The author says the test can be useful in identifying strengths and weaknesses of individuals or groups and in focusing on specific aspects of career awareness.

The Career Development Inventory has forms for junior and senior high school students as well as college and university students. The test contains five scales—career planning, career exploration, decision making, world-of-work information, and knowledge of preferred occupational group. The scales are combined to give scores in career development attitudes, career development knowledge and skills, and career orientation.

The Career Maturity Inventory is an instrument for grades 6 through 12 that measures the attitudes and competencies related to variables in the career-choice process. The test has two parts: an attitude test and a competence test. The attitude test measures attitudes toward decisiveness, involvement, independence, orientation, and compromise dimensions of career maturity. The competence test has five subtests—knowing yourself (self-appraisal), knowing about jobs (occupational information), choosing a job (goal selection), looking ahead (planning), and what should they do? (problem solving).

The College Board has a Career Skills Assessment Program for grades 9 through 14 and adults. The purpose of this assessment is to help individuals gain insight into career planning and decision making. The information helps counselors, teachers, and administrators evaluate the extent to which students have mastered fundamental career development principles. There are six content areas that have books of exercises: self-evaluation and development, career awareness, career decision making, employment seeking, work effectiveness, and personal economics.

The one problem with many instruments is that they do not require students to apply these skills to themselves. It is not enough for clients to gain some understanding of the process; they must also see how this information can be transferred to their own real world.

COMBINED PROGRAMS

The trend in career guidance is for assessment to include interest, values, and other dimensions such as aptitude, career development, and maturity. The COPSystem previously discussed in this chapter includes interest, values, and aptitude assessment. Here are some other examples of combined programs:

The Career Planning Program (CPP) of ACT is designed to help students from grade 8 to adult identify and explore personally relevant occupations and educational programs. The assessment stresses career exploration and helps individuals relate information about their interests, experiences, and abilities to the work world.

Planning Career Goals, developed by the American Institutes for Research and published by CTB/McGraw-Hill, consists of a number of separate subtests—life and career plans report, interest inventory, information measures, and ability measures. The battery is designed to assist guidance and counseling personnel in working with 8th- to 12th-grade students in career and educational planning. The system takes about 5 hours to administer and looks at the traits and preferences of the client, permitting comparisons with persons actually employed in the preferred career fields.

The World of Work Inventory, another comprehensive system for grade 8 to adulthood, covers interests, temperament, and aptitude and achievement areas. The battery is useful for needs assessment and can clarify for school counselors what types of occupational information are needed. The test information is also useful to personnel working with clients in rehabilitation, correctional, and employment placement contexts.

PROBLEMS OF INTEREST MEASUREMENT

Counselors need to be aware of a number of problem areas when using interest tests:

1. Even though there is much evidence of the stability of interests, especially from the late teens on, some clients change their interests dramatically in their adult years.
2. Tests given before grade 10 or 11 may not be accurate measures of interests. Students may not have had the background of experiences, real or vicarious.
3. Job success is usually correlated more to abilities than interests.
4. Many interest inventories are very susceptible to faking, either intentionally or unintentionally.
5. Response set may affect the validity of an individual's profile. Clients may choose options they consider more socially desirable, or acquiescence may prevail.
6. High scores are not the only valuable scores on an interest inventory. Low scores, showing what people dislike or want to avoid, are often more predictive than high scores.
7. Societal expectations and traditions may prove more important than interest in determining vocational selection. Gender bias was a major concern in interest measurement during the past several decades and needs to be considered when selecting instruments and interpreting profiles.
8. Socioeconomic class may affect the pattern of scores on an interest test. Scores for upper- and middle-class clients are more predictive than scores for lower-class clients.
9. The inventories may be geared to the professions rather than to skilled and semiskilled areas. Many inventories were criticized because they were geared exclusively to college-bound students.
10. A profile may be flat and hard to interpret. In such a situation a counselor should use other tests and techniques to determine interests.
11. Tests use different types of psychometric scoring procedures. Some interest tests use forced-choice items, in which individuals are asked to choose from a set of options. Examinees may like or dislike all of the choices but still must choose. Scoring procedures will have an impact on interpretation of results.

FUTURE TRENDS IN INTEREST MEASUREMENT

Holland (1986) predicts a movement toward more practical inventories. The movement has been stimulated by the inclusion of standard inventories within computer-assisted career systems. Holland believes that inventories will be more helpful to females, people with skilled trade interest, and older citizens (p. 262). The use of more interpretative materials and workbooks will compete with one-to-one counseling strategies. Holland recommends more study of the use of inventories for intervention. He foresees a proliferation of computer-based inventories, scoring, and interpreting systems, along with self-help workbooks. Hansen (1990) reports on the increased use of interest inventories and the expansion of their use to new populations, especially in cross-cultural contexts.

EMPLOYMENT TESTING: ROLES AND PURPOSES

Tests are used in employment contexts for placement decisions, assignment to training programs, promotion, retention, licensing, and certification. Tests can be used, for example, to select individuals for entry-level positions, make differential job assignments, select individuals for advanced and specialized positions, decide who will be promoted within an organization, decide who is eligible for training, and provide diagnostic and career development information for individuals. To be effective, tests must be valid for the intended purpose and should be the least discriminating tools for the decisions that need to be made. Tests can help ensure fair treatment of workers in an employment context.

In its catalogs of tests for business and industry, the Psychological Corporation uses a two-way grid to identify the human resource applications for the uses of tests. The horizontal dimension lists the job type, while the vertical lists the human resource application. The job types listed include clerical and administrative; accounting and financial; sales and service; supervisory, managerial, and professional; industrial and technical; and a final category, "may fit other jobs." The functions are job analysis, administrative assessment, basic skills (reading, writing, and arithmetic); general aptitude, the ability to think, learn, and succeed; specialized aptitude and ability, managerial, mechanical spatial, manual, visual; personal characteristics and style assessment; assessment for training and development, the ability to benefit and succeed, vocational/career guidance, and vocational rehabilitation.

TEST USE IN THE PRIVATE SECTOR

Employees in the private sector work primarily in manufacturing, retail trades, and service occupations. Clerical workers constitute the largest group, numbering approximately 20 million persons. Tests are used in the private sector to help make decisions in selection, placement, training, and promotion of personnel. Tests are also used to provide credentials or certification.

Types of Tests

Gatewood and Perloff (1990) report that employers use general aptitude, cognitive ability, clerical achievement, spatial and mechanical abilities, perceptual accuracy, and motor ability tests for selection and promotion. Clerical workers were tested by two-thirds to four-fifths of the employers. Testing was used more by transportation and communication industries than by manufacturing and more by large corporations (employing 1,000 or more employees) than by smaller companies. Large companies, with many different job categories, tended to rely on in-house experts or consultants to handle test development and administration.

The Bureau of National Affairs Survey (Miner, 1976) provides a good summary of trends. Of companies that used tests, more than 80% used them to screen applicants for office-clerical positions. Only 20% used tests to screen applicants for production or maintenance jobs, 14% used tests for data processing jobs, and fewer than 10% used tests to screen applicants for sales or service jobs.

Personality tests are used in some employment contexts. In general, the most widely used personality tests discussed in the text are used in industrial contexts also, such as the Myers-Briggs Type Indicator, the California Psychological Inventory, the Edwards Personal Preference Inventory, and the Guilford-Zimmerman Temperament Survey. Projective tests such as the Rorschach Ink Blot Test, the Thematic Apperception Test, and the Sentence Completion Test are reportedly used by some groups. Assessment of attitudes, stress, organizational commitment, and work environment are used to diagnose strengths and weaknesses in the organization and to monitor changes in the work force.

Scales of job satisfaction measure dimensions such as attitude toward supervision, the company, the co-workers, pay, working conditions, promotion, security, subordinates, autonomy, and esteem needs. Some of the standardized tests that are used in business and industry are described here:

> The Aptitude and Intelligence Series includes many subtests: blocks, dexterity, dimensions, factory terms, fluency, judgment, memory, motor, numbers, office terms, parts, secretary, semiskilled worker, senior clerk, skilled worker, unskilled worker, vehicle operator, writer, perceptions, precision, sales terms, tools, contact personality factor, neurotic personality factor, contact clerk, dental office assistant, dental technician, designer, engineer, factory machine operator, factory supervisor, general clerk, inspector, instructor, numbers clerk, office machine operator, office supervisor, office technical, optometric assistant, sales clerk, sales engineer, salesperson, sales supervisor, and scientist.

> The Basic Occupational Literacy Test (BOLT) has four subtests of reading and arithmetic. The reading test has four levels of difficulty and assesses vocabulary and reading comprehension. The arithmetic section measures computation and reasoning at the fundamental, intermediate, and advanced levels. The BOLT

wide-range scale is used as a quick screen to determine whether the employment counselor should give the General Aptitude Test Battery or Non-Reading Aptitude Test Battery.

The Career Attitudes and Strategies Inventory is a way to identify career influences and problems for consideration or resolution. It includes a career checkup; a self-assessment of the client's career or situation; and a survey of the beliefs, events, and forces that affect the client's career.

The Comprehensive Ability Battery (CAB) contains 20 pencil-and-paper subtests that measure a single primary-ability factor related to performance in an industrial setting. The subtests are verbal ability, numerical ability, spatial ability, perceptual completion, clerical speed and accuracy, reasoning, hidden shapes, rote memory, mechanical ability, meaningful memory, memory span, spelling, auditory ability, aesthetics judgment, organizing ideas, production of ideas, verbal fluency, originality, tracking, and drawing.

Comprehensive Personality Profile is used in employee selection and professional development situations and measures whether the individual is people- or task-oriented or patient/impatient. The primary traits assessed are emotional intensity, intuition, recognition, motivation, sensitivity, assertiveness, trust, and good impression.

The Employee Aptitude Survey Series has a number of tests such as verbal comprehension, visual pursuit, visual speed and accuracy, space use, numerical reasoning, verbal reasoning, word fluency, mechanical speed and accuracy, and symbolic reasoning.

The Employers' Test and Service Associates publishes tests such as the General Mental Ability Test, the Office Arithmetic Test, the General Clerical Test, the Stenographic Skills Test, the Mechanical Familiarity Test, the Mechanical Knowledge Test, the Sales Aptitude Test, and the Personal Adjustment Index.

The Employment Barrier Identification Scale assesses the ability of an unemployed client to gain and retain employment. It looks at job skills, education, environmental support, and personal survival skills.

The Employment Reliability Inventory is an 81-item true/false test measuring emotional maturity, conscientiousness, trustworthiness, long-term commitment, and safe job performance.

The Industrial Reading Test measures reading comprehension and is used for selecting job applicants and screening trainees for vocational and technical programs.

The Job Effectiveness Prediction System includes tests such as coding and converting, comparing and checking, filing, language usage, mathematical skill, numerical ability, reading comprehension, spelling, and verbal comprehension.

The Personnel Test for Industry (PTI) measures general ability in verbal and numerical areas and is used in the selection of workers needing competencies in these areas.

The Wesman Personnel Classification Test assesses general verbal and numerical abilities and is used for selection of employees for clerical, sales, supervisory, and managerial positions.

The Wonderlic Personnel Test measures general verbal, spatial, and numerical reasoning and is used for selection and placement purposes and to predict adjustment to jobs, turnover, and dissatisfaction on routine, simple, labor-intensive jobs.

Certification

Friedman and Williams (1982) point out that the trend toward competency testing is strong in industry, too. Job applicants are often required to complete competency testing before they submit their applications. In addition, there are statutory-based licensing examinations and certification programs. Shorthand reporters, automobile mechanics, respiratory therapists, and mental health counselors all take licensing or certification examinations. Merely passing the test is not enough; the public is concerned about continued competence and has pressed for continuing education and recertification programs.

Career Planning

Besides screening applicants or certifying applicants for placement purposes, tests are used for career planning. Many industries are interested in helping their workers define the goals they would like to achieve within the company. A testing program is designed to help workers identify interests, values, and competencies and guide them in further professional development and formal educational activities. Many corporations provide outplacement services for individuals who lose their jobs as a result of downsizing.

TEST USE IN GOVERNMENT

The federal government became involved in employment testing in 1883, when Congress created the U.S. Civil Service Commission. In 1979 the Office of Personnel Management (OPM) became involved in the testing process and established standards for job classification and competitive examinations for more than 1,000 types of jobs. The OPM has responsibility for two-thirds of the federal civilian work force, and a large percentage of these workers are selected by one of the testing programs.

Other governmental agencies develop and administer their own tests. The Department of State, for example, uses its own tests to select foreign service officers. The U.S. Employment Service (USES) has developed tests for use in local and state employment offices. The General Aptitude Test Battery (GATB) is widely used; it compares examinee scores with those of workers in more than 600 jobs. USES has also developed interest inventories and tests of proficiency in dictation, typing, and spelling.

State and local government agencies often require tests for selection purposes. Tests are frequently required of police officers and fire fighters as well as clerical workers. Local governmental agencies tend to use tests less frequently than state agencies do. However, both state and local agencies use oral and performance examinations more often than federal agencies do (Friedman & Williams, 1982). Skilled workers tend to be given tests more often than unskilled workers are, although tests are not used as the sole criterion. Education, experience, character, and residence requirements are other important factors considered in hiring.

Occupational and Professional Licensing

States often mandate occupational and professional licensing for which some type of examination is required. This is even true in education in many states, with teachers and principals required to pass licensing examinations. States often establish a licensing board for a specific occupation. Workers who take required licensing examinations include architects, acupuncturists, audiologists, chiropractors, dentists, dental hygienists, engineers, funeral directors, landscape architects, land surveyors, occupational therapists, psychologists, speech pathologists, hearing aid counselors, optometrists, registered nurses, practical nurses, pharmacists, physical therapists, physicians, physicians' assistants, podiatrists, and social workers.

TEST USE IN THE MILITARY

The military makes extensive use of tests for selection and classification purposes. The Armed Services Vocational Aptitude Battery (ASVAB) was developed in 1976 by combining the validated subtests from the various test batteries used by each of the services. One form has been developed to be used in high schools as a guidance tool for counselors and as a recruiting tool. ASVAB helps identify the proper technical training or education needed for various types of occupational areas in the armed forces. In addition, specific tests are used to select candidates for admission to the service academies, reserve officer training programs, officer candidate schools, and specialized programs such as flight training. The Cadet Evaluation Battery, the Air Force Officer Qualifying Test, the Flight Aptitude Selection Test, and the Defense Language Aptitude Test are examples.

PERSONNEL SELECTION AND CLASSIFICATION TECHNIQUES

A number of procedures and devices other than psychological tests are used in personnel selection and classification.

Biographical Data

Almost all employers require prospective employees to complete an application blank, a biographical information blank, or a life history. Employers believe that these forms provide information on what the candidate has done in the past and can be used to predict future behavior. Gatewood and Feild (1990) identify three assumptions for the use of biographical data. The best predictor of applicants' future behavior is what they have done in the past. Applicants' life experiences provide an indirect measure of their motivational characteristics. Applicants are less defensive about describing their previous behaviors on the form than they are about discussing their motivations for these behaviors. Research does indicate that biographical information has been a useful predictor of turnover and job success (Perloff, Craft, & Perloff, 1984). Biographical data also have been valuable in assessing individuals and classifying them into subgroups for better placement and use. Personnel directors sometimes divide large groups of current and former employees into categories of successful and unsuccessful workers and determine which items differentiate the two groups. Cook and Cook (1988) state that biodata instruments are cheaper than other custom-made tests but are not as valid as cognitive tests.

Interviews

The selection interview is one of the basic tools of the personnel director. The purpose of the interview is to gain information about the candidates' qualifications and experiences relevant to the available job. According to Perloff et al. (1984), limited evidence indicates that the procedure is valid and reliable. More systematic, structured, job-related interviews tend to have higher validity. The situational interview, with specific questions based on job-related critical incidents, has also proven to be a valid assessment tool. Studies of the interview show that interviewers tend to make decisions about candidates early in the interview. Negative information tends to be weighed more heavily than positive information, and visual cues tend to be more important than verbal cues. In addition, ratings are affected by how many others are being rated at the same time; clients who share similarities with the interviewer—the same race, sex, and so on—tend to be more favorably rated. Often applicants are rated the same in evaluations, either superior (leniency error), average (central tendency error), or poor (stringency error). Sometimes one or two either good or bad characteristics of an applicant tend to influence the ratings of all the other characteristics (halo error). Sometimes the interviewer allows the quality of the applicants who preceded the present applicant to influence the ratings of the present applicant (contrast effect). Interviewers at times are overconfident in their ability to evaluate applicants; as a result, they make hasty decisions.

Interviewers need training and instruction in the following skills (Gatewood & Feild, 1990, p. 481):

1. Creating an open-communication atmosphere
2. Delivering questions consistently
3. Maintaining control of the interview

4. Developing good speech behavior
5. Learning listening skills
6. Taking appropriate notes
7. Keeping the conversation flowing and avoiding leading or intimidating the intervie-wee
8. Interpreting, ignoring, or controlling the nonverbal cues of the interview

Gatewood and Feild (1990) argue that the selection interview can be valuable if the interviewers are trained in the process, panels are used whenever possible, job-related questions are used, and multiple questions are designed for each KSA (knowledge, skill, and ability) required by the job.

Assessment Center

The most widely used multiple assessment procedure in industry is the assessment center. Primarily, the center has been used to evaluate the potential of candidates for promotion to managerial positions. The center usually analyzes a candidate's performance on several standardized assessment exercises. These are usually selected or constructed from a thorough job analysis of the positions for which the assessment is to be made. According to Perloff et al. (1984), overall evidence suggests that assessment center evaluations are valid and promising predictors for all groups, regardless of sex or minority status. Cook and Cook (1988) call the assessment center the Rolls-Royce of selection methods because it is expensive and uses a wide range of assessment methods and trained assessors. However, the range of assessors and assessment methods reduces bias and gives candidates more chance to show their strengths and weaknesses. Byham and Thornton (1986) indicate that the three most widely used techniques are the in-basket exercises, assigned leaderless group discussions, and interview simulations. They emphasize that the assessment center exercises mirror the majority of day-to-day activities of individuals performing in the target jobs.

To evaluate and select the exercises, the observer needs to ask the following questions:

1. Is the exercise appropriate for the targeted job?
2. Does the exercise represent an important component of the job?
3. Have most of the important dimensions of the job been included in the exercises?
4. Are the exercises efficient and cost effective?
5. Are the exercises valid?
6. Do the exercises accomplish their purpose?

Thornton and Byham (1982) identify nine dimensions frequently measured in assessment centers: (1) the use of oral communication in individual or group situations, (2) planning and organizing strategies (setting goals, making proper assignments, and allocating resources), (3) delegating responsibilities and using subordinates effectively, (4) control (monitoring and regulating activities and responsibilities), (5) decisiveness (readiness in making decisions, rendering judgments, and taking action), (6) initiative (influencing events to achieve goals), (7) tolerance for stress, (8) adaptability (maintaining effectiveness with various tasks, responsibilities, or people), and (9) tenacity. The administrator of an assessment center should keep in mind the following guidelines:

1. Assessment should be based on clearly defined dimensions of the position or behavior in question.
2. Multiple assessment techniques should be used.
3. A variety of job-sampling techniques should be used.
4. Familiarity with the job and the organization is needed; experience in the job or role is desirable.
5. Thorough training in assessment center procedures is necessary for all observers and raters.
6. All pertinent behavior should be observed, recorded, and communicated to other raters and observers.
7. Group discussion and decision-making procedures are used to integrate observations, rate dimensions, and make predictions.
8. Clients should be assessed against clearly understood external norms, not against each other.
9. Observers should guard against first impressions and other errors commonly made in rating and observation.

Job Analysis

One of the key elements in employee assessment is job analysis. Gatewood and Feild (1990) define job analysis as a purposeful, systematic process for collecting information on the important work-related aspects of a job (p. 251). Familiar terms such as knowledge, skills, ability, effort, responsibilities, and working conditions must all be put together so that they describe the quantity and quality of the work performed. Task analysis of the worker's functions is required, including the instruction and training that are part of the job. Variables will relate to both job content and job context. Effort, responsibility, and working conditions are contextual factors; knowledge, skill, and ability are job content factors. Both how-to aspects of the job and level of performance are important. A job analysis should follow these steps:

1. Read and review existing materials and data on the job to be analyzed.
2. Have supervisors and experienced workers in the field meet and discuss the job requirements, producing a list of tasks and roles that are performed.
3. Write the tasks and job characteristics on a flip chart so those involved in the position can react to what you have written.
4. List outputs, knowledge, skills, and abilities, including use of machines, tools, equipment, and work aids needed to get the job done. Get agreement on the tasks performed.
5. Have the workers determine the percentage of time spent on each task or skill.
6. Group common tasks together.

7. Have the workers tell how they know or recognize excellent, satisfactory, or poor performance of the tasks and the job.
8. Construct an instrument to assess job performance and have supervisors and workers react to the tasks and performance standards identified.

An example of a job analysis interview appears in Figure 10.1.

A number of task inventories are available to counselors. They contain three major sections: background information on the respondents, job tasks, and other

---

What is your job title?
Where do you work?
Of what department or division are you a member?

Job Tasks
What do you do? How do you do it? Do you use special equipment?
What are the major tasks you perform on your job? What percentage of time do you spend on each task?

Knowledge Requirements
For each task you perform, what type of knowledge is necessary?
What types of formal and informal knowledge do you need to perform these tasks?
Do you need formal coursework, on-the-job training, etc.?
What level of knowledge is required?

Skill Requirement
What types of manual, mechanical, or intellectual skills are necessary to perform your job?
What types of tasks require these skills?

Ability Requirement
What types of communication skills, oral or written, are required for your job?
Do you have to prepare reports or complete records as part of your job?
What types of thinking, reasoning, or problem-solving skills are required?
What types of quantitative and mathematical abilities are required for your job?
What types of interpersonal abilities are required?
Are you responsible for supervision of other employees?
What types of physical abilities are required?

Physical Activities
What types of physical activities are required to perform your job?
How often are you engaged in physical activities?

Environmental Conditions
What types of environmental conditions do you encounter on your job?

Other
Describe a typical day.
Are there any other facets of your job that need to be described?

Figure 10.1
Schedule for a job analysis interview

miscellaneous information. The Position Analysis Questionnaire (PAQ) is one of the leading commercial measures available. It has six sections:

1. *Information input*—where and how the worker receives information about how to perform the job
2. *Mental processes*—the cognitive skills necessary for job performance
3. *Work output*—tools, equipment, and physical activities needed to perform the job
4. *Relationships with other persons*—how other people are related to and interact with the job
5. *Job context*—the physical and social environment in which the work is performed
6. *Other characteristics*—characteristics and activities not covered by previous questions

The respondent is asked to rate 194 items on the extent of use, amount of time, importance to the job, possibility of occurrence, and applicability to the job in question. The Psychological Corporation has a similar test called the Common Metric Questionnaire.

Work Keys

Work Keys is a system developed by ACT that considers light workplace skills: applied mathematics, applied technology, listening, locating information, observation, reading for information, teamwork and writing. The system has four components (ACT, 1996):

1. *Profiling*—a form of job analysis used to identify the skills and skill levels needed for particular jobs or occupations
2. *Assessment*—a document of the levels of specific Work Keys skills attained by individuals
3. *Instructional support*—information that helps educators and trainers supplement or reinforce curriculum and instruction to address the demands of the workplace
4. *Reports and research*—a way to provide the information individuals need to make career choices, evaluate training programs, and identify qualified individuals

The profiling process is conducted by an ACT authorized job specialist and involves using a subject matter specialist from the company or business to develop a comprehensive list of tasks associated with the job. The profiling team reviews and amends the list for relevance to the job, rating the importance of the tasks to the job and the relative time spent performing those tasks compared with other tasks. From those ratings the team develops a list of the most critical skills and determines the level of each Work Key skill necessary to be successful in the job.

Table 10.1 illustrates how Work Keys relates assessment to skill.

Table 10.1
Work Keys

Assessment	Type of Item	Skill
Problem solving		
Applied mathematics	Multiple choice Pencil and paper	Apply mathematical reasoning to set up and solve workplace word problems
Applied technology	Multiple choice Paper and pencil	Solve technical problems using basic principles of mechanics, electricity, fluid dynamics, and thermodynamics
Observation	Multiple choice Videotape	Pay attention to steps to be followed in a process, to safety procedures, and to quality-control standards
Communication		
Listening/writing	Constructed response Audiotape	Receive and write down information to communicate to someone else; listening scored for accuracy and completeness of response; writing scored for mechanics and style
Locating information	Multiple choice Pencil and paper	Find information on graphics such as bar graphs, tables, diagrams, floor plans, forms, charts, and instrument gauges
Reading for information	Multiple choice Pencil and paper	Read and understand memos, bulletins, notices, letters, policy manuals, and government regulations
Interpersonal teamwork	Multiple choice Videotape	Choose behavior or action that supports the team and leads toward task accomplishment

Guidelines for Employee Selection

A number of guidelines should be followed by personnel workers who are developing an employee selection process:

1. Know the legal and ethical considerations thoroughly.
2. Know basic measurement concepts.
3. Know the steps in collecting evidence of criterion-referenced validity.
4. Be able to analyze the skills, competencies, and personal qualities that relate to successful performance on the job.
5. Consider practical factors such as cost, number of employees involved, and time.
6. Locate tests that purport to measure the characteristics identified for the job.
7. Administer the tests to workers on the job as well as to new applicants.
8. Observe the workers tested and have supervisors report on the performance of these workers.
9. Analyze how the test scores and ratings relate to success on the job.

10. If evidence is favorable, formulate an operational plan to use the data for selection purposes. If evidence is not favorable, select other instruments and get additional ratings.
11. Systematically monitor and evaluate the system.

Cronbach (1984) advocates more persistent and analytical research, starting with the development of limited and measurable criteria. If the criteria are diverse and dependable, he concludes that it is far more instructive to find out what factors predict each of the criteria rather than combine the criteria into one index.

Using the MBTI in Organizations

The Myers-Briggs Type Indicator (MBTI) can be used in most business or industrial organizations as a tool to help individuals understand themselves and others and approach problems in different ways (Hirsh & Kummerow, 1990). The test can help organizations with career planning and development; improved teamwork; conflict resolution; and better individual communication with supervisors, peers, and employers. There are 16 profiles possible on the MBTI. Consider the following example:

> Individuals classified as ESTJ (Extroversion, Sensing, Thinking, Judgment) by the MBTI tend to be analytical, decisive, logical, and tough-minded and are adept at planning and organization. According to Hirsh and Kummerow (1990), such people contribute an ability to see flaws in advance; to critique problems logically; and to organize people, processes, and products.
>
> ESTJs are take-charge leaders who are able to use past experiences to solve problems. They tend to make decisions quickly. They like to work in environments that are task-oriented, organized, and structured in which meeting goals is rewarded. They like their associates to be hardworking people who want to get the job done correctly. However, these individuals do have potential problem areas. They tend to decide too quickly and may lack diplomacy in working with others to get the job done. Sometimes they may not see the need for change.
>
> Hirsh and Kummerow (1990) suggest that ESTJs need to recognize the need to consider all sides before deciding on strategies and the benefits of change. They need to make sure they show appreciation of others and also take time to reflect on their feelings and values.

Personnel Selection Inventory

The Personnel Selection Inventory (PSI) is used by many organizations in their hiring process. The system is designed to identify high-caliber employees who can contribute positively to the organization. It is based on extensive research and is designed to comply with federal EEOC guidelines on fair employment practices and the Americans with Disabilities Act. The test is written at a 7th-grade reading level.

In addition to an individual's scores, the PSI provides a report of significant behavioral indicators, pinpointing any specific area of concern that might need to be investigated. A number of noncognitive scales measure constructs such as honesty, drug avoidance, nonviolence, and tenure (likelihood that the worker will not leave the company) as well as mathematical ability. The following list shows the PSI scales:

Employee/customer relations—tendency to be courteous and cooperative with customers and co-workers

Risk—tendency to engage in dangerous or thrill-seeking behavior

Stress tolerance—experience with stress and ability to tolerate it

Safety—attitude toward safety

Work values—attitude toward work and productive on-the-job habits

Math—ability to total order, count change, figure discounts, etc.

Supervision attitude—likelihood of doing the work assigned and responding appropriately to supervision

Responsibility—probability of engaging in counterproductive or careless, irresponsible behavior

Productivity—having the potential to perform well on the job and be a productive worker

Customer service attitude—tendency to be courteous, cooperative, friendly, and attentive toward customers

Validity/candidness—extent to which an applicant tries to present socially desirable responses instead of actual attitudes and opinions

Validity/accuracy—degree to which a worker understands and carefully completes the inventory

Employee index—composite measure of the overall suitability for hire

The PSI can be scored by optical scanning, computer software, fax, or telephone. The test is available in English, French Canadian, French, and Spanish.

CURRENT TRENDS AND PERSPECTIVES

Employers are showing increased sensitivity in how they use tests for hiring purposes; they do not want to be charged with discrimination and unfair practices. Because employers must go through elaborate validation and documentation procedures when they employ tests for selection purposes, their use of such tests has declined. However, the use of tests for certification purposes has increased. Industry is moving toward multifactored assessment using references, testing, interview data, health and physical examinations, and an application blank. Interviews are now more heavily evaluated than tests; written tests are used most frequently for selecting clerical or entry-level workers. Some industries have initiated diagnostic and developmental testing. But the traditional pencil-and-paper tests have been replaced by techniques such as leaderless group discussion, in-basket exercises, and other types of simulated procedures.

Table 10.2
Major selection techniques in employment testing

Type	Strengths	Problem Areas
Cognitive tests	Easy to develop and validate Tests of reading comprehension and mathematics ability well established Large numbers of applicants can be tested by pencil and paper tests at one time Easy to score and administer	Adverse impact on minority groups and women Have less face validity than work samples
Computer-administered tests	Administration procedures standardized Security enhanced Have time to read and understand directions	Candidate's experience with the computer Might have large numbers of applicants to test and limited computer facilities Might be expensive if additional hardware or software is necessary Possible system problems or software problems Comparability with pencil and paper form of testing
Keyboarding tests	Given on either a computer or a typewriter	Differences in computer equipment used for testing Easier to correct copy on computer than typewriter Individual skilled in a particular word processing package may be affected by negative transfer Possible lack of standardization
Structured interviews	Able to tap interpersonal skills Keep interviewer on track with job-related questions Providing a guide leads to higher level of standardization	Obtaining valid and reliable ratings is difficult Does not allow for probing or follow-up Questions not always job related and appropriate for the position for which individuals are being hired

There is growing concern about the lack of job analysis data and the need for improved validation of the selection procedures used by business and industry. Licensing and certification examinations are being developed, and there is a push for periodic reassessment of competencies for licensing.

Tenopyr (1981) concludes that employment testing is controversial because of its association with the civil rights movement. She points out that there are problems with fairness models because employers cannot afford to use different tests for various subgroups or interpret tests differently for each group. "If employment testing

Type	Strengths	Problem Areas
Situational judgment inventories	Valid approach for customer service and jobs that require human interaction Give a measure of the candidate's practical intelligence Provide insight into the candidate's work ethic and judgment Inexpensive	Hard to develop Expensive to develop Responses and scores influenced by social desirability factor Need follow-up role-playing exercises to better interpret scores Responses limited by the options given
Bio data	Long history of use in business and industry Easy to administer Provide information not given by cognitive tests Combine both rational and empirical approaches on understanding the constructs	Very large number of samples needed to develop questionnaire Candidates not always truthful in their responses Response bias such as social desirability might be a factor Candidate may feel that some of the questions are inappropriate and an invasion of privacy
Physical ability tests	Show whether the candidate has the strength and stamina to do the job	ADA limits use Would require doctor's okay for testing Doctors may not know ADA provisions
Personality tests	Measure constructs not normally assessed by cognitive tests Efficient and inexpensive to administer Present a broad picture of the candidate	Lack of face validity Candidates may fake or cheat on the test Might invade privacy

were outlawed tomorrow, the effect of employment of women in business and industry would scarcely be noticed" (p. 1120).

Since so many businesses are concerned about the cost of employee theft, they often use integrity testing to assess a person's dependability, reliability, or aversion to rules. Although the polygraph can no longer be used for employee selection, other forms of integrity testing are used and have generated much controversy. Applicants are often rejected if they have low scores on integrity tests. Critics point out that these tests do not distinguish between taking small items and big items and present no proof that individuals with low scores are likely to steal. They may have high reliability, but the tests have been criticized for the apparent lack of validation evidence. The high percentage of misclassification errors and the prospect that such instruments can be perceived as an invasion of privacy make their use very controversial (Gatewood & Perloff, 1993). Table 10.2 lists the major selection techniques in employee testing.

Research evidence does not support the validity of the interview or the value of variables such as experience and education. Tenopyr (1981) states that a biodata sheet may have promise, but tests tend to be more valid and reliable than the alternative methods (p. 1123). The most commonly used test is the job knowledge test, not the aptitude test. Tenopyr concludes that a complete abandonment of employment testing and the substitution of other alternatives will not work and will be no more useful than a lottery for jobs (p. 1125). She believes that constructive use of tests can benefit everyone.

Schmidt and Hunter (1981) have found that cognitive ability tests of the kind generally used in personnel selection are valid predictors of successful performance for all jobs in all settings. They also conclude that cognitive ability tests are equally valid for minority and majority applicants and do not underestimate the expected job performance of minority groups. They quote evidence that cognitive ability tests can produce large labor cost savings since individuals with greater cognitive ability tend to have better skills and require less training.

The revision of the General Aptitude Test Battery (GATB) has concerned civil rights advocates since blacks and Hispanics tend to score on average one standard deviation lower than whites. Florez (1991) spoke in favor of not using the GATB for employment screening. He claims that the test has an adverse impact on the protected groups and that the liability pool is increased.

SUMMARY

There are many new approaches to interest and career assessment. The computer has had a tremendous impact on the administration, scoring, and interpretation of these inventories. These tests have proven to be good measures of vocational success, but many factors need to be considered. The maturity, socioeconomic class, and educational level of the client all play important roles in assessing interests. Environment and heredity issues are also involved. A client may not have had the opportunities and experiences necessary to make valid judgments. Family, societal, and peer expectations may influence an individual's pattern of behavior. Temperament may also influence an individual's preferences. The career and vocational counselor needs to have a comprehensive knowledge of the world of work as well as extensive knowledge of assessment techniques and counseling procedures.

Since the 1970s, employment testing has been a center of controversy. Laws and court decisions have had an impact on employment testing. Testing is more widely used in federal and state agencies than in business and industry. In addition, many skilled and professional workers must take certification or licensing examinations, which then become the prerequisite for hiring. Tests in business and industry are primarily used for selection purposes, most often for clerical personnel. The decline in testing has led to a movement away from objective selection procedures. Analysis of research has indicated that testing does not discriminate against minority groups and women but saves the organization money. Nevertheless, currently there is more reliance on clinical judgment and consideration of the applicant's experience and education. Personnel psychologists need to be guided by the nine specific standards for the use of tests in employment contexts.

QUESTIONS FOR DISCUSSION

1. Do you believe that interest tests are not necessary, that the best way to find out about a person's interests is to ask, "What are you interested in, or what would you like to do or be?" Defend your position.

2. Interest tests have been criticized as sexually and culturally biased. What procedures can ensure that tests are developed and used properly by workers in the field?

3. The format and mode of presentation of career guidance tests are changing. Some tests are presented on videotape or computer. For example, a test taker may see video pictures of individuals performing a job. Do you believe that these modes of test administration will prove to be more valid than the traditional pencil-and-paper approach? Which type of inventory would you prefer to take and why?

4. What career guidance tests have you taken? What impact have these tests had on your career development? When did you take these tests? How were the results presented to you? Did you agree with the results? If you were displaced from a current job, would you seek testing to help you identify other possible jobs or career fields?

5. Batteries of tests often include aptitude, values, and interest tests rather than just interest tests alone. The computerized career guidance systems often include short tests of values and aptitudes rather than just asking individuals to rate their aptitudes and values. What factors do you think an individual needs to consider in making a career choice? Are there other areas you would include in the battery? What specific tests would you use? What types of nontest information would you find important? What type of assessment program would you use with high school students? With young adults with handicaps? With clients who have midcareer crises? With older adults?

6. Many employment test experts believe that the guidelines from the courts and government are outdated and make costly demands on employers that are not justified by the latest research. Do you agree or disagree with this position? Why?

7. If you were being considered for promotion on your job, what type of assessment procedures would you consider most valid: pencil-and-paper instruments, behavioral assessments, observation, or some other approach? Why?

8. How would you set up a licensing examination for workers in your field? What things would you do to ensure that you meet all of the legal guidelines?

9. The use of tests by business and industry has decreased, yet we are hearing more about the need for accountability, worker efficiency, and competence to be competitive in the global marketplace. What do you predict the future of employment testing will be? What trends do you predict for the next 10 years?

SUGGESTED ACTIVITIES

1. Evaluate an instrument listed or discussed in this chapter and write a critical review of it. Be sure to read the evaluations of the test in the *Mental Measurement Yearbooks*, *Test Critiques*, and *A Counselor's Guide to Vocational Guidance Instruments*.

2. Administer several career guidance tests and write an interpretation. Tape or role-play the results for the client.

3. Write a position paper on one of the following topics: the role of assessment in career guidance, gender and cultural bias in interest measurement, computer-assisted career guidance testing, or the history of career guidance testing.

4. Develop a career guidance and testing program for one of the following: an elementary school, a junior high school, a senior high school, an employment agency, a counseling and testing service, a mental health agency.

5. Design some nontest techniques to assess individual interests and values. Try your assessment techniques out on a sample of individuals and write a report of your findings.

6. Study the following hypothetical case and answer the questions at the end:

   Mary is 35 years old and has gotten tired of the same job. She has experienced some job burnout and has decided to see what other types of careers she might be able to pursue. She agreed with the counselor that an interest inventory might be a good starting point for discussion. The counselor administered the COPSystem Interest Inventory and the Career Ability Placement Survey (CAPS). Mary had the following profile on the COPSystem:

Cluster	Raw Score	Percentile
1. Science, Professional	26	91
2. Science, Skilled	11	50
3. Technology, Professional	9	45
4. Technology, Skilled	4	30
5. Consumer Economics	11	50
6. Outdoor	18	70
7. Business, Professional	26	85
8. Business, Skilled	14	55
9. Clerical	1	2
10. Communication	15	45
11. Arts, Professional	17	35
12. Arts, Skilled	21	48
13. Service, Professional	30	87
14. Service, Skilled	17	50

   These are Mary's CAPS scores:

1. Mechanical Reasoning	13	83
2. Spatial Relations	15	92
3. Verbal Reasoning	24	98
4. Numerical Ability	18	92

5. Language Usage	22	83
6. Word Knowledge	41	68
7. Perceptual Speed and Accuracy	116	83
8. Manual Speed and Dexterity	230	32

   a. How would you describe Mary's pattern of interests?

   b. How would you describe Mary's pattern of aptitudes?

   c. What further information would you want to have about Mary?

   d. What further information would you want to have about the tests?

   e. The CAPS has a self-interpretive profile and guide. How would you use this with Mary?

7. Interview an individual who is working in the personnel field in business and industry. Find out what types of assessment procedures that person's company uses to hire workers and to promote workers. Report your findings to the class.

8. Conduct a task or job analysis of your current job. Get the reactions of others—that is, your co-workers and your supervisors. See if they agree. Then design assessment instruments to rate individuals in your field. Identify standardized instruments and procedures that might already be available.

9. Design an assessment program to hire workers in your field, to identify professional development needs, and to identify those who should be promoted to managerial levels.

10. Write a critical review of the literature on one of the following topics: assessment centers, job analysis, legal aspects of employment testing, leaderless group discussion, in-basket and situational testing.

ADDITIONAL READINGS

Berk, R. A. (Ed.). (1986). *Performance assessment: Methods and applications*. Baltimore: Johns Hopkins University Press.

The book includes chapters by a number of experts in each field and covers topics such as job analysis, numerical rating scales, behavior-based scales, performance tests, assessment centers, appraisal interviews, utility analysis, validity generalization and predictive bias, and performance distribution assessment. There are also chapters on the application of performance assessment to different applied fields.

Gatewood, R., & Perloff, R. (1990). Testing and industrial application. In G. Goldstein & M. Hersen (Eds.), *Handbook of psychological assessment* (2nd ed.). New York: Pergamon.

The chapter provides an overview of the many types of assessment procedures currently used within business and industry.

Holland, J. L. (1986). New directions for interest testing. In B. S. Plake & J. C. Witt (Eds.), *The future of testing*. Hillsdale, NJ: Erlbaum.

Holland discusses the usefulness, validity, and reliability of interest testing. He identifies some of the current trends as well as the critical issues and opportunities in this area.

Journal of Vocational Behavior, 33(3) (December 1988).

This is a special issue on fairness in employment testing.

Kapes, J. T., & Mastie, M. M. (1994). *A counselor's guide to vocational guidance instruments* (3rd ed.). Falls Church, VA: National Vocational Guidance Association.

This guide provides critical reviews of the major interest inventories, measures of work values, career development inventories, and instruments for special populations.

Kummerow, J. M. (Ed.). (1991). *New directions on career planning in the workplace*. Palo Alto, CA: Consulting Psychologists Press.

Two chapters provide valuable information for the career counselor: one by Kummerow on using the Strong Interest Inventory and the Myers-Briggs Type Indicator together in career counseling, one by Mirabile on competency profiling.

Lawman, R. L. (1991). *The clinical practice of career assessment: Interest, abilities, and personality*. Washington, DC: American Psychological Association.

The author explains which tests to use, what to look for, and how to give feedback.

Pfieffer Library on Training and Development Resources. San Francisco: Jossey-Bass.

The *Pfieffer Library* is available in two formats: CD-ROM or a 28-volume looseleaf set. There are six volumes of inventories, questionnaires, and surveys that contain 80 instruments on topics such as individual development, communication, problem solving, groups and teams, consulting and facilitating, and leadership.

Power, P. W. (1991). *A guide to vocational assessment* (2nd ed.). Austin, TX: Pro-Ed.

The author reviews instruments, techniques, and issues related to vocational assessment of disabled clients, including use of work samples and computers, independent living with behavioral assessment approaches, and so on.

Reardon, R. C., & Lenz, J. (1998). *The Self-Directed Search and related Holland career materials*. Odessa, FL: Psychological Assessment Resources.

The authors provide guidance for using the RIASEC theory and provide case studies for the theory with the assessment tools.

CHAPTER 11

Personality Testing

OVERVIEW

Personality includes all the special qualities people have that make them different from each other—charm, energy, disposition, attitude, temperament, cleverness—and the feelings and behavior they exhibit. Personality assessment is important in describing and understanding behavior; it is also an area of controversy.

Personality tests are a part of the affective domain and are thus not as valid and reliable as most of the aptitude and achievement tests that make up the cognitive domain. They give us a picture of the individual's typical performance. Personality tests are used in clinical settings to identify personal problems and diagnose psychopathologies as well as in counseling and guidance contexts. Just as values and interest tests are important tools in vocational guidance, so are adjustment and temperament inventories important in personal counseling. Personality tests can help individuals gain insight into their own behav-

ior, and they can be used to evaluate change after therapy, growth groups, and assertiveness training. Personality tests can help describe an individual systematically, diagnose a problem, indicate growth or change in behavior, and predict behavior. Such tests are extensively used in research studies.

Workers in the helping professions who plan to use personality tests need more training than is provided in this text. The goal here is to present an overview of the field and a conceptual framework for personality tests. Separate courses are available for individuals who want to develop proficiency in the use of projective and the other clinical-level tests. The potential user needs to have practicum experience under the supervision of an experienced examiner. Specialized in-service training is available for many tests and is valuable even for experienced examiners because of the many innovations in the field.

OBJECTIVES

The chapter should help the reader

✔ Understand the role and importance of theory in personality assessment

✔ Be familiar with the techniques of measuring personality

✔ Know the advantages and disadvantages of different formats in assessing personality

✔ Identify tests and instruments to assess specific dimensions of personality

✔ Locate and discuss sources of information related to personality assessment

✔ Be cognizant of the issues and problems in personality assessment

ROLE OF PERSONALITY THEORY

Many different theories have been developed to explain human behavior. It is not the purpose of this text to summarize these theories but to state that the examiner does need to know them. Theories give us a frame of reference and a way of conceptualizing and interpreting behavior. Many personality tests do have a base in theory, of which the test is a conceptualization.

Henry A. Murray

Personality theorist Henry A. Murray had a tremendous impact on personality assessment in the 20th century. His book *Explorations in Personality* (1938) postulated his concepts of personality. He was aware not only of the biological but also the social and environmental bases of personality. His theory looks at how individuals are affected by external forces and how their attitudes, needs, and values influence their reaction to the world around them. In Murray's theory needs are closely studied. He defined *need* as a constructor—a force that helps individuals organize their perceptions, apperceptions, intellectualizations, connotations, and actions in such a way as to move an existing, unsatisfying situation in a certain direction. He stated that needs manifest themselves by leading the organism to search for, avoid encountering, or (when encountered) attend and respond to certain kinds of presses, or environmental forces (pp. 123–124). His list of psychogenic, or secondary, needs includes abasement, achievement, acquisition, affiliation, aggression, autonomy, blame avoidance, change, cognizance, construction, counteraction, deference, dominance, exposition, excitement, harm avoidance, nurturance, passivity, play mirth, recognition, rejection, retention, sex, succor, and understanding.

Murray saw presses as determinants of behavior. Two aspects of presses are how the individual perceives a press and how the press is in reality. The interaction between needs and presses forms thema, the resulting unit or pattern of behavior. Murray and his associates developed the Thematic Apperception Test (TAT) as an outgrowth of his theories.

The Thematic Apperception Test is a projective personality test that is individually administered and consists of 20 cards with ambiguous pictures on them. The examinee is instructed to make up a story that includes what is occurring in the situation depicted in the picture, what has happened to lead up to that situation, and what will happen in the future. Some of the cards vary according to the age and sex of the examinee, and one blank card is for the examinee to make up her own story. In interpreting the results, the examiner needs to know the common plots for the pictures. If an examinee comes up with a deviation from the normal plots, this information gives some insight into the examinee's characteristic modes of functioning. In the first picture of the TAT a young boy is contemplating a violin that rests on a table in front of him. One person's story might be that the boy was daydreaming about becoming a great violinist. Therefore, he begged his parents to buy him a violin and let him take lessons. They scraped and sacrificed and finally got him the violin, but when they hear him practice, they wish they had spent the money on a haircut instead.

Groth-Marnat (1997) indicates that typical stories given to card 1 revolve around a rebellious boy being forced by his parents or an authority figure to play the violin or around a self-motivated boy who is daydreaming about becoming a violinist. Bellak and Abrams (1997) points out that this picture deals with the general issue of impulse versus control or the conflict between personal demands and external controlling agents. The stories for this picture can provide information about the client's relationships with parents—whether they are domineering, controlling, indifferent, helpful, understanding, or protective. The stories also indicate the need for achievement and how it is accomplished.

Unfortunately, there are no standard scoring procedures that all psychologists accept. Murray used qualitative methods of scoring and focused on five dimensions—the hero; motives, trends, and feelings of the hero (needs); forces of the hero's environment (press); themes and outcomes; and interests and sentiments. Murray believed that the first task is to identify which story character is the focal figure or hero. He believed that examinees identify with this character and project their needs, attitudes, and feelings onto that person.

Murray did try to quantify the degree of each psychogenic need identified in each story by counting the number of times a certain need was mentioned. The same procedure is used for presses. According to Murray's technique, the examiner would thus determine the characteristics of the hero and the patterns of needs and presses. Murray believed that these patterns then combine to make thema, but he gave rather vague instructions on how to analyze thema.

Arnold (1962) has identified five categories of thema:

1. Achievement success or failure, happiness/unhappiness, active effort or passivity
2. Right and wrong, ethical considerations, guilt
3. Human relations
4. Reaction to adversity
5. Interests and sentiments

The TAT has been used by clinicians, school psychologists, and researchers for more than 50 years. It can help access the covert and deeper structures of personality and is less susceptible to faking. With no right or wrong answers, examinees often find the situation interesting and nonthreatening. The test gives a broad measure of personality and has been used to measure cognitive style, creativity, problem-solving skills, verbal fluency, imaginative processes, family dynamics, adjustment, general intelligence, and sexual adjustment (Groth-Marnat, 1997).

Dana (1985) concludes that competent interpretation of the TAT is difficult because there is no consensus on how to score the test. In addition, responses on the TAT are affected by culture, the examiner, and purpose of the assessment. It has been one of the most frequently used assessment procedures, but the validity and reliability of the test are questionable because of unsystematic card stimuli, a lack of standard directions and administration procedures, use of various short forms, an absence of consensual scoring, and a paucity of careful training for interpretation (p. 132).

Listed here are a number of other tests based on Murray's theories:

The Adjective Checklist is a pencil-and-paper personality inventory containing 300 adjectives. It measures 37 dimensions of personality, including 15 need scales based on Murray's theory.

The Children's Apperception Test is a TAT test with 10 cards depicting animals in human social context. Examinees aged 3 to 10 are asked to tell a story for each picture.

The Children's Apperception Test—Human Figure is a TAT projective test using human figures in situations of concern to children. Examinees aged 3 to 10 are asked to tell a story for each picture.

The Edwards Personal Preference Inventory is a pencil-and-paper forced-choice personality inventory designed to measure 15 of Murray's needs. It also yields a consistency score.

Robert's Apperception Test for Children is a TAT test using 16 line drawings as stimuli for examinee storytelling. The pictures emphasize everyday contemporary events such as parent disagreement, affection, observation of nudity, and school and peer interpersonal events. The test is designed to identify emotionally disturbed children aged 6 to 15.

The Symonds Picture Story Test is a TAT test designed for adolescents.

Carl Jung

Carl Jung has also influenced personality test authors. A contemporary of Freud, Jung (1910, 1918) used Galton's word association techniques to diagnose mental illness and developed a projective test employing free association with a list of 100 words. Jung's theory has influenced the development of a major inventory, the Myers-Briggs Type Indicator (MBTI). Jung postulated that four dimensions structure an individual's personality: extroversion-introversion, sensing-intuition, thinking-feeling, and judgment-perception. The MBTI is a personality test used in personal counseling, marital counseling, educational programming, and research in the business and industrial sector. The test is available in several forms, is self-administered, and is used with high school students and adults.

Other Theory-Based Tests

The Personal Orientation Inventory (POI) is based on Maslow's theory of manifest needs and measures values and behaviors important in the development of actualized individuals. It has scales such as time ratio, support ratio, self-actualization value, existentiality, feeling reactivity, spontaneity, self-regard, self-acceptance, synergy, acceptance of aggression, and capacity for intimate contact. The inventory has been useful in evaluating therapy and assessing an individual's mental health.

The Blacky Pictures (Blum, 1950) are a projective test based on Freud's theory and consist of 11 cartoons portraying dogs in situations related to the stages of psychosexual development.

The Vocational Preference Inventory (VPI) is based on Holland's theory of vocational adjustment. A personality-type theory, the first six scales measure the six types: realistic, investigative, social, artistic, enterprising, and conventional. The VPI is a 160-item pencil-and-paper inventory in which examinees are asked to identify occupations they like or might consider.

TECHNIQUES FOR MEASURING PERSONALITY

Koppitz (1982) categorizes personality tests according to techniques—verbal, visual, drawing, manipulative, and objective.

Verbal Techniques

Verbal techniques are defined by Koppitz (1982) as those methods that involve both verbal stimuli and verbal responses (p. 276). The stimuli and responses can be transmitted orally or in writing. With this technique the examinee should have adequate to good language skills and should be able to hear or read words and express himself orally or in writing. Such tests provide a sample of the written and oral expression in addition to the content of the responses.

Projective Questions. Informal techniques such as simple projective questions can be used:

> If you were starting your program of studies over again, would you major in the same field?
>
> If you could be anything you wanted to be, what would you be?
>
> If you had three wishes, what would you wish for?
>
> What do you like most about school?
>
> What do you like least about school?

Sentence Completion. The sentence completion method is another personality test. Rotter and Rafferty (1950) published Rotter Incomplete Sentence Blank (ISB) in three forms—high school, college, and adult. Each form contains 40 items, which are the stems of sentences to be completed by the examinee. The test can be administered individually or to groups, or it can be self-administered. It can also be given orally. The stems are designed to assess attitudes toward family, peers, school, work, anxiety, guilt, and physical disability.

Koppitz (1982) uses the ISB a number of ways. She analyzes the content of the responses, the quality of language and sentence structure, vocabulary, spelling, and handwriting. Rotter provides a scoring system, which rates the completed sentences on a seven-point scale for the degree of conflict revealed. The responses also can be classified in three categories—unhealthy, neutral, and positive or healthy. Koppitz sees the ISB as a useful icebreaker with reluctant and unspontaneous teenagers but believes that it often gives little unconscious or involuntary information about the examinee.

Story Completion Technique (SCT).   There are different versions of this technique, but all are characterized by a verbal stimulus of at least one sentence. Hartshorne and May (1928) and Piaget (1932) all used SCT in their research. Thomas developed 15 stories about a hypothetical child of the same age and sex as the child being tested. Here is an example: "A boy is at the table with his parents. Father suddenly gets angry. Why?" (p. 278). The stories are designed to investigate a child's dreams, fantasies, attitudes, and defense mechanisms, and they can be analyzed for major themes. Ziotgorsky and Wiggs (1986) conclude that story completion methods are valuable instruments in the assessment of personality.

Visual Techniques

With this approach visual stimuli are presented to the examinee, who gives a verbal response. The classic example of this technique, the Rorschach, consists of 10 bilaterally symmetrical inkblots, part in black and gray and part in color. It is a projective test that asks examinees to tell what the blots remind them of. A Swiss psychiatrist, Herman Rorschach, developed this technique and described it in his monograph *Psychodiagnostik* in 1921.

The test has two phases. The first is the free association phase in which the examiner presents the first blot and asks, "What might this be?" (Erdberg, 1985). The second phase is the inquiry phase and starts after the client has gone through the 10 blots. The clinician determines the exact location of each precept and ascertains which variable, color or form, was the primary factor in what the examinee saw in the blot. The test is a perceptual-cognitive task. First, perception is involved in scanning and visualizing the blot. Then cognitive dimensions determine how the individual organizes or structures the response. The examiner considers the location of each response. Was the whole blot used in the interpretation or an unusual detail? The examiner also looks at the determinants of the perception. Was the response influenced by form, movement, color, texture, or dimensionality? The content of the responses is also coded. A number of scoring procedures are available (see Exner, 1991, 1993, 1994, 1995; Exner & Weiner, 1995). Hurt, Reznikoff, and Clarkin (1995) claim that cognitive and ideational processes are measured quite extensively by the Rorschach. Cognitive dimensions can be assessed through the examinee's appreciation of consensual reality, capacity to make use of multiple determinants in creative and novel ways, breadth of content categories, ability to integrate disparate symbolism, attention to detail, and integration of affective and ideational aspects of the response (p. 199).

The examiner must be thoroughly trained in the use of the Rorschach. Groth-Marnat (1997) concludes that a clinician can make numerous errors during administration, scoring, and interpretation. He states that the interpretations need to be checked and rechecked against the overall Rorschach configuration and additional test and biographical data.

Generally, high consistency exists in the scoring of the Rorschach, but less evidence exists of the validity of the test. Anastasi (1996) evaluates four major challenges relating to the validity of the test:

1. Color itself has no effect on response.
2. Scores are influenced by a subject's verbal aptitude.
3. Response productivity is closely tied to age, intellectual level, and amount of education.
4. Earlier validity studies were based on inadequately developed norms.

Overall, the Rorschach continues to be a widely used instrument. Clinicians find it useful because the tasks required bypass the examinee's conscious resistance and help obtain information about unconscious processes.

Other Tests Using Visual Techniques.   The previously described Thematic Apperception Test and Children's Apperception Test are other examples of the visual technique. In addition, Solomon and Starr have used visual stimuli in the School Apperception Test. The drawings in this test focus on school-oriented fantasies, attitudes, and perceptions. The Hand Test for ages 6 to adult is designed to measure attitudes and action tendencies likely to be expressed in overt behavior, particularly aggression. Ten picture cards present hands in different positions, and the examinee is asked to describe the activities portrayed on each card. The examiner analyzes the responses both qualitatively and quantitatively for potential negative behavior toward people and objects in the environment, pathological inefficiency, and social withdrawal.

Drawing Techniques

A number of widely used drawing tests are used to assess personality. Among them are the House-Tree-Person Test, the Draw-a-Person Test, the Bender Visual Motor Gestalt Test, the Draw-a-Family Test, and the Kinetic Family Drawing Test. Drawing seems to be a natural medium for expression in children, and artists have given us insights into the process. Drawing is viewed as a projective technique in which the client shares his perceptions and reactions to the world around him. The style of the drawing—how the individual represents her content—varies tremendously from person to person and drawing to drawing. How the individual approaches drawing reflects how she approaches life situations (Groth-Marnat, 1997).

Draw-a-Person Test.   This test was originally developed by Florence Goodenough to assess the intelligence of children but was expanded by Karen Machover (1949) to include a guide for evaluating personality variables. Koppitz (1968) further refined the scoring system and developed a system of identifying different indicators of emotional difficulties. Some of the general guidelines for interpreting drawings are included in Table 11.1.

Koppitz (1968) identified 30 emotional indicators in children's drawings. She advocates grouping these indicators according to the behavior they reflect. For example, poor achievement might be reflected in poor integration, a monster or a grotesque figure, omission of body, omission of arms, or omission of mouth (Koppitz, 1982, p. 285). The drawing of a hostile aggressive individual might show a big figure, transparency, crossed eyes, teeth, long arms, big hands, or genitals. Depressed, withdrawn children characteristically include tiny figures and short arms but no eyes. Other attitudes that can be identified through analysis of drawings are impulsivity, insecurity, anxiety, and shyness or timidness.

Family Drawings.   Family drawings can give insight into an individual's perception of his place within the family. In the Kinetic Family Drawing Test (KFD), the individual is asked to "draw the whole family doing something." In analyzing the drawing, the examiner looks for who is present or who is omitted or given a substitute. The size of the figures is important as well as their position, distance, and interaction with one another. Special attention should be given to the individual's self-portrayal.

The KFD is analyzed for action, symbols, and style. Action refers to the movement of energy between people and/or objects and can indicate the feeling exhibited. Symbols are interpreted according to psychoanalytic theory. Guidelines are provided in the test manual for interpreting the KFD.

The House-Tree-Person Test (HTP) requires the individual to draw a house, a tree, and a person. Hammer (1985) states that the house may represent the way the individual sees her home situation and intrafamily relationships. Tree drawings are analyzed in terms of size, shape, and the quality of the trunk, branches, leaves, and the ground on which the tree stands; these aspects represent the individual's deeper, more subconscious personal feelings. The drawing of the person is viewed as a conscious representation of the individual and her environment.

Bender Visual Motor Gestalt Test.   The Bender Visual Motor Gestalt Test consists of nine cards containing abstract designs that the examinee is asked to copy onto a blank sheet of paper. The test was designed to measure visual-motor integration and functions as a developmental test for children aged 5 to 11, the period when perceptual-motor skills develop. With older students the test can indicate problems with visual-motor perception resulting from a developmental lag or malfunctioning in the visual-motor areas.

Koppitz (1975) presents a development scale to accompany the Bender test and identifies 12 emotional indicators found in the copied designs:

1. *Confused order*—sign of mental confusion, poor planning and organization
2. *Wavy line*—poor motor coordination and/or emotional instability
3. *Dashes substituted for circles*—impulsivity or lack of interest
4. *Increase in size*—low frustration tolerance, explosiveness
5. *Large size*—impulsivity, acting-out behavior
6. *Small size*—anxiety, withdrawal, constriction, timidity
7. *Fine line*—timidity, shyness, withdrawal
8. *Careless overwork, reinforced lines*—impulsivity, aggressiveness, acting-out behavior
9. *Second attempt at drawing figures*—impulsivity, aggressiveness, acting-out behavior
10. *Expansiveness, two or more pages*—acting-out behavior
11. *Box around one or more figures*—attempt to control impulsivity, weak inner control, need for outer limits and structure
12. *Spontaneous elaboration and/or additions to designs*—unusual preoccupation with own thoughts, fears, anxieties, serious emotional problems

Manipulative Techniques

Some examinees, especially children, have trouble expressing their feelings or attitudes verbally or through drawing but can express themselves in play through manipulative materials such as puppets, toys, or clay. Koppitz (1982) states that play can become a projective technique when used with selected materials in an environment free from distractions and in the presence of an observer (p. 289). This approach is especially useful with children who have social, language, cultural, or physical disabilities. The advantages of this technique are several. Toys are natural or familiar items to children. The technique has both diagnostic and therapeutic value, and children feel comfortable in a play environment.

Kits and anatomically correct dolls are available, but many psychologists find miniature toys and cars to be as good. In addition, many different kinds of hand puppets are available in toy stores, and spontaneous play with puppets is quite often the preference of the child. Children often like to involve the observing psychologist in the puppet show.

Objective Techniques

The most popular and widely used technique to assess personality is the personality questionnaire. It can be administered to individuals or to groups and is easily administered and scored. Questionnaires exist to measure all the different dimensions of personality—attitudes, adjustment, temperament, values, motivation, moral behavior, and anxiety.

Table 11.1
General guidelines for interpreting drawings

Dimension	Interpretation
Location/Placement	
Central	Normal, reasonable, secure person
Upper right	Intellectualizing tendencies, possible inhibition of expression of feeling
Upper left	Impulsive behavior, drive toward immediate emotional satisfaction of needs, orientation toward past
High on page	High level of aspiration, extreme optimism
Low on page	Feelings of insecurity, low levels of self-esteem, depressive tendencies, defeatist attitudes
Lower edge as base	Need for support, lack of self-confidence
Size	
Unusually large	Aggressive, expansive, or grandiose tendencies, acting out potential
Unusually small	Feelings of inferiority, timidness, insecurity, ineffectiveness, inhibition, depressive behavior under stress
Pencil Pressure/ Stroke/Line Quality	
Variable	Flexible, adaptive person
Heavy	Sign of tension, high energy level, forcefulness, and possible acting out tendencies
Light, sketchy	Hesitant, indecisive, timid, insecure person; inhibited personality, low energy level
Shaded strokes	Anxiety
Long strokes	Controlled behavior, inhibition
Short strokes	Impulsive behavior
Straight uninterrupted lines	Assertive and decisive behavior
Organization and symmetry	
Bizarre	Schizoid tendencies
Boxed off	Indication of difficulty in controlling life reliance on external structure or organizations
Element encapsulated	Desire to remove an area of conflict from life
Extremely symmetrical	Obsessive-compulsive, overintellectually defensive, cold, distant, hypertensive, and perfectionist tendencies
Lacking symmetry	Insecurity, poor impulse control, unbalanced self-concept
Erasures	
Excessive	Uncertainty, indecisiveness, and restlessness, obsessive-compulsive personality
Occasional/to improve	Flexibility, satisfactory adjustment
Localized	Conflict or concern about what that area represents

Dimension	Interpretation
Detail	
Absent	Psychosomatic, hypertensive conditions or depressive and withdrawing
Excessive	Obsessive-compulsive tendencies, rigidity and/or anxiety, highly emotional
Bizarre	Indicative of psychosis
Internal organs depicted	Likelihood of romantic delusions, schizophrenic or manic conditions, poor judgment, sexual disturbance indicated by sexual organs
Outer clothing	Voyeuristic or exhibitionist tendencies
Distortions and omissions	
Distortions	Confused, psychotic or schizophrenic condition
Omissions	Conflict, denial
Perspective	
From below	Rejection, unhappiness or inferiority, withdrawal tendencies
From above	Sense of superiority, compensation for underlying feelings of inadequacy
Distant	Inaccessibility, desire to withdraw
Close	Interpersonal warmth, psychological accessibility
Shading	
Shaded area	Anxiety
Complete absence	Character disorder
Color	
Black	Depression, suppression, inhibition, inadequacy, self-deprecation
Red	Problem or danger, anger or violent reaction, need for warmth and affection
Orange	Extroversion, emotional responsiveness to outer world, life or death struggle, ambivalence
Yellow	Cheerfulness, intellectualizing tendencies, lack of inhibition, expansiveness, anxiety
Green	Regulation of affective tendencies, healthy ego, peacefulness, security
Blue	Quiet, calm, well-controlled, cold, distant, fading away or withdrawing
Purple	Inner emotional and affective stimulation, internalization of affect, bold exterior, need to control or possess
Brown	Sensuousness, security, fixations, rigidity, in touch with nature
Gray	Noninvolvement, repressions, denial, emotional neutralization
White	Passivity, emptiness, depersonalization, loss of contact with reality

Minnesota Multiphasic Personality Inventory–2.   The most widely used person-ality adjustment inventory is the Minnesota Multiphasic Personality Inventory–2 (MMPI–2). Revised in 1989, the new edition has been restandardized and audiotaped for blind, illiterate, semiliterate, or disabled individuals. Another option is the box form, with each item on a separate card. The client separates the cards into true and false categories. The test can be machine- or hand-scored. The MMPI–2 is designed to be administered to clients aged 16 and older who have had at least six years of schooling. The reading level of the examinee has to be adequate, and the intelli-gence level should be 80 or higher. Raw scores are translated into *T* scores with a mean of 50 and a standard deviation of 10. There are three major validity scales: Lie (L), Infrequency (F), and Correction (K). An additional "?" scale is a compilation of unanswered items throughout the MMPI. MMPI–2 has several new validity scales: Fb (unusual response inconsistency), TRIN (true response inconsistency), and VRI (vari-able response inconsistency). The test results are considered valid if fewer than 30 items are left unanswered and the other validity scales are within normal limits.

The L, or lie, scale consists of 15 items such as "I never get angry." The scale indi-cates whether the client is consciously or unconsciously presenting himself as a per-fectionist. The F scale consists of 64 items but does not measure a trait. Because the items are answered in a deviant direction by fewer than 10% of the normal adult population, a high score indicates that the test taker has endorsed a large number of serious psychological items.

There may be a number of reasons for high scores on this scale. A scoring error may have occurred, or the client may be a poor reader with limited comprehension. Also, the test taker might be trying to look bad on the test or be confused and have delusions. The answer pattern might be a plea for help from a patient who is exag-gerating symptoms. With an adolescent the score may express defiance, hostility, or negativism (Graham, 1990).

The K, or correction, scale measures defensiveness as a test-taking attitude. The scale has 30 items that cover a wide range of content areas. Low scores usually indi-cate a deliberate attempt to appear bad, but sometimes a self-effacing, self-critical client may actually endorse these pathological tendencies. Ten basic clinical scales of the MMPI are listed in Table 11.2.

Profile analysis is the main interpretive framework of the MMPI. Newmark (1996) indicates that the standard procedure is to interpret profiles according to the two highest clinical scales with *T* scores above 70, provided both scales are within 10 *T*-score points of each other. The resulting code reflects the number of the two scales with the highest scores, the most elevated scale listed first. A number of new scales for the MMPI have been derived by researchers and clinicians—Welsh's Anxiety Scale, Welsh's Repression Scale, Ego Strength Scale, MacAndrew Alcoholism Scale, Dependency Scale, Prejudice Scale, Low Back Pain Scale, and so on.

A number of content scales have been modified or added to MMPI–2: anxiety, fears, obsessiveness, depression, health concerns, bizarre behavior, anger, cynicism, antisocial practices, type A behavior, low self-esteem, social discomfort, family prob-lems, work interference, and negative treatment indicators. The use and interpreta-tion of the revised scales remain equivalent to the older ones. Users should be cau-

Table 11.2

Clinical scales on the Minnesota Multiphasic Personality Inventory–2

Scale	Item Total	Item Content
Hypochondriasis (Hs)	(32)	Undue concern with physical health
Depression (D)	(57)	Depression, denial of happiness and personal worth, lack of interest, withdrawal
Hysteria (Hy)	(60)	Specific somatic complaints, denial of psychological or emotional problems, discomfort in social situations
Psychopathic deviate (Pd)	(56)	Identification with culturally conventional masculine and feminine choices, aesthetic interests, activity-passivity
Paranoia (Pa)	(40)	Delusions of persecution and ideas of reference, interpersonal sensitivity, suspiciousness, moral self-righteousness
Psychasthenia (Pt)	(48)	General dissatisfaction with life, difficulty with concentration, indecisiveness, self-doubt, obsessional aspects
Schizophrenia (Sc)	(78)	Feeling of being different, feelings of isolation, bizarre thought processes, poor family relationships, sexual identity concerns, tendency to withdraw
Hypomania (Ma)	(46)	Elevated energy level, flight of ideas, elevated mood, increased motor activity, expansiveness, grandiosity
Social introversion-extroversion	(69)	Introversion-extroversion, social insecurity

tious of the supplementary and research scales, however, because their validity has not been thoroughly established in clinical settings.

California Psychological Inventory.   In contrast to the MMPI, which is used primarily with abnormal populations, the California Psychological Inventory (CPI) assesses normal personality dimensions concerning an examinee's typical behavior patterns, usual feelings, opinions, and attitudes related to social, ethical, and family matters. The CPI focuses on diagnosing and understanding interpersonal behavior within normal populations. It is a pencil-and-paper personality inventory for individuals aged 12 to 70 who have a fifth-grade or higher reading level. The four clusters of scales are presented in Table 11.3. The CPI is one of the most frequently used personality inventories and has been employed in many contexts and research studies. It is rated as one of the best personality inventories currently available.

Millon Index of Personality Styles.   The Millon Index of Personality Styles (MIPS) (Millon, 1994) is a personality inventory for use with normal adults. The cognitive mode scales (extroversing/introversing, sensing/intuiting, thinking/feeling, systematizing/innovating) correlated .70 with the MBTI. Besides measuring cognitive modes, the MIPS assesses three other dimensions. The first, motivating aims, has

Table 11.3
Scales of the California Personality Inventory

Scales	Descriptors	
Measures of poise, self-assurance, and interpersonal proclivities	Dominance	Conflict × cautious
	Capacity for status	Ambitious × unsure
	Sociability	Outgoing × shy
	Social presence	Self-assured × reserved
	Self-acceptance	Positive self × self-doubting
	Independence	Self-sufficient × seeks support
	Empathy	Empathetic × unempathetic
Normative orientation and values	Responsibility	Responsible × careless
	Socialization	Conforms × rebellious
	Good impression	Pleases others × complains about others
	Communality	Fits in × sees self different
	Well-being	Optimistic × pessimistic
	Tolerance	Fair minded × fault finding
Cognitive and intellectual functioning	Adjustment via conformity	Efficient and well organized × distracted
	Achievement via independence	Clear thinking × uninterested
	Intellectual efficiency	Keeps on task × hard time getting started
Measure of role and personal style	Psychological mindedness	Insightful and perceptive × apathetic and unmotivated
	Flexibility	Likes change × not changeable
	Femininity/Masculinity	Sensitive × unsentimental

three scales (enhancing/preserving, modifying/accommodating, individuating/nurturing). The second, interpersonal behaviors, includes five scales (retiring/outgoing, hesitating/asserting, dissenting/conforming, yielding/controlling, complaining/agreeing). The last factor is response set, which assesses negative impression, positive impression, and consistency. There is also an overall adjustment index. The test takes about 30 minutes to complete and can be hand or computer scored.

FORMAT OF TESTS

A wide variety of item formats are used to assess personality dimensions. The MMPI and CPI use a true-false format; the Adjective Checklist presents a list of descriptive words to check; the Work Environment Preference Inventory uses a Likert-type attitude format. The Edwards Personal Preference Inventory has a forced-choice format: the examinee has a choice between two options on an item. On the Allport-Vernon-Lindzey Scale of Values the examinee ranks options in one part of the test.

FACTOR ANALYTIC APPROACHES

Factor analysis is a statistical method used in test development to see how items cluster statistically. It is also used as an explanatory technique. Factor analysis helps us see how many distinguishable individual differences can be identified in a set of scores and how significant the influence of each dimension is (Cronbach, 1984, p. 283).

Cattell and his associates have developed a series of personality tests based on the factor analytic method. The Early School Personality Questionnaire (ESPQ) is read or presented by tape to children aged 6 to 8. A special answer sheet uses pictures to guide children in marking their answers. The Children's Personality Questionnaire (CPQ) is used with children ages 8 to 12, the High School Personality Questionnaire (HSPQ) with youth ages 12 to 18. The Sixteen Personality Factor Questionnaire (16PF) is used with clients aged 16 or older.

These four tests contain many of the same factors. Consequently, it is possible to look developmentally at the personality dimensions they measure. The publisher offers computer scoring and interpretation of some levels. Special interpretative reports are available on the 16PF: the Personal Career Development Profile, the Karson Clinical Report, and the Marriage Counseling Report.

Eysenck also made use of factor analysis in his test development. The Eysenck Personality Inventory (EPI) for high school students and adults is a 57-item pencil-and-paper inventory that measures two major dimensions: extroversion-introversion and neuroticism-stability. Eysenck found that these two dimensions accounted for most of the variance on personality tests. The Eysenck Personality Questionnaire (EPQ) is a 90-item pencil-and-paper inventory measuring extroversion-introversion, neuroticism-stability, and tough-mindedness or psychoticism. It also has a Lie scale and can be given to individuals aged 7 and older. The authors claim it can be used for clinical diagnosis, educational guidance, occupational counseling, personnel selection and placement, and market research.

Five-factor tests of personality have recently received much attention in the literature. The NEO Personality Inventory–Revised (NEO-PI-R) (Costa & McRae, 1992) is a 240-item test that measures five major domains—neuroticism, extroversion, openness, agreeableness, and conscientiousness. The neuroticism subscales are anxiety, angry hostility, depression, self-consciousness, impulsiveness, and vulnerability. The extroversion subscales are warmth, gregariousness, assertiveness, activity, excitement seeking, and positive emotions. The agreeableness subscales are trust, straightforwardness, altruism, compliance, modesty, and tender-mindedness. The openness subscales are fantasy, aesthetics, feelings, actions, ideas, and values. The conscientiousness subscales are competence, order, dutifulness, achievement striving, self-discipline, and deliberation. The test has several forms: R is for men and women, and S is for an observer. There is also a shorter version, the NEO Five Factor Inventory (NEO-FFI) that has only 60 items and yields just the five domain scores.

DIMENSIONS OF PERSONALITY

Many different dimensions of personality exist. Some tests attempt to assess overall personality, while others focus on one dimension. Following is a representative sample of topics and tests.

Enneagram

The enneagram is a type system with nine dimensions. Riso and Hudson (1996) postulate that this ancient system will help individuals unlock their hidden aspects so that they can become freer and better-functioning individuals. They believe that the study of one's profile leads to self-understanding and then to the understanding of others. Three levels are present in each type: healthy, average, and unhealthy. A number of questionnaires and instruments have been developed. Riso and Hudson (1996) have a paired comparison test, the Riso-Hudson Enneagram Type Indicator (see Table 11.4).

Self-Concept Scales

Self-concept has been a popular construct in theories of personality and vocational development. Some of the widely used self-concept measures are listed here:

Table 11.4
Types included on the Riso-Hudson Enneagram Type Indicator

Type	Healthy	Unhealthy
1. Reformer	Idealistic, orderly	Perfectionistic, intolerant
2. Helper	Concerned, helpful	Possessive, manipulative
3. Motivator	Self-assured, ambitious	Narcisstic, psychopathic
4. Artist	Creative, individualistic	Introverted, depressive
5. Thinker	Perceptive, analytical	Eccentric, paranoid
6. Loyalist	Likable, dependable	Masochistic, plagued by doubt
7. Generalist	Accomplished, extroverted	Excessive, manic
8. Leader	Powerful, expansive	Dictatorial, destructive
9. Peacemaker	Peaceful, reassuring	Passive, repressed

The Coopersmith Self-Esteem Inventory assesses attitudes toward self in social, academic, and personal contexts. Both short and longer versions present items (25 to 58) to be answered "like me" or "unlike me." Specific scales include general self, school-academic, home-parents, social self-peers, and lie. School and adult forms are available.

The Culture-Free Self-Esteem Inventory has three forms, A and B for children and AD for adults (Battle, 1992). The children's scales measure general self-esteem, social self-esteem, academic self-esteem, and parent-related self-esteem. The adult version measures general, social, and personal self-esteem.

The Inferred Self-Concept Scale is a 30-item scale in which parents, teachers, or counselors rate dimensions of behavior indicative of an individual's self-concept.

The Multidimensional Self-Esteem Inventory (MSEI) is a 116-item scale measuring components and levels of self-esteem. The highest level is assessed on the inventory by a global self-esteem scale. There are eight component scales at the intermediate level: competence, lovability, likeability, personal power, self-control, moral self-approval, body appearance, and body functioning. There is an identity integration scale providing a measure of global self-concept and a defensive self-enhancement scale that serves as a measure of the individual's defensiveness.

The Piers-Harris Children's Self-Concept Scale measures self-concept dimensions such as evaluation of behavior, school and intellectual status, physical appearance and attributes, anxiety, popularity, and satisfaction.

The Self-Concept Adjective Checklist is a 114-item pencil-and-paper test of self-concept. It checks physical traits, social values, and intellectual abilities. In K to 3 the stem is "I am. . . ." In grades 4 to 8 an additional stem can be used: "I would like to be. . . ."

The Self-Concept and Motivation Inventory (SCAMIN) assesses self-concept in an academic setting, measuring achievement needs, achievement investment, role expectation, and self-adequacy. The four levels are preschool-kindergarten, early elementary (grades 1 to 3), later elementary (grades 3 to 6), and secondary (grades 7 to 12).

The Self-Perception Inventory assesses how individuals see themselves and how they think others see them, such as students, adults, teachers, and family.

The Tennessee Self-Concept Scale measures identity, self-satisfaction, behavior, physical self, moral-ethical self, personal self, family self, and social self. All 100 items are to be answered on a five-point scale, from completely false to completely true. This scale measures self-concept in terms of identity, feeling, and behavior.

Self-concept measurement is reviewed comprehensively by Wylie (1979, 1990). Shavelson, Hubner, and Stanton (1976) also review some of the major instruments and propose a model of self-concept.

Many studies have related self-concept to achievement, minority group member-ship, and locus of control. Self-concept is believed to be a useful personality con-struct, although its measurement seems to have continued problems because of the lack of validity and reliability of many of the instruments.

Anxiety Tests

A number of scales have been developed to assess the anxiety level in different groups of individuals. One of the most widely used scales is the Manifest Anxiety Scale for adolescents and adults. It uses 50 true-false items to measure an individ-ual's predisposition to react with anxiety in stressful situations. A modified version for children is the Children's Manifest Anxiety Scale, which also includes an 11-item Lie scale.

The State-Trait Anxiety Scale was developed to identify the anxiety an individual feels at a particular moment versus the way he feels generally. One version is for chil-dren in grades 4 to 8, the other for seventh graders to adults. The test was designed to evaluate the individual's anxiety level to identify those who might need help in coping with anxiety. The inventory can be used with clients in counseling and ther-apy as well as for research.

PROBLEMS IN PERSONALITY ASSESSMENT

A number of problems can affect the validity of personality assessment. Many responses to assessment procedures are influenced by variables other than the per-sonality characteristics of the test takers. Psychological, sociological, linguistic, and other variables influence how the examinees respond. These systematic biases are called response set or response style. Lanyon and Goodstein (1982) identified two types of response style: (1) the tendency of the test taker to distort responses in a particular direction regardless of the stimulus content, and (2) the tendency of the test taker to answer deliberately to produce a certain image. The authors conclude that response style can be corrected through careful test construction practices, but deliberate faking is still a major problem.

Acquiescent response style is the tendency of the test taker to respond positively (true or yes) regardless of the item content. Test takers respond to ambiguous items just as they do to clearer items.

The social desirability response set is the tendency of the test taker to choose the response that she believes to be socially desirable rather than the response that more accurately reflects her behavior or feelings. Sometimes a test taker deliberately and consciously chooses the socially desirable response; the individual may be fak-ing goodness because she is defensive about her behavior. Sometimes the choice is unconsciously expressed. Extreme degrees of social desirability help to distort results and affect the validity of the interpretation. Some tests such as the Edwards

Personal Preference Inventory have attempted to control the social desirability of the items by using forced-choice item matching on the basis of social desirability.

Defensiveness also causes test takers to deliberately slant their responses toward being favorable and well-adjusted. Individuals are able on many tests to come up with fake positive profiles. Some personality tests such as the MMPI have scales that can be used to identify the test taker as a good or bad faker.

Kline (1993) mentions another problem, the influence of ability and attainment on test scores. These variables can be a major source of distortion. He points out that "personality questionnaires are, inevitably, somewhat superficial, are usually transparent and thus easy to fake, and ultimately seem too crude to encapsulate the subtlety and richness of personality" (p. 242).

SUMMARY

Many ways of assessing personality have been described, and different dimensions have been identified. It is important to know what method is best to obtain the desired client information. Personality tests have lower validity and reliability coefficients than achievement and ability tests and produce larger standard errors of measurement. Promising tests and techniques exist, but many procedures and instruments require specialized training and supervision for proper administration, scoring, and interpretation.

QUESTIONS FOR DISCUSSION

1. How important is personality theory in personality assessment? Do tests and assessment techniques have an adequate theoretical foundation?

2. What are the many different ways of measuring personality? Compare the advantages of each approach.

3. Faking is one of the major problems on personality tests. How would you structure a testing situation to minimize faking? Do you believe that everybody fakes on personality inventories? Explain your answer.

4. A wide variety of item content measures dimensions of personality, from food choices to occupations to musical preferences. How important do you think the content of the items is in assessing personality? Another factor is the format of the items. What are the advantages and disadvantages of the different formats? For what groups would each format work best?

5. Do you believe that pencil-and-paper personality inventories give a valid picture of an individual's personality? Would situational tests or observation in naturalistic, everyday settings provide more valid information?

SUGGESTED ACTIVITIES

1. Operationally define a personality construct and devise several strategies to measure the construct. Develop some preliminary instruments and give them to a sample of individuals. What was the reaction of the test takers to the form of the test? Analyze the forms. Which form or type of test was most valid? Most reliable?

2. Identify a personality test of interest to you. Critically analyze the test. Read the reviews of the test in the *Mental Measurement Yearbooks* and *Test Critiques*.

3. Interview workers in the helping professions who use tests and find out which personality tests they use and why. Report your findings to the class.

4. Review the research on one of the current issues in personality testing, and write a critical analysis of your findings.

5. Make an annotated bibliography of personality tests, specific test types, or test areas appropriate for your current or future field.

6. Read the following case and answer the questions at the end:

   Case of Salinda

   Name: Salinda

   Age: 18

   Race: African American

   Highest grade completed: 10

   Family: Mother is a single parent who works as a practical nurse in a local hospital

   Salinda's dependents: 2 children, ages 17 months and 3 months.

   Career goal: Telemarketing

   Personality Profile

   Measures of Psychosocial Development

	T Score		T Score
Trust	24	Mistrust	55
Autonomy	41	Shame and Doubt	38
Initiative	28	Guilt	64
Industry	42	Inferiority	65
Identity	59	Identity Confusion	69
Intimacy	36	Isolation	62
Generativity	24	Stagnation	61
Ego Integrity	55	Despair	65
Total Positive	38	Total Negative	60

Values Scale

Inner Oriented	*T Score:*
1. Ability Utilization	23
2. Achievement	31
3. Aesthetics	42
4. Personal Development	37
5. Altruism	40

Physical Prowess

1. Physical Prowess	57
2. Risk	56
3. Authority	46

Group Oriented

1. Social Interaction	36
2. Cultural Identity	45
3. Social Relations	50
4. Working Conditions	43
5. Variety	31

Physical Activity

1. Physical Activity	49
2. Variety	31

Material

1. Advancement	31
2. Economic Rewards	26
3. Economic Security	35
4. Prestige	33
5. Autonomy	49
6. Lifestyle	31

Checked that she was dissatisfied with her status as a student, occupation, leisure, and community.

On the Adult Career Concerns Inventory she was high on the exploration and implementation stages.

On the Myers-Briggs Type Indicator, she was ESFP.

Self-Directed Search SEC

Self-Concept
Self-Esteem Inventory

			Raw Score	*%*	*Standard Score Percentile*
1.	(32)	Total	27	63	56
2.	(16)	General	15	78	59
3.	(8)	Social	7	51	53
4.	(8)	Personal	5	50	51

a. How would you describe Salinda's personality?
b. What additional tests would you like to have Salinda take?

   c. What other types of information would you like to have to enhance your interpretation of the results?

   d. How would you present the test results to Salinda? What would you tell her?

   e. Would it make a difference in your interpretation if Salinda were Native American, Asian, Hispanic, or Caucasian?

   f. Would your interpretation be different if Salinda were seeking career counseling? Personal counseling?

ADDITIONAL READINGS

American Psychiatric Association. (1994). *Diagnostic and statistical manual of mental disorders* (4th ed.). Washington, DC: Author.

The manual describes the criteria and codes for psychiatric diagnostic classification.

Bellak, L., & Abrams, D. M. (1997). *The TAT, CAT, and SHT in clinical use* (6th ed.). Boston: Allyn & Bacon.

The book provides a history and foundations for projective testing and guides examiners in the use of the Bellak Scoring System for the apperception tests.

Bracken, B. A. (Ed.). (1996). *Handbook of self-concept*. New York: Wiley.

A chapter by Keith and Bracken contains a historical and evaluative review of self-concept instrumentation.

Butcher, J. N. (1990). *MMPI–2 in psychological treatment*. New York: Oxford.

The author discusses the use of the MMPI in psychological treatment selection and planning.

Byrne, B. M. (1996). *Measuring self-concept across the life span. Issues and instrumentation*. Washington, DC: APA.

Byrne discusses multiple models and instruments used to measure self-concept over the life span.

Graham, J. R. (1990). *MMPI–2: Assessing personality in psychopathology*. New York: Oxford.

The book is a guide to the revised MMPI–2 and discusses the new validity and content scales.

Gross, M. (1962). *The brain watchers*. New York: Random House.

The author tells of some of the misuses of personality testing and even discusses how to cheat on personality tests.

Groth-Marnat, G. (1997). *Handbook of psychological assessment* (3rd ed.). New York: Van Nostrand Reinhold.

The book contains chapters on the interpretation of projective drawings, the Thematic Apperception Test, the Rorschach, the MMPI, and the California Psychological Inventory. The author presents information on the history and development of the tests, their reliability and validity, their assets and limitations, interpretation procedures, and a bibliography of references and resources.

Handler, L., & Hilsenroth, M. J. (Eds.). (1998). *Teaching and learning personality assessment.* Mahwah, NJ: Erlbaum.

The book covers conceptual models for assessment of different tests and for teaching and learning specialized issues in assessment.

Kline, P. (1993). *The handbook of psychological testing.* New York: Routledge.

The author reviews psychometric theory and methods and discusses the major types of tests. He presents information on the use of tests and describes and evaluates some of the major instruments.

Newmark, C. S. (Ed.). (1996). *Major psychological assessment instruments* (2nd ed.). Boston: Allyn & Bacon.

The book contains chapters on the MMPI, the Rorschach, the Thematic Apperception Test, the House-Person-Tree Test, the Draw-a-Person Test, and Bender Gestalt Test along with chapters on the Kaufmann and the Wechsler scales. This is an excellent source on current research, use, and interpretation of these tests.

Rabin, A. I. (Ed.). (1986). *Projective techniques for adolescents and children.* New York: Springer.

The text has chapters on the major projective personality tests used with children, such as the Thematic Apperception Test, the Michigan Picture Test–Revised, the Separation Anxiety Test, the Rorschach, the Hand Test, and the Story and Sentence Completion Tests.

Reilley, R. R., & Reilley, B. A. (1991). *MMPI–2 tutorial workbook.* Austin, TX: Pro-Ed.

The workbook contains information on the revised test and is designed for professionals who want a refresher in the appropriate use of the test. Topics such as computer assessment, report writing, psychometric scaling, and sources of information on the MMPI–2 are presented.

Schinka, J. A., & Green, R. L. (Eds.). (1997). *Emerging issues and methods in personality assessment.* Mahwah, NJ: Erlbaum.

This book has three parts: (1) "Personality Assessment Instruments: Current Status and Future Research Directions," (2) "Continuing Issues in Personality Assessment," and (3) "Advances in Statistical Methods for Personality Assessment Research."

Wylie, R. (1990). *Self-concept instruments.* Lincoln: University of Nebraska Press.

Wylie critiques the major self-concept scales.

CHAPTER 12

Assessment of Adjustment

OVERVIEW

Tests are used as a part of the clinical assessment or in individual counseling. In both instances the tests are individualized and given one to one. The setting may be in a hospital, mental health clinic, prison, treatment facility, or counselor's office. A wide variety of tests and assessment procedures may be used. A number of problems and issues relate to the use of tests for clinical assessment and counseling.

OBJECTIVES

The chapter should help the reader become aware of

✔ The models of measuring adjustment

✔ Types of tests and techniques that can be used effectively

✔ Ethical standards, legal issues, and standards of use that need to be followed

✔ Issues and concerns about the use of tests in clinical assessment and counseling

CLINICAL ASSESSMENT

Clinical assessment is the process that counselors and psychologists use to gain information about a client. The examiner is often interested in diagnosing the problems of a client and may also want to describe the client's behavior, predict future behavior, or evaluate therapeutic interventions (Korchin & Schuldberg, 1981). Tests and assessment procedures are selected to provide information useful in decision making while taking into account the special background and characteristics of the client. The client may be a child, adolescent, or adult; a patient in a clinic or hospital; an inmate in a prison; or an outpatient in a clinic.

Types of Tests and Assessment Techniques

There is a wide variety of tests and assessment techniques. The choice of which to use is influenced partly by the theoretical orientation of the counselor, partly by the type of decision to be made. In most cases the counselor uses more than one technique, choosing among aptitude batteries, ability tests, personality tests, projective techniques, interview schedules, checklists, rating scales, and behavioral observations in natural or contrived situations. There are several reasons for appraisal:

1. To determine which DSM-IV classification is appropriate
2. To see whether neurological impairment exists
3. To help decide which type of treatment, counseling, or therapy would be most appropriate
4. To prescribe the proper instructional strategies
5. To identify the client's assets, achievement, aptitude, or personality to guide in rehabilitative, therapeutic, or educational planning
6. To determine whether an inmate should be considered for a release program
7. To evaluate the effectiveness of treatment, counseling interventions, and group sessions

Models of Clinical Assessment

One popular model of clinical assessment is the psychodiagnostic model influenced by the theories of Murray and Rapaport. The model is holistic and is intended to describe the client in a variety of ways. The model calls for the use of a number of procedures, the measurement of various areas of psychological functioning, assessment of conscious as well as unconscious levels, use of projective techniques as well as objective personality instruments, interpretation based on scorable responses and symbolic signs, and a description more personal and individualistic than normative (Holt, 1968). The counselor or psychologist is the key individual in this processes and has to organize and conceptualize the questions to be asked and decide on techniques. Clinical judgment is crucial.

A second model is psychometric and emphasizes more objective use of tests and assessment instruments. Tests must be reliable and valid for the purposes identified;

the test findings rely on the criterion validity of the tests rather than the clinical judgment of the examiner. The two positions have been in contention for several decades and are part of the controversy between clinical and statistical prediction (Meehl, 1954).

Rogers (1942) believed that assessment results were not that valuable. He argued against formal assessment, believing that no discovery about a client makes any difference in psychotherapy until the information becomes evident to the client in the course of the therapeutic encounter. Individuals holding to the humanistic approach do not use tests routinely or as a precondition to therapy. If used, the testing process includes the client as a coassessor rather than an object being studied by a detached examiner. Behavioral psychologists and counselors look for objective behavioral indicators, not tests, to measure traits, drives, motives, and unconscious wishes.

Standards for the Clinical Use of Tests

Standards for Educational and Psychological Testing lists standards that should be considered when using clinical tests. These standards are important because clinicians deal not only with the diagnostic use of tests but also with the prediction of behavior and response to treatment.

A number of standards relate to the validity of tests and test interpretations. Even though a test is used for clinical purposes, the examiner must still be constrained by the same need for criterion-referenced evidence of validity that exists with other test uses.

The standards also call for the protection of client rights. The counselor or psychologist is expected to share with clients the test results and the interpretations as well as information about the range of error for interpretations when such information would be beneficial to the client. The sharing of information is to be in words that clients can understand.

TESTS IN COUNSELING

Many counselors use tests as a tool in working with their counselees. Research has shown that standardized tests can be a valuable part of the counseling process.

Counselors tend to use tests to help their clients learn more about their own

1. Occupational or work values
2. Career goals and vocational interests
3. Career development
4. Occupational knowledge and preferences
5. Educational interests
6. Achievement, aptitude, and abilities
7. Problem-solving and coping skills

8. Study skills
9. Relationships with others
10. Attitudes and motives
11. Developmental needs
12. Attitudes toward family, spouse, marriage, and significant others

Techniques

Counselors use all of the different types of tests and techniques listed in chapters 6 through 11. They use both formal and informal methods—pencil-and-paper invento-ries, projective techniques, checklists, situational tests, interviews, simulations, inventories, and work samples. For tests to be an effective tool in counseling, coun-selors need to be skilled in helping their clients understand and interpret the results. Counselors need to be able to facilitate the appropriate use of the data in decision making. Counselors use tests in all types of settings, such as agencies, government, industry, private practice, and schools. Test use is influenced by setting as well as the background of the counselor and the test taker.

Counselors use a wide variety of tests in clinical assessment.

Standards for Use of Tests in Counseling

Professional standards provide guidelines for the use of tests in counseling. Accord-ing to the *Standards for Educational and Psychological Testing* (AERA, APA, & NCME, 1985), counselors are responsible for reviewing the following items:

1. Interpretive material provided to the test taker, to check for accuracy, clarity, and usefulness
2. Technical data, to see if separate norms should be used for males or females (an extremely important step with interest tests and an aid in discussing prior test scores and assessing the accuracy of current scores)

3. Manual, to determine the rationale for the specific combination of tests used and the justification of the interpretive relationships among the scores
4. Distributions of scores by gender, race, and ethnic group

The counselor should also caution the client not to rely solely on the test results but to consider other test scores, observations, and other relevant information on personal and social skills, values, interests, accomplishments, and experiences. The counselor should encourage multiple valid assessments of the client's abilities, interests, and personality. The counselor should look at school or work performance, participation in extracurricular activities, and hobbies. The counselor should also be sure that interpretive materials and illustrations are made relevant to the client.

CURRENT TRENDS

Korchin and Schuldberg (1981) report that there is a decline in the use of clinical testing for a variety of reasons.

Many new roles are available for the clinician such as therapy, administration, teaching, research, and community programs. Several schools of psychology and counseling are opposed to testing. Questions regarding the reliability and practicality of traditional clinical practices have been raised, and research has not supported the value of testing.

Changes also have occurred in graduate programs at universities, and testing courses are not considered as valuable as they once were. Also, problems in testing methods have occurred when the clinician assumes a secondary and passive role.

Many issues, such as invasion of privacy, have been raised concerning the use of psychological tests. The reactions to the process many times have been negative because of the cost in time and money.

BEHAVIORAL ASSESSMENT

Behavioral assessment centers on the circumstances of behavior rather than the reasons for it. The process relies greatly on observation, especially observation that requires few inferences on the part of the observer. Sometimes clients are required to keep a log of their behavior. Counselors use behavioral assessment in naturalistic and contrived settings, role playing, psychodrama, and interviews. Behavioral assessment is also used in a number of different ways, such as screening, identifying a problem, designing the intervention, monitoring progress, following up, and evaluating cases. A number of strategies are used: interviewing techniques, behavior checklists, observational schedules, self-monitoring procedures, simulation and analogue methods, physiological assessment, and computer-assisted assessment (Ollendick & Greene, 1990).

Behavioral Observation

One of the major methods of behavioral assessment is observation, normally of a specific, observable set of behaviors. Observations can be carried out in different contexts and environments, but a number of factors should be considered (Ollendick & Greene, 1990; Haynes, 1990):

1. Observers should be familiar with the behavioral categories to be studied.
2. Observers should have been trained to use videotapes, films and other audiovisual equipment.
3. Observers should have a chance to check their observations with other raters and with the standards established in the training sessions.

Several problem areas relate to this technique. First is the problem of reactivity. If the client knows he is being observed, his behavior may be quite different from when he is unaware of it. People want to play roles and put themselves in a good light. Second, when an observer has to assess a number of individuals over time, fatigue and boredom may occur. In addition, observers may have some unconscious or conscious biases that interfere with objective results. Observer expectations can also influence client behavior.

Two major types of observation are participant and nonparticipant. A group leader responsible for conducting a group but also monitoring the behaviors of individuals in the group is an example of participant observation (Haynes, 1990). In nonparticipant observation the observer does not become a part of the situation. For example, a teacher on playground duty might be able to observe a certain student without her knowing she is being observed, thereby eliminating the problem of reactivity.

Observation can be highly structured. When time sampling is part of the system, every so often the observer might classify the behavior taking place and record the person responsible for it. The procedures for coding can be simple, requiring just a check by a category, or complex, demanding analysis. Unstructured observation might describe or identify the following components:

1. Purpose and object of the observation
2. Physical environment
3. Acts or events that have taken place
4. Time dimensions
5. Actors or people observed
6. Goals of the persons observed
7. Feelings of the observer

Students of ethnographic observation follow outlines like this when they are observing. They are interested in naturalistic observation and do not usually have preconceived theories or set observational schedules to follow.

Self-Monitoring

Self-monitoring is a widely used technique in behavioral assessment. It can be used effectively as a therapeutic technique or simply as a data-collecting device to assess low-rate behaviors such as migraine headaches, high-rate or continuous behaviors such as blood pressure, and other behaviors such as eating patterns, smoking, caffeine intake, and the like. It is a reactive type of measurement technique because attention is focused on the targeted behavior and the individual knows what events are to be observed. It is a valuable strategy to provide accurate information to workers in the helping professions, and it can provide client reinforcement and feedback. The success of the technique depends on the goals of the monitoring, the quality of the instructions given, and the number of behaviors being monitored. The accuracy of this method depends on the motivation and cooperation of the client. A number of recording devices can be used—for example, pocket diaries, golf counters, tape recorders, and phone-answering devices. When using self-monitoring with a client, the counselor should follow these procedures:

1. Give explicit definitions and examples of the targeted events and explain their possible relevance to the problem at hand.
2. Give explicit monitoring instructions on how to record the behavior.
3. Illustrate the use of the form or recording device and provide practice exercises.
4. Ask the client to repeat the target definitions and self-monitoring instructions.
5. Test client understanding of the assignment.
6. Check with the client during the period specified for any questions or problems.

Simulation and Analogue Methods

Often a counselor wants to find out what a person might do in a given situation, testing a hypothesis before the situation develops in reality. This procedure can be used as an evaluation tool to see whether training has had an effect. It also is a means of giving individuals a chance to rehearse or practice a needed skill as well as a non-threatening technique in the therapeutic process. Role playing is often used to evaluate the client's social skills (Haynes, 1990). The procedures are these: (1) analyze the task the client is to do; (2) develop realistic situations; (3) provide role-playing opportunities.

The technique has the advantage of helping clients distinguish between the form and functions of the behaviors being assessed. It also allows the counselor to assess performance in highly personal and intimate situations, and it can provide a more flexible and individualized assessment.

ASSESSMENT APPROACHES

Inventories Used in Assessment

A number of other inventories are widely used for assessing individuals in the mental health field. The MMPI was discussed in the last chapter and is the most widely used adjustment test. Millon has developed several instruments, including the Millon Clinical Multiaxial Inventory (MCMI-III), which is used to assess the DSM-IV categories of personality disorders and clinical syndromes. The inventory uses 20 clinical scales, divided into three categories:

Basic Personality Patterns (DSM-IV/Axis II)
1. Schizoid (asocial)
2. Avoidant
3. Dependent (submissive)
4. Histrionic (gregarious)
5. Narcissistic
6. Antisocial (aggressive)
7. Compulsive (conforming)
8. Passive-aggressive (negativistic)

Pathological Personality Disorders
S = schizotypal (schizoid)
C = borderline (cycloid)
P = paranoid

Clinical Symptom Syndromes (DSM-IV/Axis I)

A = anxiety	B = alcohol abuse	PP = psychotic delusions
H = somatoform	T = drug abuse	CC = psychotic depression
N = hypomanic	SS = psychotic thinking	D = dysthymic

The MCMI-III has two validity indicators. The W-Weight factor is a scale that suppresses the distorting effects of either psychological defensiveness and self-enhancement or emotional complaining and self-depreciation. The V-Validity index is a scale that detects those who fail to cooperate, are unable to comprehend the items, or are too disturbed to answer the items relevantly.

Two computerized interpretations are available from the National Computer Systems and MICROTEST assessment software. The first is a clinical interpretative report that includes the profile of the client and a detailed narrative explaining the psychodynamic relationship between the client's personality patterns of behaving and feeling and the clinical symptoms she may be exhibiting (Millon & Davis, 1996).

The second is the correctional interpretive report that distinguishes the enduring personality characteristics from the more acute maladaptive symptoms. The report focuses on difficulties the client may have in adjusting to imprisonment, her trustworthiness, problems with authority, and general antisocial behavioral tendencies. The report provides implications for management and rehabilitation strategies.

The Millon Behavioral Health Inventory (MBHI) is intended to help mental health workers design a comprehensive treatment plan for adult medical patients. The MBHI provides information on the client's basic coping styles, problematic psychosocial attitudes and stressors, and information on attitudes toward treatment intervention. The 20 scales on the MBHI are classified in four areas—basic coping skills, psychogenic attitudes, psychosomatic correlates, and prognostic indexes. The scales under basic coping styles relate to the way in which the individual reacts to health care personnel, services, and medical regimens. The scales are titled introversive, cooperative, confident, respectful, inhibited, sociable, forceful, and sensitive.

The six scales under psychogenic attitudes assess problematic psychosocial attitudes and stressors; they are titled chronic tension, premorbid pessimism, social alienation, recent stress, future despair, and somatic anxiety. The three scales under psychosomatic correlates show the similarities of clients to patients with psychosomatic complications; the scales are titled allergic inclination, cardiovascular tendency, and gastrointestinal susceptibility. The three prognostic indexes identify possible treatment problems or difficulties—pain treatment responsivity, life threat reactivity, and emotional vulnerability. The total test consists of 150 true-false items and is written at the eighth-grade reading level.

The Millon Adolescent Personality Inventory (MAPI) is geared to the specific concerns and behaviors of adolescents. The MAPI provides information on the social functioning of adolescents, including information on their relationships with family and peers, self-esteem, impulse control, and social tolerance. The 22 scales are grouped under four categories—personality styles, expressed concern, behavioral correlates, and reliability and validity indexes. Here are some items similar to those asked on this test:

T F   I like to be with people who go to church regularly.

T F   I feel tense when I think of what I will be expected to do in school this year.

T F   I worry about my drug habits getting out of control.

Two types of report forms are used—one for clinical use, the other for educational or guidance use.

The Clinical Analysis Questionnaire (CAQ) (Krug, 1980) is designed to measure both normal and pathological traits and provides a multidimensional profile of the client. The test has 28 scales, 16 of which measure normal personality traits included on the Sixteen Personality Factor Questionnaire, 7 of which measure various primary aspects of depression, and 5 of which measure factors identified in the Minnesota Multiphasic Personality Inventory pool. The clinical scales are hypochondriasis, suicidal depression, agitation, anxious depression, low-energy depression, boredom and withdrawal, paranoia, psychopathic deviation, psychasthenia, and psychological inadequacy. The test can be administered to individuals aged 16 and older; it has an average reading level of 6.7. A number of second-order factors can be scored by the equations developed through factor analysis—extroversion, anxiety, tough poise, independence, superego, socialization, depression, psychoticism, and neuroticism. The test belongs to the family of factorial-derived tests discussed in the chapter on personality testing.

The Personality Assessment Inventory (PAI) is a 344-item, self-administered, objective inventory used to assess critical clinical aspects of personality. The PAI has 22 nonoverlapping full scales, 4 validity scales, and 11 clinical scales. The clinical scales measure somatic complaints, anxiety, anxiety-related disorders, depression, mania, paranoia, schizophrenia, borderline features, antisocial features, alcohol problems, and drug problems. The treatment scales involve aggression, suicidal ideation, stress, nonsupport, and treatment rejection. The validity scales cover inconsistency, infrequency, negative impression, and positive impression. A short form of the PAI consists of the first 160 items.

The Adolescent Multiphasic Personality Inventory (AMPI) is an MMPI test for adolescents (ages 10 to 19) and has a fourth-grade reading level. The AMPI has 133 items and scales that are parallel to the MMPI.

The Child and Adolescent Diagnostic Scales are self-report tests that can be scored and profiled in 5 minutes and take about 15 minutes to take. These scales measure DSM-IV dimensions such as attention deficit/hyperactivity disorder, oppositional defiant disorders, overanxious disorders, identity disorders, eating disorders, substance abuse disorders, and so on.

A number of other personality assessment inventories might be useful to mental health counselors, such as the Analysis of Coping Style, the Beck Anxiety Inventory, the Beck Depression Inventory, the Beck Hopelessness Scale, the Brief Symptoms Inventory, the DSM-IV Multiaxial Evaluation, the Eating Inventory, the Global Assessment of Functioning, the Reynolds Adolescent Depression Scale, the Rust Inventory of Schizotypal Cognitions, the Self-Description Questionnaire, the State-Trait Anxiety Scale, the Suicide Ideation Questionnaire, and the Therapeutic Reaction Scale.

Psychodiagnostic Testing

Clinicians quite often have been trained to use and interpret certain classic tests in the field such as the Wechsler tests, the Rorschach, the Thematic Apperception Test (TAT), the Sentence Completion Test, the Bender Visual Motor Gestalt Test, and the MMPI. Katz (1991) identifies the best tools for assessing different diagnostic categories:

Intellectual functioning—Wechsler tests, Bender Gestalt, Draw-a-Person (DAP), Stanford-Binet–IV

Brain damaged—Wechsler tests, Bender Gestalt, and specialized tests

Psychotic—Rorschach, MMPI-2, MCMI-III, biographical data blank

Neurotics—MMPI-2, Rorschach, TAT, DAP, PAI, MCMI-III

Sociopathic—TAT, behavior, MMPI-2, MCMI-III

Passive-aggressive—TAT, behavior, Sentence Completion

Schizoid—Rorschach, TAT, DAP, MMPI-2

Katz looks for patterns when he analyzes the test results. For psychotic individuals he might find withdrawn or disturbed behavior exhibited on a test battery. The Wechsler Adult Intelligence Scale–Revised (WAIS-R) might show variation or disturbed and odd thinking. On the MMPI-2, the client might score high on the schizophrenia, paranoia, and psychasthenia scales. On the Sentence Completion Test the sentences will show confused, illogical, and bizarre patterns. The TAT might reveal odd elements, bizarre twists, and possible anguish.

Groth-Marnat (1997) recommends that the data gained through observation, interviewing, and testing be combined to complete the diagnosis. The crucial elements in determining treatment are the individual's level of intellectual functioning, the nature of his anxiety, defensive structures, self-image, self-esteem, sexual identity, and the balance between impulse and control.

Neuropsychological Assessment Batteries

Neuropsychological assessment refers to testing for brain damage or for organicity (Goldstein, 1984). Such tests are sensitive to the condition of the brain. Brain damage most often affects the cognitive functions, such as memory. Some individuals might show loss of speed in performing skilled activities or psychomotor or perceptual-motor activities. Some have deficits in auditory or tactile perception. Others have problems with visual-spatial skills.

One of the most widely used instruments for neuropsychological assessment is the Halstead-Reitan Neuropsychological Test Battery. This test uses Wechsler intelligence scales but also includes a number of tests used originally by Halstead, some added by Reitan, and several added by others. Some tests within the battery call for tactual performance. For example, the Halstead Tactual Performance Test uses the Seguin-Goddard formboard, but the test taker is blindfolded and has to place all 10 blocks into the formboard using only a sense of touch. The test taker has to do this three times: first, with the preferred hand, then with the other, and finally with both hands. On the Klove Roughness Discrimination Test the test taker must order four blocks, each covered with a different grade of sandpaper. The blocks are presented behind a blind, and the test is scored on the time the client takes and the number of errors made with each hand.

Also included in the Halstead-Reitan Battery are visual and psychomotor scales. For example, the Reitan Aphasia Screening Test contains both language and copying tasks. The copying tasks require the test taker to make a copy of a square, a Greek cross, a triangle, and a key. The language functions measured are naming, repetition, spelling, reading, writing, calculation, narrative speech, and left-right orientation. The language section is scored by listing the number of aphasic symptoms. The Klove Grooved Pegboard Test requires the test taker to place pegs shaped like keys into a board containing recesses oriented in randomly varying directions. The test taker performs first with one hand and then the other. Some of the other tests on the scale are the Finger Tapping Test, the Halstead Category Test, the Perceptual Disorders Test, the Seashore Rhythm Test, the Speech Perception Test, the Trail Making Test, and the Visual Field Examination. The battery takes 6 to 8 hours to administer.

Another widely used battery is the Lauria-Nebraska Neuropsychological Battery. The test has 11 content scales:

1. Motor measures a wide variety of motor skills.
2. Rhythm measures nonverbal auditory perception, such as pitch discrimination and rhythmic patterns.
3. Tactile measures tactual discrimination and recognition.
4. Vision measures visual-perceptual and visual-spatial skills.
5. Receptive speech measures perception of sounds from simple to complex.

6. Expressive speech measures ability to repeat sounds, words, and word groups and to produce narrative speech.
7. Writing measures ability to analyze words into letters and to write under varying conditions.
8. Reading measures ability to make letter-to-sound transformations and to read simple material.
9. Arithmetic measures knowledge of numbers and number concepts and the ability to perform simple calculations.
10. Memory measures short-term memory and paired associate learning.
11. Intellectual processes measures sequencing, problem solving, and abstraction skills.

The test is shorter than the Halstead-Reitan and helps screen a large number of areas that may be affected by brain damage.

There is a variety of tests available from the Benton Laboratory of Neuropsychology. A kit is available, or some tests can be purchased separately. Examples include the Facial Recognition Test, the Judgment of Line Orientation Test, the Pantomime Recognitions Test, the Right-Left Orientation Test, the Serial-Digit Learning Test, the Tactile Form Recognition Test, the Temporal Orientation Test, and the Visual Form Discrimination Test.

Other new instruments include the following:

The Kaufman Short Neuropsychological Assessment Procedure (K-SNAP) was developed by H. S. Kaufman and N. L. Kaufman to measure cognitive functioning of individuals aged 11 to 85. The test measures attention and orientation, simple memory, and perceptual skills.

The Quick Neurological Screening Test (QNST-2) (1997) assesses 15 areas of neurological integration as they relate to learning. The scales are control of large and small muscles, motor planning, motor development, sense of rate and rhythm, spatial organization, visual and auditory skills, perceptual skills, and balance orientation.

The Ross Information Processing Assessment, Second Edition (RIPA-2) (1996) is designed to assess any cognitive and linguistic deficits and determine severity levels. The scales on the RIPA-2 are immediate memory, recent memory, spatial orientation, orientation to the environment, recall of general information, organization, and auditory processing and retention.

INTERVIEWS

The interview, especially the structured interview, has become an important tool in clinical assessment. The DSM-IV provides a structured guidebook. In addition to the verbal content of the interview, a clinician is often interested in a client's nonverbal behavior or cognitive style. Currently, more attention is being placed on the cognitive areas for knowing and understanding a client.

Structured interviews call for the interviewer to ask each interviewee exactly the same questions in the same manner. A specific set of questions is usually read to the client. Unstructured interviews, on the other hand, do not have a specific plan or order in which the topics are presented. Many examiners believe the best rapport is established when they use words familiar to clients and topics the clients are willing to discuss (Wiens, 1990). Consequently, the same set of questions might not be asked, and the interviewer might use more open-ended questions such as "Tell me about yourself." The advantages of the structured interview are that it assures that specific information will be collected from all clients and it does not require as much training because all interviewers have a list of questions in a prescribed order. The advantages of the unstructured interview are that it gives the interviewee a chance to determine what is important to talk about; it allows the examiner to pursue important but unanticipated topics; and it provides an opportunity to judge the interviewee's behavior in an unstructured situation.

Computerized versions of structured interviews are available. The Structured Clinical Interview for the DSM-IV provides several report options, helps clinicians screen clients on Axis I in approximately 25 minutes, and covers areas such as mood disorders, anxiety disorders, psychoactive substance abuse disorders, somatoform disorders, eating disorders, and psychotic symptoms. A sample structured interview schedule, appropriate for use in an alcoholic treatment facility, is included in Figure 12.1.

Certain general guidelines should be considered before and during an interview:

1. Have a clear idea of why the individual is being interviewed. The kinds of questions asked depend on the types of inferences, decisions, or descriptions to be made after the interview. Better information results from specific goals.
2. Be concerned about the physical setting or environment for the interview. Interviews will go better if the environment is quiet and comfortable. If the room is noisy or has poor lighting, it may detract from the quality of the information gained. Comfortable and private facilities permit the client to relax without the confidentiality and privacy of the interview being threatened.
3. Establish rapport with the interviewee. Good rapport leads the interviewee to be cooperative and motivated.
4. Be alert to the nonverbal as well as verbal behavior of the client. How a person says something may be as important as what is said.
5. Be in charge and keep the goals of the interview in mind. Have the interview schedule readily available but do not suggest answers. Give the client time to answer and do not become impatient during periods of silence.

There are a wide variety of checklists available to help clinicians organize the information gained in the interview and help structure the interview. Some examples follow:

The Mental Status Checklist provides a comprehensive examination of the mental status of the client. There are versions for children, adolescents, and adults.

The Personal History Checklist facilitates recording personal history during intake sessions for children, adolescents, and adults.

Name_____ Date _____

Address_____ Home phone _____

_____ Business phone _____

City_____ State _____ Zip _____

Race_____ Sex _____ Height_____ Weight _____ Age _____

Date of birth _____ Place of birth _____

Next of kin_____ Relationship _____

Address _____

Current employment_____ Duration _____ Salary _____

Spouse's employment _____

Other sources of income _____

Referred by _____

Health insurance _____

Current marital status _____ Number of marriages and duration _____

_____

Children (*sex and ages*) _____

Type of residence_____

Number in household_____ Head of household _____

Church membership_____ Attendance _____

Belief in higher power _____

_____

Current health problems _____

Physical handicaps _____

Serious illness/surgery _____

_____

Current medications _____

Schools attended _____

Years_____ Certificates/diplomas/degrees _____

_____

Vocational and technical training _____

Military service: _____

Army _____ Navy _____ Air Force _____ Marines _____ Coast Guard _____

Length of service _____ Rank_____ Type of discharge _____

VA history_____

Employment history:

Job description   Dates   Reasons for leaving

_____

Family history:

Brothers _____Sisters _____Birth order _____

Type of family structure _____

Father's occupation _____Mother's occupation _____

Description of mother _____

Description of father _____

Description of home life _____

_____

History of drug abuse in family _____

Figure 12.1
Outline of a structured psychosocial interview

242

Family's attitude toward substance abuse _____
_____
Current relationships with parents _____
Current relationships with siblings _____
Current relationship with spouse_____
Current relationships with children _____
Criminal justice record:
Number of arrests _____
Types _____
Number of convictions _____
Number and duration of times in jail_____
Number and duration of times in prison_____
Number of times on probation or parole _____
Cases/warrants pending_____
Current probation officer_____
Current legal status _____
Alcohol and substance abuse information:
Number of times in detoxification centers _____ Mental hospitals and/or state
hospitals _____ Jail (for substance-abuse-related offenses) _____
Hospital (for medical attention) _____ Shelters (such as Salvation Army) _____
Dates of DWI convictions _____
History of drug use:
Age of first use _____ Substances tried _____
First contact_____ First drinking experience _____
First intoxication _____ First blackout _____ Convulsions _____
Morning tremors_____ Hallucinations _____ DTs_____ Fights _____
Personality change _____
Substances regularly used_____
_____ Choice _____
Frequency of use _____
Attempts to stop substance abuse _____
_____
Support groups attended _____
Pattern of substance abuse:
Daily _____ Weekends_____ Periodic _____ Alone _____ Bars_____ Friends _____
Use in 24-hour period:
At present _____ Substances_____
At peak _____ Substances_____
Date of last drug/substance abuse and amount_____
Overdoses, withdrawals, or adverse reactions _____
_____
Attempted suicides _____
Problems caused by substance abuse:
Job _____
Family_____
Finances _____
Health_____
Sex _____
Loss of control _____

Figure 12.1 *continued*

The Personal Problems Checklist provides a list of common problems for each age group. There are versions available for adults, adolescents, and children.

Psychiatric Interviews

Workers in the helping professions consider the interview one of the most important technical instruments to find out about individuals and their social functioning. The purpose of the psychiatric interview is to help provide information to guide diagnosis and selection of a treatment plan. The questions are designed to elicit information from the physical, psychological, biochemical, anatomical, social, emotional, family, and educational aspects of a client's life (Beutler & Berren, 1995). The following areas are usually included in the interview schedule:

1. *Demographic information*—This information includes the age, sex, educational level, marital status, number of children, and employment of the client.
2. *Chief complaint*—The chief complaint should be recorded in the client's exact words. Sometimes individuals feel that there is nothing wrong with them but that their wives or husbands are sick and need to be receiving treatment.
3. *Present illness and medical history*—It is important to ascertain the background factors related to the client's present illness.
4. *Past psychiatric history*—Any information on the client's past illnesses should be recorded, including the types of disorder, any precipitating factors, and the steps taken in treatment.
5. *Mental status*—Any information on the client's appearance, cognitive functioning, affect, moods, and interpersonal style is helpful.
6. *Personal and social history*—The information itself is important, but the way the client presents it also gives the interviewer a look at how the client speaks, thinks, feels, and evaluates situations. The interviewer tries to get a complete family history, including short sketches of the individual's parents, siblings, and other relatives. All dimensions of the client's personal history are important.

There are a number of interview schedules available for adults with personality disorders. The Personality Disorder Interview (PDI) is a semistructured interview for the assessment of the DSM-IV personality disorders. The Hare Psychopathy Checklist–Revised (PCL-R) is designed to assess antisocial personality disorder in forensic and psychiatric populations. The Structured Interview of Reported Symptoms (SIRS) assesses malingering and feigning of psychiatric symptoms.

Psychological Case Study

The interview is a key component of a psychological case study, which Bromley (1986) defines as an account of a person in a situation, focusing on a relatively short, self-contained part of an individual's life and the unique aspects of that individual's personality. The purpose of the case study technique is to find a solution to the client's problem by looking at how and why a client acted as he did in a given situation. Case studies can refer to many situations and environments—for example, a case study of a business organization. In this text, however, case study refers to a reconstruction and interpretation of a major episode in a client's life.

Case studies are conducted in a context that guides the investigator in what procedures should be used and what end results should be accomplished. For example, the investigator might be concerned about whether a person should be placed on probation or whether a client should seek divorce. Bromley (1986) lists six basic rules in preparation for conducting a case study (p. 24):

1. Be sure that facts and details are accurate.
2. Have a clear idea of the aims and objectives of the study explicitly and unambiguously stated.
3. Assess the degree to which the stated aims and objectives have been accomplished.
4. Receive training in the case study method and establish rapport and a good working relationship with the client.
5. View the client in an ecological perspective—objects, persons, and events are interpreted in terms of the individual's physical, social, and symbolic environment. Remember, the case study is undertaken because the personal qualities of the client are unusual, or the psychological and situational circumstances are unusual, or both.
6. Be able to write in a good clear manner, direct and objective but not disinterested.

No set formats exist of how to write the psychological case study, but Bromley (1986) identified 14 items to be included (p. 28):

1. Demographic information about the client and a description of physical appearance
2. Lifestyle and history of the client, including routine activities, material possessions, physical health, and important life events
3. Psychological makeup of the client—attitudes, abilities, motivations, self-concept, and so on
4. Social history of the client—social role and status, social relationships, family, friendships, and loyalties
5. Moral and ethical standards of the client relative to the case
6. The client's problem under investigation in the case study
7. An account of the evidence and arguments related to the analysis of the case study
8. A detailed description of any issue that falls beyond the normal range of events
9. A review of the evidence and arguments in relation to the conclusions and recommendations made
10. A summary of the methods and procedures utilized in conducting the case study and a reminder of the context of the study, the conditions that gave rise to it, and the factors affecting any future course of the study
11. A statement of any reservations, implications, or comments important to the case
12. A title and an abstract
13. Summary and conclusion sections that include a brief statement of the problem; the methods used to study the problem; the main findings; and the conclusions, recommendations, and predictions
14. A list of references and sources used and acknowledgments

The investigator must keep in mind the reasons for conducting the case study and guard against one-sided points of view. Team approaches and case conferences enhance eliciting different points of view. The investigator must also be mindful of the target of the case study. Self-analysis is often doubly valuable. It gives the investigator insight into how the individual perceives herself and may lead the client to better self-understanding. The investigator should avoid merely cataloging behavior and personality characteristics. Human behavior is an interaction between personal characteristics and situational factors, and the case study should provide some general conclusions about the client.

Interviewing Children and Adolescents

A number of specific interview schedules are designed for use with children and adolescents. The Interview Schedule for Children (Kovacs, 1982) is a widely used interview schedule for children aged 8 to 17. The schedule takes about 40 to 60 minutes to administer, after which the interviewer rates the symptoms from the information given in the child's responses.

Another scale is the Child Assessment Schedule (Hodges, Kline, Stern, Cytryn, & McKnew, 1982). It includes questions about school, friends, activities, family, fears, worries, self-image, mood, somatic concerns, expressions of anger, and thought disorder and also has questions on delusions, hallucinations, and related symptoms. The schedule has been useful in detecting psychopathology in children.

The Trauma Symptoms Checklist for children aged 8 to 16 is available in paper-and-pencil format and has a Windows scoring and interpretation version available. The six clinical scales are anxiety, depression, anger, post-traumatic stress, dissociation, and sexual concerns. Two validity scales are also a part of the checklist: underresponse and hyperresponse.

WELLNESS

The 1991 theme for AACD (now ACA) was wellness. Wellness looks at the total person, and Hettler's model includes six dimensions—physical, spiritual, emotional, social, intellectual, and occupational. One of the most popular instruments is the Lifestyle Assessment Questionnaire. The LAQ evaluates an individual's habits and knowledge in a wide range of health and wellness dimensions. Eleven questions are in the personal data section. Section 2 concerns lifestyles and has questions on physical exercise, nutrition, and spiritual dimensions of the individual's life. Section 3 is a health risk appraisal, and Section 4 has individuals rate topics for personal growth. A computerized report form is available, and the instrument is also produced on interactive software. The report to the client is entitled "Making Wellness Work for You" and provides suggestions on how the client can make positive lifestyle changes.

Test Well: Wellness Inventory (1992) is a scale to promote awareness of wellness and published by the National Wellness Institute for adults with a minimum of a 10th-grade education. There is also a college version of the instrument. The 12 scales are physical fitness and nutrition, social awareness, medical self-care, spirituality and values, emotional management, intellectual wellness, environmental wellness, safety, occupational wellness, sexuality, and emotional awareness. There is a total wellness score.

PITFALLS

Fisher (1985) reminds professionals involved in assessment in the mental health field to look carefully at counterproductive behaviors:

1. *Being too sociable or following the "nice-guy" syndrome*—Some examiners are more concerned with being liked than being objective and professional in their tasks.
2. *Being collusive or aloof*—This is the other end of the scale.
3. *Being a technician*—Some examiners put more emphasis on the procedures and the techniques than on looking at the person as a whole.
4. *Being a rescuer*—Some examiners rush to the rescue of their clients (also called the doctor syndrome).
5. *Being an opponent*—Some examiners act as though they and their clients are on opposite sides.

SUMMARY

A wide variety of assessment models and techniques is used to assess adjustment of clients. Workers in clinical and counseling contexts use tests for a wide variety of purposes. Although the use of clinical testing has declined, many new techniques have been used in measuring and evaluating clients. Behavioral assessment techniques such as self-monitoring, behavioral observation, and simulation have been widely used in the field because they center on evaluating actual behavior in naturalistic situations.

Several new instruments and techniques, as well as renewed interest in the classical testing procedures, have resulted from computer scoring and interpretation procedures. Neuropsychological testing has been developed to identify brain damage or organicity. Traditional techniques such as the interview and the case study are primary tools of workers in the helping professions.

QUESTIONS FOR DISCUSSION

1. What do you believe the role of testing should be in a mental health setting? What should the goals and objectives be for testing in this context? Some clinicians are opposed to any type of testing in this field. Why do you agree or disagree with their position?
2. What are the advantages and disadvantages of using behavioral assessment techniques? In what types of situations would behavioral assessment procedures be more appropriate than traditional standardized testing?

3. What are the advantages and disadvantages of an interview? What are the different types of interviews and when would you use them? What are the sources of
bias operating in the interview and how would you attempt to correct bias in
interview situations?

4. What types of interviews are used in the mental health field? What are some of
the problems and issues in the use of the interview technique?

5. What are the uses of the case study? What are the advantages and disadvantages
of this approach? When would you use case studies in your work?

SUGGESTED ACTIVITIES

1. Interview psychologists and counselors working in the mental health field and
find out what tests and assessment procedures they use and why. Report your
findings to the class.

2. Critically review a test used primarily in mental health settings. Read the reviews
of the test in different journals and yearbooks.

3. Design a behavioral assessment instrument and try it out on several individuals.
Write an analysis of your experiment.

4. Design an interview schedule and try it out on several individuals. Write an analysis of the results.

5. Critically review a software package used in a mental health setting—for example, a biographic data program or a test interpretive package.

6. Write a review of the literature on a topic such as behavioral assessment, case
study approach, use of tests in clinical settings, use of tests in counseling settings, or neuropsychological testing.

7. Make an annotated bibliography of tests used in the mental health setting.

8. Study this information about Lawana and answer the questions that follow it:

Case of Lawana

Lawana is a 16-year-old who has completed her education through grade 10. She says she
doesn't have the energy or desire to go anywhere and adds that when she does go out,
she feels anxious and scared.

Background Information:

Lawana's mother is living with a Hispanic and has been married twice—the first time for
11 years, the second for 1½ years. Lawana has two sisters, ages 8 and 12, and an older
brother, age 22, who no longer lives with the family. Lawana's mother got pregnant with
Lawana during a period of separation from her first husband. Lawana learned about this
and maintains regular positive contact with her biological father. She hates her mother's
live-in boyfriend, who abuses her when he is drunk. Her mother, who has refused to
acknowledge the abuse, believes Lawana's problems are caused by racial prejudice at
school. Lawana is earning Bs and Cs in her classes.

Lawana's mother was concerned enough about Lawana's condition to arrange an appointment for her at the local mental health clinic. Lawana was tested with a number of assessment instruments. Her profile follows.

Personality Assessment Inventory

Validity

Inconsistency	52	Infrequency	50
Positive Impression	40	Negative Impression	57

Clinical

Somatic Complaints	55	Anxiety	68
Anxiety-Related Disorders	65	Depression	45
Mania	45	Paranoia	55
Schizophrenia	56	Borderline Features	57
Antisocial Features	48	Alcohol Problems	50
Drug Problems	48		

Treatment

Aggression	55	Suicidal Ideation	62
Stress	62	Nonsupport	58
Treatment Rejection	40		

Interpersonal

Dominance	48	Warmth	42

Beck Anxiety Inventory: 27 (severe)
Beck Depression Inventory: 42 (moderate)

a. How would you describe Lawana's adjustment? (Remember, on the PAI, the mean *T* score is 50 and the SD is 10.)

b. What additional information about Lawana would you like to have?

ADDITIONAL READINGS

Several good source books on tests are available for special groups and populations. PRO-ED has published an interesting assessment series: S. Joseph Weaver (1984) has edited *Testing Children*; Robert G. Harrington (1986) has edited *Testing Adolescents*; and Dennis P. Swiercinsky's (1985) collection is *Testing Adults*. Many chapters are of interest to people working in the mental health field. Others include:

Choca, J. (1991). *Interpretive guide to the Millon Multiaxial Inventory.* Washington, DC: APA.

The book shows users of the Millon how to interpret the tests and examines the design and development of the inventory.

Golden, C. J. (1990). *Clinical interpretation of psychological tests* (2nd ed.). Boston: Allyn & Bacon.

The author provides examples of the clinical application of tests such as the Wechsler scales, the Wide Range Achievement Test, the Peabody Individual Achievement Test, the MMPI-2, the 16PF, the Bender Gestalt, and the Halstead-Reitan Neuropsychological Battery.

Katz, L. (1986). *A practical guide to psychodiagnostic testing*. Springfield, IL: Thomas.

The author provides practical suggestions on how to conduct psychodiagnostic testing.

Rogers, R. (1995). *Diagnostic and structure interviewing: A handbook for psychologists*. Odessa, FL: PAR.

The handbook is designed to help workers in the social and behavioral sciences hone their interviewing skills.

Ziskin, J. (1986). "The Future of Clinical Assessment," and Dean, R. (1986). "Perspectives on the Future of Neuropsychological Assessment," both in B. S. Plake & J. C. Witt, *The Future of Testing*, vol. 2 in the Buros-Nebraska Symposium on Measurement and Testing.

The chapters present current thinking and future projections on testing in these areas.

Learning Styles

OVERVIEW

Learning style is defined as an individual's preferred mode and desired conditions to learn. People differ in how they approach learning. Mann and Sabatino (1985) state that "two individuals with identical IQs, with the same configuration of special abilities, or with exactly the same type and strength of information processing capacities may nevertheless be quite different in the ways that they perceive things, think, solve problems, recall events, come to decisions, play musical instruments, and swing baseball bats" (p. 189).

Assessing learning style has important benefits. It can help us understand how an individual learns and how he perceives, approaches, interacts, and responds to the learning environment (Keefe & Languis, 1983). Dunn, Dunn, and Price (1987) found that when students are taught with approaches and resources that complement their unique learning styles, their achievement is significantly increased and their attitudes are better. Hargrove and Poteet (1984) believe that one of the most neglected aspects of diagnostic activity with exceptional students is the determination of their unique learning styles (p. 10).

OBJECTIVES

After studying this chapter, the reader should be able to

✔ List and explain the purposes and objectives of assessing learning styles

✔ List the different types of tests to assess learning styles and identify the dimensions they measure

✔ Discuss the issues, trends, and problems in measuring learning styles

PROCESSING STYLE

Processing style, an important component of learning style, can be defined as the individual's method of inputting and outputting information. Input is the reception of sensory information from visual, auditory, or hepatic sources. (Hepatic combines the kinesthetic and tactile stimuli.) Processing involves integrating the information with previously learned information. Individuals store the information in short-term memory and then use a variety of memory strategies to store the information in long-term memory. Output involves using a vocal or motor response to a problem or task.

MODALITY ASSESSMENT

Modalities are the specific sensory or motor abilities that are our pathways to learning. Inghram (1980) states that modality assessment is divided into two types—assessment of acuity and assessment of perception. Assessment of acuity is an attempt to evaluate whether a certain pathway to learning exists. Assessment of perception evaluates the ability to discriminate visually, aurally, tactilely, or kinesthetically to store and recall a stimulus and integrate that stimulus into memory. In summarizing the research on modality preference, Reiff (1992) reports that about 30% will remember what is seen, 30% remember what is heard, and 30% use mixed modalities. The remaining 10% remember kinesthetically. Modality strengths vary with age as the child matures and gains experience; eventually, the modalities blend.

Visual Assessment

Usually perception includes five dimensions (Inghram, 1980, pp. 274–275):

1. *Visual discrimination*—the ability to identify differences and similarities in stimuli, such as among letters, numbers, words, or graphic forms
2. *Figure ground*—the ability to locate or identify a figure from a background of irrelevant stimuli, such as finding a certain word on a page
3. *Visual memory*—the ability to recall a sequence of visually presented stimuli, such as letters or numbers
4. *Visual closure*—the ability to make a whole from reduced cues, such as naming an object or scene from an incomplete drawing
5. *Visual motor integration*—the ability to utilize perceived visual stimuli to make body movements more effective and efficient, such as a football player weaving downfield to avoid tackles

Listed here are a number of instruments available to measure both visual acuity and visual perception:

The Bender Visual Motor Gestalt Test assesses the examinee's ability to reproduce visual stimuli and aids in identifying brain-injured individuals. The Bender Gestalt Test is a form of the Bender test for young children.

The Detroit Tests of Learning Aptitude measure visual attention to letters and visual discrimination.

The Developmental Test of Visual-Motor Integration assesses visual-motor function of children ages 2 to 15.

The Frostig Developmental Test of Visual Perception measures hand-eye coordination, figure/ground, form constancy, position in space, and spatial relations in children ages 4 to 8.

The Illinois Test of Psycholinguistic Abilities includes subtests on visual closure, visual sequential memory, and visual association.

The Keystone Visual Survey Test measures dimensions of visual functioning.

The Memory for Designs Test measures visual perception of individuals ages 8 and older.

The Metropolitan Readiness Test has a matching and copying subtest.

The Slosson Drawing Coordination Test is used to diagnose visual-perceptual and visual-motor coordination problems and brain damage.

The Snellen Eye Chart is used to screen visual acuity.

The Spache Binocular Reading Test is used to screen a child's visual acuity.

Visual perceptual difficulties can be informally assessed by observing a client in different contexts. Any of the following behaviors might signal trouble (Inghram, 1980, p. 281):

Holding paper too close to the face

Holding a book too near or too far away

Having poor eye-hand coordination

Stumbling

Being restless, irritable, or nervous when called on to use eyes for close work

Frowning, scowling, and squinting

Blinking eyes frequently

Shutting or covering one eye

Rubbing eyes frequently

Clients with visual perceptual difficulties may complain about different physical problems when they have to use their eyes. They may state they have a hard time reading what is required. Students with visual perception problems may be clumsy in visual motor tasks such as writing, drawing, cutting, and different types of games involving movement and coordination. Such students are easily distracted and are careless about doing assignments sequentially.

Auditory Assessment

The auditory modality has four dimensions:

1. *Auditory discrimination*—the ability of the client to distinguish among sounds, such as the sounds of letters or blends
2. *Sound/ground*—the ability to select an auditory stimulus (e.g., a theme in music) from a background of competing auditory stimuli (e.g., the accompaniment)
3. *Auditory memory*—the ability to recall the sequence of stimuli presented orally, such as following commands and remembering digits
4. *Auditory blending*—the ability to blend distinct sounds into words

Any question about auditory acuity should be referred to an audiologist. A number of standardized measures of auditory acuity can be administered by trained examiners. Examples of some of the auditory assessment instruments are included here:

The Goldman-Fristoe-Woodcock Auditory Skills Test Battery contains 12 subtests that assess auditory attention, discrimination, memory, and sound-symbol skills in individuals aged 3 to 80.

The Goldman-Fristoe-Woodcock Test of Auditory Discrimination assesses skills in auditory discrimination, auditory memory, and sound-symbol associations in individuals aged 3 to 84.

The Illinois Test of Psycholinguistic Abilities includes subtests on auditory frequency memory and sound blending.

The Oliphant Auditory Discrimination Memory Test assesses the ability of examinees in grades 1 to 8 to hear and discriminate sounds and words.

The Screening Test for Auditory Perception assesses ability of students in grades 1 through 6 to discriminate types of vowels, consonants, rhyming verses, nonrhyming words, and so on.

The Wechsler Intelligence Scale for Children—Revised and the Wechsler Adult Intelligence Scale include a digit span subtest.

The Wepman Auditory Discrimination Test assesses the ability of children aged 5 to 8 to identify similarities and differences in word pairs.

Many informal ways of identifying auditory problems are used. If the examinee has problems following directions, asks constantly to have items repeated, is distracted easily by extraneous auditory stimuli, or has pronunciation problems, she may have auditory processing problems.

Inghram (1980) identifies seven categories of auditory perception deficits (see Table 13.1).

Motor Assessment

An individual can learn through using psychomotor abilities. A number of standardized tests measure different types of sensory motor skills. Sometimes self-concept

Table 13.1
Auditory perceptual deficits

Deficit	Characteristic Behavior
Signal/ground	Has difficulty attending to what is said because of the presence of competing noise Has difficulty identifying a sound in its word context
Auditory closure	Cannot supply the missing auditory parts Has trouble in retrieving all that is said
Auditory constancy	Has difficulty in recognizing vowel or word sounds from one day to another Cannot recognize rhyming patterns Does not understand sound families
Sound discrimination	Has difficulty in distinguishing and discriminating between sounds that closely resemble each other
General auditory memory	Has difficulty remembering a sound contained in several different words Has immediate memory and can repeat but may forget the next day
Auditory attention	Is unable to remember something that has just been said by someone else Exhibits poor memory for auditory stimuli and is easily distracted
Sequential auditory memory	Cannot recall appropriate word order to constitute acceptable syntax in a sentence Cannot remember simple instructions Has difficulty in recalling appropriate word order

and academic performance can be improved through development of the individual's motor abilities. Improved coordination may improve participation in sports, games, dancing, and so on. Individuals may become more confident or more accepted and feel much better about themselves. Here are some of the tests available in this area:

The Bruininks-Oseretsky Test of Motor Proficiency assesses dimensions such as running speed, agility, balance, bilateral coordination, strength, and upper limb coordination and looks at the gross and fine motor coordination of examinees aged 4 to 14.

The Devereux Test of Extremity Coordination assesses the level of motor development in children aged 4 to 10.

The Lincoln-Oseretsky Motor Development Scale measures 36 motor development tasks in children aged 6 to 14.

The Moore Eye-Hand Coordination and Color Matching Test assesses speed of eye-hand movement and ability to match colors in individuals aged 2 and older.

The Primary Visual-Motor Test assesses visual-motor functions in copying geometrical and representative designs in children aged 4 to 8.

The Purdue Perceptual-Motor Survey assesses laterality, directionality, and perceptual-motor matching skills in children from preschool to grade 8.

The Southern California Sensory Integration Tests measure visual, tactile, and kinesthetic perception as well as motor performance in children aged 4 to 10.

Modality Preference Assessment

Certain tests and assessment instruments can be used to quickly determine the examinee's modality preference. It is important to determine not only effective modalities but also the modalities that interfere with learning. The Swassing-Barbe Modality Index (Barbe & Swassing, 1979) is used to identify a student's modality strengths. It presents a matching-to-sample task, is individually administered, and takes about 20 minutes. The examiner presents a stimulus sample (circles, triangles, squares, and hearts), and the examinee is asked to reproduce the sample. Testing is conducted with visual, auditory, and tactile stimuli.

The first test in the index is the visual test. The examinee is given several warmup items and is then shown a set of shapes, beginning with three shapes and ending with nine. The test taker is instructed to assemble the shapes in the sequence just seen. Testing is stopped when the examinee makes errors on two consecutive sets. The second test is an auditory test. The names of shapes are read aloud in sequence at the rate of one per second. The examinee is asked to assemble the sequence of shapes in the sequence just heard. The third test is a kinesthetic test. The examiner holds a shield so that the examinee can feel but cannot see the shapes. Then the examiner removes the shield and asks the examinee to reassemble the shapes in the sequence just felt. Three separate scores are tallied.

COGNITIVE STYLE

Cognitive style is another dimension of learning style. It is the preferred way in which an individual reacts to environmental stimuli; it is used to describe how individuals differ in organizing and controlling a task. Messick (1989) defines cognitive styles as information processing habits that represent an individual's typical modes of perceiving, thinking, remembering, and problem solving. Witkin (1949) identified two component styles—field dependence and field independence. Field-dependent individuals tend not to restructure situations but to accept them as experiences. They are more attentive to social cues, accept other people readily, and like to be with people. Field-independent people prefer to interpret and restructure their environmental situations. They are less attentive to social cues and prefer to work with ideas and abstract principles. Field-independent individuals are more interested in science and mathematics, like to set their own goals, are more internally oriented,

and do not require external reinforcement. Reiff (1992) reports that field-independent individuals are global, benefit from cooperative learning, and need strategies to
help organize and comprehend material. Field-independent individuals are analytical, more internally motivated, and cognitively flexible, and they like independent
projects.

Witkin, Moore, Goodenough, and Cox (1977) found that cognitive style is an
important factor in academic learning and social behavior. Three of the widely used
tests of cognitive style are listed here:

> The Children's Embedded Figures Test is a 25-item individually administered test
> of perceptual process and cognitive style for children aged 5 to 12.

> The Embedded Figures Test assesses cognitive style in perceptual tasks; it is a
> 12-item test with cards containing complex and simple figures and requiring the
> examinee to locate and trace a previously seen simple figure within a larger com-
> plex figure.

> The Group Embedded Figures Test assesses cognitive style through 25 pencil-
> and-paper items that require individuals to find 1 of 8 simple figures in complex
> designs.

Numerous cognitive styles exist. For example, Kagan (1966) identified the impul-
sive/reflective style. Examinees with an impulsive style give answers quickly, without
thinking through the situation, and often make errors. Reflective examinees are just
the opposite. Mann and Sabatino (1985) classify cognitive styles into three general
categories (p. 191):

1. A cognitive style may simply identify particular characteristics or traits that a person
   possesses in greater or lesser degree, such as authoritarianism.
2. A cognitive style may indicate placement at a particular point on a cognitive personality dimension whose opposite poles indicate opposing cognitive orientations, such
   as field independence versus field dependence or reflection versus impulsivity.
3. Certain cognitive styles place individuals within a particular cognitive category, such
   as analytical, categorical, or relational in their thinking.

Some of the cognitive control styles are leveling-sharpening, scanning-focusing,
conceptual-differential, constricted-flexible, and field articulation. Leveling-sharpening is defined by Goldstein and Blackman (1978) as representing the characteristic
degree to which current precepts and relevant memory traces interact or assimilate
in the course or registration of current precepts and memories (p. 8).

Conceptual Tempo

A popular cognitive construct, conceptual tempo or reflection-impulsivity, was studied by Kagan, Rosman, Day, Albert, and Phillips (1964); it relates to the different
speeds with which individuals make decisions. Kagan et al. used the Matching Familiar Figures Test to assess reflection-impulsivity. Individuals are presented with 12 pictures and asked to choose the one that most nearly matches a particular picture
selected by the examiner. The task requires individuals to scan the alternatives and

to make a decision. The time taken to respond is considered a measure of the individual's tendency toward reflection or impulsivity.

Reiff (1992) reports that reflective learners think longer before they answer a question and tend to make fewer errors. They spend time deliberating and analyzing the situation. Impulsive individuals fail to attend to tasks, have difficulty considering quick decisions and alternatives to problems, are less systematic in their information search, produce fewer testable hypotheses, underestimate time intervals, are impatient, and want immediate gratification.

Counselors can help reflective learners by allowing them time to thoroughly examine materials, model risk taking to show that error is natural, help them organize proofing of work, provide cooperative learning experiences, and teach them test-taking skills. Impulsive learners can be helped by organizing materials and assignments into smaller components, providing a nondistracting environment, providing explicit guidelines and directions, and structuring time into smaller segments (Reiff, 1992).

Brain Preference

Grady (1984) reports that research points toward two hemispheres of the brain. The left hemisphere takes care of linear and sequential operations; the right hemisphere is in charge of simultaneous and visual functions. He concludes that cognitive style is related to hemispheric organization: individuals tend to have a hemispheric preference or dominance (p. 1). Wonder and Donovan (1984) emphasize that the human brain's two halves have different but overlapping skills or ways of thinking. They found individuals with left preferences to be positive, analytical, linear, explicit, sequential, verbal, concrete, rational, active, and goal-oriented. Individuals with right-brain preferences were intuitive, spontaneous, emotional, nonverbal, visual, artistic, holistic, playful, diffuse, symbolic, and physical.

According to Gazzaniga (1985) and Sherrod (1985), people tend to prefer one side of the brain over the other, and that preference affects their approach and attitude toward life and work. Sherrod states that an individual's major and minor dominance could serve as a supplemental clue to a career selection. Left-brain–oriented people tend to prefer career fields such as planning, law, editing, technology, writing, and bookkeeping. Right-brain–oriented people tend to prefer roles such as policymakers, artists, poets, sculptors, politicians, playwrights, and musicians. Two brain preference instruments are identified here:

The Brain Preference Indicator uses a 36-item multiple-choice self-report format, with selected options scored for left or right brain preference.

Your Style of Learning and Thinking (SOLAT) appears in different forms for children, adolescents, and adults and attempts to measure brain preference through 40 items with three response options per item, one each representing left, right, and integrated ways of functioning.

Figure 13.1 shows sample items representative of those often included on such instruments.

SA	A	D	SD	1.	I prefer to be a listener.
SA	A	D	SD	2.	Daydreaming helps me solve problems.
SA	A	D	SD	3.	I like to do things on the spur of the moment.
SA	A	D	SD	4.	I like to follow my hunches.
SA	A	D	SD	5.	I like to take risks.
SA	A	D	SD	6.	I like to be free to learn without a lot of structure.
SA	A	D	SD	7.	I can express myself well verbally.
SA	A	D	SD	8.	I remember faces easily.
SA	A	D	SD	9.	My mood changes frequently.
SA	A	D	SD	10.	I can remember and sing songs I hear on the radio or TV.
SA	A	D	SD	11.	I like to print when I take notes.
SA	A	D	SD	12.	I like to work in groups.
SA	A	D	SD	13.	I am seldom absentminded.
SA	A	D	SD	14.	I use gestures to express my feelings.
SA	A	D	SD	15.	I prefer hands-on experiences to verbal instructions.
SA	A	D	SD	16.	I like to think before I answer so that I use the right words.
SA	A	D	SD	17.	I can rely on my intuition.
SA	A	D	SD	18.	I can remember slogans I hear.
SA	A	D	SD	19.	I like to write down the goals and activities I need to accomplish each day.
SA	A	D	SD	20.	I like to learn things by watching how others do them and then imitating.

SA = strongly agree, A = agree, D = disagree, SD = strongly disagree

Figure 13.1
Sample brain preference survey

LEARNING PERSONALITIES

Another way to look at differences in learners is through their personality structure. In educational settings one of the most widely used tests to measure personality type is the Myers-Briggs Type Indicator (MBTI). The test is based upon Jung's theory of psychological types and measures personal tendencies or preferences along four bipolar dimensions: extroversion-introversion, sensing-intuition, thinking-feeling, and judging-perceptive.

Individuals are assigned the initial letter of each bipolar dimension on which they score highest. An individual's type is the combination of the four preferences.

E represents an extrovert, who relates more easily to the outer world of people.

I represents an introvert, who relates more easily to the inner world of ideas.

S stands for sensing, preferring to work with known facts.

N stands for intuition, preferring to look for possibilities and relationships.

T stands for thinking, basing judgments on impersonal analysis and logic.

F stands for feeling, basing judgment more on personal values.

J refers to judging, preferring a planned way of life.

P refers to perceptive, preferring a flexible, spontaneous way of life.

The MBTI profile sheet presents a quick picture of 16 different combinations of the four dimensions. For example, the INFP has the following characteristics:

1. Full of enthusiasm
2. Loyal
3. Not apt to talk of a continuing relationship until a person is known well
4. Concerned about learning
5. Interested in language
6. Fond of independent projects
7. Apt to undertake too much but will somehow get it done
8. Friendly but not always sociable
9. Not concerned with physical environment
10. Not concerned about possessions

Lawrence (1982) states that individuals must follow their inclinations if the best learning is to take place.

The Murphy-Meisgeier Type Indicator for Children (1987) measures the psychological type of children in grades 2 through 8 using the same four preference scales as the MBTI. The authors provide manuals to help teachers and parents use the information from the test. Characteristics of each type of student are identified, and suggested activities are given. Teachers are told that an intuitive student needs opportunities to be creative and original, dislikes routine and taking time for precision, has a seemingly sporadic approach rather than an orderly one, and so forth. Some of the suggested activities for intuitive students are to challenge them with problem-solving activities for which there are multiple solutions; to implement role-playing activities, especially improvisation; and to reduce the number of practice examples that are required for assignments.

LEARNING STYLE INVENTORIES

Learning style can be broadly defined as the way in which an individual learns. Dunn (1983) states that learning style represents the "way individuals concentrate on, absorb, and retain new or difficult information or skills" (p. 496). Keefe and Monk (1988) define learning style as the composite of characteristic cognitive, affective, and physiological factors that serve as relatively stable indicators of how individuals perceive, interact with, and respond to learning environments (p. 3). Many learning style inventories are available. One widely used instrument is the Learning Style Inventory (LSI) (Dunn, Dunn, & Price, 1987), which looks at modality preferences as well as other factors. The test authors look at environmental elements that affect learning—sound, light, temperature, and design. An emotional dimension considers factors such as motivation, persistence, responsibility, and structure. Sociological dimensions relate to whether an individual likes to work alone, with peers, in pairs, in a team, with adults, or in a varied situation. Another level considers the physical factors, including intake of food or drink, time of day, and desire for mobility. The final dimension of the model relates to psychological variables—cerebral dominance, impulsivity, and analytical versus global approaches.

The Learning Style Profile (LSP) (Keefe, Monk, Letteri, Languis, & Dunn, 1988) is a 128-item pencil-and-paper inventory that was developed under the sponsorship of the National Association of Secondary School Principals. The subscales on the test cover cognitive, affective, and physiological dimensions of learning styles. Cognitive dimensions include perceptual preferences, field independence/dependence, simultaneous/successive, inductive/deductive, active/reflective, thinking/feeling, need for structure, sharpening/leveling, focusing/scanning, narrow/broad, reflective/impulsive, and complex/simple. Affective styles include achievement motivation, risk taking/cautiousness, social motivation, anxiety, persistence, inductive/deductive, thinking/feeling, and need for structure. Physiological dimensions are time-of-day preference; need for mobility; anxiety; and environmental elements such as sound, light, temperature, and design.

Other widely used learning style instruments are listed here:

The Canfield Learning Styles Inventory assesses individuals from grade 6 to adult in four areas—conditions (peer, organization, goal setting, competition, instructor, detail, independence, authority), content (numeric, qualitative, inanimate, people), mode (listening, reading, iconic, direct experience), and expectation.

The Learning Efficiency Test measures visual and auditory memory under both ordered and unordered recall. It measures immediate, short-term, and long-term recall.

The Learning Preference Inventory uses Jung typology: sensing-feeling, sensing-thinking, intuiting-feeling, extroversion-introversion.

The Learning Styles Inventory measures student attitude toward nine models of instruction—projects, drill and recitation, peer teaching, discussion, teaching games, independent study, programmed instruction, lecture, and simulation.

The Learning Type Measure assesses four types of learning styles based on doing/watching and feeling/thinking continuums.

Learning styles are also geared to specific subject areas. One such inventory is the Reading Style Inventory (RSI), a diagnostic reading test that identifies a student's natural learning style in reading. The test takes 20 to 30 minutes to administer and has a diskette available to test, score, and produce computerized individual or group profiles. The RSI matches an individual reading-style diagnosis with the most appropriate reading methods and materials.

Kolb (1976) has a different type of model. He postulates that learning proceeds in four stages:

1. Concrete experience that directly involves the learner
2. Reflective observation in which the learner reflects on experience from different perspectives

3. Abstract conceptualization in which the learner creates generalizations and theories

4. Active experimentation with application of theories to problem solving and decision making

Kolb's Learning Style Inventory is used to assess an individual's personal preferences along the abstract-concrete and active-reflective dimensions. He identifies four major types of learning styles:

1. Convergers, who like to solve specific problems
2. Divergers, who like to organize many relationships into a gestalt and use their imaginative ability to see commonalities
3. Assimilators, who use inductive reasoning to develop theoretical models
4. Accommodators, who like to carry out plans and conduct experiments and who are action-oriented.

Graska and Riechmann (Eisen, 1984) have a different type of conceptualization of learning style. Their instrument measures six types of learning styles—competitive, collaborative, avoidant, participant, dependent, and independent.

Mind Styles

Gregorc (1982) has still another conceptualization of learning styles. His scale is called the Gregorc Style Delineator and consists of 10 sets of four words each, which the examinee is asked to rank. The scale is designed to reveal two types of abilities for managing information: perception and ordering.

Gregorc looks at perception as the means by which an individual grasps information. It has two dimensions—abstractness and concreteness. He defines abstractedness as the quality that enables an individual to grasp, conceive, and mentally visualize data through the faculty of reason and to emotionally and intuitively register and deal with inner and subjective thoughts, ideas, concepts, feelings, drives, desires, and spiritual experiences (p. 5). He defines concreteness as the quality that enables an individual to grasp and mentally register data through the direct application of the physical senses. The second type of ability—ordering—also has two qualities: sequence and randomness. Sequence is defined as the quality that helps individuals grasp and organize information in a linear, step-by-step, methodical, predetermined order. Randomness helps individuals grasp and organize information in a nonlinear, galloping, leaping, and multifarious manner. The Gregorc Style Delineator assesses the perception and ordering abilities individuals use to adapt to their everyday environments at work, school, home, or in social interactions.

Other Instruments

The K-ABC, discussed in Chapter 7, also differentiates between serial and simultaneous information-processing styles. This information is valuable to teachers in planning instruction.

The Florida Analysis of Semantic Traits (Bailey & Siudzinski, 1986) is an individually administered scale that measures six dimensions of learning style. With one dimension the student is asked to respond to a question such as, "What do you want from your schoolwork?" or "What is important about your schoolwork?" Analysis of the response to this question indicates the type of criteria the student thinks is important. The responses are scored on a dimension from aesthetical to practical. Criteria are important motivators; when an individual's criteria are used to describe a task or outcome, the individual becomes invested in that task or outcome.

The other scales measure direction, source, reason, decision factors, and convincers. The Direction Scale measures how students focus or maintain their motivation. The two extremes are toward and away from. Toward describes people who can focus on achieving their goals. These individuals are motivated to have, get, achieve, and attain. Away-from individuals are motivated by a problem or something to get away from, to be avoided, steered clear of, or gotten rid of. These students have trouble maintaining focus on their goals and are distracted, and most respond to negative situations (p. 11).

The Source Scale is analyzed for internality and externality of the responses. The Reason Scale assesses whether the individual prefers options or procedures. Procedures people prefer following the rules. Options people are not satisfied with the way something has always been done. Another scale deals with decision factors and identifies four types. The sameness person does not like change and wants his world to remain the same. The sameness-with-exceptions person wants her world to remain about the same but will adapt as change occurs. The difference and difference-with-exception individual loves change and will force change whenever possible. The both-sameness-with-exceptions-and-difference individual likes normalcy and change and will adapt as change occurs. The last scale measures which modality convinces individuals to do something. A second part of the scale relates to the number of times individuals must experience the modality to be convinced. The information from all six scales is then translated into action strategies to improve instructional strategies and the motivation and attitude of students.

SUMMARY

Learning style and modality assessment may provide useful information for the diagnosis and description of behavior. The information can help provide strategies and methodologies for both the instructor and the learner. It is useful to know both the formal and informal procedures used to assess the different dimensions of learning style. Many of the instruments listed have questionable validity and reliability. Although they might have face validity, they have little concurrent or predictive validity. The research on learning styles is still new, but there are many implications for teaching and learning as well as for understanding interpersonal conflicts and problems.

QUESTIONS FOR DISCUSSION

1. Do you believe all instructors ought to assess the learning styles of their students and use a variety of teaching strategies? Or should the instructor specifically train individuals to cultivate new learning styles and skills?

2. What are the ways you learn best? Review the different types of learning styles discussed in this chapter, and determine the categories or types that pertain to you.

3. Many psychologists have emphasized the importance of cognitive theories and abilities in learning situations. Do you feel that cognitive styles tests provide the instructor and learner with more important information than an aptitude test or interest test does? Defend your position.

4. Do you feel that a better way of investigating differences among students is to look at personality structure rather than learning style or cognitive style? Why or why not? Would you want to give all of your students the Myers-Briggs Type Indicator? Why or why not?

5. The validity and reliability of the instruments discussed in this chapter are usually lower than for traditional types of tests. Would you still use these instruments to make instructional decisions? What would you tell the students about the tests?

SUGGESTED ACTIVITIES

1. Critique a cognitive style or learning style inventory. Take it yourself or administer it to an appropriate test taker. Does the test appear to have face validity? Does the test have construct validity? What are the reliability coefficients reported?

2. Take the Myers-Briggs Type Indicator. How could this test be used in instructional environments? Does the test provide a valid portrait of you? How could this test be used in instructional environments?

3. Make an annotated bibliography of cognitive style and learning style tests.

4. Conduct an experiment. Give one of the learning style tests to a class and an instructor. Give the class an attitude test about the class and an instructor. Divide the class into two groups: those who have the same type of learning style as the teacher and those who do not. Are there differences in the attitudes of the two groups toward the instructor and the class?

5. Recruit a volunteer and use a learning or cognitive style inventory to identify the individual's style. What would happen if you formed work, growth, or therapy groups that had persons of only one learning or personality type included? Is it better to have mixed types of individuals within a group? Conduct an experiment on this topic or read the research on the topic and write a short position paper.

6. Read the case of Quille and answer the questions that follow it.

Quille took the Personal Style Indicator (Controneo, 1983). She had the following profile:

Affiliative 90%
Creative 70%
Enterprising 30%
Ordered 5%
Investigative 35%

The instrument is an eight-item assessment instrument in which the individual is asked to rank five words based upon their importance to her (e.g., "Rank 1 the word that is most important to you and 5 to the word that is least important to you: [a] Thinker [b] Doer [c] Facilitator [d] Coordinator [e] Promoter"). Strengths for affiliatives include learning by interaction, sharing ideas with others, and discussing in peer groups or with an instructor or mentor.

Quille also took the Learning Type Measure (LTM) (McCarthy & St. Germain, 1993). The LTM is a 27-item instrument. Fifteen items involve ranking preferences (e.g., "I am usually [a] productive [b] creative [c] disorganized or [d] critical"). Twelve of them are items related to the passive/active or watching/doing continuum (e.g., "I prefer a hobby that is [a] active [b] passive"). Quille was identified most likely as an "imaginative learner." Imaginative learners are idea people, function through social interaction, need to be involved personally, and learn by listening and sharing. She scored lowest as a "common sense learner," one who needs to know how things work, seeks usability, and perceives information abstractly and processes it actively. The two styles in the middle were "analytical learner" and "dynamic learner."

On the Myers-Briggs Type Indicator, Quille was an ENFP (extraverted intuition with feeling). These individuals usually have as strengths people skills, enthusiasm and energy, adaptability, creativity, and new ideas and possibilities.

a. How would you characterize Quille's learning style?
b. What additional information would you like to have on the instruments and Quille before interpreting the assessment data?
c. The first two instruments were short and could be completed in 5 minutes or less. Would you use these instruments? Why or why not? When might you use these instruments?
d. What do these instruments say about career fields that might fit Quille's learning style?

ADDITIONAL READINGS

Fairhurst, A. M., & Fairhurst, L. L. (1995). *Effective teaching, effective learning: Making the personality connection in your classroom.* Palo Alto, CA: Consulting Psychologists Press.

The authors describe the preferred learning styles for the 16 MBTI types.

Griggs, S. A. (1991). *Learning styles counseling.* Ann Arbor, MI: ERIC Counseling and Personnel Services Clearinghouse.

The author discusses how counselors can increase their effectiveness by knowing their client's learning style and illustrates how counseling interventions can be prescribed based on learning styles. The research on learning styles in counseling and teaching is presented and strategies for consulting with teachers and parents about learning styles discussed.

Lawrence, G. D. (1997). *Looking at type and learning styles.* Gainesville, FL: CAPT.

The book focuses on learning styles of both teachers and students based upon the MBTI.

Meisgeier, C., Murphy, E., & Meisgeier, C. (1989). *A teacher's guide to type: A new perspective on individual differences in the classroom*. Palo Alto, CA: Consulting Psychologists Press.

This guide introduces teachers to type theory and suggests activities that can be used with each of the personality types.

Myers, I. B. (1980). *Gifts differing*. Palo Alto, CA: Consulting Psychologists Press.

This book provides a general overview of Jung's theory of personality types and specifically describes the 16 personality types found on the MBTI.

Reiff, J. C. (1992). *Learning style*. Washington, DC: NEA.

The author presents a conceptual framework for understanding learning styles and shows how the knowledge will help counselors and helping professionals.

CHAPTER 14

Assessment of Development

OVERVIEW

One in five American children has a developmental, learning, or emotional problem, according to the 1988 National Health Interview Study of Child Health. Some experts think the statistics should be higher because many parents and helping professionals are unable to recognize certain disorders. Counselors need to know characteristic behaviors at the different developmental stages, be able to assess problems, and recommend special educational assistance. Early competence exerts a subtle influence toward adaptation throughout life. Failure to adapt at one period of development promotes difficulty later. The chapter focuses not only on early development and developmental delays but on development through the life span. Moral development, career development, and psychosocial development are discussed.

OBJECTIVES

After studying this chapter the reader should be able to

✔ Discuss the general principles of developmental assessment

✔ Describe the major domains assessed in developmental testing

✔ Explain the advantages and disadvantages of the various assessment devices used to measure aspects of development

✔ Identify some of the major instruments used in developmental assessment

GENERAL PRINCIPLES

Developmental and readiness testing has become increasingly important in the early screening and identification of clients who might need remedial help or further assessment. Children are rapidly developing, and this must be considered in assessment and treatment (Yule, 1993). The assessment can be a valuable tool in the screening, diagnosis, placement, program planning, and evaluation of programs. Much attention has been placed on identifying preschoolers with disabilities, but many developmental theories now focus on the total life span rather than just childhood and adolescence. Developmental assessment is important in understanding cognitive, ego, interpersonal, moral, and psychosocial development as individuals progress through the various stages of their life.

The assessment needs to focus on both the client and the client's environment. The client plays an active role in shaping an environment that fulfills his basic needs. The significant individuals in the client's world need to be identified, and parents, guardians, spouses, friends, and relatives might be needed to provide input for the assessment. Attachments, separations, and losses in a client's life have a dramatic influence. While age is an important factor in assessment, social factors also must be considered (Yule, 1993).

Current functioning is influenced by previous events, and counselors need to evaluate clients with this in mind. Theories point out that conflicts are inevitable and necessary for human development, and some may never be completely resolved.

Developmental assessment focuses on these characteristics:

1. The normality of client functioning in the various domains
2. The historical factors that contributed positively or negatively to the client's functioning
3. The current state of affairs—family, school, or work factors that contribute positively and negatively to the client's functioning
4. The client's current state of wellness—her physical, psychological, and emotional health
5. The expectations of the client and her significant others
6. The client's current educational, social, and psychological needs

Yule (1993) reminds helping professionals not to treat any assessment finding in isolation but to piece it together with other data on the client's overall adjustment. Isolated symptoms should be viewed cautiously and emphasis placed on patterns of adjustment and their adaptability and flexibility. Behavior is interpreted in light of developmental norms and environmental factors.

DOMAINS

Developmental tests measure typical skills that should be mastered at certain stages. Preschool tests, for example, assess gross motor, fine motor, language, self-help,

Drawings of people provide information about a child's developmental level.

social, emotional, and cognitive skills. A number of domains are common to developmental assessment instruments across the life span:

Communication skills—verbal and nonverbal, receptive and expressive, listening and comprehension

Cognitive skills—reasoning, thinking, memory; basic achievement in reading, writing, and mathematics; problem solving

Physical development—general growth; motor and sensory; balance, locomotion, and walking

Emotional development—temperament, adjustment, emotional expression, self-concept, attitudes

Social development—peer and family relationships, friendships, interpersonal relationships

Self-care skills—basic self-care needs such as drinking, eating, toileting, dressing

Independent living skills—functioning independently in the home and community, including clothing care, cooking, transportation, shopping, money management

Work habits and adjustment skills—working independently, maintaining proper work habits, working with employers and employees, seeking and keeping jobs

Adjustment problems—aggression, hyperactivity, acting out, withdrawal, delinquency, stress, depression

METHODS OF ASSESSMENT

The four major techniques of assessment are direct testing; naturalistic observation; interviewing of parents, teachers, or guardians; and multiple measures. Direct testing is not always possible because of the developmental level of a client, a disability, wariness toward the test administrator, or the presence or nonpresence of parents in the case of young children. In these situations, the performance of individuals tends to be inconsistent.

Naturalistic observation provides an opportunity to see how a person behaves and performs in normal everyday functioning. The process is time-consuming and expensive. A number of structured observation schedules exist, and raters need to be trained to use them so that observations are consistent and properly focused.

Helping professionals use a wide variety of interviewing methods. Computerized versions are designed to elicit specific information; life history schedules help guide the collection of appropriate information from parents. Preschoolers or individuals with certain disabilities are not capable of filling out self-report forms, so interviews with parents or guardians are necessary to determine skills and adaptive behaviors not always modeled in school. The validity of personality tests such as the Personality Inventory for Children and self-concept scales such as the Inferred Self-Concept Scale that teachers or parents complete is questionable. Reliability of the data depends on the quality of the scale (content validity) and the accuracy of the people who are answering the questions.

There is a variety of informal assessment procedures that help professionals achieve a more global perspective of the problem. Sentence completion techniques can be used to zero in on important concerns at a particular stage of development (e.g., "In school, when the teacher calls upon me, I _____ _____."). Journaling is also used. Individuals are asked to tell how they feel about certain types of experiences, interventions, programs, and the like. A portfolio of these feelings can be kept. Other writing exercises such as stories and poems can also be helpful in understanding the client.

Observing individuals while they are playing games or drawing in play therapy or other informal situations can provide information on their cognitive and psychosocial development. Clients can be asked to tell a story about a particular picture or situation or to complete a story.

Self-monitoring requires the individual to keep a record of certain behaviors, feelings, or worries. A client could keep a record of the number of times he blew his cool, felt depressed, spoke out in class when not called upon, felt a craving for certain foods, and the like.

Helping professionals get more complete information when they use multiple measures. The process might be more time-consuming and expensive, but it allows the counselor to combine information from a number of different sources, individuals, and occasions.

EARLY IDENTIFICATION

Three widely used general batteries assess preschool children: the Developmental Indicators for the Assessment of Learning–Revised (DIAL-R), the Battelle Developmental Inventory, and the Denver Developmental Screening Test. DIAL-R is used to assess the cognitive, language, motor, social, and emotional development of children ages 2 to 6. In the motor area tests the child is involved in activities such as catching a bean bag, jumping, hopping, skipping, building with blocks, touching fingers, and cutting with cutting cards and scissors. The Battelle Developmental Inventory can be given from birth to 8 years and measures personal, social, adaptive, motor, communication, and cognitive skills. The Denver Developmental Screening Test assesses personal-social, fine motor, language, and gross motor skills of children from birth to age 6.

Some instruments focus on one domain. The Children's Adaptive Behavior Scale is designed to assess a child's adaptability to different social environments. The five areas covered are language development, independent functioning, family role performance, economic and vocational activity, and socialization. The Matson Evaluation of Social Skills can be used with clients aged 6 through adult and features both a teacher rating and a self-report form.

Here are some other instruments widely used for assessing preschool children:

The Bayley Scales of Infant Development, Second Edition (1993) are useful in monitoring early signs of behavioral problems.

The McCarthy Scales of Children's Abilities (MSCA) (1972) have 18 subtests and yield 5 scale scores: verbal, quantitative, perceptual performance, memory, and motor. The scales are combined to provide a general cognitive index.

The Miller Assessment for Preschoolers (1982) measures sensory-motor and cognitive abilities as well as gross and fine motor functioning. It also has a verbal index.

The Stanford-Binet Intelligence Scale–IV (1986) has 15 subtests. Verbal reasoning, abstract/visual reasoning, quantitative reasoning, and short-term memory scores are available to the examiner.

The Wechsler Preschool and Primary Scale of Intelligence–Revised (WPPSI-R) (1989) is a downward extension of the WISC. Verbal, performance, and total IQ scores can be computed.

LANGUAGE DEVELOPMENT

The time between birth and age 6 is a crucial period for language development. A number of standardized tests are available to help professionals look at qualitative and quantitative differences. Here are a few examples of tests:

The Houston Test for Language Development (HTLD) measures verbal and non-verbal communication of children from birth to age 6. The test is used for differential diagnosis of problems resulting from emotional deprivation, auditory and motor deficits, and other causes. The HTLD provides a profile of strengths and weaknesses that can be valuable when planning specific interventions.

The Reynell Developmental Language Scale (RDLS) assesses slow development in receptive and expressive language areas for children ages 1 to 7.

The Test of Adolescent Language–2 (TOAL–2) identifies problems in both the spoken and written language of adolescents. TOAL–2 provides scores in listening, speaking, reading, writing, spoken language, written language, vocabulary, grammar, receptive language, and expressive language.

The Test of Language Development (TOLD) assesses receptive and expressive vocabulary and expressive grammatical structure by using picture identification, grammatical completion, word definitions, word discrimination, and word articulation. The primary form can be given to children aged 4 to 8.11, while the intermediate form is used with children aged 8.6 to 12.11.

COGNITIVE STAGES

Piaget's theory of cognitive development involves four major stages. In the sensorimotor stage children from birth to age 2 develop schemes and organized patterns of behavior or thought through sensory and motor activities. The preoperational stage occurs between the ages of 2 and 7, when children develop the ability to conserve and decenter—that is, to overcome perceptual centration, irreversibility, and egocentrism in their logical thinking. During the concrete operational stage children between ages 7 and 11 develop the ability to use mental operations but have difficulty manipulating conditions without experience. The formal operational stage starts at age 11 or 12, when children are able to solve problems, work with abstractions, form hypotheses, and engage in mental operations. Children tend to think, perceive, organize, and understand their personal, physical, and social environments differently at various stages of development.

Two tests assess stages of development:

The Concept Assessment Kit (CAK) measures cognitive development of preschool and primary grade children. The CAK is a multiple-item task-assessment and oral-response test measuring conservation. Forms A and B measure conservation of two-dimensional space, number substance, continuous quantity, discontinuous quantity, and weight. Form C measures conservation using area and length.

The Wach Analysis of Cognitive Structures assesses the development of learning ability among young children and suggests activities to stimulate learning and growth. The inventory has 15 clusters of tasks divided into subtests consisting of manipulative, visual-sensory, and body movement actions. The test is culture-free and nonverbal and has been used with children having language, mental, and hearing deficits.

The tests focus on how we think and reason. They do not present norms and standard scores like traditional cognitive ability tests do, nor do they have the same level of validity. Some counselors believe this information also provides a frame of reference for looking at social and emotional development and is useful in instructional programming.

The case of Bobby shows how school professionals might assess development.

CASE OF BOBBY

Bobby
Race/sex: African-American male
Date of birth: 8/17/93
Grade: Kindergarten
Present school: San Pablo Elementary

Tests Used

At age 4.5 on 1/27/98:

Developmental Test of Visual-Motor Integration
Leiter International Performance Scale
Peabody Picture Vocabulary Test–Revised
Preschool Attainment Record
Stanford-Binet Intelligence Scale, Form L–M

At age 5.8 on 4/23/99:

Wechsler Preschool and Primary Scale of Intelligence–Revised

At age 5.9 on 5/15/99:
(Speech and Language Evaluation)

Bracken Basic Concept Scale
Cultural Evaluation of Language Fundamentals–Revised
Expressive One-Word Picture Vocabulary Test
Goldman-Fristoe Test of Articulation

Structured Photographic Expressive Language Test–II
Zimmerman Preschool Language Scale

At age 6.4 on 12/18/99:

Vane Kindergarten Test
Vineland Adaptive Behavior Scale
Woodcock-Johnson Test of Achievement–Revised

Reason for Referral

Bobby was originally referred to Child Find by the Speech and Hearing Center to obtain a current level of functioning. His parents noted delays in overall developmental skills and significant deficits in the use of speech and language.

Background Information

Bobby's mother reported her pregnancy was normal and without complications. However, at the age of 6 months Bobby contracted bacterial meningitis, after which his speech and language skills were severely delayed.

Review of Records

Bobby's initial evaluation by the psychologist on 1/27/98 (age 4.5) indicated a Stanford-Binet

Intelligence Scale IQ of 54, a Leiter IQ of 79, and a Peabody Picture Vocabulary Test score of 52. The examiner noted that the scores obtained appeared to be somewhat depressed due to significant difficulties in speech and language. Placement in a preschool handicapped program was recommended on 3/22/98.

A reevaluation was completed on 4/23/99. Results of Bobby's performance on the WPPSI-R were a Verbal IQ of 70, a Performance IQ of 86, and a Full Scale IQ of 75.

Speech and language assessment was completed in May 1999. Reported results include these scores:

Bracken Test of Basic Concepts	50
Cultural Evaluation of Language Fundamentals—Revised	65
Expressive One-Word Picture Vocabulary Test	61

The examiner reports that Bobby shows severe delays in expressive language and a severe phonological disorder. Participation in a program for severely language-impaired students was suggested.

Testing was also administered on 12/18/99. The Woodcock-Johnson Tests of Achievement–Revised indicated academic skills at a prereadiness level comparable to a preschool youngster below 4 years old.

Vane scoring of the human figure drawing yielded an age equivalent of 5.4, which is in the low average range.

Adaptive skills as measured through teacher ratings of the Vineland Adaptive Behavior Scale showed standard scores in the average range.

Sensory Functioning

In the fall of 1999 Bobby passed the vision screening administered at school. During the evaluation he was observed to shield his right eye during drawing activities. Observations were discussed with his parents, and periodic screenings at school were suggested.

Results of the hearing screening indicated that auditory acuity in the left ear was adequate. He failed to respond appropriately at all frequency levels presented in the right ear. Significant deficits in speech articulation and language were also reported.

Summary and Conclusions

Bobby is a 6-year, 4-month-old youngster who is placed in a full-time SLD program. He has evidenced significant deficits in acquisition of basic academic skills, and he also sustains substantial delays in speech and language. Results of formal intellectual assessments indicate that overall conceptual skills are within the borderline to low average range, but scores should be interpreted with caution due to his significant difficulties in speech and language. Current academic levels are significantly below that expected of his estimated ability.

Adaptive skills show functioning at a level more typical of a much younger child, with the most notable deficits in communication skills. Daily living and self-help skills are an area of relative strength although still rated at the preschool level.

Bobby can be expected to continue requiring a comprehensive, well-structured, individualized educational program. Preferential seating and individual presentation of instructions are suggested. Continued placement in the self-contained SLD program seems the most appropriate and least restrictive to meet his overall educational needs. A meeting of counselors, psychologists, teachers, and parents should be scheduled to consider permanent placement and review current assessment results.

PSYCHOSOCIAL DEVELOPMENT

Erikson developed a theory of personality development based upon psychoanalytical, biographical, historical, and anthropological methods of study. He postulates eight stages of psychosocial development. At each stage positive and negative forces produce conflict and a crisis that must be resolved. When the negative forces have a stronger influence than the positive factors, the outcome leads to difficulties in adjustment and development. The developmental crisis that needs to be resolved during the first year is trust versus mistrust. For 2- and 3-year-olds it is autonomy versus doubt, for 4- to 5-year-olds initiative versus guilt. Industry versus inferiority is the crisis from 6 to 11 years, identity versus role confusion peaks during adolescence, while intimacy versus isolation occurs during young adulthood. Generativity versus stagnation is the crisis during middle age, integrity versus despair during old age. The degree and direction of conflict resolution determines the overall health of the individual, but the degree of conflict resolution is relative since no stage conflict is completely resolved. One of the major instruments to assess Erikson's stages is the Measures of Psychosocial Development. The case of Anita illustrates the use of this inventory.

CASE OF ANITA

Ms. Moore was a counselor working with a group of unwed African-American teenage mothers. She was eager to find out more about the personality dynamics and conflict resolution of Anita, one of her counselees.

Anita is 16 and will be a senior in high school if she is able to pass her courses. Her pregnancy and the birth of a daughter during the school year have hampered her academically, and she is talking about dropping out of school. Anita comes from a single-parent family. Currently, her grandmother is taking care of her baby while Anita works part time at Kentucky Fried Chicken. Ms. Moore decided to administer the Measures of Psychosocial Development (MPD) since it is based upon sound personality theory and assesses adolescent and adult personality development. The MPD is a 112-item self-report inventory that

has 27 different scales: 9 positive scales (trust, autonomy, initiative, industry, identity, intimacy, generativity, ego integrity, and total positive), 9 negative scales (mistrust, shame and doubt, guilt, inferiority, identity confusion, isolation, stagnation, despair, and total negative), 9 resolution scales (one for each stage), and a total resolution scale. The test taker responds on a 5-point scale ranging from "not at all like you" to "very much like you."

The MPD is easy to score. Ms. Moore just removed the top page of the answer sheet, counted the ratings for each row of items, and recorded the scores on each of the 27 scales on the profile sheet.

Alpha reliabilities ($n = 372$) for the scales ranged from a low of .65 on trust to a high of .84 on identity confusion. The median coefficient was .74. Test-retest coefficients for 108 individuals were also reported and ranged from a high of .91 on total negative to a low of .67 on inferiority.

The MPD reports construct validity through intercorrelations of the scale, correlation of the MPD with the Inventory of Psychosocial Development and the Self-Description Questionnaire. The author claims the data support the discriminant validity of the positive scales and that there is moderate support for the negative scales and consistent evidence for convergent validity of the scale. Separate norms are presented for males and females ages 13 to 17, 18 to 24, 25 to 49, and 50 and over. The manual does not provide the means and standard deviations for any of these groups or the standard errors of measurement for the various scales. Despite separate norms, no statistical evidence indicates a gender difference. The norms use T scores with a mean of 50 and a standard deviation of 10.

Anita had the following percentile ranks on the MPD:

Positive Scales

Trust	03
Autonomy	42
Initiative	27
Industry	24
Identity	14
Intimacy	01
Generativity	11
Ego Integrity	01
Total Positive	03

Negative Scales

Mistrust	79
Shame and Doubt	50
Guilt	35
Inferiority	69
Identity Confusion	65
Isolation	92
Stagnation	38
Despair	96
Total Negative	79

Resolution Scales

Trust versus Mistrust	08
Autonomy versus Shame and Doubt	50
Initiative versus Guilt	46
Industry versus Inferiority	27
Identity versus Identity Confusion	24
Intimacy versus Isolation	01
Generativity versus Stagnation	27
Ego Integrity versus Despair	02
Total Resolution	05

The MPD manual (p. 9) states that high scorers on mistrust perceive the world as inconsistent, painful, stressful, and threatening and believe that life is unpredictable. They struggle with the burden of questioning whether others are trustworthy. Their basic mistrust may be characterized as a sense of living precariously, of feeling that good things never last or doubting that needs will be met. High scorers on isolation tend to remain alone and be self-absorbed because of fear of ego loss. Isolation occurs if a person's identity is too weak to sustain the uncertainties of intimacy. The individual may be drawn toward intimate relationships but also be frightened by them (p. 10). Commitments and responsibilities seem unreasonable or too restrictive.

High scorers on despair perceive that their lives have been filled with misdirected energies and lost opportunities. They believe there is no time to undo the mistakes of the past and to begin life anew.

MORAL DEVELOPMENT

Piaget studied the moral development of children and identified two broad stages. Kohlberg expanded the two broad stages into three levels, each with two stages. The first level is preconventional morality and usually extends to age 9. The two stages are punishment-obedience orientation and instrumental-relativist orientation. The second level is conventional morality and includes the good boy–nice girl and the law-and-order orientations. This period is typical of youth ages 9 to 20. Level 3 is postconventional morality and includes social contract and universal ethical principle orientation. A number of instruments have been developed to measure moral reasoning:

The Defining Issues Test is a pencil-and-paper instrument that presents dilemmas about which the client selects preferred responses.

The Ethical Reasoning Inventory is a paper-and-pencil inventory that consists of six dilemmas from Kohlberg's Moral Judgment Inventory. Questions are followed by two responses and sets of reasons that represent stages of Kohlberg's theory.

The Moral Judgment Interview and Scoring System uses a structured interview technique that involves a minimum of 21 questions about the client's reasoning regarding three moral dilemmas. Raters are used to match the responses against the stage criteria.

The Social Moral Reflection Measure is a group-administered version of Kohlberg's manual.

The scoring of some of these tests is tedious and time-consuming and demands careful study of the manuals and criteria for scoring. Reliability of some instruments is moderate. Gilligan (1982) believes that women have a different approach to resolving real-life dilemmas. The question about the criterion-referenced validity of these tests is whether individuals actually behave the way they say they do.

CAREER DEVELOPMENT

Super (1990) postulates a five-stage theory of career development. The first is the growth stage in which the preadolescent develops self-awareness and interests. Children role-play and fantasize about different jobs and occupations. The exploratory stage extends from early adolescence to early adulthood and has three phases: crystallization, specification, and implementation. Crystallization relates to developing ideas about fields of endeavor and appealing occupations. Specification relates to moving from general preferences to choosing a specific career or job. Implementation requires pursuing chosen fields.

The establishment stage normally takes place in early to middle adulthood and consists of developmental tasks: stabilizing, consolidating, and advancing. Individuals settle down, support their families, and develop appropriate lifestyles in the stabilizing stage. At the consolidating stage individuals are concerned with their place in an occupation or in an organization. Workers expect to move up the ladder and get ahead financially in the advancing stage. The maintenance stage extends from middle adulthood to later adulthood and consists of three developmental tasks: holding, updating, and innovating. The disengagement stage extends from the early 60s to retirement and has three phases: disengagement, retirement planning, and retirement living.

Super, Thompson, and Lindeman (1988) point out that it is common for individuals to change career paths after becoming established. This requires them to reassess life and career plans and go back to previous developmental stages and tasks.

The case of Cindy shows how testing can be used in career development.

CASE OF CINDY

Cindy is a 28-year-old Caucasian female. She has been married since June 1992 and has a six-year-old daughter. Cindy is interested in reentering the job market but is unsure about her employment qualifications and interests. She doesn't know whether to return to school, get vocational training, or begin work wherever employment is available. Cindy maintained a high C or low B average throughout high school but did not particularly like school. After graduation she was employed as a grocery clerk/cashier and a retail salesperson but stopped working when her daughter was born. Now Cindy wants to develop her job skills and explore career options. Her husband is employed as a high school teacher and has encouraged her to research her career choices.

Cindy dresses neatly, has good eye contact, and is friendly, verbal, and articulate. She understands the need for career exploration and appears focused and committed to developing an action plan.

The counselor chooses the Adult Career Concerns Inventory (ACCI) as one of the assessment instruments because it is intended for adults who are rethinking their careers. The ACCI is appropriate for both sexes, is written in American English at the eighth-grade reading level, and may be hand or machine scored. The test taker is asked to respond to 61 items on a 5-point scale indicating the amount of current concern toward the statement.

The test manual provides a developmental model for assessment and counseling. The authors present content, concurrent, and predictive validity as well as the factor structure of the instrument. Alpha coefficients are reported for two different groups and range primarily in the .80s and .90s. The authors also present the standard error of measurement.

Cindy's results on the ACCI indicate considerable concern for exploration. Specification had an average score of 5.0, while implementation and crystallization were 4.5 and 4.0 respectively. The next highest score was 4.6 on updating. The other scales had scores of 4.0 or less. The disengagement stage had the lowest scores.

Here are Cindy's other test results:

Strong Interest Inventory—General Occupational Theme Scores

Realistic: average
Investigative: moderately low
Artistic: moderately high
Social: moderately high
Enterprising: moderately low
Conventional: moderately low
Academic Comfort: moderately high
Intro/Extroversion: average

Salience Inventory:

Participation:	High salience—home and family, working
	Moderate—studying
	Low—leisure, community service
Commitment:	High salience—home and family
	Moderate—working, studying
	Low—leisure
Value Expectations:	High—home and family, community service
	Moderate—working, studying

Myers-Briggs Type Indicator:

ENFP Extrovert, Intuitive, Feeling, Perceptive

SUMMARY

Counselors' knowledge of assessing developmental readiness has become increasingly important in the early identification and screening of clients with problems. Developmental tests measure the typical skills expected in normal development. Assessment includes physical, social, cognitive, emotional, communication, self-care, and independent living skills as well as work habits and adjustment. Direct testing, naturalistic observation, interviewing, and a combination are used to assess these domains. Much emphasis is placed on the early identification of problems and preschool screening. Developmental theories provide a useful framework for understanding critical periods of development.

QUESTIONS FOR DISCUSSION

1. What are the general principles of developmental assessment?
2. List and discuss the major domains assessed in developmental testing.

3. What are the advantages and disadvantages of the various methods of developmental assessment?

4. What are some of the major instruments used in early identification?

5. What contributions have developmental stage theories made to assessment? Do you agree or disagree that developmental theories have little value in the assessment process?

6. Review the case of Bobby, Anita, or Cindy. Do you feel that the counselor used appropriate tests? Why or why not? Did the tests have sufficient reliability and validity for the purposes intended? What is your interpretation of the data and test results given? What additional information would you have found desirable?

SUGGESTED ACTIVITIES

1. Interview counselors and helping professionals about what types of developmental assessment procedures they use and why. Have them identify problems they have had in working in developmental assessment. Report your findings to the class.

2. Visit a Child Find or similar agency and inquire about the assessment procedures they use, the cooperating agencies they work with, the incidence of children with disabilities they have identified, and the type of parent education and training that is available. Report this information to the class.

3. Write a paper or give a report on assessing developmental stages, milestones of development, assessment domains, critical issues or problems in preschool assessment, or a similar topic.

4. Select a developmental screening or stage instrument and administer it to an appropriate subject. Write down your results and discuss them in class.

5. Write a critical analysis or review of one of the major developmental assessment instruments.

6. Imagine you are a school counselor. What developmental assessment tools and techniques would you use to help understand the following cases?

Mary is in ninth grade and involved in all types of school activities. She is a cheerleader, a member of the basketball team, and a member of the National Honor Society. She has increased the amount of time she spends in exercising and jogging. She does these activities every day and has placed herself on a stringent diet. She has begun to lose weight. Her mother is concerned and calls to arrange an appointment with you.

John has just started second grade. He becomes tearful when school or his teacher is mentioned. He procrastinates when getting ready for school in the morning and misses the bus some mornings. His parents have called you because they are concerned about John's behavior.

Shannon is a junior in high school. She is concerned because all her friends know what they want to do after high school but she doesn't. She thinks that something is wrong with her and feels she doesn't have the skills and abilities to do much of anything.

ADDITIONAL READINGS

Bagnatto, S. J., & Neisworth, J. (1991). *Assessment for early intervention*. New York: Guilford.

The book focuses on the competencies needed for developmental assessment and presents models of team assessment and intervention.

Blau, T. H. (1991). *The psychological examination of the child*. New York: Wiley.

The book is designed to help the examiner identify anything that might be out of order in a child's development and deals with what is important to learn about all children and their development.

Cohen, L. G., & Spenciner, L. J. (1994). *Assessment of young children*. New York: Longman.

The authors include chapters on assessing development and adaptive problems.

Reynolds, C. R., & Kamphaus, R. W. (1990). *Handbook of psychological and educational assessment of children: Intelligence and achievement*. Vol. 2: *Personality, behavior, and context*. New York: Guilford.

Volume 2 covers a broad base of the domains tested and includes evaluation and treatment of childhood disorders in development, learning, and behavior.

Vance, H. B. (Ed.). (1998). *Psychological assessment of children* (2nd ed.). New York: Wiley.

Various assessment approaches are critically analyzed.

Vernon, A. (1993). *Developmental assessment and intervention with children and adolescents*. Alexandria, VA: American Counseling Association.

The author provides strategies to assess the normal problems that children and youth face. Case studies are presented along with strategies to help diagnose and remediate the problems.

Environmental Assessment

![gray bar]

OVERVIEW

Environmental assessment contributes to the understanding of the dynamics of behavior and is used to determine the impact of environment on the development of the individual, the family, and other groups. Knowledge of a client's environment helps the counselor determine possible intervention strategies and resources that could be used effectively. Public Law 94–142 requires determination of the least restrictive environment for children with disabilities. Ecological psychology focuses on specific features of the environment and the interactive effect of individuals within systems. The focus is not only on how situational variables determine the present behavior of individuals and groups but also on how these variables influence the direction of personal and social growth over time.

OBJECTIVES

This chapter should help the reader understand

✔ The uses of environmental assessment in counseling and personality appraisal

✔ The dimensions and models of environmental assessment

✔ The instruments and techniques available to helping professionals

✔ The applications of environmental assessment in counseling and educational contexts

THEORETICAL BACKGROUND

Environmental assessment has roots in the phenomenological approaches to counseling because idiographic approaches are often used by the counselor. Counselors are interested at times in discovering the laws or factors that guide the behavior of a certain individual rather than laws pertaining to people in general. Barnett and Zucker (1990) state that this approach stresses the personal and social behaviors and constructs that have validity for the client, such as overt behaviors of concern to the individual or others; covert or internal events that can be reported; central themes, values, and goals; and the impact of behaviors and situations on the individual (p. 145). The approach is concerned with the perceptions, cognitions, and learning of the individuals involved. Wallace and Larsen (1992) point out that this perspective helps the counselor to view children in relationship to their total environment.

Environmental assessment also has roots in ecological psychology. Bandura (1986) emphasizes that in social transactions people become each other's environments (p. 335). Ecological psychology focuses on groups and their adaptation to their environment, and it is characterized by its naturalistic methodology, site specificity, systems concepts, emphasis on long time periods, transdisciplinary emphasis, and evaluation of natural experiments.

Values

A number of important values in this approach have been identified:

1. Knowledge of the environment can help us understand the behavior and adjustment of children and adults.
2. Ecological assessment helps counselors determine possible intervention strategies and resources.
3. Ecological strategies help counselors evaluate outcomes of the assessment-intervention process.
4. Environmental assessment is important to help determine the extent to which a given environment is likely to facilitate positive development.
5. Environmental assessment helps counselors determine the extent to which certain skills are required for successful placement in those environments.
6. Public Law 94–142 requires assessing environments to determine, across multiple dimensions, the extent to which they are normalized and least restrictive.

Barnett and Zucker (1990) state that child, school, family, and relevant community systems should be assessed for multiple perspectives of adjustment pertaining to the referral question, systems problems, and strengths (p. 146). They believe that it is important to consider not only how situational variables influence the present behavior of clients but also how these variables may later change clients' personal and social growth and adjustment.

Models and Dimensions

Moos (1997) has developed a model to assess the dimensions related to the psychosocial characteristics and social climates of environments. He claims that environments have unique personalities, just as people do (p. 1). His model focuses on three dimensions: relationship, personal growth, and system maintenance and change. The relationship dimensions identify the nature and intensity of the personal relationships within the environment. Key concepts in the relationship dimensions across environments are involvement, support, spontaneity, expressiveness, affiliation, and peer cohesion. Personal development dimensions are characterized by autonomy, practical orientation, personal problem orientation, independent-task orientation, competition, self-discovery, and anger and aggression. The exact nature of these dimensions, of course, depends on their underlying purposes and goals. System maintenance and change dimensions assess the extent to which the environment is orderly, is clear in its expectations, maintains control, and is responsive to change. The scales are called order and organization, clarity, and control. Moos and his co-workers have developed a number of scales to assess environments in a wide variety of settings, such as the family, school, and correctional setting.

Bailey and Wolery (1989) define the environment to include everything that surrounds us and experiences to which we are exposed. They stress seven important components:

Physical space—available space and how it is arranged

Organization and supervision of space—must be organized and well defined according to function

Materials—sufficient materials for those using the environment

Peer environment—the number and type of people sharing the environment

Organization and scheduling—level of organization of the environment, how activities are scheduled, and the roles of the people involved

Safety—environment free of hazards, with adequate supervision

Responsiveness—provides an opportunity to enhance feelings of competency and independence

Moos (1997) points out six ways of identifying the characteristics of human environments (p. 1):

1. Ecological dimensions, which include geographical, meteorological, architectural, and physical design variables
2. Behavior settings, which are characterized by both ecological and behavioral properties
3. Dimensions of organizational structure
4. Dimensions identifying the collective, personal, and/or behavioral characteristics of the people living and functioning in an environment
5. Variables relevant to the functional or reinforcement analyses of environments
6. Dimensions related to psychosocial characteristics and social climates of environments

ASSESSMENT STRATEGIES

The strategy used to assess the environment depends on the referral question or the purpose of the assessment. One of the major techniques, direct observation, is preferred to interviewing because clients may have difficulty assessing their own environment. For example, if there is a concern about safety, the observer might want to draw a diagram of the room and plot the activity and movement within the space. For convenience, observers use checklists and rating scales when assessing the salient features of the environment.

Bailey and Wolery (1989) point out that helping professionals should be aware of the complexities of environmental assessment, appreciate the dynamic and interactive nature of environments, focus on functions rather than forms, and be familiar with a variety of strategies. They believe multiple sources of information and multiple measurement strategies should be used.

FAMILY/HOME ENVIRONMENT

Research has revealed the importance of environmental factors in personal, social, and cognitive growth. The family is one of the most important environments for children and can have a tremendous impact on personal and social growth. Many instruments to assess dimensions of the family environment have been developed. Some of the observational scales used to code different dimensions of family interaction are described here:

The Affective Style Measure is used to observe families in situations in which the participants discuss problems. The observer codes their interaction in categories, such as criticism, guilt induction, and intrusiveness. The code has been found useful in predicting psychiatric disturbance in adolescents and young adults.

The Defensive and Supportive Communication Interaction System is a coding system used to observe the defensive and supportive communication in family interaction, family therapy, and marriage therapy. Some of the defensive categories coded are judgmental-dogmatism, indifference, and superiority. Some of the supportive categories coded are emphatic understanding, equality, and spontaneous problem solving.

The Developmental Environments Coding System (DECS) assesses familial variables predicted by structural-developmental theory to affect ego and moral development. Dimensions such as focusing, competitive challenging, noncompetitive sharing of perspective, avoidance, rejection of the task, distortion, support, and affective conflict are coded.

The Family Conflict and Dominance Codes measure dominance and conflict in family interaction. Family members are asked to complete a questionnaire separately and are then brought together to fill out one questionnaire that represents the family's opinion or view.

The Family Constraining and Enabling Coding System (CECS) is used to analyze transactions in family communication by measuring the frequency of communication events and their sequences. Constraining categories include cognitive constraining and affective constraining; enabling categories include cognitive enabling and affective enabling.

The Family Interaction Scales (FIS) are a coding system for observing family interaction based on the theories of Jackson and Satir. The purpose of the scales is to promote understanding of individual personal development in the family context. The six major dimensions are agreement/disagreement, clarity, topic, commitment, intensity, and relationship.

Self-report instruments are another approach to measuring the family environment. Here are some of the widely used instruments:

The Children's Version of the Family Environment Scale (CVFES) is a downward pictorial extension of the Family Environment Scale and is used with elementary schoolchildren.

The Colorado Self-Report Measure of Family Functioning is designed to provide a description of whole family functioning along 15 dimensions under three general headings—relationship, personal growth, and system maintenance.

The Conflict Tactics Scale (CTS) measures the use of reasoning, verbal aggression, and violence as modes of dealing with conflict in relationships within a family.

The Family Adaptability and Cohesion Evaluation Scales III (FACES III) measures family cohesion and adaptability and perceived and ideal family functioning.

The Family Assessment Measure (FAM) assesses dimensions of family strengths and weaknesses from three perspectives: the family as a system, dyadic relationships, and individual family members.

The Family Environment Scale (FES) measures the social environmental characteristics of the family and has three climate dimensions—relationship, personal growth, and system maintenance. The FES has 10 subscales: cohesion, expressiveness, conflict, independence, achievement orientation, intellectual-cultural orientation, active-recreational orientation, moral-religious emphasis, organization, and control.

The Family Evaluation Form (FEF) assesses dimensions of family functioning: family centeredness, conflict and tension, open communication, emotional closeness, community involvement, children's relations, children's adjustment, parenting–nurturance, parenting–independence training, parenting–effective discipline, parenting–strict/punitive discipline, parenting–negative style, husband/wife dominance, marital satisfaction, homemaker role, worker role, financial problems, and extrafamilial support.

The Family Functioning in Adolescence Questionnaire (FFAQ) measures family functioning in adolescence and has scales such as structure, affect, communication, behavior control, value transmission, and external systems.

The Family Process Scales (FPS) assess the interdependence of family members, the dynamic homeostasis in the family, and the family's ability to provide an environment that fosters healthy psychological development and a sense of well-being in its members.

The Family Relationship Questionnaire (FRQ) measures family functioning in the areas of affect, conflict, and dominance and can be used with culturally and economically different types of families.

The McMaster Family Assessment Device, Version 3 (FAD) evaluates family functioning on seven dimensions and is used to screen healthy and pathological family functioning. The FAD scales are problem solving, communication, roles, affective responsiveness, affective involvement, behavior control, and general functioning.

The Self-Report Family Inventory (SFI) assesses dimensions of the family such as health, communication, cohesion, directive leadership, and expressiveness and can be used along with observational instruments in the Beavers System approach to family assessment.

The case of Ann shows how tests of family functioning can be used.

CASE OF ANN

Ann, a 9-year-old in third grade, was not achieving up to the expectations of her mother. She believed Ann was better than a C or D student and that she was lazy and not trying in school. Ann said she likes school but can't keep up with the work and she has too much homework. Recently Ann's father, a naval officer, was sent to the Middle East on deployment for at least 6 months. Ann is the oldest of three children. Her mother mentioned the problems of being a navy wife and her sometimes stormy relationship with her husband. Ann's mother works part time as a receptionist for a local business.

One of the tests given to Ann by the counselor was the Children's Version of the Family Environment Scale. Ann had no problems taking the test, which includes 30 items. Looking at three pictures on each of 10 scales, she was asked to choose the one that looks most like her family.

The test appears to have face validity, and the pictures seem to represent the scales and constructs measured by the test. The authors report the procedures they used to establish the content validity of the items. The test-retest reliability was .80 over a four-week interval. The norms are based on a population of 158 children from the region around Buffalo, New York, grades 1 to 6. According to the authors, the sample represented approximately 26 per grade, an equal number of males and females, and a number of different nationalities. The religious grouping was primarily Roman Catholic. A norm table is available for converting raw scores to standard scores over the combined grades. No information is provided in the manual on the fixed mean and fixed standard deviation of the subscales. Table 15.1 illustrates Ann's scores.

Table 15.1
Case of Ann: Results of the Children's Version of the Family Environment Scale

Scales	Raw Score	Standard Score	Third-Grade Means
Relationship			
Cohesion	4.0	28	6.67
Expressiveness	5.0	43	5.78
Conflict	8.0	57	7.14
Achievement-Orientation	7.0	55	7.04
Personal Growth			
Independence	3.5	35	5.53
Intellectual/Cultural	2.0	22	5.89
Active/Recreational	3.0	22	7.00
Moral/Religious	8.0	53	7.32
System Maintenance			
Organization	4.5	30	7.18
Control	7.5	52	5.60

The scales with the highest raw scores were conflict (the amount of openly expressed anger, aggression, and conflict among family members), achievement-orientation (the extent to which school activities are cast into an achievement-oriented or competitive framework), and moral/religious emphasis (emphasis on ethical and religious issues and values).

The lowest raw scores were intellectual/cultural orientation (degree of interest in political, social, intellectual, and cultural activities), active/recreational orientation (extent of participation in social and recreational activities), and independence (the extent to which the family members are assertive and self-sufficient and make their own decisions).

SCHOOL ENVIRONMENT

A number of variables are important not only to the attitudes, personal success, and achievement of students but also to several nonachievement behaviors such as attendance, social interaction, number of interruptions, and level of questions (McKee & Wilt, 1990). Assessment needs to focus on seating position, classroom design and furniture arrangement, spatial density and crowding, noise, and lighting. Teacher effectiveness research has identified teacher behaviors that are related to student achievement, such as with-itness, overlapping, signal continuity and momentum, group alerting, and accountability in lessons.

Scales have been developed to measure the psychological attributes of the school environment at all levels from kindergarten to graduate school. Various forms measure the perceptions of groups such as parents, teachers, students, and administrators. Some of the major instruments are described here:

The Classroom Environment Scale measures the psychosocial environment of the school on three major dimensions—relationship, personal growth, and system maintenance and change. The scales are involvement, affiliation, teacher support, task orientation, competition, order and organization, rule clarity, teacher control, and innovation.

The College Characteristics Index (CCI) measures 30 needs derived in part from Murray's theory discussed in Chapter 11. The first nine scales are abasement, achievement, adaptability, affiliation, aggression, change, conjunctivity, counteraction, and deference.

The College Student Experiences Scale (CSEQ) assesses 14 dimensions of college activities, 8 dimensions of college environment, and 21 estimates of outcomes of colleges. Additional sections call for demographic data and opinions about college.

The Effective School Battery has a form for students and one for teachers. The teacher inventory has 12 parts—background information, involvement of parents, classroom management and teaching practices, resources, job satisfaction, training and other activities, interaction with students, school rules and discipline, how different groups get along, personal safety, personal opinion, and school climate. The student inventory has four parts: what about you, how you spend your time, your school, and what do you think.

The High School Characteristics Index (HCSI) assesses 30 dimensions of environmental press characteristic of the high school environment.

The Institutional Functioning Inventory (IFI) can be used to compare how administrators, faculty, students, trustees, and so on perceive dimensions of the college environment. The 11 scales are intellectual-aesthetic extracurriculum, freedom, human diversity, concern for improvement of society, concern for undergraduate learning, democratic governance, meeting local needs, self-study and planning, concern for advancing knowledge, concern for innovation, and institutional spirit.

The School Environment Preference Survey (SEPS) measures work-role socialization as it occurs in the traditional school. SEPS has four scales: self-subordination, traditionalism, rule conformity, and uncriticalness. The test is helpful in planning instructional strategies for students or as an aid in placement in alternative learning environments.

The case of Sam shows how counselors can test school environment issues.

CASE OF SAM

Mr. Brown, a beginning fifth-grade mathematics and science teacher, came to the counselor for help. One student, Sam, is giving the teacher fits because he acts in an inappropriate manner. The counselor decides to use the Instructional Environment Scale (TIES) (Ysseldyke & Christenson, 1987) as the instrument to help understand the situation.

The test authors state that TIES systematically describes how a student's academic behavior problems are a function of factors in the instructional environment. TIES is used to gather data on 12 components of effective instruction—instructional presentation, classroom environment, teacher expectations, cognitive emphasis, motivational practice, relevant practice, informed feedback, adaptive instruction, academic engaged time, progress evaluation, instructional planning, and student understanding.

The counselor followed the procedures outlined in the manual:

1. Conducted a classroom observation and recorded the observations on the green form
2. Interviewed Sam, the student identified by the teacher as a problem, with the structured interview schedule on page 4 of the green form
3. Interviewed Mr. Brown and completed page 1 of the green form
4. Reviewed information from the interviews and observations to see if more information was needed
5. Observed science and mathematics classes and completed the institutional rating form on the blue sheet and the summary profile sheet
6. Provided feedback to the teacher and to the student

The counselor carefully read the directions for scoring TIES and read the interpretive examples. The manual presents interrater reliabilities ranging from .83 on cognitive emphasis and motivational strategies to .96 on informed feedback and student understanding. The median coefficient was .95. The authors present evidence on the content validity of the 12 components and support each with evidence from research on effective teaching.

After observing Sam, the counselor asked the teacher whether Sam's performance was typical. Mr. Brown said that Sam put on a bigger show because he had a bigger audience. The teacher said his instructional goals and expectations were the same for all students. He did not plan for Sam separately and followed the instructional sequence as in the syllabus of the county. Mr. Brown said he taught the class as a whole. He wanted to keep all the students at the same place and did not give Sam any independent assignments or help.

In the interview with Sam the counselor asked about the mathematics and science classes Sam had just attended. Sam said he knew what the teacher wanted him to learn but did not know why he had to learn the "junk." He said, "I will never use this stuff." Sam said he did his homework once in a while if he liked the topic. The boy reported that the teacher occasionally asked him questions, but usually he could not answer them. Mr. Brown yelled at him for being lazy, not completing assignments, and not doing his work neatly. The counselor reviewed the class exercise that had just been assigned and found that Sam had completed 10 of 15 math problems, the first seven of which were correct. When the problems called for more than one operation, Sam appeared to be confused.

The counselor rated the 12 dimensions of teaching after observing the classes. Each item was rated on a four-point scale. A rating of 1 indicated that the description was not at all like the student's instructional environment, whereas a rating of 4 indicated that the description was very much like the student's instructional environment. The purpose is to identify instructional strengths and weaknesses and to identify aspects of the environment that are contributing to the student's difficulties. Domains of 1s and 2s suggest areas of difficulty in which change is needed for the student to improve academically.

The counselor rated Mr. Brown 4 on instructional presentation, classroom environment, cognitive emphasis, and teacher expectation. Ratings of 3 were given on relevant practice and academic engage time. Scores of 2 were given on motivational strategies, informed feedback, and instructional planning; 1s were assigned for student understanding, adaptive instruction, and progress evaluation.

SCHOOL CLIMATE

The impact of school reform and decentralization of authority means that much attention has been placed on school climate and environment. The National Association of Secondary School Principals developed a model to assess school climate (Howard & Keefe, 1991). Their comprehensive model consisted of four types of variables—school district and community environment, school input, school climate, and student outcomes. The school district and community environment variables were the population in the area in which the school was located and the percentage of school-aged children in the area served by the school. The school input variables were the governance of the school (private, public), percentage of minorities enrolled in the school, number of students receiving free or reduced lunches, percentage of students in remedial programs, number of activities for which budgeted resources were available, number of elective courses in the curriculum, average per-pupil expenditure, principal's attitude toward change, performance of the school's administrative team, average teacher salary, student-teacher ratio, percentage of school employees who were professionals, number of transfers in and out of the school, average daily attendance, number of students whose primary language was English, principal's perception of autonomy of action in the district, principal's perception of participation in school decisions, number of students enrolled in the school, nature of student dress rules in the school, nature of student employment rules in the school, importance of 14 selected school goals, teacher satisfaction, teacher perceptions of autonomy of action in district or school, and teacher perceptions of participation in school decisions. The two school climate variables were teacher climate and student climate; these were measured by the NASSP Climate Surveys.

There were six student outcomes: total achievement (reading and math scores), percentage of students receiving disciplinary referrals, percentage of students passing all courses, student satisfaction, student self-efficacy (measured by the Brookover Self-Concept of Ability Scale), and percentage of students completing the school year (not dropping out).

WORK ENVIRONMENT

A number of approaches measure the work environment. Sometimes the instrument measures the social-psychological dimensions of work; other times the scale might focus on measuring leadership, stress, organizational climate, or attitudes toward the bureaucratic structure. Here is a sample of work environment scales:

The Leadership Appraisal Survey evaluates how associates view their leader or supervisor and looks at leadership style and components of leadership.

The Occupational Environment Scale assesses the types of stress people experience in their work environment: role-related stress, responsibility for others, role ambiguity, role insufficiency, role overload, and boundary roles.

The Organizational Climate Index (OBI) is based on the need-press paradigm of Murray and measures the psychological climate of the work setting.

The Productivity Environmental Preference Survey (PEPS) assesses how workers prefer to function, learn, and perform their work-related or educational activities. PEPS is used for employee placement and counseling as well as to provide information for office design and layout. It has scales such as sound, temperature, light, design, motivation, responsibility, persistence, structure, self-orientation, and peer orientation. There is a computerized version of the test available for PCs.

The Rahim Organizational Conflict Inventories (ROC) measure the types of conflict and various styles of handling conflict found within an organization.

The Work Environment Scale, one of 10 social climate scales developed by Moos and his associates, measures three dimensions of work—relationship, personal growth, and system maintenance and change. The scales are involvement, peer cohesion, supervisor support, autonomy, task orientation, work pressure, clarity, control, innovation, and physical comfort. There are three forms: the real form measures workers' perceptions of existing work environments; the ideal form measures the workers' perceptions of the ideal work environment; and the expectations form measures workers' expectations about their work settings.

PERSON-ENVIRONMENT-FIT

Person-environment-fit theories stress the need to study the congruence between the client's needs, capabilities, and aspirations and environmental demands, resources, and response opportunities (Holland, 1997). Counselors look for ways in which different environmental arrangements and conditions force accommodations in behavior and study the individual-environment interactions. At times counselors focus on whether clients are functioning in the environment as predicted. Person-environment-fit has wide application and is especially important when working with preschool children, students with disabilities who need to be mainstreamed, and workers who are making career-change decisions.

Holland (1997) points out that individuals seek an environment that is reinforcing, satisfying, and congruent with their personality types. Congruence is related to factors such as job and personal satisfaction. Holland developed two instruments that measure personality types—the Self-Directed Search and the Vocational Preference Inventory. These tests are discussed in Chapter 10.

SUMMARY

Environmental assessment contributes to the understanding of the dynamics of behavior of children and adults in work, school, or other environments. The environment can be viewed in terms of physical space—how the space is organized and supervised, the materials in the environment, the people in the environment, how the environment is scheduled, its safety, its responsiveness, and so on. The environment can also be assessed from a psychosocial perspective. Research has pointed to the importance of the family/home environment to personal, social, and cognitive growth. Likewise, the school environment and specifically the classroom environment influences the achievement and self-concept of learners. Research on person-environment-fit supports the importance of the congruence between the environment and the individual's potential.

QUESTIONS FOR DISCUSSION

1. What are the theoretical roots of environmental assessment?
2. Why is environmental assessment valuable to the helping professional?
3. What are some of the major models and dimensions of environmental assessment?
4. What are some of the major strategies used to assess the environment?
5. What approaches are used to measure the family environment?
6. Compare and contrast approaches used to measure the school environments.
7. What approaches are used to measure the work environment?
8. Review the case of Ann. What should the counselor say to Ann's mother when reporting the results of this test? Would you have given Ann this test? From infor-

mation provided how would you rate this test? What tests would you have given Ann, if any? Why?

9. Review the "Case of Sam." If you were the counselor, how would you proceed to work with Mr. Brown and Sam to improve the instructional environment as well as Sam's academic performance? Discuss possible strategies with other class members.

SUGGESTED ACTIVITIES

1. Interview family counselors and find out what types of assessment instruments and techniques they use and why. Report your results to the class.

2. Interview school counselors and find out what types of assessment instruments and techniques they use to evaluate the school and classroom environment and why. Report your findings to the class.

3. Administer one of the family, work, or school environment scales; score and interpret the results; and present the report to the class.

4. Write a critical review of one of the major environment instruments.

5. Write a paper on one of the current issues in assessing the environment such as person-environment-fit or a similar topic.

6. Study the following case of Team X and answer the questions at the end:

A Fortune 500 company decided that it would change its system and use work teams. The company had a general orientation session on total quality management (TQM) but did not provide any team building or group skills training, which are crucial elements in TQM. The organization brought in a consultant to try to "fix" the teams when it appeared the experiment resulted in lower, rather than higher, productivity. The consultant administered the Campbell-Halcum Team Development Survey (TDS) to collect baseline data.

The purpose of the TDS is to stimulate a focused discussion about the team's strengths and weaknesses; to help the team identify, acknowledge, and address its problems; to give team members an opportunity to share their ideas for improving the team; to help the leader see how his or her perceptions compare with those of the rest of the team; to identify training needs; and to provide benchmark data to track the team's progress. Members respond to 93 statements using a 6-point scale ranging from "strongly agree" to "strongly disagree." A sample of the statements follows:

1. Team members resent being on this team.
2. The team has an excellent idea of the directions needed to accomplish the goals set for it.

There is also a 23-item observation scale that can be used in conjunction with the team member form. This scale uses a 6-point scale and includes statements such as "Group members respect each other."

Here are the results of the Team X group and its leader's scores:

Dimension/Scale	Team Average T Score	Chair's T Score
Resources		
Commitment	50	51
Competence	60	59
Material Resources	45	60 —
Time and Staffing	45	55 —
Information	58	60
Resource Use		
Mission Clarity	38	36
Leadership	40	38
Planning/Organization	42	40
Team Unity	62	64
Empowerment	45	52
Individual Goals	47	52
Improvement		
Conflict Resolution	58	53
Innovation	60	55
Team Assessment	48	60
Feedback	43	40
Rewards	38	40
Team Success		
Satisfaction	55	58
Performance	47	45
Overall Index	51	52

The mean *T* score is 50, and the SD is 10. The authors call 45–55 midrange, 55–60 high, and 60 or more very high, whereas 40–45 is low and 35–40 very low.

a. What would you identify as the strengths and weaknesses of the team?
b. How do the perceptions of the chair and the members correlate?
c. What implications do the data have for training and development?

ADDITIONAL READINGS

Cohen, L. G., & Spenciner, L. J. (1994). *Assessment of young children*. New York: Longman.

Chapter 43, "Observing the Child and the Environment," provides an excellent overview of the current instruments and assessment strategies used in working with preschool and elementary children.

Grotevant, H. D. (1989). *Family assessment: A guide to methods and measures*. New York: Guilford.

The authors discuss observational and self-report measures and present abstracts of major schedules and instruments used in family assessment.

Moos, R. H. (1976). *The human context: Environmental determinants of behavior*. New York: Wiley.

Moos presents his psychosocial model of assessing environments.

Touliastos, J., Perlmutter, B. F., & Straus, M. A. (Eds.). (1990). *Handbook of family measurement techniques*. Newbury Park, CA: Sage.

The authors review tests and assessment devices to measure family interaction, intimacy and values, parenthood, roles and power, and adjustment.

CHAPTER 16

The Computer in Assessment

OVERVIEW

Computer technology has been applied to all phases of testing. For more than 30 years test scoring, computing of norms, derived scores, and reliability and validity coefficients have been computerized. Computers are currently being used in the administration, scoring, and interpretation of many tests and assessment instruments. All types of instruments—personality, achievement, intelligence, aptitude, and interest—are being programmed for the computer, which is seen as a tool to facilitate and improve measurement practices. Adaptive testing and interactive testing are current practices. A test can be assembled by the computer with an agreed-upon item response methodology and can be tailored to the test taker. Professional literature has given much attention to the topic, and several special issues of professional journals have dealt with it.

OBJECTIVES

This chapter should help the reader understand

✔ What uses test developers make of computer-assisted and computer-adaptive assessments and which ones are available to counselors

✔ How pencil-and-paper and adaptive tests can be compared and evaluated

✔ Where information about adaptive tests can be found

✔ How computer-assisted and computer-adaptive tests can be evaluated

✔ What the advantages and disadvantages are of these approaches to testing

TEST ADMINISTRATION

One of the most common testing applications is computer administration of items at a terminal. Green (1984) states that tests thus administered are not very different from conventional pencil-and-paper tests. Normally, the items are multiple choice and are presented one at a time. The examinee indicates an answer by pressing a key on a keyboard or moving the cursor with a mouse. Light pens are used with some programs. Instructions are presented visually, and test takers can proceed only by pressing the key that the program requests. Practice items give the examinee a chance to become familiar with the format. On some tests examinees are required to check whether they have pressed the key they meant to press. Madsen (1986) lists seven advantages of test administration on a terminal (p. 9):

1. Relatively low equipment costs are required if the testing volume is low.
2. Computer-assisted tests reproduce closely the instructions and presentation formats of pencil-and-paper versions.
3. Testing on a terminal has proven to be as cost-effective as traditional testing after the initial equipment costs are covered.
4. Positive client response to computer-assisted testing is common.
5. Evidence is beginning to show that computer testing does not affect the reliability of the instrument over a wide range of special clients and situations.
6. The collection of ancillary test data is now possible on variables such as response time and patterns for items and scales.
7. Adaptive testing, in which selection of the next question is based on the test taker's responses to previous items, is a near perfect example of computer-assisted testing adjusted to suit the needs of individuals.

Watkins and McDermott (1991) summarize the advantages—ability to do interactive testing, more efficient use of staff time, more efficient scoring, reduced error rate, and potential assistance to persons with visual or auditory disabilities. Kline (1993) also summarizes the advantages of computer testing over traditional methods. He believes the first and greatest advantage is that computer-administered testing allows for almost immediate feedback of results. In addition, he notes, administration procedures are always the same. He also states that where skilled examiners are in short supply, the prewritten interpretation can be valuable. Kline points out that computer-administered tests can facilitate the testing of individuals with disabilities, who can use special keyboards.

As limitations, Watkins and McDermott (1991) note that computer-administered tests depersonalize the client, interface poorly with clients, reduce efficiency with difficult clients, compromise the confidentiality of clients who are possibly at risk, cannot discriminate between normal and pathological responses, and may introduce bias into testing.

Madsen (1986) also lists several limitations of computer-assisted test administration, such as increased cost and scheduling problems, problems of some test takers in using the equipment, difficult or impossible adaptation of certain types of tests and item formats, and lack of normative data for computer-assisted tests. Kline (1993) states that some subjects, particularly older adults and those with intellectual handicaps, may have difficulty with computer-administered tests. In addition, some counselors believe that a primary tenet of counseling is to establish rapport with the client, and a computer cannot do this.

Jackson (1985) points out the **differences** between standard and computerized administration (p. 7):

1. Method of presentation of stimulus material—Only one nonverbal item might be present on the screen rather than several on a page in standard administration.
2. Type of task required of the test taker as a result of computer presentation—The computer may not be programmed to review previous responses.
3. Method of recording responses
4. Method of score interpretation

One other difference is that more information can be gained through computer administration. Green (1984) indicates that the computer can time each response and produce a response rate in addition to the number of correct answers.

EQUIVALENCE OF CONVENTIONAL AND COMPUTER TESTS

Bunderson, Inouye, and Olsen (1989), in reviewing the studies on computer-based testing and conventional testing, conclude that the reliabilities of the computer and conventional tests are very similar and that computer tests tend to yield lower scores than conventional tests. Green (1984) states that when a conventional test is transferred to computer presentation, there is no assurance that the test performance will be equivalent. He concludes that time-limit and response differences could affect the total test score (p. 5). Research has indicated that when speed tests are translated from pencil-and-paper to a computer mode of presentation, responses come much faster on the computer. In their study of computer and conventional modes, Greaud and Green (1986) found a large mean difference in favor of the computer.

Because the computer normally presents one item at a time in a regular sequence, the test takers' attention is directed to each item. The computer also forces a change in how the test takers can take tests. On pencil-and-paper tests the examinee can scan the whole test, skip around, and leave out items. Most computer programs, however, force the examinee to answer questions in order and thus discourage skipping. This procedure may be a potential source of difference on personality and interest tests. Lee, Moreno, and Sympson (1984) reported that individuals taking computer versions of mathematics tests are less likely to turn away from the display and use pencil and scratch paper than are examinees with pencil-and-paper versions. Jackson (1991) concludes that advances in computer technology including touch screens, voice recognition, and rapid access to massive scored data give us a greater capacity to do justice to the complexity of personality. Watkins and McDermott (1991) state that most of the current applications are narrow in scope and application but promise increased efficiency, economy, and reliability.

Allred and Harris (1984) report that on an adjective checklist, people tested by computer are more likely to check more adjectives as applying to themselves than are individuals using conventional formats. Green (1984) concludes that conventional and computer-presented tests may yield scores that are not directly comparable. He calls for different norms for the two versions or some system of scale transformation that will permit the same norms to be used. Jackson (1985) concludes that modifications introduced by computer-aided testing require equivalence studies and sometimes restandardization of the test. He believes that it is appropriate to require test makers who publish computer-aided testing to provide evidence of the comparability of pencil-and-paper and computer formats (p. 9).

INDIVIDUALIZATION

One of the major advantages of computer presentations of ability, aptitude, and achievement tests is that the format makes possible individualization of the tasks to be measured. Item banks can be developed, and the computer can be programmed to select items from the set so that each test taker can get a different test. Two types of formats—adaptive and nonadaptive—are used. On adaptive tests the item selection is sequential—that is, the items are selected on the basis of how the test taker performed on the previous items. An estimate of the examinee's skill level is made after each item response and is the basis for selection of the next item. The method gives rough approximations and requires a number of responses before the precision improves. One advantage is the climate created by the process: high-ability individuals are not bored by lots of easy items, and low-ability test takers are not frustrated by questions that are too difficult. Green (1984) concludes that computer tests can be more precise than pencil-and-paper tests, moving estimates up and down the scale until a sufficiently accurate ability estimate is found—often after half the number of items a conventional test would need (p. 10).

In nonadaptive testing the items are selected at random from the item bank so that each test taker gets a different test form. This method has been used to simplify test security and repetitive testing. It also reduces the advantage of coaching on specific item content. This approach is useful when individuals have to be retested, such as on minimum-level skills or essential-skills tests. However, the item pool must be large so that the items presented on the retake are not likely to have been included on the first test. One problem with this approach is equivalence. If the item bank contains items that are homogeneous in content and of approximately equal difficulty, the tests will be fairly parallel and equal.

COMPUTER-AIDED PERSONALITY TESTING

Computer-aided personality testing is receiving as much attention as computer applications of testing in the cognitive areas. Jackson (1985) lists the following advantages of computer-aided personality testing (p. 5):

1. The saving of time of the counselor or psychologist
2. The possibility of using trained assistants to monitor test administration
3. The short time lag between administering the test, scoring it, and interpreting it
4. The elimination of human scoring errors
5. The programming capability of the computer to combine rules and complicated processing
6. The standardization of interpretations, eliminating different points of view
7. The potential for systematically collecting and developing normative databases
8. The ability of the computer to perform complex scoring procedures
9. The ability to use computer-based assessment with special populations for whom standard pencil-and-paper procedures are not feasible

The widespread availability of computers has made possible not only on-line presentation of stimulus material but all types of programs for scoring and interpreting the test data. Studies with computer-assisted testing of psychiatric and physically disabled patients and of individuals at all age levels have been made. Programs have been developed to aid psychiatric diagnosis; diagnosis of alcoholism, type A behavior, personal construct systems; and personal decision making and career guidance.

EVALUATING COMPUTER-BASED ADAPTIVE TESTING

Green (1984) lists five main psychometric criteria for evaluating computer-based adaptive testing—unidimensionality, reliability, validity, quality of the item parameters, and equating. Unidimensionality relates to the domain being measured. In ability and aptitude testing, items should be homogeneous and should correlate highly with the total score. The test or scale usually yields one score. However, evidence should be presented that the domain is unidimensional and measures primarily one dimension.

Reliability for these tests is computed by the use of an internal consistency reliability index. McBride and Martin (1983) found twice as many items are needed on a conventional test to get the same reliability as on a computer-adaptive test. Content, predictive, and construct validity information is also important in evaluating computer-adaptive tests. The criterion-related and construct validity of these tests is computed in the same way as for a pencil-and-paper test. It is important to look at how the content validity of the items was studied.

The quality of parameters relates to the quality of the reliability indexes of the items, and the estimate of the item parameters appears to require a large number of cases and items (Green, 1984, p. 15). Because not all items are used with each test taker, those items selected can affect reliability significantly. Items with low reliability dilute the estimate of time parameters of items with good reliability.

Green (1984) identifies two aspects to equating. Because each individual's test is unique, the tests must be certified as equivalent. This task demands that the test is unidimensional with a small error of measurement and that the item responses fit the item response theory model. The second is being able to equate the computer-adaptive test score with the conventional test score. The Educational Testing Service publication *Computer Based Testing: From Multiple Choice to Multiple Choices* (1994) gives these advantages of computer-adaptive testing:

1. Mastery levels can be demonstrated faster, and the test can be terminated (for licensure or certification) once a test taker has reached the criterion level of mastery.
2. Testing is more interesting and positive. The test provides questions at a level that is consistently appropriate and challenging to the test taker.
3. Testing time is shortened by focusing on the test taker's ability level.
4. Increased psychometric precision is possible over a broad range of proficiency.

In assessing computer-assisted and computer-adaptive tests, the form included in Figure 16.1 might be useful. Moreland (1992) summarizes four important factors in assessing computer-assisted test interpretations: the credentials of the system author, the documentation of the system, the scholarly review of the system, and the tryouts of the system.

PROFESSIONAL STANDARDS AND GUIDELINES

In *Guidelines for Computer-Based Tests and Interpretations,* the American Psychological Association (1985) suggests that automated tests be used as only one of several sources of information about clients. Shertzer (1986) recommends that professional training standards be changed so that all graduate students in the helping professions take a course in computer applications with emphasis on computer-assisted testing and become familiar with the APA guidelines. He calls for five main objectives to be gained:

1. Basic computer literacy
2. Knowledge of information sources
3. An objective and evaluative attitude toward computer-based tests
4. Understanding of the individual's right to privacy
5. Knowledge of and experience with computer-assisted testing

Because of accelerated advances in computer technology—touch screens, voice recognition, rapid access to data—our knowledge of computer hardware and software needs to keep pace. The field is evolving in its methods and standards. Green (1991) sees the standards as a living document that provides us with an important start but that will require frequent revision.

Standards for Educational and Psychological Testing (AERA, APA, & NCME, 1985) also addresses the issue of computer-assisted and computer-adaptive testing. The standards call for adaptive tests to provide estimates of the magnitude of errors of measurement based on the analysis of the results from repeated administrations using different items. Alternate form estimates of reliability are necessary to provide an independent check on the magnitude of errors in measurement in adaptive test-

Test title _____

Description of test _____

Description of scales _____

Potential uses _____

Publisher's address _____

      Phone _____

Author qualifications _____

Hardware requirements _____

      K _____

      Additional equipment _____

System availability	Trial period available	_____ Yes
_____ Apple		_____ No
_____ IBM		
_____ Other_____		

Materials provided

_____ Handbook or guidebook	_____ Videocassettes
_____ Technical manual	_____ Training package
_____ User's manual	_____ Other_____
_____ Discs	

Cost

_____ Number of uses

_____ Software cost per user

_____ Supplemental costs (other systems, additional hardware) _____

Populations to be served

_____ Primary/preschool	_____ Young adult
_____ Elementary (K–6)	_____ College/junior college
_____ Junior high (7–9)	_____ Adult
_____ High school (10–12)	_____ 65+
_____ Special populations (specify)_____	

Potential users	Sophistication required
_____ Administrators	_____ High
_____ Counselors	_____ Medium
_____ Psychologists	_____ Low
_____ Teachers	
_____ Students/examinees	

Features available on software

_____ Test scoring	_____ Measures of variability
_____ Test score interpretation	_____ Record-keeping features

Figure 16.1
Form to evaluate computer testing programs

Features available on software *(continued)*

_____ Item analysis, difficulty, discrimination   _____ Individual records
_____ Reliability information   _____ Accumulated record keeping
_____ Descriptive statistics   on individuals
_____ Group records   Tabular presentations
_____ Capability of adding other data   _____ Graphic presentations
_____ Measures of central tendency

Administration features

_____ Self-administered   _____ Can add local items
_____ Randomly generated   _____ Computer-adaptive

Technical characteristics (1 = excellent, 2 = good, 3 = poor)

_____ User friendliness   _____ Ease of operation
_____ Display   _____ Ease of input/entry
_____ Documentation   _____ Printing/graphics
_____ Storage capacity   _____ Flexibility
_____ Clarity of score   _____ Profiles
_____ Clarity of reports   _____ Error checking
_____ Ability to change scores   _____ Reading level
_____ Response time between input and feedback   _____ Help options
_____ Reliability data   _____ Internal consistency
_____ Parallel forms   _____ Standard error measurement
_____ Content validity   _____ Construct validity
_____ Predictive validity   _____ Concurrent validity

Item selection/presentation

_____ Access to directions   _____ Skipping features
_____ Type of item selection
     _____ Random   _____ Sequential
     _____ Adaptive   _____ Feedback

Display conventions

_____ Format   _____ Color
_____ Headings   _____ Highlighting
_____ Menus

Answering/scoring

_____ Answer registration methods   _____ Backup and changing answers
_____ Error hopping

Norms

_____ Computer-assisted-adaptive format   _____ Pencil-and-paper format
_____ Appropriateness   _____ Adequacy of sample
_____ Types of scores

Figure 16.1 *continued*

ing. The guidelines caution against concurrent comparisons between pencil-and-paper and adaptive forms as estimates of the alternate form reliability; however, if the variance in the methods is small, the tests can be considered parallel.

The standards also suggest that the author needs to provide in the manual the rationale and supporting evidence for procedures used in selecting items for administration, deciding when enough items have been presented, and scoring the test.

The scaling, norming, score comparability, and equating procedures used in adaptive testing need to be reported. The authors are responsible for providing specific information about the methods of equating the different forms of the test as well as studies checking the adequacy of equating procedures.

The environment for the administration of computer-adaptive tests call for the items displayed on the screen to be legible and free from glare, with the terminal properly positioned. The novelty of presentation should be watched since it might have an unknown effect on the test administration.

Green (1991) recommends that a good strategy is to use the system, enter a set of responses, and examine the results and their interpretation. Counselors should review similar systems at the same time so they can compare how the systems react to the same response pattern.

SOURCES OF INFORMATION

Many sources of information on software exist in this field. Journals publish reviews or include articles and research on computer-assisted and computer-adaptive testing. Professional organizations that address computerized testing are concerned with standards and provide useful information to users. Computer networks, reference and resource books, ERIC documents, and annotated bibliographies are plentiful. Several sources are identified at the end of this chapter.

Other resources for helping professionals include Assessment Abstracts Online at http://www.parine.com. McMinn and Scanish have developed the Rorschach Trainer Version I for Windows.

Several companies provide online administration, scoring, and interpretation of major assessment and outcome measures for use by clinicians. For examples, Optaio is a service though the Psychological Corporation. Unlimited monthly use of standardized assessment instruments is available for monitoring patient progress over time. Available instruments include the following:

Beck Anxiety Inventory

Beck Depression Inventory II

Beck Hopelessness Scale

Beck Scale for Suicide Ideation

Brown Attention Deficit Disorder Scale

Butcher Treatment Planning Inventory

Devereux Scales of Mental Disorders

Eating Inventory

Rust Inventory of Schizotypical Cognitions

ETS has developed ACCUPLACER, a system that offers colleges and universities a comprehensive program for testing, placement, advisement, and research. The placement tests for the system use computer-adaptive testing in seven assessment areas: reading comprehension, sentence skills, level of English proficiency, arithmetic, elementary algebra, college-level mathematics, and supplemental skills. CRASMS is the placement, advisement, and management component. It can be programmed to tell students their college placement scores and what they mean as well as when their first class starts and who their advisors are.

Many of the tests discussed in this book can be administered, scored, and interpreted using computer software. For example the Minnesota Multiphasic Personality Inventory, the NEO Personality Inventory–Revised, the Self-Directed Search, the Myers-Briggs Type Indicator, the Personality Assessment Inventory, and the California Psychological Inventory all have computer-assisted administration. Both the Wechsler scales and the Rorschach have computer scoring and interpretation software available.

COMPUTER OPTIONS

Several programs are available to help individuals computerize their own tests. These programs address the following:

1. *How the items are presented to the test takers*—in high-resolution text, color graphics, special characters, and even foreign alphabets
2. *How the test is designed*—conventional format (everyone gets the same item), sequential (testing continues until the examiner can make a decision), adaptive (maximum information)
3. *How the narrative score interpretation is presented*—in the test maker's own words and style or geared to the specific needs of the test taker or tester
4. *How the data is stored*
5. *How the data is scored*—including what type of statistical analysis is completed

ADVANTAGES AND DISADVANTAGES OF COMPUTER APPLICATIONS

These are some of the major advantages of computer applications:

1. Quick, easy, and economical collection of information
2. Improved scoring accuracy
3. Possible alternate formats
4. Faster feedback to the tester and test taker

5. Reduced time spent on routine tasks, such as intake, interviewing, and initial assessment
6. View of computer-assisted testing and interpretation as legitimate and important
7. Endless computer applications
8. Item response theory allowing people to get different sets of items

Disadvantages of computer applications include the following:

1. Computer interpretations are confounded because no allowances are made for the client's emotional state, physical disabilities, or other pertinent characteristics.
2. Some traditional instruments may not be easily adapted to computer formats. Computer-assisted tests have psychometric properties different from those of the paper-and-pencil tests they replace. For example, reading tests that require oral reading may be a problem, although in the future speech recognition will be sophisticated enough to be used for this purpose.
3. Normative data may be inadequate for computer-assisted or computer-adaptive tests.
4. The equipment can be expensive, and multiple scoring problems might arise with inadequate equipment.
5. Adequate client-screening procedures need to be developed to identify clients in crisis, who may be unable to concentrate or respond to a computer-assisted interview or assessment.
6. Costs in equipment, training, and time may not be worthwhile.
7. Computers lack human involvement. Some individuals see the computer as cold and inhuman. The computer does not recognize when the examinee is tired or has a limited attention span. Most of the time the program is not able to handle probes.
8. Clients may see a threat to the confidentiality of test data; computers have the potential to collect, store, and recall much intimate information.
9. The standards for obtaining these tests are not strictly monitored.
10. A big investment of money is needed by publishers to develop this type of testing.

It is important to remember that the examiner does not have access to decisions or rules the authors have developed or selected. The computer can be guided to make decisions, but someone has to program the computer, providing the information or rules for decision making. Individuals in the helping professions certainly need to develop computer literacy, but that literacy may not be sufficient to evaluate computer rules and procedures. Consequently, it is necessary to be cautious in the use of computerized reports with clients. Some individuals advocate using the computer for what it can do best—quickly process and store information—and humans for what they can do best—think, interpret, and interact.

Dramatic changes in computer technology make possible a more sophisticated diagnostic analysis of item responses and interpretive reporting of test results. Baker (1989) points out that these two areas depend more on the state of the art in psychology and artificial intelligence than on technology. New systems merge the important components of actuarial and clinical reasoning.

COMPUTER-BASED TEST INTERPRETATION

The quickest-growing computer application in assessment is computer-based test interpretation. However, some experts caution that computer-based reports eliminate the judgment of the clinician and may not be valid for the individual case (Maddux & Johnson, 1998; Tallent, 1983). There are four major types of computer applications: scoring reports, descriptive reports, actuarial reports, and computer-assisted clinical reports. The chapter on achievement testing presented a computer scoring report for one school grade on a survey achievement battery. Descriptive reports provide scale-by-scale test results, usually limited to a page or two. Actuarial reports are based on the empirical determination of the relationship between the test results and predictions that can be made from the results. These empirical judgments depend on formulas developed to diagnose, classify, or predict behavior. Computer-assisted clinical reports are based on the judgments of experts in the field related to the test. Such judgments lead to the decisions rules they develop, which are programmed into the computer report.

SOFTWARE FOR TEST DEVELOPMENT

A number of software programs have been developed to help the examiner construct tests. Here are some examples:

Iteman assesses data using the Rasch model of test analysis.

Microcat is a computerized testing system to support the entire test process. It can create and maintain an item bank, develop and print forms, and develop and administer computerized test forms in conventional or adaptive versions.

Testpak consists of two software programs—one for criterion-referenced tests, the other for norm-referenced. The programs analyze, disaggregate, and report data in combination with other student information and can produce a variety of reports for teachers, administrators, and parents. The tests are analyzed using the classical theory of test item analysis.

TRENDS AND ISSUES

Wise and Plake (1990) point out that we have gone through several generations of computer applications. Initially paper-and-pencil tests were programmed for the computer. Now new formats and types of items are possible, and computer-based simulations can be used in training and testing of problem solving. Many developments in computer and video technology in the past 25 years have occurred, and we can anticipate even greater impact on the field of testing in the future. Hanson (1986) predicts that society will be moving out of the print medium into ready access to video disk and computer-based information. She states that computers now have the capacity to give tests, compute scale scores, print results, and provide interpretive comments and diagnostic information for objective aptitude, ability, achievement, psychomotor, interest, and personality tests as well as for projective tests such as the Rorschach (p. 50). The systems, she concludes, are all self-contained and require only a client who can read a video display and type or a clerk who can assist with those tasks. Hanson believes that, with video disks storing visual and auditory information, testing applications will not necessarily be limited to data, graphics, and printed words but can be supplemented with sound and motion picture or still-frame visual materials.

Helping professionals are seeing a tremendous growth in the instruments being adopted, adapted, and created for administration by computer. Meier and Geiger (1986) conclude that confidentiality is the issue most often mentioned in discussions of ethical problems regarding computers. Sampson and Pyle (1983) have proposed ethical principles for computer-assisted testing and assessment, addressing the issue of individual rights and confidentiality. They recommend that counselors ensure that confidential data are restricted to appropriate professionals, and they propose establishing computer security and proper storage of data.

Bersoff and Hofer (1991) remind us of the many legal issues involved, such as copyright of the test, scoring procedures, norms, and correlational tables. Authors and publishers are reluctant to release the scoring and interpretation procedures, viewing them as trade secrets. Questions arise concerning the use of computer reports. For example, are counselors who are not trained in a certain test interpretation liable when they use computer interpretive reports?

Computer-adaptive testing is increasing. The National Council on Licensure Examinations reports that the Nurses Licensing Test, for example, has a computer-adaptive form. The Graduate Record Examination, the Professional Assessment of Beginning Teachers, and the examinations of the National Council of Architectural Registration Boards all have computer-adaptive forms available. The Educational Testing Service uses the Sylvan Technology Centers to administer its computer-adaptive versions of tests. Convenience is a strong argument for these types of tests: clients have a choice of time and date and have a more personalized learning experience in a controlled environment. They receive preliminary scores immediately and final results much faster. Computer-adaptive testing in this context provides equal access, sensitivity to the needs of users with disabilities, and test security. The differential item function ensures equality and fairness in testing.

Kyllonen (1997) foresees the merging of technology and theory in the development of future aptitude batteries. The process would include computer delivery, item-generation technology, multidimensional adaptive technology, comprehensive cognitive abilities measurement, and a latent factor center design. Merging of these latest advances will help develop the prototype test format for the next generation. In 1998 the APA session on testing trends had sessions on computerized test-item banking, a revolution in item analysis and test construction.

SUMMARY

Computer technology has been used in all phases of testing. Many tests now have computer-assisted versions. Computer-assisted testing allows for more efficient use of staff time, more efficient and reliable scoring, and greater flexibility in testing individuals with disabilities. Disadvantages include depersonalization of the client and poor interfaces between the client and the computer. The issue of confidentiality is also of concern. Computer-adaptive testing is becoming more widely available to assess the aptitude and achievement of test takers. Many tests provide computer-generated interpretations of tests. Helping professionals are seeing a tremendous growth in the instruments being adopted, adapted, and created for administration, scoring, and interpretation by the computer. Users need to be certain that these tests meet the professional standards for educational and psychological testing and be alert to the legal and ethical issues involved with computer testing.

QUESTIONS FOR DISCUSSION

1. Do you agree with Meier and Geiger's (1986) recommendation that all graduate students in the helping professions complete a course in computer applications in human services, with special emphasis on computer-assisted testing? Why or why not?

2. In what ways are computer-assisted assessment and traditional assessment techniques alike? In what ways are they different?

3. Should assessing be left to the computer and interpretation to the human service professional? Defend your position on this issue.

4. What do you see as future trends in this field? Do you believe that there will be marked acceptance of the new technologies and innovative approaches in computer assessment? Why or why not?

5. Adaptive testing is not a new concept but has been adapted for use with the computer. One of the advantages of computer-adaptive testing is that it saves time. Do you believe the results of such approaches will be as valid or reliable as those of traditional testing? Why or why not?

SUGGESTED ACTIVITIES

1. Take a computer-assisted test. Evaluate your experience and report the findings to the class.

2. Interview test takers who have taken computer-adaptive tests and identify their attitudes toward the experience. What aspects did they like best? What aspects did they like least?

3. Make an annotated bibliography of computer-adaptive and computer-assisted tests that are currently available in your field.

4. Get three or four computerized reports of test results. Analyze them according to criteria such as understandability, attractiveness of format, readability, and psychometric properties.

5. Devise a rating scale to evaluate computer-assisted or computer-adaptive tests and select an instrument to evaluate with your scale. Compare the traditional test form with the computerized form. Are there marked differences in the two versions?

6. Read the following case study and answer the questions at the end:

   Lu is upset to learn that her professional licensing examination is a computer-adaptive test now, which will be given at the XYZ Technology Center.

   She complains to you, her counselor: "At my age, I hate computers. I don't use one. . . . I don't want one! How can they really say that the results are the same as before? The exam use to be 6 hours, and now you say it will only take me 2 hours. How can they cover all the knowledge we are supposed to have in a 2-hour period? Also, I don't type or speak computerese. I will be at a disadvantage!"

   a. How would you answer her concerns?
   b. How would you help her prepare for the testing and alleviate her anxiety?

ADDITIONAL READINGS

The following professional journals publish information about computer-based testing:

Behavior Research Methods and Instrumentation

Computer Living

Computers in Human Behavior

Computers in Human Services

Computers in Psychiatry/Psychology

Counseling Psychologist

Educational and Psychological Measurement

International Journal of Man-Machine Studies

Journal of Counseling and Development

Journal of Educational Measurement

Journal of Occupational Psychology

Measurement and Evaluation in Counseling and Development

Psychiatric Annals

Gutkin, T. B., & Wise, S. L. (Eds.). (1991). *The computer and the decision-making process*. Hillsdale, NJ: Erlbaum.

The book has chapters on computer-assisted personality test interpretation, psychodiagnostic applications, validity of computer-based interpretation, use of computers in behavioral assessment, use in industrial/organizational psychology, legal issues, and guidelines for computer testing.

Maddux, C. D., & Johnson, L. (1998). Computer-assisted assessment. In H. Vance (Ed.), *Psychological assessment of children* (2nd ed., pp. 87–105). New York: Wiley.

The authors give a brief history of the use of computers in assessment and discuss the assessment-related tasks often performed on the computer.

Moreland, K. L. (1992). Computer-assisted psychological assessment. In M. Zeidner & R. Most (Eds.), *Psychological testing: An inside view* (pp. 343–376). Palo Alto, CA: Consulting Psychologists Press.

The chapter offers a current overview of what is happening in computer-assisted testing.

Sands, W. A., Waters, B. K., & McBride, J. R. (Eds.). (1997). *Computerized adaptive testing*. Washington, DC: American Psychological Association.

The book discusses numerous aspects of computerized adaptive testing, including second- and third-generation applications and current and future challenges.

Wainer, H. (1990). *Computerized adaptive testing: A primer*. Hillsdale, NJ: Erlbaum.

The author discusses computer history, system design and operation, item pools, item-response theory, item calibration and proficiency estimation, scaling and equating, reliability and measurement precision, validity, and future challenges.

CHAPTER 17

Alternate and Authentic Assessment Techniques

OVERVIEW

Observation is one of the primary data-gathering tools of workers in the helping professions. The main purpose of observation is to collect information that will be useful in describing, interpreting, and explaining client behavior. Sometimes an individual is observed in a natural situation such as on the job, in the classroom, or at home. At other times the individual can be observed in a contrived or a simulated situation. Observation is one of the key tools of assessment. Shertzer and Linden (1979) call it humankind's first educational tool and first method of appraisal (p. 366). Observation of test behavior is sometimes as important as the actual answers given by the individual.

The interview is also an important assessment tool for workers in the helping professions.

There has been a growing dissatisfaction with traditional testing procedures and a movement toward alternative and authentic assessment techniques. These procedures have primarily been used in assessing achievement but are currently being used in other areas.

The first part of the chapter focuses on alternate assessment techniques that are widely used by helping professionals. These are qualitative methods that have proven to be useful tools. The second part of the chapter centers on authentic assessment.

OBJECTIVES

The chapter should help the reader identify

✔ The different methods of observation and the procedures and techniques used

✔ The methods, procedures, and techniques of alternate and authentic assessment

✔ The use of rating scales, interview schedules, and checklists

✔ The use of observation in analyzing test
behavior

✔ The problems that arise in the use of
interview schedules and rating scales

OBSERVATIONAL APPROACHES

Observational techniques are used in many settings. Workers in the helping professions use observational techniques to assess client behavior in play therapy, sociodrama, psychodrama, simulated experiences, role playing, test performance, discussion groups, conferences, and interviews. The procedures vary considerably.
Observations can focus on specific behaviors that are objective and observable or on
general, overall behavior or adjustment. Observations can be a one-shot affair or a
sampling over a longer span of time. The observer can use rating or record forms,
observation schedules, or devices such as the tape recorder, video equipment, or
computers to record the data. Rating scales, anecdotal records, ranking scales, sociometric tests, client-kept records, checklists, and self-appraisal scales are some of the
varied recording methods used.

Attention		1	2	3	4	5
		Low				High
Response time		1	2	3	4	5
		Slow				Quick
Activity level		1	2	3	4	5
		Passive				Active
Security		1	2	3	4	5
	Ill at ease					Calm and collected
Anxiety		1	2	3	4	5
		Low				High
Relationship to examiner		1	2	3	4	5
		Poor				Good
Need for reinforcement		1	2	3	4	5
		Low				High
Task orientation		1	2	3	4	5
	Gives up					Sticks to task
Reaction to failure		1	2	3	4	5
		Poor				Good
Interest in test		1	2	3	4	5
		Low				High

Figure 17.1
Sample observational scale for an intelligence test

Attitudes Toward the Test	Low		Moderate			High
Interest in the test	1	2	3	4	5	6	7
Motivation to perform well	1	2	3	4	5	6	7
Attitudes Toward the Examiner						
Degree of rapport	1	2	3	4	5	6	7
Degree of cooperation	1	2	3	4	5	6	7
Degree of comfort	1	2	3	4	5	6	7
Degree of openness	1	2	3	4	5	6	7
General Behavior						
Degree of anxiety	1	2	3	4	5	6	7
Degree of self-confidence	1	2	3	4	5	6	7
Praise or reinforcement needed	1	2	3	4	5	6	7
Frustration tolerance	1	2	3	4	5	6	7
Work Style						
Attention span	1	2	3	4	5	6	7
Impulsivity	1	2	3	4	5	6	7
Persistence	1	2	3	4	5	6	7
Methodical thinking	1	2	3	4	5	6	7
Interest in being challenged	1	2	3	4	5	6	7
Response time	1	2	3	4	5	6	7
Personality Style						
Introversion	1	2	3	4	5	6	7
Reality orientation	1	2	3	4	5	6	7
Mood swing	1	2	3	4	5	6	7
Seriousness	1	2	3	4	5	6	7
Degree of spontaneity	1	2	3	4	5	6	7
Internality	1	2	3	4	5	6	7

Figure 17.2
Test observation form

Test Behavior Observational Scales

A variety of scales may be included as part of a testing package. For example, there are observation forms that examiners can use with some of the individual intelligence tests (see Figure 17.1). Some scales can be used with many types of individual tests (see Figure 17.2).

Slosson and Callisto (1984) have designed a scale called Observational Analysis to aid the examiner in the observational process. The behavioral profile calls for the examiner to check categories such as outward behavior, relationship with examiner, recall, affective tone, attitude, work habits, and expression. The authors also have a visual scanning form to be used for physical observations of the client, including observations of the head and face; arms, torso, and hands; legs and gait; and miscellaneous other categories. A posttest questionnaire requests verbal answers from the client in response to questions such as "Did you feel comfortable or uneasy about taking the test?" The system involves observation of the client in the total communication process.

Clinical Observations

The examiner may also want to observe the client in learning, performing, or social situations. Observations may be focused on a specific observable behavior, such as time on task, or may cover a wide variety of behaviors, such as affective, cognitive, psychomotor, and social. The examiner might use a checklist of whether a behavior was present or record anecdotal records of typical behavior. Clinical observation is an extremely valuable tool in working with very young children or with clients who have mental or emotional disabilities.

The examiner might be concerned with dimensions of psychomotor performance. Observation of fine motor coordination might focus on hand-eye coordination; use of fingers; angle of paper to body; reversals or rotations in copying, drawing, or writing; and handedness (Hargrove & Poteet, 1984). Observation of gross motor behavior might look at balance, activity level, body shifts, body positioning, and coordination.

Observation of social behavior can also be helpful, focusing on the relationships the client has with peers, teachers, authority figures, siblings, and parents. Dimensions of cognitive behavior might also be interesting—not only learning styles but also approaches to reasoning and ways of memorizing. Many affective components are related to learning, such as frustration and fatigue, motivation and effort, attention to task, and distractibility.

Self-Observations

On many occasions self-observations are important. A variety of types of data may be collected. Shapiro and Cole (1993) state that the simplest and most common method for collecting self-monitored data is to have the client record the occurrences of the targeted behavior. The data can be summarized over time and frequency rates compiled. Sometimes the client is asked to tally the number of incidences of the targeted behavior in time units. There are mechanical devices to help the client tally, such as golf counters and wrist counters.

A counselor is often helped in interpreting a case study by an autobiography, diary, journal, letters, themes, stories, and poems. Aiken (1985) states that most people spend quite a bit of time observing themselves. He cautions that self-observations are likely to be more biased than observations made by others (p. 325). However, individuals can be trained to be more objective and systematic in self-observation. They can be trained to keep records of their thinking, actions, and feelings. Since the data are recorded by the individual, periodic checks for accuracy might be necessary. Often the data are checked against ratings by others.

Autobiographies are used to provide insight into individual behavior, attitudes, and personality dimensions. Counselors can specify a certain format or allow individuals to arrange their thoughts however they want. Autobiographies include the facts the clients think are important about their environments. This form of expression also reveals self-concept; but it does rely on trust, and individuals may be concerned about confidentiality. Autobiographies may give insight into personality dynamics and conflicts, but counselors should interpret the data in light of other available information. One of the problems with this method is that many clients tend to overlook their limitations and weaknesses.

The two major formats are structured and unstructured. The counselor may specify the format or allow individuals to arrange their thoughts any way they want. The counselor must study the autobiography and then interpret the data along with other types of information collected. Autobiographies may give some insight into the personality dynamics and conflicts of the clients.

Logs, journals, and diaries are other approaches. These sources help counselors discern individual interests and activities, but it is difficult to get people to keep logs and diaries on a day-to-day basis. Themes, poems, letters, and stories written by the client may also provide valuable information about the individual or at least stimulate discussion in a counseling situation. Content analysis is used in looking at these data; the methodology is described in most textbooks on research methods in the social sciences.

Unstructured versus Structured Observation

One way of looking at observation is to classify it into structured and unstructured categories. Unstructured observation is open-ended. The helping professional observes the behavior of the client, recording as much as possible of whatever appears to be useful or important. After the data are collected, the observer attempts to analyze and evaluate the behavior. A different approach is the use of structured observation, in which the helping professional has already determined why the observation is to take place, what is to be observed, and how the data will be recorded. This approach is deliberately systematic. The different purposes of observation lead to different approaches.

Problems in Observation

Sometimes breakdowns happen in the tracking and recoding of observations. Barrios (1993) identified four such problems. The first is lack of a clear definition of the construct to be observed. To prevent this, the definition needs to be precise, concrete, and observable. A second problem is the demands of the scale. Sometimes the observer has to record too many behaviors. The validity and reliability of the observations can be increased if the number of behaviors, complexity of the coding, or duration of the observation is decreased. The third breakdown is caused by distractions. Occasionally some external or internal event diverts the observer's attention and focus. This could be eliminated or reduced by imposing greater structure on the observation, changing the milieu of the observation, or, in some cases, changing the observer. Mistreatment is the last type of breakdown. Sometimes observers are not treated with dignity and respect. This breakdown can be avoided by ensuring dignity, respect, and greater appreciation for the observers. They should be praised when they do a good job.

Critical Incident Approach

Flanagan (1954) proposed using another form of uncontrolled and naturalistic observation called the critical incident technique. Supervisors are asked to identify specific behaviors that are critical to job performance or that distinguish good or poor work behavior. Analysis of their input provides valuable information on the requirements for effective performance. This technique has been applied to a number of contexts. Shertzer and Linden (1979) point out that having an individual clarify critical events in his life provides insight into the personal and social factors that have affected that person's behavior. Some career planning exercises call for individuals to make a time line and record the 10 most critical events in their lives (see Figure 17.3).

Situation Tests

Situation tests are a form of controlled observation. In one classic example of the technique, Hartshorne and May (1928) studied character traits by observing children in a variety of structured situations, some of which permitted them to cheat and win at a game, copy test answers, or steal coins. The researchers found that children's honesty was highly dependent on the situation in which they were observed. For example, no child tended to be totally honest or totally dishonest. A boy who was an excellent student but a poor athlete would not cheat if asked to correct his own paper but would inflate his score in a sports situation. A girl who excelled in physical

0	5	10	15	20	25	30	35	40	45	50
			a	b	c	d		e		

a = Work experience in community agency during high school
b = Graduated from college with degree in psychology, got married, did not work
c = Divorced, took job as secretary, went part time to the university to become certified as an elementary teacher
d = Began teaching second grade
e = Felt burnt out, decided to change careers and become a guidance counselor, went back to the university for master's

Figure 17.3
Critical events exercise

performance but was a poor speller would record her physical performance correctly but cheat on scoring her spelling.

Another example occurred during World War II, when the U.S. Office of Strategic Services (OSS) had to select special agents to carry out espionage or other special intelligence assignments. The candidates were observed as they participated in a wide variety of assessment techniques, including pencil-and-paper tests, stress interviews, problem-solving exercises, and a wide variety of situational tests (OSS Assessment Staff, 1948). The candidates were rated by the assessment staff and by their own peers, but the validity of these procedures was never established because performance on the tasks was never correlated with success on assignments carried out by those selected.

Situational testing has been used in a variety of settings, including the selection of clinical psychologists (Kelly & Fiske, 1951). One variation of this technique is a leaderless group discussion in which group process becomes the means of observing individual behavior. Candidates for a position might all be invited to a session in which they are given a problem situation to solve, a controversial topic to discuss, or a plan of operation to devise. Observers focus on certain salient traits that they are looking for, such as leadership or problem-solving ability.

A simulated work experience assessment is the In-Basket Test (Frederiksen, Saunders, & Wand, 1957) in which the examinee is given a variety of materials that provide background information, from memoranda to technical reports. The examinee is then presented with a series of problems in the in basket and is asked to take action—for example, hiring or firing personnel or handling production problems. A number of versions of this approach have been developed for different groups, such as school administrators and military officers. Candidates demonstrate how they would handle each problem and are evaluated not only on their solutions but also on the processes used. Simulated tests are becoming more popular with the availability of varied computer software programs.

Brown (1983) identifies problems that arise in the scoring and interpreting of situational tests. He concludes that the data generated with this technique often have undesirable statistical properties, are based on ratings using ordinal scales, have a limited range of values, and in general are unreliable.

Unobtrusive versus Participant Observation

Often it is possible to observe an examinee through a two-way mirror. Because the observer in this situation is not seen by the examinee, ethical guidelines call for the examinee to be informed and give approval. Unfortunately, when an examinee realizes she is being observed, performance may not be typical. However, when visitors come by regularly, targeted individuals may not be aware of being observed. When there is no interaction between the observer and those being observed, and when the individual's behavior is not affected by the situation, observations are said to be unobtrusive.

Participation observation, a tool of the cultural anthropologist, involves the observer as a part of the observational situation. The observer evaluates the group or individuals while participating in the interaction. Aiken (1985) states that the observer's own behavior affects the reactions of other people in the situation (p. 32), but the technique can aid the observer to understand the dynamics of the situation.

Training Observers

Barrios (1993) points out that a key factor in getting valid and reliable data from observation is the training of observers. The first step is orientation, explaining the purpose and importance of observation. The second step is education, instruction in the definitions and recording schemes. The third step is evaluation, which involves assessing the observer's knowledge of the definitions, coding, and tracking procedures. The fourth step is application, in which observers obtain experience in a number of different situations. The fifth step is recalibration, which involves checking the accuracy and agreement of observers and correcting any deviation. The last step is termination, seeking the observers' feedback and evaluation of the process. Their contribution to the project needs to be acknowledged. Observers should be reminded of the need to maintain confidentiality.

METHODS OF DATA COLLECTION

The observer may want to focus on a single incident or on all client behavior in a given time period. The records needed depend on the purpose of the observations. The observer might take notes, dictate observations into a tape recorder, or use a checklist, rating scale, or behavior tallying or charting procedure. Decisions beforehand include the following:

1. Who will be observed
2. What will be observed
3. Where the observation will take place
4. When the observation will take place
5. How the observation will be recorded

Anecdotal Records

One method of recording is the anecdotal record, a good way to gather information about a client's social adjustment. Anecdotal records are brief accounts of behavior recorded in a log or on index cards. An anecdote is a written description of an observed event. The following information should be included (Ten Brink, 1974, p. 166):

1. Name of individual observed
2. Name of observer
3. Date and time of the observation
4. Location of the observation
5. Anecdote

6. Context
7. Interpretation

Ten Brink also includes eight procedural suggestions for recording behavioral anecdotes:

1. Focus on a single specific incident.
2. Be brief but complete.
3. Use objective behavioral descriptions.
4. Use phrases rather than sentences as long as the phrases are understandable.
5. List the behaviors in the sequence in which they occurred.
6. Evaluate what you have written. Is it a good snapshot of behavior?
7. Include direct quotations whenever possible and significant.
8. Record both positive and negative statements.

An advantage of the anecdotal record is that it does not depend upon the individual's capacity to communicate with the observer. In addition, this approach uses natural settings to observe behavior, and the systematic collection of such information can help in the understanding of a client's behavior. The major disadvantages are the time and expense of observation, the time it takes to write down the verbal description, and the questionable objectivity and reliability of the records.

Behavior Tallying and Charting.   Many times the easiest way to record certain behaviors is to tally their occurrences. Sometimes concern centers around the number of times a behavior occurs, as is the case in educational environments where precision teaching or behavior modification efforts are taking place. At other times concern focuses not only on the frequency of behavior but also on its duration. A teacher might be interested in how much time a student spends in her own seat or what percentage of time a preschooler spends crying. Time sampling might be used for behaviors that occur at high rates; that approach involves the recording of behaviors at certain times rather than continuously. Figure 17.4 illustrates a record used to assess the frequency of behavior, and Figure 17.5 shows a way of recording the duration of behavior. Before any intervention is tried, it is important to establish the base rate of the behavior to be modified in order to determine later whether the behavior has been strengthened or eliminated.

Checklists.   Checklists are a way to record the presence or absence of specific behaviors in a given situation. A checklist normally consists of statements about expected behaviors. The observer checks yes or no to indicate whether the behavior occurred. A sample checklist is shown in Figure 17.6. Piacentini (1993) suggests that they can be used to assess a broad band or can be global in design to assess specific disorders or problem areas.

Rating Scales.   Rating scales are devices that can be used to record impressions of behaviors that have been selected in advance. Such scales can help focus attention on specific behaviors. Rating scales most often consist of behaviors to be observed and require the rater to indicate the degree or frequency of behavior occurrences.

```
                                                    Date    2/1 to 2/5

    Name _____

    Observer _____


    Description of Behavior     Physically aggressive - any deliberate body
                                contact made with any part of the body,
                                hands, legs, etc.


    Days                Tallies              Total
    Monday              ////////             8
    Tuesday             //////////           10
    Wednesday           ///////              7
    Thursday            ////////////         12
    Friday              ///////////////      15
    Average =  10.4
```

Figure 17.4
Record of the frequency of behavior

Sometimes the rater is asked to rate the characteristics of the observed behavior or performance. A number of different rating scales are commonly used. Some of the formats are illustrated in Figure 17.7.

Rating scales provide a standardized format for the collection of data, ensuring systematic and comprehensive coverage of the behavior in question (Piacentini, 1993). The structured format reduces subjectivity and increases reliability. Dependence on the rater's experience and day-to-day variability are minimized. However, raters need to be trained to increase the reliability of ratings, and the scales need to be well constructed and have the proper format (Aiken, 1996).

GUIDELINES FOR OBSERVATION

Certain guidelines should be considered for observation:

1. Be objective. Be aware of personal biases and prejudices.
2. Be aware of the halo error—the tendency to be influenced by your first impression of an individual or by an exceptional trait. Such influence can be a source of bias.

Name _____

Observer _____

Description of Behavior   *Out of seat, wandering around classroom.*

Cannot state why when away from the desk.

Day	Time	Total minutes
Monday	9:10 – 9:30	20
	10:07 – 10:15	8
	11:00 – 11:07	7
	2:00 – 2:22	22
Tuesday	9:05 – 9:27	22
	9:50 – 10:03	13
	1:15 – 1:38	23
Wednesday		
Thursday		
Friday		

Average _____

Figure 17.5
Record of the duration of behavior

3. Recognize personal response tendencies—perhaps rating everyone high (generosity error), low (severity error), or in the middle (central tendency error). Be alert to only positive or negative observations.
4. Focus on relevant behaviors. Attend only to the assigned behaviors on the checklist or rating scale.
5. Be as unobtrusive as possible.
6. Observe more than once; the more observations, the better the chance of getting a complete and accurate picture.

Name_____
Observer_____
Date_____
Time observed_____

Yes	No	
____	____	Interrupted others when they were talking.
____	____	Gave compliments or encouragement when talking to others.
____	____	Argued or quarreled with others.
____	____	Swore and used vulgar language.
____	____	Took kidding without getting upset.
____	____	Looked at people directly when talking to them.
____	____	Had a short temper and got angry quickly.
____	____	Was blunt and direct and got to the point.
____	____	Expressed his/her opinion freely.
____	____	Got loud and noisy in conversation.
____	____	Disagreed and took opposite point of view.
____	____	Was nervous and tense when talking with others.
____	____	Was positive about self and others.
____	____	Spoke slowly and softly.
____	____	Made grammatical errors often.
____	____	Had difficulty pronouncing certain words.

Figure 17.6
Checklist of social behavior

7. Have more than one person observe to permit comparison of results.
8. Train observers so that all focus on and record the same behavior in the same way.
9. Instruct observers and have practice sessions in what behaviors are to be observed and how they are to be recorded.

INTERVIEWING

The interview is a form of situation test that relies heavily on observation. Types of interviews include counseling, employment, structured versus unstructured, clinical, panel, stress, medical history, and diagnostic. Interviewing demands good interpersonal and communication skills on the part of the interviewer; different individuals interviewing the same candidate often do not agree on their findings.

Standardized interviews are designed to collect the same type of information from all respondents. In a structured interview, everyone is asked the same questions in the same order, and the answers are recorded identically. Individual intelligence tests are a form of standardized, structured interview. For example, a number

Semantic Differential Type
Behavior with examiner
Reserved ____ ____ ____ ____ ____ ____ ____ Open
        1   2   3   4   5   6   7

Response to testing process
Leery ____ ____ ____ ____ ____ ____ ____ Confident
        1   2   3   4   5   6   7

Graphic Type
Reaction to test environment
Comfortable   Somewhat comfortable   Uncomfortable   Ill at ease
    1   2   3   4

Necessity to repeat questions
    Never   Occasionally   Often
    1   2   3   4   5   6   7

Numerical Type
Rapport with examinee
    1   2   3   4   5   6   7
    Low   High
Examples needed by test taker
    1   2   3   4
    Only 1   5 or more

Figure 17.7
Sample formats showing semantic differential, graphic, and numerical types of rating scales

of structured interview schedules classify children, adolescents, and adults on the DSM-IV, such as the Children's Assessment Schedule (CAS), the Diagnostic Interview for Children and Adolescents (DICA), the Interview Schedule for Children (ISC), and the Schedule for Affective Disorders and Schizophrenia for School Aged Children (K-SADS). In unscheduled interviews the interviewer sometimes varies the sequence of the questions and the order of the topics. The information is recorded on a standardized report form, however, so that the data can be compared and summarized.

Here are some advantages of interviewing:

1. Clients can be guided to answer items completely.
2. Probes can be interpreted or explained.
3. Additional information or understanding can be pursued.
4. Nonverbal behavior and cues as well as different aspects of expressive behavior can be observed.

Interviewing also has disadvantages (Shertzer & Linden, 1979):

1. Success depends on the skill of the interviewer to ask the right questions and correctly interpret the data.

2. Impressions and interpretations are subjective.
3. The communication of some individuals is inhibited, and clients may be unwilling to answer certain questions.
4. The personality of the interviewer can influence the outcome.

Guidelines for Conducting Interviews

Even though the reliability and validity of interviewing may be questionable, it is the only way to gather some types of information; the interviewer can reword questions, add questions, seek clarification of information not understood, pursue interesting topics as they arise, or change the line of questioning altogether (Ten Brink, 1974, p. 170). Here are some general guidelines:

1. Be prepared. Be familiar with the interview purpose, the schedule of questions, and the method of recording answers. Be set mentally and psychologically for the interview.
2. Practice reading the schedule. Test it on a colleague or someone from the target group.
3. Establish rapport. Show interest in the interviewee.
4. Try to put the interviewee at ease so that he will be friendly, cooperative, relaxed, and patient.
5. Explain the purpose of the interview and assure the client of confidentiality.
6. Start with questions that are nonthreatening.
7. Remember, there are certain questions in employment interviewing that are considered legally unacceptable by the Fair Employment Act: those relating to age, race, religion, marital status, arrest record and legal problems, number of children and their ages, membership clubs and organizations, occupation of spouse, and maiden name of a female applicant.
8. Do not react to what is said by agreeing or disagreeing; instead, reinforce the fact that the interviewee is answering the questions. Encourage the interviewee to express thoughts and feelings freely.
9. Guide the session with carefully planned questions so that the interview remains on target. Avoid leading questions.
10. Probe and get more details or explanations when the client does not respond to a question.
11. Change or translate words as necessary for individuals from different educational or cultural backgrounds.
12. Listen carefully, patiently, and intensively but avoid overreacting.
13. Be accepting and courteous.
14. Follow the directions for recording the information from the interview. Be as inconspicuous as possible but discuss with the respondent before the interview begins the type of data recording that will be used. If the session is not electronically recorded, take notes throughout the interview.
15. Observe nonverbal and expressive behavior—not only what is said but how it is said.

16. Check the validity of your information by rephrasing some of the questions and asking the client to expand on the information.
17. Be alert to signals that it is time to terminate the interview.

PROBLEM AREAS

Observational techniques show promise but have psychometric problems. They can be important tools in gaining information, but observers need to be well trained. In many cases observers are asked to rate certain dimensions of individual behavior. Cronbach (1984) states that the most serious rating error is leniency or generosity (p. 509). Some raters prefer to say good things about everyone rather than discriminate. The halo error occurs when an observer rates an examinee high on one dimension not clearly observed because the individual performed well on another. Sometimes interviewers are influenced by first impressions, usually by unfavorable information about the interviewee. According to Cooper (1984), five problems can affect observation (pp. 80–81):

1. Lack of agreement regarding what is to be observed. Different observers have different agendas, goals, and expectations regarding an observation.
2. Failure to achieve a reasonable degree of objectivity. What one person sees as truth may not be perceived as truth by others.
3. Effect of the observer on the behavior of the individual or group being observed. The observer may be too obtrusive.
4. Improper preparation for observation. The observer may not have a good idea of what specific behaviors will be observed or how data will be collected.
5. Generalization from an inadequate sample of behavior. More than one observation may be needed. A given observation may not have been a typical sample of an individual's behavior or performance.

AUTHENTIC ASSESSMENT

The major testing movement of the 1990s has been authentic assessment. When the multiple-choice format came under fire in the 1980s, teachers were encouraged to use other methods of educational assessment such as essays, projects, portfolios, performance tasks, and open-ended exercises. These assessment procedures are not entirely new since the National Assessment of Educational Progress initiated similar formats in 1969.

There is much confusion about the terminology (Fisher, 1993): some refer to *authentic assessment* (Wiggins, 1989), others to *performance assessment* (Stiggins, 1987). Both approaches involve assessing students by observing the things they do. Assessment involves students' demonstrating that they have achieved a given outcome.

Authentic assessment focuses on the development of assessment exercises that are not biased against any group of students and can be reliably scored and validly interpreted. Raters are needed in many cases to score the assessments. Current research on a pilot project in Vermont indicates low reliability of the scoring procedures. Miller and Seraphine (1993) conclude that authentic assessment will probably be useful in low-stake assessment such as in classroom situations. Further, they note that multiple assessments will have value but will take more time from instructors and learning and will increase the anxiety level of students, teachers, and administrators.

Authentic assessment involves authentic learning, according to Glatthorn (1998). It emphasizes real-life experiences. For example, students may be asked to write a speech that could be delivered to the county commissioners (performance assessment). If they actually presented it, the assessment used for evaluating this assignment would be authentic assessment.

Portfolio Assessment

Portfolio assessment is one of the most widely used types of alternative or authentic assessment. Many teachers keep portfolios on their students. The portfolio has several purposes:

1. To document the growth and development of the student
2. To serve as a vehicle for communication between teacher, student, and parents
3. To guide instructional planning for the student
4. To maintain a standard assessment procedure throughout the program

The teacher includes in the folder the assessment record of the child, checklists, teacher communications, writing activities, and reading assignments. Additional information such as the reading log, writing log, goal sheet, journal, teacher's notes, learning log, teacher-student conference log, and screening data might be used.

Portfolios can help show students' growth over time, their favorite or personally important work, and the evolution of one or more projects or products. The portfolio can also be used to prepare a sample of best work for employment or college admissions. It can be used for student placement decisions or to achieve alternative credit for a course. It is a helpful tool in curriculum and program evaluation.

Johnson (1996) calls the portfolio the multiple choice of performance assessment. Schools and teachers differ about the types of entries to be included as well as how they are going to be evaluated. Sometimes criteria are very structured; other times a minimum of structure is required.

Figure 17.8 shows an evaluation checklist for portfolios created in a middle school English class.

According to Johnson (1996), these are the key design elements to consider when developing portfolios: (1) specify desired outcomes and expectations, (2) create rubrics and criteria defining quality of work, and (3) involve students in decisions about how portfolios should be structured and evaluated.

Figure 17.8
Evaluation checklist for portfolios

Student_____Date_____
Class_____Teacher_____

Mechanics
_____Correct spelling
_____Correct grammar
_____Appropriate word usage
_____Subject-verb agreement
_____Correct punctuation
_____Other_____

Structure
_____Well organized
_____Coherent
_____Paragraph unity
_____Appropriate topic sentences
_____Logical conclusions

Style
_____Style appropriate for purposes
_____Tone fits topic

Teacher action
____Rewrite and resubmit
____Correct errors noted and resubmit
____Correct errors and place in portfolio
____Read comments and place in portfolio

Outside rater
____Meets school criteria

The portfolio approach demonstrates both the learning process and the product. The process gives a teacher or counselor a portrait of the problem-solving techniques used by the student. The student also has the opportunity to demonstrate what she knows and can do. In any field portfolios encourage self-reflection and metacognitive strategies. Nevertheless, although the portfolio process has a high degree of realism and creativity, its validity and reliability are often questioned.

Guidelines for Good Assessment Systems

The National Council of Teachers of Mathematics (1993) listed six standards for alternative or authentic assessment in mathematics; the principles also apply to other content areas:

1. Assessment should reflect the mathematics that are most important for students.
2. Assessment should enhance mathematics learning.

3. Assessment should promote equity by giving each student optional opportunities to demonstrate mathematical power and by helping each student meet the profession's high expectations.

4. All aspects of the mathematics assessment process should be open to review and scrutiny.

5. Evidence from assessment activities should yield valid inferences about students' mathematics learning.

6. Every aspect of an assessment process should be consistent with the purpose of the assessment.

The National Council for Measurement in Education (1994) provided criteria for evaluating alternative assessment procedures. The purpose of the assessment needs to be identified. Multiple measures should be used, and the process should have technical rigor. The process must be cost-effective, of educational value, and equitable to all students. The information should be useful to decision makers.

Gooding (1994) has seven criteria that should be reflected in a good evaluation system. The assessment needs to be longitudinal and assess student learning over time. It should be authentic and focus on knowledge and skills the learner needs for success outside of school. The objectives of the assessment should be communicated effectively so that they are known by teachers, parents, and students. The assessment should be nonbiased and fair to individuals from different learning backgrounds and cultures. It should be process-oriented and require students to produce a product or performance. It should be student-oriented, involving students in self-assessment and evaluation. Learners should be required to produce knowledge and apply it when solving problems.

Issues and Problems

One of the big challenges for helping professionals in the authentic assessment movement is to help teachers link assessment to ongoing instruction. Teachers need a better understanding of their classroom practices and the ethical aspects, reasoning, and consequences of good/poor instruction. Teacher training institutions must help preservice interns to improve their assessment skills.

Math teachers, for example, need to consider that mathematics assessment may demand substantial linguistic ability and thus be unfair to people who are lacking those skills. Since performance-based assessment uses only a small number of tasks, these tasks may favor one group over another. Students must be provided with assessment alternatives that are appropriate to their ethnicity, gender, disability, or language. The use of portfolio assessment requires teachers to adapt to ever-changing curricular and instructional demands (CRESST, 1994).

This brief overview suggests what might happen soon in the professions. Licensing and certification tests might need to become more authentic. Many examinations for skilled and craft trades are performance-based.

SUMMARY

Observational techniques are widely used in assessing and evaluating clients. Counselors and psychologists use observational techniques to assess a client's behavior in play therapy, sociodrama, psychodrama, simulated experiences, role playing, test performance, discussion groups, conferences, and interviews and in job, home, or school situations. Sometimes observation is a secondary part of a testing situation. On most individual tests the examiner rates the test taker's behavior as well as his answers. Observational techniques show promise but do have psychometric problems that interfere with their validity and reliability.

QUESTIONS FOR DISCUSSION

1. What are the major types and sources of errors likely to arise in observational situations? How can you eliminate or reduce these sources of error?

2. Some individuals advocate the use of unobtrusive observation, claiming that clients will tend to perform in more natural and typical ways. Think of situations in which unobtrusive observation is not possible. How can you enhance the validity of your observations when it is impossible for you to be unobtrusive? Should contrived situations be used?

3. Interview some counselors and psychologists. Ask them how much time they spend using observational techniques and find out whether they use structured or unstructured observation. What instruments or schedules do they use? How valid and reliable do they feel the observations are?

4. When would you make use of self-observational techniques? What training or instructions would you give a client before assigning self-observation? What psychometric problems do you see with these techniques?

5. Compare structured and unstructured interviews. In what situations or contexts would you use each type? Individual standardized tests are considered a form of structured interview. Is it appropriate to deviate from the sequence established by the test authors? What are some factors to consider when interviewing a client?

SUGGESTED ACTIVITIES

1. Choose a type of behavior that is of interest to you and prepare an operational definition of the behavior. Construct a checklist to record the number of times that the behavior occurs in a given situation.

2. Go to the library and find a copy of *Mirrors of Behavior* (Simon & Boyer, 1974). Choose one of the categorical scales included in the volume and try it out in the appropriate environment. Report on the usability of the scale and comment on the reliability and validity as well as the problems one might encounter in using the scale.

3. Review the different observational checklists that are part of many individual tests. What commonalities exist among these scales? What differences? How observable are the behaviors or constructs to be rated by the examiner?

4. Collect some career autobiographies from a group of individuals. Determine a system to analyze the results. Discuss the rationale for your analysis and the results from your study. How did the instructions you gave in the sample influence the results?

5. Review some of the standardized rating scales that are widely used in your field. What scales have higher reliability—structured or unstructured, self-rating or rating by other scales, categorical or summary type? Report your findings to the class.

6. Study the case of Alicia and answer the questions at the end.

Alicia is in a community college outreach program and is participating in a 2-week session designed to help students develop skills and see the importance of staying in school and going on to postsecondary education. The program is for rural, underachieving, minority students.

The following are entries in Alicia's journal:

Monday: Yesterday when I first got their we went to the dorms got our name log then we went and put our clothes in the dorms. Then I went outside to mess with the boys and we had fun with one of the counselors. We played basket in the gym and I had lots of fun. I also like this boy name Rod but me and him both can't talk to each other because he has a girlfriend and I have a boyfriend. I guess I have to put that in the closet. Well get back to real business I think this program so far have done me some good because sometimes other people can learn things better than others. I ihig over her I catch on easy so you know how that is. Because I really want to learn more because up their in life it's gonabe hard down that long road and because we are black you know they think black people can't be or do anything and tha's why am going to pay atton and make something out of my self. also I think this program is good for us because it keeps you off the streets Keeps you away from drugs it keeps you from lots of things think about. they alway told me my 15 years I been on this earth can't do a thing when you just sit around doing nothing. Also I want to go to college and be in a marching band and major in mathematics. Because me an person that likes to need losts of people and fun things like that you know. Well kind of ran out of words to say But I will always remember to stay in school BECAUSE IF YOU BELIEVE YOU WILL ACHIEVE.

Tuesday: Today's Tuesday, so far so good I got up this moing thank God for waking me up. Well let me get on withit took me a shower put on some clothes and went to breakfast. Well breakfast was pretty good this morning. I got full and started on my way to go back to my room and got my books fo my class we went to reading class we was learning about verbs and good stuff like that then we came to Study Hall and did the homework our english teach gave us it was not much but it was rough. Well sitting her in Study Hall listen to thes boys trip on each other one boy told this other boy that he looked like a snaping turtule that mess was funny to. also Miss Pam told one of my friends that she write to big and told one boy he write to bad She coud not read nothing he say. they she asked one boy how to spell it was that he was not using his studing time all they do is paly stand and tell jokes so I don't pay them no mind. Oh when we was comming to Study Hall we was so sorry we did not want to take the stairs so we took the elavater now tell me is that sorry or what. Well I am running out of words to say gotta go See YA *Wednesday*: Today is Wednesday I got up this moing went to the bathroom and brush my teeth. Then I went to my room and putsome clothes on then went to brakfast and got full. Then I went to Reading class and learned a little bit then we went to Study Hall then we started triping you know we started tell jokes and stuff like that we tried to tell Miss Pam that we did not have any work to do but she fooded us She made us work asnway. Then she made us take a test and some of us did not study and probely flunk the test you know. Also I think Shon is very nice because he is always smiling and that's the way I like to see pople smiling all the time. Also when I was going to Study hall I touch rod on his arm I like that you know how that is to touch someone you really want to get to. Well we know some flunk Because he told everybody that he miss eight and he told Miss Pam that he want to take the test over becausse she could not read it with his bad handwriting. Of I flunk the test too. I miss five I think I need to study. Know let me get to yesterday we had so much fund we was in the gym and the boys was playing basketball and Chad and Rod and all of them I was cheering for all of the exspecally Rod I like him as you can see. Oh By the way our team did not win because they say we cheated but we didn't we won fare and squar. After we got finished with the relay we ate snacks then we went to take a shower then went to bed well got to go. See YA when I see YA Peace

a. What are the major themes in Alicia's journal?
b. What kind of system would you develop to analyze these journals?
c. What kind of impact do you think the program had on Alicia? Why?

ADDITIONAL READINGS

Read current issues of the *Journal of Behavioral Assessment, Behavioral Assessment*, and *Journal of Abnormal Child Psychology*. These journals publish research on observational techniques and instruments.

Aiken, L. R. (1996). *Rating scales and checklists.* New York: Wiley.

Aiken provides information on how to design, construct, administer, and score rating scales.

Johnson, B. (1996). *The performance assessment handbook.* Vol. 1: *Portfolios and Socratic seminars.* Vol. 2: *Performances and exhibitions.* Princeton, NJ: Eye on Education.

The author gives examples of the use of portfolios, performances, exhibitions, and Socratic seminars in education.

Goldstein, G., & Hersen, M. (1990). *Handbook of psychological assessment* (2nd ed.). New York: Pergamon.

Three chapters on interviewing and two on behavioral assessment provide good information.

Simon, A., & Boyer, E. G. (Eds.). (1974). *Mirrors for behavior III: An anthology of observational instruments.* Wyncote, PA: Communications Material Center.

CHAPTER 18

Working with Special Populations

OVERVIEW

Everyone has different conceptions of exceptional and special needs examinees. Haring (1982) described exceptional people as those who differ from the norm so significantly and so repeatedly as to impair their success in very basic social, personal, or educational activities. They are described by professionals as disabled, impaired, disordered, or exceptional.

Haring (1982) defined *disabled* as any person whose functioning is reduced as a result of physical deficit or one who experiences problems in learning or social adjustment. Examples of physical deficits include limb loss, crippling conditions, or damage to the brain. The term *impaired*, according to Haring, is more commonly used to refer to sensory deficits. Blindness or deafness are two examples. *Disordered*, another descriptor, refers to problems in learning or social behavior. Emotional disturbance is an example of a behavior disorder; a language disorder denotes difficulty in comprehension or production of language.

In this chapter we will use the term *disabled* to refer to special needs individuals with physical, intellectual, and/or emotional deficits as compared with the general population. People with special needs also include linguistic minorities and the gifted and talented.

OBJECTIVES

After studying this chapter, the reader should be able to

✔ Discuss the standards and ethical considerations in testing special needs populations

✔ Identify the major tests and assessment techniques used with these groups

✔ List the goals and objectives and explain the issues and problems of testing special needs examinees

STANDARDS FOR TESTING PEOPLE WITH DISABLING CONDITIONS

Standards for Educational and Psychological Testing (AERA, APA, & NCME, 1985) identifies standards for testing people with disabling conditions. The majority are primarily intended for test authors who are modifying tests to use with special needs groups.

Test authors are required to have psychometric expertise and experience in working with these groups, and test publishers should caution examiners about the use and interpretation of the test with special needs clients until it has been fully validated. Authors should conduct pilot tests on people who have similar disabilities to check the appropriateness and feasibility of the modifications and should include a careful statement of steps taken to modify the test so that users will be able to identify any changes that may alter its validity.

Test authors should use empirical procedures to establish time limits for modified forms and explore the effects of fatigue. They also should provide validity and reliability information for both the modified and unmodified forms.

Clearly, it is important for the user to study the manual and evaluate the technical information to determine whether the modifications are valid and reliable for the group in question. In addition, counselors and psychologists working with clients who have special needs should know what alternate tests and modes are available and appropriate for these persons. Clients need to be informed of the availability of these other instruments and be given a chance to take them. Those who are interpreting the test results need to know which set of norms should be used. Regular norms are used when the examiner needs to compare the disabled individual's test performance with the general population. Special norms are appropriate when the examiner is looking at how the individual performs in relation to peers with the same disabling conditions.

The needs of impaired examinees should be considered carefully. Hearing impaired individuals need interpreters who sign the instructions and/or items for them. Some tests have videocassettes with the directions and items presented in sign language. For visually impaired individuals, large print versions, Braille forms, and forms on cassette recorders are available. Most national testing programs have provisions for special needs individuals to have more time to complete tests.

Both content and format of tests have to be revised for people with special needs. Most publishers have expert panels who review the appropriateness of test items to eliminate bias.

Testing Linguistic Minorities

For many non-English-speaking groups, English is a second or third language. Tests written in English may become tests of language proficiency for these individuals rather than measures of other constructs. Of course, it is sometimes important and necessary to have tests that measure English proficiency—especially for educational diagnosis and placement. Tests not meant to measure proficiency in English are sometimes translated into the appropriate native language. However, there may be problems in translation, and the content and words might not be appropriate or meaningful to the group being tested.

Standards for Educational and Psychological Testing (AERA et al., 1985) includes seven standards relating to the testing of linguistic minorities. The selection and use of appropriate tests need to be reviewed carefully. A number of standards are intended primarily for the test authors and publishers but should be taken into consideration by the test user. If the test is modified, the changes should be spelled out in the manual in addition to specifications for test use. The reliability and validity of the test for the intended linguistic group are also important. If two versions of dual-language tests exist, evidence of the comparability of the forms should be included. The standards also caution users not to require a greater level of proficiency on the test in English than the job or profession requires—a significant concern in developing and selecting employment, certification, and licensing examinations. Another standard is extremely important to users; it cautions them not to judge English language proficiency on the basis of test information alone. Many language skills are not adequately measured by multiple-choice examinations. The counselor needs to use observation techniques and perhaps informal checklists to assess proficiency more completely.

The *Code for Fair Testing Practices in Education* (APA, 1988) calls for tests to be developed in ways that make them fair for test takers of different race, gender, or ethnic background or those with disabling conditions. Test users are asked to evaluate the procedures used by test developers to avoid potentially insensitive content or language; review the performance of test takers of different races, gender, and ethnic background when samples of sufficient size are available; and evaluate how performance differences may be caused by inappropriate characteristics of tests. When necessary and feasible, test administrators are to use appropriately modified forms of tests or administration procedures for test takers with disabling conditions and then interpret standard norms with care in light of the modifications made.

Public Law 94–142

Public Law 94–142, the Education for All Handicapped Children Act, exemplifies the current philosophical and social attitudes toward people with special needs. Passed by Congress in 1975 and amended in 1990 by substituting the word *disabled* for *handicapped*, the law guarantees disabled children 3 to 21 years old appropriate educational opportunities in the least restrictive environment. The law also sets standards for the types of assessment materials and procedures used. Assessment must not discriminate against a child on the basis of race or culture. Furthermore, test and assessment materials should do the following:

1. Be provided and administered in the examinee's language or other mode of communication
2. Be validated for the specific purpose for which they are to be used
3. Be administered by trained personnel according to specifications in the manual

4. Yield useful information in specific areas of educational need
5. Give an accurate picture of what is to be assessed, such as aptitude and achievement, rather than reflect the examinee's impaired skills
6. Be used and interpreted by a multidisciplinary team of persons, including at least one teacher or specialist in the area of the disability

The targeted student should be assessed in all areas related to the suspected disability; the testing should not be confined to academic performance but should also include health, vision, general intelligence, communication skills, and emotional status. In other words, a single criterion cannot determine the most appropriate educational program for a test taker.

PRESCHOOL EVALUATIONS

In recent years there has been an effort to identify children with disabilities prior to kindergarten. Bailey and Wolery (1989) point out five important assessment domains for this group: cognitive skills, motor skills, communication skills, play and social skills, and self-care skills.

An annotated list of preschool assessment instruments and tests is provided here:

The Bayley Scales of Infant Development are used to assess the mental and psychomotor development of children from 2 to 30 months of age and to aid in the diagnosis of normal or retarded development.

The Cattell Infant Intelligence Scale measures intellectual development of children from 3 to 30 months by assessing verbalizations and motor control.

The Dallas Preschool Screening Test is used to assess the learning disabilities of children between the ages of 3 and 6: it measures auditory, language, motor, visual, psychological, and articulation development.

The Denver Developmental Screening Test (DDST) is used to evaluate a child's personal, social, fine motor, gross motor, language, and adaptive abilities. The test is appropriate for use as a screening tool with children from birth to age 6.

The Developmental Assessment for the Severely Handicapped is an observation scale used to assess the progress of severely disabled children from birth to 9 years of age developmentally. The scale provides information on the sensory-motor, language, preacademic, daily living, and socio-emotional areas used to establish individual education programs.

The Kent Infant Development Scale (KID Scale) uses a 252-item inventory to assess the developmental age of infants and young children chronologically or developmentally under 1 year of age. The test measures cognitive, language, motor, self-help, and social skills.

DuBose (1982) reminds us that neither Gesell nor Piaget studied children who were impaired or were developing more slowly than their peers. This paucity of developmental information makes it harder for examiners to assess preschool children with disabilities. Some of the behaviors to be noted and considered are described in Table 18.1.

Public Law 99–457, the Education of the Handicapped Act Amendments of 1986, focuses on identifying and developing programs for infants and toddlers with disabilities. The purpose of the law is to facilitate the development and implementation of statewide interagency programs of early intervention services that are comprehensive, coordinated, and multidisciplinary. The law defines individuals with disabilities as those who are mentally retarded; hard of hearing; deaf; speech, language, or visually impaired; seriously emotionally disturbed; or orthopedically impaired. It also includes other health impaired individuals and those with specific learning disabilities who require special education and related services. Under the legislation, families with children in these categories should be provided with multidisciplinary assessment of unique needs and identification of services appropriate to meet their

Table 18.1
Performance characteristics of preschool children with disabilities

Disability	Behavior
Deafness	Language skill acquisition affected severely Communication skills qualitatively different Social skill acquisition delayed Cognitive skills not necessarily affected Motor skills not necessarily affected
Blindness	Gross and fine motor coordination affected severely Awareness of spatial relationships, object permanence affected Self-care and social skills delayed Verbal and cognitive skills development hampered Sensory motor skill development hampered Language patterns and development restricted
Physical impairment	Motor skills poorly developed Some form of visual impairment with some disabilities (e.g., cerebral palsy) Possible auditory or perceptual problems Possible speech problems Delayed skill acquisition in all domains
Social-emotional-behavioral problems	Poor communication skills Possible delay in motor behavior Possible visual problems and hearing loss in autistic children
Mental disability	All areas of development affected Sensory perception problems

unique needs. The targeted group is children from birth to age 2 who are experiencing developmental delays, as measured by appropriate diagnostic instruments and procedures, in one or more of the following areas: cognitive development, physical development, language and speech development, psychosocial development, and self-help skills. Also included are children with a diagnosed physical or mental condition that has a high probability of resulting in developmental delay. The key is early identification. Rossetti (1990) points out the need for the involvement of teams of specialists—speech therapists, occupational therapists, physical therapists, and psychologists—in assessing this group.

TYPES OF DISABILITIES AND DISORDERS

Communication Disorders

A communication disorder is defined as a significant deviation in speech or language from norms based on sex, age, and cultural, ethnic, or social expectations (Haring, 1982, p. 82). Speech pathologists are responsible for the assessment of clients with communication disorders and may use a number of different assessment approaches. Psychologists and counselors testing these individuals may find that examinees are unable to say words correctly or to formulate ideas according to accepted standards. The examiners need to concentrate their attention on what these clients have to say and reward client efforts with warmth and positive reinforcement. Here are some other good practices:

1. Demonstrate acceptance and positive regard for the client as an individual.
2. Try to remove any distracting stimuli from the testing environment.
3. Keep instructions and directions simple. Repeat or rephrase questions when appropriate.
4. Be alert to facial expressions, gestures, and tone of voice.
5. Allow the examinee to nod, point, or otherwise indicate the answer nonverbally.

Intellectual Disabilities

Tests of intelligence have been primarily used to assess whether the examinee has a moderate, severe, or profound intellectual disability. Mildly retarded individuals usually score 2 to 3 standard deviations below the mean and range between 55 and 69 on IQ tests. The moderately retarded score 3 to 4 standard deviations below the mean and range between 40 and 54 on IQ tests. Severely retarded individuals score 4 to 5 standard deviations below the mean and have IQs of less than 25.

The testing of severely disabled individuals presents a challenge to the examiner because of the intensity of their physical, mental, or emotional problems. These individuals do not respond well to even the most pronounced stimuli and sometimes have temper tantrums. They also lack even the most rudimentary form of verbal control. Assessment of these individuals may have to be done over a period of time in both natural and contrived situations. DuBose (1982) advocates that behaviors be assessed across several settings to ensure generalization and that conditions be modified for specific severe disabilities. Items used should call for behaviors that are observable and measurable. The American Association on Mental Retardation (AAMR) (1992) definition of being mentally retarded includes three criteria: scoring 2.5 standard deviations below the mean on the Wechsler or Binet scales, showing deficits in adaptive behavior, and exhibiting these symptoms by age 18.

Adaptive Behavior.   Adaptive behavior is defined as a person's ability to deal effectively with personal and social demands and expectations. For example, the public school version of the AAMD Adaptive Behavior Scale addresses independent functioning, physical development, economic activity, language development, number and time concepts, vocational activity, self-direction, responsibility, and socialization.

The second part of the scale covers destructive behavior, antisocial behavior, nonconforming behavior, untrustworthiness, withdrawn behaviors, odd mannerisms, interpersonal manners, vocal habits, eccentric habits, psychological disturbances, and use of medication.

Many adaptive behavior schedules have been developed and used to assess the characteristics of special populations, especially individuals with possible mental retardation, emotional disturbance, or other learning disabilities. Evaluation provides diagnostic and prescriptive information for the educational programming and guidance of these individuals. Aman, Hammer, and Rojan (1993) advocate a multimodal assessment of mental retardation, including the use of direct observation, adaptive behavior scales such as the AAMD's or the Vineland Adaptive Behavior Scale, IQ tests, and behavior rating scales such as the Behavior Disturbance Scale of the Psychopathology Instrument for Mentally Retarded Youth.

Here are some other instruments measuring adaptive behavior:

The Adaptive Behavior Inventory is designed for use with individuals aged 5 to 18. The scales are independent functioning, physical development, economic activity, language development, numbers and time, domestic activities, prevocational/vocational activity, self-direction, responsibility, and socialization

The Adaptive Behavior Scales: Residential and Community, Second Edition (ABS) are designed for use with clients between ages 18 and 80. They assess the individual's ability to cope with the social demands of the environment and determine the strength and weaknesses among adaptive assets or liabilities of individuals with developmental disabilities.

The Adaptive Behavior Scales: School, Second Edition are designed to be used with children between ages 3.0 and 18.11. The scales are personal self-sufficiency, community self-sufficiency, personal-self responsibility, social adjustment, and personal adjustment.

Behavior Disorders

Behavior disorders are sometimes labeled as emotional disturbance. Disagreement exists over classification and acceptable standards. The DSM–IV lists disorders that examiners need to be familiar with when working with diverse groups: attention deficit disorders (with or without hyperactivity), conduct disorders, anxiety disorders, eating disorders, stereotyped movement disorders, pervasive developmental disorders, disorders with physical manifestations, and others. Examiners need to recognize the major symptoms of the different types of behavior, which can vary from extreme withdrawal to extreme acting out and aggressive behavior.

Psychologists or examiners rely on many techniques to screen for intervention and program placement of those identified as having behavior disorders. Observation and rating procedures have been used to assess individual functioning in a natural setting. Reports from family, peers, teachers, and parents are valuable also, and sometimes standardized tests are used.

These are some of the general tests and scales used to assess individuals in this category:

Burks's Behavior Rating Scales are used to identify patterns of behavior problems in children and to aid in deferential diagnosis.

The Child Diagnostic Screening Battery and Adolescent Diagnostic Screening Battery are used with children in clinical settings to identify all possible DSM–IV diagnoses. The tests have forms for parents or guardians and for the clinician.

The Diagnostic Inventory of Personality and Symptoms uses the DSM–IV as the framework for the items and scales used.

The Louisville Behavior Checklist measures social-emotional behaviors indicative of psychopathological disorders in children and is used by examiners when interviewing parents.

Here are some general guidelines for testing individuals with behavior disorders:

1. Have a carefully structured environment for testing.
2. Reinforce appropriate behavior.
3. Be fair and consistent.
4. Be sensitive and try to understand individual frustrations, hopes, and fears.
5. Keep directions and routines simple and establish reasonable rules.

Autism and Pervasive Development Disorders.   Autism and pervasive development disorders are characterized by qualitative impairment in communication, language, and symbolic development and are marked by a restrictive repertoire of activities and interests. Most autistic persons have some degree of mental retardation. They suffer from multiple problems in speech, language, and communication. They sometimes exhibit tantrums, aggressive outbursts, and noncompliance. Marcus and Schopler (1993) recommend multimodal assessment for these individuals, including diagnostic instruments such as the Childhood Autism Rating Scale (CARS) and the Autism Behavior Checklist (ABC), among others.

Developmental-educational assessment should also be completed, using scales such as the Psychoeducational Profile–Revised (PEP-R). To meet the challenge of working with this group, the test authors have altered sequences of items so that stressful language items are balanced by more enjoyable visual and motor tasks. The scale permits alternative methods of communication to enable appropriate assessment of individuals with autism. The test has two sections: the first assesses developmental functions; the second identifies unusual or atypical behavior.

The Adult Psychoeducational Profile (APEP) is used with moderately to severely handicapped older autistic persons. Communication and language assessment instruments for this group include the Peabody Picture Vocabulary Test. Social, family, and medical information is also included in the assessment.

The following tests are used especially for autism:

The Autism Screening Instrument for Educational Planning provides an assessment and educational planning system for autism and developmental delay. The scale looks at sensory, relating, body concept, language, and social self-help; samples vocal behavior; assesses interaction and communication; and determines learning rate.

The Behavior Observation Scale for Autism assesses the presence of behaviors characteristic of autism.

The Gilliam Autism Rating Scale helps identify and diagnose autism in individuals aged 3 to 23 and estimates the severity of the problem. The scales are stereotyped behaviors, communication, social interaction, and developmental disturbances.

Anxiety Disorders. Anxiety disorders take different forms in childhood and adolescence but are characterized by intense subjective distress and maladaptive patterns of cognition and behavior. For children and adolescents these might be separation anxiety, overanxiety, and avoidant disorders. For adults they may take the form of generalized anxiety disorders, panic disorder, phobic disorders, and the like. Strauss (1993) suggests the use of multimodal assessment such as structured interviews, self-report inventories, parent and teacher checklists, client observations, and physiological measurements. Major self-report inventories include the Children's Manifest Anxiety Scale–Revised and the Fear Survey Schedule for Children–Revised. A number of rating scales contain items dealing with anxiety and withdrawal.

One of the most widely used tests to measure anxiety in adolescents and adults is the State-Trait Anxiety Scale. It provides two different types of assessment of anxiety: how individuals feel at a particular time (state) and how individuals normally perceive a situation.

Conduct Disorders. Individuals with conduct disorders show patterns of antisocial behavior, often exhibit impaired functioning at home and school, and are viewed as unmanageable by parents and teachers. The child or adolescent may exhibit the following behaviors: stealing, truancy, property destruction, use of weapons, physical cruelty, arson, and similar actions. Helping professionals assess the disorder using a variety of techniques, including self-report inventories such as the MMPI and Millon or reports by others such as the Sutter-Eyberg Student Behavior Inventory. There are a number of direct evaluative systems, such as the Parent Daily Report. Peer evaluations are also sought through sociometric techniques. Kazdin (1993) reports that each method has its strengths, methodological weaknesses, and sources of bias. Therefore, he advocates the use of multiple measures for accurate assessment.

Attention Deficit Disorder.   Although its cause is unknown, attention deficit disorder involves multiple areas of functioning and is a complex and chronic disorder of the brain. Rapport (1993) recommends multimodal assessment, which includes structured and semistructured interviews such as the Diagnostic Interview for Children and Adolescents (DICA) and the Diagnostic Interview Schedule for Children (DISC), checklists and rating forms such as the Child Behavior Checklist (CBC) and narrow band rating scales and checklists such as the Child's Learning Profile (CLP), observations of classroom behavior, intellectual and achievement testing, and neurocognitive testing such as the Continuous Performance Test (CPT) or the Matching Familiar Figures Test (MFFT).

One of the newer scales is by Brown (1996), the Brown Attention Deficit Disorder Scale (ADDS), designed to assess attention deficit disorder in adolescents and adults. The five scales are activating and organizing work, sustaining attention and concentration, sustaining energy and effort, managing affective interference, and utilizing working memory and assessing recall. The Connors's Rating Scale–Revised (1996) assesses a broad range of psychopathological and problem behaviors, including attention deficit disorder. It has two forms: a short form for teachers, which measures oppositional behavior, cognitive inattention problems, and hyperactivity; and a long form for parents and helping professionals, with 59 items.

Eating Disorders.   Two major eating disorders, anorexia nervosa and bulimia, are characterized by a morbid overconcern with weight and physical appearance. In anorexia nervosa the client starves herself to the point of emaciation, strives for thinness, and fears becoming fat. Bulimia clients also strive for thinness but have strong urges to overeat, which leads to binges followed by self-induced vomiting, laxatives, fasting, and similar behavior. Gardner and Parker (1993) advocate multimodal assessment, starting with an initial interview. Sometimes a medical examination is necessary to determine if weight loss is due to some underlying physical disorder. Gardner and Parker (1993) provide an outline of a clinical interview checklist that includes items dealing with demographic features and treatment history, weight-controlling behavior, binge eating and eating behavior, attitudes toward weight and shape, physical symptoms, and psychological and interpersonal factors.

There are a number of self-report inventories, such as the Eating Disorders Inventory-2, which assesses features common in anorexia nervosa and bulimia nervosa. The scales are drive for thinness, ineffectiveness, body dissatisfaction, maturity fear, interceptive awareness, impulse regulation, social insecurity, and asceticism. The inventory also assesses three dimensions of eating behavior important in recognizing and treating eating-related disorders: cognitive control of eating, disinhibition, and hunger.

Hearing Impairment

Individuals differ in their degree of impairment as well as the age of onset of the impairment. Audiologists screen individuals with hearing losses that range from mild to profound and can be caused by a number of factors. Normally, examinees with hearing deficits have a pattern of retarded speech and language development and problems in social development. Some have poor control of their impulses and do not have a strongly developed sense of responsibility. They often misinterpret the feelings and behaviors of others and may be significantly behind their peers in educational achievement.

Intelligence tests that do not demand oral language are preferable for this group. Examiners must be careful in reaching conclusions during observations. Individuals who exhibit behavior characteristic of learning disabled, behavior disordered, or mentally retarded persons may be suffering from a hearing loss that leads to those similar behaviors. Simeonsson (1986) identified three major purposes for assessment of hearing impaired individuals: to understand cognitive competency and achievement discrepancy, cognitive and linguistic discrepancy, and personal and social functioning.

Many individual differences exist within this group, and it is important to take into consideration the etiology of the impairment as well as the developmental history of the individual. The following guidelines pertain to assessment of hearing impaired persons:

Be sure that any individual with problems speaking or understanding spoken language has a hearing evaluation.

Keep the test environment controlled and free from distraction; an individual with a mild hearing loss may be distracted by extraneous noise.

Avoid visual distractions, especially if the examinee is reading lips.

If necessary, have an interpreter help communicate with the examinee.

Allow the interpreter and the deaf person to arrange seating to enhance the lines of communication.

Have more than one test or approach to measure the construct in question.

Bradley-Johnson and Evans (1991) point out that testing should be supplemented with interviews, review of school records, and use of classroom observation. Vance (1998) recommends assessing adaptive behavior of all students with disabilities or suspected disabilities along with observations conducted in different settings.

Visual Impairment

Visual impairment may be caused by injury or disease that reduces the individual's central vision, accommodation, binocular vision, peripheral vision, or color vision. The impairment affects normal patterns of cognitive, affective, and psychomotor development. Visually impaired preadolescents and adolescents quite often have problems in social development that cause lower self-concepts. Psychologists and educators assess aptitude and achievement of the visually impaired by adapting standard instruments to meet their needs. Chase (1986) points out that test administrators need to become familiar with the nature of visual disorders and their impact on development. Testers must be aware of the following:

1. The effects of distracting noise in a testing situation
2. The need for additional time to complete tasks if the test is in Braille or large type
3. The need to structure the testing environment and let the examinee become familiar with objects by handling them
4. The need to describe the setting for the examinee
5. The need for several breaks or multiple sessions

Specialized tests are available for assessing children and adults with visual impairments. The Hill Performance Test of Selected Positional Concepts measures the spatial concepts of visually impaired children aged 6 to 10. The Reynell-Zinkin Scales provide a profile of six areas for children up to 5 years old: social adaptation, sensorimotor, exploration of environment, response to sound and verbal comprehension, expressive language, and nonverbal communication. The Hepatic Intelligence Scale is a performance-based scale for the blind and partially sighted aged 16 and older and has six tests: digit symbol, object assembly, block design, object completion, pattern board, and bead arithmetic.

Gifted and Talented Persons

Often educators think of a gifted individual as a person with a high level of intellectual ability. Terman (1954) operationally defined gifted as those individuals who score in the top 1% on the Stanford-Binet or have IQs of 130 or above. The U.S. Office of Education (1978) definition implies that the gifted individual possesses high performance capabilities in areas such as intellect, creativity, academics, leadership, or the performing or visual arts and requires services or activities not ordinarily provided by a school.

Examiners of gifted and talented individuals have relied on group and individual intelligence tests; survey achievement batteries; and the ratings of teachers, parents, and even students themselves. Some of the scales used to assess the gifted and talented are listed here:

The Creativity Attitude Survey for grades 4 to 6 assesses confidence in one's own ideas, appreciation of fantasy, theoretical and aesthetic orientation, openness to impulse expression, and desire for novelty.

The Creativity Checklist is given to counselors, parents, and teachers to rate eight dimensions of creative behavior, such as fluency, flexibility, resourcefulness, constructural skill, ingenuity, and independence. It can be used with individuals from kindergarten to adulthood.

The Gifted and Talented Evaluation Scales contain a 50-item rating scale of behaviors characteristic of gifted and talented students. It is completed by teachers and parents or those having knowledge of the students. The scale is for students ages 5 to 18.

The Gifted and Talented Screening Form asks parents and teachers to rate individuals on academic performance, creativity, intelligence, psychomotor ability, and visual-performing arts. The scale is used in grades K through 9.

The Group Inventory for Finding Creative Talent (GIFT) surveys the creative interests and attitudes of students in grades K through 6.

The Group Inventory for Finding Interests: Gifted and Talented Screening Form assesses the creative interests and attitudes of students in grades 6 through 12.

The Scales for Rating the Behavioral Characteristics of Superior Students are completed by teachers, parents, or guidance counselors to measure various dimensions of gifted behavior—learning, motivation, creativity, leadership, art, music, drama, planning, precise communication, and expressive communication.

The Screening Assessment for Gifted Students has two forms, one for elementary students aged 5.0 to 8-11 and one for middle- or upper-grade students aged 7.0 to 12.11. Student aptitude is measured by a reasoning test, achievement by an information test. The middle- and upper-grade version measures creativity with a divergent production subtest.

Thinking Creatively in Action and Movement (TCAM) is a nonverbal movement test used to assess the creativity of children aged 3 to 8.

Thinking Creatively with Sounds and Words measures the ability of individuals to create images for words and sounds. There are two forms, one for grades 3 through 12 and one for adults.

The Torrance Tests of Creative Thinking assess the ability of individuals to visualize and transform words and meanings.

The Watson-Glaser Critical Thinking Appraisal measures the individual's ability to think critically and includes dimensions such as inferences, recognition of assumptions, deduction, interpretation, and evaluation of arguments.

Examiners testing gifted individuals should not be influenced by stereotypical attitudes. Who is tested and what tests are given depend partly on the operational definition of gifted. It can pertain to exceptional academic achievement, extraordinary creativity, special talents, superior intelligence, or some other variable. Examiners should remember that gifted and talented students can have the same testing problems that other students have. They may not want to do well because of peer pressure, they may be bored and frustrated, or they may come from disadvantaged environments and be overlooked by teachers and administrators.

SUMMARY

Psychometric criteria have an important role in diagnosing mental retardation, learning disabilities, and giftedness, and they are used as a secondary tool in diagnosing behavioral and emotional disorders. Clinical judgment is also considered an important factor in the diagnosis of exceptionality, especially for communication impairment and behavior and emotional disorders. Biomedical information is extremely important when studying visual, auditory, and motor impairment. Examiners need to be aware of the specific standards and guidelines for testing special populations. They need to be experienced and knowledgeable in working with the special group in question.

QUESTIONS FOR DISCUSSION

1. How might the following examiner variables affect the validity of the test results? (a) Personal bias and expectation, (b) Difficulty understanding what the examinee says, (c) Lack of knowledge of the particular handicap, (d) Lack of experience testing and working with the particular exceptionality, (e) Lack of special communication skills (e.g., American Sign Language)

2. Do you think it is acceptable to adapt and modify a standardized test to accommodate the special needs of the examinee? Why or why not?

3. How important is the testing environment in the testing of exceptional individuals? How would the following factors affect the validity of the test results? (a) Lighting in the room, (b) Noise level of the testing environment, (c) Physical features of the room, (d) Artificial nature of the setting, (e) Positioning needs of the examinee

4. How do labels and diagnostic criteria affect the types of tests given and the validity of the results? Critics have faulted the designations for not reflecting the presence of a disability or the degree of impairment. How should the examiner address this problem?

5. A large number of individuals are impaired in more than one area. What procedures should the examiner follow to ensure proper diagnosis and/or placement?

SUGGESTED ACTIVITIES

1. Interview psychologists who work with special populations and find out what tests they use and why. Report your findings to the class.

2. Review a videotape of a testing session of an individual with a disability. Were there deviations from standard procedures? In what ways did the examiner test the individual differently from the norm?

3. Interview special needs individuals and find out their experiences with and reactions to testing. Report your findings to the class.

4. Locate public laws and court decisions related to assessing exceptional individuals. Write a summary of the legislation and the court decisions.

5. Locate a test that has been adapted and standardized for use with a special population. Compare the adaptation with the original version. How was the test modified? Why? How do the two sets of norms compare?

6. Study the following five brief cases and answer these questions about each:

   a. How would you classify the person?
   b. What additional information would you like to have about him or her?
   c. What methods would you use to assess the person or individuals like him or her?

   Mary, a 12-year-old female, has dropped from 100 to 75 pounds in the last 6 months. She refuses to eat with the family. Fights take place at meal time because of her eating habits.

   Jonathan had a full scale IQ of 91 on the WISC-III with a Verbal score of 82 and Performance of 106. He was easily frustrated and impulsive in the tasks he was required to do. He couldn't sit still except on the performance items that interested him. His teacher checked "poor" on the following items on a learning profile checklist:

   Quality or neatness of handwriting

   Completeness of assignments

   Quality of reading skills

   Quality of speaking skills

   She also noted that he completes his work in a hasty, careless fashion.

   Robert is an 11-year-old boy from a blended family. He lives with his mother, stepfather, and the stepfather's two children. He had a 121 Full Scale IQ on the WISC-III. His grades were excellent, but lately his disruptive and aggressive behavior has led to frequent suspensions and lower grades. His mother reports that he is unmanageable at home and is increasingly oppositional and angry. When he gets angry, he breaks dishes and starts fires. At school he has been accused of stealing money. When he gets angry, he beats up any student who happens to be near him.

   Mindy is a 9-year-old girl who is normal in intelligence but refuses to go to school. She says she is afraid to leave home because she worries that her mother will leave her or die. She tells her mother she can teach her at home. She often enters her parents' bedroom at night and sleeps on the floor.

   Allan's mother is concerned because he shows a lack of affection and little interest in interacting with his peers and parents. His language appears to be delayed. The counselor observing Allan in class noted he had problems communicating and interacting with his classmates.

ADDITIONAL READINGS

Aylward, G. P. (1994). *Practitioners' guide to developmental and psychological testing.*

The author discusses psychological tests used to assess children with developmental delays, poor school performance, and behavioral problems.

Bradley-Johnson, S., & Evans, L. D. (1994). *Psychoeducational assessment of hearing-impaired students: Infancy through adulthood* (2nd ed.). Austin, TX: PRO-ED.

The authors discuss issues and procedures related to the assessment of hearing impaired students and review the tests and subtests commonly used with this population. They present a checklist of procedures to use before, during, and after testing.

Hamayan, E. V., & Damico, J. S. (1991). *Limiting bias in the assessment of bilingual students.* Austin, TX: PRO-ED.

Problems in the education and assessment of students with limited English proficiency are identified.

Mash, E. J., & Terdal, L. G. (Eds.). (1997). *Assessment of childhood disorders* (3rd ed.). New York: Guilford.

The book discusses assessment of behavior disorders, emotional and social disorders, developmental and health-related disorders, children at risk, and problems of adolescence.

Rossetti, L. M. (1990). *Infant-toddler assessment.* Austin, TX: PRO-ED.

The author discusses the assessment of high-risk infants and toddlers and includes sample questionnaires and evaluation instruments.

Simeonsson, R. J. (1986). *Psychological and developmental assessment of special children.* Boston: Allyn & Bacon.

This text identifies dimensions and issues in assessing special children and provides general strategies and instruments for use with this group. The assessment of hearing impaired, visually impaired, motor impaired, autistic, hospitalized, and chronically ill children is discussed.

Vance, H. B. (Ed.). (1998). *Psychological assessment of children* (2nd ed.). New York: Wiley.

Part 3 of the text focuses on assessing special populations. There are chapters on developmental assessment of infants and preschoolers, culturally and linguistically diverse children and youth, diagnosis and assessment of autistic disorders, vocational assessment of special needs learners, and assessing children with mental retardation.

Multicultural Assessment

OVERVIEW

Assessment instruments are often criticized for being biased and unfair for use with minorities. One problem that confuses the issue is the broad range of meanings for ethnicity and diversity. *Ethnicity* often is defined as patterns of behavioral roles, social interaction, social customs, language usage, and values shared by a particular group. Rotherman and Phinney (1986) found that studying four dimensions of social patterns helps in differentiating and understanding various ethnic groups: interdependence versus independence, active achievement versus passive acceptance, authoritarianism versus equalitarianism, and expressive versus restrained styles of communication. The 1990 U.S. census identifies four major ethnic groups: African Americans, who constitute 12.1% of the population; Hispanics 9%, Asian Americans 2.9%, and Native Americans .5%.

The American Psychological Association (1992) has published a set of guidelines for providers of psychological services to ethnically, linguistically, and culturally diverse populations. The nine guidelines emphasize that counselors need to understand their own ethnicity and culture and the impact they have on individuals from different backgrounds. Examiners need to orient the client before testing and, whenever possible, provide information in writing as well as orally. They need to be aware of relevant research and practice issues related to the ethnic or cultural group to be assessed and respect these values and beliefs.

According to the standards, the helping professional should document relevant factors such as the number of generations the individual's family has been in this country, her fluency in English, her level of education, and her level of stress related to verbalization. Most examiners are Caucasian and use standard English.

OBJECTIVES

After completing this chapter, the reader should be able to

✔ List and discuss the standards for multicultural assessment

✔ Identify factors that help in understanding various ethnic groups

✔ Describe assessment instruments, techniques, and procedures that are appropriate for use with various ethnic groups

✔ Explain the trends and issues in multicultural assessment

STANDARDS FOR MULTICULTURAL ASSESSMENT

The Association for Assessment in Counseling (1993) has identified 34 standards relevant to multicultural assessment from five of the major sets of standards. Ten standards concern the selection of assessment instruments according to content. Nine relate to the use of information about the reliability, validity, and norming of the instruments to be selected. Four involve the administration and scoring of the assessment instruments, and 11 cover the use and interpretation of the assessment results. The major theme of these standards is the selection of appropriate instruments.

Content Considerations

The *Code of Fair Testing Practices in Education* (APA, 1988) includes two standards in the area of content. The first standard stresses defining the purpose of testing and the population to be tested and then selecting a test appropriate for that purpose and population. The second standard covers the importance of evaluating the test for any potentially insensitive content or language.

The *ACA Responsibilities of Users of Standardized Tests* (ACA, 1989) contributes four standards: the examiner is to determine the limitations to testing created by the individual's age, racial, sexual, ethnic, and cultural background; give attention to how the test is designed to handle variation of motivation, working speed, language facility, and experiential background; determine whether one common or several different tests are required for accurate measurement of groups with special characteristics; and determine whether persons of groups that use different languages should be tested in either or both languages.

Four standards are taken from the *Standards for Educational and Psychological Measurement* (1985). When recommending a test for use with linguistically diverse test takers, the test publisher should provide information necessary for appropriate test use and interpretation. Counselors need to review the interpretive materials from the test to make sure that case studies and examples are not limited to illustrations of people in traditional roles. The type and content of the items need to be studied in relation to the cultural background and prior experiences of the ethnic group to be tested. Research should be conducted to explore whether the item or test performance differences for a particular kind of test are related to age, ethnic, cultural, and gender factors. The test and items should be appropriate and unbiased.

Technical Considerations

The *Code of Fair Testing Practices in Education* (APA, 1988) calls for examiners to make sure the test content and norming groups are appropriate for test takers from different racial, ethnic, or linguistic backgrounds. The counselor is to select tests that have been developed in ways that attempt to make them as reliable and valid as possible for test takers of different race, gender, or ethnic backgrounds. Counselors should review the data from the manual on the performance of these test takers. The groups must be of sufficient size.

Responsibilities of Users of Standardized Tests (AACD, 1989) also emphasizes the importance of considering the reliability and interpretability of the test and determining whether the standardization and norming procedures are relevant to the local population and use of the data.

Standards for Educational and Psychological Tests (AERA, APA, & NCME, 1985) emphasizes the importance of reviewing the criterion-related evidence of validity when recommending decisions that have an actuarial as well as a clinical impact. Since many tests are translated from one language or dialect to another, the reliability and validity for the uses intended in the linguistic groups must be established. The examiner also needs to review any studies of the magnitude of predictive bias due to differential prediction for groups for which previous research has established a substantial prior probability of differential prediction for the type of test in question.

Administration and Scoring

Responsibilities of Users of Standardized Tests (AACD, 1989) emphasizes the need for the examiner to demonstrate verbal clarity, calmness, empathy for the examinees, and impartiality toward all being tested but to consider potential effects of examiner-examinee differences in ethnic and cultural background, attitudes, and values. *Standards of Educational and Psychological Testing* (AERA et al., 1985) reminds examiners that linguistic modification recommended by the test publishers should be described in detail in the test manual. Testing should be designed to minimize threats to the reliability and validity of the test that can arise from language differences.

Use and Interpretation

The *Code of Fair Testing Practices in Education* (APA, 1988) reminds examiners that when interpreting the scores of these groups, they must take into consideration differences between the norms and the scores of test takers and the familiarity of the test takers with the specific questions on the test. In addition, parents and guardians need to know their rights and what procedures they need to follow if they have problems with the assessment.

Responsibilities of Users of Standardized Tests (AACD, 1989) notes that the socioeconomic status, gender, subculture, and other factors may affect an individual's test performance. The counselor needs to use the norms for the group to which the client belongs.

Standards for Educational and Psychological Testing (AERA et al., 1985) explains that in educational, clinical, and counseling situations, test administrators and users should not attempt to evaluate test takers whose special characteristics such as age, disability, or linguistic, generational, or cultural backgrounds are outside the range of their academic training or supervised experience.

Multicultural Counseling Competencies and Standards (Sue, Arrendondo, & McDavis, 1992) includes three standards related to multicultural assessment:

1. Culturally skilled counselors must be aware of the potential bias of assessment instruments and, when interpreting findings, keep in mind the client's cultural and linguistic characteristics.
2. They also need an awareness and understanding of how culture and ethnicity may affect personality formation, vocational choices, manifestations of psychological disorders, help-seeking behavior, and the appropriateness of counseling approaches.
3. Counselors must not only understand the technical aspects of the instruments but also be aware of the cultural limitations.

The bottom line is that counselors need not only training and experience in assessing these clients but the cultural awareness to protect the welfare of the diverse clients with whom they are working. *Ethical Standards of ACA* (ACA, 1993) instructs counselors to provide specific orientation or information to the examinees prior to and following test administration so that the results of testing may be placed in proper perspective with other relevant factors such as the effects of socioeconomic, ethnic, and cultural factors on test scores. Counselors then proceed with caution when attempting to evaluate and interpret the performance of minority group members or other persons who are not represented in the norming groups on which the instrument was standardized.

TEST BIAS

Test bias is a complex issue. Valencia and Aburto (1991) argue that the major concern during the 1970s and 1980s was whether IQ tests were biased against racial and ethnic minorities. Jensen (1980) claims bias is strictly statistical and can be defined as the systematic error of individuals' scores that is connected to group membership and bias in context for racial or ethnic groups. An item or subtest is labeled *biased* when empirical evidence shows that it is more difficult for one group member than another, the general ability level of the two groups is held constant, and no reasonable rationale exists to explain the group differences on the same items. Jensen says that test fairness/unfairness relates more to moral philosophy than to psychometrics.

Reynolds and Brown (1984) list six dimensions of bias—inappropriate content, inappropriate standardization samples, examiner and language bias, inequitable social consequences, measurement of different constructs, and differential predictive validity.

Bilingual children with limited English skills have trouble understanding oral and written directions in addition to the vocabulary and the syntax of the test items. Often they have a hard time giving correct verbal responses, and they may have trouble discriminating among sounds that are not a part of their primary language.

Test Taker Bias Factors

Oakland (1982) advises awareness of points of bias during assessment of culturally different or minority group individuals. Some potential bias centers around the test taker (pp. 153–154):

Language—The examinee's ability to understand and communicate in English is very important. Conventional measures that require a high level of competence in English are not appropriate.

Test wiseness—The examiner cannot assume that examinees can understand directions, comply with proper test taking procedures, and be involved and attentive during testing.

Motivation and anxiety—The examiner may find an examinee who refuses to cooperate or is too anxious. The examiner needs to consider the attitudinal characteristics of examinees and attempt to get them to do their best.

Cultural differences—Minority examinees may come from restricted environments in expectations, language experiences, formal and informal learning experiences, and upbringing. The examiner needs to understand the background of the examinees and whether the test is appropriate.

Examiner Bias Factors

The examiner may introduce bias in several ways. The examiner needs to recognize personal bias and how it may influence interpretation of results. This requires treating each individual with dignity and respect and pursuing the best interests of the examinee. Baruth and Manning (1991) have identified some of the common barriers to effective multicultural counseling:

1. The counselor makes erroneous assumptions about cultural assimilation
2. There is a difference in class and cultural values
3. There are language differences and both cultural or socioeconomic class misunderstandings
4. The counselor believes stereotypes about culturally different people
5. The counselor fails to understand the culture
6. There is little understanding of the client's reasoning structures
7. There is a lack of cultural relativity among counselors

DEVELOPING GREATER MULTICULTURAL UNDERSTANDING

In developing an action plan to increase their multicultural understanding, counselors can use research on the multicultural counseling process, case studies in the literature, experiences of other counselors they are working with, their own experiences with culturally different clients, and other firsthand experiences with various ethnic groups (Dragus, 1989; Nutall, Romero, & Kalesnik, 1992). For counselors the first step is to develop greater self-awareness and comprehension of their own cultural group. They need to comprehend their own environmental experiences in the mainstream culture and reflect on their sensitivity toward their personal beliefs and values. Specific training in working with certain groups provides greater confidence and knowledge of the group.

Counselors need to develop an awareness and comprehension of the history and experiences of the cultural group with which the client is currently identifying or encountering. In general, the counselor must develop perceptual sensitivity toward the client's personal beliefs and values (Baruth & Manning, 1991).

Ethical Principles

Ethical standards of working with culturally diverse clients require counselors to have cultural knowledge based on research and experience. They also must understand their own cultural background and be able to go beyond their own biases and prejudices. Counselors must respect the diverse values and beliefs of clients as they affect their view of the world and psychosocial functioning. Counselors must also be aware of the impact of social, environmental, and political conditions on problems and interventions. They must be advocates and stand against racism and discrimination. In assessment they need to use multisource, multilevel, and multimethod approaches to assess the capabilities, potentials, and limitations of the clients (APA, 1992). During assessment and counseling, counselors need to be careful and active listeners, be genuine, and demonstrate verbally and nonverbally that they understand what they are communicating. They want to show that they care about clients and their situations and are working to help them achieve a realistic solution.

Testing Principles

When testing culturally and ethnically different clients, the examiner must do the following:

1. Become familiar with the characteristics and learning styles of different groups
2. Avoid stereotypes
3. Treat all clients equally and with respect and dignity
4. Be sure that the tests are valid and appropriate for the cultural group

Etic and Emic Perspectives

Etic perspective emphasizes the universal qualities among human beings by examining and comparing many cultures from a position outside those cultures. Emic perspective is culture-specific and examines behavior from within a culture, using criteria relative to the internal characteristics of that culture (Dana, 1993). From the etic perspective, assessment involves comparing individuals' scores to a norming group and comparing different individuals from different cultures on a construct assumed to be universal across all cultures.

Dana (1993) includes as etic measures a broad spectrum of instruments to measure psychopathology, personality measures, and major tests of intelligence and cognitive functioning. Included as etic personality measures are the California Psychological Inventory and the Eysenck Personality Questionnaire. Included in the intelligence/cognitive functioning area are the Wechsler Intelligence Scales, the System of Multicultural Pluralistic Assessment, the Kaufman Assessment Battery for Children, the McCarthy Scales of Children's Abilities, and the Stanford-Binet Intelligence Scale. Other single construct tests for identification of psychopathology are the State-Trait Anxiety Scale, the Beck Depression Inventory, and the Michigan Alcoholism Screening Test. The MMPI is also on this list; it has been translated into 150 languages and has reported applications in 50 countries. The other tests listed have also been translated into other languages, mainly Spanish.

Emic methods include behavior observations, case studies, studies of life events, picture story techniques, inkblot techniques, word association, sentence completion, and drawings. Most of these methods are classified as projective. These tests can provide a personality description of the individual that reflects the data and mirrors the culture and ethnic group (Dana, 1993). The analysis demands that the examiner have more knowledge of the culture but aids the understanding of the individual in a cultural context.

Thematic apperception test versions include the following:

Michigan Picture Story Test—designed for Hispanic American and African American children and adolescents

Tell Me a Story Test (TEMAS)—designed for Spanish-speaking populations

Themes Concerning Blacks Test—20 charcoal drawings depicting aspects of African American culture and lifestyle

Thompson Modification of the TAT—10-card version for African Americans

Sentence completion methods have been used with many different cultures. The items can be designed to assess the social norms, roles, and values of clients from different cultures. Here are examples of some of the items:

The thing I like most about America is _____.

Anglos _____.

If I could be from another culture or ethnic group, I _____.

There are not always formal scoring systems for the different emic tests.

Acculturation

The degree of acculturation to the dominant society and the extent to which the original culture has been retained provide valuable information in interpreting assessment results. Dana (1993) has developed a checklist to record acculturation information. One item relates to the phase of the acculturation process and has five levels: precontact, contact, conflict, crisis, or adaptation. Another item relates to the mode and has four categories: assimilation, bicultural, traditional, marginal. Dana also looks at group membership—whether the group consists of native peoples, immigrants, refugees, ethnic groups, or sojourners. The sociocultural pattern is recorded by looking at settlement patterns, status, status mobility, support network, and group acceptability.

For Americans, two instruments can provide information on the moderating variables that affect assessment interpretation: the Developmental Inventory of Black Consciousness (DIB-C) and the Racial Identity Attitude Scale (RIAS). The DIB-C has four stages: preconsciousness, confrontation, internalization, and integration. The RIAS also has four: preencounter, encounter, immersion-emersion, and internalization. Another useful scale is the African Self-Consciousness Scale (ASC), which has four dimensions: awareness of black identity; recognition of survival priorities and affirmative practices, customs, and values; active participation in defense of survival, liberation, and the like; and recognition of racial oppression (Baldwin & Bell, 1985).

Dana (1993) advises counselors to use moderator variables whenever there is evidence that a client is not representative of an Anglo-American cultural background. A counselor can get an idea of whether the client is identifying with a culture of origin rather than with the dominant Anglo-American culture by soliciting the information found in Figure 19.1.

---

1. What is your country of origin?
2. What was your reason for coming to the United States?
3. How long have you been in the United States?
4. Was any parent, grandparent, or relative in this country before you came?
5. What language do you speak in your home?
6. What languages can you speak? How well?
7. Is your family in the United States?
8. Do you have friends from your country here?
9. Are there people from your country living near you?
10. Where do you live? A house, apartment, room?
11. What education or schooling did you complete?
12. Are you currently going to school or taking classes somewhere?
13. Are you currently working? Where? What do you do on the job?
14. What type of work did you do before coming to this country?
15. Have you had any problems since coming here?
16. Have you had any conflicts on the job, at school, or at home?
17. What kind of problems have you had adjusting to life in the United States?

Figure 19.1
Interview schedule for assessing multicultural clients

Strategies

Since each client is unique, the examiner needs to be alert to important behavioral signals. Certain behavior may affect the reliability and validity of the test. Appropriate examiner responses are summarized in Table 19.1.

Table 19.1
Critical behavior indicators and possible examiner responses

Behavior	Response
Is silent	Establish rapport. Give nonverbal and performance test first, get other indexes of individual behavior
Says "don't know"	Don't assume client cannot respond
Is shy and reserved, lowers eyes	Observe client in other situations, spend time establishing rapport, start with nonverbal and untimed tests, provide reinforcement, try to motivate client
Uses wit or popular language	Be firm and positive, be sure examinee knows why the test/instrument is being given
Interrupts the test or asks questions	Be firm but allow some dialogue, be sure the examinee knows the purpose of the test
Is inattentive and restless	Structure test environment, keep examinee involved
Is uncertain about how to respond	Rephrase question, make meaning clear
Watches the examiner rather than listens to the questions	Be firm, be sure questions are clear, be sure there are no distractions in test situation If the responses are inappropriate, question further
Performs poorly on timed tests	Recognize a culture not oriented to the value of time, avoid drawing conclusions about individual performance until untimed measures have been tried
Shows poor knowledge of vocabulary	Try other ways of measuring the examinee's expressive vocabulary, question individual in primary language
Is ur..notivated to take test	Explain purpose and value of test to client and family, try techniques to motivate client performance
Scores poorly on information items	Recognize that some items might be biased and not a part of the examinee's culture, ask examinee to clarify any unusual responses
Is afraid of embarrassing or dishonoring family	Initiate test-wise session, practice session, or some type of warmup
Is quiet and does not ask questions or interact	Establish rapport, explain examiner's role and purpose of the test, ask client to repeat the question if no answer is given or the answer is inappropriate
Is afraid of a male examiner	Observe examinee, establish rapport before testing

When working with minority and culturally different groups, the helping professional must have basic knowledge of the trends and issues related to the treatment
of these groups, the culture of the individuals being tested, tests and assessment
procedures appropriate for the groups, and agency and institutional sources of referral and support for the individuals being assessed.

A variety of modes and tests can be used, ranging from nonverbal culture-free
tests in the language of linguistic minorities to tests in standard English. The examiner, we have already discussed, needs to know the client's level of assimilation into
the mainstream culture. Understanding the client's educational level and background, language facility, and receptive and expressive vocabulary can help guide
test selection.

SUMMARY

Many factors can bias the assessment of multicultural groups and individuals and
lead to possible sources of misinterpretation. Legal and professional standards call
for nonbiased, nondiscriminatory assessment, validation of tests for a specific purpose, and use of multiple sources of information and multiple windows to view and
understand diversity. Emic approaches provide this window and increase the credi-
bility of the assessment. Moderating variables such as the degree of assimilation of
the majority culture are also important in understanding the individual.

QUESTIONS FOR DISCUSSION

1. How might the following examiner variables affect the validity of the test results?
   (a) Personal bias and expectations of counselor of a certain ethnic group, (b)
   Lack of experience of the counselor in working with a certain ethnic group, (c)
   Lack of knowledge of the client's first language, (d) Lack of knowledge of the
   specific ethnic group

2. Do you think it is acceptable to adapt and modify a standardized test to accommodate the ethnic group being represented by the client? Why or why not?

3. What personality characteristics do counselors need to have when testing a
   member of a minority group?

4. Compare and contrast your culture with that of another ethnic group. What are
   the similarities? What are the differences?

5. What are the different dimensions of bias that an examiner must be alert to?

SUGGESTED ACTIVITIES

1. Interview a psychologist who assesses a number of multicultural clients and find out what tests he uses and why. Report your findings to the class.

2. Make an annotated bibliography of tests designed for administration to one of the following groups: Hispanics, Asian Americans, African Americans, or Native Americans.

3. Interview counselors who work with diverse groups and find out how they developed their cultural knowledge and awareness.

4. Locate public laws and court decisions related to assessing minority group members. Write a summary of the legislation and court decisions.

5. Locate a test that has been adapted for a certain minority or ethnic group. How was the test modified? How do the two sets of norms compare? How does the reliability compare?

6. Imagine that you are a counselor. Study the following brief case studies and answer the questions at the end of each.

John is a 15-year-old African American male. Assessment using Gardner's Typology shows that he has high musical and kinesthetic intelligence. His family moved into the city from a suburban area because of the father's job change. He attends an inner-city high school with a magnet program in engineering and mathematics because his parents don't want him to be bused to another school 30 minutes away. The school he attends has limited programs in fine arts and music and few resources. One of John's friends was shot by a gang in a shopping center, and another classmate died from a drug overdose. John has started to withdraw and shows signs of depression. He becomes sick on school days. His parents want you to test John and help him.

a. What type of assessment procedures and instruments would you use with John?
b. What factors and issues do you feel need to be addressed?
c. What additional information would you like to have about John?

Claudia is a 14-year-old bilingual Latina referred to the child study team because of her truancy, lack of motivation, and negative attitude toward her teachers and school. She has been placed in an English As a Second Language class with many students who have negative motivation and poor skills. Often she tells her parents she is going to school but instead skips and goes to the local mall. However, she does well academically when she is in class. One of her teachers says: "She is like all of the other problem students we have in this program: no interest, no discipline, and no motivation."

a. What type of tests would you give and why?
b. What factors might tend to bias Claudia's test results?
c. What additional information about Claudia would you want to have?

Tobeka, a 6-year-old African American, has entered first grade but is having considerable academic difficulties. She has been referred for a multifactor evaluation by the school's multidisciplinary team. Her mother has refused to let Tobeka be tested until she can examine the tests that will be used. You have met with the mother to explain why the tests will be given and have discussed what tests will be administered.

a. What factors were involved?
b. What test standards were involved?
c. What was your ethical responsibility?

Janie, an 8-year-old Native American of the Penobscot tribe, has been referred to a multi-disciplinary team by her guidance counselor and teachers for evaluation of her avoidant behavior and assessment of her intellectual potential. She refuses to participate in her reading group, cries often, and usually fails to follow directions. Her teacher says Janie isolates herself from others in the class and refuses to participate. Her mother has indicated that the other students made fun of Janie.

a. What issues should you consider before you meet with Janie?
b. What important professional standards for multicultural assessment should be considered in this case?
c. What assessment techniques and procedures would you use?

ADDITIONAL READING

Canino, I. A., & Spurlock, J. (1994). *Culturally diverse children and adolescents: Assessment, diagnosis, and treatment*. New York: Guilford.

The authors guide clinicians in learning how to determine the impact of cultural differences, poverty, discrimination, and acculturation issues when assessing children and adolescents. The book has numerous clinical vignettes to illustrate the constructs.

Dana, R. H. (1993). *Multicultural assessment perspectives for professional psychology*. Boston: Allyn & Bacon.

The author presents a comprehensive model for multicultural assessment and a specific review of instrumentation used to assess African Americans, Hispanics, Asian Americans, and Native Americans.

Geisinger, K. F. (1992). *Psychological testing of Hispanics*. Washington, DC: American Psychological Association.

The author discusses differential psychology and psychological testing of Hispanics.

Hilliard, A. G. (Ed.). (1991). *Testing African American students*. Morristown, NJ: Aaron.

The contributors discuss issues such as African American culture and psychological assessment, the impact of testing on African Americans, and issues in professional practice.

Rogers, M. R. (1998). Assessment of culturally linguistically diverse children and youth. In H. B. Vance (Ed.), *Psychological assessment of children* (pp. 358–384). New York: Wiley.

Rogers discusses professional preparation as well as psychometric considerations important in assessing children.

Test-Taking Skills

OVERVIEW

Test-taking skills have become an important topic in the field of measurement and research. Much controversy has centered around whether coaching can help individuals raise their test scores, particularly by reducing anxiety. This controversy has focused on programs to help students improve their performance on the Scholastic Aptitude Test (SAT). Goldman (1971) concludes that coaching is of help to at least some individuals and is likely to be of greater assistance to underachievers and persons who are rusty in the particular area being tested.

OBJECTIVES

This chapter should enable the reader to

✔ List and discuss the different strategies to help individuals maximize their test performance

✔ Identify and analyze the different factors related to test performance

✔ Evaluate the sources of help available to assist individuals in improving their test performance

TEST ANXIETY

Test anxiety is the general feeling of uneasiness, tension, or foreboding that some individuals experience in testing situations. Excessive anxiety can have a detrimental effect on individual performance (Sarason, 1980; Tobias, 1979; Tyron, 1980). When individuals feel pressure to make high scores on a test, their anxiety level may increase (Deffenbacher, 1978). In reviewing the literature on anxiety and test performance, Goldman (1971) found that individuals with high levels of anxiety tend to do worse on cognitive tests. Wine (1980) concluded that individuals with high test anxiety worry about not doing as well as they would like to do on a test. This mindset leads to their failure to concentrate on or attend to the test. Individuals with low test anxiety, on the other hand, do not worry and are able to concentrate on their test performance. Zeidner and Most (1992) conclude that maximum performance tests (e.g., problem-solving, situational, and critical-thinking exercises) tend to evoke anxiety in the test takers. High anxiety levels impede performance and lead to cognitive interference and task-irrelevant thinking (Saklofske, Kowalchuk, & Schwean, 1992). Spielberger and Vagg (1995) conclude that test anxiety is a situation-specific trait, with worry and emotionality its major components. Worry is not correlated with achievement while emotionality is.

Measures of Test Anxiety

Several published instruments are designed to measure test anxiety. The Test Anxiety Inventory is a 20-item pencil-and-paper test to measure two major components of test anxiety: worry and emotionality. The inventory can be given to students and adults in grade 10 and higher and is similar in structure to the A-Trait Scale of the State-Trait Anxiety Scale. It can also be self-administered.

The Rocky Mountain Behavioral Science Institute publishes two test anxiety scales—the Suinn Test Anxiety Behavior Scale (STABS) and the Test Anxiety Profile (TAP) by Oetting and Cole. The STABS is a 50-item pencil-and-paper test for individuals in grade 7 to adulthood. Clients rate their anxiety concerns on a 5-point scale, ranging from "not at all" to "very much." The test items concern clients' experiences related to academic testing situations. The TAP is a 77-item pencil-and-paper test measuring individual feelings about six academic testing situations: multiple-choice exams, mathematics exams, essay exams, unannounced tests, talking in front of a class, and tests with time limits.

The classic test in the field is the Children's Test Anxiety Scale (CTAS), which contains 30 items. Feld and Lewis (1969) have identified four components discovered through factor analysis of the CTAS—test anxiety, remote school concerns, poor self-evaluation, and somatic signs of anxiety. Test anxiety is measured by questions such as "Do you worry a lot before you take a test?" and "While you are taking a test, do you usually think you are doing poor work?" To assess remote school concerns, the test includes questions such as "When you are in bed at night, do you sometimes worry about how you are going to do in class the next day?" and "After you have taken a test, do you worry about how well you did on the test?" Poor self-evaluation is measured by questions such as "When the teacher is teaching you about reading, do you feel that other children in the class understand him or her better than you?" and "Do you sometimes dream at night that other boys and girls in your class can do things you cannot do?" To measure somatic signs of anxiety, there are questions such as "When you are taking a test, does the hand you write with shake a little?" and "When the teacher says that she is going to find out how much you have learned, do you get a funny feeling in your stomach?"

Strategies to Help Test Anxiety

Gonzales (1995) concludes from his research that reduction in test anxiety leads to improvement in academic performances of students. Cognitive therapeutic approaches and systematic desensitization are found to be effective. Cognitive therapy focuses in this case on the worry aspect of the testing situation, desensitization on the emotional part. Hembree (1988) reviews the correlates, causes, effects, and treatment of test anxiety. The test examiner must be attentive to the examinee's needs. Examinees should be motivated to do their best on tests but should not be made anxious. Sometimes, however, pressure comes not from the psychologist, counselor, or teacher but from the parents. Currently in our educational system tests have assumed too much importance in some states. They are used as the sole criterion to judge whether a student should be promoted to the next grade or allowed to move from one level to another.

The examiner should consider these strategies in test administration:

1. To be sure examinees understand test instructions, check with them, asking whether they understand. In a group test, circulate around the room to see if students are following directions and recording their answers properly.
2. To establish rapport and an environment that is relaxed and as stress-free as possible, before the test create a learning-oriented environment. Examinees may need to be taught more effective study habits and may need more time to prepare for tests. Tests can be an interesting learning experience as well as a motivational one. At test time be friendly and positive but follow standardized procedures. Ensure that examinees have the proper physical facilities, space to work, proper lighting, ventilation, and so on.
3. To remove some of the pressure from major tests and exams, conduct group or class sessions on how to take a test, give the examinees practice tests, and provide a list of guidebooks and study guides that are available for an upcoming test.

Relaxation Techniques

The object of relaxation exercises is to help test takers practice mind calming. The following is an example of what a test administrator might say before a test:

Sit down and get very comfortable. Close your eyes and take a deep breath. Exhale and let your body and mind relax completely. Breathe in again, and as you breathe out, feel even more relaxed. Forget about everything except what I am saying. Listen carefully. Continue to breathe deeply and slowly. You should begin to feel more and more relaxed.

You are sitting in a lounge chair on the beach. It is not too warm or too cold. The temperature is just right. Everything is very peaceful and pleasant. You see the waves coming onto the beach. They are a beautiful blue, and the sun is a brilliant yellow. You feel nice and warm and relaxed all over. Take a deep breath in the nice clear air. You lose track of time. The sky becomes a deeper blue. . . .

Now that you are relaxed, think positively of yourself. Say, "I can remember all I need to know on the test." Say it several times. Say, "I will know the right answers." Say, "I am alert; my mind is powerful."

Stress Reduction

Learning can be increased if stress is reduced. Stress is defined as a force that can cause strain or distortion in the individual. Teaching test-taking skills is one approach to reducing stress on tests; another approach is to improve students' knowledge base. One way to do this is to help teachers improve the quality of their instruction. Effective teachers use analytical and synthetic approaches to the subject matter, organize their material to make it clear, and establish rapport with their students (Whitman, Spendlove, & Clark, 1986, p. 1). Teachers bring more than knowledge to the classroom; they also play the role of motivators, experts, and judges.

Feedback is an important factor in improving future performance and alleviating stress. Five steps are essential to effective feedback:

1. Help students know where they stand.
2. Set specific objectives and state the evaluative criteria for successful performance.
3. Provide written comments on papers, tests, and homework assignments.
4. Test frequently.
5. Talk individually with the learners about the quality of their work.

After reviewing the research, Whitman et al. concluded that the frequency and quality of teachers' contact with students both in and out of the classroom influence how students learn. Positive teacher-learner relationships have been linked with learner satisfaction with school, educational aspirations, and academic achievement.

Teachers need to be alerted to dimensions of stress and know how to help learners develop skills to cope more effectively with its negative aspects. They should identify learners with severe anxiety and refer them to professional mental health counselors. A counselor might provide sessions for students on study skills, time management, self-confidence, and relaxation techniques.

IMPROVING TEST SCORES

As we have discussed, two of the main approaches to improving test scores are better content preparation and better test-taking skills. Counselors can help individuals become more familiar with types of items and testing procedures. The goal of any consulting session is ultimately a valid performance measure of the individual who is being tested.

Coaching

Coaching is a method used by administrators, teachers, and counselors to help test takers improve their test performance. Prell and Prell (1986) state that although there is no universally accepted definition for coaching, the term is popularly used to mean training test takers to answer specific types of questions and provide the information required by a specific test. Coaching is sometimes referred to as teaching to the test.

The topic of coaching has been the object of much attention lately. Considerable controversy has surrounded coaching to improve performance on the SAT. Alderman and Powers (1980) reported that almost one-third of the high schools surveyed offered special programs for students taking the SAT. Many commercial seminars are also available. Researchers have reported that short high school training programs help examinees gain on average 10 points on the SAT verbal section and 15 points on the mathematics section (Messick, 1980; Messick & Yungeblut, 1981). It should be understood, however, that gains of 20 to 30 points result from getting just two to three more items correct. Stockwell, Schaffer, and Lowenstein (1991) wrote about the phenomenon in their book, *The SAT Coaching Coverup: How Coaching Courses Can Raise Scores by 100 Points and Why ETS Denies the Evidence*. Cronbach (1984) concludes that the research stimulated by the SAT controversy indicates the following factors:

1. Many different types of coaching programs are in operation in the schools.
2. A key variable in the success of such programs is client motivation and prior preparation.
3. Because most studies have not used true experimental designs, it is difficult to compare an experimental group with a control group.

Of significance are concerns about the social, philosophical, and ethical aspects of coaching. Some social scientists believe that individuals from lower socioeconomic groups are at a disadvantage because they cannot afford to participate in such programs. Wigdor and Garner (1982) conclude that there may be a considerable advantage to preparing test takers for an examination if it measures abilities and knowledge that are educationally worthwhile.

Strategies to Increase Test Wiseness

Millman, Bishop, and Ebel (1965) define test wiseness as "a subject's capacity to utilize the characteristics and formats of the test and/or test-taking situation to receive a high score" (p. 710). They note that test wiseness is independent of the examinee's knowledge of the subject matter that the items are designed to measure. Millman et al. (1965) identify two major dimensions of test wiseness—elements dependent on the test construction or purpose, and elements independent of that construction or purpose. Four major categories of concern for increasing test wiseness are use of time, avoidance of errors, strategies for guessing, and use of deductive reasoning.

Spielberger and Vagg (1995) conclude that the most effective treatment of test-anxious students is to allow students to discuss and practice their newly learning coping skills. Treatment provided in groups is more effective than what individuals receive in a one-to-one session. Most students who suffer from test anxiety need instruction on how to study as well as on how to take tests. Vagg and Spielberger advocate a two-stage strategy. First, focus on reducing the test anxiety during the test. Then help students use their existing coping skills more effectively.

In her publication for the Educational Testing Service, *Everything You Wanted to Know About Test-Wiseness*, Ford (1973) expands upon the concepts of Millman et al. and adds instructions specific to different types of item formats. She presents a number of general test-taking strategies related to understanding and following directions, knowing how to record responses on tests, using time effectively, and figuring out answers. Here are some general strategies that can be used to increase test wiseness:

1. Use available practice examinations and brochures describing the test. Practice generally has a positive effect on the test performance, building the confidence of the test takers and improving their ability to perform.
2. Have practice sessions on understanding instructions and developing listening skills. Discuss the problems that arise, and give examinees practice with instructions for different types of test formats and answer sheets.
3. Advise examinees on using time efficiently. They should first scan the test to see the scope of what has to be done. They should answer questions they know, going back to the more difficult and time-consuming questions. And they should allow time to check their answers to see whether they have been recorded properly.

In general, test takers feel more knowledgeable and have less anxiety when they receive instructions about how to take a test. Such sessions reduce errors caused by unfamiliarity with test procedures and lead to scores that better reflect an examinee's knowledge and abilities.

Special strategies apply to each type of item format. For example, test takers on multiple-choice tests are cautioned to examine carefully all of the options or responses before attempting to choose the correct answer. If the examinee stops when she sees a correct answer—say, option A—she could miss reading options B, C, D, and E, which might also be correct. Option E might read, "All of the above." At other times options may be similar and vary only slightly; usually these options can be eliminated. The examinee has a better chance of getting a higher score if options known to be incorrect can be eliminated and the choice is made from among the remaining alternatives. Sometimes an option resembles the stem—uses the same names, words, or phrases; usually such options should be selected. Correct answers are often longer and perhaps stated more precisely or specifically than the other alternatives.

Prell and Prell (1986) conclude that the most important aspect of test wiseness is its relationship to test validity. Test wiseness is considered a source of variance on tests that reduces the validity. The goal is to maximize the variance due to the knowledge and abilities measured by the test and not penalize test takers who are not test wise. Urman (1983) found that a lack of test wiseness can penalize test takers and that the bias against test takers who are not test wise extends to standardized tests. Prell and Prell (1986) conclude that student performance on tests will become a more accurate reflection of actual knowledge as test wiseness techniques are taught to students.

Application of Test Wiseness to Teacher-Made Tests

More attention has focused recently on training in test wiseness to help improve test takers' performance on standardized tests, but that knowledge will also help, even more dramatically, with teacher-made tests. Chiodo (1986) provides rules that instructors should follow to reduce student anxiety and improve test wiseness of students on teacher-made examinations:

1. Review the scope of the exam. The instructor should tell the learners in advance the general areas that the test will cover and the relative importance of each.
2. Use practice tests. The instructor should give the learners samples of the types of items they will face and sample answers for essay and short-answer questions. Sample items help learners become familiar with the language the instructor uses.
3. Be clear about time limits. Learners need to know how long the test will take and whether extra time will be allowed.
4. Announce what materials and equipment the learners need to bring to the testing situation—pencils, calculators, notebooks, bluebooks, and the like.
5. Review the grading procedures. Test takers need to know how the test will be scored and interpreted and how much the test will count.
6. Review the policies on makeup exams and retakes. The instructor needs to spell out the rules prior to the testing period. Test takers should know whether they may take a makeup test if they have a legitimate reason for missing class or whether they may retake the test if they do not do well.
7. Provide study help. Students might benefit from a study guide for the test or some formal review sessions.
8. Make some provisions for last-minute questions. Some test takers come up with questions on the day of the test or even during the testing. The instructor needs to have established a procedure for handling these questions.
9. Allow for breaks during long exams. Test takers should have a chance to stand up or stretch or go to the rest room if needed.

10. Coach students on test-taking skills. The examiner should remind learners to survey the whole exam before they start and plan their time efficiently. Test takers need to understand the directions and be reminded to answer those questions they are sure of first.

WORKSHOP ON TEST-TAKING SKILLS

A workshop or seminar for individuals on test-taking strategies might last for several sessions, depending on the test to be taken. These sessions should focus on behavior before the test, behavior during the test, general strategies for taking tests, specific strategies for certain types of items or domains, and content review. Here is an outline of a possible series of workshops on test-taking strategies:

    A.   SESSION 1—Behavior before the test
        1.   Get psychologically ready for the test.
        2.   Attend any orientation sessions.
        3.   Read informational brochures on the test.
        4.   Check domains and objectives to be measured.
        5.   Determine review and study strategies.
        6.   Secure study guides and previous exams if available.
        7.   Check into availability of review or study groups.
        8.   Think positively; pep yourself up.
    B.   SESSION 2—Day of the test
        1.   Get a good rest, eat properly, dress comfortably.
        2.   Be early, don't rush, allow time.
        3.   Try relaxation techniques.
        4.   Concentrate on task, avoid being distracted, block feelings of anxiety.
        5.   Develop a positive mindset toward the test.
    C.   SESSION 3—Behavior during the test
        1.   If permitted, skim the test before starting to gain a general overview of the tasks to be accomplished.
        2.   Decide how much time to allocate to each part of the test.
        3.   Go through the test and answer all the questions you know.
        4.   Leave the hard or time-consuming questions until the last, but don't skip too many questions.
        5.   Keep an eye on the time.
        6.   Read the test critically.
        7.   Read directions carefully as well as sample questions and answers.
        8.   Double-check your answers.
        9.   Check to see whether you recorded your answers correctly.
      10.   Identify clues in the item stems of questions.
      11.   Identify clues in the options or answer choices.
      12.   Know the rules for guessing.
      13.   Know how standardized tests arrange items.

    D. SESSION 4—Objective test/multiple choice
1. Work quickly and accurately but read the whole item.
2. Read the directions carefully.
3. Watch for more than one correct answer and options such as "all of the above."
4. Read every word in the stem of an item and don't skim.
5. Eliminate implausible options.
6. Look for key words or clues that may be in the item.
7. Don't be afraid to guess.
8. Don't be afraid to change your answer.
9. Be confident and don't get flustered.
10. Know how to answer verbal analogy items.
11. Know how to answer reading comprehension items.
12. Know how to answer mathematical and quantitative reasoning items.

OTHER FACTORS

A number of factors can affect test-taking behavior and thus test scores:

1. Anxiety
2. Bluffing
3. Changing answers
4. Past experience
5. Response set and positional preferences
6. Reading comprehension
7. Speaking ability, enunciation, and voice
8. Spelling and grammar
9. Penmanship and fluency

Anxiety was discussed earlier in this chapter and can affect all four major types of tests—objective, essay, oral, and performance. Bluffing occurs mainly on essay or oral examinations and can bias an individual's score. Test takers with good verbal facility quite often can express themselves well but must be sure to spend some time organizing their answers, using good topic sentences or opening statements.

Changing answers is another factor. Many people believe that their first choices are best and do not change their answers. In general, however, research has shown that it does pay to check over responses. Reiling and Taylor (1972) found that students who changed their answers tended to improve their scores.

Past experience can also influence results. Many test takers are exposed to a test type or item type with which they have had no experience. Goldman (1971) has suggested that alternate forms, if available, be given to examinees in this situation. Sometimes testing in general has not been a part of an individual's cultural or educational experiences. This type of test taker might profit from attending sessions on how to take tests.

Response set and positional preferences affect individual performance, especially on personality tests. In general, a good standardized test in the cognitive area randomizes correct answers. If 100 items have four options each, each option should serve as the correct answer approximately 25 percent of the time.

Teacher-made tests often reveal unconscious patterns, such as having more items true rather than false. Examinees should be informed that correct answers will follow a random pattern, and any guessing should take that pattern into consideration.

A major criticism of group tests is that they demand reading comprehension skills. Most test authors, however, try to keep the verbal level of the item simple so that the items measure knowledge or application rather than reading comprehension. Counselors should check an examinee's reading level before arbitrarily administering a test. In some cases a test may have to be administered orally, or a nonverbal test may have to be given.

Voice, enunciation, and oral expression are also factors that can affect an individual's performance on an oral test. Many times, practice or rehearsal sessions and role playing can help individuals learn to present themselves better on oral examinations.

Spelling and grammar, penmanship, and fluency are important factors on essay tests. Errors in spelling and grammar detract from the ideas being presented and influence rate judgment negatively. On the other hand, good penmanship and fluent expression create a positive expectation in raters and encourage high ratings.

INFORMATION ON TEST TAKING

One of the major sources of information on test taking is the test publisher. Many publishers have brochures, study guides, and practice exercises available for their tests. A representative bibliography is included at the end of the chapter. The quality of publisher aids varies, however; some are well done, some are not. The following outline should guide the helping professional who must develop an awareness brochure for a scholastic aptitude test:

A. General statement and misconceptions about preparing for tests
  1. The test measures innate ability, and there is no way to prepare for the test.
  2. A system can be developed to help improve test scores.
B. General statement of what research says about different factors related to test performance
  1. Previous educational experiences are an important factor in test performance.
  2. Generic skills in verbal reasoning and fluency and mathematical analysis and reasoning—the skills necessary for success in academic programs—are measured by scholastic aptitude tests.

    C.   General statement of what type of preparation has helped individuals improve their test performance

        1.   Test companies and educational publishers often have sample tests and study guides available for test takers.

        2.   Special short- or long-term courses in a given area might be considered.

        3.   Courses in test-taking strategies might be of help to some individuals.

    D.   General statements about test-taking strategies

        1.   Test performance is only one indicator of potential; previous achievement and other factors are also valid indicators. Therefore, test takers ought not be overwhelmed by the importance of the test.

        2.   Test takers should become knowledgeable about the tests they plan to take.

        3.   Test takers should practice taking sample tests.

        4.   Test takers should develop the proper mental and psychological mindset.

        5.   Test takers should develop time management skills and apply the principles to taking tests.

        6.   Test takers should learn strategies for problem solving and guessing on tests.

        7.   Test takers should learn to be careful and check their work.

    E.   Specific strategies for answering verbal and mathematical types of questions should be discussed.

    F.   An annotated bibliography of resource information (books, guides, and audiovisuals) should be available.

Most test publishers provide brochures on how to take tests, practice tests, purposes and scope of the test, and so on. For example, for the National Teachers Examination ETS has available a bulletin of information, a descriptive booklet on the NTE Core Battery, and descriptive leaflets for the specialty area tests. These guides include a previously administered form of the test, rationale for the answers, test-taking strategies, and an explanation of scoring procedures. They also include a separate answer sheet and answer key. ETS (1988) has developed a test-taking tip sheet to provide general information on test taking. Other tip sheets have been developed on analytical, reading, verbal, and quantitative questions and preparing for achievement tests. The tip sheet provides the following suggestions on test taking:

Be a Good Consumer

1. Get information about tests from the test publisher. Often there are copies of tests that have been previously given available.
2. Know what the test covers and does not cover.
3. Plan to be successful the first time you take the test.

Before the Test

1. Become familiar with the types of questions.
2. Assess your strengths and weaknesses.

3. Develop practice and study strategies.
4. Become familiar with the directions and organization of the test.
5. Learn whether you will be penalized for guessing.
6. Study your guessing pattern.

During the Test
1. Arrive at the test site early.
2. Work carefully.
3. Answer the questions immediately.
4. Decide what questions you might get if you have enough time and the questions you will not get because you have no idea of the answer.
5. Answer every question if there is no penalty for guessing.
6. Keep focused. Don't let others distract you.

After the Test
1. Cancel your test performance if you had unforeseen health, family, or emotional problems.
2. Review your results on the test along with your goals and aptitude.
3. Plan to take the test again if necessary.

Test Alert

Test Alert (1990) is an instructional program of test-taking strategies published by Riverside Publishing Company. The purpose of the program is to introduce primary school students to effective techniques for taking standardized tests. The goal of Test Alert is to help students achieve test scores that accurately reflect their achievement. The program focuses on strategies for test taking, not on a review of the content being tested. Level A is for grades 1 and 2 and is organized into five lessons, one for each day of the school week. Each lesson takes 35 to 45 minutes. The five lessons are Good Listening, Good Guessing, A Closer Look at Numbers, A Closer Look at Words, and Using Clues. Level B is for grades 3 and 4, Level C for grades 5 and 6. The 10 lessons at levels B and C each take approximately 45 minutes. A list of strategy categories follows:

Mechanics of Test Taking
Lesson 1   Reordering Information and Answers
Lesson 2   Pacing Yourself
Lesson 3   Making Good Guesses

Reading Strategies
Lesson 4   Recognizing Main Ideas
Lesson 5   Drawing Conclusions

Mathematics Strategies
Lesson 6   Improving Computation Skills
Lesson 7   Solving Word Problems
Lesson 8   Understanding Math Units

Language Strategies
Lesson 9   Ordering Ideas
Lesson 10   Developing Paragraphs

The lessons include a focus exercise that is an entertaining activity to demonstrate the major concepts of the lesson. Discussion questions, activity booklets, and a teacher's guide are available. The session ends with a trial test in which questions are presented in both timed and untimed formats.

SUMMARY

Often we neglect to prepare individuals properly to take tests. We fail to teach not only test-taking skills but also study skills. Many tests now have practice exams and study guides. Practice in test taking is helpful for those with limited recent experience. The goal of tests is to obtain a true measure of individual performance. Factors such as self-concept, self-confidence, and achievement motivation can affect actual test performance as well as participation in test-taking programs.

QUESTIONS FOR DISCUSSION

1. Should counselors, psychologists, and teachers make sure that sessions on test-taking skills are conducted prior to all major examinations? Why or why not?

2. Study guides have been published for all of the major national testing programs. How would you go about evaluating these guides? Would you recommend a specific one or series, or would you just tell the client that a number of sources are available in most bookstores? Explain your approach.

3. If an individual came to you for advice about a $1,400 series of seminars in preparation for the Graduate Record Examination , what would you tell that person?

4. Do you think that anxiety plays a significant role in test performance? Should we try to assess anxiety before and during testing situations? Why or why not?

5. Have you taken seminars in test-taking strategies or sessions on how to improve your performance on a nationally administered examination? What was your evaluation of the seminar or session? Do you believe your performance improved as a result of the seminar?

SUGGESTED ACTIVITIES

1. Read *How to Take a Test: Doing Your Best* by John E. Dobbin (Princeton, NJ: Educational Testing Service) and report your reaction to the class.

2. Critically review the kit designed to help elementary school students improve their skills in taking standardized tests, *It's Good to Know* (Princeton, NJ: Educational Testing Service).

3. Many computer programs are available to help individuals prepare for standardized tests. Review one of these programs. Was it more effective than a book or programmed text designed to accomplish the same purpose?

4. Prepare an annotated bibliography of sources to help an individual prepare to take one of the major standardized tests.

5. Administer one of the tests designed to measure test anxiety, and discuss the results with the class.

6. Try one of the relaxation techniques with a class or group of students prior to a major test. What was their reaction to the experience?

7. Read the following brief cases and answer the questions at the end of each.

Carolyn needs to take the SAT to complete her file so she will be considered for admission to the college for which she is applying. She says, "I don't have time to go to the test prep sessions at school. It's just an aptitude test, and either I have it or I don't."

a. Do you agree with Carolyn?
b. What approach would you use to help her?

Helen is a 20-year-old college senior enrolled in elementary education. She has a 3.0 grade point average on a 4-point system. She has to take 2 years of a modern language and is currently taking Spanish 200. Whenever she has a test in class, she becomes nauseous and faints. She does not report the same feeling when she takes tests in other courses.

a. What do you think is Helen's problem?
b. What approach would you use to help her?

Jorge is from Mexico and had the equivalent of a high school education. He has worked as a short-order cook in a fast food business for the past 5 years and wants to better himself. He wants to enter the local state university and major in business but has been told that he has to take the SAT or ACT. He has been out of school for 7 years and is quite concerned that he won't be admitted.

a. What is Jorge's problem?
b. How would you help him?

Mary is a 43-year-old displaced homemaker. She has raised her family and was a full-time mother and housewife until her recent divorce. She now wants to become economically independent. She graduated from college with a degree in history when she was 20 years old. To get a current teaching certificate, she is required to take a teacher examination. She failed her first attempt, must take the test over again, and is seeking help.

a. What do you hypothesize is her problem?
b. What strategies would you use to help her?

ADDITIONAL READINGS

Dobbin, J. E. (1986). *How to take a test: Doing your best*. Princeton, NJ: ETS.

Written in nontechnical language and covering topics such as study techniques, practical test-taking strategies, rules of thumb about guessing, and interpretation of scores, the book also provides practice in answering reading comprehension, sentence completion, synonym and antonym, analogy, and mathematics questions.

Educational Testing Service. *On your own: Preparing to take a standardized test* [Video]. Princeton, NJ: Author.

This interactive video program intersperses test-taking tips with interactive classroom exercises. (Order from Info-Disc Corporation, 4 Professional Drive, Suite 134, Gaithersburg, MD 20879.)

Hembree, R. (1988). Correlates, causes, effects and treatment of test anxiety. *Review of Educational Research, 58*(1), 47–77.

Hembree critically reviews the research literature on test anxiety and identifies significant findings.

Reitz, R. (Ed.). (1989). *Test anxiety*. Bloomington, IN: Phi Delta Kappa.

The book is a collection of articles on components of test anxiety, attributes of test-anxious students, assessment of treatment strategies, and test anxiety treatment programs.

Sapp, M. (1993). *Test anxiety*. Lanham, MD: University Press of America.

Sapp reviews research design and instruments used in anxiety research.

Spielberger, C. D., & Vagg, P. R. (Eds.). (1995). *Test anxiety: Theory, assessment and treatment*. Washington, DC: Taylor & Francis.

The text has four sections: text anxiety theory and measurement, antecedents and correlates and the consequences of anxiety, research on the treatment of anxiety, and theory-based treatment of test anxiety.

Tyron, G. S. (1980). The measurement and treatment of test anxiety. *Review of Educational Research, 50*, 343–372.

Representative test-taking guides are listed here.

School Testing Programs

OVERVIEW

Schools are among the biggest consumers of tests; each year hundreds of millions of standardized tests are administered by school personnel. The annual cost has been estimated at more than 1 billion for 20 million school days. Teachers use testing extensively for instructional, diagnostic, motivational, and grading purposes and construct many of their own tests in addition to using many standardized tests. This chapter does not focus on teacher-made tests but looks at goals and purposes of school testing programs, the procedures and personnel involved, and the types of tests normally used.

OBJECTIVES

After studying the chapter, the reader should be able to

✔ Discuss the goals of a school testing program

✔ List and explain the procedures for selecting tests

✔ Identify who should be involved in a testing program

✔ Discuss the roles and responsibilities of school personnel involved in testing programs

✔ List and describe what types of tests should be used and why

✔ Identify the issues and problems involved with school testing programs

GOALS AND PURPOSES OF A TESTING PROGRAM

Teachers, counselors, and administrators need all types of information about students. They need to know about their cognitive and scholastic abilities, their interests, their achievement, and their problems. In school contexts many goals, purposes, and people are involved in a testing program. Here are some of the possible goals of a school testing program:

1. To identify the readiness of kindergarten and first-grade students
2. To determine whether students have mastered the basic and essential skills required by the school system and state, federal and professional organizations
3. To place individuals in educational programs
4. To identify individuals with special needs
5. To evaluate the curriculum and specific programs of study
6. To help individuals make their educational and vocational decisions
7. To assess the scholastic aptitude and cognitive skills of individual students
8. To measure achievement in specific courses and subject areas

STEPS IN PLANNING A TESTING PROGRAM

A number of steps should be followed in designing a school testing program. The first step is to identify the types of information needed to make decisions; data should be valuable and necessary. The test user should look at what is needed, when and where it is needed, and who will use it. For example, is the test to be used for selection, placement or grouping, or diagnosis? For one of these purposes, a test is usually administered near the beginning of the school year. A test used to measure achievement gains or program evaluation might be scheduled at both the beginning and the end of the school year.

The second step is to identify the types of tests to be given and establish procedures for selecting them. The third step is to identify the responsibilities of the staff in the testing program and to make sure the program is coordinated so those who need the test data are provided with the results. The fourth step is to disseminate the test results to the appropriate individuals so that proper decision making and evaluation can take place. The fifth step is to develop an evaluation strategy to continuously monitor the testing program.

Personnel Involved

Mehrens and Lehman (1986) state that the school testing program should be a cooperative venture from the planning stage through the recording, interpretation, and dissemination of results stages (p. 428). The program should not be planned only by the superintendent's staff, the building principal, the school psychologist, or the guidance counselor nor by a combination of these individuals. It is preferable to get more groups involved in decision making, including parents, students, teachers, and representatives from local postsecondary institutions as well as the administrative leaders in the school district. Widespread involvement promotes acceptance of the program and helps each group understand its stake in the process. Teachers might be concerned about getting valid information for instructional decisions, whereas principals might want information with which to evaluate the curriculum. Students might want tests that will help them in their educational and vocational decision making.

Selecting the Test

After a committee has established the different types of tests to be administered, the instruments must be selected. Especially in nonachievement areas, this is usually the responsibility of counselors and psychologists who are trained in testing. Teachers and curriculum supervisors might be involved in the selection or the development of essential skills or basic skills tests, under the guidance of a staff member who is an expert on measurement. It is important that the chairperson or coordinator of the selection subcommittee be familiar with ethical and legal standards, technical standards for educational and psychological tests, and sources of test information.

Scope of Responsibilities

The scope of responsibilities in this process is large because the test information is used for so many different purposes. The committee must decide what type of tests should be given, when, how often, and to whom. In addition, the committee must determine who is responsible for administering the program and the tests, scoring the tests, and reporting and disseminating the results. The committee has to consider a number of dimensions before a testing program can be fully implemented. It might be helpful to develop a list of topics that need to be resolved or clarified and then create a responsibility chart like the one illustrated in Figure 21.1.

Administration

Normally, a person who is trained as a psychologist or counselor is given the responsibility for administering a testing program. The individual should be competent in testing and assessment, communication skills, public relations, administering people and programs, and training and in-service education.

Many administrative duties are required of this individual, who will oversee the ordering, distribution, administration, scoring, interpreting, and reporting of the testing program. In addition, the individual has to provide the in-service training for teachers and personnel involved with the tests.

	Issue	Decision Maker	Date	Product/Outcome
1.	What are the purposes of the testing program?	Full committee	9/1–10/15	Position paper
2.	What types of tests should be used?	Subcommittees	10/15–11/1	Report or plan
3.	What specific tests should be selected?	Subcommittees	11/1–12/1	Plan or list
4.	Who will administer and score the tests?	Full committee	12/1–12/15	Procedure
5.	Where and when will tests be administered?	Full committee and subcommittees	12/16–1/15	Schedule
6.	How will the results be used, reported, and recorded?	Subcommittees on dissemination and records	1/16–1/30	Plan and forms
7.	What training is necessary to implement the program?	Subcommittee on in-service training	1/31–2/15	In-service training program
8.	How can the results be used to stimulate research and evaluation activities?	Research and evaluation subcommittees	2/16–3/1	Research/evaluation plan
9.	What will be the strategies to get the testing plan adopted, accepted, and implemented?	Full committee	3/1–4/1	Marketing plan and board approval

Figure 21.1
School testing program responsibility chart

CATEGORIES OF TESTS

The type of test used in school testing programs is sometimes a function of state as well as school system requirements. Some states mandate certain testing and ban other types, such as intelligence testing. A typical program is delineated in Figure 21.2.

The primary type of test used in school testing programs is the achievement test. Some school districts administer survey achievement batteries at the beginning and end of each school year in the elementary grades and use the results as one criterion for promotion.

Many schools give criterion-referenced achievement tests that they develop within the district and call minimum-level and essential skills tests. Students are expected to obtain a certain level of performance to be promoted from one grade to

Test/Inventory	Grade Level												
	K	1	2	3	4	5	6	7	8	9	10	11	12
Readiness/screening	x												
Essential skills	x	x	x	x	x	x	x						
Survey achievement		x	x	x	x	x	x	x	x				
Scholastic aptitude				x		x							
State assessment				x		x			x			x	
Minimum level skills								x	x	x	x	x	x
General interest								x					
General aptitude battery								x					
Subject area achievement										x	x	x	x
Multifactor aptitude battery										x			
Career maturity										x			
Career interest/career values											x		
Armed Services Vocational Aptitude Battery (ASVAB)											x		
Advanced placement												x	
Preliminary Scholastic Aptitude Test (PSAT)												x	
Scholastic Aptitude Test (SAT)													x
American College Testing Program (ACT)													x
National Merit													x
Interest													x

Figure 21.2
Typical school testing program

the next; that is, students are expected to demonstrate mastery of certain performance objectives at each grade level. The school might require a score of 75% on the items on one objective for the student to be given credit for mastering that objective. On the elementary level, these tests usually assess reading, mathematics, and writing skills. On the secondary level, students generally take subject area achievement tests or minimum-level skills tests in a specific content field—for example, American history, algebra 1, or chemistry.

Many states require examinations in basic skills in the third, fifth, eighth, and eleventh grades. Normally, the tests measure skills in reading, writing, and mathematics. Some states use the national assessment model, which measures 10 subject areas, 2 areas per year. The following tests also measure student skills:

	%												1 2 3 4 GRADES
WORD ATTACK	67												
VOCABULARY	95												
COMPREHENSION	73												A A A
TOTAL READING	89												A
SPELLING	30												D D C
LANGUAGE MECHANICS	35												
LANGUAGE EXPRESSION	55												C B C
TOTAL LANGUAGE	45												
MATH COMPUTATION	97												
MATH CONCEPTS	72												
TOTAL MATH	95												B A B
TOTAL BATTERY	80												
SCIENCE	50												B B B
SOCIAL STUDIES	49												B C B

DAN Y GR 2

Achievement test results can be used to help teachers plan effective instructional strategies to increase achievement.

The American College Testing Service offers a program called the Comprehensive Assessment Program (CAP), which provides the school district with materials to assess achievement, ability, and attitude.

The Developing Cognitive Abilities Test indicates whether students are working at, above, or below anticipated levels of performance.

The High School Subjects Tests and the Assessment of Writing provide end-of-course examinations.

The National Achievement Test measures achievement K–12 and assesses dimensions of reading, language, mathematics, reference skills, social studies, and science. The Career Survey is also part of the program in grades 7 through 12.

The School Attitude Measure assesses dimensions of academic self-concept, instructional mastery, control over performance, and student motivation.

Scholastic Aptitude Tests

Many school districts still administer scholastic aptitude tests. Some districts use these tests only as a rough screening for the gifted program; others give scholastic aptitude tests with survey achievement tests. Many teachers, counselors, and parents find the test information useful because it describes students' cognitive abilities. The tests are also useful in identifying underachievers and in locating students who are talented and gifted but who have not been previously identified. Nonetheless, in some districts and states scholastic aptitude tests are banned because of their misuse and cultural bias.

Multifactor Aptitude Tests

The state or district often requires administration of a multifactor aptitude test at least once for each student in grades 9 through 12. The Armed Services Vocational Aptitude Battery is the most widely used aptitude test in the high schools. The General Aptitude Test Battery is often administered to high school students by a state employment counselor. Some schools administer aptitude tests that are a part of vocational or career guidance systems, such as the Career Aptitude Placement Series. The information gained is helpful to students who are thinking about their educational and vocational plans.

Career Guidance Tests

A wide variety of career guidance tests are used in the schools, especially at the secondary level. General interest batteries are often given both in junior and senior high schools. In addition to interest tests, schools often administer work values, career maturity, and decision inventories. The results from these tests are helpful not only to the individual student but also to the counseling staff in planning career guidance activities. Along with achievement and aptitude information, the results from career guidance tests aid districts in evaluating the educational and vocational needs of students.

The American College Testing Service has developed a system called Work Keys to assess the abilities of noncollege students so that businesses can better evaluate these individuals. The assessment includes performance tests, records of education, training, and work experience.

DEVELOPMENTAL MODEL

Schools need to design systems that are appropriate to their needs. The sample model included in Figure 21.2 looks only at standardized and external testing but does not represent the full picture. A complete testing program must include other dimensions, such as a method to identify and plan for students who have special needs and a way to assess areas of development not measured by standardized tests. For examples of the types of testing some school districts use to assess exceptional students, see Table 21.1.

Table 21.1
Identification of exceptional students

Exceptionality	Tests and Procedures
Mental disability	Slosson Intelligence Test (score of 75 or below) Public school version of the American Association of Mental Deficiency Adaptive Behavior Scale Devereux Behavior Rating Scale Wechsler Intelligence Scale for Children (WISC), Wechsler Preschool and Primary Scale of Intelligence (WPPSI), or Stanford-Binet Leiter International Performance Scale Peabody Picture Vocabulary Test Vision, hearing, speech, and language screening Medical, social, and psychological data
Emotional disability	California Test of Personality Wide Range Achievement Test Slosson Intelligence Test Draw-a-Person Test, Kinetic Family Drawing Test Children's Apperception Test Burks's Behavior Rating Scales Behavioral observations Complete social history Documented and dated evidence of two conferences Documented and dated evidence of two interventions or adjustments that have been tried but have not been successful Vision, hearing, speech, and language screening
Specific learning disabilities	Slosson Intelligence Test WISC, WPPSI, Stanford-Binet Peabody Picture Vocabulary Test Wide Range Achievement Test Bender Visual Motor Gestalt Test Survey achievement test results Peabody Individual Achievement Test Behavioral observations Documented and dated alternatives attempted Summaries of two conferences held Vision, hearing, speech, and language screening Woodcock-Johnson Psychoeducational Battery Work samples Attendance record Social, psychological, and medical history
Gifted	Slosson Intelligence Test Renzulli Rating Scale WISC, WPPSI, Stanford-Binet Survey achievement test results

A school system might also be concerned about physical development of its students from K to 12 and want a systematic check on their vision, hearing, speech, and physical fitness. The information from needs assessments can help school personnel determine individual and group needs.

Needs Assessments

A number of different instruments have been designed to assess the needs of students. Some measure primarily social, psychological, and emotional needs. Others measure guidance and instructional needs. A variety of such instruments is available from major publishers, but many schools prefer to develop their own based on specific programs and community characteristics. An example of a career guidance needs assessment instrument is given in Figure 21.3.

Read each phrase and then decide the importance of that activity to you. Circle the appropriate number to the left of each phrase, using the scale that follows. Also circle the item number of any area in which you would like to have assistance from the counselor.

  0 if you feel the item is not important
  1 if you feel the item is of some importance to you
  2 if you feel the item is of moderate importance to you
  3 if you feel the item is of great importance to you

0 1 2 3   1.   Knowing what jobs are available locally that I can enter immediately after graduating from high school

0 1 2 3   2.   Knowing how to apply for a job

0 1 2 3   3.   Knowing how to write a résumé

0 1 2 3   4.   Knowing how to dress for and what to say in an interview

0 1 2 3   5.   Learning more about my career interests

0 1 2 3   6.   Learning more about the training and education required in my career interest areas

0 1 2 3   7.   Talking with people employed in my career interest areas

0 1 2 3   8.   Arranging for work experience in my career interest fields

0 1 2 3   9.   Learning more about my values and the way they relate to my career choice

0 1 2 3   10. Learning about what courses I should take if I want to enter certain career fields

---

Figure 21.3
Example of a career guidance needs assessment instrument

EVALUATION OF SCHOOL PROGRAMS

Most elementary and secondary schools apply for accreditation from their regional accreditation agency. In the process schools are required to complete self-studies and may opt to survey students, teachers, and parents. The National Study of School Evaluation has developed evaluative criteria for elementary and secondary schools and made available three different instruments that can be used to evaluate the school programs—the Parent Opinion Inventory, the Student Opinion Inventory, and the Teacher Opinion Inventory.

The Teacher Opinion Inventory is a two-part instrument designed to accomplish three goals: (1) to assess teacher opinion about many facets of the school; (2) to provide teacher recommendations for improvement; and (3) to provide valuable data for the school administrator to use in decision making about program development, policy formulation, administrative organization, faculty development, and community relations.

The first part of the instrument consists of 64 multiple-choice items covering five major categories: organization and administration; curriculum and instruction; student discipline, counseling, and advisement; school and community relations; and job satisfaction. Here is a sample item to illustrate the format of the multiple-choice section:

Are you satisfied or dissatisfied with the way students are treated by teachers?

a. Very satisfied
b. Satisfied
c. Neither satisfied nor dissatisfied
d. Dissatisfied
e. Very dissatisfied

The second part consists of eight open-ended questions similar to this one:

What curricular changes would you like to see implemented in your school?

The Student Opinion Inventory was developed to accomplish two goals: (1) to assess student attitude toward many facets of school and (2) to provide student recommendations for improvement. The inventory uses six scales: student-teacher, student-counselor, student-administrator, student-curriculum and instruction, student-participation, and student-school image. There are 35 multiple-choice questions; here is one example:

How much help do your teachers give you in the selection of courses?

a. All the help I need
b. Most of the help I need
c. About half the help I need
d. Little of the help I need
e. None of the help I need

There are 12 open-ended questions like this one:

If you think you need more help at school, what kind of help do you need that you are not getting?

The Parent Opinion Inventory has 53 multiple-choice questions and 11 subscales:

1. Intra-student–body relationships
2. School information services
3. Parent involvement
4. Educational objectives
5. Intra-school problems
6. School program factors
7. Innovative programs
8. Student activities
9. Support services
10. Auxiliary services
11. General psychological climate

The following example is similar to the multiple-choice questions on the parent inventory:

> The school system needs to make numerous curriculum and educational changes to keep up with other schools in the state.
> a. Strongly agree
> b. Agree
> c. Disagree
> d. Strongly disagree
> e. No opinion

The open-ended questions are like this one:

> What do you think our schools should be trying to do?

One feature of the battery is that there are common items across all three instruments so that the opinions of the school administration and staff, students, and parents can be compared. Comparisons are possible on both the multiple-choice and open-ended items.

A number of other instruments that have value in helping school personnel evaluate different components of the school are available. The Effective School Battery measures dimensions of the school's psychosocial climate as viewed by teachers and students. Psychosocial climate involves constructs such as staff morale, fairness and clarity of rules, and relations with parents and the community. The test also measures population characteristics such as the family educational background of the students, the attachment of the students to the schools, and the extent to which students believe in rules.

The teacher form measures job satisfaction, participation in continuing professional development, and attitudes toward education. It includes scales such as these:

1. *Safety*—how safe teachers report the school environment to be
2. *Morale*—how enthusiastic the teachers are and how confident in the school
3. *Planning and action*—how innovative and experimental the school programs are
4. *Administration*—how teachers view the administration
5. *Resources*—how teachers view the adequacy of supplies and resources

6. *Parent/community involvement*—how the school uses community resources in its programs

7. *Student influence*—how the students participate in school decisions

8. *Use of grades as sanctions*—how teachers use grades as sanctions in response to student misconduct

On the student form there are six scales—safety, respect for students, planning and action, fairness of rules, clarity of rules, and student influence.

On the profile of teacher characteristics, dimensions such as job satisfaction, interaction with students, personal security, classroom orderliness, professional development, nonauthoritarian attitude, and pro-integration attitudes are plotted. On the profile of student characteristics, information about the educational background of the parents is also summarized.

ISSUES AND CONCERNS

A number of legal as well as philosophical issues and concerns relate to test programs. Many states have imposed external testing programs and have, in effect, controlled what is being taught and when. Some citizens argue that the curriculum decisions should be made at the local level with citizen input. Testing in primary grades has become a controversial issue. Some states have eliminated standardized testing and state assessment testing in grades K to 3.

When both external and internal testing programs are used, much duplication of effort can result. Kubiszyn and Borich (1987) point out that many districts tend to administer more than one test to measure the same thing or to achieve the same purpose. This problem is compounded when tests are required by local, state, and federal agencies. A systematic evaluation of the types of tests given can help determine whether information is redundant. The evaluator might develop a worksheet and make an analysis of the tests being given, listing each measurement objective in a separate column for each grade level and then identifying the tests that meet each objective. The beginning of a sample worksheet is shown here:

Grade 3: Objective 1	*Grade 3: Objective 2*
Measure vocabulary development	*Measure reading comprehension*
Stanford Achievement Test	Stanford Achievement Test
Minimum level skills test	Minimum level skills test
State assessment test	State assessment test
Reading skill packet test	Mathematics skill packet test

This example shows four tests being used to measure each of the first two objectives. Testing takes up a significant portion of instructional time, and needless duplication is certainly to be avoided.

Vermont has developed a plan that combines mixed methods of assessment. The state will assess students in the fourth and eighth grades in writing and mathematics in three ways: (1) a uniform test, primarily performance-based rather than multiple choice; (2) a portfolio that includes materials collected by the teacher from students during the course of the year; and (3) a "best piece" that represents what a student considers her best effort of the year.

Portfolios are viewed as providing more complete information about students' abilities than conventional testing. There are some practical problems, however, that need to be evaluated to see if the process is achieving its goals. The use of portfolio assessment requires teachers to adapt to ever-changing curriculum and instructional demands. The validity and reliability of the process is a problem. Performance-based assessments quite often only use a small number of tasks that may favor one group or another. As a result, scoring reliability is low. The process is time consuming, and policymakers need to weigh the costs against the benefits of the proposed assessment changes as well as their educational value before they are implemented. Performance assessment needs to make sure that the purpose of the assessment is clearly identified and multiple measures are used (NCME, 1994). The performance assessment should have technical rigor, be cost-effective, protect students' rights, be equitable, and provide information for decision making.

GOALS 2000 EDUCATION STRATEGIES

The Goals 2000 educational strategies were developed by an advisory committee during the Bush administration. Major goals include the following:

1. All children in the United States will start school ready to learn.
2. The high school graduation rate will increase to at least 90%.
3. American students will leave grades 4, 8, and 12 having demonstrated competency in challenging subject matter, including English, mathematics, science, history, and geography. Every school in the United States will ensure that all students learn to use their minds, so that they may be prepared for responsible citizenship, further learning, and productive employment in our modern economy.
4. U.S. students will be first in the world in science and mathematics achievement.
5. Every adult American will be literate and possess the skills and knowledge necessary to compete in a global economy and exercise the rights and responsibilities of citizenship.
6. Every school in America will be free of drugs and violence and will offer a disciplined environment conducive to learning.

Goals 2000 in Florida, for example, calls for school districts to devise evaluation plans and procedures on a local level. Other groups of citizens and educators are advocating national examinations.

State Comprehensive Assessment Tests and Standards-Based Curricula

Many states have developed comprehensive assessment tests—for example, the standards-driven Florida Comprehensive Assessment Test (FCAT) administered to fifth, eighth, and tenth graders. Florida also administers a writing test, Florida Writes, in grades 4, 8, and 10 and the High School Competency Test in grade 11.

The trend in K–12 education is to implement a standards-based curriculum based on state, national, and professional standards. According to Kendall and Marzano (1996), these standards identify what students should know and do. Assessment is a valuable component of the model. But is the curriculum based on important standards, and do the assessments measure student mastery of the curriculum? In particular, do performance results indicate that learning is taking place (Glatthorn, 1998)? All these questions must be addressed.

School Improvement

The school improvement movement has led to the development of several instruments to evaluate the effectiveness of reform. One such assessment is Sizing Up Your School System: The District Effectiveness Audit (Buttram, Corcoran, & Hansen, 1989) published by Research for Better Schools. The audit focuses on dimensions such as goal setting, curriculum, quality assurance, resource allocation, work environment, school improvement, and community relations. Another set of scales, by the same publisher, is the Dimensions of Excellence Scales: Survey for School Improvement (Dusewicy & Beyer, 1991). The eight scales cover school climate, leadership, teacher behavior, curriculum, monitoring and assessment, student discipline, staff development, and parent involvement. There are three versions—a school staff survey, a student survey, and a parent survey.

The educational reform movement and Goals 2000 have led to focusing on a new design for assessment and evaluation. One such approach is alternate or authentic assessment. The authentic assessment procedures have raised a number of questions. Do racial, cultural, and socioeconomic class gaps narrow or widen with the use of performance assessment? Should choices of alternatives be provided that address differences in ethnicity, gender, or abilities, or should the same sample of behavior be collected for all students?

Here are some general procedures to follow when designing an authentic student assessment in mathematics (NCTM, 1993):

1. Identify the big ideas.
2. Identify the expected knowledge of the concepts and skills, know-how, effort, and context related to each big idea. The statement should enhance the learning of math.
3. Collect or create several examples of problem situations and questions about those situations that could be used to assess students' capabilities in relation to the standard. The assessment should promote equity by giving each student the opportunity to demonstrate math power and by helping each student meet professional expectations.
4. Develop scoring procedures to judge student performance and review them.
5. Report the results of student performance.
6. Conduct an equity review of the whole process and its consequences and evaluate the process to see if it is consistent.

SUMMARY

Schools spend millions of dollars on tests each year. School testing programs are given to screen, group, and place students; to make selections; to measure growth; and to facilitate the accomplishment of educational goals. Test selection should involve a careful study of the goals and include in the planning all the public involved in using the information gained from the tests. Achievement, scholastic aptitude, general aptitude, and career guidance tests are part of most school testing programs. At times counselors also need information from the affective domain and find attitude and opinion batteries useful in addition to different types of needs assessments.

QUESTIONS FOR DISCUSSION

1. Study Figure 21.2, a sample school testing program. What tests would you add or drop? Why?

2. Study Table 21.1, which lists tests and procedures for identifying exceptional students. Do you see any tests that would be inappropriate for the use suggested in the table? For example, would you use the Slosson Intelligence Test as an initial screen to identify mentally disabled individuals?

3. Teachers may feel that they are under tremendous pressure because of achievement testing. They may dislike the standardized achievement battery selected for their district because it does not measure what they are teaching. In such a situation what steps should the district administrators take to ensure the best test selection and gain the support of district teachers?

4. What types of nonintellectual or noncognitive tests should be included in the school testing program?

5. Should intelligence tests or scholastic aptitude tests be given to students every two to three years along with achievement tests? Why or why not? Should all students be required to take some type of personality test, such as the California Test of Personality? Why or why not?

SUGGESTED ACTIVITIES

1. Visit a nearby school and find out what tests are part of that school's testing program.

2. Go to the library and find *School Attitude Measures*, published by the Instructional Objectives Exchange. A number of school attitude inventories are included in the book. Administer one to a friend. Record the results and report them to the class.

3. Assume that you are a school's director of testing and have just received the printout that follows. It summarizes the performance of the school's first-grade students on a recently administered test. In addition to these numbers, you know that the district requires a passing score of 80%. Draft the communication pieces that you would send to teachers, parents, and students.

Objective	Students Tested	Number Failed	Number Passed	Percent Passed
Recognize basic vocabulary	156	24	132	84.6
Recognize Dolch words	156	0	156	100.0
Identify word meanings in context	156	6	150	96.1
Identify rhyming words	156	8	148	94.8
Identify long/short vowels	156	30	126	80.8
Write uppercase and lowercase alphabet	156	5	151	96.7
Discriminate beginning sounds	156	18	138	88.4
Associate ending sounds	156	46	110	70.5

4. Review the school report card for High School X. If you were asked to summarize the information for the Parent-Teacher Association, what would you say?

School Report Card

	School Percent	District Percent	State Percent
White	78	53	60
Black	14	41	23
Hispanic	3	2	14
Asian	5	3	2
Indian	0	1	1

By Gender	Male Percent	Female Percent
	49	51

	School Percent	District Percent	State Percent
School Attendance Rate	85	92	91
School Mobility	33	45	34

(beginning of year compared with enrollment at end of year)

	School Percent	District Percent	State Percent
Students with mild disabilities (SLD, EMR, Visual, Physical)	5.0	7.0	6.0
Students with moderate disabilities	1.0	2.0	1.0
Limited English Proficiency	1.0	2.0	5.0

Dropouts	Male No.	Female No.	School Percent	District Percent	State Percent
White	40	25	4.0	5.0	4.0
Black	14	7	8.0	4.0	5.0
Hispanic	0	2	4.0	5.0	6.0
Asian	0	2	2.0	2.0	2.0
Indian	0	0	0.0	6.0	6.0
Suspended from school					
White	162	136	16.0	16.0	11.0
Black	69	56	37.0	21.0	20.0
Hispanic	7	9	25.0	20.0	11.0
Asian	11	8	16.0	10.0	6.0
Indian	0	0	0.0	14.0	13.0

Staff	No.
Teachers	98
Administrators	8
Support Staff	40

Degree	School Percent	District Percent	State Percent
Bachelor's	59	58	55
Master's	40	40	41
Specialist	0	1	3
Doctorate	1	1	1

Teaching Experience	Percent	Racial/Ethnic Group	Percent
First Year	0	White	88
1–3	16	Black	8
4–9	19	Hispanic	2
10–19	19	Asian	2
20+	40	Indian	0

High School Competency Test Grade 11

Communications (Passing Percentage)

	School	District	State
White	95	94	95
Black	80	82	78
Hispanic	82	83	79
Asian	96	83	86
Indian	70	86	89
Unknown	67	76	78
Mathematics			
White	89	86	87
Black	61	53	54
Hispanic	56	73	67
Asian	71	84	86
Indian	70	71	79
Unknown	67	56	62
SAT Average	900	996	880

Expenditure per Student

Regular	$3400	$3581	$3826
Exceptional	9020	7417	8429
At Risk	3600	3497	4294
Vocational	4400	5111	4590
Whites			

5. Write a position paper on one of the issues related to school testing programs.

6. Interview the counselor responsible for administering the school testing program and report your findings to the class.

ADDITIONAL READINGS

Buros Institute of Mental Measurements. (1994). *Psychological assessment in schools*. Lincoln, NB: Author.

The publication discusses tests most frequently used in the assessment of youth.

Crestline, published by CSE/CRESST, 10920 Wilshire Boulevard, Suite 900, Los Angeles, CA 90024-6511; http//:www.cse.ucla.edu

Crestline is the newsletter of the National Center for Research on Evaluation, Standards, and Student Testing.

Glatthorn, A. A. (1998). *Performance assessment and standards-based curricula: The achievement cycle.* Larchmont, NY: Eye on Education.

The book is a very readable introduction to standards-based curricula and authentic learning.

Jaegar, R. M. (1994, April). What parents want to know about schools: A report on school report cards. *Evaluation Perspectives*, *4*(2), 2–3.

Plake, B. S., & Witt, J. C. (Eds.). (1986). *The future of testing, Vol. 2* (Buros-Nebraska Symposium on Measurement and Testing Service). Hillsdale, NJ: Erlbaum.

Read two chapters in Part II, "Educational and Academic/Professional Directions": Nancy Cole's "Future Directions for Educational Achievement and Ability Testing" and Ronald Berk's "Minimum Competency Testing: Status and Potential."

CHAPTER 222

Communicating Test Results to Clients, Parents, and Professionals

OVERVIEW

Test results are valuable only if they are used. The responsible test administrator reports test data to the client with concern for the client's need for information and awareness of the client's cognitive level. Results must be communicated in a way that test takers and other targeted individuals can understand.

The first part of the chapter deals with communication of test results, which may be between the examiner and the client, parents,

teachers, lawyers, police, employers, social workers, and other professionals.

The second part of the chapter deals with the role of the tester as consultant. Consultation may be necessary to help the examiner gain more information about the client. It may also be intended to help the parent, teacher, or other professional better understand the assessment results.

OBJECTIVES

The purpose of this chapter is to

✔ Understand the guidelines and standards for communicating test results

✔ Be familiar with different methods and techniques of reporting and disseminating test results

✔ Identify some problem areas in disseminating results and some possible approaches

✔ List and discuss the models and techniques used in consulting with parents, teachers, and professionals

✔ Recognize the importance of communication skills

GUIDELINES FOR COMMUNICATING TEST RESULTS

The AACD (1980) position paper on the responsibilities of users of standardized tests lists four key elements: the counselor must know the test manual, know the limits of the test, know informed consent procedures, and protect the client's right to privacy.

As we have discussed in previous chapters, examiners need to know the information in the test manual and be prepared to explain difficult concepts. It is important to get clients to understand the limits of a test. When appropriate, the standard error of measurement can help to emphasize that the test results are not absolute; they provide approximations of where true scores might fall. Test results can be influenced by various sources of bias, which may affect the interpretation of the scores. The test taker needs to understand that test data represent just one source of information.

Shertzer and Linden (1979) provide a good summary of the principles needed to guide test interpretation:

1. Select the most valid test available for the purpose.
2. Be skilled and competent in interpreting the test results.
3. Interpret test data in light of the other available information.
4. Present results in terms of probabilities rather than certainties.
5. Be certain that test data help meet a need, and present the results objectively and impersonally. Encourage the client to make his own interpretations and express his own reactions.
6. Interpret with special care results from tests in which clients can vary their responses at will.
7. Realize that the client may react emotionally and even irrationally to the test results, and temper the approach with knowledge of the individual.
8. Use both group and individual approaches to help clients engage in self-appraisal and planning. (p. 501)

Goldman (1971) believes that the counselor needs to look at the process, and he agrees that the first key step is selecting the correct test. In addition, counselors constantly need to sharpen their interviewing skills. The posttest interview gives an opportunity to deal with interpretation and use it in planning and decision making. Counselors need to keep up with the literature on reporting test results.

Lien (1971) adds several other dimensions that should be considered:

1. Be sure that both the examiner and examinee have a clear and immediate goal in mind that serves as the basis of the test report.
2. Avoid specific reporting of derived scores such as standard scores and percentile ranks, if possible.
3. Concentrate on increasing understanding rather than posing as an expert.
4. Recognize that the client may be helped to understand the data but not necessarily accept the results.
5. Never compare one client with another.
6. Be sure that your client or others needing the test information understand the interpretation.

Garfield and Prediger (1982) suggest certain steps and procedures that a counselor should consider in interpreting test results; these are included in the checklist in Figure 22.1.

Informed Consent

Certain responsibilities relate to informed consent. The test taker should be informed about what will be done with the test results and who will use them. The examiner should also discuss with the test taker any circumstances that could have affected the validity or reliability of the results. The consent of the examinee must be obtained before test results are used for any purpose other than that advanced prior to the testing. The examiner also needs to protect the examinee's right of privacy, and all information needs to be accurate.

Prior to Testing

_____ Read in the manual the suggestions for interpreting the test.
_____ Check to see whether interpretation procedures are substantiated by the psychometric evidence found in the manual.
_____ Review with the client the purposes of the testing.
_____ Explain the strengths and limitations of the test.
_____ Explain how the test is scored.
_____ Discuss who receives the test results and how they are used.

During the Reporting Session

_____ Have client discuss personal reactions to and feelings about the test.
_____ Examine whether any factors such as race, age, sex, or handicapping conditions have influenced the test results.
_____ Seek additional information to explain any discrepancies or inconsistencies that become evident.
_____ Translate the results into language the client can understand.
_____ Emphasize strengths and objectively discuss weaknesses.
_____ Allow sufficient time for client to assimilate the results.
_____ Listen attentively to what client says.
_____ Observe nonverbal as well as verbal cues.
_____ Check to see whether the examinee understands the test results.
_____ Correct any misconceptions.
_____ Encourage client to further research or study the meaning of the results.
_____ Provide some alternatives for the test taker to consider, based on the test information.
_____ Schedule follow-up sessions, if needed, to facilitate understanding, planning, or decision making.

Figure 22.1
Checklist of steps and procedures for test interpretation

STANDARDS FOR REPORTING TEST RESULTS

Professional standards and codes of ethics emphasize the importance of how test results are reported. Some of these standards focus on requirements of test authors and publishers. The test manual, for example, should contain information that will facilitate test interpretation. As a matter of fact, all test materials, including computerized reports, should be designed to facilitate test interpretation. Other standards focus on special types of tests, such as certification and licensing examinations. Reports are to be given promptly to applicants. Test takers who fail should be told their scores and the cutoff score required to pass the test. Applicants should be informed of their performance on all parts of the test for which scores are produced. In addition, rules and procedures used to combine scores or other assessments to determine the overall outcome should be reported to the test taker.

Furthermore, the rights of the test taker must be taken into consideration, and there are procedures to handle test irregularities. Some testing organizations offer the test taker the option of prompt and free retesting or arbitration of the dispute.

Standards call for the clinician to share with clients the test results and interpretations. The clinician is directed to provide information about the range of error for such interpretations when that information will be beneficial to the client. The test information is to be expressed in language that the client or client's legal representative can understand.

METHODS OF REPORTING TEST RESULTS

There are five major methods of reporting test results: individual sessions, group sessions, written reports, programmed and interactive approaches, and video approaches. The role and function of the test taker and counselor vary with each approach.

Individual Sessions

Counselors often use individual interpretation sessions to present test results to clients. How the scores are reported is a function of the counselor's theoretical orientation. Counselors who are more client-centered are apt to present clients with raw and derived scores and encourage the clients to join the process of interpreting the scores. Counselors might direct attention to how the clients feel about their scores and interpretations. Counselors who are more direct may review the purpose of the testing, present the results, clarify what the scores mean, and discuss the implications of the results.

When a client interprets and reacts to his own scores, the counselor may gain new insight into the client. By participating in the discussion of the test results, the client may become more accepting of the results and may use the information in decision making. Some counselors argue that the more the client participates, the more understanding and learning takes place. Other counselors believe that individual sessions are time consuming and unproductive.

Oral Reports.   Quite often the examiner customarily makes an oral report to parents and guardians. The complexity of the report depends upon the familiarity of the parents or client with the concepts and terms used, and it is the responsibility of the counselor to translate the information into language the parents can understand. To maximize the effectiveness of the report, parents and guardians need to do the following (Shore, Brice, & Love, 1992, p. 110):

1. ask for definitions of unfamiliar terms
2. request examples to support any generalizations that the examiner makes
3. offer examples of the examinee's behavior that contradict test results
4. have the examiner repeat the parts they didn't understand when presented
5. ask for a summary before leaving the session

Parents should make a list of questions to ask the examiner, such as the following:

1. What tests did my child take?
2. What were my child's strengths on each test? Weaknesses?
3. Are there any recommendations or suggestions on how I might help my child?

Group Sessions

Group sessions are used frequently to provide interpretation of client test results. Clients with particular learning or personality styles prefer group and social interaction; such clients often learn from each other as well as from the counselor. Most tests now provide interpretive material that the counselor can highlight effectively and efficiently in group sessions. This approach is usually more economical. The counselor can work with a small or large group and can use overhead transparencies, filmstrips and tapes, or videotapes to present material. Such aids are less likely in a one-to-one situation. The use of group sessions does not preclude offering individual sessions if a client needs further help processing the information.

Written Reports

More test publishers are providing some sort of written report of the test results. With many tests clients score themselves, plot the scores on a profile, and have immediate interpretation of the results. School districts often provide parents with interpretive reports of their children's performance on survey achievement testing. Both the language and interpretation are simplified.

Written reports are not valuable to all individuals. Many students and parents have problems reading and understanding test reports even when the language is simple. Many written reports present profiles of scores that are helpful for test takers who have difficulty visualizing test results. Some individuals find written reports impersonal and dislike them. Many computerized forms of test interpretation are available now. Computerized reports may be effective in presenting basic facts but probably are ineffective in changing a person's established belief system.

Interactive Approaches

Interactive approaches are another method of presenting test results. With the advent of computer-assisted testing, clients can be provided with immediate results. Many of the computerized guidance information systems, such as CHOICES, are of this interactive type. Holland's Self-Directed Search is a guided exercise that provides the user with useful career information.

Computer-assisted administration of instruments allows for more branching in the programming and immediate feedback. The individual can start over again and see what happens with different choices. This approach relies on written text and visual stimuli. Clients often are freer in responding to a computer than to a counselor and usually rate computer assessment very positively. A few test takers are overwhelmed by the computer and fear they cannot operate a program. Other clients are philosophically opposed to the impersonal nature of the computer.

Video Approaches

A current trend is to combine the technology of the computer with that of video equipment. Scores on certain scales can key individualized reports back to clients, providing audio as well as visual presentation. The presentation can appear more professional and be checked for accuracy before it is used with clients. In addition, the analysis can be more complete and thorough since the rules are built into the program.

PROBLEM AREAS

Counselors may face a number of problems in disseminating test information. Some of the more common problems are discussed here.

Acceptance

The goal of the feedback session with clients quite often is getting them to accept the test results and incorporate that information into their decision making. Negative results frequently prompt resistance: test takers don't want to change their self-concepts to align with test data and often resist accepting valid information about themselves.

Counselors can enhance acceptance of the test information in the following ways:

1. Involve clients in decision making and general selection of tests before testing.
2. Establish rapport with clients so that they trust the counselor and are relaxed in the sessions.

3. Spend sufficient time with clients in interpreting the results, not overwhelming them with too much data.
4. Translate the results into language that clients can understand.
5. Show the validity of the information for the decision(s) to be made.

Readiness of the Client

The critical factor in the acceptance of the data is client readiness. Test takers who believe that they have a specific need for counseling about the test results and want to learn what meaning data have for them will more readily accept the information presented. If the information is damaging to a client's self-concept or ego, the counselor might have to work on getting that client to extend her acceptance. The counselor can use these techniques to help the client become ready:

1. Have several sessions prior to the report session to build understanding and acceptance.
2. Allow the client to bring up the topic; don't immediately begin the session with test interpretation.
3. Focus on the test rather than on the client.
4. Try to engage the client actively in the learning and planning process both before and after the testing.

Negative Results

Often the results are not what the client wanted, desired, or expected. The client may have failed to pass a certification or licensing examination or to achieve the minimum score for admission to college. Certain results are a threat to the client's self-concept. On a personality test a client may turn up with high scores on the lie scale and become defensive. Or the client may tend to be overly truthful and may have a high score on a neuroticism scale. The test administrator should consider the following:

1. Explaining the rationale for cutoff scores and the validity of the established procedures
2. Gaining an understanding of the test taker's perceptions and feelings, seeing the whole person complete with irrationalities and blind spots
3. Accepting the test taker's right to argue with test implications without necessarily agreeing with the test taker
4. Being genuine and expressing personal feeling, perhaps disagreeing with the client's views and goals, and pointing out the consequences of a particular course of action
5. Identifying other information about the client that supports or does not support the test data
6. Discussing the implications of the data and the importance of that information for decision making

Flat Profiles

Many times an individual's pattern of scores has no highs or lows but is just a flat profile. On aptitude and achievement tests this indicates a similar level of performance in all areas. It might be above average, average, or below average. On interest or career guidance inventories, especially if the client is undecided about future goals, the data may not be extremely helpful. Response set might be a factor on a test, with the individual ranking everything high, average, or low. Holland (1979) believes there are major problems in counseling individuals with flat profiles. In the case of flat profiles on interest and career guidance tests, counselors can ask clients to read the descriptions of the six Holland types and rank the three types most characteristic of themselves (Miller, 1985) and discuss the clients' expectations, relevant past experiences, previous work activities, and misconceptions and stereotypes.

In the case of flat profiles on aptitude and achievement tests, counselors can look at the interests, values, and career goals and assure the clients that their profiles are not abnormal.

The counselor should discuss what an individual considers her strengths to be and what she can do acceptably. A good procedure is to investigate the individual's performance on previous tests to determine whether this pattern is typical.

Motivation and Attitude

Test results are more significant to clients who are motivated to take a test, come in and discuss the results, and have a positive attitude toward the value of the data. Some clients have a negative attitude toward testing prior to the test and maintain that attitude afterward. Some clients become negative after they see that the test results are not what they expected.

Workers in the helping professions should recognize that tests can aid clients in developing more realistic expectations about themselves and can be valuable in decision making. However, some clients put too much weight on the results and become overdependent on test data to solve their problems. Other clients use test results as a way of escaping their feelings and problems. Counselors interpreting test results need to be aware of not only a client's motivation to take or not take a test but also his attitude toward the test. Other important information includes the immediate goal for the interpretation of the test results and the client's desire to be involved in decision making about the type of test to be taken and the dissemination of test results.

COMMUNICATION OF TEST RESULTS TO THE PUBLIC

When test results are released to the news media, those responsible for releasing the results should provide information to help minimize the probabilities of misinterpretation. A current movement toward accountability has influenced schools' use and reporting of test data. Administrators like to use standardized and criterion-referenced test data to show that the schools are accomplishing the educational goals of society. However, many people have trouble understanding the concepts used in measurement and the many different types of derived scores that test makers report. Test data, when properly presented, can be useful tools in interpreting the school system for the community. Shertzer and Linden (1979) advocate that emphasis be placed on interpretive reporting of group results to show what the scores signify in terms of progress toward the realization of school objectives and vocational plans (p. 504).

Communication with the public should follow these general guidelines:

1. Communication should take place before and after testing. News releases can announce a test, and letters and cards can be sent to the parents or guardians. An example of such a letter appears in Figure 22.2. Reports of test results can be made through the local media or can be presented at PTA or community meetings.
2. Because most citizens are not familiar with test jargon and statistical terms, the results should be presented as simply as possible while still remaining accurate and honest.
3. Percentile bands or stanines can be reported graphically or visually using handouts, transparencies, or slides.
4. Data should be presented in summary form—for example, by grade rather than by teacher.
5. Statistical and measurement terms can be defined in nontechnical language with examples provided.
6. The public is not stupid and should not be treated with condescension.

Any oral or written report should include the following components:

1. A general description of the tests or testing program
2. Uses of the test results
3. Types of skills and competencies measured
4. Types of scores reported and their meaning
5. Types of norms used
6. Definitions and examples of the summary statistics and measurement concepts needed to understand the presentation
7. The results with appropriate comparisons (national, state, district, and school; year-to-year changes; or grade-by-grade changes)
8. Factors that might have influenced the results

An oral presentation requires time for questions. The examiner should be prepared to answer the following types of questions about major issues:

Are these tests biased against minority and disadvantaged students?

Why do we test so much?

Why are some schools in the system achieving higher results than others in the system?

Are teachers influenced by the test results?

Dear Ocean School Parents and Guardians:

Can you believe it? We have only 9 weeks left in the school year! The time has passed quickly, but there is still much to accomplish. We are confident that with your cooperation we will attain the goals set for this year. We want this to be the best year ever for our children.

As you may know, our school board has adopted promotional criteria for students in grades K through 8. The criteria are based in part on the Stanford Achievement Test and the Essential Skills Tests. We will begin administering the Stanford Achievement Test next week. The first day of testing will be Monday, April 5. The test will be given over a 2-week period. This time includes makeup testing for children who might be absent, although we hope that every child will be present on testing days and will arrive at school on time. Nonetheless, we do not want any children who are ill to take the tests, so those students will have an opportunity to be tested later.

The Essential Skills Tests will be administered in early May. These tests measure a child's progress in mathematics and reading. We will send home a reminder before the tests.

You can help your child(ren) do well on these tests by following some simple suggestions.
1. Each child should have a good night's rest prior to a testing day. We suggest 10 hours of sleep.
2. Each child should have a good, well-balanced breakfast before coming to school on a testing day.
3. Conflicts and arguments should be avoided. A child's emotional state has great influence on performance.
4. No child should feel anxious about the test. Pressure has a negative effect.

If you have any questions or suggestions, please do not hesitate to contact the school office, in person or by telephone. We have appreciated your assistance and support throughout the year.

Sincerely yours,
Ocean School Guidance Counselor

Figure 22.2
Sample letter of information for parents

THE TESTER AS CONSULTANT: LEGAL CONSIDERATIONS

When testers act as counselors, they need to be aware of legal requirements, which can be very specific in many situations. The Buckley Amendments became the Family Education Rights and Privacy Act (PL 93–380) and gave parents the opportunity to see all the information affecting the evaluation, placement, or programming of their children. The law covers all personally identifiable educational records collected, maintained, or used. Parents have the right to demand changes in a record if they find the information to be inaccurate, and their consent must be obtained before test scores and records can be released. These rights transfer to the individual at age 18 or to students attending postsecondary schools. Schools are responsible for informing parents of their right to access records and are required to hold a hearing if errors are thought to be included in records (see also Chapter 24).

When a client is being assessed for placement, the examiner should remember that the parents probably have useful information. In the screening and placement of students under PL 94–142, the counselor must document contact with the parents and the information received from them. The counselor is required to provide the parents with written notice of any proposed change in client identification, evaluation, or placement. Each evaluation procedure and test to be used must be described in writing. Communication must be in a form that is understandable to the parents and in their native language. If the parents are deaf, the information must be transmitted in sign language.

ETHICAL STANDARDS FOR CONSULTATION

Principle 8 of the American Psychological Association's *Ethical Principles of Psychologists* (1992) calls for psychologists to make every effort to promote the welfare and best interests of their clients and to guard against the misuse of assessment results. Principle 5 states that psychologists have a primary obligation to respect the confidentiality of information obtained in the course of their work and should reveal information to others only with the consent of the individual involved or that person's legal representative. The exception to this principle occurs when its exercise would result in clear danger to the individual or to others.

CONSULTING WITH PARENTS

Parents are an important resource in improving children's capacity to cope with the demands of their environment. When parents want to be involved, helping professionals should identify the skills, values, and possibilities of the parents relative to helping their children. *Principles for Professional Ethics* (NASP, 1978) calls for psychologists to recognize the importance of parental support and obtain it prior to working with a child. Psychologists should secure continued parental involvement through frank and prompt reporting of evaluation findings. They are responsible for telling parents what records consist of, what kind of information goes into the report, who receives the report, and what steps are used to protect the information.

Dustin and Ehly (1984) propose a simple five-step model that involves establishing rapport or phase-in, obtaining information and identifying the problem, providing information for implementation, conducting follow-up and evaluation, and terminating the relationship. The counselor discusses the implications for the child, helps establish goals for the parents, and selects strategies that will be most beneficial to the client and family.

The *Code of Fair Testing Practices in Education* (APA, 1988) states that the counselor should tell test takers or their parents or guardians how the test scores will be kept on file and indicate to whom and under what circumstances test scores will be released. Parents should also be informed how to register complaints and have problems resolved about testing. Counselors need to provide parents and guardians with information about the rights of the test taker and discuss whether they can obtain copies of tests and completed answer sheets, retake tests, have tests rescored, or cancel scores.

Brown, Wyne, Blackburn, and Powell (1979) propose a more elaborate model consisting of seven steps that can be modified to convey test results to parents:

1. Establish a good working relationship.
2. Assess the family and parent dynamics and environment.
3. Check on the validity of assumptions about the family and parents.
4. Explain the test results.
5. Discuss the implications for the child.
6. Establish goals for the parents and select strategies.
7. Involve the child in the conference with the parents.

The consultation can be done with a single parent, a couple, or a group of parents.

Explaining Test Results to Parents

Most parents have little knowledge about testing. Even if various facets of the testing program are explained initially, the examiner should review for parents the purposes of the testing using nontechnical language. Actual test results might be visually presented through graphs and profiles to help parents understand. Reports need to be comprehensible as well as informational. In reporting specific types of scores, the examiner should be sure that parents understand the type of score being discussed. They should be told the limitations of the test, and the standard error of measurement should be explained. The AACD standards suggest that the examiner discuss the qualifications necessary to interpret and use standardized tests and identify sources of bias that might operate in the situation.

The examiner should walk the parent through the interpretation, being patient and understanding but honest. Working with parents may identify a need for parent education in some group sessions on measurement topics and issues. Goldman (1971) points out that those who work with children and adolescents find that parents rather than the children are most in need of the information provided by tests (p. 438). However, he believes that counselors cannot assume parents will be reasonable and objective about the test report; they may have unreasonable aspirations, blind spots, and defense mechanisms themselves or about their children. It is important to spend enough time with parents, perhaps more than one session, to deal with their feelings and attitudes.

Sattler (1992) proposes a four-stage model for working with parents:

Initial phase of the interview—It is important to have both parents or guardians present at the report session to permit the counselor a more objective assessment of the facts and a chance to get the parents or guardians to share the responsibilities of the test results. The examiner needs to establish rapport and recognize that parents may have experienced many frustrations and hardships in their family life. They should be encouraged to talk; what they have to say is important. The examiner should assess parents' interest in the test results, their attitudes toward their child's condition, their handling of problems with the child, and their goals and expectations for the child.

Communicating diagnostic findings—The examiner should set the ground rules for the information sharing and should refuse to side with either parent or child. Parents should be encouraged to participate in the session and should be warned that some of the information shared might at times arouse conflict, hostility, or anxiety. They should be free to express their feelings, just as the examiner is honest in portraying the results. The hope is that the parents will develop realistic perceptions and expectations for their child.

Discussion of specific recommendations—The examiner should check to see that parents have fully understood the test results and their implications. The parents may want specific recommendations or program suggestions, and the examiner should be prepared to provide these.

Termination of the interview—Parents may be unable or unwilling to accept the results of the evaluation. The examiner should accept that difficulty and perhaps provide the names of other professionals or agencies in case the parents want to get a second opinion. The examiner should also be available to see the parents again if necessary and desirable.

Parent-Examiner Conferences

In preparing for a parent conference, the examiner should gather all pertinent information, including a report of the standardized tests taken by the child and an interpretation of the results. The examiner should also be prepared to record additional information from the parents that might facilitate work with the child. Parents might be asked to describe how the student feels about school, teachers, counselors, testing, grading, or peers. They might also elaborate on the student's special interests. The examiner might have on display the work of other students so that the parents can see not only what books and materials are being used but also what level of work is expected. The examiner should end the conference on a positive note, thanking the parents for their interest and scheduling another appointment if necessary.

Types of Questions Parents Ask About Tests

Parents ask a number of questions about test scores and reports. Here are some typical questions and some points to include in a response:

What is a standardized test? This term refers to conditions under which the test was developed, resulting in a number of standards of performance that are representative of a wide sample of test takers. It also refers to conditions under which the test is administered, usually in a uniform manner so that all test takers receive the same directions, same time to take the test, and so on.

How was the test administered? It was administered by individuals trained and experienced in giving tests, such as teachers, counselors, and psychologists.

How are the tests scored, reported, and recorded? Tests are usually sent back to the publisher to be computer scored. Individual and group reports are sent back to the school district or examiner. Many testing services provide labels on which results are recorded and which can be fastened to the cumulative record or file of the individual. Individual profiles and test summaries are sent to parents; class, grade, and district profiles are sent to the schools.

Often parents ask questions about specific scores used on different tests. The examiner should be prepared to explain scores such as national percentile ranks, grade equivalent scores, stanines, local norms, and standard scores. Specific questions may relate to many areas:

What do these scores really mean?

What is wrong with grade equivalent scores?

Why are our school's scores below the national norms?

Why do you test so much?

How do you use the scores?

How accurately do the tests predict success?

Is there really a relation between the scores and a child's achievement in class?

How much do scores vary and why?

What is scholastic aptitude?

What is intelligence?

What kinds of questions were asked on this test?

Who will see the test results?

Can test scores be improved with coaching?

Is the test fair to members of my race, gender, or ethnic group?

Other Areas of Concern to Parents

Parents also may want to know what to do if they disagree with the results of the testing. For example, the examiner says the child is not ready for kindergarten and the parents think the child is, or the parents think the child should be placed in the gifted program and the examiner doesn't agree. They could be advised of avenues they might take, such as pursuing an independent evaluation on their own, recognizing that the school district may not reimburse them for the evaluation and that it may be difficult to have the client tested with the same tests. Shore et al. (1992) remind parents that the people involved in the process are trying to do what is in the best interest of the test taker. Parents should use the information gained from the assessment and discussion with the examiner to make an informed decision about what is best for their child.

Parents may want to know whether test results really matter. The examiner should elaborate on the testing objectives and point out that our society is concerned with accountability. In addition, test results are often a major criterion for promotion or admission to a specific program. Parents should take test results seriously and be supportive of testing programs. They should encourage their children to do their best and praise them for doing as well as they can. Parents' attitudes toward a testing program influence how children view that program.

Parents are sometimes concerned about the anxiety caused by tests and want to know about techniques to help reduce that anxiety. Many bookstores offer audiotapes detailing relaxation techniques. The examiner needs to emphasize that some anxiety is useful, but too much is a problem. Parents should be warned to respond to test anxiety in a realistic manner and not to overreact to test scores.

Parents might ask whether the tests are culturally biased. Many attempts have been made to eliminate as much bias as possible in most test instruments. The essential skills and minimum-level skills tests are based upon what the students are supposed to learn in schools. Scores would be biased only if individuals did not have an equal opportunity to learn the material included on these tests. Standardized tests use panels of experts to review the items for sexual bias, cultural bias, and bias for individuals with disabilities. On scholastic aptitude tests the item responses for various groups are compared to see if there are differences in how minority and majority groups respond to the test items. However, even with these attempts, some bias might still be operating in the testing situation and may distort a person's true score.

Parents may be concerned about whether scores are fixed or changeable. They need to be reminded that a test measures a sample of behavior at a particular time, using items from a given domain. Tests scores do change; they can go up and down. There may be some ups and downs in the child's test profile from year to year or subtest to subtest. Sometimes a poor performance happens because a student may not be skilled in the areas measured by the test. Most children perform better in some areas than in others. Parents need to understand the dynamics at work and refrain from hasty value judgments.

Parents may also be concerned about whether students ought to be given their own test results. In most cases students should be provided feedback on their performance in words and terms they can understand. The information can help them understand their own strengths and weaknesses and make more realistic educational and vocational choices.

Parents may wonder whether their children are overachievers or underachievers. Overachievers are students who achieve better in the classroom than scholastic aptitude tests predict. These students usually have a positive attitude toward school, internal orientation, and high motivation. The label has been greatly criticized by educators and psychologists from a theoretical and practical standpoint. Underachievers perform below the prediction of a scholastic aptitude test. Many learning disabled students have normal aptitude but achieve a standard deviation or more below the average for their grade or age.

The Informing Interview

In the informing interview the counselor attempts to communicate assessment results with the parents or guardians. The goal of this session may be partly educational and motivational for the parents and partly therapeutic (Gabel, Oster, & Botnik, 1986). When problems identified are mild or less deviant, parents are more accepting of the results and are less anxious. When the problems are severe, the parents or guardians may become angry and defensive or blame themselves and others. When parents are defensive, communication is usually ineffective.

Gabel et al. (1986) suggest that the initial statement and explanation of the problem should be in nontechnical terms. Later the counselor may use medical and psychological terms as support for the assessment. Certain terms, such as mental retardation and brain damage, might stand as an emotional block to communication if not adequately clarified and explained.

The counselor needs to be alert to what questions the parents asked as well as what questions they did not ask. What questions were they really asking? What questions should they be asking? The counselor may want to address practical questions that concern the client such as schooling, therapy, and counseling needs and the like.

Parents as Test Interpreters

Testing companies usually provide self-interpretative report forms for parents, but most parents still have questions about what the test scores mean. A workshop for parents might help them understand and interpret test results properly. Boehm and White (1982) provide four guidelines for parents who present test results to their children (pp. 138–139):

1. Inform the child about areas of strength or areas needing development.
2. Find out whether the child understands what the test scores mean (e.g., children often confuse the meaning of percentile with percentage).
3. Avoid judgment of an individual's worth. The student whose score is high is no better as a person than the student whose score is low.
4. For a student who is having difficulty, offer to find out the reasons and try to help.

Overall, parents need to maintain open communication with their children. Test results should be shared constructively, and steps should be outlined to help with any problem area. Parents also need to listen to their children's view of a test or test result.

Consulting with Teachers

Teachers may also need consultation about test use and interpretation. They have to administer and score both local and standardized tests, and they need to know the practical implications of the scores for their students.

Again, the first step for the examiner is to establish a working relationship. Brown, Pryzwansky, and Schulte (1995) call for a relationship of mutual trust, open communication, genuineness, and positive regard. The teacher is seeking ways to help a student and wants to have the test results interpreted in language that is easy to understand. The consultation is quite often for the purpose of establishing a plan of action for a particular student.

Caplan and Caplan (1993) have identified four types of problems that arise in teacher consultation:

1. The teacher lacks skills and competencies needed to work with students.
2. The teacher is not objective and unbiased.
3. The teacher lacks confidence and perceives personal deficiencies.
4. The teacher lacks the ability to conceptualize the student's problem.

The NEA and NCME have asserted that student assessment is an essential part of teaching and that good teachers cannot exist without good student assessment. Teachers need to acquire skills and abilities to select, develop, apply, use, communicate, and evaluate student assessment information.

Problems that can interfere with the success of the consultation process might be identified by observing the teacher in class or by listening carefully to what the teacher has to say:

"Mary has a low IQ. It's impossible to motivate her."

"John comes from a bad family. He'll be just like his brothers and not amount to anything."

"Dick scored at the 34th percentile. He did not do well at all."

Part of the problem may be that the teacher does not know enough about basic measurement concepts. This topic could be addressed in a group situation, perhaps through in-service education. If the teacher is biased, the examiner may have to use confrontation and report the objective data collected through observation and feedback. Teacher expectations have a tremendous influence on what happens in the classroom; they should be realistic and communicated regularly and effectively.

Goals should be set for teacher consultation; they help focus attention on strategies. The collaborative model of consultation calls for strategies to be developed jointly by the consultant and teacher. The theoretical orientation of the consultant partly determines the strategies to be used. Neo-client theory might stress human relation skills such as problem solving and effective communication, whereas behavior theory might focus on selective use of reinforcement strategies.

The National Association of School Psychologists (1978) calls for establishing professional relationships with school personnel. Standard IV relates to the need of the school psychologist to have a working understanding of the goals, processes, and legal requirements of the educational system and to be familiar with the organization, instructional materials, and teaching strategies of the school. Effective communication skills are essential, and the school psychologist is reminded that the findings and recommendations need to be put into language that is readily understood by the school staff.

Indirect Delivery Model

Gutkin and Curtis (1982) propose an indirect service model that includes steps that will help teachers and parents and other professionals understand, interpret, and use assessment results more effectively:

1. Develop an open, trusting relationship. Rapport must be established.
2. Establish a collaborative, coordinate relationship. Both parties should have equal authority in the decision-making process.
3. Involve the consultee in the consultation process. The consultant is responsible for helping consultees become active in the process.
4. Encourage the consultee to accept or reject suggestions. The consultee cannot be forced to accept strategies.
5. Maintain a voluntary relationship. Principals should not force teachers into consultation.
6. Maintain confidentiality. The information shared should be kept confidential.

In this model the consultant may plan to collect data from observations, interviews, and standardized tests if both the consultant and consultee believe the information would be useful. Any tests selected and administered should address specific problems identified in the case.

Problem-Solving Consulting Model

A problem-solving approach helps the parties involved clarify and define the problem of the client and facilitate the analysis of forces that will lead to more effective problem solving. Helping professionals can brainstorm alternate strategies, evaluate and choose among the alternatives, and then specify the responsibilities of the consultee and consultant. The strategy then must be implemented and evaluated for effectiveness. The process can be recycled if necessary and the steps repeated (Gutkin & Curtis, 1982, p. 805).

For situations in which the purpose of the consultation focuses on mental health issues, Caplan (1963, 1970, 1993) and Caplan and Caplan (1993) have proposed a model that includes the focus as well as the goal of consultation. The two major goals are remediation and prevention. The focus may be on individual cases or on administrative programs. Caplan (1970) advocates a consultee-centered case consultation because the primary goal is to improve the consultee's capacity to function effectively in this category of case in order to benefit many similar clients in the future. Because of the educational emphasis, the consultant uses the discussion of the current case situation, not basically to understand the client but to understand and remedy the consultee's work difficulties as manifested in this example (p. 125).

CONSULTING WITH OTHER PROFESSIONALS

Many times an examiner is required to communicate test results to other professionals, such as principals, psychologists, social workers, correctional officers, and judicial staff members. Not all of these professionals understand test information. Again, it is important to work cooperatively to establish good rapport and a working relationship based on mutual respect and recognition of joint proficiencies. Communication skills remain an important variable.

Explanations should be clear and unambiguous. The APA's (1992) *Ethical Principles of Psychologists* (Principle 8) calls for the examiner to indicate any reservations regarding test validity or reliability because of assessment circumstances or inappropriate norms. Psychologists and counselors are cautioned to ensure that assessment results and interpretations are not misused by others.

When reporting to other professionals, examiners are faced with a variety of decisions. Goldman (1971) provides some basic guidelines for presenting test information to other professions:

1. Find out exactly what information the recipient needs, what she plans to do with it, and what qualifications she has.
2. Make sure ethical and legal procedures are followed, such as securing a client's written permission to release information.
3. Check to see whether procedures have been established for test information. Normally a policy is already in force.
4. Aim the report as directly as possible to the particular question asked. This practice saves time and provides clear communication of needed information.

EVALUATION OF THE CONSULTANT

Parents, teachers, and other professionals might be asked to evaluate the work of the consultant. Questions such as these are helpful:

1. Did the consultant help you better understand the problem that prompted the testing?
2. Did the consultant help you understand the test results better?
3. Did the consultant provide you with practical suggestions for using the test results?
4. Were you satisfied with the consultant's style in relating to you?
5. Were you happy with the services provided by the consultant?
6. What could be done to improve the services?

A checklist or rating form for consultees might pose questions like these:

1. How many times have you met with the consultant this year?
   1 2 3 4 5 6 7 8 9 10 times or more
2. How helpful was the consultant to you?
   Not helpful 1 2 3 4 5 6 7 Extremely helpful
3. How knowledgeable was the consultant about testing?
   Slightly 1 2 3 4 5 6 7 Extremely

SUMMARY

Dissemination of test results is a function of communication. Knowledge of what to communicate requires a thorough background in test interpretation and an understanding of the test manual and the purposes of the test. Group and individual counseling sessions need to be planned prior to testing as well as after testing has been completed. In many types of testing programs, parents and the community need to be informed. It is advantageous to develop a systematic program to inform test users, parents, teachers, and the public about testing. The examiner needs a thorough knowledge of ethical and legal aspects and must be able to translate the test results into language clients can understand.

Consultation demands not only a knowledge of the problem situation but different models of interaction. The consultant needs to know the ethical and legal standards as well as strategies to work with teachers, parents, and other professionals. Communication skills are an important part of the consultation process. In addition, the consultant should include in the process a mechanism for evaluation of his services.

QUESTIONS FOR DISCUSSION

1. Which type of test interpretation do you feel is more accurate—group versus individual, computer-based narratives, or standard test profiles?
2. Do you agree that individuals interpreting tests should be extremely careful about interpretation of test results for women, older individuals, minority group members, and individuals with disabilities? Why or why not? Does the type of test influence the need for caution?
3. What role do you believe counseling theory should have in the interpretation of test results? Should the interpretation be based on a given theory? Defend your position.
4. What are the major problem areas in disseminating results to parents? The community? The test taker? How would you go about evaluating the effectiveness of dissemination efforts?

5. If you could choose the way you were to receive your test results, what system would you choose? Why?

6. Clients value tests more if they see the need for the test information. Are the attitudes of the test taker more important than the system chosen for interpreting results?

7. What do you think are the main issues and problems that consultants face in working with parents, teachers, and other professionals regarding test results?

8. How important is the role of the consultant for people in the helping professions? What skills does a consultant need?

9. How would you handle a teacher or parent who became excessively dependent on your services and solutions? What should the role of the consultant be in such a case?

10. What model of consultation would you choose if you were asked to work with individuals on testing problems or results? What factors would influence your choice? Would underlying psychological theories be a factor in your decision?

11. Goldman (1971) states that parents are most in need of the information provided by tests. Do you agree with this statement? What kind of program should be established to help parents better understand the test results of their children?

SUGGESTED ACTIVITIES

1. Review the literature on methods and techniques of test interpretation.

2. Talk with the persons responsible for test interpretation and dissemination in several school districts. Assemble a notebook or folder of the sample news releases and examples of the districts' letters to parents, students, and teachers.

3. Interview psychologists and counselors who use tests frequently. Find out the systems they use to report test results to their clients and their approaches to problems such as flat profiles, individuals who are disappointed with test results, and so on. Report your findings to the class.

4. Devise a rating scale to evaluate different types of media presentations for disseminating test results.

5. Videotape how you would handle test interpretation sessions with a client who (a) is not ready to accept the results, (b) had a flat profile with all low scores, or (c) who has a really negative attitude toward testing.

6. Devise a workshop for a group of individuals in your field who work with tests and need help communicating test results.

7. Interview workers in the helping professions who use tests and find out how much time they spend in consultation. Have them discuss the model of consultation they use. Ask them what steps they follow in the consultation process.

Also, ask them what types of problems they have had in their roles as consultants. Report your results to the class.

8. Compare the major models of consultation on test results. Identify studies and articles in the literature that deal with test results and test problems.

9. Set up a model consultation program for a consultant who is working with teachers, parents, or other professionals on testing problems and results.

10. Role-play a situation in which you have to consult a helping professional on testing problems or results. Examples: A teacher might want to know how she can help her students improve their test scores. She is afraid that she will lose her job if the class does not do well on achievement tests. Or a doctor might want to know whether a child shows any signs of learning disabilities and how that information could be relayed to the child's parents.

11. Write a paper on the skills a consultant needs to be effective with testing problems and results.

12. Design an instrument to evaluate the work of a consultant on testing problems.

13. Review these brief case studies and answer the questions that follow:

Maria's mother was very concerned when she received her second grader's scores on the Comprehensive Test of Basic Skills. Maria scored at the 99th percentile on math but only at the 81st on reading. Maria was at the 94th percentile on the word attack scale and the 95th on vocabulary but at the 45th on language and 54th on science. Maria had been tested for the gifted program and was accepted by virtue of a 133 score on the Stanford-Binet. Her mother can't make any sense out of the test scores and wants the teachers and counselors to help her daughter improve them.

a. What approach would you use with Maria's mother?
b. What would you tell her about the test results?

You have been asked to be a consultant on a training and development project. The project involves work with unemployed workers; you are to help explain how to use and interpret different career instruments. The previous consultant who left recently had convinced the project managers to use the Self-Directed Search (SDS) and the Myers-Briggs Type Indicator (MBTI).

a. How would you go about developing your role as a consultant?
b. What steps would you follow?
c. The project participants want you to consult with them on how to interpret the two tests. One individual wants you to guide him through the process of analyzing, interpreting, and reporting back to the client the results on the SDS and MBTI. His case concerns Albert Smith, a 23-year-old Caucasian male who dropped out of school in the 10th grade. He is enrolled in a high school equivalency program in conjunction with the project. Albert has had numerous jobs in the food service industry but has not been able to hold on to them. He has a wife and three children and realizes that he needs further training and education to support his family. On the MBTI he is an ISFJ. On the SDS, he is an ARS. How would you proceed?

ADDITIONAL READINGS

Brown, D., Pryzwansky, W. B., & Schulte, A. C. (1995). *Psychological consultation: Introduction to theory and practice* (3rd ed.). Boston: Allyn & Bacon.

The text examines different theories and approaches to consultation. Chapters deal with evaluation, ethical and legal considerations, and training consultants. The last chapter contains a good discussion of issues in consultation.

Caplan, G., & Caplan, R. B. (1993). *Mental health consultation and collaboration*. New York: Basic Books.

The authors stress the theory and practice of mental health consultation and discuss the nature and purpose of mental health collaboration.

Gutkin, T. B., & Curtis, M. J. (1982). School-based consultation: Theory and techniques. In C. R. Reynolds & T. B. Gutkin (Eds.), *The handbook of school psychology* (pp. 519–561). New York: Wiley.

This chapter is especially valuable for individuals who work in the schools.

Harmon, L. W. (1989). Counseling. In R. Linn (Ed.), *Educational measurement* (3rd ed., pp. 527–544). New York: Macmillan.

The chapter discusses and illustrates some measurement applications to counseling and issues related to such applications.

Lyman, H. B. (1989). *Test scores and what they mean* (5th ed.). Upper Saddle River, NJ: Prentice Hall.

The text presents information about the interpretation of test scores.

Miller, M. J. (1985). Counseling region 99 clients. *Journal of Employment Counseling, 22*, 70–76.

Miller offers a strategy for clients who possess a flat profile and are positioned in region 99 in the "World of Work Map."

Shore, M. F., Brice, P. J., & Love, B. G. (1992). *When your child needs testing: What parents, teachers, and other helpers need to know about psychological testing*. New York: Crossroad.

The authors consider these questions: why psychological testing, how do I begin, what should the child be told, what about the results, what if I disagree, and what about confidentiality?

Written Test Reports

OVERVIEW

Many times a counselor is required to complete a written report of test results. The type of report depends in part on the purpose of the testing, in part on who will receive the test report. The information age has been affected by widespread use of the computer. Many tests now have computer-generated test reports and software packages available to assist professionals in writing test reports.

OBJECTIVES

After studying this chapter, the reader should be able to

✔ List and discuss ways to format and write test reports for various groups

✔ Identify the proper language and writing style to be used in reports

✔ Discuss the use of computer-generated reports

✔ Locate and evaluate computer-generated reports

PURPOSES OF WRITTEN REPORTS

Counselors do not always agree about what written reports should do. According to Ownby (1997), most authors agree that the report should serve at least four purposes—describe the client who is being assessed and the client's problem, provide a record of the evaluation results for future use, serve as a means of communication to persons wanting or needing the results, and recommend an appropriate course of action. Ownby also recommends that counselors consider the context of the report while writing it as well as the referring agent, the client's environment, and the broader context in which interventions are to be made.

CONTENT OF A REPORT

The content of a report depends on the recipients and the purposes of the report (Goldman, 1971; Shore, Brice, & Love, 1992). The information should be communicated in a way that is understandable, usable, adequate, and economical. Normally a test report includes eight components:

1. *Demographic information*—name and address of examinee, date of birth/chronological age, date of examination, race, sex, grade/school, parents or guardians, examiner
2. *Reason for referral and relevant background information*—problem indicated by client; person(s) referring client; relevant educational, social, medical information; family information and history; previous testing results; other personal information
3. *Behavioral observations of the client*—during testing, in nontesting situations, in classroom or work settings
4. *Test results*—tests given; total, scale, and subscale scores; range and spread of scores; basal and ceiling age levels; test items passed or failed
5. *Diagnostic impressions*—strengths and weaknesses affecting performance, diagnostic interpretations
6. *Recommendations*—specific answers to referral questions, predictions, cautions, recommendations
7. *Summary*—brief integrated statement of test findings
8. *Signature*—of the test administrator/report writer

The cases of John and Allen illustrate written reports.

CASE OF JOHN

Student: John
Race/sex: White/male
Chronological age: 7.8
School: Middletown
Dates of evaluation: 10/8/99, 10/15/99, 12/3/99
Date of report: 12/3/99

Reason for Referral

John was referred for psychoeducational evaluation because of poor progress in class.

Background Information

John has a history of poor academic achievement. Last year he was frequently absent from school but now attends regularly. The Department of Health and Rehabilitative Services has been involved with the family.

John is having great difficulty doing the work required of him. He does not appear to understand what he is asked to do. Often his response has nothing to do with the question. He wants to please and will fill his paper with attempts to respond. His writing gives evidence of a tendency to reverse and transpose letters and numbers. He does succeed better in math than in reading. He has a concept of numbers and can do simple addition and subtraction.

Behavioral Observations

John is a friendly boy. He was shy at first but quickly warmed up. His effort and cooperation were good. John seemed to have great difficulty understanding what was said to him. He tends to agree with any suggestion without weighing its merits. John had problems naming common objects. He had difficulty expressing himself. Often John covered his mouth with his hands or looked down while he spoke as if to give people a reason not to understand him.

During the evaluation, John's affect was somewhat flat. He showed hardly any emotion. Both weeks that John was seen, he had bruises around his face and could not adequately explain their presence.

In class, John was quiet and kept to himself. He tried to work diligently. The teacher overlooked occasions when John copied from other children. He seems to enjoy praise and peer recognition.

Tests Administered

Goodenough Draw-a-Person Test
Peabody Picture Vocabulary Test
Test of Nonverbal Intelligence
Wechsler Intelligence Scale for Children–
    III (WISC)
Woodcock-Johnson Test of Achievement

Analysis of Test Results

John's scores on the WISC placed him in the borderline range of intellectual ability. A significant discrepancy exists between his verbal and performance scores in favor of the latter. Thus, it can be hypothesized that he performs better with concrete stimuli rather than on totally verbal tasks.

This possibility was evaluated by administering the Test of Nonverbal Intelligence and the Peabody Picture Vocabulary Test. These tests also suggest that John has a verbal language deficit and can function better nonverbally. Moreover, the pattern of John's subtests suggests that lack of experience and emotional factors may be depressing his performance. Present test scores should be considered as indicators of current functioning and not as long-range predictors of future progress.

Academically, John is functioning as well as can be expected. He has a very significant deficit in reading achievement, and his fund of general knowledge is weak. John cannot yet recognize all the letters of the alphabet or consistently spell his name correctly.

Summary

John is functioning in the borderline range of intelligence. Indications are that his performance may be depressed. He seems to be demonstrating a severe language processing deficit. He has great difficulty with reading and oral information. He is capable of doing some simple math, however.

Recommendations

Based on all available data, an appropriate exceptional student education placement should be discussed.

CASE OF ALLEN

Student: Allen
Race/sex: White/male
Date of birth: 8/3/93
Chronological age: 5.7
School: #33
Grade: Kindergarten
Date: 3/27/99

Tests Used

Behavioral observation
California Test of Personality (CTP)
Developmental Test of Visual–Motor
    Integration (VMI)
Peabody Picture Vocabulary Test–Revised
Sentence Completion Form for Children
Wechsler Preschool and Primary Scale
    of Intelligence–Revised (WPPSI)
Woodcock-Johnson Memory Scale

Reason for Referral

Allen was evaluated at the request of the child study team in consideration of severe behavioral difficulties experienced within the classroom. An estimate of his current intellectual functioning was also needed.

Background Information

Allen currently resides with his biological mother. No other children live in the home. According to information in the child study team packet, Allen has a short attention span, often seeks attention at inappropriate times, is often disruptive and physically aggressive toward peers, and generally experiences behavioral difficulties within the classroom. He refuses to come into the school, runs off, and talks back. He shows little self-control and is argumentative and aggressive. He recently transferred from another school within the district.

Burks's Behavior Rating Scale was completed prior to this evaluation. Of the 19 subscales, 6 were found in the very significant range—poor impulse control, excessive suffering, poor anger control, excessive sense of persecution, excessive resistance, and poor social conformity. There were six other areas in the significant range—poor ego strength, poor coordination, poor intellectuality, poor attention, poor sense of identity, and excessive aggressiveness. A number of incident reports and behavioral observations are included in the child study team's packet. Allen often has temper tantrums, shows a great deal of disrespect (even to the principal of the school), and has not responded well to any interventions that have occurred thus far. He is quite oppositional and defiant and refuses to comply with school rules.

Hearing and vision screening were passed prior to this evaluation.

Behavioral Observations

Allen was observed prior to the evaluation. He entered the cafeteria and was instructed to sit down in his regular seat. He immediately refused to sit there and wanted to sit somewhere else. He said that other students could sit at other tables and was quite verbally oppositional to his teacher. He also stuck out his tongue at the teacher and growled. A number of verbal interventions occurred in which the supervising teacher attempted to modify Allen's inappropriate behavior. In each case Allen responded either verbally or nonverbally in an oppositional manner. He did comply with a number of minor requests. As a rule, his behavior was attention seeking, oppositional, and defiant. At the end of the observation Allen began to jab a straw at another student. When instructed to stop, he refused to give the straw to a teacher, crawled under the table, and refused to comply with the teacher's request. At that time he apparently became quite upset but calmed down after some teacher interaction.

During the evaluation, Allen repeated many of these behaviors. When brought to the testing room, he immediately became quite upset and lay on the floor crying. He cried for approximately 5 minutes, refused to be tested, crawled to the door, and began kicking the door. He began to call names and yell. This behavior was not reinforced, and he calmed down about 5 minutes later. He appeared to respond well to lack of reinforcement for negative behavior. Stickers and gum were used as reinforcers for test performance.

Even with reinforcers, Allen had a very short attention span and tended to give up easily. He was quite distractible and often wanted to perform tasks other than the ones at hand. He required a good deal of verbal reinforcement and praise to maintain a productive work level. He was quite easily frustrated, particularly with nonverbal reasoning tasks.

Test Results

Intelligence testing on the WPPSI revealed a full scale IQ of 102, which estimates cognitive functioning in the average range. He earned a significantly higher performance IQ (111) than verbal IQ (94). This significant difference may be due to a variety of factors. Within the current evaluation, Allen tended to give up easily on verbal items and seemed to enjoy the nonacademic play characteristics of the nonverbal, manipulative items. Considering the short attention span and ease of distractibility noted earlier, Allen does demonstrate that he can work effectively when the stimulus materials are interesting and the tasks are short.

A wide degree of scatter was noted within Allen's profile; his individual subtest scores vary from the low average to superior ranges. He demonstrated his best abilities on tasks reflecting perceptual organization and planning and visual-motor control. However, Allen does have difficulty with tasks requiring attention and concentration, which are related to academics. In addition, the overall pattern of scores reflected a significant degree of emotionality, as did the oppositional, defiant, and impulsive behavior exhibited during testing. Individual differences should be interpreted with caution because of these behavioral manifestations.

The Peabody was administered in order to assess receptive vocabulary. Allen obtained a standard score of 108, which represents an average performance for his chronological age. His skills in this language area represent an approximate age equivalent of 6.2 years.

The VMI presents tasks of copying geometric forms. On this test of visual-motor skills, Allen demonstrated skills at the 71st percentile, representing above-average skills for his chronological age. Consequently, abilities in this area represent a relative strength.

The Woodcock-Johnson Memory Scale assessed short-term memory through auditory processing of verbally presented sentences and digits (repeated backwards). Allen attained a standard score of 92, representing an average performance.

Personality dynamics were assessed through the CTP, Sentence Completion Form, and behavioral observations. Allen reflected significant emotionality throughout the evaluation. He is a young man with a quite unsatisfactory adjustment to the school environment. He recognized that he has significant difficulty with peer interactions, primarily because of a lack of social skills and a good deal of egocentrism. He does not believe that he experiences warmth and nurturance from his environment. At one level Allen desires to reach out to the environment in an affectionate manner. However, this desire is blocked by lack of skills and a tendency to act out his feelings. These dynamics were quite apparent throughout the testing situation. Allen was initially quite hostile and aggressive. When he was not rejected because of his behavior, he appeared to be sincerely interested in pleasing the examiner. Allen also related that he likes his classroom teacher a great deal, although he has continual difficulty within and outside the classroom. The difficulty in forming functional relationships may be due to fears or guilt, although these aspects need exploration within the therapeutic milieu. In any event, emotional indicators were reflected, representing a significant degree of severity.

Diagnostic Impressions

Allen appears to be functioning in the average range of cognitive skills. He does demonstrate a better nonverbal ability (in the high average range) than verbal ability (in the average range). He does have a wide degree of scatter, which may reflect attentional difficulties as well as oppositional behavior toward the tasks presented. Consequently, the results of this intellectual evaluation should be interpreted with caution. An analysis of Allen's learning abilities reveals adequately developed receptive vocabulary, short-term memory, and visual-motor skills. No difficulties were noted in any of these areas.

Emotionality is the primary concern with Allen. Throughout observations and actual testing, he demonstrated aggressive, oppositional, and defiant behavior. He seems to have a great desire for acceptance and nurturance, but he lacks skills and impulse controls necessary to sustain relationships other than punitive ones. These dynamics may be due to a variety of factors in the clinical history and may be best explored within a therapeutic setting. In terms of behavioral management, Allen responded quite well to the nonreinforcement of defiant and angry behavior as well as positive reinforcement of appropriate on-task behavior.

Allen would benefit from spending time in a highly structured classroom environment, directing attention to his emotional difficulties. Attention should also be given to the acquisition of basic skills including those in the social/interactional as well as the academic areas. Allen and his parents are currently involved in family therapy at a local clinic. This should certainly continue, and Allen would probably benefit from a long-term relationship in a therapeutic milieu. Temper tantrums as well as oppositional and defiant behavior should not be reinforced, within practical limitations. Appropriate behavior as well as on-task and successful academic attempts should be reinforced. Through interventions, Allen may begin to achieve at a rate that is more commensurate with his overall cognitive abilities.

Relative Strengths

1. Planning ability, perceptual organization, visual-motor control (WPPSI)
2. Perceptual ability, visual-motor organization (WPPSI)
3. Memory, attention, and finger and manual dexterity (WPPSI)
4. General range in knowledge and information (WPPSI)
5. Visual-motor skills (VMI)

Process Deficits

None

Relative Weaknesses

1. Numerical reasoning ability (WPPSI)
2. Verbal social knowledge and practical judgment (WPPSI)

Emotional Indicators

1. Distractibility, poor attention, oppositional and defiant behavior (observations during testing)
2. Oppositional and defiant behavior, rebelliousness (behavioral observations outside the testing situation)
3. Poor personal, social, and overall adjustment (CTP)
4. Poor peer relationships, denial (sentence completion)
5. Subtest scatter, verbal/performance discrepancy (WPPSI)
6. Poor impulse control, excessive suffering, poor anger control, excessive sense of persecution, excessive resistance, and poor social conformity (Burks's)

FACTORS AFFECTING THE TEST REPORT

Certain factors should be kept in mind when writing a test report. The first consideration might be the focus of the report. Will it be a test-oriented focus, concentrating on the objective test results, the items, the scales, and the technical aspects of the examinee's performance? Or will the report focus on the examinee and her characteristics? The decision depends partially on the purpose of the testing and on addressing the referral questions.

The examiner must then decide what material should be included and excluded. Quite often a tremendous amount of information is available. The examiner should have a good understanding of the self-concept, attitudes, interests, motivations, and family background of the examinee and should cite the supporting evidence of diagnostic impressions, attempting to depict the client's individuality and uniqueness. Some judgments are difficult because they are necessarily more subjective. With consistent evidence from a number of sources, the examiner can be more sure of interpretations and conclusions.

Sattler (1992) emphasizes that everything observed from the initial encounter to the end of the contact with the client constitutes data for analysis. The examination is to be viewed not merely as a question-and-answer session but as an opportunity for interaction between the client and the examiner, which is as much a part of the examination as are the test questions and the examinee's responses.

Katz (1991) identifies six common problems in psychological report writing:

1. *Overuse of jargon*—Jargon may relate to a certain theory or to psychological testing. Many individuals who are not versed in the particular theory or the technical language will have trouble understanding what is being said. Furthermore, unless operational definitions are included, certain words and terms cause problems because individuals have different concepts of the same term.
2. *Focus on test results rather than the individual*—In this situation test findings are extensively reported but are not related to the behavior of the individual and very few practical suggestions or inferences are reported.
3. *Downplay of test results*—Sometimes a report departs too far from the test findings. It may include more social history of the individual but little evidence from the test results, and the inferences may be based on observations and background information rather than on test information.
4. *Poor organization of the report*—Sometimes each test or subtest is reported, but the test results are not integrated as a whole. At other times historical information is interspersed with the test results, making it hard to separate the components.
5. *Failure of the examiner to take a position*—Examiners often are reluctant to make specific diagnoses or treatment recommendations even when the data are there to support them.
6. *Poor written communication skills*—Sometimes a report is poorly written and shows deficiencies in spelling, grammar, syntax, and vocabulary usage.

Tallent (1994) identifies five major categories of problems that are somewhat similar to those just listed: content, interpretation, examiner attitude and orientation, problems of communication, and science and the profession.

WRITING THE REPORT

The goal is to communicate clearly the results of the testing. The examiner should include the purposes of the testing, specific problems or decisions that gave rise to the testing, behavioral descriptions, and sources of information. The examiner should not include hearsay, unverified opinions, generalized statements, or potentially harmful or damaging information.

Tallent (1958) points out that the style of the report can interfere with effective communication, and he identifies three styles. In the Barnum style the report writer includes many universalities and ambiguities and presents a great deal of hoopla with little substance. In the Aunt Fanny style the writer includes information that is true about all test takers, including their Aunt Fanny. The Madison Avenue style contains information to sell an idea or conclusion and is meant to placate someone or to express possible hostility.

Katz (1991) lists eight general guidelines for good report writing:

1. Get to it. It is better to write your report the day of testing or at least within 24 hours of seeing the client. Otherwise, observations and impressions can be forgotten.
2. Remember the basics. Certain basic information must be included, such as date, identifying biographical data, tests administered, behavioral observations, categories of test results, diagnostic prescriptions, recommendations, and a summary.
3. Have in mind the proper organization for the desired report.
4. Keep in mind how long the report should be; aim for clarity and accuracy but keep brevity in mind. Many people might ignore or slight a 10-page report but will read a 2-page report completely and carefully.
5. Say what needs to be said. Examiners should report their findings clearly and directly, using straightforward statements and including specific recommendations. If findings are tentative and nonconclusive, the report should so state.
6. Try to make the report readable and interesting. Carefully choose words and sentences.
7. Ask for feedback. Ask those who read and use the report to give their reaction to it. Feedback helps to improve areas of weakness and reveals areas of strength.
8. Know who is going to read or receive the report. Ethical principles call for the report to be in a language that can be understood by the parties using the report. Consumers of test reports possess a wide variety of skills, interests, and knowledge of educational and psychological tests. (pp. 143–149)

Organizing the Report

One of the crucial issues in psychological test report writing is organization. Klopfer (1960) identifies different patterns of organization:

1. *Theory-oriented report*—The examiner uses a certain personality or psychometric theory as the frame of reference.
2. *Test-oriented report*—The examiner focuses primarily on test information, explaining it in detail and telling how interpretations were derived.
3. *Problem-oriented report*—The examiner focuses on the particular question asked in referral.
4. *Person-centered report*—The examiner focuses on the examinee rather than the sources of information.
5. *Ego-psychological report*—The examiner focuses on the assets and strengths of the individual as he copes with life demands.

Technical Aspects

The writer needs to be familiar with the *Publication Manual of the American Psychological Association-Fourth Edition* (APA, 1994). It describes the mechanical aspects of writing style in sections on punctuation, spelling, capitalization, italics, abbreviations, footnotes, and references. For example, the APA guide permits the use of abbreviations that appear as word entries in *Webster's New Collegiate Dictionary*, such as IQ. Other abbreviations, even if used frequently by journal authors, should always be explained fully when first used. Care should be used even then. For example, SAT is used to designate both the Stanford Achievement Test and the Scholastic

Aptitude Test of the College Entrance Examination Board. Even psychologists and counselors may get somewhat confused by isolated or listed abbreviations.

Language

The writer should be specific and concrete rather than abstract and ambiguous. Abstract ideas quite often present problems to readers, who may not be quite sure of meaning. Ambiguous sentences are often misinterpreted because they imply different meanings to different individuals. The sentence "Mary lacks mechanical aptitude" leaves the reader to interpret "lacks" and "mechanical aptitude." It would be better to say "Mary is unable to use the screwdriver or put washers on the bolts." Similarly, in the sentence "John is an extrovert," who is to define an extrovert? It would be better to say, "John likes to be with people and be the center of attention. He talks and laughs loudly and makes sure he introduces himself to everyone in the room."

The examiner should present factual test data directly and accurately, basing interpretations and recommendations on reliable and valid data. It is quite easy to overgeneralize from limited test information. For example, consider the statement "The examinee is tall for his age and may feel a deficit in his affiliation need." The subject may have a low score on the affiliation scale of the Edwards Personal Preference Schedule, but it is not necessarily a result of his being tall for his age.

Informational statements should also be precise. The sentence "Her IQ was approximately 125 on the WISC-III" leaves the reader unsure. The score is a specific number and can be kept precise by citing the standard error of measurement—for example, an IQ of 125 (± 5).

Revising and Editing the Report

The first draft of the report should be checked for errors and clarity. The following questions address potential problem areas:

1. Do the sentences convey the intended information?
2. Is information presented in an objective manner?
3. Are statements clear, simple, and precise?
4. Are recommendations based upon reliable and sufficient data?
5. Are data factual?
6. Were client records and files reviewed?
7. Are the test results a valid and reliable indicator of client behavior and performance?
8. Are inferences and generalizations based on factual supporting data?
9. Have factors such as previous test results; anecdotal records; behavioral observations; parent, spouse, teacher, or peer reports and observations; medical history; grades; work history; and educational attainment been considered in the synthesis, analysis, and evaluation of current test information?
10. Is the case overstated? Are irrelevant statements eliminated?
11. Is the report organized into logical parts with smooth transitions from part to part, paragraph to paragraph?

12. Are technical details, technical vocabulary, and fancy words minimized? Are terms defined and translated into a commonsense vocabulary?
13. Are sources of information documented?

Figure 23.1 presents a checklist for evaluating a test report.

Read the case of Theodore and decide if it meets the standards of the checklist in Figure 23.1.

Demographic information

_____ Name of examinee
_____ Address of examinee
_____ Chronological age
_____ Date of birth
_____ Gender
_____ Race
_____ Information about parent or guardian
_____ Highest grade of education completed
_____ School(s) attended
_____ Date of testing
_____ Name of examiner
_____ Occupation of parents or guardian
_____ Occupation of examinee if available

Reason for referral

_____ Self-referral
_____ Referral by others (teacher, parents, spouse, etc.)
_____ Follow-up session

Background information

_____ Relevant educational information
_____ Relevant social information
_____ Relevant medical information
_____ Relevant personal information
_____ Relevant family information

Behavioral observations

_____ Observation of examinee before testing
_____ Observations during testing
_____ Observations after testing
_____ Observations in nontesting situations
_____ Observations during feedback or report session

Tests used

_____ Tests given described
_____ Scales and subscales reported
_____ Standard error of measurement given for scores
_____ Basal age and ceiling
_____ Skills mastered
_____ Norms used mentioned, if appropriate
_____ Range of scores reported
_____ Description of any deviations in administration and scoring
_____ Appropriate norms used
_____ Appropriate, valid, and reliable tests used

Diagnostic impressions

_____ Strengths affecting performance
_____ Weaknesses affecting performance
_____ Diagnostic impressions

Recommendations

_____ Specific answers to referral problem(s)
_____ Predictions based on scores
_____ Cautions based on scores
_____ Practical and useful recommendations made

Writing mechanics and style

_____ Well-organized report
_____ Proper grammar
_____ Correct mechanics
_____ Easy to read
_____ Jargon avoided
_____ Technical vocabulary minimized
_____ Summary provided
_____ Report presented objectively

Figure 23.1
Checklist for evaluating a test report

CASE OF THEODORE

Theodore was referred for psychological evaluation in an effort to assess his current level of functioning.

Context

Theodore is living with his aunt. She was awarded custody because Theodore's mother is a crack cocaine user. He is the middle of three children. He has a younger and an older sister. He attends a local Head Start school. He is 5 years old. At school he is a behavioral problem, fighting, cursing, and throwing temper tantrums when he does not get his own way. He cries a lot at home and requires constant and energetic supervision at school and at home he requires a great deal of constant and energetic supervision. When he is bad, he is not allowed to watch TV and has to stay in the house. When he is good, he gets lots of hugs and kisses.

He says he likes to draw and tell stories, but he does not have the motor coordination to draw and the verbal skills to tell stories. Theodore can recite his ABCs with only minor pronunciation difficulties and is able to correctly count to 7. During the testing he could not keep still and tipped over the same table eight times the same way during the half hour he was being examined.

Tests Administered

He was administered the Slosson Intelligence Test and the Children's Apperception Test—Animal Figures and the Draw-a-Person Test. The examiner could not obtain a basal age for Theodore on the Slosson. He said he could tell good stories but could not even tell the animals in the CAT plates. He was unable or did not want to draw a person. He became frustrated during the testing but continued to state he could draw and he could tell stories.

Summary

Theodore appears to be very developmentally delayed. He lacks recognition skills and gets frustrated because he is unable to express himself. Theodore's vocabulary is limited and his cognitive development delayed.

Recommendation

The Ritalin prescribed by the psychiatrist seems to be working. Theodore should continue with his early educational activities at Head Start. His aunt should take a course in parenting or join some support group of parents with children similar to Theodore. Raising a special needs child who has communication problems leads to frustration of both Theodore and his aunt.

Diagnostic Impressions

Axis I	314.01 Attention deficit/hyperactivity disorder, combined type
	315.90 Learning disorder, not otherwise specified
Axis II	319.00 Mental retardation, severity unspecified
Axis III	292.89 Toxic effects of cocaine
Axis IV	Psychosocial stressors: severe neglect by biological parents, including prenatally and neonatally
Axis V	GAS.40 Major impairment in testing, communication, school, and home

COMPUTER-GENERATED REPORTS

More tests are offering computer-generated test reports and interpretations. This service saves the examiner time and permits complex analyses. The ability of the computer to summarize results from schools, classes, or other types of groups has been widely accepted and used. However, social scientists are becoming concerned about the ethical issues in the clinical use of interpretation of computerized test results (Zachary & Pope, 1983). Computerized instruments are used in many fields and may not always be consistent with professional guidelines.

Matarazzo (1983) identifies four of the major concerns:

1. Are there real advantages to computerized interpretation of tests?
2. Will these interpretive reports reach the hands of inexperienced or unqualified individuals who will respond to the halo effect of objectivity projected by a computerized report?
3. Will publishers and developers of computerized interpretive programs reveal their decision rules (their classification or assessment standards) for professional review?
4. Will these computer reviews be sufficiently validated?

Advantages of Computerized Interpretation Programs

A number of advantages can be claimed for computerized interpretive programs. Roid (1986) lists five:

1. Accuracy of scoring and retrieval of norms from complex norm tables
2. Time saved by clinicians
3. Ability of the computer to follow complex decision rules in a fraction of a second
4. Ability to show moderating effects on test interpretation (i.e., that certain age or ethnic groups have different ranges or patterns of scores)
5. Ability to complete elaborate profile and statistical analyses

Types of Computer Interpretive Programs

Moreland (1992) has identified two types of commercially available programs besides the scoring only and descriptive types: the clinician-modeled and clinical actuarial. Computerized scoring packages are available for many tests, presenting results on labels or short profile sheets for individuals.

Descriptive scoring gives individuals not only test results but also descriptive phrases, such as "average," "above average," "indicates mastery of." Such programs present certain descriptive words and phrases based upon quantitative criteria. A report, for example, might summarize the results on a given test. The first section might list in descending order the interest clusters measured on the test, with higher scores indicating stronger preferences. The report might use symbols such as 1, 2, or 0 to indicate a positive, negative, or neutral preference.

In the clinician-modeled approach the computer is used to generate an interpretation based upon the interpretive decisions of a renowned clinician or groups of expert clinicians. The information is programmed into the computer. A number of programs are available for the Minnesota Multiphasic Personality Inventory, and Miller (1984) has used this approach with the Louisville Behavior Checklist. Tape recordings of his actual case interpretations were studied, and objective decision rules were extracted from this information.

Computerized actuarial systems have been developed by a number of researchers. McDermott (1980) devised a computer program to identify intelligence, achievement, and adaptive behavior scores that related to quantitative judgments about learning disability status. Barclay (1983) used 25 years of multivariate statistical research on self, peers, and teacher ratings of elementary students to design a computerized interpretive program that provides a narrative, diagnostic, and prescriptive report useful to teachers, school psychologists, and other school personnel. Roid (1986) reports that the most widely used actuarial programs are those developed for use with the Minnesota Multiphasic Personality Inventory–II. The Sixteen Personality Factor Test has reports tailored to be used in vocational counseling as well as marriage counseling. The Strong Interest Inventory is just one more example of a test using this approach.

Computer interpretation can become very sophisticated because of the logic and memory used to study test patterns and verifiable behaviors or characteristics of examinees. Multivariate statistical analysis can be used to discriminate or distinguish among examinees in various criterion groups and assess the probabilities of group membership quickly and accurately. The computer can aid also in integrating information from a number of sources and tests. It has the ability to analyze patterns of data across situations, individuals, periods of time, and events.

Evaluation

Evaluation of the programs is essential and necessary. Professional standards address computerized interpretations of test results. Many problems arise in the interpretation of these programs because of the lack of information from the test publishers and authors. Here are some of the questions that should be asked of qualified professionals:

1. Does the author present documentation on the validity and reliability of the method?
2. Does the author present information for the examiner about the procedures used in the development of the interpretive program?
3. Is the format attractive?
4. Is the presentation clear and precise?
5. Does research compare traditional, clinical, and actuarial interpretation?
6. Is the procedure cost-effective?
7. Are the limitations and problems of this approach discussed by the author?
8. Is the role of the counselor or psychologist spelled out in the manual? What is the role of clinical judgment in using computerized interpretations?

9. Are possible misinterpretations discussed?
10. What are the equipment demands? What size and type of computer can be used?
11. Are backup disks and a hotline available?

SUMMARY

Written test reports are widely used in presenting and interpreting results of testing. The purpose of such a report is to provide a record of the client's performance and to communicate the results, observations, interpretations, and recommendations to a targeted individual or group. The goal of evaluation may vary, but some general guidelines need to be followed in all report writing:

1. Write the results objectively and straightforwardly.
2. Edit the report carefully, correcting spelling, grammar, and punctuation errors and clarifying expressions.
3. Watch how things are said, avoiding jargon, technical language, stereotypical phrases, and ambiguous or abstract terms.
4. Write the report so that it is interesting and readable.
5. Draw appropriate inferences and provide realistic recommendations.

Computer interpretations are becoming more popular, and much software is available. Many promising types of reports are being generated, but problems arise when these computerized interpretative reports are used by inexperienced or unqualified individuals without the proper background knowledge of the tests.

QUESTIONS FOR DISCUSSION

1. What steps and procedures should an examiner follow to get feedback from consumers of test reports? How valuable is this type of feedback?

2. Written reports have been criticized for being too mechanical, rigid, and impersonal. Do you believe this criticism is more justified with computerized test reports than with examiner reports? Compare the advantages and disadvantages of both type of reports.

3. Should students in the helping professions have a required course in technical writing that includes a unit on writing test reports? Why or why not? What steps can test examiners take to improve the quality of their test reports?

4. What, if anything, is wrong with the following statements found in test reports? How would you edit each statement? (a) Amy appeared to be emotionally disturbed. (b) The CAT, CPQ, and CTP were administered to Amy. (c) Amy did not know her colors. (d) Amy did not have good psychomotor coordination. (e) Amy was a pretty good student in her class. (f) Amy gave concrete and fabricated explanations to the questions asked. (g) Amy gave distant, highly personalized,

slang, and neologistic responses on the Word Association Test. (h) Qualitative analysis suggests that anxiety, obsessiveness, and excessive compulsivity may have had the effect of lowering Amy's score on the Wechsler.

5. Should there be a common format for test reports, or should it depend on the purpose of the report and the recipient?

SUGGESTED ACTIVITIES

1. Administer one of the tests discussed in the text and write a report of the results for the test taker.

2. Devise a checklist to evaluate a written test report and use it to critique one of the reports included in the text.

3. Edit the following statements and explain any changes: (a) John's IQ was indicated to be 79. (b) Items that reflect Mary's attitude toward school were not high. (c) Dick's lack of attention and interest may have contributed to his flat profile on the aptitude test. (d) In contrast, Jane's preference for social reinforcement was below average.

4. Write a critical review of the literature on one of the following topics—computerized test reports, reliability and effectiveness of test reports, common errors in written test reports, professional ethics and test reports.

5. Make an annotated bibliography of sources on test report writing.

6. Devise a workshop for teaching people in the helping professions to improve their test report writing skills.

7. Critique several computerized test reports.

8. Read the following case and answer the questions at the end:

Yvonne was evaluated with the following instruments: Differential Aptitude Test, Myers-Briggs Type Indicator, FIRO-B, Strong Interest Inventory, Self-Directed Search, 16PF, COP-System Interest Inventory.

Yvonne scored at the 80th percentile on the verbal section of the DAT, which suggested that her capability to understand ideas expressed in words and her ability to think and reason with words are above average. She scored at the 40th percentile on the numerical section of the instrument. This suggests that her numerical capability is average.

She was an ISFJ (Introverted, Sensing, Feeling, Judging) on the Myers-Briggs and can be characterized as being systematic, painstaking, and thorough. This type of individual is very hardworking and adapts well to facts.

On the FIRO-B her scores suggest that she operates within a select or exclusive group of friends. She may be somewhat uncomfortable in social situations, especially if she is not familiar with the people.

Her interest inventory scores indicate that she appears to have general interests in medical service, social service, writing, communication, sales, politics, and business management.

Her 16PF results indicate that she would like to excel in activities of a journalistic nature, including writer, editor, and reporter.

Yvonne is a middle-aged woman with a college degree in Christian education and minors in speech and English. Her interest in academic areas is very high. Her aptitude scores suggest that she can be successful in advanced college work, especially if she remediates math areas. She seems to be a woman who is selective of the company she keeps.

Specific occupations that may be suitable for Yvonne include broadcast work, print media, writing editor, reporter, media specialist, guidance counselor, social worker, special education teacher, speech pathologist, English teacher, recreation leader, nurse, physician's assistant, emergency medical technician, nursing home administrator, travel agent, salesperson, human resource worker, or school administrator.

a. What problems do you find in this report?

b. What needs to be done to improve it?

c. What additional information about Yvonne would you like to have?

d. For whom do you think the report was written?

ADDITIONAL READINGS

Fisher, C. T. (1985). *Individualized psychological assessment*. Monterey, CA: Brooks/Cole.

Fisher describes the individualized approach in testing and provides sample reports and information on report writing.

Katz, L. (1991). *A practical guide to psychodiagnostic testing* (2nd ed.). Springfield, IL: Thomas.

The guide has an excellent chapter on writing test reports.

Ownby, R. L. (1997). *Psychological reports: A guide to report writing in professional psychology* (3rd ed.). Brandon, VT: CPPC.

Ownby provides guidelines for writing psychological reports and provides several examples.

Tallent, N. (1993). *Psychological report writing* (4th ed.). Upper Saddle River, NJ: Prentice Hall.

The book discusses the purposes and context of the psychological report and covers topics such as pitfalls in reporting, responsibility, effectiveness, the content of psychological reports, and conceptualizing the psychological report.

Zuckerman, E. L. (1995). *The clinician's thesaurus: A guidebook for writing psychological reports and their evaluations* (4th ed.). Brandon, VT: CPPC.

The book helps test administrators identify appropriate questions to elicit information about specific symptomatic behavior in the mental, cognitive, and emotional domains.

Legal and Ethical Concerns and Issues in Testing

OVERVIEW

Codes of ethics provide a framework for responsible test use. There are probably as many codes of ethics as there are professional societies; but to become dynamic helping professionals, individuals must be committed to the ethical standards of their profession and follow them in their practice. A code of ethics expresses the values on which helping professionals build their practice. *Ethical Principles of Psychologists* (APA, 1992) includes six general principles: to maintain high competence in one's work; promote integrity in the science, teaching, and practice of psychology; uphold professional standards of conduct and accept responsibility for one's behavior; afford appropriate respect to the fundamental rights, dignity, and worth of all people; contribute to the welfare of those with whom one interacts professionally; and be aware of one's professional and scientific responsibilities to the community and the society in which one works and lives. These principles are translated into specific ethical standards and principles, which will be the focus of this chapter.

There are also a number of laws on both the state and national levels that affect testing and testing practices. Professionals need to be familiar with the laws as well as with the court decisions that interpret them.

OBJECTIVES

After reading this chapter, the reader should be able to

✔ List and discuss the major codes of professional ethics as they apply to tests and testing practices

✔ Compare and contrast the commonalities and differences among the different codes

✔ Identify the important federal and state legislation that affects tests and testing practices

✔ Discuss the court decisions and their impact on tests and testing practices

✔ Demonstrate knowledge of legal and ethical issues in evaluation and assessment

NBCC CODE OF ETHICS

The National Board of Certified Counselors (NBCC, 1989) identifies in Section C of its code 15 standards dealing with measurement and evaluation. The first deals logically with orientation. The counselor must orient the examinee before and after the administration of assessment instruments. During orientation the counselor must inform the client of the explicit use of the test results.

The counselor is responsible for the appropriate selection of the assessment instruments to be used. She must ensure the validity and reliability of the instrument. Instruments that are biased or otherwise inappropriate will provide invalid information for decision making.

The counselor must be guarded when making statements to the public about specific instruments and techniques. False claims and unwarranted connotations often result from misunderstanding or poor communication.

Counselors must recognize their limitations and only perform techniques or administer assessment instruments for which they have received appropriate training.

Counselors must record when tests are not administered under standard conditions or when irregularities or unusual behavior arise during testing. The behavior might invalidate the results. The code deems unsupervised or inadequately supervised tests as not meeting ethical standards. The exception are tests such as interest inventories, which are often designed to be self-administered and self-scored.

Counselors must maintain test security. Coaching and dissemination of test items and materials can invalidate the test results. Counselors, however, must discuss the conditions that might provide more favorable results, such as telling test takers that they can guess without penalty.

Counselors must understand the technical limitations of an instrument when interpreting the results. They need to schedule periodic review and/or retesting of the client to help prevent stereotyping.

The counselor must be concerned about the welfare of test takers. Who receives the results and how they will be used are important considerations. Interpretations must be made in light of any limitations in the instruments or norming group.

Computer-generated test administration and scoring programs may be used if the counselor is sure that this type of testing will provide the client with accurate results. Developers must check computer-based interpretations for validity before they are marketed.

Counselors using tests or making decisions based on test results need appropriate training and skills in educational and psychological measurement, validation criteria, test research, and guidelines for test development and use.

If the tests report insufficient technical data, counselors must explicitly state to examinees the specific purposes for the use of such instruments and why they are being used.

Counselors need to be cautious when evaluating or interpreting the performances of minority group members or other individuals not represented in the standardized sample. Counselors need to recognize that test results only give a picture of the test taker at one moment in time and may become obsolete.

AMERICAN PSYCHOLOGICAL ASSOCIATION STANDARDS

Ethical Principles of Psychologists (APA, 1992) lists 10 standards for evaluation, diagnosis, and intervention. The first is that psychologists should only perform evaluations, diagnostic services, or interventions within the context of a defined professional relationship and that their assessments, recommendations, and reports are based on information and techniques (such as interviewing test takers) sufficient to substantiate their findings.

The psychologist must have competence in the tests and assessment techniques used and select appropriate instruments and techniques for assessment. The psychologist is to refrain from misusing techniques, results, and interventions and should prevent others from misusing the information these test results provide.

If psychologists are involved in test development, they are responsible for conducting research with tests and other assessment techniques using scientific procedures and current professional knowledge for test design, standardization, validation, reduction of bias, and recommendations for use.

Psychologists should recognize the limitations to the certainty with which they diagnose or make judgments or predictions about individuals. They need to consider that in some situations they might be required to adjust administration or interpretation because of factors such as the age, gender, national origin, religion, sexual orientation, disability, language, or socioeconomic status of the individual.

Psychologists must consider the various characteristics of the individual being assessed that might affect their judgments or reduce the accuracy of their interpretation.

They also have a responsibility of not promoting the use of psychological assessment techniques by unqualified examiners.

The freshness of results is a factor. Psychologists do not base their assessment, intervention decisions, or recommendations on outdated test results and measures that are not useful for the current purpose.

Individuals offering assessment or scoring services to other professionals should make sure their procedures are appropriate, valid, and reliable.

Results need to be explained in a language that can be understood by the individual who is being assessed. Appropriate explanations of results must be given by the psychologists.

The last standard holds the psychologist responsible for making reasonable efforts to maintain the integrity and security of tests and other assessment techniques consistent with the law, contractual obligations, and the code of ethics.

ACA CODE OF ETHICS

The American Counseling Association (ACA, 1993) likewise has a code of ethics that has a specific section on measurement and evaluation. The preamble reminds counselors that the primary purpose of educational and psychological testing is to provide descriptive measures that are objective and interpretable in either comparative or absolute terms. Counselors must recognize that there are a wide variety of assessment procedures and that test results provide only one of many sources of information for counseling decisions. The standards are similar to those of the APA and NBCC. Standards deal with orientation; test selection; dissemination of results to the public; competence in administration, scoring, and interpretation; following standardized procedures in test administration; problems of prior coaching; the purpose of testing and the explicit prior understanding of the client; cautious evaluation and interpretation of the performance of minority group members or others not represented in the norming group; and unauthorized reproduction or modifications of tests without the permission of the author and publisher. Counselors are reminded that they need to be cautious when interpreting the results of a research instrument without sufficient data on its validity, reliability, and interpretability.

CODES OF PROFESSIONAL RESPONSIBILITY

A number of professional responsibility codes have been developed by organizations or consortia concerned with measurement and assessment issues. The National Council of Measurement in Education (NCME, 1995) has published Draft 3 of its *Code of Professional Responsibility in Educational Measurement* (CPR). An ad hoc committee of the council developed the code to promote professionally responsible practices in educational assessment.

The CPR provides a framework of eight major areas of assessment standards that need to be addressed, including responsibilities of those who

1. Select assessment products and services
2. Market and sell assessment products and services
3. Educate others about assessment
4. Develop assessment products and services
5. Administer assessments
6. Score assessments
7. Interpret, use, and communicate assessment results
8. Evaluate programs and conduct research on assessments

Each section includes more specific standards. In section 7, for example, those who interpret, use, and communicate assessment results are to provide all needed information about the assessment, its purposes, and its uses for the proper interpretation of the results; provide an understandable discussion of all reported scores, including proper interpretations; promote the use of multiple sources of information about persons or programs in making educational decisions; communicate the adequacy and appropriateness of any norms or standards being used in the interpretation of assessment results; discourage unsubstantiated claims, inappropriate interpretations, or otherwise false and misleading statements about assessment results and any likely misinterpretations; and protect the privacy rights of individuals and institutions.

NCME and the American Association of School Administrators, the National Association of Elementary School Principals, and the National Association of Secondary School Principals (1994) have developed a set of standards for administrator training programs that use ethical standards as one criterion for determining competency. Administrators are to demonstrate a working knowledge of the *Competency Standards in Student Assessment*. One key element is the ability to recognize unethical, illegal, and otherwise inappropriate assessment methods and uses of assessment information. As with other standards, the administrator should understand and be able to apply the basic concepts of assessment and measurement theory; understand the purposes of different kinds of assessment (i.e., achievement, ability, and diagnostic); understand measurement terminology and be able to express that terminology in nontechnical terms; recognize appropriate and inappropriate uses of assessment techniques or results and understand and follow ethical guidelines for assessment; know the mechanics of constructing various types of assessment that are both appropriate and useful; interpret and use assessment information appropriately; know how interpretations of assessments may be moderated by students' socioeconomic, cultural, linguistic, and other background factors; be able to evaluate an assessment strategy or program; and finally be able to use computer-based assessment tools that collect input, mediating, and outcome variables that are related to student learning, instruction, and performance.

Throughout this text, references have been made to some of the other major sources of professional codes for test users. A list of these codes follows:

American Association for Counseling and Development (now American Counseling Association) and Association for Measurement and Evaluation in Counseling and Development (now Association for Assessment in Counseling). (1989). *Responsibilities of users of standardized tests*. Alexandria, VA: Author.

American Educational Research Association. (1992, October). Ethical standards of the American Educational Research Association. *Educational Researcher, 21*(7).

American Educational Research Association, American Psychological Association, and National Council on Measurement in Education. (1995). *Standards for educational and psychological tests*. Washington, DC: Author.

Joint Committee on Testing Practices. (1988). *Code of fair testing practices in education*. Washington, DC: Author.

National Association of College Admission Counselors. (1988). *Statement of principles of good practice*. Alexandria, VA: Author.

National Council on Measurement in Education. (1995). *Code of professional responsibilities in educational measurement*. Washington, DC: APA.

RESPONSIBLE TEST USE

In each of the following situations, read the scenario and decide what ethical standards are in question:

1. The Browns decide to start a computerized dating service and mail clients the NEO Personality Inventory. They score the tests and match clients on the basis of their personality types, using the premise that opposites attract when they match the profiles. The clients are sent a profile sheet of their test results.

2. Jan came to the United States last year from Poland and has been staying with his relatives in New York. He was hit by a taxi when he was crossing a street and received a concussion and other possible head injuries. His lawyer wanted a psychological evaluation. Although Jan is not fluent in English, the examiner administered the Lauria-Nebraska Neuropsychological Battery.

3. Robin learns that the CDC Company uses the Sixteen Personality Factor Questionnaire for screening customer representatives and decides to get a copy of the test and manual to study before applying for the position. When she calls the company, she finds out that she has to complete a form to be registered with the company and get the material. She knows that she does not have the qualifications for the job, so she asks one of her professors to order the materials for her. The professor does so. Robin studies the test and scoring keys and decides how she will answer the test questions to make herself look like the right type of person for the job.

4. A psychology professor has convinced the student services committee to give all first-year students the Minnesota Multiphasic Personality Inventory–2. During orientation week, all new students were administered the test but not told its purpose, only that they would be required to take a wide variety of types of tests including achievement, aptitude, interest, and personality. The professor had some student assistants score the tests. He found that he had no time to review the results, so he simply had the test information filed in students' cumulative folders.

LEGAL ASPECTS

Counselors not only need to keep up to date on current legislation that affects their practice; they also must stay current with the decisions made in the courts. A number of major pieces of legislation have had implications for testing practices and procedures. Legal rights come from not only the Constitution of the United States, state constitutions, and federal and state laws but also from interpretations by the courts. This section briefly discusses some of the major pieces of federal legislation, followed by some important court decisions brought by individuals or groups who believed they had been harmed by testing practices.

Family Educational Rights and Privacy Act of 1974 (Buckley Amendment)

The Family Educational Rights and Privacy Act of 1974 protects parents' right to examine their children's academic records and stipulate the terms under which others may have access to them. If there is test information in the records, parents have a right to see these scores as well.

Public Law 94-142

Public Law 94-142 was passed by Congress and signed into law on November 25, 1975. The legislation was an effort to reduce the disparities in educational opportunities between exceptional children and nonexceptional children. The law directs educators to develop extensive identification procedures, provide special education in the least restrictive environment, ensure nondiscriminatory testing and evaluation, and form individualized programs for each child with disabilities. The law was passed to ensure that all exceptional children have access to an appropriate education and related services to meet their unique needs, to ensure protection of their rights, and to assist schools in providing that education.

The law requires that parents give their consent before a child is tested. Parents must be fully informed of all information relevant to the activity for which consent is sought in their native language or other mode of communication. Parents must be fully informed about a particular test to be given and agree in writing to the procedure. Parents have the right to inspect the test protocols. Parents are entitled to inspect and review the educational records of their child related to identification, evaluation, and placement.

Tests and other evaluation materials must be in the child's native language or other mode of communication unless it is clearly not feasible to do so. The tests must have been validated for the specific purpose for which they are to be used. Tests have to be administered by trained personnel in conformance with instructions provided by test authors and publishers. Tests must be chosen and administered to ensure that they will accurately reflect a child's aptitude and achievement level. The philosophy and practice call for multiple criteria in determining appropriate placement. Evaluation must be done by a multidisciplinary team including at least one teacher or other specialist with knowledge of the area of disability. The child is assessed in all areas related to the suspected disability.

Public Law 98-524

Public Law 98-524, the Carl D. Perkins Vocational and Technical Act, was passed by Congress and signed into law on October 19, 1984. It was intended to serve individuals who are inadequately served under vocational education programs—especially individuals who are disadvantaged or handicapped, men and women entering non-traditional occupations, adults in need of training and retraining, single parents or homemakers, individuals with limited English proficiency, and individuals incarcerated in correctional institutions. The law extends the provisions of the Vocational Education Act of 1963 by mandating vocational assessment, counseling, support, and transitional services for students identified as handicapped and disadvantaged. "Disadvantaged" was limited to economic and academic rather than cultural.

Public Law 99-457

Public Law 99-457 is an amendment to Public Law 94-142 that extends the right to a free and appropriate education to all children aged 3 and above. The law allows states to develop early intervention services for children with developmental delays. Each family involved in the program must have an Individualized Family Service Plan (IFSP).

Public Law 101-476

Public Law 101-476, the Education of the Handicapped Act Amendments of 1990, was signed into law on October 30, 1990. It was later renamed the Individuals with Disabilities Education Act (IDEA). The act focuses on helping youth with disabilities in the transition from school to vocational rehabilitation, employment, postsecondary education, work, or adult services. Parents have access to all relevant records concerning the identification, evaluation, and educational placement of the child. Parents also have the opportunity to obtain their own independent educational evaluation of the child.

Public Law 101-336

Public Law 101-336, the Americans with Disabilities Act (ADA), was passed by Congress and signed into law on July 26, 1990. The law broadly expands the civil rights laws that apply to women and minorities to more than 43 million Americans who have some form of disability. The law has certain provisions related to testing. Under the reasonable accommodation section, it states:

> A private entity offering an examination is responsible for selecting and administering the examination in a place and manner that ensures that the examination accurately reflects an individual's aptitude and achievement level, or other factors the examination purports to measure, rather than reflecting an individual's impaired sensory, manual, or speaking skills, except where those skills are factors that the examination purports to measure.

The test must assess an essential requirement of the job. It would be invalid if the particular disability would adversely affect test performance on an employment test. Accommodating individuals with disabilities on tests is not necessarily a simple process. Fischer (1994) points out that to comply with ADA, individually modified forms of the standard instrument must be prepared to accommodate a disabled examinee. Although ADA requires reasonable accommodation, the code of ethics and standards for testing requires a much higher standard if the resulting test scores are to be meaningful (p. 23).

EMPLOYMENT LAWS

Title VII of the Civil Rights Act of 1964 as amended in 1972, 1978, and 1991 outlaws discrimination in employment based on race, color, religion, gender, pregnancy, or national origin. The Age Discrimination in Employment Act of 1967 outlaws discrimination against those who are age 40 and above. The Equal Pay Act of 1967 outlaws discrimination in pay based on the gender of the worker, and the Vietnam Era Veterans Readjustment Act of 1974 outlaws discrimination against Vietnam-era veterans.

The Tower amendment to the Equal Employment Act (1966) provides that an employer may give and act upon the results of

> any professionally developed ability test provided that such test is not designed, intended, or used to discriminate because of race. Professionally developed ability test is defined to mean a test which fairly measures the knowledge or skills required by the particular job or class of jobs which the applicant seeks or which fairly affords the employer a chance to measure the applicant's ability to perform a particular job or class of jobs. (Equal Employment Opportunity Commission, 1976)

In 1970 the EEOC redefined discrimination in terms of the effects of selection procedures resulting in adverse impact. Any paper-and-pencil or performance measure including all formal, scored, quantified, or standardized techniques used as a basis for any employment decision that adversely affects hiring, promotion, transfer, or any other employment or membership opportunity of classes protected by Title VII constitutes discrimination unless the test has been validated and evidences a high degree of utility and the person giving or acting on the results can demonstrate that alternative suitable hiring, transfer, or promotion procedures are unavailable.

The Civil Rights Act of 1991 prohibits score adjustment or differential test cutoffs by race. Congress saw score adjustment as violating the principle of fairness.

COURT DECISIONS ON EDUCATIONAL TESTING

Following are a few of the major court decisions on the use of testing in education:

Larry P. v. Riles (1974, 1979, 1984) involved as plaintiffs black elementary school students from the San Francisco United School District, who claimed that they had been improperly placed in classes for the educable mentally retarded

(EMR). The placement had been made on the basis of their scores on an intelligence test that they claimed was inappropriate for use with black students. The district EMR students were 28.5% white and 66% black. The court concluded that the schools had been using an inappropriate test for the placement of blacks in EMR programs and that the test could not be used. The school in the future would have to submit a written statement declaring that tests were not discriminatory and had been validated for EMR placement decisions and provide statistics on the scores of white students and African American students.

Diana v. California State Board of Education (1973, 1979) concerned the appropriate use of intelligence tests with Mexican American students. These students tended to score poorly and were placed in EMR classes. The out-of-court agreement required the schools to test students both in their first language and in English and restricted the administration of many of the verbal sections of the tests.

Debra P. v. Turlington (1979, 1981, 1983, 1984) questioned the fairness of the Florida State Student Assessment Test. The plaintiffs, 10 African American students, argued that they had been denied due process because they had not been given adequate time to prepare for the test and that the test was used to segregate students by race. The court found the test was not discriminatory. The court concluded that it was the responsibility of the school systems when using a test for granting high school diplomas to show that the test covers only material that was actually taught to the students.

Sharif v. New York State Educational Department (1989) concerned the use of Scholastic Aptitude Test (SAT) scores as the sole basis for awarding state merit scholarships. The plaintiffs claimed that the state was discriminating against girls who were competing for the award. The court ruled that New York could not use the SAT scores alone as a basis for awarding scholarships and needed to have other criteria such as grades or some statewide achievement test data.

COURT DECISIONS ON EMPLOYMENT TESTING

Here are some of the major court decisions related to tests and testing practices:

United States v. Georgia Power (1973) first acknowledged the possibility of the unreliability of differential validity.

Griggs v. Duke Power Company (1971) required a 2-step process for the case to be considered by the courts. First, the plaintiff has to establish a prima facie case of discrimination. Second, the employer must establish that the test is a "reasonable measure of job performance." A paper-and-pencil test given to prospective coal handlers was struck down.

Washington v. Davis (1976) accepted a selection rule with an adverse impact because the test predicted final marks in police training and was a logical criterion measure.

Bakke v. California (1978) struck down the quota system for minority groups in professional schools.

Golden Rule Insurance Company v. Richard L. Mathias (1980) focused on the out-of-court agreement between the Educational Testing Service and the Golden Rule Insurance Company. The plaintiffs claimed that the test developed by ETS used to license insurance agents was not job-related and unfairly discriminated against blacks.

Contreras v. City of Los Angeles (1981) held that the employer's burden is satisfied by showing it used professionally acceptable methods and that the test was predictive or significantly correlated with important elements of work behavior that comprised or were relevant to the job.

Berkman v. City of New York (1987) struck down an arbitrary conversion process to enhance scores for female firefighter applicants even though the underlying tests did not predict job performance.

Watson v. Fort Worth Bank and Trust (1988) ruled that adverse impact does not apply to subjective criteria. The plaintiff had to identify a specific criterion that produces an adverse impact and show reliable and probative statistical evidence to support an inference of discrimination. The employer needs only to offer a legitimate business reason for the criterion. Employers are not required even when defending standardized tests to introduce formal validation studies showing that particular criteria predict actual on-the-job performance.

Cronbach (1984) identified three crucial questions that need to be considered when using tests in employment contexts:

1. Can an adverse impact be shown, such as a greater rejection rate for eligible blacks than for eligible whites?
2. Is the selection rule valid? Was it used as the basis of selection for the job? Are the criterion, content, and construct validity available?
3. Can an alternative selection procedure be used that has less impact?

The Golden Rule Procedure, named for the court case described previously, calls for simple but specifically prescribed procedures for item analysis, item selection, and monitoring of results of the testing program for minority groups. Ethnic and racial data are collected on the candidates who take the test, and analysis of the test items is completed separately by race or ethnic group and educational level. The percentage of each group passing the items is used to classify the test items. Items for which the correct answer rates of ethnic or minority groups and white examinees are most similar have priority for inclusion on the test. The procedure calls for ongoing analysis of the test items and emphasizes keeping the reading level no higher than grade 12 ability.

_____ I have the educational and experiential background to administer the tests
I have selected to use.

_____ The tests are valid for the purposes I identified.

_____ I have sufficient information about the examinee's cultural, linguistic,
social, and educational background.

_____ I have received informed consent from the client if of age.

_____ I have received informed consent from a minor's parents or guardian.

_____ I have discussed the reasons for the test with the client.

_____ The client sees the value of the testing.

_____ I have explained the limitations of the tests to be given.

_____ I have discussed how the test results will be used.

_____ I have discussed how the data will be stored and who will have access to
the data.

_____ I will promise to seek written approval to share confidential information.

_____ I will provide feedback in language that the client can understand.

Figure 24.1
Legal/ethical checklist

CURRENT TRENDS AND PERSPECTIVES

Employers are showing increased sensitivity in how they use tests for hiring purposes; they do not want to be charged with discrimination and unfair practices. Because employers must go through elaborate validation and documentation procedures when they use tests for selection purposes, the use of tests for those purposes has declined. However, the use of tests for certification and licensing purposes has increased.

Tenopyr (1981) concludes that employment testing has been a storm of controversy because of its association with the civil rights movement. She points out that there are problems with fairness models because employers cannot afford to use different tests for various subgroups or interpret tests differently for each group.

Counselors should be alert to legal and ethical standards at all times. Figure 24.1 presents a legal/ethical checklist.

SUMMARY

Since the 1970s, employment and school testing have been the focus of controversy. Laws and court decisions have had an impact on testing practice. The overall effect has probably been fairer tests and testing practices for minority groups. The role of tests is constantly being redefined by the courts. Helping professionals need to be guided by the code of ethics of their organization, be familiar with the laws and court interpretations, and be careful, critical consumers of assessment practices and procedures.

QUESTIONS FOR DISCUSSION

1. Many employment test experts believe that the guidelines from the courts and legislatures are outdated and make costly demands on employers that are not justified by the latest research. Do you agree or disagree with this position? Why?

2. Do you think that equity for minority group members can be obtained through item selection by test makers following the Golden Rule Procedure? Is the procedure a threat to the validity of the test? Why or why not?

3. Are codes of ethics something every group advocates but very few members follow?

4. What position would you take if your code of professional ethics conflicted with a recent ruling of the court?

5. Do you feel ethical behavior is more situation-specific than a general trait?

SUGGESTED ACTIVITIES

1. Interview the affirmative action officer at your place of work or at the school you are attending. What are her views on testing? Report your findings to the class.

2. Make a content analysis of two or three of the codes of ethics as they relate to testing. How are they alike? How are they different?

3. Stage a mock trial on one of the major issues in testing, such as due process, appropriateness of certain tests for a particular function, misuse of tests, appropriateness of a certain test for a minority group member, and the like.

4. Discuss some of the cases presented in the section on responsible test use.

5. See if any cases in your local court system have involved testing issues.

6. Study the following cases and answer the questions at the end of each:

A private liberal arts college is working toward getting regional accreditation. The school has usually admitted a large percentage of students from the bottom half of their high school classes, including any student with a 2.0 grade average on a 4.0 scale. The college does not require the SAT or ACT. The admissions committee has been under pressure to increase the academic respectability of the college by changing the standards to require scores of 400 on both the verbal and quantitative sections of the SAT. The committee was told that enrollment would increase if the school used an established assessment test and that fewer students would drop out.

a. What are the testing issues in this situation?
b. What factors or testing practices are involved?
c. If you were a consultant invited by the college to help the admissions committee in the selection and retention of students, what would you advise?

To remain competitive, Memorial Hospital has decided it needs to cut its budget by downsizing among semiskilled workers such as orderlies, custodians, cafeteria personnel, stockroom clerks, fileroom clerks, and so on. The hospital would like to help these workers qualify for higher-level jobs so they can remain with the organization. Looking at the attrition rate, hospital administrators know they will need workers with advanced technical skills and will have to recruit from the outside to fill these positions if they have no one qualified internally. The personnel department has decided to give all the targeted workers who will lose their positions the Wide Range Achievement Test and the Wonderlic Personnel Test and select those with the highest scores to be retrained. Of the workers 80% are women and minority group members.

a. What are the ethical and legal issues related to this case?
b. What testing factors are involved?
c. If you were a consultant hired by the hospital to help identify workers to be retrained and do outplacement counseling for those who are to be let go, what would you advise Memorial to do?

ADDITIONAL READINGS

American Psychological Association. (1993). *Responsible test use. Case studies for assessing human behavior*. Washington, DC: Test User Training Work Group of the Joint Committee on Testing Practices.

The workbook contains 78 cases to train professionals to use tests wisely. Cases are from seven different settings, ranging from counseling to speech-language-hearing contexts, and cover 86 elements of proper test use.

Tucker, B. P., & Goldstein, B. A. (1991). *The educational rights of children with disabilities. A guide to federal law*. Horsham, PA: LRP.

The authors provide an overview of the Education for All Handicapped Children Act. Chapter 15 lists the procedures for testing and evaluation.

CHAPTER 225

Current Trends and Issues

OVERVIEW

The public perspective toward testing has changed many times during this century. People are concerned about the use of testing and its consequences. Glaser and Bond (1981) argue that changes have been stimulated by legal, social, political, and scientific advances. Plake and Witt (1986) conclude that the field of testing and measurement is a conservative science that has experienced many advances in technology. There are seeds for change as evidenced by the fairness in testing and authentic assessment movements. Glaser and Bond (1981) point out that creative advances in knowledge result from unrestricted free inquiry. Indeed, the critics of testing have demanded changes that were positive and needed.

OBJECTIVES

This chapter should enable the reader to identify

✔ Current trends and issues in testing
✔ Future trends and issues in testing

COMPETENCY TESTING AND THE REFORM MOVEMENT

Assessment is part of everyone's life—in school, careers, licensing, and counseling. In nearly all cases the group administering a test operates under the following premises:

A test can be designed to measure competence.

A test can be selected that measures abilities, knowledge, and skills necessary to perform a particular job at the minimum level of competence.

A test is capable of screening out those who lack the necessary level of competence.

Schools have been charged to train students to become workers capable of learning, with the ability to acquire knowledge independently and use it to solve unforeseen problems. Because business and industry are finding that workers lack necessary job skills, they are demanding reform in the schools. At the same time new forms of assessment, such as authentic assessment, curriculum-based assessment, direct assessment, and alternative assessment, are becoming popular.

Many issues are involved in choosing which style of testing to use. The standards-based curriculum and assessment movement leads to questions such as (1) who is going to be in charge of the assessment, (2) what is going to be affected by the results, and (3) what stakes are involved in the process? There are more questions involved as well. Who is going to design the assessment: local teachers or national policymakers? Will several types of assessments be used or just one stand-alone index?

Minimum-level competency testing affects all areas of education and life. More than 800 occupations and professions require licensing or minimum-level competency examinations (Shimberg, 1982). Thus, the focus on educational reform has become a national trend. Florida and Georgia were the first states to establish minimum competency programs. By the 1980s, 49 states had such programs, while today 46 states have them. Of this group, 34 use standardized norm-referenced tests, 34 use criterion-referenced tests—meaning that some states use both. Passing such state tests is a requirement for high school graduation in 18 states (Burger & Burger, 1994).

It is easy to see why minimum-competency testing is often considered a solution to the lack of job skills. According to Burger and Burger (1994), studies by the National Commission on Excellence in Education show the following:

1. About 75 million adults are considered functionally illiterate as measured by tests of everyday reading, writing, and comprehension.
2. About 13% of all 17-year-olds are functionally illiterate—as many as 40% in minority groups.
3. Scores on the College Board Scholastic Aptitude Test have declined from 1963 to 1980. The average verbal score fell more than 50 points, and the average mathematics score nearly 40 points.

4. The number and proportion of students who demonstrate superior achievement have declined.

5. Many 17-year-olds lack higher cognitive skills. About 40% cannot draw inferences from written material, only 20% were able to write a persuasive essay, and only 33% could solve a mathematics problem requiring several steps.

6. Between 1975 and 1980, 25% of all mathematics courses were remedial, an increase of 72%.

7. Business, industry, and military leaders state they are to spend millions of dollars on remedial education and training programs. (pp. 8–9)

Minimum-competency testing programs have common characteristics (Pipho, 1978). The tests emphasize the acquisition of minimum skills or competencies, most often academic skills such as reading, mathematics, and writing and/or survival skills such as following directions, filling out an employment application, or balancing a checkbook. An absolute performance for pass-fail decisions is set so that the examiner can separate competent from incompetent candidates. The tests are used for educational and instructional decisions about an individual—graduation, promotion, retention, or appropriate instructional strategies.

Perkins (1982) offers an excellent summary of the pros and cons of minimum-competency testing, listing 26 benefits and 24 costs. Because we have already identified benefits, we will list here some of the disadvantages:

1. Leads to an erosion of liberal education
2. Leads to teaching for the test
3. Promotes further stigmatization of the underachiever
4. Encourages labeling of students
5. Causes more dropouts
6. Places the burden of failure on students
7. Ignores the needs of gifted students and average students by emphasizing minimum standards

The National Commission on Testing and Public Policy (1990) found that too many tests emphasize lower-order thinking skills and devour valuable instructional time. Pressure to show improved reading and mathematics scores tends to turn teaching these critical subjects into test preparation in which students read isolated paragraphs and practice answering questions. According to the commission, tests should measure what students are ready to learn next, not what they are unable to learn. Goals 2000 emphasize the importance of students' being able to use higher-order cognitive skills. Thus, testing practices are changing from multiple choice to alternate assessment procedures so that higher-order thinking skills can be assessed.

Other issues related to minimum-competency testing include possible bias against various groups and a question of whether students with disabilities should be expected to meet the same standards as other students. Hambleton and Eignor (1980) have identified five trouble spots in minimum-competency testing: identifying the set of competencies, establishing the performance standard, collecting appropriate validity evidence, computing the reliability of scores and decisions, and equating the scores on alternate test forms.

About 68% of the states in 1990 required minimum-competency testing for teachers, responding to the public belief that colleges and universities in some cases have granted diplomas to graduates who were not competent. Teacher competency tests can include basic skills, instructional content, and teaching methodology. In Florida, principals have been required to pass a competency test since 1987.

Testing programs have been a target for legal cases. For example, *Debra P. v. Turlington* called for the state to demonstrate that the competencies measured were actually part of classroom instruction in Florida. Nevertheless, as of 1990, 47 of the 50 states had statewide student testing and about half of the states expanded their programs to include more grades, subject areas, and higher-order skills.

The public currently supports minimum-competency testing; opposition is equated with supports assessment to identify the incompetence of schools and educational systems. This reform movement has intensified during the 1990s. State mandates for educational change demand immediate action and long-term planning, at least until discontent about incompetence has abated and the meaning of high school and college diplomas has been restored.

LICENSURE AND CERTIFICATION EXAMINATIONS

As we have discussed, licensing and certification examinations are related to the minimum-competency movement; they now constitute a major use of testing in our country. The purpose of this testing is to ensure that applicants have the knowledge and skill for practice in their fields. Most licensing requires successful completion of an approved educational program. The examination functions as an additional check on candidate preparation. It also provides feedback on the quality of educational programs, forcing some schools to improve their curriculum. In addition, candidates are often required to provide evidence of good character and knowledge of ethics in their fields.

The validity of these examinations is a crucial issue. Kane (1986) points out that "the interpretation of licensure examination scores as predictors of future performance in practice is appealing because it implies a high degree of utility for the licensure process" (p. 155). He sees two important components of validity—the need for evidence that the abilities measured are crucial for practice in the field, and the need for test scores to reflect competence in the critical abilities identified as crucial for the job.

Establishing valid criteria that can be generalized to cover the wide variety of licensure situations fairly is a technical problem that requires more research. Conversely, the fact that many applicants may test well does not necessarily mean they will perform a job well if they do not use their knowledge and skills effectively.

Kane (1986) considers licensure a matter of public policy shaped by public expectations. He identifies five questions relevant to policy decisions about licensing examinations:

1. What types of situations occur most frequently in practice or have the most serious potential consequences?
2. What abilities, including knowledge and skills, are needed to deal with these situations effectively?
3. How well are these abilities taught and assessed in educational programs preparing practitioners?
4. How well does the examination assess competencies in critical abilities, and what sources of variance other than differences in competence (e.g., reading level, response bias) influence examination scores?
5. What are the implications of setting standards at different levels? (p. 179)

The public will probably demand even more examinations and want more input into the activities of licensing and certifying agencies.

TRUTH IN TESTING

The truth in testing movement was a product of the 1970s, partly motivated by the accountability movement. Proponents believe that test makers should be more accountable for the intellectual quality and social consequences of the tests they produce. New York passed a law on truth in testing (effective in 1980) that required disclosure of the questions and answers determining examinees' scores on postsecondary and professional admissions tests within 30 days of the release of the test scores. Nairn and associates' report (1980) on the Educational Testing Service stimulated interest in this legislation. They concluded that ETS has not protected and represented the public interest and found that admissions tests such as the SAT have little predictive validity for how well students will do in school, noting that such tests are biased against minority groups and students from lower socioeconomic levels. Their findings also indicated that coaching can boost test scores on aptitude and admissions tests.

Most professional testing organizations oppose truth in testing legislation. The APA's Committee on Psychological Tests and Assessment has raised two areas of concern: disclosure of items from low-volume tests or tests with finite items, and test interpretation that depends on a long history of research. Nevertheless, although the truth in testing law has been expensive for test publishers, it has led to more positive public attitudes toward testing.

INVASION OF PRIVACY

Invasion of privacy has been one of the major issues in testing. Some people are concerned about the confidentiality of the results. Others are offended by some of the questions, while still others are concerned about how the questions will be used. Some individuals feel that they are coerced into responding to items if their school or company gives the test. Computer-assisted and -adaptive testing and computer data banks and retrieval systems have renewed interest in this issue.

Legal statutes and current standards of professional organizations remind us of the rights of the test taker. Tests must not include questions that require clients to reveal the following information:

1. Political affiliation
2. Mental and psychological problems potentially embarrassing to clients and their families
3. Sexual behavior and attitudes
4. Illegal, antisocial, self-incriminating, and demeaning behavior
5. Critical appraisals of individuals with whom respondents have close family relationships
6. Legally recognized privileges and analogous relationships, such as those of lawyers, physicians, and ministers
7. Income (per PL 95–561)

The public is concerned about the type of information gathered, its use, and its storage. Ethical procedures require informed consent before tests are given, an explanation of why the tests are administered, the type of information they yield, who will get a copy of the results, and how the information will be stored or filed.

FAIRNESS TO MINORITY GROUPS

One of the major concerns relating to admissions, achievement, and intelligence testing has been the question of fairness to minority groups. A disproportionate number of minority students do achieve low or failing scores on minimum-competency examinations and earn lower scores on the SAT. According to Mehrens and Lehman (1986), "if a test does tend to discriminate (differentiate) between races, sexes, or other subcultures, and if the differential scores are not related to what is being predicted (such as on-the-job success), then the test is unfair" (p. 471). This issue has been raised not only in selection for higher education and in minimum-competency testing but also in employment testing. Some of the key issues were discussed in Chapter 24.

Testing requirements for athletes have been the subject of some controversy. As of 1994, for an athlete to be eligible to participate in college sports, the NCAA requires a combined SAT of 700 or an ACT of 17, with a grade-point average of 2.0. Some academics still feel that there is a double standard for athletes, whose requirements for admission are lower than the requirements for regular students.

A 1969 article by Arthur Jensen stimulated much debate; he stated that "genetic factors are strongly implicated in the average Negro-White intelligence difference" (p. 82). Herrnstein (1971) and Herrnstein and Murray (1994) have also concluded that data on IQ and social class differences indicate a pattern of inherited stratification. Despite these claims, the items on IQ tests continue to be criticized for being unfair to minority groups. Some states, such as California, have banned the use of IQ tests in making assignments to special education classes. The relative importance of heredity and environment will continue to be debated as steps are taken through test development and student intervention to eliminate bias and improve minority group performance on tests.

There are also public concerns about gender bias in testing. Some observers believe that girls are discriminated against on the Scholastic Aptitude Tests, and a disproportionately small number of females are semifinalists on the National Merit Examination.

HOSTILE GATEKEEPER

The National Commission on Testing and Public Policy (1990) calls for a broad overhaul of educational and employment tests. The commission argues that tests developed to screen out students and job applicants are inconsistent with today's best policies. Our current testing system has been labeled by a Ford Foundation–funded study as a "hostile gatekeeper" (NCTPP, 1990). The report concludes that schools and businesses increasingly rely on multiple-choice tests to make critical judgments about individuals and institutions, causing limited opportunity—particularly for women and minority groups. The report calls for schools and businesses to shift to alternate forms of assessment to measure performance. They also advocate a national board to oversee and monitor the use of standardized tests.

HOW ASSESSMENT IS CHANGING

The Past

Educational and psychological tests have become a widely accepted social enterprise in the twentieth century because of their utility in dealing with large numbers of people and their association with technology. After the success of the Army Alpha in World War I, many tests were developed between 1920 and 1940. Buros's first bibliography in 1937 contained 44 pages (as compared with 1,322 in the *Thirteenth Mental Measurements Yearbooks*) and included many tests of questionable validity and reliability. Testing during this period was occasionally criticized, but for the most part tests were well accepted and results rarely questioned.

Political and philosophical movements influenced the 1950s, 1960s, and 1970s. Schools were desegregated, and concern grew about ethnic, cultural, and gender bias in testing. The misuses of testing were exposed, and some states banned the use of IQ tests. Legislation was enacted to protect the rights of individuals with disabilities and to foster equal opportunity. Also, programs supported ethnic heritage, women's rights, and sexual equity.

The Present

Current test use reflects the philosophy of the beginnings of the testing movement: "If it exists, it can be measured." ETS (1993) states in *Testing in America's Schools* that the volume of testing in U.S. schools has increased markedly since the 1970s and probably will continue unless alternative assessments under development begin to take the place of traditional standardized tests. Philosophical and political ideology has shifted toward a conservative point of view—from humanistic approaches in education to emphasis on basic skills. Accordingly, more emphasis has been placed on accountability, which has led to increased use of licensing and minimum-level competency testing. Society is relying even more heavily on testing than it did in the past. The testing companies have accommodated the changes dictated by laws, such as the truth in testing law, and by legislation to eliminate cultural, ethnic, and sexual bias. The technology of testing has been stimulated by these political and social events as well as the impact of the computer. More sophisticated procedures can select items and generate criterion validity. Nonclassical psychometric models are currently being widely used. The information age has led to a greater concern for who has access to information, how it is stored, and how the rights of the individual will be protected.

The Future

Influenced by technology and society, the future will bring changes in the practices and procedures used in testing. Preliminary studies and research indicate that computer-adaptive and computer-assisted testing will be used more extensively. Cost-effective and labor-saving, the computer is able to collect psychological data along with traditional test information, providing immediate feedback and remediation. More tests that use multiple input and output devices for displaying results continue to be developed. Tests have already been transferred from pencil-and-paper format to computer format. Different types of items now are being devised that are unique to the potential of the computer. Video disk technology, CD-ROM, and virtual reality technology can simulate real situations. Instead of depending upon words, an item on an interest test can give a visual display of an occupation.

The use of the Internet for counseling and assessment activities will increase. The National Career Development Association (1997) has published extensive guidelines for career assessment in this area:

1. Evaluating on-line inventories or tests to assure that their psychological properties are the same in computer delivery as they are in print form
2. Abiding by the same ethical guidelines when administering or interpreting on-line instruments, face-to-face interviews, and print forms
3. Protecting the confidentiality of results
4. Referring clients to a qualified counselor in their particular geographical area
5. Validating on-line instruments for self-help use, if appropriate

There are other issues concerning e-mail and Internet use. Joint committees of professional organizations are working on technical standards, clarification of response bias with electronic surveys and testing, and standards for use of technology in general. Other issues relate to electronic testing, comprehensive data integration, video conferencing, and better technology (Landberg, 1998).

More tests will have computer-generated reports. Fewer helping professionals will be involved in test administration, scoring, and interpretation; the computer will replace them and change their role.

The future will see continued reliance on tests as the primary means of establishing mastery of competencies. Selection tests and large-scale admissions programs will be under increased scrutiny. Various groups in undergraduate education have advocated dropping the Scholastic Aptitude Test as an admissions requirement. Selection tests have had questionable predictive validity; the best single predictor of future achievement is past achievement. SAT results may increase the efficiency of prediction slightly, but studies have shown that 50% or more of the variance related to success in college is unaccounted for by the predictors used.

Schools, states, and institutions will share more in the future. Consortia of states now are working together to construct criterion-referenced and minimum-level skills tests. More reliance on using and refining tests and item banks already available will be generated. Alternate assessment and performance testing will be refined and will have freer formats. Glaser (1994) states that students will be able to observe and reflect on their own performance so they can judge their own level of achievement and develop self-direction. Assessment programs will be judged in terms of the contributions they make to encourage students and teachers to devote their energies to certain content, concepts, and student performance.

The future will move toward assessing cognitive aspects of intelligence. Cognitive interpretation is practical for helping psychologists and teachers derive individually prescribed programs. Also more emphasis will be placed on the development of multiple intelligences in school and counseling. Gardner (1993), Sternberg (1986), and others working in this field will have an increased influence on theory development and test use. Certain questions will be important. How do individuals make sense of the information they receive? What are the implications of these constructs for validity theory? Evidence might be collected, such as the meaning of the message as interpreted by the recipient, the acquired knowledge that the individual uses to understand the message, the actual circumstances in which the message is received, and so on (Moss, 1998).

In personality measurement, behavioral assessment techniques will become more widely used, and traditional pencil-and-paper inventories will diminish in importance. Certain clinicians will probably be reluctant to change, even though many studies have already indicated that the old standby tests lack validity and reliability.

Professional licensing and certification examinations will include performance assessment. Test items must reflect qualities and skills needed for job performance, not just knowledge demonstrated on pencil-and-paper tests.

In general, the theoretical framework for testing is changing. Key concepts in classical theory were correction for attenuation, the Spearman-Brown formula, the reliability index, the Kuder-Richardson formulas, and Guttman's lower bounds to reliability. Classical theory was founded on the premise that the measurement error, a random latent variable, is part of the observed score. Item response theory (IRT) has become a popular alternative to the classical theory of test scoring and item analysis. IRT focuses on adaptive testing, analyzing item locations and respondent values as points on the scale of the quantitative variable. Binet, for example, judged mental age not by the number of items correct but by the highest item the child got right.

Test authors and test publishers will need to withdraw some tests from public access since they do not meet the standards set by professional organizations. Test companies will need to revise problem tests so that they conform to ethical and professional standards or discontinue them. If the test industry does not voluntarily address this issue, the public and the professions will demand compliance.

Movements come in cycles. Criticism of testing will increase again, especially when studies look at the long-term effects of accountability. States have mandated testing but have not put funds into research to establish the validity of tests. More court cases and judicial opinions will be forthcoming, and the values and priorities of the legislature will change. The future will probably question whether established policies have led to better practice, quality education, or more competent professionals in the work force.

The history of testing has included misuses, abuses, and controversies. Many states require teachers as well as counselors and psychologists to take a number of semester hours in testing and demonstrate their testing competencies. However, this requirement does not yet pertain to all professionals who make heavy use of testing. Future movements will ensure the competency of all workers who use tests.

Helping professionals need to look at their role in the future. More discussions of tests focus on consequential validity: what were the consequences of the test used? Professionals need to develop the knowledge, skills, and competencies to be good consumers of tests. Measurement writers stress the need for a decision-making model for using tests and emphasize that tests are only one source of information, the results of which are not absolute. Many leaders in the field advocate using a multimodal approach to get information needed for decision making.

Unfortunately, leaders in the field sometimes forget what they espouse. They base their judgments on attitudes, past training and practices, and feelings rather than on disinterested, objective analysis. Helping professionals need to remember the steps of the scientific method and encourage freedom of thought and divergent opinions. They must be able to step back and take another look. Too often test experts take refuge in their factor and discriminant analysis and fail to consider the practical significance of the results. Helping professionals must be competent, knowledgeable, scientific, analytical, and evaluative. In most businesses the consumer is right, and consumer wishes and desires are honored. In testing, the consumer must be protected.

SUMMARY

Trends and issues in testing are influenced by political, social, economic, and technological developments in our world. Current issues receiving much attention are standards-based assessment, licensure and certification, truth in testing, invasion of privacy, and fairness of tests for minority groups. The history of testing has included criticism from within and without. Some of these controversies periodically resurface. In this information age, the roles and functions of testing are changing. Computer-assisted and -adaptive testing are becoming widely used and accepted. All changes have implications for the competencies needed by those who test. Helping professionals must always keep in mind the ethical and professional standards in the field when they select, use, and interpret tests.

QUESTIONS FOR DISCUSSION

1. What are the major issues and controversies in testing today? Which are the most critical? Why?

2. What do you predict will be the issues and controversies in testing 10 years from now? 20 years from now? Why?

3. Discuss the major issues in testing and analyze the factors impinging on those issues. Are the forces legal, educational, political, psychological, social, or psychometric? What force do you think is most influential?

4. What do you predict will be the future trends in testing?

5. Some critics think that there is too much use and reliance on testing today. Do you agree or disagree with this position? Why?

SUGGESTED ACTIVITIES

1. Write a position paper on one of the issues in the field of testing.

2. Write a critical review of the literature on one of the trends or innovations in testing.

3. Interview workers in the helping professions and have them identify what they think are the current issues, trends, and controversies. Report your findings to the class.

4. Conduct a survey of workers in the helping professions to learn their attitudes toward testing and the current issues and trends. Construct your instrument, administer it, and analyze the results. Report the results to the class.

ADDITIONAL READINGS

Conferences such as those sponsored by the Educational Testing Service and the Buros Institute are held annually, and their proceedings are usually published. Additionally, many yearbooks deal in testing, and journals in the field have special publications. For example, *Issues of Educational Measurement* is an excellent source of issues and trends. Newsletters of professional organizations and the ERIC Center on Assessment and Evaluation are excellent sources. To stay current and well informed about appraisal procedures and issues, helping professionals need to be aware of these sources as well as information in newspapers and magazines and on television.

Appendix A: Tests

AAMD Adaptive Behavior Scale
Nihira, K., Foster, R., Shellhaas, M., Leland, H., Lambert, N. M., & Windmiller, M. (1975). Monterey, CA: CTB/McGraw-Hill.

ACCUPLACER
College Board. (1998). New York: Author.

ACT Interest Inventory
American College Testing Program. (1988). Iowa City: Author.

Adaptive Behavior Inventory
Brown, L., & Leigh, J. E. (1986). San Antonio, TX: PRO-ED.

Adaptive Behavior Scales
Lambert, N., Kazve, N., & Leland, H. (1993). San Antonio, TX: PRO-ED.

Adjective Checklist
Gough, H. G., & Heilbrun, A., Jr. (1980). Palo Alto, CA: Consulting Psychologists Press.

Adolescent Multiphasic Personality Inventory
Duthie, B. (1985). Richland, WA: Pacific Psychological.

Adult Career Concerns Inventory
Super, D. E., Thompson, A. S., & Lindeman, R. H. (1988). Palo Alto, CA: Consulting Psychologists Press.

Adult Language Assessment Scale
Duncan, S. E., & DeAvila, E. A. (1991). Monterey, CA: Publishers Test Service.

Adult Psychoeducational Profile
Mesibou, G., et al. (1982). Hillsborough, NJ: Orange Industries.

Advanced Placement Program
Educational Testing Service. (1950 to date). Princeton, NJ: Author.

Advanced Progressive Matrices
Raven, J. C. (1962). London: Lewis.

Affective Style Measure
Doane, J. A. (1981). Los Angeles: UCLA Family Project.

African Self-Consciousness Scale
Baldwin, J. A., & Bell, Y. R. (1985). *Western Journal of Black Studies, 9*(2), 65–68.

Algebra Prognostic Test
Hanna, G., and Orleans, J. B. (1982). San Antonio, TX: Psychological Corporation.

Allport-Vernon-Lindzey Scale of Values
Allport, G. W., Vernon, P. E., & Lindzey, G. (1970). Chicago: Riverside.

Analysis of Coping Style
Boyd, H. F., & Johnson, G. O. (1981). San Antonio, TX: Psychological Corporation.

Aptitude and Intelligence Series
Industrial Psychology. (1960). New York: Author.

Armed Services Vocational Aptitude Battery
U.S. Military Enlistment Command. (1984). Washington, DC: U.S. Department of Defense.

Arthur Point Scale of Performance Tests
Arthur, G. (1947). San Antonio, TX: Psychological Corporation.

Assessment of Writing
CTB/McGraw-Hill. (1993). Monterey, CA: Author.

Autism Behavior Checklist
Riley, A. M. (1984). Tucson: Communication Skill Builders.

Autism Screening Instrument for Educational Planning
Krug, D. A., Arick, J. R., & Aomond, P. J. (1993). Austin, TX: PRO-ED.

Basic Achievement Skills Individual Screener
Psychological Corporation. (1982). San Antonio, TX: Author.

Basic Occupational Literacy Test
U.S. Employment Service. (1974). Washington, DC: U.S. Department of Labor.

Basic Skills Assessment Program
Educational Testing Service. (1979). Monterey, CA: CTB/McGraw-Hill.

Battelle Developmental Inventory
Newburg, J., Stock, J., Wnek, L., Guidobaldi, J., & Suinick, J. (1984). Allen, TX: DLM.

Bayley Scales of Infant Development
Bayley, N. (1969). San Antonio, TX: Psychological Corporation.

Beck Anxiety Inventory
Beck, A. T. (1993). San Antonio, TX: Psychological Corporation.

Beck Depression Inventory
Beck, A. T. (1987). San Antonio, TX: Psychological Corporation.

Beck Hopelessness Scale
Beck, A. T. (1987). San Antonio, TX: Psychological Corporation.

Beck Scale for Suicide Ideation
Beck, A. T., & Steer, R. A. (1990). San Antonio, TX: Psychological Corporation.

Behavior Observation Scale for Autism
Freeman, B. J. (1978). Los Angeles: Author.

Bender Gestalt Test
Koppitz, E. M. (1975). Orlando, FL: Grune & Stratton.

Bender Visual Motor Gestalt Test
Bender, L. (1964). New York: American Orthopsychiatric Association.

Bennett Mechanical Comprehension Test
Bennett, G., & Owens, W. A. (1980). San Antonio, TX: Psychological Corporation.

Bernreuter Personality Inventory
Bernreuter, R. G. (1938). Palo Alto, CA: Consulting Psychologists Press.

Blacky Pictures
Blum, G. S. (1950). Ann Arbor, MI: Psychodynamic Instruments.

Body Cathexis Scale
Secord, P. F., & Jouard, S. M. (1953). *Journal of Consulting Psychologists, 17*(5), 343–347.

Bracken Basic Concept Scale
Bracken, B. A. (1984). San Antonio, TX: Psychological Corporation.

Brain Preference Indicator
Wonder, J., & Donovan, P. (1984). New York: Morrow.

Brief Symptoms Inventory
DeRogatis, L. R., & Spencer, P. M. (1975). Riverwood, MD: Clinical Psychometric Research.

Brookover Self-Concept of Ability Scale
Brookover, W. B. (1983). Princeton, NJ: Author.

Brown Attention Deficit Disorder Scale
Brown, T. E. (1996). San Antonio, TX: PRO-ED.

Bruininks-Oseretsky Test of Motor Proficiency
Bruininks, R. H. (1978). Circle Pines, MN: American Guidance Service.

Burks's Behavior Rating Scales
Burks, H. F. (1969). Los Angeles: Western Psychological Services.

California Psychological Inventory
Gough, H. G. (1987). Palo Alto, CA: Consulting Psychologists Press.

California Test of Personality
Tiegs, E. W. Clark, W. W., & Thorpe, L. P. (1989). Los Angeles: California Test Bureau.

Campbell-Halcum Team Development Survey
Halcum, G., & Campbell, D. (1992). Minneapolis: NCS Assessments.

Campbell Interest and Skills Survey
Campbell, D. P. (1994). Minneapolis: National Computer Systems.

Canfield Learning Styles Inventory
Canfield, A. A. (1980). LaCrescenta, CA: Humanics Media.

Career Ability Placement Survey
Knapp, L. F., & Knapp, R. R. (1984). San Diego: Educational & Industrial Testing Service.

Career Assessment Inventory
Johansson, C. B. (1982). Minneapolis: National Computer Systems, PAS Division.

Career Attitudes and Strategies Inventory
Holland, J. L., & Gottfriedson, L. (1994). Odessa, FL: Psychological Assessment Resources.

Career Awareness Inventory
Fadale, L. M. (1975). Bensenville, IL: Scholastic Testing Service.

Career Development Inventory
Super, D. E., Thompson, A. S., Lindeman, R. H., Jordaan, J. P., & Myers, R. A. (1981). Palo Alto, CA: Consulting Psychologists Press.

Career Maturity Inventory
Crites, J. O. (1973). Monterey, CA: CTB/McGraw-Hill.

Career Planning Program
American College Testing Program. (1974). Iowa City: Author.

Career-Related Experience Inventory
Liptak, J. (1992). Indianapolis: Jist Works.

Career Skills Assessment Program
College Board Publications. (1978). Princeton, NJ: Author.

Career Survey
American Testronics. (1986). Iowa City: Author.

Cattell Infant Intelligence Scale
Cattell, P. (1960). San Antonio, TX: Psychological Corporation.

Child and Adolescent Diagnostic Scales
Duthie, B. (1989). Richland, WA: Pacific Psychological.

Child Assessment Schedule
Hodges, K. (1985). Durham, NC: Duke University, Department of Psychiatry.

Child Behavior Checklist
Achenbach, T. H., & Edenbrock, C. (1991). Burlington: University of Vermont, Department of Psychiatry.

Child Diagnostic Screening Battery
Smith, J. J., & Eisenberg, J. M. (1984). Towson, MD: Reason House.

Childhood Autism Rating Scale
Schopler, F., Reichler, R. J., & Renner, B. R. (1986). Los Angeles: Western Psychological Services.

Children's Adaptive Behavior Scale
Richmond, B. O., & Kicklighter, R. H. (1980). Atlanta: Humanics.

Children's Apperception Test
Bellak, L., & Bellak, S. S. (1974). Larchmont, NY: CPS.

Children's Assessment Schedule
Hodges, K., et al. *Journal of Abnormal Psychology, 10,* 307–324.

Children's Embedded Figures Test
Karp, S. A., & Konstadt, N. (1971). Palo Alto, CA: Consulting Psychologists Press.

Children's Manifest Anxiety Scale
Castaneda, A., McCandless, B. R., & Palermo, D. C. (1956). *Child Development, 27,* 317–326.

Children's Personality Questionnaire
Porter, R. B., & Cattell, R. B. (1982). Champaign, IL: Institute of Personality and Ability Testing.

Children's Test Anxiety Scale
Sarason, S. B., Davidson, K. S., Lighthall, F. F., Waite, R. R., & Rugbush, B. K. (1960). *Anxiety in elementary school children.* New York: Wiley.

Children's Version of the Family Environment Scale
Pineo, C., Simons, N., & Slawinowski, M. (1984). East Aurora, NY: Slosson.

Child's Learning Profile
DePaul, G. J., Rapport, M. D., & Barriello, L. M. (1989). Unpublished.

Classroom Environment Scale
Moos, R. H., & Trickett, E. J. (1974). Palo Alto, CA: Consulting Psychologists Press.

Clerical Aptitude Test
Kobal, A., Wrightstone, J. W., & MacElroy, A. J. (1950). Murfreesboro, TN: Psychometric Affiliates.

Clinical Analysis Questionnaire
Krug, S. E. (1980). Champaign, IL: IPAT.

Cognitive Assessment System
Das, J. P., & Naglieri, J. A. (1997). Chicago: Riverside.

College Characteristics Index
Stern, G., et al. (1962). Syracuse, NY: Evaluation Research Associates.

College-Level Examination Program
College Board. (1981). New York: Author.

College Student Experiences Scale
Pace, C. R. (1983). Los Angeles: Higher Education Research Institute.

Colorado Self-Report Measure of Family Functioning
Bloom, B. L. (1985). Boulder: University of Colorado, Department of Psychology.

Coloured Progressive Matrices
Raven, J. C. (1983). London: Lewis.

Common Metric Questionnaire
Harvey, R. J. (1990). San Antonio, TX: Psychological Corporation.

Comprehensive Ability Battery
  Hakstian, A. R., & Cattell, R. B. (1982). Champaign, IL: Institute for Personality and Ability Testing.

Comprehensive Test of Basic Skills
  California Test Bureau. (1981). Monterey, CA: CTB/McGraw-Hill.

Computer Operator Aptitude Battery
  Holloway, A. J. (1974). Chicago: Science Research Associates.

Computer Programmer Aptitude Battery
  Palormo, J. M. (1974). Chicago: Science Research Associates.

Concept Assessment Kit
  Goldschmid, M. L., & Bentler, P. M. (1968). San Diego: Educational and Industrial Testing.

Conflict Tactics Scale
  Straus, M. A. (1979). Durham, NH: Family Research Laboratory.

Connors's Rating Scale
  Connors, C. K. (1997). Austin, TX: PRO-ED.

Continuous Performance Test
  Connors, C. K. (1994). Odessa, FL: Psychological Assessment Resources.

Coopersmith's Self-Esteem Inventory
  Coopersmith, S. (1981). Palo Alto, CA: Consulting Psychologists Press.

COPSystem Career Occupational Preference System
  Knapp, R. R., & Knapp, L. F. (1983). San Diego: Educational and Industrial Testing Service.

COPSystem Interest Inventory
  Knapp, R. R., & Knapp, L. F. (1982). San Diego: Educational and Industrial Testing Service.

Crawford Small Parts Dexterity Test
  Crawford, J. (1956). San Antonio, TX: Psychological Corporation.

Creativity Attitude Survey
  Schaefer, C. E. (1971). Creve Cove, MO: Psychologists and Educators.

Creativity Checklist
  Johnson, D. L. (1979). Chicago: Stoelting.

Criterion Test of Basic Skills
  Lundell, K., Brown, W., & Evans, J. (1976). Novato, CA: Academic Therapy Publications.

Cultural Evaluation of Language Fundamentals
  Semel, E. (1995). San Antonio, TX: Psychological Corporation.

Culture-Fair Intelligence Tests
  Cattell, R. B., & Cattell, A. K. S. (1977). Champaign, IL: Institute for Personality and Ability Testing.

Culture-Free Self-Esteem Inventory
  Battle, J. (1992). Austin, TX: PRO-ED.

Curtis Verbal-Clerical Skills Tests
  Curtis, J. W. (1965). Murfreesboro, TN: Psychometric Affiliates.

Dallas Preschool Screening Test
  Percival, R. R. (1972). Richardson, TX: Dallas Educational Services.

Defensive and Supportive Communication Interaction System
  Alexander, J. F. (no date). Salt Lake City, UT: Author.

Defining Issues Test
  Rest, J. (1979). Minneapolis: University of Minnesota, Center for the Study of Ethical Development.

Denver Developmental Screening Test
  Frankenburg, W. F. (1970). Denver: Ladoca Publishing Foundation.

Dependency Scale
  Golightly, C. (1970). Princeton, NJ: ETS.

Detroit Tests of Learning Aptitude
  Hammill, D. D. (1985). Austin, TX: PRO-ED.

Developing Cognitive Abilities Test
  Beggs, D. L., & Mouw, J. T. (1989). Chicago: American Testronics.

Developmental Assessment for the Severely Handicapped
  Dykes, M. K. (1980). Austin, TX: Exceptional Resources.

Developmental Environments Coding System
  Powers, S. J. (1982). Amherst, MA: Author.

Developmental Indicators for the Assessment of Learning
  Mardell-Czudnowsky, C., & Goldenberg. D. (1990). Circle Pines, MN: American Guidance Services.

Developmental Inventory of Black Consciousness
Milliones, J. (1980). *Psychotherapy, 17,* 175–182.

Developmental Test of Visual-Motor Integration
Beery, K. E., & Buktenica, N. A. (1967). Cleveland: Modern Curriculum Press.

Devereux Behavior Rating Scale
Naglieri, J. A., LeBuffe, P. A., & Pieffer, S. I. (1993). San Antonio, TX: Psychological Corporation.

Devereux Scales of Mental Disorders
Naglieri, J. A., et al. (1994). San Antonio, TX: Psychological Corporation.

Devereux Test of Extremity Coordination
Devereux Foundation. (1973). Devon, PA: Author.

Diagnostic Interview for Children and Adolescents
Herjanic, B., & Reich, W. (1982). *Journal of Abnormal Child Psychology*, 10, 307–324.

Diagnostic Interview Schedule for Children
Shaffer, D. Schwab-Stone, M., Fisher, P., Cohen, P., et al. (1993).

Diagnostic Inventory of Personality and Symptoms
Vincent, K. R. (1977). Richland, WA: Pacific Psychological.

Differential Aptitude Test Battery
Bennett, G. K., Seashore, H. G., & Wesman, A. G. (1982). San Antonio, TX: Psychological Corporation.

Dimensions of Excellence Scales
Dusewicy, R. A., & Beyer, F. S. (1991). Philadelphia: Research for Better Schools.

Draw-a-Family Test
Hulse, W. C. (1951). *Journal of Child Behavior, 3,* 152–174.

Draw-a-Person Test
Naglieri, J. A. (1988). San Antonio, TX: Psychological Corporation.

Draw-a-Person Test
Urban, W. H. (1963). Los Angeles: Western Psychological Services.

Early School Personality Questionnaire
Cattell, R. B., & Coan, R. W. (1982). Champaign, IL: Institute for Personality and Ability Testing.

Eating Disorders Inventory
Garner, D. M., Olmsted, M. P., & Polivy, J. (1991). Odessa, FL: Psychological Assessment Resources.

Eating Inventory
Stunkard, A. J., & Messick, S. (1994). San Antonio, TX: Psychological Corporation.

Edwards Personal Preference Inventory
Edwards, A. L. (1959). San Antonio, TX: Psychological Corporation.

Effective School Battery
Gottfredson, G. D. (1984). Odessa, FL: Psychological Assessment Resources.

Ego Strength Scale
Jacobs, M. A. (1968). Newton, MA: Author; Epstein, S. (1983). Princeton, NJ: ETS Test Collection Library.

Embedded Figures Test
Witkin, H. A. (1971). Palo Alto, CA: Consulting Psychologists Press.

Employee Aptitude Survey Series
Grimsley, G., Ruch, F. L., Warren, N. D., & Ford, J. S. (1963). Bay Village, OH: Psychological Services.

Employment Barrier Identification Scale
McKee, J. M. (1981). Tuscaloosa, AL: Behavior Science Press.

Everyday Skills Test
California Test Bureau. (1975). Monterey, CA: CTB/McGraw-Hill.

Expressive One-Word Picture Vocabulary Test
Gardner, M. F. (1990). Novato, CA: Academic Therapy.

Eysenck Personality Inventory
Eysenck, H. J., & Eysenck, S. B. G. (1969). San Diego: Educational and Industrial Testing Service.

Eysenck Personality Questionnaire
Eysenck, H. J., & Eysenck, S. B. G. (1976). San Diego: Educational and Industrial Testing Service.

Facial Recognition Test
Benton, A. L., et al. (1983). New York: Oxford University Press.

Family Adaptability and Cohesion Evaluation Scales
Olson, D. H., Portner, J., & Lavee, Y. (1985). St. Paul: University of Minnesota, Family Social Science.

Family Assessment Measure
Skinner, H. A., Steinhauer, P. D., & Santa-Barbara, J. (1984). Toronto: Addictions Research Foundation.

Family Conflict and Dominance Codes
Henggeler, S. W., & Tavormina, J. B. (1980). *Journal of Genetic Psychology*, *137*, 211–222.

Family Constraining and Enabling Coding System
Hauser, S., et al. (1987). Cambridge, MA: Harvard Medical School, Family Development Project.

Family Evaluation Form
Emery, R. S., Weintraub, S., & Neale, J. M. (1984). Stony Brook: State University of New York: Department of Psychology.

Family Functioning in Adolescence Questionnaire
Roelofse, R., & Middleton, M. (1985). *Journal of Adolescence*, *8*, 33–45.

Family Process Scales
Barbarin, O. A., & Gilbert, R. (1985). Ann Arbor: University of Michigan, Family Development Project.

Family Relationship Questionnaire
Henggeler, S. W., & Tavormina, J. B. (1980). Memphis, TN: Memphis State University, Department of Psychology.

Fear Survey Schedule for Children
Schere, M. W., & Nakamura, C. Y. (1968). Blacksburg, VA: Virginia Polytechnic Institute, Department of Psychology.

Finger Tapping Test
Benton, A. (1983). Fairlawn, NJ: Oxford University Press.

FIRO-B
Schutz, W. (1977). Odessa, FL: Psychological Assessment Resources.

Florida Analysis of Semantic Traits
Bailey, R. C., & Suidzinski, R. M. (1986). Dallas: Bali Screening Company.

Florida Comprehensive Assessment Test
Florida Department of Education. (1988). Tallahassee: Author.

Frostig Developmental Test of Visual Perception
Frostig, M. (1966). Palo Alto, CA: Consulting Psychologists Press.

Gates-McKillop-Horowitz Reading Diagnostic Test
Gates, A. I., McKillop, A. S., & Horowitz, E. C. (1981). New York: Teachers College Press.

General Aptitude Test Battery
U.S. Employment Service, Division of Testing. (1967). Salem, OR: Author.

General Clerical Test
Psychological Corporation. (1972). San Antonio, TX: Author.

General Educational Development Test
General Educational Development Testing Service. (1987). Washington, DC: American Council on Education.

General Educational Performance Index
Seaman, D. F., & Seaman, A. (1980). Austin, TX: Steck-Vaughn.

General Mental Ability Scale
Trevor, H. S., & Stoufer, G. (1983). Chambersburg, PA: Employers' Tests and Services Associates.

Gesell Maturity Scale
Gesell, A., & Amatruda. (1949). New York: Psychological Corporation.

Gifted and Talented Evaluation Scale
Gilliam, J. E., Carpenter, B. O., & Christenson, J. R. (1996). Austin, TX: PRO-ED.

Gifted and Talented Screening Form
Johnson, D. L. (1980). Chicago: Stoelting.

Gilliam Autism Rating Scale
Gilliam, J. E. (1995). Austin, TX: PRO-ED.

Goldman-Fristoe Test of Articulation
Goldman, R., & Fristoe, M. (1972). Circle Pines, MN: American Guidance Service.

Goldman-Fristoe-Woodcock Auditory Skills Test Battery
Goldman, R., Fristoe, M., & Woodcock, R. W. (1976). Circle Pines, MN: American Guidance Service.

Goldman-Fristoe-Woodcock Test of Auditory Discrimination
Goldman, R. (1970). Circle Pines, MN: American Guidance Services.

Goodenough-Harris Draw-a-Man Test
Goodenough, D. L., & Harris, D. B. (1963). San Antonio, TX: Psychological Corporation.

Graves Design Judgment Test
Graves, M. (1965). San Antonio, TX: Psychological Corporation.

Gregorc Style Delineator
Gregorc, A. F. (1982). Maynard, MA: Gabriel Systems.

Group Embedded Figures Test
Oltman, P. K., Raskin, E., Witkin, H. A. (1971). Palo Alto, CA: Consulting Psychologists Press.

Group Inventory for Finding Creative Talent
Rimm, S. B. (1980). Watertown, WI: Educational Assessment Services.

Group Inventory for Finding Interests
Rimm, S. B., & Davis, G. A. (1980). Watertown, WI: Educational Assessment Services.

Guilford-Zimmerman Temperament Survey
Guilford, J. P., & Zimmerman, W. S. (1949). Palo Alto, CA: Consulting Psychologists Press.

Hall Occupational Orientation Inventory
Hall, L. C., & Tarrier, R. B. (1976). Bensenville, IL: Scholastic Testing Service.

Halstead Category Test
Reitan, R. M. (1974). Odessa, FL: Psychological Assessment Resources.

Halstead-Reitan Neuropsychological Test Battery
Reitan, R. M. (1979). Tucson: Reitan Neuropsychology Laboratory.

Halstead Tactual Performance Test
Reitan, R. M. (1979). Tucson: Neuropsychological Laboratory.

Hand-Tool Dexterity Test
Bennett, G. K. (1965). San Antonio, TX: Psychological Corporation.

Hare Psychopathy Checklist
Hare, R. D. (1991). North Tonawando, NY: Multi-Health System.

Harrington-O'Shea Career Decision-Making System
Harrington, T. F., & O'Shea, A. J. (1982). Circle Pines, MN: American Guidance Service.

Hay Aptitude Test Battery
Hay, E. N. (1982). Northfield, IL: Wonderlic Personnel Test.

Hepatic Intelligence Scale
Shurrager, H. C., & Shurrager, P. S. (1964). Wood Dale, IL: Stoelting.

High School Characteristics Index
Stern, G., et al. (1962). Syracuse, NY: Evaluation Research Associates.

High School Personality Questionnaire
Cattell, R. B., Cattell, M. D., & Johns, E. (1984). Champaign, IL: Institute for Personality and Ability Testing.

Hill Performance Test of Selected Positional Concepts
Hill, E. (1981). Wood Dale, IL: Stoelting.

House-Tree-Person Test
Buck, J. N. (1970). Los Angeles: Western Psychological Services.

Houston Test for Language Development
Crabtree, M. (1963). Wood Dale, IL: Stoelting.

Illinois Test of Psycholinguistic Abilities
Kirk, S. A., McCarthy, J. J., & Kirk, W. D. (1968). Champaign: University of Illinois Press.

In-Basket Test
Frederiksen, N., Saunders, D. R., & Wand, B. (1957). *Psychological Monographs, 71*(9).

Industrial Reading Test
Psychological Corporation. (1978). San Antonio, TX: Author.

Inferred Self-Concept Scale
McDaniel, E. L. (1973). Los Angeles: Western Psychological Services.

Institutional Functioning Inventory
McGrath, E. J., et al. (1983). Princeton, NJ: Educational Testing Service.

Instructional Environment Scale
Ysseldyke, J. E., & Christensen, S. L. (1987). Austin, TX: PRO-ED.

Integrated Assessment System
Psychological Corporation. (1992). San Antonio, TX: Author.

Interest Determination, Exploration, and Assessment System
Johansson, C. B. (1980). Minneapolis: National Computer Systems, PAS Division.

Interview Schedule for Children
Kovacs, M. (1985). *Psychopharmacology Bulletin, 21,* 991–994.

Inventory of Psychosocial Development
Constantinople, A. (1965). Poughkeepsie, NY: Vassar College, Department of Psychology.

Iowa Tests of Basic Skills
Hieronymus, A. N., Lindquist, E. F., & Hoover, H. D. (1978). Chicago: Riverside.

Iowa Tests of Educational Development
Lindquist, E. F., & Feldt, L. S. (1982). Chicago: Science Research Associates.

Jackson Vocational Interest Survey
Jackson, D. N. (1977). Port Huron, MI: Research Psychologists Press.

Jesness Behavior Checklist
Jesness, C. F. (1984). Palo Alto, CA: Consulting Psychologists Press.

Job Effectiveness Prediction System
Personnel Decisions Research Institute for Life Office Management Association. (1978). Atlanta: Life Office Management Association.

Judgment of Line Orientation Test
Benton, A. (1983). Fairlawn, NJ: Oxford University Press.

Judgment of Occupational Behavior—Orientation
Cutler, A., Ferry, F., Kauk, R., & Robinett, R. (1972). Belmont, CA: CFKR Career Materials.

Kaufman Assessment Battery for Children
Kaufman, A. S., & Kaufman, N. L. (1983). Circle Pines, MN: American Guidance Service.

Kaufman Short Neuropsychological Assessment Procedure
Kaufman, A. S., & Kaufman, N. L. (1994). Circle Pines, MN: American Guidance Service.

Kent Infant Development Scale
Reuter, J. M., & Katoff, L. (1981). Kent, OH: Kent Developmental Metrics.

Keymath Diagnostic Arithmetic Test
Connolly, A., Nachtman, W., & Pritchett, E. M. (1999). Circle Pines, MN: American Guidance Service.

Keystone Visual Survey Test
Keystone View. (1974). Davenport, IA: Author.

Kinetic Family Drawing Test
Burns, R. C., & Kaufman, S. H. (1972). *Actions, styles, and symbols in kinetic family drawings.* New York: Bruner/Mazel.

Klove Grooved Pegboard Test
Klove, H. (1965). Lafayette, IN: Lafayette Instruments.

Klove Roughness Discrimination Test
Klove, H. (1965). Lafayette, IN: Lafayette Instruments.

Kohs's Block Design Test
Kohs, S. C. (1919). Chicago: Stoelting.

Kuder General Interest Survey
Kuder, G. F. (1976). Chicago: Science Research Associates.

Kuder Occupational Interest Survey
Kuder, G. F. (1979). Chicago: Science Research Associates.

Kuder Preference Record
Kuder, G. F. (1976). Chicago: Science Research Associates.

Kwalwasser Music Talent Test
Kwalwasser, J. (1953). Miami: Belwin-Mills.

Lauria-Nebraska Neuropsychological Battery
Golden, C. J., Purisch, A. D., & Hammeke, T. A. (1985). Los Angeles: Western Psychological Services.

Law School Admissions Test
Law School Admissions Council. (1988). Washington, DC: Law School Admissions Service.

Leadership Appraisal Survey
Hall, J. (1986). Woodlands, TX: Telemetrics International.

Learning Efficiency Test
Webster, R. E. (1981). Novato, CA: Academic Therapy Publications.

Learning Preference Inventory
Silver, H. F., & Hanson, J. R. (1978). Moorestown, NJ: Hanson, Silver, Strong, & Associates.

Learning Style Inventory
Brown, J. F., & Cooper, R. M. (1993). Freeport, NJ: Educational Activities.

Learning Style Inventory
Kolb, D. A. (1976). Boston: McBer.

Learning Style Profile
  Keefe, J. W., & Monk, J. S. (1988). Reston, VA: National Association of Secondary School Principals.

Learning Styles Inventory
  Dunn, R., Dunn, K., & Price, G. E. (1987). Lawrence, KS: Price Systems.

Learning Styles Inventory
  Renzulli, J. S., & Smith, L. H. (1978). Mansfield Center, CN: Creative Learning Press.

Learning Type Measure
  McCarthy, B., & St. Germain, C. (1993). Barrington, IL: Excel.

Leiter International Performance Scale
  Leiter, R. G. (1952). Chicago: Stoelting.

Lifestyle Assessment Questionnaire
  Eisenrath, D. (1989). Stevens Point, WI: National Wellness Institute.

Lincoln-Oseretsky Motor Development Scale
  Sloan, W. (1956). Chicago: Stoelting.

Louisville Behavior Checklist
  Miller, L. C. (1984). Los Angeles: Western Psychological Services.

Low Back Pain Scale
  Fairbank, J. (1980). *Physiotherapy, 66,* 271–272.

MacAndrew Alcoholism Scale
  MacAndrew. (1965). *Quarterly Journal of Studies on Alcohol, 26,* 238–296.

Manifest Anxiety Scale
  Taylor, J. A. (1953). *Journal of Abnormal Psychology, 48,* 265–270.

Matching Familiar Figures Test
  Kagan, J., Rosman, B. L., Day, D., Albert, J., & Phillips, W. (1964). Information processing in the child: Significance of analytic and reflective attitudes. *Psychological Monographs, 78*(1).

McCarthy Scales of Children's Abilities
  McCarthy, D. (1972). San Antonio, TX: Psychological Corporation.

McMaster Family Assessment Device
  Epstein, N. B., Baldwin, L. M., & Bishop, D. S. (1982). Providence, RI: Brown University/Butler Hospital Family Research Project.

Measures of Psychosocial Development
  Hawley, G. A. (1985). Odessa, FL: Psychological Assessment Resources.

Mechanical Aptitude Test
  Kobal, A., Wrightstone, J. W., Kunze, K. R., & MacElroy, A. J. (1952). Murfreesboro, TN: Psychometric Affiliates.

Mechanical Familiarity Test
  Employers' Tests and Services Associates. (1993). Chambersburg, PA: Author.

Mechanical Knowledge Test
  Employers' Tests and Services Associates. (1993). Chambersburg, PA: Author.

Meier Art Test: Aesthetic Perception
Meier Art Test: Judgment
  Meier, N. C. (1963). Iowa City: University of Iowa, Bureau of Educational Research and Service.

Memory for Designs Test
  Graham, F. K., & Kendall, B. S. (1960). Missoula, MT: Psychological Test Specialists.

Mental Status Checklist
  Schinka, J. A. (1998). Odessa, FL: Psychological Assessment Resources.

Metropolitan Achievement Test
  Balow, I. H., Farr, R., Hogan, T. P., & Prescott, G. A. (1984). San Antonio, TX: Psychological Corporation.

Metropolitan Readiness Test
  Nurss, J. R., & McGauvran, M. E. (1986). San Antonio, TX: Psychological Corporation.

Michigan Alcoholism Screening Test
  Selzer, M. L. (1971). *American Journal of Psychiatry, 127,* 1653–1658.

Michigan Picture Story Test
  Hutt, M. L. (1980). Orlando, FL: Grune & Stratton.

Miller Assessment for Preschoolers
  Miller, L. J. (1982). San Antonio, TX: Psychological Corporation.

Miller's Analogies Test
  Miller, W. S. (1975). San Antonio, TX: Psychological Corporation.

Millon Adolescent Personality Inventory
Millon, T., Green, C. J., & Meagher, R. B., Jr. (1982). Minneapolis: National Computer System, PAS Division.

Millon Behavioral Health Inventory
Millon, T., Green, C. J., & Meagher, R. B., Jr. (1982). Minneapolis: National Computer System, PAS Division.

Millon Clinical Multiaxial Inventory
Millon, T. (1987). Minneapolis: National Computer System, PAS Division.

Millon Index of Personality Styles
Millon, T. (1994). San Antonio, TX: Psychological Corporation.

Minnesota Clerical Test
Andrew, D. M., Peterson, D. G., & Longstaff, H. P. (1959). San Antonio, TX: Psychological Corporation.

Minnesota Importance Questionnaire
Vocational Psychology Research. (1981). Minneapolis: University of Minnesota, Vocational Psychology Research.

Minnesota Manual Dexterity Test
Lafayette Instrument Company. (1969). Lafayette, IN: Author.

Minnesota Multiphasic Personality Inventory
Hathaway, S. R., & McKinley, C. (1992). Minneapolis: University of Minnesota Press.

Minnesota Paper Formboard
Likert, R., & Quasha, W. H. (1970). San Antonio, TX: Psychological Corporation.

Minnesota Rate of Manipulation Test
University of Minnesota, Employment Stabilization Research Institute. (1969). Circle Pines, MN: American Guidance Service.

Minnesota Spatial Relations Test
American Guidance Service Test Division. (1930). Circle Pines, MN: Author.

Moore Eye-Hand Coordination and Color Matching Test
Moore, J. E. (1968). Atlanta: Moore & Associates.

Moral Judgment Interview and Scoring System
Kohlberg, L. (1987). New York: Cambridge University Press.

Multidimensional Self-Esteem Inventory
O'Brien, E. J., & Epstein, S. (1988). Odessa, FL: Psychological Assessment Resources.

Multiscore
Riverside Publishing Company. (1984). Chicago: Author.

Murphy-Meisgeier Type Indicator for Children
Meisgeier, C., & Murphy, E. (1987). Palo Alto, CA: Consulting Psychologists Press.

Musical Aptitude Profile
Gordon, E. (1965). Chicago: Riverside.

Myers-Briggs Type Indicator
Myers, I. B., & Briggs, K. S. (1985). Palo Alto, CA: Consulting Psychologists Press.

National Achievement Test
Psychometric Affiliates. (1983). Murfreesboro, TN: Author.

National Educational Development Series
Thurstone, T. G. (1994). Park Ridge, IL: SRA/London House.

NEO Five Factor Inventory–Revised
Costa, P. T., & McCrae, R. R. (1989). Odessa, FL: Psychological Assessment Resources.

NEO Personality Inventory–Revised
Costa, P. T., Jr., & McCrae, R. R. (1992). Odessa, FL: Psychological Assessment Resources.

Nowicki-Strickland Locus of Control Scale
Nowicki, S., & Strickland, B. R. (1973). *Journal of Consulting Psychology, 40*, 148–154.

Observational Analysis
Slosson, S. W., & Callisto, T. A. (1984). East Aurora, NY: Slosson Educational Publications.

Occupational Environment Scale
Osipow, S. H., & Spokane, A. R. (1993). Odessa, FL: Psychological Assessment Resources.

Occupational Stress Inventory
Osipow, S. H., & Spokane, A. R. (1987). Odessa, FL: Psychological Assessment Resources.

O'Connor Finger Dexterity Test
O'Connor, J. (1926). Chicago: Stoelting.

O'Connor Tweezer Dexterity Test
O'Connor, J. (1928). Chicago: Stoelting.

Office Arithmetic Test
   Hadley, S. T., & Stouffer, G. A. (1984). Chambersburg, PA: Employers' Tests and Services Associates.

Office Skills Test
   Hadley, S. T., & Stouffer, G. A. (1984). Chambersburg, PA: Employers' Tests and Services Associates.

Ohio Vocational Education Achievement Testing Program
   Ohio Vocational Achievement Tests Series. (1987). Columbus: Ohio State University, Vocational Instructional Materials Laboratory.

Ohio Vocational Interest Survey
   D'Costa, A. G., Winefordner, D. W., Odgers, J. G., & Koons, P. B., Jr. (1981). San Antonio, TX: Psychological Corporation.

Oliphant Auditory Discrimination Memory Test
   Oliphant, G. (1971). Cambridge, MA: Educators Publishing Service.

Organizational Climate Index
   Stern, G., et al. (1962). Syracuse, NY: Evaluation Research Associates.

Otis-Lennon School Ability Test
   Otis, A. S., & Lennon, R. T. (1982). San Antonio, TX: Psychological Corporation.

Pantomime Recognitions Test
   Benton, A. L., et al. (1983). Fairlawn, NJ: Oxford University Press.

Parent Daily Report
   Patterson, G. R., & Reid, J. B. (1987). *Behavioral Assessment, 9,* 97–109.

Parent Opinion Inventory
   National Study of School Evaluation. (1981). Falls Church, VA: Author.

Peabody Individual Achievement Test
   Dunn, L. M., & Markwardt, F. C., Jr. (1970). Circle Pines, MN: American Guidance Service.

Peabody Picture Vocabulary Test
   Dunn, L. M., & Dunn, L. M. (1997). Circle Pines, MN: American Guidance Service.

Perceptual Disorders Test
   Halstead Russell Neuropsychological Evaluation System. (1993). Los Angeles: Western Psychological Services.

Personal Adjustment Index
   Employers' Tests and Services Associates. (1993). Chambersburg, PA: Author.

Personal History Checklist
   Schinka, J. A. (1988). Odessa, FL: Psychological Assessment Resources.

Personal Orientation Inventory
   Shostrom, E. L. (1968). San Diego: Educational and Industrial Testing Service.

Personal Problems Checklist
   Schinka, J. A. (1998). Odessa, FL: Psychological Assessment Resources.

Personal Style Indicator
   Controneo, K. (1983). Athens, GA: Academic Excellence Leadership Project.

Personality Disorder Interview
   Widiger, T. A., Mangive, S., Corbin, E. M., Ellis, M. A., & Thomas, G. V. (1994). Odessa, FL: Psychological Assessment Resources.

Personality Inventory for Children
   Wirt, R. D. (1982). Los Angeles: Western Psychological Services.

Personnel Selection Inventory
   London House. (1996). Park Ridge, IL: McGraw-Hill/London House.

Personnel Test for Industry
   Wesman, A. G., & Doppelt, J. E. (1969). San Antonio, TX: Psychological Corporation.

Piers-Harris Children's Self-Concept Scale
   Piers, E. V., & Harris, D. B. (1984). Los Angeles: Western Psychological Services.

Planning Career Goals
   American Institutes for Research. (1976). Monterey, CA: CTB/McGraw-Hill.

Porteous Maze Test
   Porteous, S. D. (1965). San Antonio, TX: Psychological Corporation.

Position Analysis Questionnaire
   McCormick, P. R., Jeanneret, P. R., & Meacham, R. C. (1969). West Lafayette, IN: Purdue Research Foundation.

Primary Mental Abilities Test
   Thurstone, L. L., & Thurstone, T. G. (1974). Chicago: Science Research Associates.

Primary Test of Cognitive Skills
Huttenlocher, J., & Levine, S. C. (1990). Monterey, CA: CTB/McGraw-Hill.

Primary Visual-Motor Test
Haworth, M. R. (1970). Orlando, FL: Grune & Stratton.

Productivity Environmental Preference Survey
Dunn, R., Dunn, K., & Price, G. E. (1981). Lawrence, KS: Price Systems.

Programmer Aptitude Competence Test System
Haverly, C. A., & Seiner, P. (1970). Denville, NJ: Haverly Systems.

PSI Basic Skills Tests for Business, Industry, and Government
Ruch, W. W., Shub, A. N., Moinat, S. M., & Dye, D. A. (1983). Bay Village, OH: Psychological Services.

Psychopathology Instrument for Mentally Retarded Youth
Senatore, V., Matwon, J. L., & Kazdin, A. E. (1985). *American Journal of Mental Deficiency, 89,* 459–466.

Purdue Pegboard Test
Tiffin, J. (1968). Chicago: Science Research Associates.

Purdue Perceptual-Motor Survey
Roach, E. G., & Kephart, N. C. (1966). San Antonio, TX: Psychological Corporation.

Quick Neurological Screening Test
Mutti, M. Sterling, H. M., & Spaulding, N. O. (1997). San Antonio, TX: Psychological Corporation.

Racial Identity Attitude Scale
Helms, J. E. (1990). New York: Greenwood.

Rahim Organizational Conflict Inventories
Rahim, A. (1983). Palo Alto, CA: Consulting Psychologists Press.

Raven's Progressive Matrices
Raven, J. C. (1960, Standard; 1965, Coloured). San Antonio, TX: Psychological Corporation.

Reading Style Inventory
Learning Research Associates. (1986). Roslyn Heights, NY: Author.

Reitan Aphasia Screening Test
Reitan, R. M. (1984). Tucson: Neuropsychology Press.

Renzulli Rating Scale
Renzulli, J. S. (1981). Mansfield Center, CT: Creative Learning Press.

Revised Hamilton Rating Scale for Depression
Hamilton, M. (1960). *Journal of Neurology, Neurosurgery, and Psychiatry, 23,* 56–62.

Reynell Developmental Language Scale
Reynell, J. K. (1977). Windsor, UK: NFER-Nelson.

Reynell-Zinkin Scales
Reynell, J., & Zinkin, P. (1990). Windsor, UK: NFER-Nelson.

Reynolds Adolescent Depression Scale
Reynolds, W. M. (1987). San Antonio, TX: Psychological Corporation.

Riso-Hudson Enneagram Type Indicator
Riso, R. (1987). Boston: Houghton Mifflin.

Riverside Curriculum Assessment System
Riverside Publishing Company. (1991). Chicago: Author.

Roberts's Apperception Test for Children
Roberts, G. E., & McArthur, D. S. (1982). Los Angeles: Western Psychological Services.

Rokeach Value Survey
Rokeach, M. (1973). Sunnyvale, CA: Halgren Tests.

Rorschach Ink Blot Test
Rorschach, H. (1945). Bern, Switzerland: Huber.

Ross Information Processing Assessment
Ross, D. G. (1996). Austin, TX: PRO-ED.

Rotter Incomplete Sentence Blank
Rotter, J. B., & Rafferty, J. E. (1950). San Antonio, TX: Psychological Corporation.

Rust Inventory of Schizotypical Cognitions
Rust, J. (1987). San Antonio, TX: Psychological Corporation.

Sales Aptitude Test
Hadley, S. T., & Souffer, G. A. (1983). Chambersburg, PA: Employers' Tests and Services Associates.

Salience Inventory
Super, D. E., & Nevill, D. D. (1985). Palo Alto, CA: Consulting Psychologists Press.

Scales for Rating the Behavioral Characteristics of Superior Students
Renzulli, J. S., Smith, L. H., White, A. J., Callahan, C. M., & Hartman, R. K. (1976). Mansfield Center, CN: Creative Learning Press.

Schedule for Affective Disorders and Schizophrenia for School Aged Children
Puig-Antich, J., & Chambers, W. (1978). Los Angeles: Western Psychological Services.

School and College Ability Tests
Educational Testing Service. (1980). Princeton, NJ: Author.

School Apperception Test
Solomon, I. L., & Starr, B. D. (1968). New York: Springer.

School Attitude Measure
Wick, J. (1990). Iowa City: American College Testing.

School Environment Preference Survey
Gordon, L. (1978). San Diego: Edits.

Screening Assessment for Gifted Students
Johnson, C. K., & Corn, A. L. (1992). Austin, TX: PRO-ED.

Screening Test for Auditory Perception
Kimmel, G. M., & Wild, J. (1981). Novato, CA: Academic Therapy Publications.

Seashore Measures of Musical Talents
Seashore, C. E. (1960). San Antonio, TX: Psychological Corporation.

Self-Concept Adjective Checklist
Politte, A. J. (1971). Creve Coeur, MO: Psychologists and Educators.

Self-Description Questionnaire
Marsh, H. W. (1988). San Antonio, TX: Psychological Corporation.

Self-Directed Search
Holland, J. L. (1985). Odessa, FL: Psychological Assessment Resources.

Self-Perception Inventory
Martin, W. T. (1969). Chesterfield, MO: Psychologists and Educators.

Self-Report Family Inventory
Beavers, W. R., Hampon, R., & Hulgus, Y. (1985). Dallas: Southwest Family Institute.

Sentence Completion Test
Irvin, F. S. (1979). Creve Coeur, MO: Psychologists and Educators.

Sequential Tests of Educational Progress
Educational Testing Service. (1979). Monterey, CA: CTB/McGraw-Hill.

Serial-Digit Learning Test
Benton, A. L. (1983). New York: Oxford University Press.

Sixteen Personality Factor Questionnaire
Cattell, R. B., & IPAT Staff. (1994). Champaign, IL: Institute for Personality and Ability Testing.

Sizing Up Your School System
Buttram, J. L., Corcoran, T. B., & Hansen, B. J. (1989). Philadelphia: Research for Better Schools.

Slosson Drawing Coordination Test
Slosson, R. L. (1967). East Aurora, NY: Slosson Educational Publications.

Slosson Intelligence Test
Slosson, R. L. (1981). East Aurora, NY: Slosson Educational Publications.

Social Moral Reflection Measure
Gibbs, J. C. (1984). Princeton, NJ: ETS.

Southern California Sensory Integration Tests
Ayers, A. J. (1972). Los Angeles: Western Psychological Services.

Spache Binocular Reading Test
Spache, G. D. (1961). Davenport, IA: Keystone View.

Speech Perception Test
Halstead-Russell Neuropsychological System. (1993). Los Angeles: Western Psychological Services.

SRA Achievement Series
Naslund, R. A., Thorpe, L. P., & Lefever, D. W. (1981). Chicago: Science Research Associates.

SRA Clerical Aptitude Test
Richardson, Bellows, Henry, & Company. (1973). Chicago: Science Research Associates.

SRA Mechanical Aptitude Test
Richardson, Bellows, Henry, & Company. (1970). Chicago: Science Research Associates.

SRA Test of Mechanical Concepts
Stanard, S. J., & Bode, K. A. (1976). Chicago: Science Research Associates.

Stanford Achievement Test
Gardner, E. F., Rudman, H. C., Karlsen, B., & Merwin, J. C. (1997). San Antonio, TX: Psychological Corporation.

Stanford-Binet Intelligence Scale
Thorndike, R. L., Hagen, E. P., & Sattler, J. M. (1986). Chicago: Riverside.

Stanford Measurement Series (8th ed.)
Psychological Corporation. (1989). San Antonio, TX: Author.

State-Trait Anxiety Scale
Spielberger, C. D. (1983). Palo Alto, CA: Consulting Psychologists Press.

Stenographic Skills Test
Hadley, S. T., & Stouffer, G. A. (1984). Chambersburg, PA: Employers' Tests and Services Associates.

Stromberg Dexterity Test
Stromberg, E. L. (1951). San Antonio, TX: Psychological Corporation.

Strong Interest Inventory
Strong, E. K., Jr., Hansen, J. C., & Campbell, D. P. (1994). Palo Alto, CA: Consulting Psychologists Press.

Structured Interview of Reported Symptoms
Rogers, R., Bagby, M., & Dickens, E. (1992). Odessa, FL: PAR.

Structured Photographic Expressive Language Test
O'Hara, E., & Kresheck, J. O. (1983). Sandwich, IL: Janelle.

Student Opinion Inventory
National Study of School Evaluation. (1981). Falls Church, VA: Author.

Suicide Ideation Questionnaire
Reynolds, W. M. (1987). San Antonio, TX: Psychological Corporation.

Suinn Test Anxiety Behavior Scale
Rocky Mountain Behavioral Science Institute. (1971). Fort Collins, CO: Author.

Sutter-Eyberg Student Behavior Inventory
Sutter, J., & Eyberg, S. (1992). Sarasota, FL: Professional Resources Press.

Swassing-Barbe Modality Index
Swassing, R., & Barbe, R. (1979). Columbus, OH: Zaner-Bloser.

Symonds Picture-Story Test
Symonds, P. M. (1948). New York: Teachers College Press.

System of Multicultural Pluralistic Assessment
Mercer, J. R., & Lewis, J. E. (1979). San Antonio, TX: Psychological Corporation.

Teacher Opinion Inventory
National Study of School Evaluation. (1981). Falls Church, VA: Author.

Tell Me a Story Test
Constantino, G., Malgady, R. G., & Rogler, L. H. (1988). Los Angeles: Western Psychological Services.

Temporal Orientation Test
Benton, A. L. (1983). New York: Oxford University Press.

Test Anxiety Inventory
Spielberger, C. D. (1980). Palo Alto, CA: Consulting Psychologists Press.

Test Anxiety Profile
Oetting, E. R., & Cole, C. W. (1980). Fort Collins, CO: Rocky Mountain Behavioral Science Institute.

Test of Adolescent Language
Hammill, D. D. (1994). Austin, TX: PRO-ED.

Test of Adult Basic Education
CTB/McGraw-Hill. (1987). Palo Alto, CA: Author.

Test of Cognitive Skills
California Test Bureau. (1976). Monterey, CA: CTB/McGraw-Hill.

Test of Language Development
Hammill, D. D., & Newcomer, P. L. (1988). Austin, TX: PRO-ED.

Test of Nonverbal Intelligence
Brown, L., Sherbenu, R. J., & Dollar, S. J. (1982). Austin, TX: PRO-ED.

Tests of Achievement and Proficiency
Scannell, D. P., Haugh, U. M., Schild, A. H., & Ulmer, G. Chicago: Riverside.

Test Well: Wellness Inventory
National Wellness Institute. (1992). Stevens Point, WI: Author.

Thematic Apperception Test
Murray, H. A. (1943). Cambridge, MA: Harvard University Press.

Themes Concerning Blacks Test
Williams, R. L. (1972). St. Louis: St. Louis University, Department of Black Studies.

Therapeutic Reaction Scale
Thomas, D. E. (1984). ERIC Document 255 782.

Thinking Creatively in Action and Movement
Torrance, E. P. (1981). Bensenville, IL: Scholastic Testing Service.

Thinking Creatively with Sounds and Words
Torrance, E. P., Khantena, J., & Cunnington, B. F. (1973). Bensenville, IL: Scholastic Testing Service.

Thompson Modification of the TAT
Thompson, R. E., & Bachrach, A. J. (1949). Cambridge: Harvard University Press.

Torrance Tests of Creative Thinking
Torrance, E. P. (1974). Bensenville, IL: Scholastic Testing Service.

Trail Making Test
Benton, A. (1983). Fairlawn, NJ: Oxford University Press.

Trauma Symptoms Checklist
Briere, J. N. (1992). New York: Garland.

Universal Nonverbal Intelligence Test
Bracken, B. A., & McCallum, R. S. (1998). Chicago: Riverside.

USES Clerical Skills Test
U.S. Employment Service. (1968). Washington, DC: U.S. Department of Labor.

USES Interest Inventory
U.S. Employment Service. (1981). Washington, DC: U.S. Department of Labor.

Valpar Component Work Sample System
Valpar International Corporation. (1993). Tucson: Author.

Values Scale
Super, D. L., & Nevill, D. D. (1985). Palo Alto, CA: Consulting Psychologists Press.

Vane Kindergarten Test
Vane, J. P. (1968). Brandon, VT: CPPC.

Vineland Adaptive Behavior Scale
Sparrow, S. S., Balla, D. A., & Cicchetti, D. V. (1985). Circle Pines, MN: American Guidance Service.

Visual Form Discrimination Test
Wepman, J. M. (1975). Los Angeles: Western Psychological Services.

Vocational Interest, Experience, and Skills Assessment
American College Testing Program. (1983). Iowa City: Author.

Vocational Preference Inventory
Holland, J. L. (1985). Odessa, FL: Psychological Assessment Resources.

Wach Analysis of Cognitive Structures
Wach, H., & Vaughan. (1977). Los Angeles: Western Psychological Services.

Watson-Glaser Critical Thinking Appraisal
Watson, G., & Glaser, E. M. (1980). San Antonio, TX: Psychological Corporation.

Wechsler Adult Intelligence Scale
Wechsler, D. (1981). San Antonio, TX: Psychological Corporation.

Wechsler Bellevue Intelligence Scale
Wechsler, D. (1939). San Antonio, TX: Psychological Corporation.

Wechsler Individual Achievement Test
Psychological Corporation. (1992). San Antonio, TX: Author.

Wechsler Intelligence Scale for Children
Wechsler, D. (1991). San Antonio, TX: Psychological Corporation.

Wechsler Preschool and Primary Scale of Intelligence
Wechsler, D. (1967). San Antonio, TX: Psychological Corporation.

Welsh's Anxiety Scale
Welsh, G. S. (1965). *Journal of Clinical Psychology, 21,* 34–47.

Welsh's Repression Scale
Welsh, G. S. (1965). *Journal of Clinical Psychology, 21,* 34–47.

Wepman Auditory Discrimination Test
Wepman, J. M. (1973). Los Angeles: Western Psychological Services.

Wesman Personnel Classification Test
Wesman, A. G. (1965). San Antonio, TX: Psychological Corporation.

Wide Range Achievement Test
Jastak, S., & Wilkinson, G. S. (1984). Wilmington, DE: Jastak Assessment Systems.

Wonderlic Personnel Test
Wonderlic, E. F. (1981). Northfield, IL: Wonderlic Personnel Test.

Woodcock-Johnson Psycho-Educational Battery
Woodcock, R. W., & Johnson, M. B. (1977). Allen, TX: DLM.

Woodcock-Johnson Test of Achievement
Woodcock, R. W., & Johnson, M. B. (1990). Chicago: Riverside.

Woodworth Personal Data Sheet
Woodworth, R. W. (1920). Chicago: Stoelting.

Work Environment Preference Inventory
Gordon, L. (1973). San Antonio, TX: Psychological Corporation.

Work Environment Scale
Insel, P., & Moos, R. H. (1974). Palo Alto, CA: Consulting Psychologists Press.

Work Keys
American College Testing. (1996). Iowa City: Author.

Work Values Inventory
Super, D. E. (1970). Chicago: Riverside.

World of Work Inventory
Ripley, R. E., & Hudson, K. (1977). Scottsdale, AZ: World of Work.

Your Style of Learning and Thinking
Torrance, E. P., & Reynolds, R. L. (1980). Athens: Georgia Studies of Creative Thinking.

Zimmerman Preschool Language Scale
Zimmerman, I. L., Steiner, V. G., & Pond, R. E. (1995). San Antonio, TX: Psychological Corporation.

Appendix B: Test Publishers and Distributors

Academic Therapy Publications
20 Commercial Boulevard
Novato, CA 94949-6191

American College Testing Program
2201 North Dodge Street
P.O. Box 168
Iowa City, IA 52243

American Guidance Service
4201 Woodland Road
P.O. Box 99
Circle Pines, MN 55014-1796

Behavior Science Press
P.O. Box 020938
Tuscaloosa, AL 35402

Belwin-Mills Publishing Company
15800 Northwest 48th Avenue
Miami, FL 33014

College Board Publications
45 Columbus Avenue
New York, NY 10023

Consulting Psychologists Press
3803 Bayshore Road
P.O. Box 10096
Palo Alto, CA 94303

Creative Learning Press
P.O. Box 320
Mansfield Center, CT 06250

CTB/Macmillan/McGraw-Hill
Publishers Test Service
20 Ryan Ranch Road
Monterey, CA 93940-5703

Dallas Educational Services
P.O. Box 831254
Richardson, TX 75083

Devereux Foundation
19 South Waterloo Road
P.O. Box 400
Devon, PA 19333

Educational and Industrial Test
Services
P.O. Box 7234
San Diego, CA 92167

Educational Testing Services
Publication Order Service
P.O. Box 6736
Princeton, NJ 08541-6736

Educators Publishing Service
75 Moulton Street
Cambridge, MA 02238

Employers' Tests & Services Associates
341 Garfield Street
Chambersburg, PA 17201

ERIC Document Reproduction
Service
P.O. Box 190
Arlington, VA 22210

Gesell Developmental Test Materials
P.O. Box 272391
Houston, TX 77277

Grune & Stratton
Orlando, FL 32887

Harrison G. Gough Institute of
Personality and Research
University of California
Berkeley, CA 94720

Haverly Systems
78 Broadway
P.O. Box 919
Denville, NJ 07834

Humanics Limited
1482 Mecaslin Street, N.W.
Atlanta, GA 30357-0400

Humanics Media
5457 Pine Cone Road
La Crescenta, CA 91214

Industrial Psychology
515 Madison Avenue
New York, NY 10022

Institute for Personality and Ability
Testing
1602 Coronado Drive
P.O. Box 1188
Champaign, IL 61824-1188

IOX Assessment Associates
11411 West Jefferson Boulevard
Culver City, CA 90230

Jastak Assessment/Wide Range
P.O. Box 3410
Wilmington, DE 19804-0250

Kent Developmental Metrics
1325 South Water Street
P.O. Box 845
Kent, OH 44240-3178

Ladoca Publishing Foundation
Laradon Hall Training and Residential Center
East 51st Avenue and Lincoln
Street
Denver, CO 80216

Lafayette Instrument Company
P.O. Box 5729
Lafayette, IN 47903

Life Office Management Association
5770 Powers Ferry Road
Atlanta, GA 30327

McGraw-Hill/London House
9701 West Higgins Road
Rosemont, IL 60018-4720

Meeting Street School
Easter Seal Society of Rhode
    Island
667 Waterman Avenue
East Providence, RI 02914

National Computer Systems
10901 Bren Road East
Minnetonka, MN 55343

Pacific Psychological
710 George Washington Way
Suite G
Richland, WA 99352

Person-O-Metrics
Evaluation and Development Ser-
    vices
20504 Williamsburg Road
Dearborn Heights, MI 48127

PRO-ED
8700 Shoal Creek Boulevard
Austin, TX 78758-6897

Psychological Assessment
    Resources
P.O. Box 998
Odessa, FL 33556

Psychological Corporation
555 Academic Court
San Antonio, TX 78204-2498

Psychological Services Bureau
P.O. Box 327
St. Thomas, PA 17252-0327

Psychological Services
370 Lake Forest Road
Bay Village, Ohio 44140

Psychological Test Specialists
P.O. Box 9229
Missoula, MT 59807

Psychometric Affiliates
P.O. Box 807
Murfreesboro, TN 37133

Reason House
1402 York Road #207
Lutherville, MD 21093-6024

Research Psychologists Press
1110 Military Street
P.O. Box 984
Port Huron, MI 48060

Riverside Publishing Company
425 Springlake Drive
Itasca, IL 60143-2079

Rocky Mountain Behavioral Sci-
    ence Institute
P.O. Box 1066
Fort Collins, CO 80522

Scholastic Testing Service
480 Meyer Road
P.O. Box 1056
Bensenville, IL 60106-1617

Sheridan Psychological Services
P.O. Box 6106
Orange, CA 92667

Slosson Educational Publications
P.O. Box 280
East Aurora, NY 14052-0280

Stoelting Company
Oakwood Center
620 Wheat Lane
Wood Dale, IL 60191

U.S. Department of Labor
Division of Testing
200 Constitution Avenue
Employment and Training Admin-
    istration
Washington, DC 20213

U.S. Military Entrance Processing
    Command
2500 Green Bay Road
North Chicago, IL 60064

Valpar International Corporation
P.O. Box 5767
Tucson, AZ 85703

Western Psychological Services
12031 Wilshire Boulevard
Los Angeles, CA 90025-1251

Wonderlic Personnel Test
1509 North Milwaukee Avenue
Libertyville, IL 60048-1380

Glossary

Ability test An ability test measures the present level of functioning and can provide an estimate of the future performance of an individual on specific tasks or domains in cognitive or psychomotor areas. See also *achievement test* and *aptitude test*.

Accountability Both students and teachers are being required to show that students have mastered course or grade objectives. Minimum-level skills, essential skills, survival skills, and other types of achievement tests are used to provide evidence of mastery.

Achievement test An achievement test measures the degree or extent of the knowledge, information, skills, and competencies that a person has acquired through training, instruction, or experience. There are survey achievement tests as well as subject-related tests.

Acquiescence response set Some test takers have a tendency to select positive responses (e.g., "true" or "yes") on attitude and personality tests.

Adaptive testing This procedure adjusts the test questions presented according to an individual's responses to previous items on the test. Test items can thus be geared to the individual's ability or achievement levels, and test takers may start and finish at different levels.

Adjustment test An adjustment test is one of the major types of personality tests. Such tests measure the ability of an individual to function normally in society and achieve personal needs.

Affective domain The affective domain covers dimensions of personality such as attitudes, motives, emotional behavior, temperament, and personality traits.

Age norms Age norms for a particular test provide the median score made by test takers of a given chronological age. In addition to intellectual and social age, many tests provide information on typical characteristic behavior of individuals at given age levels.

Alternate forms For many achievement and aptitude tests it is necessary to have more than one form of the tests available. Alternate forms are constructed according to the same blueprint—that is, with the same set of objectives, the same type of items, and similar difficulty and discrimination values for the test items. The two forms also have similar statistical characteristics; the means, standard deviations, and correlations with other measures should all be approximately equal.

Alternate-forms reliability This type of reliability requires correlating the scores of individuals on one form with the scores they made on the second form. This coefficient provides evidence of the equivalence of the two forms as well as the stability of the individual's performance.

Alternative assessment Alternative assessment emphasizes assessing performance of the test taker through portfolios, interviews, observations, work samples, and the like instead of through multiple-choice norm- or criterion-referenced examinations.

Anecdotal records Anecdotal records require a series of observations on an individual(s). The observer should provide an objective description of the behavior observed and an interpretation of the situation. School psychologists are often required to record two observations of the child along with test information.

Aptitude test An aptitude test is used to provide an estimate of future performance on tasks that may or may not be similar to the tasks measured on the test. Aptitude tests are used to assess the educational readiness of individuals to learn or become proficient in a given area if education or training is provided. Aptitude tests may contain the same type of items as achievement tests.

485

Arithmetic mean See *mean*.

Assessment procedures Assessment procedures are the methods that enable one to appraise or estimate the attributes of a person, group, or programs. The tools of assessment can include checklists, inventories, observational schedules, needs assessments, rating scales, and all types of tests.

Attenuation Attenuation is a phenomenon that takes place in the statistical determination of correlation and regression. The correlation or regression is reduced because of the imperfect reliability of one or both of the measures being correlated or compared.

Attitude Attitude is a dimension of the affective domain and one aspect of an individual's personality. Attitude is reflected in reactions to events, other individuals, objects, or institutions.

Authentic assessment This type of assessment focuses on assessing realistic tasks or activities that relate to the performance on a domain or set of constructs being measured.

Basal age Basal age is the age at which the test taker passes all of the items on a given test.

Basic skills Many achievement tests are designed to measure the basic skills required to be successful in school; these are usually reading, writing, and arithmetic competencies. Such skills are necessary for the student to learn other subjects, such as science and social studies.

Battery A battery is a set of tests usually standardized on the same population. Survey achievement tests are one example of a battery. A battery facilitates comparison of a test taker's performance in different areas.

Behavioral assessment Behavioral assessment focuses on the more objective and observable components of behavior and uses a wide variety of techniques, such as observation, checklists, and self-monitoring.

Behavioral objectives Behavioral objectives require counselors and teachers to specify desired behavioral outcomes in objective, observable forms and to identify the conditions of measurement.

Bias Bias in testing results in scores that are higher or lower than they would be if the measurement were more reliable and valid. The error caused by bias is systematic rather than random.

Bimodal distribution A bimodal distribution is a frequency distribution with two modes or high points.

Biographic inventory A biographic inventory is a questionnaire or survey instrument used to obtain information about the individual's educational, social, medical, and work experiences. It is one of the tools used by counselors and employment psychologists.

Buckley Amendment The Buckley Amendment is federal legislation that gives individuals and their parents or guardians access to information, including the results of standardized tests.

Ceiling Ceiling is the level or point at which a test taker fails a test or subtest.

Central tendency Central tendency relates to the typical or average score in a distribution. The three measures of central tendency are the mean, median, and mode. Any one of these statistics summarizes the typical or average performance of a group.

Central tendency error An error of central tendency occurs when the rater avoids all the extreme judgments, both high and low, and rates all items in the middle.

Checklist A checklist is a list of words, phrases, or statements describing the behavior of an individual or situation. The rater checks the presence or absence of the item.

Coaching Coaching occurs prior to the administration of a test and involves short-term instructional activities designed to help test takers increase their test scores. Sessions often include instruction on test-taking strategies and control of test anxiety.

Coefficient alpha Coefficient alpha is a reliability coefficient that measures the internal consistency of a test. The coefficient is the expected correlation of one test form with an alternate form that contains the same number of items.

Coefficient of determination The coefficient of determination is computed by squaring the correlation coefficient. It provides an estimate of the proportion of variance in one variable that is predictable from the other variable.

Coefficient of equivalence The coefficient of equivalence is used to compute the reliability of alternate forms of a test, based either upon two administrations or on a single administration with odd and even items constituting separate forms.

Coefficient of internal consistency The coefficient of internal consistency is based upon one testing and provides an estimate of the homogeneity of test items. The split-half and Kuder-Richardson methods provide coefficients of internal consistency.

Coefficient of stability A coefficient of stability provides a picture of how consistent an individual's scores are over a period of time. The test-retest method and alternate forms provide some information on the stability of scores over time.

Cognitive domain The cognitive domain encompasses the different levels individuals use in perceiving, thinking, and remembering. These levels are knowledge, comprehension, application, synthesis, analysis, and evaluation.

Cognitive style Cognitive style refers to the strategies or approaches an individual prefers to use in cognitive activities. Some of the styles discussed in the text are internal and external locus of control, field independence–field dependence, and reflectivity-impulsivity.

Competency test A competency test is an achievement test that assesses a test taker's level of knowledge or skill in some defined domain.

Computer-assisted testing Computer-assisted testing refers to testing that is presented on the computer rather than in a test booklet.

Computer-based interpretation Computer-based interpretation is a method of providing the interpretation of test scores according to algorithms built into the computer program. The test user is provided with score reports and narrative statements about the results.

Concurrent validity Concurrent validity is one type of criterion-referenced validity. Test scores are compared with a criterion measure obtained at about the same time, and the coefficient describes their relationship.

Confidence interval The confidence interval, or confidence band, is marked by two points that define with specified probability the range that includes an individual's true score.

Consequential validity Consequential validity focuses on the consequences of giving a test and relates to all phases—administration, scoring, interpretation, construction, uses, etc.

Construct A construct is a theory or concept used to explain data in an orderly way. In a psychometric sense it is a psychological attribute or trait.

Construct validity Construct validity is the extent to which a test measures the intended psychological trait or attribute.

Content validity Content validity is the degree to which a test measures a defined body of knowledge. This type of validity is extremely important for achievement tests.

Correlation Correlation is a statistic used to measure the strength and direction of the association between two sets of scores. Coefficients range from +1.00 to -1.00. A correlation of +1.00 indicates a perfect positive relationship between the scores, a correlation of .00 indicates no relationship between the scores, and a correlation of -1.00 indicates an inverse relationship.

Covariation Covariation refers to the variance that two or more tests or variables have in common.

Criterion-referenced tests Criterion-referenced tests are designed to assess a rather limited range of objectives or goals. They are usually used as mastery tests to assess whether an individual can demonstrate a specific skill or objective.

Criterion-referenced validity Criterion-referenced validity is based on the correlation of test scores with some type of criterion measure.

Cronbach's alpha Cronbach's alpha is a procedure for estimating the internal consistency of a test based on parts of the test. It is one of the procedures used to compute reliability.

Crystallized intelligence Crystallized intelligence is one of the types of intelligence in Cattell's model. The term refers to the part of intelligence acquired through experience and education.

Culture-fair tests Culture-fair tests are designed to be fair to all types of cultural and socioeconomic groups. These tests attempt to include only content to which all groups have been exposed during maturation.

Decision theory Test users are interested in making decisions and predictions on the basis of test results. Such predictions can be classified as positive, false positive, negative, and false negative. Decision theory is also used in selecting a test—to identify the types of information needed and the types of information already available.

Derived scores A derived score is a score into which a raw score is converted by some type of mathematical operation. Percentile ranks, standard scores, stanines, and grade-equivalent scores are all derived scores.

Descriptive statistics Descriptive statistics are used to summarize characteristics of a group of scores—for example, central tendency and dispersion or variability of scores. The mean, median, mode, variance, and standard deviation are descriptive statistics.

Deviation IQ The deviation IQ is the score that compares an individual with her age or grade group. The fixed mean is usually 100, and the standard deviation is 15.

Diagnostic tests A diagnostic test is an achievement test, most often in mathematics and reading, used to identify the strengths and weaknesses of the individual. Such tests include a wide range of items on a given skill or objective.

Differential prediction Differential prediction is used in situations of criterion-referenced validity. It indicates the degree to which a test that is used to predict individual attainment yields different predictions for the same criteria for groups with different demographic characteristics, prior experience, or treatment.

Domain sampling Domain sampling refers to a given area from which sample items are taken. Often criterion-referenced tests are called domain-referenced tests. The three major domains are cognitive, affective, and psychomotor.

Equivalence reliability Equivalence reliability estimates the extent to which two or more forms of a test are consistent. In split-half reliability, the test is subdivided into two parts—for example, odd items versus even items. In parallel forms the scores from Form X of a test are correlated with the scores from Form Y to provide an estimate of the equivalence of the forms.

Equivalent forms Test makers may construct more than one form of a test to measure the same objectives with items of similar difficulty.

Error of measurement Error of measurement refers to the discrepancy between an individual's observed score and his true score.

Evaluation Evaluation is the process an individual uses to judge information from one or more sources. That process may focus on test data as well as observations and other sources.

Factor The term *factor* can describe a psychological construct, such as verbal, spatial, or numerical aptitude. It can also represent the covariance of various subtests that tend to cluster together; that is, it represents their intercorrelations or intersections.

Factor analysis Factor analysis is a statistical multivariate procedure used to analyze the intercorrelations or covariance of variables. The method results in the identification of a reduced number of factors needed to explain the intercorrelations of variables.

False negative A false negative is a type of error in which an individual is predicted to fail but actually succeeds if given a chance.

Field dependence Field dependence is one of the dimensions of cognitive style that relates to an individual's dependence on body cues in space perception.

Field independence Field independence is a dimension of cognitive style that relates to an individual's dependence on body cues in space perception but independence from the surrounding visual field.

Fluid intelligence Fluid intelligence is one of the two types of intelligence identified by Cattell. It is the inherited dimension of intelligence and includes problem-solving and thinking ability.

Forced choice Some interest and personality tests use the forced choice method, whereby the test taker is required to select one or more items from two or more similar or related options. This method helps to control for response set.

Frequency distribution A frequency distribution is a way of organizing and arranging data in a table. Scores are usually grouped in fewer intervals to summarize overall performance.

g factor The g factor is a generalized intelligence factor that is measured in most intelligence tests; tests that yield one score are following the g-factor approach. Spearman was the leading theorist of this conceptual model.

Grade-equivalent scores Grade-equivalent scores are a type of derived test score used primarily by survey achievement tests. A raw score is translated into the grade level for which the achieved score is the real or estimated mean or median.

Group test A group test can be given to more than one test taker in a single setting by one test administrator.

Halo effect Halo effect is the tendency of a rater to let the ratings in other areas of a scale influence the ratings in areas that cannot be observed or are difficult to rate.

Histogram A histogram is a bar graph that provides a picture or description of scores.

In-basket technique The in-basket technique requires the examinee to take action on a series of problem situations presented through correspondence, memos, and other documents found in a sample in-basket.

Informed consent Informed consent requires test takers to give their consent before being tested; it is legally and ethically required. Test takers are to be told what the purposes of the test are, who will have access to the scores, and how the results will be used.

Intelligence test An intelligence test measures dimensions of aptitude and ability that are needed for success in educational and vocational fields. There are both individual and group tests.

Interest inventory An interest inventory assesses an individual's likes and dislikes, preferences, and interests. This information is then related to occupational fields and clusters and can sometimes be compared to individuals working in given occupational fields.

Internal consistency Internal consistency is a method of estimating reliability that is computed from a single administration of a test. The coefficients reflect the degree to which the items are measuring the same construct and are homogeneous. Cronbach's alpha and the Kuder-Richardson formulas are measures of the internal consistency of a test.

Interpretative report Most interest, aptitude, and achievement tests provide not only a summary of the test scores but also information that helps test takers interpret and understand those scores.

Interval scale The interval scale is one of the four measurement scales and can be used to classify and order measurements. It plots equal distances between score points but does not have a true zero point. Examples of interval scales include IQ, Celsius, and Fahrenheit scales.

Ipsative measurement Ipsative measurement is a type of item format, such as forced choice or ranking, in which the variables (options or items) are compared with each other. Ipsative comparisons are only intraindividual and are not appropriate for normative interpretation.

Item bias An item is said to be biased when the average expected score on the item for the group in question is substantially higher or lower than it is for the overall population and when this difference results from factors that the item is not intended to measure.

Item response theory (IRT) IRT is an alternative theory to classical measurement theory and was developed from concepts originating in the 19th century in mathematics and psychology. An early example is how Binet placed the items on his test and is today in a modified way the basis of computer-adaptive testing.

Job analysis   The general process of identifying the abilities, competencies, knowledge, and skills needed to perform jobs is called job analysis.

Kuder-Richardson 20/21   The KR 20 and 21 formulas are used to compute reliability in one administration of a test. They are internal consistency measures. KR 20 provides an estimate equal to the mean of all possible split-half coefficients. KR 21 can be substituted for KR 20 if the item difficulty levels are similar.

Least restrictive environment   Public Law 94-142 calls for the placement of each handicapped individual in the most normal situation in which that individual can be successful.

Leniency error   When a person is rated higher on an item than she should be rated, an error of leniency is operating.

Likert scale   A Likert scale is an attitude scale that asks people to rate the intensity of their agreement with certain statements.

Locus of control   Rotter identifies a cognitive and perceptual style that relates to how individuals perceive themselves as being controlled. The two ends of the continuum are external and internal, with external indicating reliance on external reinforcement and a belief in chance and fate.

Mean   The mean is the arithmetic average of a set of scores. It is equal to the sum of the scores divided by the number of scores. The mean is one of three statistics used to indicate central tendency.

Measurement   Measurement is the process used to assign numerals to objects or constructs according to rules so that the numbers have quantitative meaning.

Median   The median is the 50th percentile or the midpoint of a distribution.

Minimum-level competency test   A minimum-level competency test measures the essential or minimum skills that school systems and states have defined as a standard to be met.

Mode   The mode is the most frequently occurring score or number in a set of scores.

National norms   National norms give the average or median performance of a probability sample representative of the whole country. Most survey achievement batteries and scholastic aptitude tests report national norms.

Nominal scale   The nominal scale is a scale that can be used to classify data into mutually exclusive and exhaustive categories.

Nonverbal test   In a nonverbal test the test taker is not required to respond to the tasks verbally, and items are not presented in a written format. The examinee may be shown pictures and asked to point to a specific one. Or the test taker may be asked to manipulate materials, copy block or bead designs, assemble puzzles, and so on.

Norm groups   Norm groups are composed of the individuals on whom a test is standardized. These groups provide the basis for interpreting scores.

Norm-referenced test   A norm-referenced test presents score interpretation based on a comparison of individual performance with that of other individuals in specified groups.

Normal curve   The normal curve is a smooth bell-shaped curve that is symmetrical around the mean; the curve can be computed with the use of an equation. Most educational and psychological variables, such as achievement and intelligence, have a normal bell-shaped distribution.

Objective test   An objective test has a predetermined scoring key. Multiple-choice tests are an example of such a test.

Observational techniques   Observational techniques are used to look at the behavior of the test taker—sometimes during the examination, sometimes in naturalistic situations. In behavior assessment self-observation is sometimes used; the client is asked to keep a log or diary of his behavior. Situational tests require raters to observe individual behavior during the test.

Ordinal scale   An ordinal scale requires an individual to rank order measurements.

Parallel forms   See *alternate* or *equivalent forms.*

Percentile rank Percentile rank places a score in a distribution by identifying the percentage of scores that fall at or below the given score. A percentile rank is a type of derived score used on most norm-referenced tests.

Performance test A performance test requires the test taker to engage in some process, such as manipulating physical objects, rather than marking an answer on an answer sheet.

Personality inventory A personality inventory measures one or more dimensions of personality, such as attitude, adjustment, temperament, and values. The test taker is usually presented with a wide variety of behaviors and asked if they are characteristic of him.

Portfolio Portfolio is a collection of products produced by the person, such as the papers, themes, tests, and book reports of a student in language arts or a collection of products produced by a person in a fine arts class.

Predictive validity Predictive validity is a form of criterion-referenced validity in which test scores are compared with performance that is measured sometime in the future. The predictor variable is the test, and the criterion variable is the future performance, often on the job or in school.

Predictor A predictor is a measurable characteristic—such as a test score, previous performance, rating, or observation—that is correlated with a criterion variable to indicate future success or failure.

Primary standards Primary standards are the essential and fundamental characteristics that should be met by all tests before they are used.

Profile A profile is a graphic representation of individual or group scores. It provides a picture of the relative magnitude of scores.

Projective techniques Projective techniques are one method of assessing personality. The test taker gives free response to a series of stimuli, such as inkblots, pictures, or incomplete sentences. It is assumed that individuals will project their own perceptions, feelings, and attitudes in their answers.

Psychomotor test A psychomotor test measures fine and gross motor skills. The psychomotor domain—unlike the cognitive and affective domains—organizes and classifies psychomotor behaviors in terms of the amount of concentration required.

Public Law 94-142 Public Law 94-142, entitled the Education of All Handicapped Children Act, was passed in 1975 and established the requirements for free and appropriate education for all handicapped children. It also restricts the use of tests and assessment procedures with handicapped individuals.

Questionnaire A questionnaire is similar to a structured interview; it contains a list of questions on a topic or issue. A questionnaire is usually administered to a group of individuals to find out about their attitudes, beliefs, behaviors, and so on.

Range Range is a statistic used to measure the variable or spread of the scores. It is the difference between the highest and lowest score in a distribution.

Rapport Rapport is a warm and friendly relationship or interpersonal environment. An examiner wants to ensure valid results by establishing this type of positive environment and thereby encouraging the proper motivation and cooperation of the test taker.

Rating scale A rating scale is a measure that requires the rater to estimate the value of a person or thing or assess the presence of some trait or characteristic. Sometimes the scale calls for self-ratings; at other times ratings are given by peers, teachers, parents, and so on.

Ratio scale The ratio scale has equal units of measurement and has a true zero point. Time, height, and weight are examples of measurements that use the ratio scale. Most educational and psychological variables cannot be measured on the ratio scale.

Raw score Raw score is the unadjusted number of correct answers.

Readiness test A readiness test measures the extent to which the test taker has acquired the skills and knowledge necessary to learn a more complex skill.

Regression Regression is a statistical technique used to help individuals predict x when they know y and the relationship between x and y. A linear equation can be compared to predict criterion scores with one or more predictor variables.

Reliability Reliability refers to the degree to which test scores are consistent, dependable, or repeatable. Reliability is a function of the degree to which test scores are free from errors of measurement.

Response set Response set refers to the tendency of a test taker to respond to test items in a stereotyped or fixed way. The test taker may consciously or unconsciously choose the most socially desirable answers or perhaps true rather than false options.

Scatter plot A scatter plot is a bivariate graph that shows the paired values of two variables being correlated.

Scholastic aptitude test A scholastic aptitude test measures the cognitive skills necessary for success in school. It is used to predict how well individuals will do in educational contexts.

Screening test A screening test makes broad categorizations as a first step in a selection or diagnostic process in school or industry.

Situational test A situational test is a performance test in which an individual is placed in a realistic but contrived situation and then is rated on his role competence and problem-solving abilities.

Skewness Skewness is the degree of asymmetry in a frequency distribution. In positively skewed distributions the scores are piled up at the lower end of the distribution, to the left of the mode. In a negatively skewed distribution the scores are piled up at the high end of the distribution, to the right of the mode.

Social desirability response set The social desirability response set is active when an individual tries to portray herself in a socially desirable light. The individual fakes "good" instead of putting down what is truly descriptive of her behavior.

Spearman-Brown prophecy formula The Spearman-Brown formula is used to estimate the relia-

bility of a test if the test length is increased. Theoretically, a longer test samples more behavior and covers more items from the measured domain, thereby increasing the reliability of the test.

Speeded test A speeded test measures performance by the number of tasks performed in a given time period. Clerical speed and accuracy, typing, and coding tests are examples of this type of test.

Split-half reliability Split-half reliability is a method of computing the reliability of a test from one administration of the test. An internal analysis coefficient is obtained by using one-half of the items on the test for one score and the other half for the second score. These scores are then correlated and corrected for a full-length test, using the Spearman-Brown formula. The method provides an estimate of the alternate-form reliability.

Standard deviation The standard deviation is the square root of the variance; it is a statistic that describes the spread or dispersion of scores. Standard deviation is used with a derived score as an index of how far above or below the mean the score falls.

Standard error of measurement The standard error of measurement is the standard deviation of the errors of measurement associated with the test scores for a specific group of test takers.

Standard score A standard score describes the location of an individual's score within a set of scores. Its distance from the mean is expressed in terms of standard deviation units. Such a score is used in norm-referenced measurement contexts.

Standardized test A standardized test is administered under standard directions and conditions.

Standards-based assessment Standards-based assessment is based upon state or national standards and is characterized by emphasis on what students should be able to do as a results of their schooling. Items on tests emphasize what students should be able to demonstrate in real-world situations.

Stanines Stanines are a 9-point scale having a mean of 5 and a standard deviation of 2. All but stanines 1 and 9 are one-half standard deviation in width. They are used to describe an individual's position relative to the norming group.

Statistics Statistics are an area of mathematics focusing on the collection, organization, and interpretation of numerical data. A statistic is a number used to describe some characteristic, such as the central tendency or variability of a set of scores.

Subtest A subtest is a grouping of items measuring the same function.

T score A T score is a derived score on a scale usually having a mean score of 50 and a standard deviation of 10.

Test anxiety Test anxiety is a psychological state of stress and fear caused by testing situations. Although some anxiety may be beneficial, extreme test anxiety can disrupt performance.

Test-retest reliability Test-retest methods require giving the same test to the same group of examinees on two different occasions and correlating the two sets of scores. The resulting coefficient gives an indication of the stability of the results.

True score The true score in classical test theory is the average of the scores earned by an individual on an unlimited number of perfectly parallel forms of the same test.

Usability Usability refers to the practical factors that must be considered in selecting a test—for example, cost, time, ease of administration, and ease of scoring.

User's guide The user's guide contains a statement of the purpose of the test, its content, and appropriate uses. The guide often contains information on how to administer, score, and interpret the test.

Validity Validity is the degree to which a certain inference from a test is appropriate or meaningful.

Variance Variance is the average squared deviation from the mean or the standard deviation squared. The statistic is a measure of variability or dispersion of the scores.

Verbal test A verbal test is a test requiring oral or written responses to test items.

z score A z score is a type of standard score in which the mean is 0 and the standard deviation is 1. A z score represents the raw score in standard deviation units.

References

Aiken, L. R. (1985). *Psychological testing and assessment* (3rd ed.). Boston: Allyn & Bacon.

Aiken, L. R. (1996). *Rating scales and checklists.* New York: Wiley.

Alderman, D. L., & Powers, D. E. (1980). The effects of special preparation on SAT-verbal scores. *American Educational Research Journal, 17,* 239–253.

Allred, L. J., & Harris, W. G. (1984). Personal communication, cited in B. F. Green (1984), *Computer-based ability testing.* Washington, DC: American Psychological Association, Scientific Affairs Office.

Aman, M. G., Hammer, D., & Rojahn, J. (1993). Mental retardation. In T. H. Ollendick & M. Hersen (Eds.), *Handbook of child and adolescent assessment.* Boston: Allyn & Bacon.

American Association for Counseling and Development (AACD). (1980). *Responsibilities of users of standardized tests.* APGA Policy Statement. Falls Church, VA: Author.

American Association of Mental Retardation. (1993). *Manual on terminology and classification in mental retardation.* Washington, DC: Author.

American Association of School Administrators, National Association of Elementary Principals, National Association of Secondary School Principals, and National Council on Measurement in Education. (1994). Competency standards in student assessment for educational administrators. *Educational Measurement, 13*(1), 44–47.

American Counseling Association. (1993). *Code of ethics.* Alexandria, VA: Author.

American Educational Research Association, American Psychological Association, and National Council on Measurement in Education. (1985). *Standards for educational and psychological testing.* Washington, DC: American Psychological Association.

American Psychiatric Association. (1994). *Diagnostic and statistical manual of mental disorders* (4th ed.). Washington, DC: Author.

American Psychological Association. (1988). *Code of fair testing practices.* Washington, DC: Author.

American Psychological Association. (1992). *Ethical principles of psychologists* (rev. ed.). Washington, DC: Author.

American Psychological Association. (1994). *Publication manual of the American Psychological Association* (4th ed.). Washington, DC: Author.

Anastasi, A. (1993). A century of psychological testing: Origins, problems, and progress. In T. K. Fagan & G. R. Vander Bos (Eds.), *Exploring applied psychology: Origins and critical analysis* (pp. 11–36). Washington, DC: American Psychological Association.

Anastasi, A. (1997). *Psychological testing* (7th ed.). Upper Saddle River, NJ: Prentice Hall.

Arnold, M. B. (1962). *Story sequence analysis: A method of measuring and predicting achievement.* New York: Columbia University Press.

Aylward, G. P. (1994). *Practitioner's guide to developmental and psychological testing.* Austin, TX: PRO-ED.

Bailey, D., & Wolery, M. (1989). *Assessing infants and preschoolers with handicaps.* Upper Saddle River, NJ: Merrill/Prentice Hall.

Bailey, R. C., & Siudzinski, R. M. (1986). *The FAST profile instruction and reference manual: The Florida Analysis of Semantic Traits Profile.* Dallas: BALI Screening Company.

Baker, F. B. (1989). Computer technology in test construction and processing. In R. L. Linn, *Educational measurement* (3rd ed.). New York: Macmillan.

Baldwin, J. A., & Bell, Y. R. (1985). The African Self-Consciousness Scales: An Africentric personality questionnaire. *Western Journal of Black Studies, 9*(2), 65–68.

Bandura, A. (1986). *Social foundations of thought and action: A social cognitive theory*. Upper Saddle River, NJ: Prentice Hall.

Bannatyne, A. (1971). *Language, reading, and learning disabilities*. Springfield, IL: Thomas.

Bannatyne, A. (1974). Diagnosis: A note on the recategorization of the WISC scaled score. *Journal of Learning Disabilities, 7*, 272–273.

Barbe, W. B., & Swassing, R. H. (1979). *Teaching through modality strengths: Concepts and practices*. Columbus, OH: Zaner-Bloser.

Barclay, J. R. (1983). *Barclay Classroom Assessment System manual*. Los Angeles: Western Psychological Services.

Barnett, D., & Zucker, K. R. (1990). *The personal and social assessment of children*. Boston: Allyn & Bacon.

Barrios, B. A. (1993). Direct observation. In T. H. Ollendick & M. Hersen (Eds.), *Handbook of child and adolescent assessment*. Boston: Allyn & Bacon.

Baruth, L. G., & Manning, M. L. (1991). *Multicultural counseling and psychotherapy. A life-span perspective*. Upper Saddle River, NJ: Merrill/Prentice Hall.

Bellak, L. (1975). *The TAT, CAT, and SAT in clinical use*. New York: Grune & Stratton.

Bellak, L. (1992). *The TAT, CAT, and SAT in clinical use* (rev. ed.). New York: Grune & Stratton.

Bellak, L. (1997). *The TAT, CAT, and SAT in clinical use* (rev. ed.). New York: Grune & Stratton.

Bennett, G. K., Seashore, H. G., & Wesman, A. O. (1977). *Counseling from profiles: A casebook for the DAT* (2nd ed.). New York: Psychological Corporation.

Bersoff, D. N., & Hofer, P. J. (1991). Legal issues in computerized testing. In T. B. Gutkin & S. L. Wise (Eds.), *The computer and the decision-making process*. Hillsdale, NJ: Erlbaum.

Beutler, L. E., & Berren, M. R. (Eds.). (1995). *Integrative assessment of adult personality*. New York: Guilford.

Binet, A., & Simon, T. (1916). *The development of intelligence in children* (E. S. Kite, Trans.). Baltimore: Williams & Wilkins.

Bishop, J. H. (1988). Employment testing and incentives to learn. *Journal of Vocational Behavior, 33*(3), 404–423.

Boehm, A. E., & White, M. A. (1982). *The parents' handbook on school testing*. New York: Teachers College Press.

Bracken, B. A., & McCallum, R. S. (1998). *Universal nonverbal intelligence test*. Chicago: Riverside.

Bradley-Johnson, S., & Evans, C. D. (1991). *Psychoeducational assessment of hearing-impaired students: Infancy through adulthood*. Austin, TX: PRO-ED.

Bromley, D. B. (1986). *The case-study method in psychology and related disciplines*. New York: Wiley.

Brown, D., Pryzwansky, W. B., & Schulte, A. C. (1995). *Psychological consultation: Introduction to theory and practice* (3rd ed.). Boston: Allyn & Bacon.

Brown, D., Wyne, M. D., Blackburn, J. E., & Powell, W. C. (1979). *Consultation: Strategy for improving education*. Boston: Allyn & Bacon.

Brown, F. G. (1983). *Principles of educational and psychological testing* (3rd ed.). New York: Holt, Rinehart, & Winston.

Brown, D., Brooks, L., & Associates. (1996). *Career choice and development* (3rd ed.). San Francisco: Jossey-Bass.

Bunderson, C. V., Inouye, D. K., & Olsen, J. B. (1989). The four generations of computerized educational measurement. In R. L. Linn (Ed.), *Educational measurement* (3rd ed.). New York: Macmillan.

Buttram, J. L., Corcoran, T. B., Hansen, B. J. (1989). *Sizing up your school system: The district effectiveness audit*. Philadelphia: Research for Better Schools.

Byham, W. C., & Thornton, G. C., III. (1986). Assessment centers. In R. A. Burke (Ed.), *Performance assessment*. Baltimore: Johns Hopkins University Press.

Campbell, D. T., & Fiske, D. W. (1959). Convergent and discriminant validation by the multitrait and multimethod matrix. *Psychological Bulletin, 56*, 81–105.

Caplan, G. (1963). Types of mental health consultation. *American Journal of Orthopsychiatry, 33,* 470–481.

Caplan, G. (1964). *Principles of preventive psychology.* New York: Basic Books.

Caplan, G. (1970). *The theory and practice of mental health consultation.* New York: Basic Books.

Caplan, G., & Caplan, R. B. (1993). *Mental health consultation and collaboration.* San Francisco: Jossey-Bass.

Carroll, J. B. (1997). The three stratum theory of cognitive abilities. In D. P. Flanagan, J. L. Genshaft, & P. L. Harrison (Eds.), *Contemporary intellectual assessment* (pp. 122–130). New York: Guilford.

Cattell, R. B. (1963). Theory of fluid and crystallized intelligence: A critical experiment. *Journal of Educational Psychology, 54,* 1–22.

Chase, J. B. (1986). Psychoeducational assessment of visually impaired learners. In P. J. Lazarus (Ed.), *Psychoeducational evaluation of children and adolescents.* New York: Grune & Stratton.

Chiodo, J. J. (1986). The effects of exam anxiety on grandma's health. *Chronicle of Higher Education, 32*(23), 68.

Chun, K. T., Cobb, C. S., & French, J. R., Jr. (1975). *Measures of psychological assessment: A guide to 3000 original sources and their application.* Ann Arbor, MI: Institute for Social Research.

Connolly, A. J. (1988). *Manual for the Keymath—Revised.* Circle Pines, MN: American Guidance Services.

Cook, M., & Cook, M. (1988). *Personnel selection and productivity.* Chicago: Dryden.

Cooper, J. M. (1984). Observation skills. In J. M. Cooper (Ed.), *Developing skills for instructional supervision.* New York: Longman.

CRESST. (1994, February). *Portfolio assessment.* Los Angeles: Author.

Cronbach, L. J. (1951). Coefficient alpha and the internal structure of tests. *Psychometrika, 16,* 297–334.

Cronbach, L. J. (1971). Test validation. In R. L. Thorndike (Ed.), *Educational measurement* (2nd ed., pp. 443–507). Washington, DC: American Council on Education.

Dana, R. H. (1985). Thematic Apperception Test (TAT). In C. S. Newmark (Ed.), *Major psychological assessment instruments.* Boston: Allyn & Bacon.

Dana, R. H. (1993). *Multicultural assessment perspectives for professional psychology.* Boston: Allyn & Bacon.

Das, J. P., & Naglieri, J. A. (1996). *The cognitive assessment system.* Chicago: Riverside.

Deffenbacher, J. L. (1978). Worry, emotionality, and task-generated interference in test anxiety: An empirical test of attentional theory. *Journal of Educational Psychology, 70,* 248–254.

Draguns, J. G. (1989). Dilemmas and choices in crosscultural counseling: The universal versus the culturally distinctive. In P. B. Pedersen, J. G. Draguns, J. Lonner, & J. E. Trimble (Eds.), *Counseling across cultures* (3rd ed.). Honolulu: University of Hawaii Press.

DuBose, R. F. (1982). Assessment of severely impaired young children: Problems and recommendations. In J. T. Neisworth (Ed.), *Assessment in special education.* Rockville, MD: Aspen Systems.

Dunn, R. (1983). Learning style and its relation to exceptionality at both ends of the spectrum. *Exceptional Children, 40,* 496–506.

Dunn, R., Dunn, K., & Price, G. E. (1983). *Learning style inventory.* Lawrence, KS: Price Systems.

Dustin, D., & Ehly, S. (1984). Skills for effective consultation. *School Counselor, 31,* 23–29.

Educational Testing Service. (1988). *Test-taking tip sheet: General.* Princeton, NJ: Author.

Educational Testing Service. (1993). *Testing in America's schools.* Princeton, NJ: Author.

Educational Testing Service. (1994). *Computer-based testing: From multiple choice to multiple choices.* Princeton, NJ: Author.

Eisen, J. (1984). Researchers examine learning styles. *APA Monitor, 15*(5), 34.

English, H. B., & English, A. C. (1958). *A comprehensive dictionary of psychological and psychoanalytical terms.* New York: Longman.

Equal Employment Opportunity Commission, Civil Service Commission, Departments of Labor and Justice. (1996). Uniform guidelines on employee selection procedures. *Federal Register, 43,* 38289–33309.

Erdberg, P. (1985). The Rorschach. In C. S. Newmark (Ed.), *Major psychological assessment instruments.* Boston: Allyn & Bacon.

Exner, J. (1991). *The Rorschach: A comprehensive system.* Vol. 2: *Current research and advanced interpretation.* New York: Wiley.

Exner, J. (1993). *The Rorschach: A comprehensive system.* Vol. 1: *Basic foundations* (3rd ed.). New York: Wiley.

Exner, J., & Weiner, I. B. (1995). *The Rorschach: A comprehensive system.* Vol. 3: *Assessment of children and adolescents* (2nd ed.). New York: Wiley.

Feld, S. C., & Lewis, J. (1969). The assessment of achievement anxieties in children. In C. P. Smith (Ed.), *Achievement-related motives in children.* New York: Russell Sage Foundation.

Fischer, R. J. (1994). The Americans with Disabilities Act: Implications for measurement. *Educational Measurement, 13*(3), 17–26, 37.

Fisher, C. T. (1985). *Individualized psychological assessment.* Monterey, CA: Brooks/Cole.

Fisher, T. H. (1993). Perspectives on alternate assessment: What's happening nationally. *Research Bulletin—Florida Educational Research Council, 25*(1), 11–16.

Flanagan, J. C. (1954). The critical incidents technique. *Psychological Bulletin, 51,* 327–358.

Florez, J. (1991, January, February). Quoted in, Assessing instruments. *Science Agenda, 4,* 6–7.

Ford, V. (1973). *Everything you wanted to know about test-wiseness.* Princeton, NJ: Educational Testing Service.

Frederiksen, N., Saunders, D. R., & Wand, B. (1957). The in-basket test. *Psychological Monograph, 71*(9).

Friedman, T., & Williams, E. B. (1982). Current uses of tests for employment. In A. K. Wigdon & W. R. Garner (Eds.), *Ability testing: Uses, consequences, and controversies* (Part 2). Washington, DC: National Academy Press.

Fuchs, D., & Fuchs, L. S. (1986). Test procedure bias: A meta-analysis of examiner familiar effects. *Review of Educational Research, 56*(2), 243–262.

Gabel, S., Oster, G. D., & Botnik, S. M. (1986). *Understanding psychological testing in children.* New York: Plenum.

Gardner, H. (1983). *Frames of mind: The theory of multiple intelligence.* Cambridge: Cambridge University Press.

Gardner, H. (1993). *Multiple intelligences: The theory in practice.* New York: Basic Books.

Gardner, P. M., & Parker, P. (1993). Eating disorders. In T. H. Ollendick & M. Hersen (Eds.), *Handbook of child and adolescent assessment.* Boston: Allyn & Bacon.

Garfield, N. J., & Prediger, D. J. (1982). Testing competencies and responsibilities: A checklist for counselors. In J. T. Kapes & M. M. Mastie (Eds.), *A counselor's guide to vocational guidance instruments.* Falls Church, VA: National Vocational Guidance Association, American Personnel and Guidance Association.

Gatewood, R. D., & Feild, H. S. (1990). *Human resource selection.* Chicago: Dryden.

Gatewood, R., & Perloff, R. (1990). Testing and industrial application. In G. Goldsten & M. Hersen (Eds.), *Handbook of psychological assessment.* New York: Pergamon.

Gazzaniga, M. S. (1985). *Social brain: Discovering the networks of the mind.* New York: Basic Books.

Gilligan, C. (1982). *In a different voice: Psychological theory and women's development.* Cambridge: Harvard University Press.

Glaser, R. (1994). Criterion referenced tests. Part II: Unfinished business. *Educational Measurement, 13*(4), 27–30.

Glaser, R., & Bond, L. (1981). Testing: Concepts, policy, practice, and research. *American Psychologist, 36*(10), 997–1000.

Glatthorn, A. A. (1998). *Performance assessment and standards-based curricula.* Larchmont, NY: Eye on Education.

Goldman, L. (1971). *Using tests in counseling* (2nd ed.). Pacific Palisades, CA: Goodyear.

Goldstein, G. (1984). Comprehensive neuropsychological assessment batteries. In G. Goldstein & M. Hersen (Eds.), *Handbook of psychological assessment*. New York: Pergamon.

Goldstein, K. M., & Blackman, S. (1978). *Cognitive styles: Five approaches to theory and research*. New York: Wiley.

Gonzales, H. P. (1995). Systematic desensitization, study skills counseling and anxiety coping training in the treatment of anxiety. In C. D. Spielberger & P. R. Vagg (Eds.), *Test anxiety: Theory, assessment and treatment* (pp. 117–132). Washington, DC: Taylor & Francis.

Gooding, K. (1994, April). Teaching to the test: The influence of alternative modes of assessment on teachers' instructional strategies. Paper presented at the annual meeting of the American Educational Research Association, New Orleans.

Grady, M. P. (1984). *Teaching and brain research*. New York: Longman.

Graham, J. R. (1990). *MMPI-2 in psychological treatment*. New York: Oxford University Press.

Graziano, W. G., Varca, P. E., & Levy, J. C. (1982). Race of examiner effects and the validity of intelligence tests. *Review of Educational Research*, *52*(4), 469–497.

Greaud, V. A., & Green, B. F. (1986). Equivalence of conventional and computer presentation of speeded tests. *Applied Psychological Measurement*, *10*, 23–34.

Green, B. F. (1984). *Computer-based ability testing*. Washington, DC: American Psychological Association, Scientific Affairs Office.

Green, B. F. (1991). Guidelines for computer testing. In T. B. Gutkin & S. L. Wise (Eds.), *The computer and the decision-making process*. Hillsdale, NJ: Erlbaum.

Gregorc, A. F. (1982). *Gregorc Style Delineator: Developmental, technical, and administrative manual*. Maynard, MA: Gabriel Systems.

Griggs, S. A. (1991). *Learning styles counseling*. Ann Arbor, MI: ERIC Counseling and Personnel Services Clearinghouse.

Groth-Marnat, G. (1984). *Handbook of psychological assessment*. New York: Wiley.

Groth-Marnat, G. (1990). *Handbook of psychological assessment* (2nd ed.). New York: Wiley.

Groth-Marnat, G. (1997). *Handbook of psychological assessment* (3rd ed.). New York: Van Nostrand Reinhold.

Guilford, J. P. (1967). *The nature of human intelligence*. New York: McGraw-Hill.

Gutkin, T. B., & Curtis, M. J. (1982). School-based consultation: Theory and techniques. In C. R. Reynolds & T. B. Gutkin (Eds.), *Handbook of school psychology*. New York: Wiley.

Hambleton, R. K., & Eignor, D. R. (1980). Competency test development, validation, and standard setting. In R. M. Jaeger & C. K. Tittle (Eds.), *Minimum competency testing: Motives, models, measures, and consequences*. Berkeley, CA: McCutchan.

Hammer, A. L. (1992). Test evaluation and quality. In M. Zeidner & R. Most (Eds.), *Psychological testing: An inside view*. Palo Alto, CA: Consulting Psychologists Press.

Hammer, E. F. (1985). The House-Tree-Person Test. In C. S. Newmark (Ed.), *Major psychological instruments*. Boston: Allyn & Bacon.

Hansen, J. C. (1990). Interest inventories. In G. Goldstein & M. Hersen (Eds.), *Handbook of psychological assessment* (2nd ed.). New York: Pergamon.

Hansen, J. C. (1986). Computers and beyond in the career decision-making process. *Measurement and Evaluation in Counseling and Development*, *19*(1), 48–52.

Hargrove, L. J., & Poteet, J. A. (1984). *Assessment in special education: The educational evaluation*. Upper Saddle River, NJ: Prentice Hall.

Haring, N. G. (Ed.). (1982). *Exceptional children and youth* (3rd ed.). Upper Saddle River, NJ: Merrill/Prentice Hall.

Harrington, T. F., & O'Shea, A. J. (1993). *The Harrington & O'Shea Career Descision Making System, Revised*. Circle Pines, MN: American Guidance Service.

Hartshorne, H., & May, M. A. (1928). *Studies in deceit* (Vol. 2). New York: Macmillan.

Haymes, S. N. (1990). Behavioral assessment of adults. In G. Goldstein & M. Hersen (Eds.),

Handbook of psychological assessment (pp. 423–466). New York: Pergamon.

Hembree, R. (1988). Correlates, causes, effects and treatment of test anxiety. *Review of Educational Research, 58*(1), 47–77.

Herr, E. L., & Cramer, S. H. (1984). *Career counseling through the life span* (2nd ed.). Boston: Little, Brown.

Herrnstein, R. J. (1971, September). IQ. *Atlantic Monthly*, pp. 43–64.

Herrnstein, R. J., & Murray, C. (1994). *The bell curve*. New York: Free Press.

Hirsh, S., & Kummerow, J. (1990). *Introduction to type in organizations* (2nd ed.). Palo Alto, CA: Consulting Psychologists Press.

Hodges, K., Kline, J., Stern, L., Cytryn, L., & McKnew, D. (1982). The development of a child assessment interview for research and clinical use. *Journal of Abnormal Child Psychology, 10*, 173–189.

Hodges, K., & Zeeman, J. (1993). Interviewing. In T. H. Ollendick & M. Hersen (Eds.), *Handbook of child and adolescent assessment*. Boston: Allyn & Bacon.

Holland, J. L. (1979). *Professional manual for the self-directed search*. Palo Alto, CA: Consulting Psychologists Press.

Holland, J. L. (1985). *Self-directed search*. Odessa, FL: Psychological Assessment Resources.

Holland, J. L. (1986). New directions for interest testing. In B. S. Plake & J. C. Witt (Eds.), *The future of testing*. Hillsdale, NJ: Erlbaum.

Holland, J. L. (1997). *Making vocational choices* (3rd ed.). Upper Saddle River, NJ: Prentice Hall.

Holt, R. R. (Ed.). (1968). *Diagnostic psychological testing* (rev. ed.). New York: International Universities Press.

Horn, J. L. (1989). Cognitive diversity: A framework for learning. In P. L. Ackerman, R. J. Sternberg, & R. Glaser (Eds.), *Learning and individual differences: Advances in theory and research*. New York: Freeman.

Howard, E. R., & Keefe, J. W. (1991). *The Case-IMS School Improvement Process*. Reston, VA: National Association of Secondary School Principals.

Hurt, S. W., Reznikoff, M., & Clarkin, J. F. (1995). The Rorschach. In L. E. Beutler & M. R. Berren (Eds.), *Integrative assessment of adult personality*. New York: Guilford.

Impara, J. C., & Plake, B. S. (Eds.). (1998) *The thirteenth mental measurements yearbook*. Lincoln: University of Nebraska Press.

Inghram, C. F. (1980). *Fundamentals of educational assessment*. New York: Van Nostrand.

Jackson, D. N. (1985). *Computer-based personality testing*. Washington, DC: American Psychological Association, Scientific Affairs Office.

Jackson, D. N. (1991). Computer-assisted personality test interpretation: The dawn of discovery. In T. B. Gutkin & S. L. Wise (Eds.), *The computer and the decision-making process*. Hillsdale, NJ: Erlbaum.

Jensen, A. R. (1980). *Bias in mental testing*. New York: Free Press.

Jensen, A. R. (1988). Armed Services Vocational Aptitude Battery. In J. T. Kapes & M. M. Mastie (Eds.), *A counselor's guide to career assessment instruments*. Alexandria, VA: National Career Development Association.

Johnson, B. (1996). *The performance assessment handbook*. Vol 2: *Performances and exhibitions*. Princeton, NJ: Eye on Education.

Johnson, M. E., & Holland, A. L. (1986). Measuring clients' expectations: The 15 Personal Problems Inventory. *Measurement and Evaluation in Counseling and Development, 19*(3), 151–156.

Joint Committee on Testing Practices. (1988). *Code of fair testing practices*. Washington, DC: American Psychological Association.

Jung, C. G. (1910). The association method. *American Journal of Psychology, 21*, 219–269.

Jung, C. G. (1918). *Studies in word association*. London: Heinemann.

Kachigan, S. K. (1986). *Statistical analysis: An interdisciplinary introduction to univariate and multivariate methods*. New York: Radius.

Kagan, J. (1966). Reflection-impulsivity: The generality and dynamics of conceptual tempo. *Journal of Abnormal Psychology, 71*, 17–24.

Kagan, J., Rosman, B. L., Day, D., Albert, J., & Phillips, W. (1964). Information processing in the child: Significance of analytic and reflective attitudes. *Psychological Monograph*, *78*, 1.

Kamphaus, R. W. (1993). *Clinical assessment of children's intelligence: A handbook for professional practice*. Boston: Allyn & Bacon.

Kamphaus, R. W., & Frick, P. J. (1996). *Clinical assessment of child and adolescent personality and behavior*. Boston: Allyn & Bacon.

Kamphaus, R. W., Petoskey, M. D. & Morgan, A. W. (1997). A history of intelligence test interpretation. In D. P. Flanagan, J. L. Genshaft, & P. L. Harrison (Eds.), *Contemporary intellectual assessment* (pp. 32–48). New York: Guilford.

Kane, M. T. (1986). The future of testing for licensure and certification examinations. In B. S. Plake & J. C. Witt (Eds.), *The future of testing*. Hillsdale, NJ: Erlbaum.

Kapes, J. T., & Mastie, M. M. (1994). *A counselor's guide to career assessment instruments* (3rd ed.). Alexandria, VA: American Counseling Association.

Katz, L. (1991). *A practical guide to psychodiagnostic testing* (2nd ed.). Springfield, IL: Thomas.

Kaufman, A. S. (1976). Verbal-performance IQ discrepancies on the WISC-R. *Journal of Consulting and Clinical Psychology*, *44*, 739–744.

Kaufman, A. S. (1990) *Assessing adolescent and adult intelligence*. Boston: Allyn & Bacon.

Kaufman, A. S., Kamphaus, R. W., & Kaufman, N. L. (1985). The Kaufman Assessment Battery for Children (K-ABC). In C. S. Newmark (Ed.), *Major psychological assessment instruments*. Boston: Allyn & Bacon.

Kaufman, A. S., & Kaufman, N. L. (1983). *Kaufman Assessment Battery for Children*. Circle Pines, MN: American Guidance Service.

Kazdin, A. E. (1993). Conduct disorders. In T. H. Ollendick & M. Hersen (Eds.), *Handbook of child and adolescent assessment*. Boston: Allyn & Bacon.

Keefe, J. W., & Languis, M. L. (1983, August). Operational definitions. Paper presented to NASSP Learning Styles Task Force, Reston, VA.

Keefe, J. W., & Monk, J. S. (1988). *Manual to Learning Style Profile*. Reston, VA: National Association of Secondary School Principals.

Keesling, J. W., & Healy, C. C. (1988). USES General Aptitude Battery. In J. T. Kapes & M. M. Mastie (Eds.), *A counselor's guide to career instruments* (2nd ed.). Alexandria, VA: National Career Development Association.

Kellerman, H., & Burry, A. (1991). *Handbook of psychodynamic testing: An analysis of personality in the psychological report*. Boston: Allyn & Bacon.

Kelly, E. L., & Fiske, D. W. (1951). *The prediction of performance in clinical psychology*. Ann Arbor: University of Michigan Press.

Kendall, L. S., & Marzano, R. J. (1996). *Content knowledge*. Aurora, CO: Midcontinent Regional Educational Laboratory.

Kline, P. (1993). *Handbook of psychological testing*. New York: Routledge.

Klopfer, W. G. (1960). *The psychological report: Use and communication of psychological findings*. New York: Grune & Stratton.

Kolb, D. A. (1976). *Learning Style Inventory*. Boston: McBer.

Koppitz, E. M. (1968). *Psychological evaluation of children's human figure drawings*. New York: Grune & Stratton.

Koppitz, E. M. (1975). *The Bender Gestalt Test for Young Children*. Vol. 2: *Research and applications, 1963–1973*. New York: Grune & Stratton.

Koppitz, E. M. (1982). Personality assessment in the schools. In C. R. Reynolds & T. B. Gutkin (Eds.), *Handbook of school psychology* (pp. 273–295). New York: Wiley.

Korchin, S. J., & Schuldberg, D. (1981). The future of clinical assessment. *American Psychologist*, *36*(10), 1147–1158.

Kovacs, M. (1982). The longitudinal study of child and adolescent psychopathology. Part 1: The semi-structured psychiatric interview schedule for children. Unpublished manuscript.

Krechevsky, M. (1994). *Project Spectrum preschool assessment handbook*. Cambridge: Harvard Project Zero.

Krug, S. E. (1980). *Clinical analysis questionnaire.* Champaign, IL: Institute for Personality & Ability Testing.

Kubiszyn, T., & Borich, G. (1987). *Educational testing and measurement* (2nd ed.). Glenview, IL: Scott, Foresman.

Kuder, G. F., & Richardson, M. (1937). The theory of the estimation test reliability. *Psychometrika, 2,* 151–160.

Kyllonen, P. C. (1997). Smart testing. In R. F. Dillon (Ed.), *Handbook on testing* (pp. 347–371). Westport, CT: Greenwood.

La Greca, A. M., & Stringer, S. A. (1985). The Wechsler Intelligence Scale for Children—Revised. In C. S. Newmark (Ed.), *Major psychological assessment instruments.* Boston: Allyn & Bacon.

Landberg, D. J. (1998). What is your face in cyberspace? *News Notes of the American Association for Assessment in Counseling, 32,* 7.

Lanyon, R. I., & Goodstein, L. D. (1982). *Personality assessment* (2nd ed.). New York: Wiley.

Lawrence, G. (1982). *People types and tiger stripes* (2nd ed.). Palo Alto, CA: Consulting Psychologists Press.

Lawrence, G. D. (1997). *Looking at type and learning styles.* Gainesville, FL: Center for Applied Personality Type.

Lee, J. A., Moreno, K. E., & Sympson, J. B. (1984, April). The effects of mode of test administration on test performance. Paper presented at the annual meeting of the Eastern Psychological Association, Baltimore.

Lien, A. J. (1971). *Measurement and evaluation of learning* (2nd ed.). Dubuque, IA: Brown.

Linn, R. (1982). Ability testing: Individual differences, prediction and differential prediction. In A. K. Wigdor & W. R. Gainer (Eds.), *Ability testing: Uses, consequences, and controversies* (Part 2). Washington, DC: National Academy Press.

Loehlin, J. C., Lindzey, G., & Spohler, J. N. (1975). *Race differences in intelligence.* San Francisco: Freeman.

Lyman, H. B. (1998). *Test scores and what they mean* (6th ed.). Boston: Allyn & Bacon.

Machover, K. (1949). *Personality projection in the drawing of the human figure.* Springfield, IL: Thomas.

Maddux, C. D., & Johnson, L. (1998). Computer assisted assessment. In H. B. Vance (Ed.), *Psychological assessment of children* (2nd ed., pp. 87–105). New York: Wiley.

Madsen, D. H. (1986). Computer applications for test administration and scoring. *Measurement and Evaluation in Counseling and Development, 19*(1), 6–14.

Mann, L., & Sabatino, D. A. (1985). *Foundations of cognitive process in remedial and special education.* Rockville, MD: Aspen Systems.

Marcus, L. M., & Schopler, E. (1993). Pervasive developmental disorders. In T. H. Ollendick & M. Hersen (Eds.), *Handbook of child and adolescent assessment.* Boston: Allyn & Bacon.

Matarazzo, J. D. (1983). Computerized psychological testing [Editorial comment]. *Science, 221*(4608).

Matey, C. (1984). Leiter International Performance Scale. In D. J. Keyser & R. C. Sweetland (Eds.), *Test critiques* (vol. 1, pp. 411–420). Kansas City, MO: Test Corporation of America.

McBride, J. R., & Martin, J. T. (1983). Reliability and validity of adaptive ability tests in a military setting. In D. J. Weiss (Ed.), *New horizons in testing.* New York: Academic Press.

McDaniel, C., & Gysbers, N. C. (1992). *Counseling for career development: Theories, resources, and practices.* San Francisco: Jossey-Bass.

McDermott, P. A. (1980). A systems-actuarial method for differential diagnosis of handicapped children. *Journal of Special Education, 50,* 223–228.

McKee, P., & Wilt, R. (1990). Effective teaching: A review of instructional and environmental variables. In T. B. Gutkin & C. R. Reynolds (Eds.), *Handbook of school psychology* (2nd ed.). New York: Wiley.

Meehl, P. E. (1954). *Clinical versus statistical prediction.* Minneapolis: University of Minnesota Press.

Mehrens, W. A., & Lehman, I. J. (1986). *Using standardized tests in education* (4th ed.). New York: Longman.

Meier, S. T., & Geiger, S. M. (1986). Implications of computer-assisted testing and assessment for professional practice and training. *Measurement and Evaluation in Counseling & Development*, *19*(1), 29–34.

Merz, W. R., Sr. (1984). Kaufman Assessment Battery for Children. In D. J. Keyser & R. C. Sweetland (Eds.), *Test critiques* (vol. 1, pp. 393–405). Kansas City, MO: Test Corporation of America.

Messick, S. (1980). *The effectiveness of coaching for the SAT: Review and reanalysis of research from the fifties to the FTC.* Princeton, NJ: Educational Testing Service.

Messick, S. (1989). Validity. In R. L. Linn (Ed.), *Educational measurement* (3rd ed.). New York: Collier Macmillan.

Messick, S., & Yungeblut, A. (1981). Time and methods in coaching for the SAT. *Psychological Bulletin, 89*, 191–216.

Meyer, P., & Davis, S. (1992). *The CPI application guide.* Palo Alto, CA: Consulting Psychologists Press.

Miller, M. D., & Seraphine, A. E. (1993). Can test scores remain authentic when teaching to the test? *Research Bulletin—Florida Educational Research Council, 25*(1), 21–29.

Millman, J., Bishop, C. H., & Ebel, R. L. (1965). An analysis of test-wiseness. *Educational and Psychological Measurement, 25*, 707–726.

Millon, T., & Davis, R. D. (1996). *Disorders of personality: DSM-IV and beyond.* New York: Wiley.

Miner, M. G. (1976). *Selection procedures and personnel records.* (Personnel Policies Forum Survey No. 112). Washington, DC: Bureau of National Affairs.

Mitchell, J. V., Jr. (Ed.). (1985). *Ninth mental measurements yearbook.* Lincoln: University of Nebraska Press, Buros Institute of Mental Measurements.

Moos, R. (1987). *Social climate scales: A user's guide* (2nd ed.). Palo Alto, CA: Consulting Psychologists Press.

Moss, P. A. (1998). The role of consequences in validity theory. *Educational Measurement, 17*(23), 6–12.

Moreland, K. L. (1992). Computer assisted psychological assessment. In M. Zeidner & R. Most (Eds.), *Psychological testing: An inside view.* Palo Alto, CA: Consulting Psychologists Press.

Munsterberge, F. (1955). Relationships between some background factors and children's interpersonal behavior. Unpublished doctoral dissertation, Ohio State University, Columbus.

Murphy, L. L., Conoley, J., & Impara, J. C. (1994). *Tests in print IV.* Lincoln, NE: Buros Institute.

Murray, H. A. (1938). *Explorations in personality.* New York: Oxford University Press.

Nairn, A., and Associates. (1980). *The reign of ETS: The corporation that makes up minds.* Washington, DC: Author.

National Association of School Psychologists. (1992). *Principles for professional ethics.* Silver Spring, MD: Author.

National Association of School Psychologists. (1980). *Standards for the provision of school psychological services.* Washington, DC: Author.

National Board for Certified Counselors. (1989). *Code of ethics.* Alexandria, VA: Author.

National Commission on Testing and Public Policy. (1990). *From gatekeeper to gateway: Transforming testing in America.* Washington, DC: Author.

National Council of Measurement in Education. (1993). *Code of professional responsibility.* Washington, DC: Author.

National Council of Measurement in Education. (1994, February). *Alternate assessment standards.* Washington, DC: Author.

National Council on Measurement in Education. (1995). *Code of professional responsibilities in education.* Washington, DC: Author.

National Council of Measurement in Education, National Association of School Administrators, & National Association of Secondary School Principals. (1994). *Standards of student assessment.* Washington, DC: Author.

National Council of Teachers of Mathematics. (1993). *Assessment standards for school mathematics.* Reston, VA: Author.

Nevo, B., & Jaeger, R. S. (1993). *Educational and psychological testing: The test taker's outlook.* Toronto: Hogrefe & Huber.

Newmark, C. S. (Ed.). (1996). *Major psychological assessment instruments*. Boston: Allyn & Bacon.

Newmark, C. S., & McCord, David. (1996). The MMPI-2. In C. S. Newmark (Ed.), *Major psychological assessment instruments* (2nd ed.). Boston: Allyn & Bacon.

Nowicki, S., & Strickland, B. (1973). Nowicki-Strickland Locus of Control. *Journal of Consulting and Clinical Psychology, 40*, 148–154.

Nuttall, E. V., Romero, J., & Kalesnik, J. (1992). *Assessing and screening preschoolers: Psychological and educational dimensions*. Boston: Allyn & Bacon.

Oakland, T. (1982). Nonbiased assessment of minority group children. In J. T. Neisworth (Ed.), *Assessment in special education*. Rockville, MD: Aspen Systems.

Oakland, T. D., & Parmelee, R. (1985). Mental measurement of minority group children. In B. B. Wolman (Ed.), *Handbook of intelligence: Theories, measurements, and applications*. New York: Wiley.

Ollendick, T. W., & Greene, R. (1990). Behavioral assessment of children. In G. Goldstein & M. Hersen (Eds.), *Handbook of psychological assessment* (2nd ed., pp. 403–422). New York: Pergamon.

OSS Assessment Staff. (1948). *Assessment of men*. New York: Holt, Rinehart, & Winston.

Ownby, R. L. (1997). *Psychological reports: A guide to report writing in professional psychology* (3rd ed.). Brandon, VT: CPPC.

Pennock-Roman, M. (1988). Differential Aptitude Test. In J. T. Kapes & M. M. Mastie (Eds.), *A counselor's guide to career assessment instruments* (2nd ed.). Alexandria, VA: National Career Development Association.

Perkins, M. R. (1982). Minimum competency testing: What? why? why not? *Educational Measurement, 1*(4), 5–9, 26.

Perloff, R., Craft, J. A., & Perloff, E. (1984). Testing and industrial application. In G. Goldstein & M. Hersen (Eds.), *Handbook of psychological assessment*. New York: Pergamon.

Piacentini, J. (1993). Checklists and rating scales. In T. H. Ollendick & M. Hersen (Eds.), *Handbook of child and adolescent assessment*. Boston: Allyn & Bacon.

Piaget, J. (1970). *The science of education and the psychology of the child*. New York: Orion.

Pipho, C. (1978). Minimum competency testing in 1978: A look at standards. *Phi Delta Kappan, 59*, 585–588.

Plake, B. S., & Witt, J. C. (Eds.). (1986). *Buros-Nebraska Symposium on Measurement and Testing*. Vol. 2: *The future of testing*. Hillsdale, NJ: Erlbaum.

Prell, J. M., & Prell, P. A. (1986, November). Improving test scores—teaching test-wiseness: A review of the literature. *Research Bulletin of the Center on Evaluation, Development, and Research*. Bloomington, IL: Phi Delta Kappa.

Rapport, M. D. (1993). Attention deficit hyperactivity disorders. In T. H. Ollendick & M. Hersen (Eds.), *Handbook of child and adolescent assessment*. Boston: Allyn & Bacon.

Reiff, J. C. (1992). *Learning styles*. Washington, DC: National Education Association.

Reiling, E., & Taylor, R. (1972). A new approach to the problem of changing initial responses to multiple choice questions. *Journal of Educational Measurement, 8*, 177–181.

Reynolds, C. R., & Brown, R. T. (1984). Bias in mental testing. In C. R. Reynolds & R. T. Brown (Eds.), *Perspectives on bias in mental testing*. New York: Plenum.

Riso, D. R. (1990). *Understanding the enneagram*. Boston: Houghton Mifflin.

Riso, D. R. (1994). *Using the enneagram for personal growth*. Boston: Houghton Mifflin.

Rogers, C. R. (1942). *Counseling and psychotherapy*. Boston: Houghton Mifflin.

Roid, G. H. (1986). Computer technology in testing. In B. S. Plake & J. C. Witt (Eds.), *The future of testing*. Hillsdale, NJ: Erlbaum.

Rossetti, L. M. (1990). *Infant-toddler assessment*. Austin, TX: PRO-ED.

Rotter, J. B. (1966). Generalized expectancies for internal versus external control of reinforcement. *Psychological Monographs, 80*, 609.

Rotter, J. B., & Rafferty, J. E. (1950). *Manual: The Rotter Incomplete Sentence Blank.* New York: Psychological Corporation.

Saklofske, D. H., Kowalchuk, V. L., & Schwean, V. C. (1992). Influences on testing and test results. In M. Zeidner & R. Most (Eds.), *Psychological testing: An inside view.* Palo Alto, CA: Consulting Psychologists Press.

Sampson, J. P., Jr., & Pyle, K. R. (1983). Ethical issues involved with the use of computer assisted counseling, testing, and guidance systems. *Personnel and Guidance Journal, 61,* 283–287.

Sarason, I. G. (Ed.). (1980). *Test anxiety: Theory, research, and application.* Hillsdale, NJ: Erlbaum.

Sattler, J. M. (1988). *Assessment of children* (3rd ed.). San Diego: Author.

Sattler, J. M. (1992). *Assessment of children's intelligence and special abilities* (3rd ed.). Boston: Allyn & Bacon.

Schmidt, F. L., & Hunter, J. E. (1981). Employment testing: Old theories and new research findings. *American Psychologist, 36*(10), 1128–1137.

Shapiro, E. S., & Cole, C. L. (1993). Self-monitoring. In T. H. Ollendick & M. Hersen (Eds.), *Handbook of child and adolescent assessment.* Boston: Allyn & Bacon.

Shavelson, R. J., Hubner, J. J., & Stanton, G. C. (1976). Self-concept: Validation of construct interpretations. *Review of Educational Research, 46,* 407–442.

Sherrod, B. (1985, November). Jobs for left brainers; jobs for right brainers. *Career World,* 19–21.

Shertzer, B. (1986). Integrating computer-assisted testing and assessment in the counseling process: A reaction. *Measurement and Evaluation in Counseling and Development, 19*(1), 27–28.

Shertzer, B., & Linden, J. D. (1979). *Fundamentals of individual appraisal: Assessment techniques for counselors.* Boston: Houghton Mifflin.

Shimberg, B. (1981). Testing for licensure and certification. *American Psychologist, 36*(10), 1138–1146.

Shore, M. F., Brice, P. J., & Love, B. G. (1992). *When your child needs testing: What parents, teachers, and other helpers need to know about psychological testing.* New York: Crossroad.

Simeonsson, R. J. (1986). *Psychological and developmental assessment of special children.* Boston: Allyn & Bacon.

Simon, A., & Boyer, E. G. (1974). *Mirrors for behavior III: An anthology of observation instruments.* Wyncote, PA: Communications Materials Center.

Slosson, S. W., & Callisto, T. A. (1984). *Observational analysis.* East Aurora, NY: Slosson.

Spearman, C. (1927). *The abilities of man.* London: Macmillan.

Spielberger, C. D., & Vagg, P. R. (Eds.). (1995). *Test anxiety: Theory, assessment, and treatment.* Washington, DC: Taylor & Francis.

Sternberg, R. J. (1980). Factor theories of intelligence are all right almost. *Educational Researcher, 9,* 6–13.

Sternberg, R. J. (1985). *Beyond IQ: A triarchic theory of human intelligence.* Cambridge: Cambridge University Press.

Sternberg, R. J. (1986). *Intelligence applied: Understanding and increasing your intellectual skills.* San Diego: Harcourt Brace Jovanovich.

Sternberg, R. J. (1990). T & T is an explosive combination: Technology and testing. *Educational Psychologist, 25*(3, 4), 201–222.

Stiggins, R. (1987). Design and development of performance assessments. *Educational Measurement, 6*(3), 32–42.

Stockwell, S., Schaeffer, B., & Lowenstein, J. (1991). *SAT coaching coverup: How coaching courses can raise scores by 100 points or more and why ETS denies the evidence.* Cambridge, MA: Fair Test.

Stoddard, G. D. (1943). *The meaning of intelligence.* New York: Macmillan.

Strauss, C. C. (1993). Anxiety disorders. In T. H. Ollendick & M. Hersen (Eds.), *Handbook of child and adolescent assessment.* Boston: Allyn & Bacon.

Strong, E. R. (1927). Vocational Interest Test. *Educational Record, 8,* 107–121.

Sue, D. W., Arrendondo, P., & McDavis, R. J. (1992). Multicultural counseling competencies and standards: A call to the profession. *Journal of Counseling and Development, 70.*

Super, D. E., & Crites, J. O. (1962). *Appraising vocational fitness by means of psychological tests* (rev. ed.). New York: Harper & Row.

Super, D. E., Thompson, A. S., & Lindeman, R. H. (1988). *Manual to Adult Career Concerns Inventory.* Palo Alto, CA: Consulting Psychologists Press.

Tallent, N. (1958). On individualizing the psychologist's clinical evaluation. *Journal of Clinical Psychology, 14,* 243–244.

Tallent, N. (1993). *Psychological report writing* (4th ed.). Upper Saddle River, NJ: Prentice Hall.

Taylor, J. A. (1953). A personality scale of manifest anxiety. *Journal of Abnormal and Social Psychology, 45,* 285–290.

Ten Brink, T. D. (1974). *Evaluation: A practical guide for teachers.* New York: McGraw-Hill.

Tenopyr, M. L. (1981). The realities of employment testing. *American Psychologist, 36* (10), 1120–1127.

Terman, L. M. (1954). The discovery and encouragement of exceptional talent. *American Psychologist, 9,* 221–230.

Test Alert. (1990). Chicago: Riverside.

Test Users Training Work Group of the Joint Committee on Testing Practices. (1993). *Responsible test use.* Washington, DC: American Psychological Association.

Thomas, M. (1937). Méthode des histoires à compléter pour le dépiste des complexes et des conflits affectifs enfantins. *Archives Psychologie, 26,* 209–284.

Thorndike, E. L. (1927). *The measurement of intelligence.* New York: Teachers College Press.

Thorndike, R. L., & Hagen, E. P. (1959). *Ten thousand careers.* New York: Wiley.

Thurstone, L. L. (1938). *Primary mental abilities* (Psychometric Monograph No. 1). Chicago: University of Chicago Press.

Tobias, S. (1979). Anxiety research in educational psychology. *Journal of Educational Psychology, 71,* 573–582.

Tucker, B. P., & Goldstein, B. A. (1991). *The educational rights of children with disabilities: A guide to federal law.* Horsham, PA: LRP.

Tyron, G. S. (1980). The measurement and treatment of test anxiety. *Review of Educational Research, 50,* 343–372.

Urman, H. (1983). The effect of test-wiseness training on the achievement of third or fifth grade students. Paper presented at the annual meeting of the National Council on Measurement in Education, Montreal.

Valencia, R. R., & Aburto, S. (1991). The uses and abuses of educational testing: Chicanos as a case in point. In R. R. Valencia (Ed.), *Chicano school failure and success: Research and policy agendas for the 1990s.* Basingstoke, England: Falmer.

Vance, H. B. (Ed.). (1998). *Psychological assessment of children* (2nd ed.). New York: Wiley.

Vernon, P. E. (1960). *The structure of human abilities* (rev. ed.). London: Methuen.

Viadero, D. (1990, June 20). Georgia ends performance-based tests for teachers. *Education week,* 18.

Wallace, G., & Larsen, S. C. (1992). *Educational assessment of learning problems: Testing for teaching* (2nd ed.). Boston: Allyn & Bacon.

Watkins, M. W., & McDermott, P. A. (1991). Psychodiagnostic computing: From interpretive programs to expert systems. In T. B. Gutkin & S. L. Wise (Eds.), *The computer and the decision-making process.* Hillsdale, NJ: Erlbaum.

Wechsler, D. (1958). *The measurement of adult intelligence.* Baltimore: Williams & Wilkins.

Weins, A. N. (1990). Structured clinical interview. In G. Goldstein & M. Hersen (Eds.), *Handbook of psychological assessment* (2nd ed.). New York: Pergamon.

Whitman, N. A., Spendlove, D. C., & Clark, C. H. (1986). *Increasing students' learning: A faculty guide to reducing stress among students* (ASHE-ERIC Executive Higher Education Report No. 4).

Wigdor, A. K., & Garner, W. R. (Eds.). (1982). *Ability testing: Uses, consequences, and controversies* (2 vols.). Washington, DC: National Academy Press.

Wiggins, G. P. (1993). *Assessing student performance: Exploring the purposes and limits of testing.* San Francisco: Jossey-Bass.

Wine, J. D. (1980). Cognitive-attentional theory of test anxiety. In I. G. Sarason (Ed.), *Text anxiety: Theory, research and application.* Hillsdale, NJ: Erlbaum.

Wise, S. L., & Plake, B. S. (1990). Computer-based testing in higher education. *Measurement and Evaluation in Counseling and Development, 23,* 3–10.

Witkin, H. A. (1949). Perception of body position and of the position of the visual field. *Psychological Monographs, 63*(1, no. 302).

Witkin, H. A., Moore, C. A., Goodenough, D. R., & Cox, P. W. (1977). Field-dependent and field-independent cognitive styles and their educational implications. *Review of Educational Research, 47,* 1–64.

Wolman, B. B. (Ed.). (1985). *Handbook of intelligence.* New York: Wiley.

Wonder, J., & Donovan, P. (1984). *Whole brain thinking: Working from both sides of the brain to achieve peak job performance.* New York: Morrow.

Wylie, R. C. (1990). *Self-concept instruments.* Lincoln: University of Nebraska Press.

Ysseldyke, J. E., & Christenson, S. L. (1987). *Instructional environment scale.* Austin, TX: PRO-ED.

Yule, W. (1993). Developmental perspective and psychopathology and influences in child behavioral assessment. In T. H. Ollendick & M. Hersen, *Handbook of child and adolescent assessment* (pp. 15–25). Boston: Allyn & Bacon.

Zachary, R. A., & Pope, K. S. (1983). Legal and ethical issues in the clinical use of computerized testing. In M. D. Schwartz (Ed.), *Using computers in clinical practice.* New York: Haworth.

Zeidner, M., & Most, R. (1992). *Psychological testing: An inside view.* Palo Alto, CA: Consulting Psychologists Press.

Ziotogorski, Z., & Wiggs, E. Story and sentence-completion. In A. I. Rabin (Ed.). *Projective techniques* (pp. 195–211). New York: Springer.

Name Index

Abrams, D. M., 207, 226
Aburto, S., 356
Aiken, L. R., 112, 158, 318, 322, 335
Albert, J., 257
Alderman, D. L., 369
Allred, L. J., 301
Aman, M. G., 343
Anastasi, A., 11, 145, 211
Andrew, D. M., 147
Arnold, M. B., 207
Arrendondo, P., 356
Aylward, G. P., 352

Bagnatto, S. J., 281
Bailey, D., 285, 286, 340
Bailey, R. C., 263
Baker, F. B., 309
Bandura, A., 284
Bannatyne, A., 122
Barbe, W. B., 256
Barnett, D., 284
Barrios, B. A., 319, 322
Baruth, L. G., 357, 358
Battle, J., 221
Bellak, L., 207, 226
Bennett, G. K., 142
Berk, R. A., 173, 203
Berren, M. R., 244
Bersoff, D. N., 311
Beutler, L. E., 244
Beyer, F. S., 394
Binet, A., 8, 112
Bishop, C. H., 369, 370
Blackburn, J. E., 410
Blackman, S., 257
Blau, T. H., 281
Blum, L. H., 209
Boehm, A. E., 414
Bond, L., 455
Borich, G., 392

Botnik, S. M., 414
Boyer, E. G., 335
Bracken, B. A., 130, 226
Bradley-Johnson, S., 347, 352
Brennan, R. L., 57
Brice, P. J., 403, 421, 424
Bromley, D. B., 244, 245
Brown, D., 346, 410, 415, 421
Brown, F. G., 152, 321
Brown, R. T., 356
Bunderson, C. V., 301
Burger, P. L., 456
Burger, S. E., 456
Buros, O. K., 11
Butcher, J. N., 226
Buttram, J. L., 394
Byham, W. C., 191
Byrne, B. M., 226

Callisto, T. A., 317
Campbell, D. T., 43
Canino, I. A., 364
Caplan, G., 415, 416, 421
Caplan, R. B., 415, 416, 421
Carroll, J. B., 114
Cattell, A. K. S., 131
Cattell, R. B., 9, 112, 113, 131
Charcot, J., 8
Chase, J. B., 348
Chiodo, J. J., 371
Choca, J., 249
Christenson, S. L., 291
Chun, B. A., 68
Clark, C. H., 368
Clarkin, J. F., 210
Clemans, W. V., 91
Cobb, C. S., 68
Cohen, L. G., 281, 296
Cole, C. L., 318
Conoley, J. C., 74, 75
Cook, M., 190, 191

Cooper, J. M., 329
Corcoran, K., 68
Corcoran, T. B., 394
Costa, P. T., 219
Cox, P. W., 257
Craft, J. A., 190, 191
Cramer, S. H., 151
Crites, J. O., 152, 180
Cronbach, L. J., 43, 48, 196, 219, 329, 369, 451
Crosby-Milenburg, C., 74
Curtis, M. J., 416, 421
Cytryn, L., 246

Damico, J. S., 352
Dana, R. H., 208, 358–360, 364
Das, J. P., 130
Davidson, J. E., 137
Davidson, M. L., 110
Davis, R. D., 236
Day, D., 257
Dean, R., 250
DeAvila, E. A., 164
Deffenbacher, J. L., 366
Detterman, D. K., 137
Dobbin, J. E., 379
Donovan, P., 258
Dragus, J. G., 358
DuBois, P. H., 11
DuBose, R. F., 341, 343
Duncan, S. F., 164
Dunn, G. E., 251
Dunn, K., 260
Dunn, R., 260, 261
Dusewicy, R. A. , 394
Dustin, D., 409

Ebel, R. L., 369, 370
Ehly, S., 409
Eignor, D. R., 457
Eisen, J., 262

English, A. C., 176
English, H. B., 176
Erdberg, P., 210
Erikson, E. H., 275
Evans, C. D., 347, 352
Exner, J., 210

Fabriano, E., 74
Fagan, T. K., 11
Fairhurst, A. M., 265
Fairhurst, L. L., 265
Farr, B., 162
Farr, F., 162
Farr, R., 173
Feild, H. S., 190–192
Feld, S. C., 366
Feldt, L. S., 57
Fischer, R. J., 68, 449
Fisher, C. T., 247, 439
Fisher, T. H., 329
Fiske, D. W., 43, 321
Fitzherbert, A., 7
Flanagan, D. P., 136
Flanagan, J. C., 320
Florez, J., 200
Frederiksen, N., 321
French, J. R., Jr., 68
Freud, S., 8
Friedman, T., 188, 189
Fuchs, D., 88
Fuchs, L. S., 88

Gabel, S., 414
Galton, F., 112
Gardner, H., 111, 113, 117, 118, 136, 463
Gardner, P. M., 9, 346
Garfield, N. J., 401
Garner, W. R., 369
Gatewood, R. D., 186, 190–192, 199, 203
Gazzaniga, M. S., 258
Geiger, S. M., 311, 312
Geisinger, K. F., 364
Genshaft, J. L., 136
Gilligan, C., 277
Glaser, R., 455, 463
Glatthorn, A. A., 330, 394, 398
Golden, C. J., 249
Goldman, B. A., 68

Goldman, L., 86, 365, 366, 373, 400, 410, 417, 419, 424
Goldstein, B. A., 452
Goldstein, G., 203, 239, 335
Goldstein, K. M., 257
Gonzales, H. P., 367
Goodenough, D. R., 257
Goodenough, F., 212
Gooding, K., 332
Goodstein, L. D., 222
Grady, M. P., 258
Graham, J. R., 216, 226
Graska, A. F., 262
Graziano, W. G., 87
Greaud, V. A., 301
Green, B. F., 300–304, 307
Green, R. L., 227
Greene, J., 173
Greene, R., 233, 234
Gregorc, A. F., 262
Griggs, S. A., 265
Gross, M., 226
Grotevant, H. D., 296
Groth-Marnat, G., 121, 207, 208, 211, 212, 226, 238
Guilford, J. P., 113
Gutkin, T. B., 314, 416, 421
Gysbers, N. C., 151

Hagen, E. P., 111, 131, 152
Hall, L. C.,, 181
Hamayan, E. V., 352
Hambleton, R. K., 173, 457
Hammer, A. L., 94
Hammer, D., 343
Hammer, E. F., 212
Handler, L., 227
Hansen, B. J., 394
Hansen, J. C., 185, 311
Hargrove, L. J., 251, 318
Haring, N. G., 337
Harmon, L. W., 421
Harrington, R. G., 249
Harrington, T. F., 145
Harris, W. G., 301
Hartshorne, H., 320
Haynes, S., 234, 235
Healy, C. C., 143
Hembree, R., 367, 379
Herr, E. L., 151

Herrnstein, R. J., 132, 460
Hersen, M., 335
Hilliard, A. G., 364
Hilsenroth, M. J., 227
Hirsh, S., 196
Hodges, K., 246
Hofer, P. J., 311
Holland, A. L., 31
Holland, J. L., 177, 185, 203, 294, 406
Holt, R. R., 230
Horn, J. L., 111, 113, 114
Howard, E. R., 292
Huarte, J., 7
Hubner, J. J., 221
Hudson, R., 220
Hunter, J. E., 200
Hurt, S. W., 210
Huttenlocher, J., 132

Impara, J. C., 75
Inghram, C. F., 252–254
Inouye, D. K., 301

Jackson, D. N., 301, 302
Jaeger, R. M., 34, 398
Jaeger, R. S., 88, 91
Jastak, J. F., 33
Jastak, S., 33
Jensen, A. R., 132, 136, 142, 356, 460
Johnson, B., 330, 335
Johnson, L., 314
Johnson, M. E., 31
Jung, C., 208

Kachigan, S. K., 31, 35
Kagan, J., 257
Kalesnik, J., 358
Kamphaus, R. W., 123, 133, 136, 173, 281
Kane, M. T., 458
Kapes, J. T., 154, 179, 204
Katz, L., 238, 250, 430, 439
Kaufman, A. S., 121–123, 127, 136
Kaufman, H. S., 240
Kaufman, N. L., 122, 123, 127, 240
Kazdin, A. E., 346
Keefe, J. W., 251, 261, 292
Keesling, J., 143

Kelly, E. L., 321
Kendall, L. S., 394
Kline, J., 246
Kline, P., 223, 227, 300
Klopfer, W. G., 431
Kohlberg, L., 277
Kolb, D. A., 261
Koppitz, E. M., 209, 210, 212, 213
Korchin, S. J., 230, 233
Kovacs, M., 246
Kowalchuk, V. L., 77, 78, 79, 84, 86, 366
Kramer, J. J., 74
Krechevsky, M., 118
Krug, S. E., 237
Kubiszyn, T., 392
Kummerow, J. M., 196, 204
Kyllonen, P. C., 311

La Greca, A. M., 121
Landberg, D. J., 463
Languis, M. L., 251, 261
Lanyon, R. I., 222
Larsen, S. C., 284
Lawman, R. L., 204
Lawrence, G. D., 266
Lee, J. A., 301
Lehman, I. J., 382, 460
Lennon, R. T., 131
Lenz, J., 204
Letteri, C. A., 261
Levine, S. C., 132
Levy, J. C., 87
Lewis, J., 366
Lien, A. J., 400
Lindeman, R. H., 278
Linden, J. D., 12, 176, 315, 320, 327, 400, 407
Linden, K. W., 12
Lindzey, G., 133
Linn, R. L., 57, 142
Loehlin, J. C., 133
Longstaff, J. P., 147
Love, B. G., 403, 421, 424
Lowenstein, J., 369
Lowman, R. L., 154
Lyman, H. B., 110, 421

Machover, K., 212
Maddux, C. D., 310, 314

Madsen, D. H., 300
Mann, L., 251, 257
Manning, M. L., 357, 358
Marcus, L. M., 344
Martin, J. T., 303
Marzano, R. J., 394
Mash, E. J., 352
Mastie, M. M., 154, 179, 204
Matarazzo, J. D., 435
Matey, C., 129
May, M. A., 320
McBride, J. R., 303, 314
McCallum, R. S., 130
McDaniel, C., 147, 151
McDavis, R. J., 356
McDermott, P. A., 300, 301, 436
McGrew, K. S., 136
McKee, P., 289
McKnew, D., 246
McRae, R. R., 219
Meehl, P. E., 231
Mehrens, W. A., 382, 460
Meier, S. T., 311, 312
Meisgeier, C., 266
Merz, W. R., Sr., 127
Messick, S., 57, 256, 369
Miller, M. D., 330, 406, 436
Miller, M. J., 421
Millman, J., 173, 369, 370
Millon, T., 217, 236
Miner, M. G., 186
Mitchell, D. F., 68
Monk, J. S., 261
Moore, C. A., 257
Moos, R. H., 285, 297
Moreland, K. L., 304, 314, 435
Moreno, K. E., 301
Morgan, A. W., 133
Moss, P. A., 463
Most, R., 12, 57, 110, 366
Murphy, E., 266
Murphy, L. L., 75
Murray, C., 132, 460
Murray, H. A., 206–208
Myers, I. B., 266

Naglieri, J. A., 130
Neisworth, J., 281
Nevo, B., 88, 91
Newmark, C. S., 216, 227

Norusis, M. J., 35
Nutall, E. V., 358

Oakland, T. D., 87, 173, 357
O'Brien, N., 74
Ollendick, T. W., 233, 234
Olsen, J. B., 301
Oster, G. D., 414
Otis, A. D., 8
Otis, A. S., 131
Ownby, R. L., 424, 439

Palmgreen, P., 68
Parker, P., 346
Parmelee, R., 87
Pennock-Roman, M., 142
Perkins, M. R., 457
Perlmutter, B. F., 68, 297
Perloff, E., 190, 191
Perloff, R., 186, 190, 191, 199, 203
Peterson, D. J., 147
Petoskey, M. D., 133
Phillips, W., 257
Phinney, J. S., 353
Piacentini, J., 323, 324
Piaget, J., 116, 132, 277
Pinel, P., 8
Pipho, C., 457
Plake, B. S., 75, 203, 250, 310, 398, 455
Plato, 6
Pope, K. S., 435
Popham, W. J., 96
Poteet, J. A., 251, 318
Powell, W. C., 410
Power, P. W., 204
Powers, D. E., 369
Prediger, D. J., 401
Prell, J. M., 369, 371
Prell, P. A., 369, 371
Price, G. E., 260
Pryzwansky, W. B., 415, 421
Pyle, K. R., 311

Rabin, A. I., 227
Rafferty, J. E., 209
Rapport, M. D., 346
Ravens, J. C., 129, 130
Reardon, R. C., 204
Reiff, J. C., 252, 257, 258, 266

Reiling, E., 373
Reilley, B. A., 227
Reilley, R. R., 227
Reitz, R., 379
Reynolds, C. R., 173, 281, 356, 421
Reznikoff, M., 210
Riechmann, W., 262
Riso, D. R., 220
Rogers, C. R., 231, 250
Rogers, M. R., 364
Roid, G. H., 435, 436
Rojan, J., 343
Romero, J., 358
Rorschach, H., 210
Rosman, B. L., 257
Rossetti, L. M., 342, 352
Rotherman, M. J., 353
Rotter, J. B., 16, 209
Rubin, R. B., 68

Sabatino, D. A., 251, 257
Saklofske, D. H., 77, 78, 79, 84, 86, 366
Sampson, J. P., Jr., 311
Sands, W. A., 314
Sapp, M., 379
Sarason, I. G., 366
Sattler, J. M., 88, 91, 111, 411, 429
Saunders, D. R., 321
Schaffer, B., 369
Schinka, J. A., 227
Schmidt, F. L., 200
Schopler, E., 344
Schuldberg, D., 230, 233
Schulte, A. C., 415, 421
Schwean, V. C., 77, 78, 79, 84, 86, 366
Seashore, H. G., 142
Seguin, E., 7
Seraphine, A. E., 330
Shapiro, E. S., 318
Shavelson, R. J., 221
Sherrod, B., 258
Shertzer, B., 176, 304, 315, 320, 327, 400, 407
Sheskin, D. J., 35
Shimberg, B., 456
Shore, M. F., 403, 421, 424
Simeonsson, R. J., 347, 352

Simon, A., 335
Simon, T., 112
Siudzinski, R. M., 263
Slosson, S. W., 317
Socrates, 6
Solomon, I. L., 211
Spearman, C., 9, 112, 132
Spencer, H., 112
Spenciner, L. J., 281, 296
Spendlove, D. C., 368
Spielberger, C. D., 366, 370, 379
Spohler, J. N., 133
Spurlock, J., 364
Stanton, G. C., 221
Starr, B., 211
Stern, L., 246
Sternberg, R. J., 111, 115, 116, 132, 133, 137, 463
Stiggins, R., 329
Stockwell, S., 369
Stoddard, G. D., 112
Straus, M. A., 68, 297
Strauss, C. C., 345
Stringer, S. A., 121
Strong, E. K., 176
Sue, D. W., 356
Super, D. E., 152, 180, 277, 278
Swassing, R. H., 256
Swiercinsky, D. P., 249
Sympson, J. B., 301
Sypher, H. E., 68

Tallent, N., 310, 430, 439
Tarrier, R. B., 181
Taylor, R., 373
Ten Brink, T. D., 322, 328
Tenopyr, M. L., 198–200, 452
Terdal, L. G., 352
Terman, L. M., 348
Thompson, A. S., 278
Thorndike, E. L., 9, 113, 132
Thorndike, R. L., 9, 111, 131, 152
Thornton, III, G. C., 191
Thurstone, L. L., 9, 112, 132
Tobias, S., 366
Touliastos, J., 297
Touliato, J., 68
Tucker, B. P., 454
Tyron, G. S., 366, 379

Urman, H., 371

Vagg, P. R., 366, 370, 379
Valencia, R. R., 356
Vance, H. B., 281, 314, 347, 352, 364
Vanden Bos, G. R., 11
Varca, P. E., 87
Vernon, A., 281
Vernon, P. E., 9, 113, 114, 132

Wagner, R. K., 132, 133, 137
Wainer, H., 314
Wallace, G., 284
Wand, B., 321
Waters, B. K., 314
Watkins, M. W., 300, 301
Weaver, S. J., 249
Wechsler, D., 112
Weiner, I. B., 210
Wesman, A. O., 142
White, M. A., 414
Whitman, N. A., 368
Wiens, A. N., 241
Wigdor, A. K., 369
Wiggins, G. P., 173, 329
Wiggs, 210
Williams, E. B., 188, 189
Wilt, R., 289
Wise, S. L., 310, 314
Witkin, H. A., 256, 257
Witt, J. C., 203, 250, 398, 455
Wolery, M., 285, 286, 340
Wonder, J., 258
Wundt, W., 8
Wylie, R. C., 221, 227
Wyne, M. D., 410

Ysseldyke, J. E., 291
Yule, W., 268
Yungeblut, A., 369

Zachary, R. A., 435
Zeidner, M., 12, 57, 110, 366
Ziotgorsky, Z., 210
Ziskin, J., 250
Zucker, K. R., 284
Zuckerman, E. L., 439

Subject Index

Abbreviations and test report writing, 431–432
Ability testing and 1990 Gallup Poll, 9. *See also* Aptitude testing; Intelligence testing
Abstracts, 65
Abuses/misuses of testing, 3
ACA Responsibilities of Users of Standardized Tests, 354
Acceptance of test information, 404–405
Acceptance of tests, factors leading to widespread, 8
Accommodation, 117
Acculturation, 359–360
ACCUPLACER, 308
Achievement testing
class profile, analysis of, 169–170
objectives, 156
overview, 155
school testing programs, 384–386
subject area tests, 160–161
types of achievement tests
adult achievement tests, 163–164
authentic and alternate assessment, 162–163
criterion-referenced tests, 157–158
curriculum-based measurement, 163
diagnostic tests, 164–165
individual achievement tests, 161–162
item banks, 158
minimum-level skills tests, 158–159
National Assessment of Educational Progress, 160

state assessment tests, 159–160
survey achievement tests, 156–157
using the results, 165–169
Achievement Tests and Measurement Devices-Vol. 1-5, 74
Acquiescent response style, 222
Acuity, assessment of, 252
Adaptive behavior, 117, 343
Adjustment problems, 270. *See also* Clinical assessment
Administration of tests
activities, suggested, 89–90
administrators, help for, 52
anxiety, test, 367
checklist of activities during testing, 84–85
competency, 5, 72
computer-assisted/adaptive testing, 300–301
discussion questions, 89
ease of administration, 52
evaluating and reviewing tests, 69
feedback from the test takers, 88
modes of test administration, 82–83
multicultural assessment, 355
objectives, 77
overview, 77
posttesting procedures, 85
behavior, recording test, 86
examiner and bias, 86–88
problems/issues in test administration, 86
pretesting procedures
awareness and orientation, 81–84
Code of Ethics, 78–79

examiner knowledge, 79
management details, 80
training test administrators, 80–81
school testing programs, 383
Standards for Educational and Psychological Testing, 78
Admissions tests, 145–147
Adolescents, interviewing, 246
Adult achievement tests, 163–164
Advanced Placement Programs, 2, 5, 160, 385
Age scores, 102, 104
Alternate assessment
future of, 463
growing use of, 162–163
objectives, 315–316
observational approaches, 316
clinical observations, 318
critical incident, 320
data collection, methods of, 322–324
guidelines for, 324–326
interviewing, 326–329
problem areas, 319–320, 329
scales, test behavior observational, 316–318
self-observations, 318–319
situation tests, 320–321
training observers, 322
unobtrusive vs. participant, 321–322
unstructured vs. structured, 319
overview, 315
reliability, 46, 48
American Association for Counseling and Development (AACD), 3, 78, 79, 400, 410, 445

American Association on Mental Retardation (AAMR), 343
American Chemical Society, 161
American College Test (ACT), 5, 100, 145, 160, 386, 387
American Counseling Association, 3, 444
American Educational Research Association (AERA), 39, 52–53, 63, 445. *See also* *Standards for Educational and Psychological Testing*
American Institutes for Research, 183
American Psychological Association (APA), 63, 68, 353, 409, 443–445, 459
American Psychologist, 68
American Sign Language, 83
Anecdotal records, 322–323
Anorexia nervosa, 346
Anxiety
   disorders, 345
   test anxiety
      defining, 366
      measures of, 366–367
      relaxation techniques, 367–368
      strategies to help, 367
      stress reduction, 368
      tests measuring, 222
Appropriateness of test for the examinee, 72
Aptitude testing. *See also* Career and employment testing
   issues and problem areas, 151–152
   multiaptitude batteries
      admissions tests, 145–147
      Armed Services Vocational Aptitude Battery, 140–142, 189, 387
      Career Ability Placement Survey, 49, 143–144
      Differential Aptitude Test Battery, 142–143
      General Aptitude Test Battery, 143, 188, 200, 387
   objectives, 139

overview, 139
scholastic aptitude tests, 386–387
specialized batteries
   artistic aptitude, 150
   clerical ability, 147–148
   computer aptitude, 151
   mechanical ability, 148–149
   musical aptitude, 150–151
   psychomotor ability, 149–150
uses for, 140
Armed services. *See* Military, the
Artistic aptitude and specialized batteries, 150
Assessing Adolescent and Adult Intelligence (Kaufman), 136
Assessing Student Performance: Exploring the Purpose and Limits of Testing (Wiggins), 173
Assessment, changes in, 462–464. *See also* Alternate assessment; Authentic assessment ; *Test/testing listings; individual subject headings*
Assessment Abstracts Online, 307
Assessment center, 191–192
Assessment for Early Intervention (Bagnatto & Neisworth), 281
Assessment of Childhood Disorders (Mash & Terdal), 352
Assessment of Children's Intelligence and Special Abilities (Sattler), 91
Assessment of Young Children (Cohen & Spenciner), 281, 296
Assimilation, 117
Association for Assessment in Counseling, 445
Association for Measurement and Evaluation in Counseling and Development, 445
Association of Assessment in Counseling of the Ameri-

can Counseling Association, 68
Asymmetrical curves, 22
Attention deficit disorder, 346
Attitude of clients about tests, 406
Attitudes and expectations of the examiner, 88
Audiotape-administered tests, 83
Auditory assessment and learning styles, 254, 255
Authentic assessment
   defining, 329–330
   future of, 463
   growing use of, 162–163
   guidelines for, 331–332
   issues and problems, 332
   mathematics, 394
   objectives, 315–316
   overview, 315
   portfolio assessment, 330–332
Autism, 344–345
Autobiographies, 318–319

Behavior. *See also* Environmental assessment; Observation
   adaptive, 117, 343
   assessing
      defining behavioral assessment, 233
      observation, 234
      self-monitoring, 234–235
      simulation and analogue methods, 235
   checklists, 323
   disorders
      anxiety, 345
      attention deficit, 346
      autism, 344–345
      conduct, 345–346
      eating, 346–347
   rating scales, 323–324
   tallying and charting, 323, 324
   test, 86
   written test results, 425, 427
Behavioral Assessment, 335
Behavior Research Methods and Instrumentation, 313
Bell Curve, The (Herrnstein & Murray), 132

Benton Laboratory of Neuropsychology, 240

Beyond IQ: A Triarchic Theory of Human Intelligence (Sternberg), 137

"Beyond Standardized Tests," 65

Bias
cultural, 413
evaluating and reviewing tests, 69, 72
examiners, 86–88
gender, 461
IQ (intelligence quotient), 133
multicultural assessment and test, 356–357

Bias in Mental Testing (Jensen), 136

Bibliographies, test collection, 65, 66

Biographical data and personnel selection/classification techniques, 190

Biomodal distribution, 23–24

Bivariate distribution, 30

Body/kinesthetic intelligence, 118

Brain preference, 258–259

Brain Watchers, The (Gross), 226

Bridge of the World of Work, 143

Bulimia, 346–347

Bureau of National Affairs Survey, 186

Buros-Nebraska Symposium on Measurement and Testing (Plake & Witt), 398

Career and employment testing. *See also* Aptitude testing
combined programs, 183–184
court decisions, 450–451
current trends and perspectives, 197–200
development, assessment of, 182–183, 277–279
government, test use in the, 188–189
instruments, career development, 182–183
interest inventories

Career Occupational Preference System, 178–179
future trends, 185
other interest inventories, 179–180
problems with, 184
Self-Directed Search, 176–177
Strong Interest Inventory, 177–178
techniques used to measure interest, 180–181
interpreting tests, guidelines for, 182
military, test use in the, 140–142, 189
objectives, 175–176
overview, 175
personality testing, 186
personnel selection and classification techniques, 189
assessment center, 191–192
biographical data, 190
guidelines for employee selection, 195–196
interviews, 190–191
job analysis, 192–194
Myers-Briggs Type Indicator, 196
Personnel Selection Inventory, 196–197
work keys, 194–195
private sector, 185
certification, 188
planning, career, 188
types of tests, 186–188
roles and purposes of, 185
school testing programs, 387
values, 181–182

Career Cluster Booklets, 179

Cattell's fluid and crystallized intelligence, 113–114

Center for the Study of Evaluation, Standards and Student Testing (CRESST), 66

Central tendency, measures of
comparisons of, 25
mean, 24, 32, 100–101
median, 25, 32
mode, 23–24, 32

Certification, occupational and professional, 5, 188–189, 332, 458–459, 463

Cheating, 87

Children, interviewing, 246. *See also* Development, assessment of

Civil Service Commission, U.S., 188

Class intervals, 18–20

Class model for scoring tests, 94

Class profile, analysis of, 169–170

Clerical ability and specialized batteries, 147–148

Clinical assessment
assessment approaches
inventories, 235–238
neuropsychological assessment, 239–240
psychodiagnostic testing, 230, 238–239
behavioral assessment
defining, 233
observation, 234
self-monitoring, 234–235
simulation and analogue methods, 235
counseling, tests in, 231–233
current trends, 233
interviews
checklists available to help clinicians, 241
children and adolescents, 246
Diagnostic and Statistical Manual of Mental Disorders (DSM-IV), 240–241
forms, 242–243
guidelines for before and during, 241
psychiatric, 244
psychological case study, 244–246
models of, 230–231
objectives, 229
observation, 318
overview, 229
pitfalls, 247
Standards for Educational and Psychological Testing, 231

Clinical assessment *continued*
  types of tests and assessment
    techniques, 230
  wellness, 246
*Clinical Assessment of Children's
  Intelligence: A Handbook
  for Professional Practice*
  (Kamphaus), 136
*Clinical Interpretation of Psycho-
  logical Tests* (Golden),
  249
*Clinical Interpretation of the
  Woodcock-Johnson Tests of
  Cognitive Abilities*
  (McGrew), 136
*Clinical Practice of Career Assess-
  ment: Interest, Abilities,
  and Personality* (Lawman),
  154, 204
Clinician-modeled approach for
  written test reports, 436
*Clinician's Thesaurus: A Guide-
  book for Writing Psychological Reports and Their
  Evaluations* (Zuckerman),
  439
Coaching to improve test scores,
  369
Code of Ethics, 78–79
*Code of Fair Testing Practices in
  Education,* 96, 339, 354,
  355, 410, 445
*Code of Professional Responsibili-
  ties in Educational Measurement* (CPR), 444, 446
Codes of professional responsibility, 444–446
Coefficients, reliability
  alternative forms, 46, 48
  internal consistency methods,
    47–48
  split-half reliability, 46
  standard error of measurement,
    48–49
  test-retest, 28–29, 45–46, 48
*CogAT Interpretive Guide for
  Teachers, A,* 131
Cognition
  anxiety, test, 367

development, assessment of,
    269, 272–274
  future of, 463
  learning styles
    brain preference, 258–259
    conceptual tempo, 257–258
    defining, 256
  Piaget's theory of cognitive
    development, 116–117, 272
College Board, 160, 183
College Majors Finder, 177
*Committee to Screen Career
  Guidance Instruments,*
  179
Communication disorders, 342
*Communication Research Mea-
  sures: A Sourcebook*
  (Rubin & Palmgreen), 68
Communication skills and devel-
  opmental tests, 269
Compendia of nonstandardized
  instruments, 68
Competency
  administration of tests, 5, 72
  certification and licensing exam-
    inations, 188
  Florida's competency require-
    ments for school coun-
    selors, 10
  humanistic education to com-
    petency-based approaches,
    change from, 8–9
  minimum-level competency
    testing, 155, 158–159,
    456–458
  reform movement, 456–458
  test users, 3–6
*Competency Standards in Student
  Assessment,* 445
*Computer and the Decision-Mak-
  ing Process* (Gutkin &
  Wise), 314
Computer aptitude, specialized
  batteries and, 151
Computer-assisted/adaptive testing, 9, 82
  administration, test, 300–301
  advantages/disadvantages of,
    308–309

current trends/issues, 310–311
  equivalence of conventional
    and, 301–302
  ethics, 311
  evaluating, 303–306
  future of, 463
  individualization, 302
  informational sources,
    307–308
  interpretation, test, 310
  legal issues, 311
  objectives, 299
  overview, 299
  personality testing, 302–303
  privacy, invasion of, 460
  programs available, 308
  reliability, 303
  software for test development,
    310
*Standards for Educational and
    Psychological Testing,* 304,
    307
  test results, communicating,
    404
  written test reports, 435–437
*Computer Based Testing: From
  Multiple Choice to Multiple
  Choices,* 304
Computerized Adaptive Testing
  (Sands, Waters & McBride),
  314
Computerized Adaptive Testing
  (Wainer), 314
Computer Living, 313
Computers in Human Behavior,
  313
Computers in Human Services,
  313
*Computers in Psychiatry/Psychol-
  ogy,* 313
Conceptual tempo, 257–258
Concrete operational period, 117,
  272
Concurrent validity, 40, 42, 44
Conduct disorders, 345–346
Conferences and test results, par-
  ent-examiner, 411
Consent, informed, 401, 460
Consequential validity, 43

Conservative orientation, political philosophy changing from liberal to, 8–9
Construct validity, 42–44
Consultant, the tester as. *See also* Parents, consulting with
ethical standards for consultation, 409
evaluation of the consultant, 417–418
legal considerations, 408–409
with other professionals, 417
with teachers, 415–417
Contemporary Intellectual Assessment: Theories, Tests, and Issues (Flanagan & Genshaft), 136
Content validity, 39–40, 44, 69
Contextual factors in testing, 88
Convergent validity, 43
Conversion tables, 105–106
COPSystem Career Brief Kit, 179
COPSystem Comprehensive Career Guide, 179
Cost of testing, 51
Council for the Accreditation of Counseling and Related Education Programs (CACREP), 9–10
Counseling, tests in, 231–233. *See also* Clinical assessment
Counseling From Profiles (Bennett, Seashore & Wesman), 142
Counseling Psychologist, 313
Counselor's Guide to Vocational Guidance Instruments (Kapes & Mastie), 154, 179, 204
Court decisions
educational testing
Debra P. vs. Turlington (1979, 1981, 1984), 450, 458
Diana vs. California State Board of Education (1973, 1979), 450
Larry P. vs. Riles (1974, 1979, 1984), 449–450

Sharif vs. New York State Educational Department (1989), 450
employment testing
Bakke vs. California (1978), 451
Berkman vs. City of New York (1987), 451
Contrearas vs. City of Los Angeles (1981), 451
Golden Rule Insurance Company vs. Richard L. Mathias (1980), 451
Griggs vs. Duke Power Company (1971), 450
United States vs. Georgia Power (1973), 450
Washington vs. Davis (1976), 451
Watson vs. Fort Worth Bank and Trust (1988), 451
Crestline, 398
Criterion-Referenced Measurement: The State of the Art (Berk), 173
Criterion-referenced tests
defining, 155
purposes of, 157–158
scoring and interpreting tests, 96, 97
symmetry and skewness, 22
validity, 40–42, 44
Critical incident approach, 320
Crystallized intelligence, 9, 113–114
Cultural bias, 413
Culturally Diverse Children and Adolescents: Assessment Diagnosis and Treatment (Canino & Spurlock), 364
Cumulative model for scoring tests, 94
Current trends/issues in testing. *See* Testing, current trends/issues in
Curriculum-based measurement (CBM), 163
Curves for a test
normal curve, 31–32, 100–101

smoothed curve, 20–21
symmetry and skewness, 21–23

Data collection, 2, 322–324
Deafness, 341
Decision-making (locating and selecting tests)
additional information, obtaining, 61, 63
available information, identifying, 61, 62
decisions and judgments to be made, 60
locating appropriate tests, 63–69
reviewing and evaluating tests, 69–70
three-step model, 2
type of information needed, identifying, 60–61
Defensiveness, 223
Desensitization, systematic, 367
Development, assessment of
age scores, 102, 104
career and employment testing, 182–183, 277–279
cognitive stages, 269, 272–274
domains, 268–270
early identification, 271
general principles, 268
grade equivalent and placement scores, 103
language, 272
methods of assessment, 270–271
moral development, 277
norms, 103–105
objectives, 267
overview, 267
psychosocial development, 275–276
school testing programs, 387–389
scoring and interpreting tests
age scores, 102, 104
grade equivalent and placement scores, 103
norms, 103–105

Developmental Assessment and Intervention With Children and Adolescents (Vernon), 281

Diagnostic and Statistical Manual of Mental Disorders-4th Edition (DSM-IV), 226, 235–236, 240–241, 344

Diagnostic and Structure Interviewing: A Handbook for Psychologists (Rogers), 250

Diagnostic tests, 155, 164–165

Dictionary of Occupational Titles (DOT), 143, 177

Difficulty of the items and test reliability, 50

Directory of Selected National Testing Programs, 74

Directory of Unpublished Experimental Mental Measures (Goldman & Mitchell), 68

Discrimination in employment, 449

Domains and developmental tests, 268–270

Drawing techniques for measuring personality, 211–215

DSM-IV. *See Diagnostic and Statistical Manual of Mental Disorders-4th Edition*

Eating disorders, 346–347

Ecological psychology, 283

Education, U.S. Office of, 100–101

Educational and Psychological Measurement, 313

Educational and Psychological Testing: The Test Taker's Outlook (Nevo & Jaeger), 88, 91

Educational Measurement (Clemans), 91

Educational Measurement (Feldt & Brennan), 57

Educational Measurement (Linn), 173, 421

Educational Psychologist, 137

Educational Researcher (Buros), 11, 68, 445

Educational Testing Service (ETS), 146, 304, 308, 311, 375, 459

Effective Teaching, Effective Learning: Making the Personality Connection in Your Classroom (Fairhurst & Fairhurst), 265

Ego-psychological report, 431

Emerging Issues and Methods in Personality Assessment (Schinka & Green), 227

Emic perspective, 358–359

Emotional development, 269, 388

Emotions and written test results, 429

Employers' Test and Service Associates, 187

Employment laws, 449. *See also* Aptitude testing; Career and employment testing

Employment Service, U.S. (USES), 188–189

Enneagram, 220

Environmental assessment
family/home, 286–289
objectives, 283
overview, 283
person-environment-fit, 293–294
school environment, 289–293
strategies, assessment, 286
theoretical background, 284–285
work environment, 293

Equal Employment Opportunity Commission (EEOC), 449

Equilibration, 117

ERIC/AE Digests, 63, 69

ERIC Clearinghouse on Assessment and Evaluation, 63

Erikson's stages of psychosocial development, 275

Error, false positive, 42. *See also* Reliability; Validity

Essay tests, 374

Ethical Principles of Psychologists, 88, 409, 417, 441, 443

Ethics and testing
American Counseling Association, 444
American Psychological Association, 443–444
codes of professional responsibility, 444–446
computer-assisted/adaptive testing, 311
consent, informed, 401, 460
consultant, the tester as, 409
current trends and perspectives, 452
examiner, ethical standards of the, 88
multicultural assessment, 358
National Board of Certified Counselors, 442–443
objectives, 441
overview, 441
responsible test use, 446

Ethnicity, 353. *See also* Multicultural assessment

Etic perspective, 358–359

Evaluating and reviewing tests, 2, 69–70, 72

Evaluation Perspectives (Jaegar), 398

Everything You Wanted to Know About Test-Wiseness (Ford), 370

Examinee characteristics and evaluating tests, 70

Examiners. *See also* Administration of tests
bias, 86–88
evaluating tests and characteristics of, 70
failure of the examiner to take a position, 430
pretesting procedures and knowledge of, 79
problems in test administration, 86–88
rapport with the examinees, 84

Explorations in Personality (Murray), 206

Exploring Applied Psychology: Origins and Critical

Analysis (Fagan & Vanden Bos), 11
Expressed interests, 180

Factor analysis, 31, 219–220
Fair Test Examiner, 65
False positive error, 42
Family Assessment: A Guide to Methods and Measures (Grotevant), 296
Family drawings, 212
Family/home environment, 286–289
Feedback
　interpretive, 5, 71–72
　stress reduction, 368
　test takers giving, 88
Finding Information About Psychological Tests: A Guide for Locating and Using Both Published and Unpublished Tests, 75
Flat profiles on aptitude/achievement tests, 406
Fluid intelligence, 9, 113–114
Ford Foundation, 461
Formal operational period, 117, 272
Format of the test, 51
Frames of Mind: The Theory of Multiple Intelligence (Gardner), 136
Frequency distribution, 17–19
Frequency polygon, 19, 21, 22
"Future of Clinical Assessment" (Ziskin), 250
Future of Testing, The (Plake & Witt), 203, 250

Gardner's theory of multiple intelligences, 117–118
Gender bias and testing, 461
Genetics and intelligence, 132, 460
Gifted and talented students, 348–349, 388
Gifts Differing (Myers), 266
Goals 2000 educational strategies, 393–394, 457

Golden Rule Procedure, 451
Government and career/employment testing, 188–189
Grade equivalent scores, 103, 104
Graphic presentations of test data, 19–21
Group-administered tests, 50, 82, 374, 403. *See also* group intelligence tests *under* Intelligence testing
Guessing, 87
Guide for Occupational Exploration, 143
Guide to Vocational Assessment, A (Power), 204
Guilford's model of intelligence, 113
Gutman's lower bounds to reliability, 464

Handbook of Family Measurement Techniques (Touliastos, Straus & Perlmutter), 68, 297
Handbook of Parametric and Nonparametric Statistical Procedures (Sheskin), 35
Handbook of Psychological and Educational Assessment of Children (Reynolds & Kamphaus), 173
Handbook of Psychological and Educational Assessment of Children: Intelligence and Achievement. Vol. 2 (Reynolds), 281
Handbook of Psychological Assessment (Goldstein & Hersen), 203, 335
Handbook of Psychological Assessment (Groth-Marnat), 226
Handbook of Psychological Testing (Kline), 227
Handbook of School Psychology (Reynolds & Gutkin), 421
Handbook of Self-Concept (Bracken), 226
Hearing impairment, 341, 347

Heredity and intelligence, 132, 460
Hierarchical theory, 113, 114
Histograms, 19, 20
Historical context of testing, 6–10
History of Psychological Testing, The (DuBois), 11
Home/family environment, 286–289
Hostile gatekeeper, 461
How to Take a Test (Dobbin), 378
Human Context: Environmental Determinants of Behavior (Moos), 297
Humanistic approach, 8–9, 231

Independent living skills, 269
Index to Tests Used in Educational Dissertations (Fabriano), 74
Indirect delivery model for communicating test results, 416
Individual achievement tests, 155, 161–162
Individual interpretation sessions to present test results to clients, 402–403
Individualization and computer-assisted/adaptive testing, 302
Individualized family service plan (IFSP), 448
Individualized Psychological Assessment (Fisher), 439
Infant-Toddler Assessment (Rossetti), 352
Inferential statistics, 32–33
Informed consent, 401, 460
Informing interview for communication of assessment results, 414
Integrity of testing, maintaining, 5
Intellectual disabilities, 342–343
Intelligence testing. *See also* IQ (intellligence quotient)
　current trends/issues, 132–133
　definitions of intelligence, 112
　group intelligence tests (representative sample)

Intelligence testing, *continued*
    Advanced Progressive Matrices, 130
    Cognitive Abilities Test, 131, 132
    Culture-Fair Intelligence Tests, 131, 132
    Otis-Lennon School Ability Test, 131
    Primary Test of Cognitive Skills, 132
    School and College Ability Tests, 131
    Test of Cognitive Skills, 131–132
    Universal Nonverbal Intelligence Test, 130–131
    individual scales (representative sample)
    Advanced Progressive Matrices, 129
    Arthur Point Scale of Performance Tests-Revised Form II, 129
    Cognitive Assessment System, 130
    Coloured Progressive Matrices, 129
    Kaufman Adolescent and Adult Intelligence Test, 127
    Kaufman Assessment Battery for Children, 122–127, 262, 359
    Leiter International Performance Scale, 128–129
    Peabody Picture Vocabulary Test, 126, 129, 345
    Raven's Progressive Matrices, 129
    Slosson Intelligence Test (SIT), 17, 26, 129
    Stanford-Binet Intelligence Scale, 127–128, 271, 359
    Test of Nonverbal Intelligence-2 (TONI-2), 129
    Wechsler scales, 118–122
    models of intelligence
    Cattell's fluid and crystallized intelligence, 113–114

    debates over the nature of intelligence, 9, 113
    Gardner's theory of multiple intelligences, 117–118
    Guilford's model of intelligence, 113
    hierarchical theory, 113, 114
    Piaget's theory of cognitive development, 116–117, 272
    Primary Mental Abilities Test, 112–113
    Sternberg's cognitive approaches to intelligence, 115–116
    two-factor theory of intelligence, 112
    objectives, 111
    overview, 111
Interactive approaches for reporting test results, 404
Interest inventories
    Career Occupational Preference System, 178–179
    future trends, 185
    other interest inventories, 179–180
    problems with, 184
    Self-Directed Search, 176–177, 308
    Strong Interest Inventory, 177–178
    techniques used to measure interest, 180–181
Internal consistency methods, 47–48
International Journal of Man-Machine Studies, 313
International Perspectives on Academic Assessment (Oakland & Hambleton), 173
Internet, the, 63, 307, 462–463
Interpretation, ease of, 52
Interpretive feedback, 5, 71–72
Interpretive Guide to the Millon Multiaxial Inventory (Choca), 249
Interval scale, 15–16

Interviews
    clinical assessment
    checklists available to help clinicians, 241
    children and adolescents, 246
    Diagnostic and Statistical Manual of Mental Disorders (DSM-IV), 240–241
    forms, 242–243
    guidelines for before and during, 241
    psychiatric, 244
    psychological case study, 244–246
    informing, 414
    observational approaches, 326–329
    personnel selection/classification techniques, 190–191
Ipsative model for scoring test, 95
IQ (intelligence quotient)
    Bell Curve, The, 132
    bias, 133
    deviation IQs, 100
    disabilities, intellectual, 342–343
    gifted and talented persons, 348
    historical context, 7
    minority groups, 460–461
    sensory discrimination and motor control, 7
Issues of Educational Measurement, 466
Item banks, 158
Item response theory (IRT), 464

Jargon and psychological report writing, 430
Job analysis, 192–194, 198. *See also* Aptitude testing; Career and employment testing
Joint Committee on Testing Practices, 445
Journal of Abnormal Child Psychology, 335
Journal of Behavioral Assessment, 335
Journal of Counseling and Development, 68, 313

Journal of Educational Measurement, 313
Journal of Employment Counseling, 421
Journal of Occupational Psychology, 313
Journals, professional
  authentic/alternate assessment, 335
  computer-assisted/adaptive testing, 307, 313
  evaluation of, 64
  measurement, listing of those focusing on, 66–67
  occasional articles on test/testing issues, 68
Jung, Carl, 208

Kaufman Assessment Battery for Children (K-ABC), 122–127, 262, 359

Language
  development, 272
  dialect of the examiner and test taker, 88
  minorities, linguistic, 338–339
  written test reports, 432
Learning disabilities, 388, 414
Learning Style (Reiff), 266
Learning styles
  cognitive style
    brain preference, 258–259
    conceptual tempo, 257–258
    defining, 256
  inventories, 260–263
  modality assessment
    auditory, 254, 255
    motor skills, 254–256
    preference assessment, 256
    visual, 252–253
  objectives, 251
  overview, 251
  personalities, 259–260
  processing style, 252
Learning Styles Counseling (Griggs), 265
Legal issues in testing, 446

Americans with Disabilities Act (ADA), 448–449
Carl D. Perkins Vocational and Technical Act of 1984, 447–448
computer-assisted/adaptive testing, 311
consent, informed, 401, 460
consultant, the tester as, 408–409
court decisions, 449–451
current trends and perspectives, 452, 453
Education of the Handicapped Act Amendments of 1990, 448
employment laws, 449
Family Educational Rights and Privacy Act of 1974, 447
Individuals with Disabilities Education Act (IDEA), 448
objectives, 441
overview, 441
privacy, invasion of, 460
Public Law 94-142, 447
Public Law 98-524, 447–448
Public Law 99-457, 448
Public Law 101-336, 448–449
Public Law 101-476, 448
Vocational Education Act of 1963, 448
Legislation
  Age Discrimination in Employment Act of 1967, 449
  Americans with Disabilities Act (ADA), 448–449
  Carl D. Perkins Vocational and Technical Act of 1984, 447–448
  Civil Rights Act of 1964, 449
  Civil Rights Act of 1991, 449
  Education for All Handicapped Children Act in 1975, 2, 283, 339–341, 409, 447
  Education of the Handicapped Act Amendments of 1990, 448
  Equal Pay Act of 1967, 449

Family Educational Rights and Privacy Act of 1974, 408–409, 447
Individuals with Disabilities Education Act (IDEA), 448
National Defense Education Act, 2
Public Law 93-380, 408–409
Public Law 94-142, 2, 283, 339–341, 409, 447
Public Law 98-524, 447–448
Public Law 99-457, 448
Public Law 101-336, 448–449
Public Law 101-476, 448
Tower Amendment to Equal Employment Act of 1966, 449
Vietnam Era Veterans Readjustment Act of 1974, 449
Vocational Education Act of 1963, 448
Leisure Activity Finder, 177
Length of the test and test reliability, 49–50
Licensing, occupational and professional, 5, 188–189, 332, 458–459, 463
Limiting Bias in the Assessment of Bilingual Students (Hamayan & Damico), 352
Linguistic minorities, 338–339
Locating and selecting tests
  criteria for selecting a test, 70–72
  decision theory model
    additional information, obtaining, 61, 63
    available information, identifying, 61, 62
    decisions and judgments to be made, 60
    locating appropriate tests, 63–69
    reviewing and evaluating tests, 69–70
    type of information needed, identifying, 60–61
  objectives, 59
  overview, 59

Logical/mathematical intelligence, 117–118
Looking at Type and Learning Styles (Lawrence), 266

Major Psychological Assessment Instruments (Newmark), 227
Making Vocational Choices: A Theory of Vocational Personalities and Work Environments (Holland), 177
Manipulative materials used to measure personality, 213
Manuals, usefulness of test, 52–54
Mathematics
　arithmetic subtest (Wechsler scales), 119
　authentic assessment, 394
　standards and guidelines, professional, 331–332
Mean, 24, 32, 100–101
Measurement and Evaluation in Counseling and Development, 313
Measurement concepts. *See also* Statistical concepts
　objectives, 37
　overview, 37
　practical features to be considered
　　administration, ease of, 52
　　administrators, help for, 52
　　cost of testing, 51
　　format of the test, 51
　　interpretation, ease of, 52
　　manual, usefulness of test, 52–54
　　readability, 51
　　scoring, ease of, 52
　　time of testing, 51
　reliability
　　coefficients, 45–49
　　defining, 43–44
　　factors influencing, 49–50
　　test development, steps in, 38–39
　validity
　　consequential, 43

construct, 42–44
　content, 39–40, 44
　criterion-related validity, 40–42, 44
　defining, 39
Measurement Update, 63
Measures for Clinical Practice-Vol. 1: Couples and Families (Fischer & Corcoran), 68
Measures of Psychological Assessment: A Guide to 3,000 Original Sources and Their Application (Chun & Cobb), 68
Measuring Self-Concept Across the Life Span (Byrne), 226
Mechanical ability and specialized batteries, 148–149
Median, 25, 32
Memory, 112, 116
Mental health. *See also* Clinical assessment
　mental retardation, 343–344
　preschoolers, 341
　school testing programs, 388
Mental Health Consultation and Collaboration (Caplan & Caplan), 421
Mental Measurements Yearbook, 63, 68, 179
Mental processing subtests on the K-ABC, 123
Mental retardation, 343–344
MICROTEST assessment software, 236
Military, the
　Army Alpha in World War I, 461
　career/employment testing, 140–142, 189
　mean and standard deviation in testing, 100
　personality testing, 8
　school testing programs, 387
　situation tests, 321
Mind styles, 262
Minimum-level competency testing, 155, 158–159, 456–458

Minorities. *See also* Multicultural assessment; Special populations, working with
　fairness to minority groups, 460–461
　white test administrators, 87
Mirrors for Behavior III: An Anthology of Observational Instruments (Simon & Boyer), 335
MMPI-2: Assessing Personality in Psychopathology (Graham), 226
MMPI-2 in Psychological Treatment (Butcher), 226
MMPI-2 Tutorial Workbook (Reilley & Reilley), 227
Modality assessment
　auditory, 254, 255
　motor skills, 254–256
　preference assessment, 256
　visual, 252–253
Mode, 23–24, 32
Modern Mental Measurement: A Historical Perspective (Linden & Linden), 12
Moral development, 277. *See also* Ethics and testing
Motivation to take a test, 406
Motor skills, 7, 254–256
Multiaptitude batteries
　admissions tests, 145–147
　Armed Services Vocational Aptitude Battery, 140–142, 189, 387
　Career Ability Placement Survey, 49, 143–144
　Differential Aptitude Test Battery, 142–143
　General Aptitude Test Battery, 143, 188, 200, 387
Multicultural assessment
　bias, test, 356–357
　objectives, 354
　overview, 353
　scoring and interpreting tests, 355
Standards for Educational and Psychological Testing

administration and scoring, 355

content considerations, 354–355

technical considerations, 355

use and interpretation, 355–356

understanding, developing greater, 357

acculturation, 359–360

ethical principles, 358

etic and emic perspectives, 358–359

strategies for, 361–362

testing principles, 358

Multicultural Assessment Perspectives for Professional Psychology (Dana), 364

Multicultural Counseling Competencies and Standards, 356

Multifactor aptitude tests, 387

Multiple intelligences, 114, 117–118

Multiple Intelligences: The Theory in Practice (Gardner), 136

Multiscore, 158

Multivariate statistical analysis, 436

Murray, Henry A., 206–208

Musical aptitude and specialized batteries, 150–151

Musical/rhythmic intelligence, 118

National Assessment of Educational Progress (NAEP), 157, 160, 329

National Association of College Admission Counselors (NACAC), 5, 446

National Association of Elementary School Principals, 445

National Association of School Psychologists, 79, 415–416

National Association of Secondary School Principals, 261, 292, 445

National Board of Certified Counselors, 78–79, 442–443

National Career Development Association, 462

National Center for Fair and Open Testing, 65

National Center on Post Secondary Teaching, Learning, and Assessment (NCP-STLA), 66

National Commission on Excellence in Education, 456

National Commission on Testing and Public Policy (1990), 457, 461

National Computer Systems, 236

National Council of Architectural Registration Boards, 311

National Council on Licensure Examinations, 311

National Council on Measurement in Education (NCME), 63, 68, 332, 445, 446

National Educational Development Series, 157

National Health Interview Study of Child Health (1988), 267

National Study of School Evaluation, 390

National Teachers Examination, 375

Needs assessments, 389

Negative attitudes toward testing, 3

Negative test results, client's response to, 405

Neuropsychological assessment, 239–240

New Directions on Career Planning in the Workplace (Kummerow), 204

Nominal scale, 14–15

Nonclassical psychometric models, 462

Nonparticipant observation, 234

Normal curve, 31–32, 100–101

Norm-referenced tests interpretation of, 96–97

percentiles, 97–98

standard scores, 98–101

Norms, 5, 103–105

Number in the testing group and evaluating tests, 69

Observation, 316

behavioral assessment, 234

clinical observations, 318

critical incident, 320

data collection, methods of, 322–324

development, assessment of, 270–271

guidelines for, 324–326

interviewing, 326–329

main purpose of, 315

problem areas, 319–320, 329

scales, test behavior observational, 316–318

self-observations, 318–319

situation tests, 320–321

training observers, 322

unobtrusive *vs.* participant, 321–322

unstructured *vs.* structured, 319

Occupational Finder, 177

Office of Personnel Management (OPM), 188

Office of Strategic Services, U.S. (OSS), 321

On Your Own: Preparing to Take a Standardized Test, 378

Oral examinations, 374

Oral reports for reporting test results, 403

Ordinal scale, 15

Organization and Piaget's theory of cognitive development, 117

Organization of the written report, 430, 431

Pantomime, 83

Parents, consulting with bias, cultural, 413

Code of Fair Testing Practices in Education, 410

conferences, parent-examiner, 411

disagreement with results of testing, parents', 412–413

explaining test results to, 410–411

indirect delivery model, 416

Parents, consulting with, *continued*
  informing interview, 414
  overachievers/underachievers, students who are, 413–414
  Principles for Professional Ethics, 409
  problem-solving consulting model, 416–417
  questions parents ask about tests, 411–412
  test interpreters, parents as, 414
Participant observation, 234, 321–322
Past experiences and test-taking skills, 373
Pearson product moment correlation, 28–31
Peer evaluations, 346
Percentiles, 97–98, 104
Perception, 113, 252
Performance assessment, 329 *See also* Authentic assessment
Performance Assessment: Methods and Applications (Berk), 203
Performance Assessment and Standards-Based Curricula: The Achievement Cycle (Glatthorn), 398
Performance Assessment Handbook. Vol. I & II (Johnson), 335
Performance components, 115
Personal development dimensions, 285
Personality testing
  computer-assisted/adaptive testing, 302–303
  dimensions of personality
    anxiety tests, 222
    enneagram, 220
    self-concept scales, 220–222
  employment context, 186
  factor analytic approaches, 219–220
  format of tests, 218–219
  learning styles, 259–260
  military, the, 8

objectives, 206
overview, 205
problems involved, 222–223
reliability of, 270
sten scores, 100
techniques for measuring personality
  drawing, 211–215
  manipulative materials, 213
  questionnaires, 213, 216–218
  verbal, 209–210
  visual, 210–211
theories
  Jung, Carl, 208
  Murray, Henry A., 206–208
  other theory-based tests, 209
Person-centered report, 431
Person-environment-fit theories, 293–294
Personnel selection and classification techniques, 189
  assessment center, 191–192
  biographical data, 190
  guidelines for employee selection, 195–196
  interviews, 190–191
  job analysis, 192–194
  Myers-Briggs Type Indicator, 196
  Personnel Selection Inventory, 196–197
  Work Keys, 194–195
"Perspectives on the Future of Neuropsychological Assessment" (Dean), 250
Pervasive development disorders, 344–345
Pfieffer Library on Training and Development Resources, 204
Physical development and developmental tests, 269
Physical impairment, 341
Piaget's theory of cognitive development, 116–117, 272
Placement programs, 2
Placement scores, 103
Political philosophy, change from a liberal to a conservative, 8–9

Portfolio and Performance Assessment (Farr), 173
Portfolio assessment, 330–332
Posttesting procedures, 85
  behavior, recording test, 86
  bias and examiners, 86–88
  problems/issues in test administration, 86
Practical Guide to Psychodiagnostic Testing (Katz), 250, 439
Practitioner's Guide to Developmental and Psychological Testing (Aylward), 352
Praise and encouragement, use of, 87
Predictive validity, 40–42, 44, 69
Preference assessment, 256
Preoperational stage, 117, 272
Preparation and the decison-making process, 2
Preparing for Testing with the (CogAT), 131
Preschool children. *See also* Development, assessment of
  instruments used for assessing, 271
  special populations, working with, 340–342
Pretesting procedures
  awareness and orientation, 81–84
  Code of Ethics, 78–79
  examiner knowledge, 79
  management details, 80
  training test administrators, 80–81
Principles for Professional Ethics, 79, 409
Privacy, invasion of, 459–460
Problem-oriented report, 431
Problem-solving consulting model for communicating test results, 416–417
Processing style, 252
Professional groups/organizations, 65, 161, 307
Professional Manual, 177

Professional responsibility, codes of, 444–446

Profiles to aid in interpretation of the results, 106–107

Profiling and Work Keys system, 194

Projective questions, 209

Projective Techniques for Adolescents and Children (Rabin), 227

Projective tests, 186, 208–211, 238–239

Psychiatric Annals, 313

Psychiatric interviews, 244. *See also* Clinical assessment

Psychodiagnostic testing, 230, 238–239

Psychodiagnostik, 210

Psychoeducational Assessment of Hearing-Impaired Students: Infancy Through Adulthood (Bradley-Johnson), 352

Psychological and Developmental Assessment of Special Children (Simeonsson), 352

Psychological and Educational Tests: A Selected Annotated Guide (Crosby-Milenburg), 74

Psychological Assessment in Schools, 398

Psychological Assessment of Children (Vance), 281, 314, 352, 364

Psychological case study, 244–246. *See also* Clinical assessment

Psychological Consultation: Introduction to Theory and Practice (Brown, Pryzwansky & Schulte), 421

Psychological Corporation, 142, 146, 194, 307

Psychological Examination of the Child (Blau), 281

Psychological Reports: A Guide to Report Writing in Professional Psychology (Ownby), 439

Psychological report writing. *See* Written test results

Psychological Report Writing (Tallent), 439

Psychological Testing: An Inside View (Zeidner & Most), 12, 57, 110, 314

Psychological Testing of Hispanics (Geisinger), 364

Psychometric knowledge, 4, 230–231

Psychomotor abilities, 149–150, 254–256

Psychosocial development, 275–276

Public, communicating test results to the, 406–408

Publication Manual of the American Psychological Association-4th Edition, 431

Questionnaires, personality, 213, 216–218

Range, 26

Rasch model of test analysis, 310

Rating scales, 323–324

Rating Scales and Checklists (Aiken), 335

Ratio scale, 16

Raw scores, 104

Readability of the test, 51

Readiness of the client for test results, 405

Reading projects, Title 1 or Chapter 1, 101

Reasoning, 112, 116

Reflection-impulsivity, 257–258

Reform movement and competency testing, 456–458

Regression analysis, 29

Relationship, measures of factor analysis, 31

Pearson product moment correlation, 28–31

regression, 29

Relationship dimensions, 285

Relaxation techniques for test anxiety, 367–368

Reliability
alternate assessment, 46, 48
coefficients
alternative forms, 46, 48
internal consistency methods, 47–48
split-half reliability, 46
standard error of measurement, 48–49
test-retest, 28–29, 45–46, 48
computer-assisted/adaptive testing, 303
defining, 43–44
evaluating and reviewing tests, 69
factors influencing, 49–50
Gutman's lower bounds to, 464
moral reasoning instruments, 277
personality testing, 270
selection, test, 71

Reports of the AMEG, 179

Response set/positional preferences affecting individual performance, 374

Responsibilities of Users of Standardized Tests, 355–356, 445

Responsible Test Use, 91

Review of Educational Research, 137, 379

Rocky Mountain Behavioral Science Institute, 366

Role playing, 235

SAT Coaching Coverup: How Coaching Courses Can Raise Scores by 100 Points and Why ETS Denies the Evidence (Cronbach), 65, 369

Scales of measurement
interval scale, 15–16
nominal scale, 14–15
ordinal scale, 15
ratio scale, 16

Scholastic aptitude tests, 386–387

School environment/climate, 289–293

School improvement movement, 394
School testing programs
  categories of tests
    achievement tests, 384–386
    career guidance tests, 387
    multifactor aptitude tests, 387
    scholastic aptitude tests, 386–387
    typical program, 385
  developmental model, 387–389
  evaluation of, 390–392
  Goals 2000 educational strategies, 393–394
  goals/purposes of, 382
  issues and concerns, 392–393
  military, the, 387
  objectives, 381
  overview, 381
  planning
    administration, 383
    personnel involved, 382–383
    responsibilities, scope of, 383, 384
    selecting the test, 383
Scoring and interpreting tests. See also Measurement concepts; Statistical concepts; Test results, communicating; Written test results
  accuracy of scoring, 5
  comparison of different types of test scores, 104
  conversion tables, 105–106
  criterion-referenced interpretation, 96, 97
  developmental intraindividual comparison, 101
    age scores, 102, 104
    grade equivalent and placement scores, 103
    norms, 103–105
  ease of scoring, 52
  examples of test scoring, 95–96
  improving test scores
    coaching, 369
    wiseness, test, 369–372
  interpreting scores, 96
Jesness Scale, 23

Kaufman Assessment Battery for Children (K-ABC), 124–125
models of scoring, 94–95
multicultural assessment, 355
norm-referenced interpretation, 96–97
  percentiles, 97–98
  standard scores, 98–101
objectives, 93
overview, 93
profiles, 106–107
reliability of the scoring, 50
standards for scoring, 94
Wechsler scales, 121–122
Selection, test. See Locating and selecting tests
Self-administered tests, 82
Self-care skills, 269
Self-Concept Instruments (Wylie), 227
Self-concept scales, 220–222
Self-Directed Search and Related Holland Career Materials (Reardon & Lenz), 204
Self-monitoring, 234–235, 270
Self-observations, 318–319
Self-report instruments, 287
Sensorimotor period, 117, 272
Sensory discrimination and motor control, 7
Sequential processing, 123
"Sex Bias in College Admissions Tests," 65
Sex of the examiner, 88
Simulation methods, 235
Situation tests, 320–321
Social desirability response set, 222–223
Social development and developmental tests, 269
Social-emotional-behavioral problems with preschoolers, 341
Spatial relations, 113, 148–149
Spearman-Brown prophecy formula, 46, 50, 464
Specialized aptitude batteries
  artistic aptitude, 150
  clerical ability, 147–148

computer aptitude, 151
mechanical ability, 148–149
musical aptitude, 150–151
psychomotor ability, 149–150
Special populations, working with
  objectives, 337
  overview, 337
  preschoolers, 340–342
  standards for
    Education for All Handicapped Children Act in 1975, 339–340
    linguistic minorities, 338–339
    Standards for Educational and Psychological Testing, 338, 339
  types of disabilities and disorders
    behavior disorders, 344–347
    communication disorders, 342
    gifted and talented persons, 348–349
    hearing impairment, 347
    intellectual disabilities, 342–343
    visual impairment, 348
Split-half reliability, 46
SPSS for Windows: Base System for User's Guide (Norusis), 35
Standard deviation, 26–28, 100–101
Standard error of measurement (SEM), 48–49
Standards and guidelines, professional. See also Ethics and testing; Standards for Educational and Psychological Testing
  ethical standards of the examiner, 88
  mathematics, 331–332
  scoring and interpreting tests, 94
  special populations, working with
    Education for All Handicapped Children Act in 1975, 339–340

linguistic minorities, 338–339
test results, communicating, 402
Standard scores
    comparison with other scores, 104
    IQs, deviation, 100
    mean and standard deviation, 100–101
    stanines, 100, 101, 104
    sten scores, 100, 101
    T scores, 99
    z scores, 98–99
Standards for Educational and Psychological Testing. See also Standards and guidelines, professional
    administration, standards for, 78
    clinical assessment, 231
    computer-assisted/adaptive testing, 304, 307
    counseling, tests in, 232
    manuals, usefulness of test, 54
    multicultural assessment
        administration and scoring, 355
        content considerations, 354–355
        technical considerations, 355
        use and interpretation, 355–356
    norms, 103
    special populations, working with, 338, 339
    validity
        construct, 42
        defining, 39
        standard error of measurement, 49
Standards for Educational and Psychological Tests, 445
Stanines, 100, 101, 104
State comprehensive assessment tests and standards-based curricula, 159–160, 393–394
State Department, U.S., 188
Statement of Principles of Good Practice, 446

Statistical Analysis: An Interdisciplinary Introduction to Univariate and Multivariate Methods (Kachigan), 35
Statistical concepts. *See also* Measurement concepts
    central tendency, measures of
        comparisons of, 25
        mean, 24
        median, 25
        mode, 23–24
    inferential statistics, 32–33
    normal curve, 31–32
    objectives, 13
    overview, 13
    relationship, measures of
        factor analysis, 31
        Pearson product moment correlation, 28–31
        regression, 29
    role of statistics, 14
    scales of measurement
        interval scale, 15–16
        nominal scale, 14–15
        ordinal scale, 15
        ratio scale, 16
    variability, measures of, 25
        range, 26
        standard deviation, 26–28
        variance, 26
    visual picture of what scores look like
        frequency distribution, 17–19
        graphic presentations, 19–21
        Nowicki-Strickland Locus of Control Scale, 16–17
        smoothed curve, 20–21
        symmetry and skewness, 21–23
Statistics: A Spectator Sport (Jaeger), 34
Sten scores, 100, 101
Sternberg's cognitive approaches to intelligence, 115–116
Straight Talk About Mental Tests (Jensen), 136
Stress reduction and test anxiety, 368
Structured observation, 319

Subject area tests, 155, 160–161
Supplement to the Eleventh Mental Measurements Yearbook (Conoley & Kramer), 74
Survey achievement tests, 155, 156–157

TAT, CAT and SHT in Clinical Use, The (Bellak & Abrams), 226
Teacher-made examinations and test-wiseness, 371–372
Teachers, consulting with, 415–417
Teacher's Guide to Type: A New Perspective on Individual Differences in the Classroom (Meisgeier & Murphy), 266
Teaching and Learning Personality Assessment (Handler & Hilsenroth), 227
Technical aspects of test report writing, 431–432
Technology affecting the testing movement, 9
Test Alert, 376–377
Test Anxiety (Reitz), 379
Test Anxiety (Sapp), 379
Test Anxiety: Theory, Assessment and Treatment (Spielberger & Yagg), 379
Test Anxiety (Reitz), 379
Test Anxiety (Sapp), 379
Test behavior, 86
Test bias, 356–357. *See also* Bias
Test Critiques, 63, 68
Test development, steps in, 38–39
Testing, current trends/issues in
    changes in assessment, 461–464
    career and employment testing, 197–200
    clinical assessment, 233
    competency testing and the reform movement, 456–458
    computer-assisted/adaptive testing, 310–311
    hostile gatekeeper, 461

Testing, current trends/issues in, *continued*
intelligence testing, 132–133
legal and ethical aspects, 452, 453
licensure and certification examinations, 458–459
minority groups, fairness to, 460–461
objectives, 455
overview, 455
privacy, invasion of, 459–460
truth in testing, 459
Testing Adolescents (Harrington), 249
Testing Adults (Swiercinsky), 249
Testing African American Students (Hilliard), 364
Testing Children (Weaver), 249
Testing in America's Schools, 462
Testing Information Sources for Educators (Fabriano & O'Brien), 74
Test-oriented report, 431
Test publishers and distributors, 483–484
Test results, communicating. *See also* Consultant, the tester as; Written test results
evaluating and reviewing tests, 69
focus on test results rather than the individual, 430
guidelines for, 400–401
methods of
group sessions, 403
individual sessions, 402–403
interactive approaches, 404
oral reports, 403
video approaches, 404
written reports, 403–404
objectives, 399
overview, 399
problem areas
acceptance, 404–405
flat profiles, 406
motivation and attitude, 406
negative results, 405
readiness of the client, 405

to the public, 406–408
standards for, 402
Test-retest reliability coefficient, 28–29, 45–46, 48
Test Scores and What They Mean (Lyman), 110, 421
Test selection. *See* Locating and selecting tests
Tests in Print IV (Murphy, Conoley & Impara), 63, 75
Tests/measures, individual
Adaptive Behavior Scales, 343
Adolescent Diagnostic Screening Battery, 344
Adolescent Multiphasic Personality Inventory (AMPI), 238
Adult Language Assessment Scale (AdultLAS), 164
Adult Psychoeducational Profile (APEP), 345
Advanced Progressive Matrices (APM), 129, 130
Affective Style Measure, 286
Air Corps Test Battery, 152
Aptitude and Intelligence Series, 186
Armed Services Vocational Aptitude Battery (ASVAB), 140–142, 189, 385, 387
Army Alpha, 6, 8, 130
Army General Classification Test, 100
Arthur Point Scale of Performance Tests-Revised Form II, 129
Attention Deficit Disorder Scale (ADDS), 346
Autism Behavior Checklist (ABC), 345
Autism Screening Instrument for Educational Planning, 345
Basic Achievement Skills Individual Screener (BASIS), 161
Basic Occupational Literacy Test (BOLT), 186–187
Basic Skills Assessment Program (BSAP), 159

Battelle Developmental Inventory, 271
Bayley Scales of Infant Development, 9, 271, 340
Beck Anxiety Inventory, 307
Beck Depression Inventory, 9, 238, 307, 359
Beck Hopelessness Scale, 9, 238, 307
Beck Scale for Suicide Ideation, 307
Behavior Observation Scale for Autism, 345
Bender Visual Motor Gestalt Test, 212–213, 238, 253
Bennett Mechanical Comprehension Test, 147
Blacky Pictures, 209
Block design test (Wechsler scales), 120
Brain Preference Indicator, 258
Brown Attention Deficit Disorder Scale, 307, 346
Bruininks-Oseretsky Test of Motor Proficiency, 255
Burks's Behavior Rating Scales, 344, 388
Butcher Treatment Planning Inventory, 307
California Achievement Test (CAT), 9, 156
California Psychological Inventory (CPI), 186, 217, 218, 308, 359
Campbell Interest and Skills Survey (CISS), 179
Canfield Learning Styles Inventory, 261
Career Ability Placement Survey (CAPS), 49, 143–144
Career Assessment Inventory (CAI), 179
Career Attitudes and Strategies Inventory, 188
Career Awareness Inventory, 182
Career Development Inventory, 182–183
Career Maturity Inventory, 183

Career Occupational Preference System (COPSystem), 178–179

Career Planning Program (CPP), 183

Cattell Infant Intelligence Scale, 340

Child and Adolescent Diagnostic Scales, 238

Child Assessment Schedule, 246

Child Behavior Checklist (CBC), 9, 346

Child Diagnostic Screening Battery, 344

Childhood Autism Rating Scale (CARS), 345

Children's Assessment Schedule (CAS), 327

Children's Embedded Figures Test, 257

Children's Manifest Anxiety Scale-Revised, 345

Children's Personality Questionnaire (CPQ), 100, 219

Children's Test Anxiety Scale (CTAS), 366

Children's Version of the Family Environment Scale (CVFES), 287

Child's Learning Profile (CLP), 346

Classroom Environment Scale, 290

Clinical Analysis Questionnaire (CAQ), 237

Coding test (Wechsler scales), 120

Cognitive Abilities Test (CogAT), 131, 132

Cognitive Assessment System (CAS), 130

College Characteristics Index (CCI), 290

College-Level Examination Program (CLEP), 2, 5, 160

College Student Experiences Scale (CSEQ), 290

Colorado Self-Report Measure of Family Functioning, 287

Coloured Progressive Matrices (CPM), 129

Common Metric Questionnaire, 194

Comprehension subtest (Wechsler scales), 119

Comprehensive Ability Battery (CAB), 187

Comprehensive Personality Profile, 187–188

Comprehensive Test of Basic Skills (CTBS/4), 156

Concept Assessment Kit (CAK), 272

Conflict Tactics Scale (CTS), 287

Connors's Rating Scale-Revised, 346

Continuous Performance Test (CPT), 346

Coopersmith Self-Esteem Inventory, 221

COPSystem Interest Inventory, 106

Crawford Small Parts Dexterity Test (CSPDT), 149

Creativity Attitude Survey, 348

Creativity Checklist, 349

Criterion Test of Basic Skills, 158

Culture-Fair Intelligence Tests, 131, 132

Culture-Free Self-Esteem Inventory, 221

Curtis Verbal-Clerical Skills Test, 147

Dallas Preschool Screening Test, 340

Defensive and Supportive Communication Interaction System, 286

Defining Issues Test, 277

Denver Developmental Screening Test (DDST), 271, 340

Detroit Tests of Learning Aptitude, 253

Developing Cognitive Abilities Test, 386

Developmental Assessment for the Severely Handicapped, 340

Developmental Environments Coding System (DECS), 286

Developmental Indicators for the Assessment of Learning-Revised (DIAL-R), 271

Developmental Inventory of Black Consciousness (DIB-C), 360

Developmental Test of Visual-Motor Integration, 253

Devereux Scales of Mental Disorders, 308

Devereux Test of Extremity Coordination, 255

Diagnostic Interview for Children and Adolescents (DICA), 327, 346

Diagnostic Interview Schedule for Children (DISC), 346

Diagnostic Inventory of Personality and Symptoms, 344

Differential Aptitude Test Battery, 142–143

Digit span test (Wechsler scales), 119

Digit symbol test (Wechsler scales), 120

Dimensions of Excellence Scales: Survey for School Improvement, 394

Direction Scale, The, 263

Draw-a-Person Test, 212

Early School Personality Questionnaire (ESPQ), 100, 219

Eating Disorders Inventory-2, 346–347

Eating Inventory, 308

Edwards Personal Preference Inventory, 186

Effective School Battery, 290

Embedded Figures Test, 257

Employee Aptitude Survey Series, 187

Employment Barrier Identification Scale, 187

Employment Reliability Inventory, 187

Tests/measures, individual, *continued*

Ethical Reasoning Inventory, 277

Everyday Skills Test (EDST), 159

Eysenck Neuroticism and Extroversion Scales, 43

Eysenck Personality Questionnaire (EPQ), 219, 359

Family Adaptability and Cohesion Evaluation Scales III (FACES III), 287

Family Assessment Measure (FAM), 287

Family Conflict and Dominance Codes, 286–287

Family Constraining and Enabling Coding System (CECS), 287

Family Environment Scale (FES), 287

Family Evaluation Form (FEF), 287

Family Functioning in Adolescence Questionnaire (FFAQ), 288

Family Process Scales (FPS), 288

Family Relationship Questionnaire (FRQ), 288

Fear Survey Schedule for Children-Revised, 345

Florida Analysis of Semantic Traits, 263

Florida Comprehensive Assessment Test (FCAT), 159, 393–394

Frostig Developmenal Test of Visual Perception, 253

Gates-McKillop-Horowitz Reading Diagnostic Test, 165

General Aptitude Test Battery (GATB), 143, 188, 200, 387

General Clerical Test, 147

General Educational Development Test, 163

General Educational Performance Index, 164

Gifted and Talented Evaluation Scales, 349

Gifted and Talented Screening Form, 349

Gilliam Autism Rating Scale, 345

Goldman-Fristoe-Woodcock Auditory Skills Test Battery, 254

Goodenough-Harris Drawi-a-Man Test, 126

Graduate Management Admission Test (GMAT), 146

Graduate Record Examination (GRE), 145–146, 311

Graves Design Judgment Test, 150

Gregorc Style Delineator, 262

Group Embedded Figures Test, 257

Group Inventory for Finding Creative Talent (GIFT), 349

Group Inventory for Finding Interests: Gifted and Talented Screening Form, 349

Guilford-Zimmerman Temperament Survey, 43, 186

Hall Occupational Orientation Inventory, 181

Halstead-Reitan Neuropsychological Test Battery, 239

Hamilton Rating Scale for Depression-Revised, 9

Hand-Tool Dexterity Test, 149

Hare Psychopathy Checklist-Revised (PCL-R), 244

Harrington-O'Shea Career Decision-Making System-Revised (COM-R), 179

Hay Aptitude Test Battery, 147

Hepatic Intelligence Scale, 348

High School Characteristics Index (HCSI), 290

High School Personality Questionnaire (HSPQ), 100, 219

High School Subjects Tests, 386

Hill Performance Test of Selected Positional Concepts, 348

Holland's Self-Directed Search, 404

House-Tree-Person Test (HTP), 212

Houston Test for Language Development (HTLD), 272

Illinois Test of Psycholinguistic Abilities, 253, 254

In-Basket Test, 321

Industrial Reading Test, 187

Inferred Self-Concept Scale, 221, 270

Information test (Wechsler scales), 119

Institutional Functioning Inventory (IFI), 290

Instructional Environment Scale (TIES), 291

Instructional Objectives Exchange (IOX), 158

Integrated Assessment System (IAS), 162

Interest Determination, Exploration, and Assessment System, 180

Interview Schedule for Children (ISC), 246, 327

Iowa Test of Basic Skills (ITBS), 9, 156, 162

Iowa Tests of Educational Development, 100, 162

Jackson Vocational Interest Survey (JVIS), 180

Jesness Behavior Checklist, 17, 23

Job Effectiveness Prediction System, 187

Judgment of Occupational Behavior-Orientation (JOB-O), 180

Kaufman Adolescent and Adult Intelligence Test (KAIT), 127

Kaufman Assessment Battery for Children (K-ABC), 122–127, 262, 359

Kaufman Short Neuropsychological Assessment Procedure (K-SNAP), 240

Kent Infant Development Scale (KID), 340

Keymath Diagnostic Arithmetic Test (KMDAT), 161, 164
Keystone Visual Survey Test, 253
Kinetic Family Drawing Test (KFD), 212
Klove Roughness Discrimination Test, 239
Kolb's Learning Style Inventory, 262
Kuder General Interest Survey (Form E), 180
Kuder Occupational Interest Survey (Form DD), 180
Kuder Preference Record-Vocational, 176
Kuder-Richardson formulas (KR20 and KR21), 47, 464
Kwalwasser Music Talent Test, 150
Lauria-Nebraska Neuropsychological Battery, 239–240, 446
Law School Admissions Test (LSAT), 146
Leadership Appraisal Survey, 293
Learning Efficiency Test, 261
Learning Preference Inventory, 261
Learning Style Inventory (LSI), 260, 261
Learning Style Profile (LSP), 261
Leiter International Performance Scale (LIPS), 128–129
Lincoln-Oseretsky Motor Development Scale, 255
Louisville Behavior Checklist, 344
Matching Familiar Figures Test (MFFT), 346
Maze test (Wechsler scales), 120
McCarthy Scales of Children's Abilities (MSCA), 271, 359
McMaster Family Assessment Device (FAD), 288
Medical College Admissions Test (MCAT), 146
Meier Art Test, 150

Memory for Designs Test, 253
Metropolitan Achievement Test, 46, 157
Metropolitan Readiness Test, 253
Michigan Alcoholism Screening Test, 359
Miller Assessment for Preschoolers, 271
Miller's Analogies Test (MAT), 146
Million Index of Personality Styles (MIPS), 217–218
Millon Adolescent Personality Inventory (MAPI), 237
Millon Behavioral Health Inventory (MBHI), 236–237
Millon Clinical Multiaxial Inventory (MCMI-III), 235
Minnesota Importance Questionnaire, 181
Minnesota Manual Dexterity Test, 149
Minnesota Multiphasic Personality Inventory-2 (MMPI-2), 216–217, 235–238, 308, 359, 436, 446
Minnesota Paper Formboard, 148–149
Minnesota Rate of Manipulation Test, 149
Minnesota Spatial Relations Test, 148–149
Moore Eye-Hand Coordination and Color Matching Test, 255
Moral Judgment Interview and Scoring System, 277
Multidimensional Self-Esteem Inventory (MSEI), 42, 43, 45, 221
Murphy-Meisgeier Type Indicator for Children, 260
Myers-Briggs Type Indicator (MBTI), 177, 186, 196, 208, 259–260, 308
National Achievement Test, 386
National Merit Scholarship Qualifying Test (NMSQT), 5

NEO Personality Inventory–Revised (NEO-PI-R), 42, 219, 220, 308
Nowicki-Strickland Locus of Control Scale (LOC), 16, 17, 18, 21, 22, 26
NTE Core Battery, 375
Nurses Licensing Test, 311
Object assembly test (Wechsler scales), 120
Observational Analysis, 317
Occupational Environment Scale, 293
O'Connor Finger Dexterity Test, 149
O'Connor Tweezer Dexterity Test, 149
Office Skills Test, 147
Ohio Vocational Education Achievement Testing Program, 161
Ohio Vocational Interest Survey: 2nd Edition (OVIS-II), 180
Oliphant Auditory Discrimination Memory Test, 254
Organizational Climate Index (OBI), 293
Otis-Lennon School Ability Test (OLSAT), 131
Parent Daily Report, 346
Parent Opinion Inventory, 390, 391
Peabody Individual Achievement Test (PIAT), 161–164
Peabody Picture Vocabulary Test, 126, 129, 345
Performance scale (Wechsler scales), 120, 121
Personality Assessment Inventory (PAI), 237–238, 308
Personality Disorder Interview (PDI), 244
Personality Inventory for Children, 270
Personal Orientation Inventory (POI), 209
Personal Preference Inventory, 223

Tests/measures, individual, *continued*

Personnel Research Institute Clerical Battery, 148

Personnel Selection Inventory (PSI), 196–197

Personnel Test for Industry (PTI), 187

Picture arrangement/completion (Wechsler scales), 120

Piers-Harris Children's Self-Concept Scale, 221

Planning Career Goals, 183–184

Preliminary American College Test (P-ACT), 5

Preliminary Scholastic Aptitude Test (PSAT), 5, 145

Primary Mental Abilities Test, 112–113

Primary Test of Cognitive Skills (PTCS), 132

Primary Visual-Motor Test, 256

Productivity Environmental Preference Survey (PEPS), 293

Professional Assessment of Beginning Teachers, 311

Programmer Aptitude Competence Test System (PACTS), 151

PSI Basic Skills Tests for Business, Industry, and Government, 148

Psychoeducational Profile-Revised (PEP-R), 345

Psychopathology Instrument for Mentally Retarded Youth, 343

Purdue Pegboard Test, 149–150

Purdue Perceptual-Motor Survey, 256

Quick Neurological Screening Test (QNST-2), 240

Racial Identity Attitude Scale (RIAS), 360

Rahim Organizational Conflict Inventories (ROC), 293

Raven's Progressive Matrices, 129

Reading Style Inventory (RSI), 261

Reynell Developmental Language Scale (RDLS), 272

Reynell-Zinkin Scales, 348

Riso-Hudson Enneagram Type Indicator, 220

Riverside Curriculum Assessment System, 161

Rorschach Ink Blot Test, 186, 210–211, 238, 308, 311

Rorschach Trainer Version I for Windows, 307

Ross Information Processing Assessment-2nd Edition (RIPA-2), 240

Rust Inventory of Schizotypical Cognitions, 308

Salience Inventory, 181

Scales for Rating the Behavioral Characteristics of Superior Students, 349

Schedule for Affective Disorders and Schizophrenia for School Aged Children (K-SADS), 327

Scholastic Aptitude Test (SAT), 5, 145, 365, 369, 431–432

School and College Ability Tests (SCAT), 131

School Attitude Measure, 386

School Environment Preference Survey (SEPS), 290

Screening Assessment for Gifted Students, 349

Screening Test for Auditory Perception, 254

Seashore Measures of Musical Talents, 150

Self-Concept Adjective Checklist, 221

Self-Concept and Motivation Inventory (SCAMIN), 221

Self-Directed Search (SDS), 176–177, 308

Self-Perception Inventory, 221

Self-Report Family Inventory (SFI), 288

Sentence Completion Test, 186, 209–210, 238

Sequential Tests of Educational Progress (STEP), 157

Sixteen Personality Factor Questionnaire (16PF), 100, 219

Sizing Up Your School System: The District Effectiveness Audit, 394

Slosson Drawing Coordination Test, 253

Slosson Intelligence Test (SIT), 17, 26, 129

Snellen Eye Chart, 253

Social Moral Reflection Measure, 277

Source Scale, The, 263

Southern California Sensory Integration Tests, 256

Spache Binocular Reading Test, 253

SRA Achievement Series (ACH 1-2), 157

SRA Clerical Aptitude Test, 148

SRA Mechanical Aptitude Test, 148

SRA Test of Mechanical Concepts, 148

Stanford Achievement Test-9th Edition (SAT9), 157, 431

Stanford-Binet Intelligence Scale, 127–128, 271, 359

State-Trait Anxiety Scale, 222, 345, 359

Sternberg Triarchic Abilities Test, 116

Story Completion Technique (SCT), 210

Strong Interest Inventory (SII), 177–178

Structured Clinical Interview for the DSM-IV, 241

Structured Interview of Reported Symptoms (SIRS), 244

Student Opinion Inventory, 390

Suinn Test Anxiety Behavior Scale (STABS), 366

Sutter-Eyberg Student Behavior Inventory, 346
System of Multicultural Pluralistic Assessment, 359
Teacher Opinion Inventory, 390
Tennessee Self-Concept Scale, 221
Test Anxiety Inventory, 366
Test of Adolescent Language-2 (Total-2), 272
Test of Adult Basic Education (TABE), 164
Test of Cognitive Skills (TCS-2), 131–132
Test of English As a Foreign Language (TOEFL), 5
Test of Language Development (TOLD), 272
Test of Nonverbal Intelligence-2 (TONI-2), 129
Tests of Achievement and Proficiency, 162
Thematic Apperception Test (TAT), 186, 206–208, 211, 238
Thinking Creatively in Action and Movement (TCAM), 349
Thinking Creatively with Sounds and Words, 349
Torrance Tests of Creative Thinking, 349
Trauma Symptoms Checklist, 246
Universal Nonverbal Intelligence Test (UNIT), 130–131
USES Clerical Skills Test, 148
Valpar Component Work Sample System, 150
Verbal scale (Wechsler scales), 119, 121
Vineland Adaptive Behavior Scale, 343
Vocabulary test (Wechsler scales), 119
Vocational Interest, Experience, and Skills Assessment (VIESA), 180

Vocational Preference Inventory (VPI), 209
Wach Analysis of Cognitive Structures, 273
Watson-Glaser Critical Thinking Appraisal, 349
Wechsler scales, 118–122, 162, 238, 254, 271, 308, 359
Wellness Inventory, 246
Wepman Auditory Discrimination Test, 254
Wide Range Achievement Test (WRAT), 33, 162–164
Wonderlic Personnel Test, 188
Woodcock-Johnson Psycho-Educational Battery (WJPEB), 164
Woodcock-Johnson Test of Achievement (WJTA), 162
Work Environment Scale, 293
Work Keys, 194–195, 387
Work Values Inventory (WVI), 182
World of Work Inventory, 184
Your Style of Learning and Thinking (SOLAT), 258
Test-taking skills
    anxiety, test
        defining, 366
        measures of, 366–367
        relaxation techniques, 367–368
        strategies to help, 367
        stress reduction, 368
    changing answers, 373
    essay tests, 374
    group tests, 374
    information on test taking, 374–377
    objectives, 365
    oral examinations, 374
    overview, 365
    past experiences, 373
    scores, improving test
        coaching, 369
        wiseness, strategies to increase test, 369–372
    workshop on, 372–373

Test use and selection. See also Locating and selecting tests
    competencies required of test users, 3–6
    decision-making model, 2
    evaluating and reviewing tests, 69
    Florida's competency requirements for school counselors, 10
    historical contexts, 6–10
    objectives, 1
    overview, 1
    uses of tests, 3
    value of testing, 2–3
Test User Qualifications Working Group, 4
Test wiseness, 369–372
Theory-oriented report, 431
Thirteenth Mental Measurements Yearbook (Impara & Plake), 9, 75, 461
Training administrators/observers, 80–81, 322
Trait and factors approach, 151–152
Trial of Wits: Discovering the Great Differences of Wits Among Men and What Sorts of Learning Suit Best With Each Genius (Huarte), 7
Truth in testing movement, 459
T scores, 99, 105
Two-factor theory of intelligence, 112

Unobtrusive observation, 321–322
Unstructured observation, 319
User's Guide, 177, 178
Using Test Results for Decision Making: A Guide for Parents and Students, 142–143

Validity
    consequential, 43
    construct, 42–44
    content, 39–40, 44
    criterion-related, 40–42, 44

Validity, *continued*
  defining, 39
  evaluating and reviewing tests,
    69
  selection, test, 70–71
Value of testing, 2–3
Values and testing, 181–182, 284
Variability, measures of
  range, 26
  standard deviation, 26–28,
    100–101
  variance, 26
Variance, 26
Venn diagrams, 29, 31
Verbal ability, 112, 117, 209–210
Vermont and school testing pro-
    grams, 392–393
Victorian era, 8
Video approaches for reporting
    test results, 404
Videotape-administered tests, 83
Vision
  impairments, visual, 341, 348
  intelligence, visual/spatial, 118
  learning styles and visual assess-
    ment, 252–253
  personality, visual techniques
    for measuring, 210–211
Visual picture of what scores look
    like
  frequency distribution, 17–19
  graphic presentations, 19–21
  Nowicki-Strickland Locus of
    Control Scale, 16–17

smoothed curve, 20–21
symmetry and skewness, 21–23
Vocational issues, 6. *See also* Apti-
    tude testing; Career and
    employment testing

Wellness, 246
*What is Intelligence? Contempo-
    rary Viewpoints on Its
    Nature and Definition*
    (Sternberg & Detterman),
    137
*When Your Child Needs Testing:
    What Parents, Teachers,
    and Other Helpers Need to
    Know About Psychological
    Testing* (Shore, Brice &
    Love), 421
White test administrators and
    minority students, 87. *See
    also* Multicultural assess-
    ment
Wiseness, test, 369–372
Word fluency, 112
Work. *See also* Aptitude testing;
    Career and employment
    testing
  environment, 293
  habits and developmental tests,
    269
World War I & II, 8, 321
Written test results, 403–404
  computer-generated reports,
    435–437

content of a report
  analysis of test results,
    425–428
  background information,
    425, 426–427
  behavioral observations,
    425, 427
  diagnostic impressions, 428
  eight components, 424
  emotional indicators, 429
  referral, reason for, 425,
    426
  strengths/weaknesses, rela-
    tive, 429
  tests administered, 425, 426
factors affecting the test result,
    429–430
objectives, 423
overview, 423
purposes of, 424
writing the report
  case study, 434
  guidelines for good report
    writing, 430–431
  language, 432
  organizing the report, 430,
    431
  revising and editing the
    report, 432–433
  technical aspects, 431–432

You and Your Career, 177

z scores, 98–99

Test Index

AAMD Adaptive Behavior Scale, 343
ACCUPLACER, 308
ACT Interest Inventory, 180
Adaptive Behavior Inventory, 343
Adaptive Behavior Scales, 343, 388
Adjective Checklist, 208, 218
Adolescent Multiphasic Personality Inventory, 238
Adult Career Concerns Inventory, 278–279
Adult Language Assessment Scale, 164
Adult Psychoeducational Profile, 345
Advanced Placement Programs, 2, 5, 160, 385
Advanced Progressive Matrices, 129, 130
Affective Style Measure, 286
African Self-Consciousness Scale, 360
Air Corps Test Battery, 152
Air Force Officer Qualification Test, 189
Allport-Vernon-Lindzey Scale of Values, 219
American College Testing Program, 5, 100, 145
Analysis of Coping Style, 238
Analysis of Learning Potential, 100
Aptitude and Intelligence Series, 186
Armed Services Vocational Aptitude Battery, 140–142, 189, 385, 387
Army Alpha, 6, 8, 130
Army Beta, 6, 8, 130
Army General Classification Test, 100

Arthur Point Scale of Performance Tests, 129
Assessment of Writing, 386
Autism Behavior Checklist, 345
Autism Screening Instrument for Educational Planning, 345

Basic Achievement Skills Individual Screener, 161
Basic Occupational Literacy Test, 186–187
Basic Skills Assessment Program, 159
Battelle Developmental Inventory, 271
Bayley Scales of Infant Development, 7, 9, 271, 340
Beck Anxiety Inventory, 307
Beck Depression Inventory, 9, 238, 307, 359
Beck Hopelessness Scale, 9, 238, 307
Beck Scale for Suicide Ideation, 307
Behavior Observation Scale for Autism, 345
Bender Gestalt Test, 6, 238
Bender Visual Motor Gestalt Test, 6, 211, 238, 253, 388
Bennett Mechanical Comprehension Test, 147
Bernreuter Personality Inventory, 6
Binet and Simon Intelligence Scale, 6
Blacky Pictures, 209
Bracken Basic Concept Scale, 273, 274
Brain Preference Indicator, 258
Brief Symptoms Inventory, 238

Brookover Self-Concept of Ability Scale, 293
Brown Attention Deficit Disorder Scale, 307, 346
Bruininks-Oseretsky Test of Motor Proficiency, 255
Burks's Behavior Rating Scales, 344, 388
Butcher Treatment Planning Inventory, 307

Cadet Evaluation Battery, 189
California Achievement Test, 9, 156
California Psychological Inventory, 186, 217, 218, 308, 359
California Test of Mental Maturity, 61
California Test of Personality, 388, 426
Campbell-Halcum Team Development Survey, 295–296
Campbell Interest and Skills Survey, 179
Canfield Learning Styles Inventory, 261
Career Ability Placement Survey, 49, 143–144
Career Aptitude Placement Series, 387
Career Assessment Inventory, 179
Career Attitudes and Strategies Inventory, 187
Career Awareness Inventory, 182
Career Development Inventory, 182–183
Career Maturity Inventory, 183
Career Occupational Preference System, 178–179
Career Planning Program, 183

Career-Related Experience Inventory, 180

Career Skills Assessment Program, 183

Cattell Infant Intelligence Scale, 6, 340

Child and Adolescent Diagnostic Scales, 238

Child Assessment Schedule, 246

Child Behavior Checklist, 9

Child Diagnostic Screening Battery, 344

Childhood Autism Rating Scale, 345

Children's Adaptive Behavior Scale, 271

Children's Apperception Test, 208, 211, 388, 414

Children's Assessment Schedule, 327

Children's Embedded Figures Test, 257

Children's Manifest Anxiety Scale, 222, 345

Children's Personality Questionnaire, 100, 219

Children's Test Anxiety Scale, 366

Children's Version of the Family Environment Scale, 287, 289

Child's Learning Profile, 346

Classroom Environment Scale, 290

Clerical Aptitude Test, 147

Clinical Analysis Questionnaire, 237

Cognitive Abilities Test 131, 132

Cognitive Assessment System, 130

College Board Achievement Tests, 160

College Characteristics Index, 290

College-Level Examination Program, 2, 5, 160

College Student Experiences Scale, 290

Colorado Self-Report Measure of Family Functioning, 287

Coloured Progressive Matrices, 129

Common Metric Questionnaire, 194

Comprehensive Ability Battery, 187

Comprehensive Assessment Program, 386

Comprehensive Personality Profile, 187

Comprehensive Test of Basic Skills, 156, 420

Computer Operator Aptitude Battery, 151

Computer Programmer Aptitude Battery, 151

Concept Assessment Kit, 272

Conflict Tactics Scale, 287

Connors's Rating Scale, 346

Continuous Performance Test, 257, 346

Coopersmith's Self-Esteem Inventory, 221

COPSystem Career Occupational Preference System, 178

COPSystem Interest Inventory, 106

Crawford Small Parts Dexterity Test, 149

Creativity Attitude Survey, 348

Creativity Checklist, 349

Criterion Test of Basic Skills, 158

Cultural Evaluation of Language Fundamentals, 273, 274

Culture-Fair Intelligence Tests, 131

Culture-Free Self-Esteem Inventory, 221

Curtis Verbal-Clerical Skills Test, 147

Dallas Preschool Screening Test, 340

Defense Language Aptitude Tests 189

Defensive and Supportive Communication Interaction System, 286

Defining Issues Test, 277

Denver Developmental Screening Test, 271, 340

Dependency Scale, 216

Detroit Tests of Learning Aptitude, 253

Developing Cognitive Abilities Test, 386

Developmental Assessment for the Severely Handicapped, 340

Developmental Environments Coding System, 286

Developmental Indicators for the Assessment of Learning, 271

Developmental Inventory of Black Consciousness, 360

Developmental Test of Visual-Motor Integration, 253, 273, 426

Devereux Behavior Rating Scale, 388

Devereux Scales of Mental Disorders, 308

Devereux Test of Extremity Coordination, 255

Diagnostic Interview for Children and Adolescents, 327, 346

Diagnostic Interview Schedule for Children, 346

Diagnostic Inventory of Personality and Symptoms, 344

Differential Aptitude Test Battery, 61, 140, 142–143

Dimensions of Excellence Scales, 394

Direction Scale, 263

Draw-a-Family Test, 211

Draw-a-Person Test, 211, 212, 238, 388

DSM-IV Multiaxial Evaluation, 238

Early School Personality Questionnaire, 100, 219

Eating Disorders Inventory, 346

Eating Inventory, 238, 308

Edwards Personal Preference Inventory, 186, 208, 219

Effective School Battery, 290

Ego Strength Scale, 216

Embedded Figures Test, 257

Employee Aptitude Survey Series, 187

Employment Barrier Identification Scale, 187

Ethical Reasoning Inventory, 277

Employment Reliability Inventory, 187

Everyday Skills Test, 159

Expressive One-Word Picture Vocabulary Test, 273, 274

Eysenck Neuroticism and Extroversion Scales, 43

Eysenck Personality Inventory, 219

Eysenck Personality Questionnaire, 219, 359

Facial Recognition Test, 240

Family Adaptability and Cohesion Evaluation Scales, 287

Family Assessment Measure, 287

Family Conflict and Dominance Codes, 286–287

Family Constraining and Enabling Coding System, 287

Family Evaluation Form, 287

Family Environment Scale, 287

Family Functioning in Adolescence Questionnaire, 288

Family Interaction Scales, 287

Family Process Scales, 288

Family Relationship Questionnaire, 288

Fear Survey Schedule for Children, 345

Finger Tapping Test, 239

FIRO-B, 438

Flight Aptitude Selection Test, 189

Florida Analysis of Semantic Traits 263

Florida Comprehensive Assessment Test, 159, 393–394

Frostig Developmental Test of Visual Perception, 253

Gates-McKillop-Horowitz Reading Diagnostic Test, 165

General Aptitude Test Battery, 6, 140, 143, 188

General Clerical Test, 147

General Educational Development Test, 163

General Educational Performance Index, 164

Gesell Maturity Scale, 6

Gifted and Talented Evaluation Scales, 349

Gifted and Talented Screening Form, 349

Gilliam Autism Rating Scale, 345

Global Assessment of Functioning, 238

Goldman-Fristoe Test of Articulation, 254, 273

Goldman-Fristoe-Woodcock Auditory Skills Test Battery, 254

Goldman-Fristoe-Woodcock Test of Auditory Discrimination, 254

Goodenough Draw-a-Man Test, 6

Goodenough-Harris Draw-a-Man Test, 126

Graduate Management Admissions Test, 146

Graduate Record Examinations, 6, 100, 145–146

Graves Design Judgment Test, 150

Gregorc Style Delineator, 262

Group Embedded Figures Test, 257

Group Inventory for Finding Creative Talent, 349

Group Inventory for Finding Interests, 349

Guilford-Zimmerman Temperament Survey, 43, 186

Hall Occupational Orientation Inventory, 181

Halstead Category Test, 239

Halstead-Reitan Neuropsychological Test Battery, 239

Halstead Tactual Performance Test, 239

Hand Test, 211

Hand-Tool Dexterity Test, 149

Hare Psychopathy Checklist, 244

Harrington-O'Shea Career Decision-Making System, 179

Hay Aptitude Test Battery, 147

Hepatic Intelligence Scale, 348

High School Characteristics Index, 290

High School Personality Questionnaire, 100, 219

High School Subjects Test, 386

Hill Performance Test of Selected Positional Concepts, 348

House-Tree-Person Test, 211, 212

Houston Test for Language Development, 272

IAS Language Arts, 162

Illinois Test of Psycholinguistic Abilities, 7, 253, 254

In-Basket Test, 321

Industrial Reading Test, 187

Inferred Self-Concept Scale, 221

Institutional Functioning Inventory, 290

Instructional Environment Scale, 291, 292

Instructional Objectives Exchange, 158

Interest Determination, Exploration, and Assessment System, 180

Interview Schedule for Children, 246

Iowa Every-Pupil Test, 6

Iowa Tests of Basic Skills, 9, 156, 162

Iowa Tests of Educational Development, 100, 162

Iteman, 310

Jackson Vocational Interest Survey, 180

Jesness Behavior Checklist, 16, 17, 22, 23

Job Effectiveness Prediction System, 187

Judgment of Occupational Behavior—Orientation, 180

Jung Word Association Test, 6

Kaufman Adolescent and Adult Intelligence Test, 127

Kaufman Assessment Battery for Children, 7, 122–127, 262, 359

Kaufman Short Neuropsychological Assessment Procedure, 240

Kent Infant Development Scale, 340

Keymath Diagnostic Arithmetic Test, 161, 164
Keystone Visual Survey Test, 253
Kinetic Family Drawing Test, 212, 388
Klove Grooved Pegboard Test, 239
Klove Roughness Discrimination Test, 239
Kohs's Block Design Test, 6
Kuder General Interest Survey, 180
Kuder Occupational Interest Survey, 7, 180
Kuder Preference Record, 6, 176
Kwalwasser Music Talent Test, 150

Lauria-Nebraska Neuropsychological Battery, 239–240, 446
Law School Admissions Test, 146
Leadership Appraisal Survey, 293
Learning Efficiency Test, 261
Learning Preference Inventory, 261
Learning Style Inventory, 260–261
Learning Style Profile, 261
Learning Styles Inventory, 260
Learning Type Measure, 261
Leiter International Performance Scale, 6, 128–129, 273, 388
Lifestyle Assessment Questionnaire, 246
Lincoln-Oseretsky Motor Development Scale, 255
Louisville Behavior Checklist, 344, 436
Low Back Pain Scale, 216

MacAndrew Alcoholism Scale, 216
Manifest Anxiety Scale, 222
Matching Familiar Figures Test, 257, 346
McCarthy Scales of Children's Abilities, 7, 271, 359
McMaster Family Assessment Device, 288
Measures of Psychosocial Development, 275, 276
Mechanical Aptitude Test, 148

Mechanical Familiarity Test, 187
Mechanical Knowledge Test, 187
Medical College Admissions Test, 146
Meier Art Test: Aesthetic Perception, 150
Meier Art Test: Judgment, 150
Memory for Designs Test, 253
Mental Status Checklist, 241
Metropolitan Achievement Test, 46, 49, 157
Metropolitan Readiness Test, 253
Michigan Alcoholism Screening Test, 359
Michigan Picture Story Test, 359
Microcat, 310
Miller Assessment for Preschoolers, 271
Miller's Analogies Test, 146
Millon Adolescent Personality Inventory, 51, 237
Millon Behavioral Health Inventory, 236–237
Millon Clinical Multiaxial Inventory, 235–236, 238
Millon Index of Personality Styles, 217
Minnesota Clerical Test, 147
Minnesota Importance Questionnaire, 181
Minnesota Manual Dexterity Test, 149
Minnesota Multiphasic Personality Inventory, 6, 7, 216–217, 218, 238, 308, 346, 359, 436, 446
Minnesota Paper Formboard, 148–149
Minnesota Rate of Manipulation Test, 149
Minnesota Spatial Relations Test, 148
Moore Eye-Hand Coordination and Color Matching Test, 255
Moral Judgment Interview and Scoring System, 277
Morrison's School Mastery Tests, 6
Multidimensional Self-Esteem Inventory, 42, 43, 45, 221
Multiscore, 158

Murphy-Meisgeier Type Indicator for Children, 260
Musical Aptitude Profile, 151
Myers-Briggs Type Indicator 186, 196, 208, 259–260, 279, 308, 420

NASSP Climate Surveys, 292
National Achievement Test, 386
National Merit Scholarship Qualifying Test, 5, 385
National Teacher Examination, 375–376
NEO Personality Inventory, 42, 45, 219, 308, 446
Nowicki-Strickland Locus of Control Scale, 16, 17, 18, 21, 22, 26

Observational Analysis, 317
Occupational Environment Scale, 293
O'Connor Finger Dexterity Test, 149
O'Connor Tweezer Dexterity Test, 149
Office Arithmetic Test, 187
Office Skills Test, 147
Ohio Vocational Education Achievement Testing Program, 161
Ohio Vocational Interest Survey, 180
Oliphant Auditory Discrimination Memory Test, 254
Organizational Climate Index, 293
Otis Absolute Point Scale, 6
Otis-Lennon School Ability Test, 61, 131

Pantomime Recognitions Test, 240
Parent Daily Report, 346
Parent Opinion Inventory, 390–391
Peabody Individual Achievement Test, 161, 163, 164, 388
Peabody Picture Vocabulary Test, 7, 129, 273, 345, 388, 425, 426, 427
Perceptual Disorders Test, 239
Personal Adjustment Index, 187

Personal History Checklist, 241
Personal Orientation Inventory, 209
Personal Problems Checklist, 244
Personality Assessment Inventory, 237–238, 308
Personality Disorder Interview, 244
Personality Inventory for Children, 270
Personality Style Indicator, 265
Personnel Research Institute Clerical Battery, 148
Personnel Selection Inventory, 196–197
Personnel Test for Industry, 187
Piers-Harris Children's Self-Concept Scale, 221
Planning Career Goals, 183
Porteous Maze Test, 6
Position Analysis Questionnaire, 194
Prejudice Scale, 216
Preliminary American College Test, 5
Preliminary Scholastic Aptitude Test, 5, 145
Preschool Attainment Record, 273
Primary Mental Abilities Test, 112
Primary Test of Cognitive Skills, 132
Primary Visual-Motor Test, 256
Productivity Environmental Preference Survey, 293
Professional Assessment of Beginning Teachers, 311
Programmer Aptitude Competence Test System, 151
PSI Basic Skills Tests for Business, Industry, and Government, 148
Psychoeducational Profile, 345
Psychopathology Instrument for Mentally Retarded Youth, 343
Purdue Pegboard Test, 149–150
Purdue Perceptual-Motor Survey, 256

Quick Neurological Screening Test, 240

Racial Identity Attitude Scale, 360
Rahim Organizational Conflict Inventories, 293
Raven's Progressive Matrices, 129
Reading Style Inventory, 261
Reason Scale, 263
Reitan Aphasia Screening Test, 239
Renzulli Rating Scale, 388
Revised Hamilton Rating Scale for Depression, 9
Reynell Developmental Language Scale, 272
Reynell-Zinkin Scales, 348
Reynolds Adolescent Depression Scale, 238
Right-Left Orientation Test, 340
Riso-Hudson Enneagram Type Indicator, 220
Riverside Curriculum Assessment System, 161
Roberts's Apperception Test for Children, 208
Rokeach Value Survey, 7
Rorschach Ink Blot Test, 6, 186, 210–211, 238, 308
Ross Information Processing Assessment, 240
Rotter Incomplete Sentence Blank, 209–210
Rust Inventory of Schizotypical Cognitions, 238, 308

Sales Aptitude Test, 187
Salience Inventory, 181
Scales for Rating the Behavioral Characteristics of Superior Students, 349
Schedule for Affective Disorders and Schizophrenia for School Aged Children, 327
Scholastic Aptitude Test, 5, 7, 145, 385, 450
School and College Ability Tests, 61, 131
School Attitude Measure, 386
School Environment Preference Survey, 290
Screening Assessment for Gifted Students, 349

Screening Test for Auditory Perception, 254
Seashore Measures of Musical Talents, 6, 150
Seashore Rhythm Test, 239
Self-Concept Adjective Checklist, 221
Self-Concept and Motivation Inventory, 221
Self-Description Questionnaire, 238
Self-Perception Inventory, 221
Self-Report Family Inventory, 288
Sentence Completion Test, 238, 426, 428
Sequential Tests of Educational Progress, 157
Serial Digit Learning Test, 240
Sixteen Personality Factor Questionnaire, 100, 219, 436, 439, 446
Sizing Up Your School System, 394
Slosson Drawing Coordination Test, 253
Slosson Intelligence Test, 16, 17, 18, 19, 20, 21, 26, 129, 388
Snellen Eye Chart, 253
Social Moral Reflection Measure, 277
Source Scale, 263
Southern California Sensory Integration Tests, 256
Spache Binocular Reading Test, 253
Speech Perception Test, 239
SRA Achievement Series, 157
SRA Clerical Aptitude Test, 148
SRA Mechanical Aptitude Test, 148
SRA Test of Mechanical Concepts, 148
Standard Progressive Matrices, 129
Stanford Achievement Test, 6, 103, 108–110, 111, 127–128, 271, 273, 359, 388
Stanford-Binet Intelligence Scale, 6, 7, 100, 111, 127–128, 271, 273, 359, 388
State-Trait Anxiety Scale 222, 238, 345, 359

Stenographic Skills Test, 187

Stenquist Test of Mechanical Abilities, 6

Sternberg Triarchic Abilities Test, 116

Stone Arithmetic Test, 6

Stromberg Dexterity Test, 150

Strong Interest Inventory, 176, 177, 178

Strong Vocational Interest Blank, 6, 176

Structured Clinical Interview for the DSM-IV, 241

Structured Interview of Reported Symptoms, 244

Structured Photographic Expressive Language Test, 273

Student Opinion Inventory, 390–391

Suicide Ideation Questionnaire, 238

Suinn Test Anxiety Behavior Scale, 366

Sutter-Eyberg Student Behavior Inventory, 346

Swassing-Barbe Modality Index, 256

Symonds Picture-Story Test, 208

System of Multicultural Pluralistic Assessment, 359

Tactile Form Recognition Test, 240

Teacher Opinion Inventory, 390–391

Tell Me a Story Test, 359

Temporal Orientation Test, 240

Tennessee Self-Concept Scale, 221

Test Anxiety Inventory, 366

Test Anxiety Profile, 366

Test of Adolescent Language, 272

Test of Adult Basic Education, 164

Test of Cognitive Skills, 131–132

Test of English As a Foreign Language, 5

Test of Language Development, 272

Test of Nonverbal Intelligence, 129, 425

Testpak, 310

Tests of Achievement and Proficiency, 162

Test Well: Wellness Inventory, 246

Thematic Apperception Test, 206–208, 211, 238

Themes Concerning Blacks Test, 359

Therapeutic Reaction Scale, 238

Thinking Creatively in Action and Movement, 349

Thinking Creatively with Sounds and Words, 349

Thompson Modification of the TAT, 359

Thorndike Handwriting, Language, Spelling, and Arithmetic Tests, 6

Torrance Tests of Creative Thinking, 349

Trail Making Test, 239

Trauma Symptoms Checklist, 246

Universal Nonverbal Intelligence Test, 130–131

USES Clerical Skills Test, 188–189

Valpar Component Work Sample System, 150

Values Scale, 181

Vane Kindergarten Test, 273

Vineland Adaptive Behavior Scale, 273, 343

Visual Field Examination, 239

Visual Form Discrimination Test, 240

Vocational Interest, Experience, and Skills Assessment, 180

Vocational Preference Inventory, 46, 209

Wach Analysis of Cognitive Structures, 273

Watson-Glaser Critical Thinking Appraisal, 349

Wechsler Adult Intelligence Scale, 7, 94, 100, 119–122, 238

Wechsler Bellevue Intelligence Scale, 6

Wechsler Individual Achievement Test, 7, 162

Wechsler Intelligence Scale for Children, 6, 94, 100, 119–122, 133, 238, 254, 359, 388, 425

Wechsler Preschool and Primary Scale of Intelligence, 7, 100, 118–122, 238, 271, 273, 388, 426, 427, 429

Welsh's Anxiety Scale, 216

Welsh's Repression Scale, 216

Wepman Auditory Discrimination Test, 254

Wesman Personnel Classification Test, 187–188

Wide Range Achievement Test, 33, 162, 163, 164, 388

Wonderlic Personnel Test, 188

Woodcock-Johnson Psycho-Educational Battery, 164

Woodcock-Johnson Test of Achievement, 162, 428

Woodworth Personal Data Sheet, 6, 8

Work Environment Preference Inventory, 218

Work Environment Scale, 293

Work Keys, 194–195, 387

Work Values Inventory, 182

World of Work Inventory, 184

Your Style of Learning and Thinking, 258

Zimmerman Preschool Language Scale, 273